Graeco-Roman New Comedy has traditionally provided a source for legal historians examining the language and operation of law both in Athens in the fourth century and in Rome in the second century BC. Drawing on the recent work of legal historians and anthropologists on the one hand, and traditional philologists on the other, Adele Scafuro provides the first comprehensive treatment in English of one crucial area of this vast field, namely, the way legal disputes are settled outside of court in Athens, both on and off the comic stage. Beginning with a close examination of pre-trial scenarios (e.g. summonses, arrests, arbitrations, family councils) in the Attic orators and looking for comparable ones in sources for pre-classical Roman law, Dr. Scafuro then turns to the plays of Greek New Comedy and their adaptations by Plautus and Terence. There she identifies similar scenarios especially in disputes concerning sexual violations, the marriages of heiresses, and divorces. While Dr. Scafuro's study makes original contributions to the study of extra-judicial dispute settlement in Athens and in pre-classical Rome it is designed for readers unfamiliar with Athenian and Roman law and shows how the recognition of legal procedures may be a useful tool for broader cultural and literary interpretations of New Comedy texts.

THE FORENSIC STAGE

THE FORENSIC STAGE

Settling Disputes in Graeco-Roman New Comedy

ADELE C. SCAFURO

Associate Professor of Classics, Brown University

CAMBRIDGE
UNIVERSITY PRESS

PPUBLISHED BY THE PRESS SYNDICATE OF THE UNIVERSITY OF CAMBRIDGE
The Pitt Building, Trumpington Street, Cambridge, United Kingdom

CAMBRIDGE UNIVERSITY PRESS
The Edinburgh Building, Cambridge CB2 2RU, UK
40 West 20th Street, New York NY 10011–4211, USA
477 Williamstown Road, Port Melbourne, VIC 3207, Australia
Ruiz de Alarcón 13, 28014 Madrid, Spain
Dock House, The Waterfront, Cape Town 8001, South Africa

http://www.cambridge.org

First published 1997
First paperback edition 2004

Typeset in Baskerville 11/12½

A catalogue record for this book is available from the British Library

Library of Congress cataloguing in publication data

Scafuro, Adele C.
The forensic stage: settling disputes in Graeco-Roman new comedy / Adele C. Scafuro.
p. cm.
Includes bibliographical references and index.
ISBN 0 521 44383 0 (hardback)
1. Classical drama (Comedy) – History and criticism. 2. Dispute resolution (Law)
3. Law and literature. 4. Law, Greek. 5. Law, Roman. I. Title
PA3028.S33 1997 96–37394 CIP
880–dc21

ISBN 0 521 44383 0 hardback
ISBN 0 521 60707 8 paperback

For my mother, father, and three sisters.

Contents

Preface

Although purposefully conceived, this book was born by accident. In 1987–89, I was blessed with a cornucopia of fellowships: a Fulbright Summer Fellowship at the American Academy in Rome, a year at the Center for Hellenic Studies in Washington D.C., and six months as an Alexander von Humboldt Fellow at Technische Universität in Berlin. I thank these institutions for the opportunities and resources they provided for intellectual growth. In Rome, seeds germinated as I wrote a scene by scene commentary on Terence's *Andria*; it is not too much of an exaggeration to say that almost every question I address in this book evolved out of that study. Upon returning to teaching duties at Brown in fall 1989, I resumed work on a manuscript, all but complete before my departure for Berlin, on identification scenarios in New Comedy and the orators. It needed an introduction and I knew exactly what topics I wanted to address. I had realized the significance of the pre-eminence of procedural over substantive law in the Athenian legal system and I felt that that order of priorities needed examination in New Comedy. I wrote by hand in the nooks and crannies of non-teaching time, shoved squibs into files and crammed them into a drawer. In the summer of 1990, I opened the drawer, typed the files, and was appalled to see that my 'introduction' extended to well over 400 pages. That 'introduction' eventually became this book – born by accident but purposefully conceived.

I thank William Wyatt, chairman of the Classics Department at Brown University and Jane Chaplin, a former undergraduate at Brown and now an Assistant Professor at Middlebury College, for being the first readers of the first 'public draft' in 1991. Without their kind encouragement, that draft would never have seen the light of another day. In early 1992, with the further encouragement of Richard Hunter, I submitted the manuscript to Cambridge University

Press. I thank the Syndics of the Press for generously accepting so gangly a manuscript in the spring of that year and for waiting for its final delivery in August 1996. Pauline Hire, Anne Rex and Susan Beer of the Press have given the manuscript careful attention during the months of production.

Law and New Comedy did not become a focus of my studies until the mid-eighties. When our colleague Alison Goddard Elliott fell seriously ill in spring 1984, I stepped in to teach several classes for her course, "Love in Antiquity," precisely at the moment when New Comedy appeared on the syllabus. I thank Alison for encouraging fledgling thoughts during the months before her death in the fall of that year. Her image was often before me as I wrote the first draft. I owe earlier debts of thanks to my graduate teachers, especially to Victor Bers, Thomas Cole, Jeffrey Henderson, and Gordon Williams, and an even earlier one to James Hoffman Day.

The range of material treated in this book is vast (Graeco-Roman New Comedy, Athenian law, Roman law). My doctoral dissertation in Greek historiography at least provided me with some experience of hopping back and forth between the Greek and Roman territory of Polybios and Livy, and I have never been able to untie a passion for literature (its passions and styles) from the oxymoronic pursuit of nailing the ever fluid historical record. So a study of law and literature has been a healthy, combative, and desirable marriage. I look to Ugo Enrico Paoli as predecessor, far more learned than I, but kindred soul in his passion for language. Since I am not a specialist in any of the areas covered by this book, I thank all those who have helped me with their expertise. Portions of this book were read by V. Bers, A. L. Boegehold, E. Cohen, J. DeBrohun, A. S. Gratwick, E. M. Harris, J. Henderson, R. Hunter, A. Kelly, D. Konstan, T. McGinn, C. Patterson, J. Penwill, M. Putnam, S. Raval, J. Rowley, L. Rubinstein, E. Stehle, and T. Tuozzo. I thank these readers, and the anonymous readers of Cambridge University Press, for all their criticisms. Many of these scholars have shared pertinent unpublished work with me or have allowed me to read work in advance of publication or its dissemination in the United States; so, too, I thank E. Cantarella, E. Carawan, S. Lambert, S. Todd, and R. Wallace. A. S. Gratwick kindly allowed me to quote from his unpublished 1969 Oxford dissertation. I have benefited much from discussion of particular problems with all the scholars named in this paragraph. With the exception of a few revised pages from the introduction and from chapters 5, 6 and 8, no part of this study has been previously published. I have, however, presented portions of every chapter to various audiences both here in the United States and abroad. I thank members of those audiences for their critical assessments.

I am acutely aware, at the finish of this study – and more so now than when I first undertook it – of how much I do not know. In particular, I do not wish the autodidactic acquisition of Roman law upon my worst enemy. I hope that some of the criticism directed toward this book might take the form of summoning forth new, interesting, and more comprehensible studies of Roman law designed for intelligent adults who are not lawyers. Some such works are available now, but alas, far too few. It is regrettable that knowledge of what is arguably the greatest intellectual construct of antiquity is fading from our universities and law schools both in Europe and the United States.

Brown University has been a good environment in which to conduct research and write while teaching. Various university funds have provided me assistance over the last seven years, enabling me to travel to Cambridge in spring 1993 and to have research and editorial assistance at various times from Z. Cunha, A. Hollingsworth, A. Kugler, H. Melchert, and J. Rowley. E. Coogan, Senior Library Associate Specialist at Brown, made heroic efforts to satisfy constant requests with promptness from Inter-Library Loan. Ruthann Whitten, Administrative Assistant to the Classics Department, with good humor and understanding, has kept the department running smoothly in its day-to-day operations so that working in one's office remains a pleasurable experience. Students, ever challenging, have been a joy: I owe them special thanks, both graduate students and undergraduates, who have sat through numerous classes where, under the guise of different course titles, technicalities of law and language often preoccupied their teacher. My colleagues have been the best possible; proximity to A. L. Boegehold and D. Konstan made law and comedy all but inevitable. Both have gone beyond the duty of good colleagues, reading portions of various drafts on a moment's notice, discussing difficult passages, keeping their doors open.

Finally, I thank my father, not quite retired from his law practice as he approaches his eightieth year, for enduring endless questions on legal procedures in American courts. To him, my mother, and three sisters, I owe special thanks, for tolerating my long absences, and even more, my occasional presence.

Providence, Rhode Island
Thanksgiving Day, 1996

Author's note on terminology, transliteration, translation, and texts

Four categories of terminology need to be explained: idiosyncratic usages of the author, periodization, Greek and Latin terms, and conventions of analytic scholarship.

I use "New Comedy" as a blanket term for both Greek New Comedy and Roman Comedy.[1] When I mean to specify the one or the other, I use the ethnic adjective. "Analytic scholarship" refers to the work and methods of those classical philologists who have engaged in the close examination of Latin plays in order to reconstruct the Greek originals, to conjecture Plautine or Terentian originality in their treatment of Greek models, and to diagnose earlier and later accretions to the Latin plays. Other idiosyncratic usages are no doubt present in this book; context or explicit exegesis, I hope, will clarify.

Chronological periodization is, by and large, conventional. In the Greek spectrum, the period of the Attic orators belongs to "classical Athens"; the period of Greek New Comedy belongs to the Hellenistic age, commencing with the death of Alexander the Great (323 BC) and ending with the battle of Actium (31 BC).[2] In the Roman spectrum, the period during which Plautus and Terence wrote is the "mid-Republic"; the "Gracchan revolution" can be used as the commencement of the "late Republic." Temporal references such as these are always somewhat arbitrary and inaccurate (e.g., at least two poets of Greek New Comedy were writing before the death of Alexander); my purpose in using the ready-made framework is, in the main, to identify a chunk of time, although there is a purposeful,

[1] "New Comedy" (νέα κωμῳδία) is conventionally used to distinguish the plays of Menander and Greek contemporaries and epigoni from those of the earlier poets of Old and Middle Comedy; the invention of the triad has been attributed to Kallimakhos and Aristophanes of Byzantium; see Henrichs 1993: 183 n. 26 for citation of relevant bibliography.

[2] For this traditional chronological framework and controversy over the use of the term "Hellenistic," see Henrichs 1993: 172, n. 3 with citation of relevant bibliography.

if slight, disputatious point in not lumping together the last two centuries of the Republic into a monolithic slab (see "Introduction").

I allude, on occasion, to four periods of Roman law. "Archaic' refers to the period of the *XII Tables*. "Pre-classical" refers to the "formative period' (roughly the last 150 years of the Republic and the first century of the Empire) when "the law of the *XII Tables* is giving way to a more flexible system."[3] "Classical" refers to the 150 years, beginning with the reign of Hadrian (AD 117–138) and extending to the post-Severan period of military anarchy (AD 235–84), when "the law had reached a stable maturity" and when the greatest of the jurists carried on their work of elaborating and consolidating the law.[4] The "post-classical" age takes its start with the accession of Diocletian and Maximian (AD 284) and extends to the beginning of Justinian's reign in AD 527. During the archaic period, the system of procedural law known as the *legis actiones* ("actions based on the law") was dominant; toward the end of that period, the formulary system begins to make its appearance and then flourishes during the pre-classical age.[5] Plautus is difficult to insert into these schemata – he appears on the cusp of the archaic and pre-classical age, at the very time when the first formulary remedies were becoming available.

Greek and Latin terms appear frequently in the pages of this book. The meanings of many of these words, so embedded in cultural customs and institutions, often chameleon in context, can be controversial, even among specialists. Greek words such as *polis* (often translated as "city-state"), *oikos* (often translated as "household"), *nothos* ("bastard"), *hubris* ("outrage"), *dikastes* ("judge / juror"), and *dikasterion* ("lawcourt") come immediately to mind.[6] I usually offer a simple translation on first occurrence, with more detailed discussion where context requires it; thereafter, I have preferred to use the Greek or Latin term. References italicized in the index will indicate

[3] Jolowicz and Nicholas 1972: 5. [4] Jolowicz and Nicholas 1972: 6.

[5] For brief discussion of the periods of Roman law and for different dates for the introduction of the formulary system, see chapter 2.2.b and n. 44. Tellegen-Couperus 1993 provides an accessible, up-to-date, and brief history of Roman law.

[6] For controversial discussions, see Hansen 1991: 55–64 on *polis*; Foxhall 1989 and MacDowell 1989 on *oikos*; Patterson 1990 on *nothos*; Fisher 1992 on *hubris*. *Dikastes* has no precise English equivalent; see chapter 1.3 and Todd 1993: 69. *Dikasterion* is a lawcourt, but the term has multiple uses; I quote from Boegehold's (1995: xxiv) glossary: "(1) A panel of dikasts selected by lot, typically numbering 201, 401, or 501 men at Athens. (2) Any building or place where such a panel decided a case at law. (3) τὰ δικαστήρια: The buildings and procedures taken together as they were used at trials; (4) The whole system of popular courts."

to the reader where the word is translated, defined, or discussed in this book.[7]

I have followed one convention of analytic scholarship when presenting reconstructions of the Greek originals of Roman plays: I use the Roman character's name in quotation marks when I refer to the character in the hypothesized Greek original. A description of analytic methods appears in the opening of Appendix 5.

In using transliterated spellings of Greek words, I have tried to be consistent, except where common usage made it personally unthinkable (e.g., Menander, Lysias). Transliteration was a decision I made early on, so as to keep separate a Pamphilus, Syrus, or Moschion of Roman Comedy from a Pamphilos, Suros, or Moskhion of Greek. But consistency here, too, has been problematic, as anyone knows who goes back and forth between Greek and Latin texts covering the same geographic territory.

The translations in this book are my own unless I have indicated otherwise. I have regularly used D. M. MacDowell's (1990) translation of Dem. 21 (*Demosthenes Against Meidias [Oration 21]*, edited with introduction, translation and commentary by Dougls M. MacDowell) and Zulueta's (1953) translation of Gaius' *Institutes* (*The Institute of Gaius. Part I.* Text with critical notes and translation by Francis De Zulueta) by permission of Oxford University Press. I have also regularly used the translation of the *Digest* executed by Watson and *alii* (1985) and which I have cited, in shorthand fashion, as 'Watson' (*The Digest of Justinian* edited by Theodor Mommsen with the aid of Paul Krueger. English edition edited by Alan Watson. Copyright © 1985 by the University of Pennsylvania Press). I thank the publisher for permission to reprint portions of this edition.

I have worked from standard Greek and Latin texts, using Oxford editions of Menander, Plautus, Terence, Lysias, and Demosthenes, and Teubner editions of the other Attic orators. Editions of legal sources and fragmentary Greek and Latin literature are cited under "Abbreviations."

[7] Cartledge, Millett, and Todd 1990 and Todd 1993 provide excellent glossaries for Greek legal terms; Rhodes' (1984) glossary is useful for titles of magistrates; Boegehold's (1995) glossary has greater emphasis on physical apparatus and personnel of lawcourts. Roman law textbooks are, by and large, not so "reader-friendly." Two helpful aids can be pointed out: each of the four volumes of Watson's translation (1985) of the *Digest* is prefaced with a glossary; Fisk's translation (1940: 429–40) of Wenger's *Institutionen des römischen Zivilprozessrechts* provides a German-to-English (and vice versa) glossary of legal terms.

Abbreviations

Abbreviations of periodicals follow the conventions of the relevant volume of *L'Année philologique.*

AP	Aristotle's *Athenaion Politeia.* Ed. M. Chambers (1986). Leipzig.
Bruns[7]	Bruns, C. G. (1909), ed., *Fontes iuris romani antiqui*, 2 vols., 7th edn. by O. Gradenwitz. Tübingen. (Note: only vol. 1 is cited; bare numbers refer to pages.)
B–S	Baiter, J. G. and Sauppe, H. (1839–50), eds., *Oratores Attici.* 2 vols. Zürich.
CGFP	Austin, C. (1973), ed., *Comicorum Graecorum Fragmenta in Papyris Reperta.* Berlin and New York.
Coll.	*Mosaicarum et Romanarum legum collatio* = *FIRA* ii. 543ff.
D.	*Digest of Justinian.*
EP	Lenel, O. (1927), *Das Edictum Perpetuum.* 3rd edn. Leipzig.
FGrHist	Jacoby, F. (1923–58), ed., *Die Fragmenta der griechischen Historiker.* Berlin and Leiden.
FIRA	Riccobono, S. et al. (1968–69), *Fontes iuris romani antejustiniani.* 3 vols. 2nd edn. Florence.
FV	*Fragmentum Vaticanum* = *FIRA* ii. 463ff.
Gaius	Gaius, *Institutes.*
h.t.	*hoc titulo* ("in this title', used in juristic references to avoid repetition of book and title numbers).
Harp.	*Harpokrationis Lexicon in decem oratores Atticos*, edited by W. Dindorf (1969), Groningen. Reprint of Oxford (1853) edn.
K–A	R. Kassel and C. Austin (1983–), eds., *Poetae Comici Graeci.* Berlin and New York.

K–G	Kühner, R. and Gerth, B. (1966), *Ausführliche Grammatik der griechischen Sprache.* 4 vols. in 2 parts. Darmstadt. Reprint of 3rd edn. (1890–1904) Hannover and Leipzig.
K–T	Körte, A. (1959), ed., *Menander, Reliquiae*, vol. 2: *Reliquiae apud veteres scriptores servatae.* Revised and augmented by A. Thierfelder. 2nd edn. Leipzig.
Lex. Cant.	*Lexicon Rhetoricum Cantabrigiense.* Edited by E. O. Houtsma (1870); selected by K. Latte for publication in *Lexica Graeca Minora* (1965). Hildesheim.
Lex Seg.	*Lexica Segueriana* = *Anecdota Graeca*, vol. 1. Edited by I. Bekker (1965) Graz. Reprint of Berlin (1814) edn.
LSJ	Liddell, H. G., Scott, R. and Jones, H. S. (1940), eds., *A Greek-English Lexicon.* 9th edn. Oxford (with Suppl. 1968).
Nauck²	Nauck, A. (1964), ed., *Tragicorum Graecorum Fragmenta*, 2nd edn. with Suppl. by B. Snell. Hildesheim.
OLD	(1968–82), *Oxford Latin Dictionary.* Oxford.
Paul. *Sent.*	*Pauli Sententiae* = *FIRA* ii. 319ff.
*ORF*³	Malcovati, H. (1953), ed., *Oratorum Romanorum Fragmenta.* 3rd edn. Torino.
PA	J. Kirchner, *Prosopographia Attica*, 2 vols., Berlin, 1901–03.
Pollux	*Pollucis Onomasticon.* Edited by E. Bethe (1967) Stuttgart.
RE	Pauly, A. F. von, Wissowa, G., and Kroll, W. (1894–1972), eds., *Realencyclopädie der classischen Altertumwissenschaft.* 66 vols. in 34. (Note: references are by author, title of article, and col. no.; authors are not cited again in the bibliography.)
Ribbeck	Ribbeck, O. (1871–73), ed., *Scaenicae Romanorum Poesis Fragmenta.* Vol. 1: *Tragicorum Fragmenta.* vol. 2: *Comicorum Fragmenta.* Reprint (1962), Hildesheim.
Ruschenbusch	Ruschenbusch, E. (1966), ΣΟΛΩΝΟΣ ΝΟΜΟΙ. *Die Fragmente des solonischen Gesetzeswerkes mit einer Text- und Überlieferungsgeschichte.* Wiesbaden (*Historia* Einzelschriften 9).
Sandbach *App.*	Appendix of recently edited papyri of Menander in Sandbach, F. H., ed. (1990), *Menandri Reliquiae*

	Selectae. Revised edition, with added appendix. First edn. (1972), Oxford.
Schroeder	Schroeder, O., ed. (1915), *Novae Comoediae Fragmenta in Papyris Reperta, exceptis Menandreis*. Bonn.
S–M	Szegedy-Maszak, A. (1981), *The Nomoi of Theophrastus*. New York. Reprinted 1987, Salem, New Hampshire.
TrGF	Snell, B., Kannicht, R., Radt, S., eds. (1971–), *Tragicorum Graecorum Fragmenta*. Göttingen.
Watson	Watson, A. (1985), ed., *The* Digest *of Justinian*. 4 vols. Eng. trans. with Latin text edited by Mommsen and Krüger. Philadelphia.
Wehrli	Wehrli, F. (1944–59), ed., *Die Schule des Aristoteles*. 10 vols. 2nd edn. (1967–9). Basel.
Zulueta	Zulueta, F. de (1953), *The Institutes of Gaius*. 2 vols.: 1: Latin text with Eng. trans.; 2: Commentary.

ABBREVIATIONS OF PLAYS

Menander

Duskolos	*Dusk.*
Epitrepontes	*Epitr.*
Misoumenos	*Mis.*
Perikeiromene	*Perik.*
Sikyonios	*Sik.*
Fabula incerta	*Fab. inc.*

Plautus

Amphitruo	*Amph.*
Asinaria	*Asin.*
Aulularia	*Aul.*
Bacchides	*Bacch.*
Captivi	*Capt.*
Casina	*Cas.*
Cistellaria	*Cist.*
Curculio	*Curc.*
Epidicus	*Epid.*
Menaechmi	*Men.*

Mercator	*Merc.*
Miles Gloriosus	*Miles*
Mostellaria	*Most.*
Persa	*Pers.*
Poenulus	*Poen.*
Pseudolus	*Pseud.*
Rudens	*Rud.*
Stichus	*Stich.*
Trinummus	*Trin.*
Truculentus	*Truc.*
Vidularia	*Vid.*

Terence

Andria	*And.*
Heauton Timorumenos	*HT*
Eunuchus	*Eun.*
Phormio	*Ph.*
Hecyra	*Hec.*
Adelphoe	*Ad.*

Introduction

1 THE GENERAL ARGUMENT

Legal historians and philologists use New Comedy as a source to illustrate (and sometimes to prove) the existence and functioning of particular laws in Athenian and Roman society. Their investigations appear to have an ancient pedigree: the Peripatetic Eumelos in the third book of his treatise *Concerning Ancient Comedy* (Περὶ τῆς ἀρχαίας κωμωιδίας) reported that "no one after the arkhonship of Eukleides is to have a share in the *polis*, unless he prove that both his parents are *astoi*; but those before Eukleides are to be left unexamined."[1] While we do not know in what precise context Eumelos cited this important law, it is tempting to imagine the Peripatetic writing in his study, adding notes on Athenian law in order to explain some more or less obscure point – possibly of chronology – in one of the texts of Old Comedy. Modern legal historians have had two traditional and overlapping spheres of interest in New Comedy – indeed, the first is (but has not always been) a prerequisite for the second: (1) they have examined the corpus of New Comedy in order to categorize its information about law and to develop methodologies for its proper use;[2] and (2) they have focused on particular subjects of law (e.g.,

[1] *FGrHist* 77 F2: Schol. Aiskhin. *Timarkh.* 39: Εὔμηλος ὁ Περιπατητικὸς ἐν τῶι τρίτωι Περὶ τῆς ἀρχαίας κωμωιδίας φησὶ Νικομένη τινὰ ψήφισμα θέσθαι μηδένα τῶν μετ᾽ Εὐκλείδην ἄρχοντα μετέχειν τῆς πόλεως, ἂν μὴ ἄμφω τοὺς γονέας ἀστοὺς ἐπιδείξηται, τοὺς δὲ πρὸ Εὐκλείδου ἀνεξετάστως ἀφεῖσθαι.

[2] For an early survey of works of this sort produced in the nineteenth century, see the introduction to Fredershausen 1906, and for more recent surveys, Paoli 1976: 32–37 (= 1962); Witt 1971: 224–27; Rotelli 1972: 97–100. The work of Emilio Costa (1890 and 1893) on Plautus and Terence contains valuable collections of legal terminology; caution, however, is warranted in using Costa's analysis of Plautine passages: the author ascribes all legal scenarios to Roman practice without consideration of their relationship to Greek models and uses Plautine phraseology to reconstruct legal formulations that are not elsewhere attested (see, e.g., his argument on Roman summonses on p. 447).

sale, theft, marriage, adultery, divorce, and the epiklerate system) which surface in the multifarious plots of New Comedy and have tried to establish their Greek or Roman provenance.[3]

In the last century, chauvinistic attitudes and unsound methods (mis-)informed much of this work. The methodical study of Athenian law which commenced in the opening decades of the nineteenth century had used Plautus as a source for Athenian law without subjecting that attribution to scrutiny. At the end of the same century, Mommsen and his contemporaries in Roman studies were putting Plautus squarely in the service of establishing Roman law. The "Roman thesis" had been given its biggest boost in 1890 with the publication of Emilio Costa's *Il diritto privato romano nelle commedie di Plauto.* Costa collected and categorized passages in Plautus according to the laws and procedures to which he thought they referred. For Costa, all was Roman law and society; Plautus' comedies could thus be used as an independent source of law. Costa's absolutism, while it found many followers, had the merit of provoking opposition to its presuppositions.[4] The ensuing decade of debate was dominated, not surprisingly, by Roman jurists. The stakes were (and still are) high: if it could be demonstrated that Roman Comedy depicted Roman law and procedure – and not simply Roman terminology – then jurists had in their possession a treasure trove of evidence for a period ill-represented by their sources. No immediate *opinio communis* emerged from the acrimonious debate.

Meanwhile, philologists of the nineteenth century had been addressing the same question, but on a much broader scale: what was the relationship of Latin plays to Greek models? Were the Roman dramatists mere translators and slavish imitators? What might constitute "originality" in such a genre? Roman allusions, alliteration, puns and jokes were assiduously sought. Theories of

[3] E.g., sale: Pringsheim 1950, Watson 1965b; theft: Huvelin 1915; marriage: Watson 1967; adultery: Paoli 1950; divorce: Taubenschlag 1926, Watson 1967, N. Lewis 1982; the epiklerate system: Paoli 1943 and 1946, Karabelias 1975, MacDowell 1982.

[4] Supporters of the Roman thesis: e.g., Bekker 1892: 53–118 and Pernard 1900; both argued that Terence as well as Plautus represented Roman law. The "opposition" was led by Dareste who attacked Costa's work in 1892: 145–54. Girard 1893 thought that the Greek originals should be taken into account and that Plautus' use as a source of Roman law should be limited to questions of detail, especially of procedure, where Roman juridical terminology is found. Schwind 1901 maintained (with superficial argumentation) that Terence presents Athenian law throughout his plays. For later criticism of Costa, see the works cited in n. 2.

"contamination" – the combining of plots from two models – exploded as a means both to explain inconsistencies in Latin plays and to confer the title of originality on their composers.[5] The end of the century saw the publication of a work impelled by a different motive, Friedrich Leo's *Plautinische Forschungen*; in it, he provided a method for the examination of individual Plautine passages with a view to discovering their Roman or Greek origins.[6] Lowe has fairly summed up Leo's contribution:

> Before the first papyrus discoveries brought to light substantial fragments of Menander's plays, parallels were collected from extant Greek literature for many aspects of Plautus' subject matter, thought, and dramatic technique, notably by F. Leo in the masterly chapter on "Plautus und seine Originale" in *Plautinische Forschungen*. Leo recognized that not all apparently Greek elements in Plautus were necessarily derived from his Greek model (*P.F.*² p. 103), but in practice he was rather too ready to assume that they were. Like other German scholars of this period, Leo was grudging in his estimate of Plautus' ability to invent new dramatic action, although he paid generous tribute to his creative genius in the sphere of language and meter; he described him as essentially a translator, even if a very free translator, and his plays as inferior to their Greek models.[7]

Important work sometimes wins accolades, often provokes criticism, and, best of all, promotes better scholarship. Leo's work, as Costa's before him, prompted all three. His treatment of Plautus was the first work of a philological nature to have an effect on jurists, small at the outset, but spiralling and lasting. Fredershausen criticized his teacher's philhellenic tendencies but nonetheless refined the comparative method and extended it to the juridical field; his work, the 1906 Göttingen dissertation and an essay in *Hermes* published six years later, remain valuable today. Eventually, the need to consider both the Roman law and its relation to the Greek model would become a rule of thumb for jurists who plunged into the texts of Roman Comedy.[8] In the philological sphere, the best criticism

5 For a review of nineteenth-century analytic scholarship, see Lowe 1992: 152–53 with citation of relevant bibliography.

6 The first edition was published in 1895; the second in 1912.

7 Lowe 1992: 153, with nn. 6 and 7.

8 Leo's comparative method (his practice rather than his generalizations) and the refinements developed by Frederhausen 1906 were exploited by Partsch 1910 and Huvelin 1915. The method is presented as common sense rule of thumb, e.g., by Pringsheim 1950: 419. More recently, the work of both Leo and Fraenkel is used, e.g., by Paoli 1962 (with less attention to Fraenkel) and Rotelli 1972 (with more attention to Fraenkel). That Leo's work had such tentacles is all the more remarkable in view of a comment he made in his history of Latin literature (1913: 144): "es sind nur wenige plautinische Einlagen, die unvermischt römisches

was provided by another of Leo's pupils, Eduard Fraenkel, in his renowned work, published in 1922, *Plautinisches im Plautus.* Once again, we can turn to Lowe for an assessment:

Whereas demonstrably Roman subject matter had previously seemed the only reliable criterion of Plautine authorship, Fraenkel was able to expand the range of criteria to include many characteristically Plautine features of thought and style. In particular he showed that many more apparently Greek motifs than Leo had supposed were probably in fact Plautus' invention, including comic allusions to Greek myth. Fraenkel further showed that these characteristically Plautine motifs were particularly associated with certain characters, especially the scheming slave, and convincingly argued that by such superficial changes, together with his metrical innovations, Plautus could substantially modify the characterization, and thus the whole emphasis of a play.[9]

It was decades, however, before the philological methods of Leo and his students filtered, in a substantial way, into the work of jurists. In a series of essays published between the nineteen-forties and sixties and culminating in the publication in 1962 of his monograph, *Comici latini e diritto attico*, Ugo Enrico Paoli amalgamated much of the best philological and juristic scholarship.[10] In an essay first published in 1951, we can hear the teasing chidings of that eloquent scholar:

Ces juristes, qui ont donné la chasse aux termes juridiques romains comme les enfants le font avec les papillons, ont été les dupes d'une mascarade littéraire: ils ne se sont pas aperçus que sous la toge d' Appius Claudius se cachait Solon, et ils ont pris pour droit romain du meilleur cru ce qui n'était que du droit attique. Faut-il répéter le proverbe que l'habit ne fait pas le moine? Personne ne peut m' empêcher au carnaval de me déguiser en Chinois; cependant, mes chers collègues, je reste, tel que je suis, un italien de Florence, même si mon habit a été confectionné par le meilleur tailleur de Pékin ou de Schanghaï.[11]

Recht enthalten. Das allermeist hat nur den römischen Schein, durch man hindurchsehen muss, um an der griechischen Kern zu kommen." British legal scholars appear to have lagged behind continental peers in the first decades of this century: A. F. Murison, writing as Emeritus Professor of Roman Law in the University of London in 1933, provides a convivial and learned survey of law in the Roman poets, but with mere lip-service to underlying problems (p. 639: "The dramatists . . . do not, I believe, confound Greek and Roman law, and I should say that the difficulty in determining this has sometimes been exaggerated").

9 Lowe 1992: 155.

10 Many of these articles, together with the monograph, were reprinted in *Altri studi di diritto greco e romano* (1976).

11 Paoli 1976: 126 (= 1951). It probably needs no pointing out that Paoli applies the costume metaphor to depict the Roman dramatists' use of Roman legal terminology – i.e., they

Other jurists had identified the path wrongly taken, but no one had more clearly pointed the way out of the forest created by literal equation of Roman Comedy with Roman law and procedure. While Paoli's redirection of that path perhaps at times over-compensated for the mistakes of predecessors, he did succeed in re-defining the method: when examining the legal scenarios of Roman Comedy, one must take into account their models; Greek legal scenarios must be reconstructed with the assistance of the evidence of Attic orators.[12] A battery of questions must then be posed to determine what it is the Roman dramatist has given us. Paoli thought there was no generalized solution to the question, "how do Roman dramatists treat Greek legal scenarios?" Each individual instance must be considered separately.

Since the publication of Paoli's work, important papyrus texts of Menander have emerged from Egypt.[13] In 1972, Sandbach published many of these in his Oxford edition of the Greek dramatist. In 1973, his and Gomme's commentary on Menander appeared, a masterly critical description of the papyrus texts and a mine of linguistic usage and legal practices of the classical and Hellenistic age. In 1983, a new edition of comic fragments by Kassel and Austin (*Poetae Comici Graeci*) began to appear. In 1990, a revised edition of Sandbach's text of Menander appeared, with an appendix containing new fragments of the Greek dramatist. The publication of these texts in the past three decades has coincided with the appearance of numerous important works on Athenian law: the "handbooks" produced by Harrison (1968–71), MacDowell (1978), and Todd (1993), Hansen's studies of *eisangelia* (1975) and of *apagoge* and related procedures (1976), Thür's study of challenges for examination under torture (1977), Rhodes' commentary on the Aristotelian *Athenaion Politeia* (1981), numerous essays of Humphreys on legal

adapt the technical language of Greek models to their own language (cf. Paoli 1976: 64–65 [= 1962]). No doubt Paoli's choice of metaphor (including his pretence of oriental disguise) was enhanced by his delivery in French. The use of the metaphor, however, to refer to *comoedia palliata*, comedies in which Roman actors wear Greek garb, perhaps betrays Paoli's "Leontic" bias.

12 Paoli's insistence on first-hand use of the orators as comparanda might seem to us today an obvious method of approach; it was not always so: numerous Roman jurists at the turn of the century appear to have relied upon legal handbooks such as that of Beauchet for their knowledge of Athenian law. The practice is still visible (*mutatis mutandis*) in this century.

13 Paoli had available V. Martin's (1959) *editio princeps* of *Duskolos* as well as Diano's 1960 edition. For a useful list of the publication dates of Menandrian *editiones principes* from 1898 through 1971, see Gomme and Sandbach 1973: 50–51.

process and social relations (e.g., 1983 and 1985), and Boegehold's history and analysis of monuments, literature, and documents relating to Athenian lawcourts and procedures (1995).[14] In the field of Roman law, numerous books by Watson, elucidating substantive law in the later Republic, have regularly exploited texts of Roman Comedy; more recently, Plautus makes frequent appearances in Treggiari's massive study of Roman marriage (1991).

Both literary critics and philologists, especially in the last three decades, have used the "law" to illuminate the Athenian and Roman society that may be represented in New Comedy;[15] they have used it, too, as a guidepost to mark points at which Roman adaptors have departed from their Greek originals.[16] The boundary between the pursuits of the two – legal historians, on the one hand, and literary critics and philologists, on the other – is usually quite clear, at least in the abstract: legal historians elucidate the "law," literary critics and philologists the texts of New Comedy. In fact, the boundary between the two, when both consider the same texts, is not always easy to draw: legal historians often elucidate texts, and literary critics and philologists have assisted in showing the way law operated in Athenian and Roman society. Law, after all, does not operate in the abstract, but in the everyday lives of men and women. Such a perception may in itself reflect a shift in emphasis that has taken place in classical studies in the twentieth century. As one legal historian and papyrologist has observed: "In the study of history the shift is from wars and politics to economy and society. In law it is from legal theory and formal principles to everyday practices, the day-to-day operation of the law as dictated by convention and custom – what jurists now refer to as 'law in action'."[17]

For all the wealth of new texts, commentaries, explications of the law, and studies of "law in action," there has been no comprehensive study of law and New Comedy since Paoli's 1962 monograph. I hope this book might fill some part of that gap. It certainly is not intended to fill it entirely, for it is not a comprehensive survey of Athenian and

[14] This is a short list of recent work in Athenian law which the author has found helpful in thinking over the Athenian material presented here; numerous other useful works have appeared in the 1990s and many are cited in the course of this book.

[15] The commentary on Menander by Gomme and Sandbach (1973) is the most outstanding contribution here. Important (and pioneering when it was first published) is Fantham 1975.

[16] Gratwick's 1969 dissertation on the *Poenulus* and Rieth's 1943 *habilitationsschrift* on *Adelphoe* (published by Gaiser in 1964) are perhaps the best examples of analytic scholarship informed by Athenian and Roman law.

[17] N. Lewis 1982: 174.

Roman legal institutions as they appear in New Comedy. I have focused on the ways in which disputes are settled in New Comedy; issues of substantive law have therefore been subsumed to issues of procedure – but the former have not been ignored.[18] I use the methods, to be explained shortly, of legal historians and philologists, to determine the possibly Greek or Roman or hybrid provenance of certain legal scenarios and I tackle many traditionally problematic Plautine passages. I place this book therefore squarely within the juridical and philological traditions of New Comedy scholarship. In accordance with these traditions, I have aimed to elucidate texts of New Comedy in two ways: first, by providing a work of reference for readers of that genre who may not recognize certain legal scenarios; and secondly, by suggesting how the recognition of such scenarios may be a useful tool for broader interpretations of New Comedy texts.

The ultimate aims of my inquiry (to which the aims expressed in the last paragraph are subsidiary) are to distinguish the Attic kernel – if there is one and if it can be reasonably known – of any relevant procedural episode and to pose the question: what does this instance, combined with other similar instances, tell us about the ways disputes were settled in Athens? In analyzing the data that are presented in this book, I became convinced that New Comedy's dramatizations of formal and informal methods of settling disputes, particularly those which are used before a case comes to trial, can supplement (but neither replace nor stand independently of) the accounts of pre-trial dispute settlements which we find in fourth-century orators. The resulting picture tells us something interesting, if simple, about the operation of law in Attic society: that litigants

[18] Procedure is indeed the organizing principle of this book, and in this respect, it uses one of the traditional approaches to the study of Athenian law. The great nineteenth-century work on Athenian law took procedure as its organizing principle – Meier and Schoemann's *Der attische Process* (1824, second edition 1883–87). While Beauchet's work in 1897 (*L'Histoire du Droit privé de la République Athénienne*) focused on substantive law and tried to limit itself to that amorphous animal, "private law," Lipsius' grand work (*Das attische Recht und Rechtsverfahren*), produced at the opening of this century, stood on the shoulders of Meier and Schoemann and once again made procedure the guiding principle. Harrison (1968–71) combined the principles of Beauchet and Lipsius, and produced one volume on substantive law and another, published posthumously, on procedure. The focus on procedure has flourished in recent decades; note, e.g., numerous works of M. H. Hansen and the critical assessments of general textbooks of Athenian law by Todd 1993: 14–17 and by Todd and Millett 1990: 5–7. For a more detailed review of studies of Greek law from the eighteenth century to the present time, see Talamanca 1994, with attention to the differences among philologists, historians, and jurists from a continental perspective.

often stage their conduct to achieve a particular effect, that "staginess" was routine both inside and outside the dikasterion. While I believe that I have presented the data of New Comedy's legal scenarios in a straightforward way, I have harnessed that presentation to my view of the way the legal system operated in Athens.

I have aimed this book at serious readers of New Comedy, among whom I include cultural, social, and legal historians; indeed, I hope the latter triadic tribe of readers will view it as a contribution to the study of "law in action." I do not establish the existence of any new laws or formal court procedures in this study. But I think I have been able to demonstrate certain important aspects of dispute settlement in Athens: above all, the manifest application of intimidation to settle disputes out of court and the prevalent use of private arbitration and family councils. I do not use New Comedy to establish the existence of these scenarios, but I do use its texts to fill out the picture of "law in action" that is adumbrated in the accounts of pre-trial activities provided by the speakers of Attic orations.

Athenian lawcourts played a significant role in regulating public and private conflict. In a recent study of the types of actions that could be brought before the courts, one historian has noted that a large percentage of the *graphai* (indictments for public offenses) and *dikai* (private lawsuits) brought or threatened stood in a series of court actions: "In some cases the series of actions is an attempt to try the same crime under a number of different heads; in all cases the repeated appearance of the same parties in the courts bears witness to the way in which the Athenian law courts were a public stage upon which private enmities were played out."[19] In particular, the initiation of a private suit under such circumstances was loaded with manipulative value; indeed, so many cases evolve out of long-standing family disputes or quite personal vendettas that a court summons, when viewed as part of a series of moves and counter-moves, is simply one more move.[20] An anthropologist has noted in regard to such phenomena that "it is not so much that quarrels are

[19] Osborne: 1985: 52. See further, chapters 1.1 and 2.1.

[20] Viewing pre-trial activities in the framework of game-theory is not uncommon; see D. Cohen 1995: 88–90 and 98 for Athens, Frier, n. 25 below, for late Republican Rome. Application of this language need not imply – as it does not in my usage or Frier's – a belief that the society in which the game-playing takes place can be characterized as primarily a feuding one where "the principal objective of this game is honor" (Cohen 1995: 88); for brief critique of this view, see chapter 3, n. 39. I combine language of game-playing with that of theater (i.e., the moves in the game can be "plotted" – they often have a "script" and might be rehearsed in advance); cf. Cohen 1995: 139, "courtroom drama is but one act

never wholly resolved, but rather that cases have their sources in the ceaseless flow of social life, and in turn, contribute to that flow."[21]

It is particularly the last statement that may be regarded as the starting point for this study – with emphasis on its latter part. The lawcourts as one platform of dispute settlement in Athens contributed to social life in diverse ways – and in diverse parts of the *polis*. They provided occasion for public spectacle, for the public iteration of an oath, year after year, by 6,000 adult Athenian men standing on the Hill of Ardettos – conceivably a fifth of the citizen population in fourth-century Athens – to offer courtroom verdicts in accordance with the laws and decrees of the *polis*. They provided formalized protocols for announcing the initiation of the legal process (e.g., by a summons or an arrest) without the aid of *polis* magistrates, for using witnesses both inside and outside the courtroom, for settling disputes – even without dikastic panels handing down a verdict. They provided an agonistic arena where courtroom decisions might reconstitute personal relationships (e.g., in estate cases) and so furnish a new status quo from whence a renewal of conflict might emerge – inside or outside the courtroom. Finally, they provided a public stage on which the scripts of prosecutors, plaintiffs, defendants, *sunegoroi* (advocates), and witnesses – with all the well-known topoi appropriate for specific roles and arguments – might be acted out before mass laymen juries and spectators – perhaps on 200 days a year.[22] In brief, the courts provided a meta-grammar of protocols for settlement, a yardstick by which violent departures might be measured, albeit a yardstick which itself was subject to alteration and manipulation. In examining the dispute settlement process in Athens, not only must its extensive sociological topography be taken into account, so too must its forensic and procedural meta-grammar – regardless of the particular "place of judgment."

The general argument of this book is that the complications and resolutions of the plots of New Comedy are centered on disputes and their settlements and that these are articulated by characters who exhibit a forensic disposition; that their behavior is influenced by the pervasive effect of Athenian law and its sanctions upon their daily

in a single play." For eloquent critique of game and stage analogies in contemporary social theory, see Geertz 1980.

[21] Epstein 1967: 230, cited by Osborne 1985: 52, n. 52 and D. Cohen 1995: 20.

[22] For estimates of the citizen population of Athens and the number of court days, see Hansen 1991: 90–94 and 186, respectively.

lives; that this pervasive effect shows up especially in their development of forensic strategies in their interactions with one another; that these strategies are identifiable in established scenarios and amount to a code of conduct which is marked by formulations of social intercourse that are not straightforward but are masked by more oblique forms of communication, by the acting of roles to achieve one's ends, by the striving to be persuasive that one's ends are justifiable and indeed obtainable. The forensic scenarios of New Comedy are a reflection of the litigious activity of fourth-century Athenians, known to us through the speeches of fourth-century orators and codified for us in such works as the *Rhetorike pros Alexandron* and Aristotle's *Rhetorike.* By identifying and recognizing forensic scenarios and strategies as essential components of New Comedy, we shall obtain a new perspective from which to understand the genre. We shall in fact be identifying the ways in which these characters think and formulate their actions.

My focus in studying New Comedy is on Athens and Athenian methods of dispute settlement. Might it be possible, alternatively or additionally, to use the scenarios of Roman plays to create a portrait of pre-trial tactics in Rome? Unfortunately, there is no contemporary source comparable to the Attic orators which might confirm that the pre-trial scenarios of Roman Comedy have a reality based on actual practices of the early second century BC.[23] An inferential argument might be made, however, by adverting to practices in Cicero's lifetime that are depicted in his orations. Frier, borrowing the language of Giddens and Goffman, has observed in his study of *pro Caecina* that, at a certain point in the wrangling between Caecina and Aebutius over a disputed estate,

> private law became not only the means to an end, but also a large part of the end itself, in the sense that both parties consciously and overtly prepared their positions in lawsuits, without necessarily committing themselves thereby to carrying one out; while their normal, more purely social ambitions were ostensibly retired into the "back region" of their interactions. Each party began to think, both of himself and of his opponent, no longer as "ordinary" Romans, but rather as potential adversaries in a court of law. In essence, they began behaving less as "ordinary" Romans, and more as incumbents of a special social role or position.[24]

[23] Two fragments from second-century orators that might provide some notion (albeit limited) of practice are: Cato fr. 206 *ORF*^{3} and C. Titius fr. 2 *ORF*^{3}.

[24] Frier 1985: 29.

He continues:

Even as "potential litigants," Caecina and Aebutius had already crossed the boundary into the judicial system of Rome; they had assumed roles (in which they would persist as actual litigants) that were properly a part of that system. Because a judicial system is formalistic and rule-oriented, and because its procedures often appear to pit adversaries against one another, the interactions associated with it frequently have a game-like quality. Caecina and Aebutius could seem to have been engaged in playing an elaborate game, continually testing one another for strong and weak points, moving from issue to issue in the search for tactical advantage. Such games are quite common in the preparatory phases of lawsuits; similar episodes are referred to in the other private orations of Cicero.[25]

On the basis of such observations, it might be possible to read back such practices into Plautine Rome and to maintain that the pre-trial conduct acted out by characters on the Roman stage is indeed reflective of actual (Roman) practice.[26] The conduct of potential litigants who lived a century and a quarter after Plautus, it might be argued, is not likely to have altered to such a degree as to bear little or no resemblance to Plautine counterparts. That argument, while not unattractive, is complicated (not vitiated) by three factors. First, Roman comedies are based on Greek models; their origin cannot be left out of account. Secondly, while it is tempting to see the last two centuries of the Republic as a unified and exciting period during which the legal system underwent enormous alteration with the introduction of the formulary system of law and with the increased reliance upon the praetor's edict, few of those changes are evident in Plautus.[27] There was a far broader array of legal remedies available to potential litigants in the first century BC than there had been for litigants in the first decades of the second century. In brief, the litigants of Cicero's era had more pawns to move about on their legal chessboards. Thirdly, Roman playwrights and their audiences had frequent opportunity for social intercourse and legal transactions with Greeks in Italy; Romans of the early second century BC

[25] Frier 1985: 30–31, with nn. 73–74, citing *Quinc.* 19 ff.; *Rosc. Com.* 56; *Tull.* 13 ff. and adding: "This type of confrontation, in which parties seek through discussion an outcome preferred by both, is called a 'negotiated game': A. Rapaport, *Two-Person Game Theory* (1966) 94 ff. Unlike the typical trial, it is not a zero-sum game; both parties may conceivably gain a better position."

[26] Cf. Kelly 1966: 61–66.

[27] See Watson 1974b: 1–2 on the unified character of the last two centuries of the Roman Republic; the same author comments on the "infancy" of the Edict in the time of Plautus on pp. 35–37.

were thus more or less well-acquainted with Greek game-playing. While the former may have shared – whether by coincidence or conscious appropriation – many of their strategies with the latter, we might usefully expand an old adage and say, familiarity breeds not only contempt, but also competition. Athenian legal scenarios provided Roman playwrights not only the possibility of adaptation, but also public opportunity for parody and one-upmanship – with little regard for reality. With these qualifying factors in mind, we can at least conclude that the pre-trial conduct exhibited by characters on the Roman stage would strike a familiar chord with Roman spectators of the second century BC. But clearly, caution will be required whether one uses Roman Comedy to extract Athenian or Roman pre-trial tactics.

My aim, as mentioned, has been to reconstruct Athenian practice. In the course of so doing, however, there is much to be learned about Plautine dramaturgy – perhaps more so than about Roman socio-legal practice. Indeed, the detailed examinations of particular Plautine scenarios presented here and there throughout this book show Plautus' propensity for disrupting legal scenarios.[28] For the Roman playwright, the law is often an opportunity for comic and dramatic exploitation rather than for mirroring the psychological games of potential litigants. Terence, a more fastidious poet than his rambunctious predecessor, has a perhaps more sophisticated attitude toward the law. This becomes evident in a number of legal jokes – a small treasure trove which has not always been fully appreciated.[29]

Literary critics, when they turn away from the legal and social background of New Comedy, frequently have devoted attention to examining the ethical bases of the conduct of the characters in New Comedy;[30] occasionally, the hierarchy of Aristotelian ethical values has insinuated itself into such evaluations. One consequence of such ethically oriented studies of Menander and Terence in particular is that the comedies are viewed as replicas of their authors' presumed

[28] See esp. chapter 4.1.b, sections 3 and 4 (Plautus' depiction of arbitration), App. 4 (the summonses of *Rudens* and *Persa*), and App. 5, Addenda 2 and 4.

[29] See App. 5, cat. nos. VII. 3, VIII. 9, add. 6. and 12. There are, of course, legal jokes elsewhere in Terence, e.g., in the prologues: see chapter 1, n. 18.

[30] The number of such interpretations of single plays and fragments is enormous, as a glance at the titles in any of the numerous bibliographies of New Comedy will indicate. As for more comprehensive works, that of Barigazzi 1965 and the survey of Gaiser 1967 may be singled out; briefer overviews are provided by Webster 1974: 43–55 in his chapter "The ethical code" and by R. L. Hunter 1985: 137–51 in his chapter "The didactic element."

ethical positions and valuations, as if their authors' purpose were didactic, to present, in the end, an example of conduct worthy of imitation, the depiction of a problem that involved a correct and ethical solution for those perceptive enough to grasp it.[31] So deeply has the ethical evaluation of New Comedy extended, that one criterion for dating Menandrian plays has sometimes been the measure of their ethical involvement combined with an assessment of the maturity of their stagecraft: well-structured plays that show compassionate characters and that demonstrate the ethical basis for the solution of problems of human relationships are presumed to be late plays.[32] The supposition rests on a combination of two assumptions: first, the Aristotelian view that the goal of human existence is the good life and second, a scholarly elaboration of this view, namely, that the articulation of the Aristotelian goal is achieved by poets later rather than earlier in their playwriting careers. The *telos*, therefore, of a good poet is to convey the good life and, necessarily, that *telos* is achieved by the mature poet rather than by the neophyte.

I do not think that the primary or exclusive concern of Menander – or of Terence – was to promulgate an ethical position. Characters in New Comedy, like human beings in real life, often use and exploit ethical positions to achieve their ends. Aristotle's *Rhetorike* is ancient testimony to the multiplicity of ways in which this might be done. In the forensic arena, sometimes the appropriation of an ethical position is genuine, sometimes not; sometimes the end is justifiable, sometimes not; success is all-important – even when defeat is all but guaranteed. Aristotle's rhetorical works ought not to be forgotten, however troublesome they may appear because of their moral ambiguity, behind the prettier and more explicit morality of his

[31] This is especially true of a number of interpretations of Terence's *Adelphoe* and of reconstructions of the Menandrian original of that play, among which the most celebrated (and attacked) is that of Rieth 1964.

[32] See, e.g., Fantham 1971: 94–96, esp. 95, comparing Menander's *HT* and *Ad. b*: "If the Ἀδελφοί B was indeed an earlier play, this may also explain the moral anomalies of the finale; comedy has triumphed over Ethos, and the high moral philosophical level found in Acts 1–4 is not sustained, because Menander has not yet reached the level of skill whereby he can satisfy the demands of stagecraft and of his own moral theories." Turner 1977: 126 in a discussion of *Misoumenos*, acknowledging that matters of technique are of "differing subjective appreciation," lists three technical criteria for dating Menander's plays to his early, middle, and late periods; as a fourth criterion, he tentatively suggests "the stress laid on *to anthropinon* as a fourth characteristic of developed technique."

The external testimonies (which are few) for the chronology of Menander's plays are collected and assessed by Körte *RE* s.v. "Menandros" no. 9, cols. 710–11 and Mette 1965: 19–22.

ethical works.[33] By insisting that we take account of the tradition of rhetoric as an ally of forensic strategies when we examine New Comedy, I am not thereby insisting that we discount the tradition of ethics: both must be treated as the dual legacy of fifth- and fourth-century Athens.

2 METHOD AND PROBLEMS

The general argument outlined above is based on an investigation of fourth-century Athenian law and its operation in New Comedy. Anyone at all familiar with the terrain of Athenian law and New Comedy will recognize immediately that a number of problematic assumptions appear to have been made. These might be summed up as the following: there can be a correlation between what we know of the operation of law on the basis of fourth-century Attic texts (mostly but not exclusively oratory) and the way law appears to operate both in the texts of Greek plays written in the late fourth and early third centuries and in the texts of Roman "adaptors" written in the second century. These assumptions demand the examination of two basic questions: (1) what do we know of Athenian law and lawcourts during the period in which Greek plays of New Comedy were written? and (2) can we use Roman adaptations written in the second century BC as evidence for Athenian procedures of dispute settlement which appeared in Greek originals composed in the late fourth and third centuries BC? We shall take up these questions separately.

While Athenian lawcourts are said to have been shut down under Antipater's regime in 322, they did not cease their operations forever.[34] With the restoration of the democracy in 318, the courts were again functioning. After the collapse of that government a year later and under the rule of Demetrios of Phaleron, the popular dikasteria may have been curtailed, but we have no certain evidence

33 For recent treatments of the problematic relationship between ethics and rhetoric in the *Rhetorike*, see the essays of Engberg-Pedersen, Irwin, and Halliwell in Rorty 1996.

34 Suda, s.v. "Demades" (a corrupt text?), reports that the orator died during the rule of Antipater ὃς κατέλυσε τὰ δικαστήρια καὶ τοὺς ῥητορικοὺς ἀγῶνας ("who terminated the lawcourts and the orators' debates"; Adler's text with Kiessling's emendation of οὗτος and transposition). See Boegehold 1995: 41, n. 61, who points out that κατέλυσε means "no more than 'terminate < for a while >' "; he compares *AP* 35. 2, where the author uses the same verb "in recounting what happened to the courts in the time of the Thirty." Boegehold 1995: 41–42 provides a brief survey of the dikasteria after 322 and includes an account of material remains.

for this.[35] *Duskolos*, the only text of Menander to which a didascalic notice is attached, won a victory at the Lenaia during the arkhonship of Demogenes and so is dated to 317/16.[36] In that play, Knemon claims that if all men were cut after his own fashion, "there would be no dikasteria, no arrests, no war."[37] In 307/6 Demetrios Poliorketes restored the "ancestral constitution."[38] While we are uncertain whether the dikasteria functioned without interruption during the next twenty turbulent years, two inscriptions indicate that they were in fact operating in 288/7 and 286/5.[39] Material evidence from excavations in the Agora, moreover, indicates that the dikasteria continued to hear cases during the third century; a large court complex (the Square Peristyle), probably constructed at the end of the fourth century but left unfinished, shows signs of dikastic use during ensuing decades of the third century.[40]

The evidence for the functioning of the lawcourts during the period of New Comedy is scrappy indeed; nevertheless, there is enough to justify the assumption that the legal scenarios and allusions to the legal system that we find in Menander are not the dramatist's nostalgic reminiscences of democratic days of yore.[41]

35 Boegehold 1995: 41, citing Demetrios of Phaleron F 141a (Wehrli), suggests that he may have increased the number of dikasts in an *eisangelia* from one thousand to fifteen hundred; he points out, however, that "such tribunals were not the same as popular courts." It is sometimes thought (e.g., Harrell [1936] 9 and n. 39) that Demetrios abolished official arbitration, but the evidence (*Lex. Cant.* s.v. *mē ousa dikē*) does not support that inference (see Lipsius 228 n. 39 and 233).

36 ἐπὶ Δημογένους is an emendation for ἐπὶ διδυμογενης; see Gomme and Sandbach 1973: 128–29 for the date.

37 *Duskolos* 743–45: εἰ τοιοῦτ]οι πάντες ἦσαν, οὔτε τὰ δικαστήρια / ἦν ἄν, οὔθ' αὑτοὺς ἀπῆγον εἰς τὰ δεσμωτήρια, / οὔτε πόλεμος ἦν, ἔχων δ' ἂν μέτρι' ἕκαστος ἠγάπα. See further, n. 41 below.

38 Plut. *Demetrios* 8. See Habicht 1979 for a study of political changes in Athens from 294 to 230.

39 The inscriptions are cited by Boegehold 1995: 42 and appear in his catalogue as nos. 93 (= *IG* II² 663. 24–30) and 94 (= *IG* II² 1163. 2–14). In the first (a restored text), the thesmothetai are to introduce a *dokimasia* (scrutiny) "when they man the people's courts"; in the second, Phuleus is commended because "he superintends honestly and in accordance with the laws the allotments of the lawcourts and other things that the laws and ordinances enjoin" (trans. Boegehold).

40 Boegehold 1995: 42 summarizes the evidence. Aside from *psephoi* from mid-third century contexts, lead tokens, and an inscribed *ekhinos* lid of *c.* 300 BC, the most important material remains might be the Square Peristyle, which Boegehold describes as "an ambitious attempt to bring the whole dikastic system within the confines of a single structure." Townsend 1995 studies the structure and associated finds in detail; see esp. p. 78 for attestation of the use of the building and pp. 90–103 for its date and identification. The structure was dismantled in the early second century BC.

41 Aside from *Dusk.* 743–45 (n. 37 above), Menander refers to courtroom activities in: *Asp.* 270–73; *Dusk.* 472; *Epitr.* 417–18; *Kolax* 132; *Misgune* frr. 278 (the *parastasis* or "court fee" is mentioned) and 279 K–T, *Sam.* 508–13; *Sik.* 133–34 (also 180 with its tantalizing reference

That the system of substantive law and procedures of the late fourth and third centuries would remain constant and exactly replicate those of the earlier fourth century is dubious – but at the same time, there is no evidence of real change.[42] We can probably identify areas where there would be great proximity. Among these, we can safely assume that men continued to arrest alleged *kakourgoi* (malefactors), to summon opponents to court, to bring suits and lodge indictments. Political crimes, offenses against the democracy such as those which formerly could be brought to account by the *graphe paranomōn* (an indictment against the proposer of an illegal decree) would of course be dead.[43] But many issues of substantive law would not change: property would still have to be protected, inheritance disputes would need to be settled, personal injuries lawfully requited, homicide would still be homicide. And we should not expect any change in the less formal modes of dispute settlement, such as private arbitrations and reconciliations – if anything, we might expect a greater reliance on them. Nor should we expect the "sociological conduct" of potential and actual litigants to have changed from their conduct only one or two generations earlier: litigants would still seek the support of relatives and close friends in times of trouble, they would still seek to preserve the values of family and *oikos*.[44] For the reasons suggested here, I feel confident that the scenarios of dispute settlement that we find in fourth-century Attic orators can be correlated with the scenarios we find in Greek New Comedy.

Now we must address the second issue: can we use Roman adaptations written in the second century BC as evidence for Athenian procedures of dispute settlement which appeared in Greek

to "three obols," which, however, appears in too lacunose a passage to enable us to see an allusion to jury pay); fr. 840 K–T. References to *apagoge* (arrest) appear in Alexis frr. 78. 4–8 and 130. 5–6 K–A and in Men. *Sik.* 272. None of the plays except *Duskolos* can be dated with certainty. Some of the allusions cited here are discussed in App. 5, cat. nos. III. 2 and 4; VIII. 1 and 2; IX. 1 and 2.

42 Procedural changes are noted by ancient sources and lexicographers, but none are clearly demonstrable: (1) Theophrastos (F 17 S–M = Harp. s.v. Ardettos) reports that the custom of swearing the dikastic oath at Ardettos fell out of use (for different interpretations, see Boegehold 1995: 41, n. 61); (2) Pollux 8. 102 reports that the Eleven were renamed *nomophulakes*, which modern interpreters have conjectured as due to confusion with *desmophulakes*; see *FGrHist* 328 F 64 and bibl. refs., cited by Jacoby in III b I pp. 337–38 and II pp. 241–42, n. 4. On the modern view that Demetrios may have abolished official arbitration, see n. 35 above. The most important administrative change may have been the building of the Square Peristyle (see n. 40).

43 See Ruschenbusch 1957: 272–74.

44 See chapter 7.1.a for an argument against radical changes in *oikos* values in the late fourth century.

originals composed in the late fourth and third centuries BC? Before I enter upon a more technical description of method, we must give some consideration to the fictive nature of the genre. Under this rubric, we should momentarily put aside the issue of Roman adaptations, and simply consider how far it is justifiable to use even Menander as a source of law for Athens. My view on this issue is conservative: instances of practices which appear to be legally endorsed (on the assumption that unlawful practices would not pass unremarked in comedy) cannot be used as an independent source of law; if the instance is not supported by other evidence, for example, by evidence that emerges from a critical examination of the Attic orators, then we can at most say, "while such and such a practice may have been endorsed by law, it might simply have been sanctioned by custom."[45]

When we turn to legal scenarios or terminology in Roman comedies, we can apply Paoli's method – although we might want to refine it further. At the end of his 1962 monograph, he summed up his results:[46]

(1) There can be no generalized conclusion about the way Roman dramatists treated Athenian law (e.g., statements such as "they always Romanized" or "they always maintained the original's Greek law"); each individual passage has its own particular problems which can only be resolved by a consideration of which Roman law and which Athenian law might be represented.

(2) The appearance of Roman juridical terms in a passage is not sufficient reason to claim that that passage is based on Roman law since it might be a simple disguise for the underlying Athenian law.

(3) The Roman dramatist's concern for his audience's ability to comprehend might induce him to suppress legal details which are not necessary to the plot of his play and to replace them, when possible, with Roman legal terminology.

(4) A legal situation which is necessary to the plot of a play, such as

[45] Brown 1983 takes a similarly conservative stance in his objections to MacDowell's 1982 treatment of *Aspis*; I do not agree, however, with all the assumptions that underlie Brown's critique. In particular, I give more credit to the Athenian audience for knowing their own laws – certainly not all of them, but laws that would have relevance to their daily lives. Because Menandrian characters do not explicitly articulate their intentions, it does not mean that they are not informed by a layman's knowledge of the law – and Athenian law, to a great extent, was "layman's law."

[46] I have paraphrased here Paoli's conclusions (1976: 76–77 [= 1962]).

the legal obligations owed by kin to an *epikleros* in the *Phormio*, cannot be Romanized.

(5) Where it has been demonstrated that a passage represents Athenian law – e.g., the representation of an Athenian arrest (*apagoge*) by a Roman summons (*in ius vocatio*) – the Romanization might go beyond simple translation.

In actual practice, these tenets can be quite elastic, especially in determining what would have been essential to the Greek original and what constitutes intelligibility to the Roman audience.[47] In regard to the first issue (determining what is essential for the Greek original), the methods of Fraenkel, somewhat underplayed by Paoli, must be applied. Additionally, the possibility of deeper, structural innovations must be considered, and likewise aspects of specifically Plautine dramaturgy – albeit both are areas of controversy in current scholarship. Concerning the second issue (intelligibility), we may well ask: how intelligible did the Roman dramatists think their legal scenarios should be for their Roman audiences? Terence provides us a clear instance in the *Phormio* of a dramatist attempting to make a foreign practice intelligible to his Roman audience:[48]

> *lex est ut orbae, qui sint genere proxumi,*
> *is nubant, et illos ducere eadem haec lex iubet.* (125–26)

There is a law that fatherless girls must be wed to their nearest kinsmen, and this same law requires the nearest kinsmen to marry them.

We know as a fact that the epiklerate system was a Greek and not a Roman institution, and the dramatist's explanation makes the practice intelligible to his audience.[49] "Intelligibility" usually becomes an issue when modern interpreters do not know for certain whether an episode in a Roman comedy represents Roman law; in such cases, interpreters who want to claim the passage as evidence for Roman law will use an argument of intelligibility: "even though we have no other evidence for practice *X* in Rome at this time,

[47] The criteria I use to determine whether a legal scenario appeared in the Greek original are explained in App. 5; particular problems are delineated in chapter 2.2.c, App. 4, and App. 5, Addenda.

[48] Some scholars claim that *Casina* 67–74 is another instance where a Roman dramatist tries to make a foreign practice intelligible to his audience, but I am not convinced. See MacCary and Willcock 1976 ad loc.

[49] The *epikleros* (heiress without a father or brothers) presented problems elsewhere to Roman dramatists. Caecilius turned the *epikleros* of Men. *Plokion* (fr. 333 OCT) into a richly dowered wife (fr. 143 Ribbeck). See App. 5, add. 10, for examples of other *uxores dotatae* who may have been *epikleroi* in the originals. *Epikleroi* are discussed in chapters 2.1 and 7.1.

nevertheless, it must be Roman because Plautus would not have presented a practice that his audience could not comprehend."[50] The argument is obviously flawed: one might argue in response that the Roman audience could be expected to have knowledge of Greek practices since large Greek communities were present in Italy; or one might argue that because the plays are set in non-Roman cities, the audience is prepared for inconcinnities with Roman practice. But the fact is, we simply cannot solve the problem when we do not know the Roman law. We are usually much better informed about Athenian law in the fourth century than we are about Roman law in the early second century BC. This is a problem which arises frequently in the pages of this book. I hope I have indicated clearly the boundaries of our knowledge; for some, I shall perhaps have crossed too frequently into the realm of speculation. But when I have, I have marked the passage, and that, I think, is a clear advance on many of my predecessors in this frustrating field.

3 SUMMARY

I have divided this study into three parts: *Pre-Trial Plays*, *Reconciliation and its Rhetoric*, and *Playing on the Boundaries of the Law*. Part I is founded upon the notion, adumbrated in the first chapter and detailed in the second, that much of the threatening conduct of potential litigants – both in fourth-century Athens and on the stage of New Comedy – is contrived or staged to coerce opponents to accept out-of-court settlements. I therefore focus upon a number of scenarios of pre-trial intimidation: summonses, arrests, and threats of these procedures or of legally endorsed self-help remedies. The conduct of characters in New Comedy mirrors the conduct of Athenian litigants who narrate their pre-trial manipulative activities and that of their adversaries in fourth-century Attic orations. Forensic discourse is a stylized code, comprehensible to its historical audience. A summons to go to court in Athens may often have been negotiable on the spot; the lodging of a private suit may often have been perceived as an invitation to settle in private; indeed, most disputants in the orators who enter into private arbitration do so after a lawsuit has been initiated.

In Part II, I examine scenarios of arbitration and reconciliation (chapters 3–7). I begin by considering arbitration in Athens and

[50] See, e.g., Watson 1967: 56 n. 1; 1965b: 46–47.

Rome on the basis of "legal sources" (chapter 3) and New Comedy texts (chapter 4).[51] The presentation of Athenian private arbitration and reconciliation in chapter 3 and Appendix 2 is the most detailed study of those procedures available in English. I offer a new interpretation of the evidence, arguing that fourth-century private arbitration must be understood, not in isolation, but in the context of other methods of dispute settlement and especially in juxtaposition with official arbitration. The institution of the latter procedure at the end of the fifth century had an effect upon its older sibling: private arbitrations may no longer have been used to execute legally binding agreements. Nonetheless, such settlements remained popular – Athenians seem to have liked non-final solutions to their private problems. Disputes might be ended – but they might also be renewed and resolved, over and over again, outside the court system. Arbitrations and reconciliations are the most common "procedural" scenarios of dispute settlement in New Comedy. Sometimes they have a decidedly legal cast; more often they appear as informal reconciliations between friends or adversaries. Except perhaps for the rather grand arbitration of *Epitrepontes* and the abortive one of *Rudens*, these scenarios have gone largely unrecognized by readers of New Comedy. One particular type of arbitration appears rather frequently in New Comedy: the meetings of family members who decide the fate of young rapists and their victims; the victim's family, following a perhaps common scenario of Athenian forensic life, might threaten a lawsuit if compensation is not at hand. I study the resolution of sexual offenses in Athens and Rome in two chapters, on the basis, once again, of "legal sources" (chapter 5) and New Comedy texts (chapter 6). In the final chapter of this section, I examine the kinds of argument that may have been used by disputants outside of the courtroom, with particular attention to quarrels concerning divorces and *epikleroi*.

In Part III, I examine means of resolving disputes that are either illegal or beyond the law's surveillance. Here I identify scenarios of

[51] I use the phrase "legal sources" guardedly when referring to sources of information about "what the law was" in both Athens and mid-Republican Rome. Aside from the few inscriptions recording laws, there are no real legal sources for Athens; we are for the most part constrained to unearth laws and procedures from the abbreviated *AP* and the dirt of rhetorical strategies in the orators. For a brief overview of Athenian "legal sources," see Todd 1993: 30–48; problems concerning the use of laws cited or paraphrased in the orators are noted here and there throughout this book. Roman "legal sources" for our period are briefly discussed in chapter 3. 1.

framing and entrapment both in the orators and in New Comedy. I show how the scenario of entrapment in crime can be transformed into entrapment in a moral offense – the ease of that transformation is a function of the forensic disposition of the characters in New Comedy, a reflection of the legal system's effect on the conduct of the individuals it regulates. Modern readers of New Comedy frequently designate such scenarios as these as generic "intrigues." My aim in delineating them is to create a more specific context for them, to show that they are embedded in the same modes of social conduct as are observable in the portrayals of certain disreputable and litigious characters in the orators.

PART I

Pre-trial plays

CHAPTER I

The staging of dispute settlement

Many characters of New Comedy exhibit what may be called a "forensic disposition." Manifesting itself in the ease with which they call upon the law – for debate, for intimidating others, for assistance in their difficulties – it aligns them with many of the litigants who surface vividly in the speeches of fourth-century Attic orators: disparagers of *philopragmones* (busybodies), but *philodikoi* (lawsuit lovers) nonetheless.[1] This disposition – in short, a flair for calling upon the law at the drop of a hat – appears in more and less overt ways throughout New Comedy.

More overtly, it reveals itself as characters easily discuss and debate the intricacies of such laws as those pertaining to *epikleroi* (heiresses without fathers or brothers), as they seek the advice of legal experts for drawing up documents or for promoting their understanding of the law, as they act as arbitrators of their neighbors' disputes, call on witnesses to testify to contractual agreements or wrongful acts, offer to torture slaves for evidence and sometimes march the tortured victims across the stage. They threaten suits against their adversaries, frame their friends and enemies to gain their ends, complain of the litigious conduct of others, and sometimes fear their own conduct will be seen in that same unflattering light.[2] The texts of fourth-century Attic orators could easily have

[1] For discussion of the topos and relevant citations from the orators, see Wyse 1904: 176; Dover 1974: 187–90; and MacDowell 1990: 304 and 355. Cf. Lys. 10. 2–3: "Not even if I had heard any other of the forbidden terms would I have entered the courtroom against him – for I believe it is an indecent and exceedingly litigious characteristic (*aneleutheron gar kai lian philodikon*) for a man to sue for slander"; and Ter. *Ph.* 620–23: "'Look here, Phormio,' I said, 'why don't we reconcile our differences gracefully rather than shamefully? For my master is a decent and non-litigious fellow (*erus liberalis est et fugitans litium*)'."

[2] References to the various scenarios cited thus far: (1) *epikleroi* in New Comedy: chapters 2.1 and 7.1 ; (2) legal experts: Men. *Sik.* 138–40; *Asp.* 184–86; Pl. *Stich.* 128, 503–4; Ter. *Ph.* 446–59 (see App. 5, cat. no. VIII. 9); (3) arbitrators in New Comedy: chapter 4; (4) witnesses, e.g., to a deposit: Pl. *Bacch.* 336; to theft: the *advocati* in *Poen.* III (see App. 5, add. 4); to

supplied material for any number of these situations and characters: e.g., the backroom manipulations over the estate of an *epikleros* in Isaios 10 *Arist.*; the ever victimized Mantitheos of [Dem.] 40 *Boiot.* who claims, as the last straw, that his half-brothers have suborned a witness to say that he bought Mantitheos' share of the family homestead; the defendant of Lysias 4 *Trauma* who is charged with the premeditated wounding of a man in a fight that allegedly arose over a former (?) slave girl whom the two men had agreed to buy and share together; and the former Corinthian courtesan Neaira of [Dem.] 59 who together with her quasi-husband Stephanos allegedly perpetrated offenses that led their blundering victims to seek various modes of redress both inside and outside the formal court system of Athens.[3] But of course the orators need not have supplied any such material for the writers of New Comedy – the material was supplied by the living fabric of Athenian culture, the everyday life lived by Menander and his contemporaries.[4]

So pervasive is the forensic disposition that required attendance in a court of law becomes the lie of choice for characters of New Comedy explaining absences to an inquisitive wife or inconvenient visitor (*Merc.* 279–81 and 326; *Pseud.* 645). Advocacy in court becomes almost a motif in entrance monologues as characters thus explain extended absences from the stage (*Cas.* 563–73; *Men.* 571–95).[5] Chaerea enters the stage in *Eunuchus* II 3 cursing an un-

assaults: chapter 2, n. 106; (5) slave torture: App. 5, add. 11; (6) catalogue of threatened suits and self-help remedies: App. 5; (7) "framing" and "entrapping" scenarios: chapter 8; (8) complaints of litigious conduct: Pl. *Men.* 571–95 (a Plautine passage; see Fraenkel 1960: 152–54); *Pers.* 62–76 (App. 5, add. 2 and 13); (9) fear of reputation for litigiousness: Ter. *And.* 810–16 (App. 5, cat. no. IX. 12).

[3] (1) On the situation of the *epikleros* in Is. 10, see Paoli 1976 (= 1946): 373; for a comparison of the situation in Is. 10 with that in *Aspis*, see Schaps 1979: 30 and chapter 7.1.b at n. 42. (2) Cf. the scenario in [Dem.] 40. 59 with Pl. *Most.* III 1. (3) Battles over beloved courtesans in New Comedy are too popular to need noting here. (4) The diverse forensic activities engendered by the alleged offenses of Neaira and Stephanos will be discussed under various headings in many of the chapters below.

[4] Cf. Introduction, "Method and Problems."

[5] The characters in the Greek originals of *Men.* and *Cas.* may have offered similar reasons (though not the extended monologue of *Men.*) for their delayed entrances. The notion of advocacy as articulated in *Men.* 571–95 has been adapted to Roman practice and explicitly depends on the Roman *patronus-cliens* relationship. While Greek practice (*sunegoria*) might be referred to in *Cas.* 563–73 (so Fraenkel 1960: 152–54, followed by MacCary and Willcock 1976) where the *advocatus* is *cognatus* to the defendant, strict translation from the Greek model is not a necessary inference. Athenian advocacy is not limited, as is commonly thought, to aiding relatives of the litigant (see, e.g., And. 1. 150 and Hyp. 3. 11–13 and chapters 3 and 4 of Rubinstein forthcoming); nor is there any reason to restrict Roman *advocati* (as "pleaders") to non-kinsmen.

fortunate encounter: a long-winded old man had asked Chaerea to remind his father to appear in court as *advocatus*; the lengthy interview prevented the young man from following his new love interest down the street (*Eun.* 326–44). Exits are similarly motivated: Apoecides, characterized as a man "who knows the law inside out" (*Epid.* 292: *iura qui et leges tenet*, and cf. 522–23) leaves the stage to act as advocate for a friend (422). Terence perhaps both parodies the convention and exploits it for ironic characterization when he has Chremes exit briefly to postpone an appointment for arbitration (*HT* 498–502); his absence from the stage allows Menedemus to speak a six-line encomiastic monologue on the subject of his friend's extraordinary capacity for judging the affairs of others (502–07).[6]

Less overtly, the forensic disposition of New Comedy reveals itself in argumentation that borrows the strategies of forensic discourse: above all, in a readiness to formulate attacks and defenses – even where criminality is not at issue, to rehearse evidence and to supply proofs, to apply, in fact, the whole battery of persuasion's arsenal. Fathers attack and defend their sons as if adolescent misconduct were a criminal offense.[7] Sons, cousins, brothers, and friends – sometimes with outside and expert assistance – supply defenses and alibis for themselves and for each other.[8] The intended or actual father-in-law is quick to bring charges against his daughter's fiancé or husband.[9] Slaves offer justifications for their choice of action, preparing self-defenses even as they transgress the limits of acceptable behavior.[10] Daughters also have forensic voices as they justify

6 The passage is probably Menandrian; see App. 6.2, nn. 88–89.

7 *E.g.*, Ter. *Ad.* 84–104: While Demea imputes to Aeschinus unlawful behavior (in general, 85, and in particular, in the description of Aeschinus breaking and entering a house, assaulting its occupants, and abducting a woman, 88–90), Micio sidesteps the issue of criminality, changes the terms of the debate, and defends his adopted son against a charge of scandalous conduct (*flagitium*, 101). Donatus (ad *Ad.* 101. 1–3) perceptively notes the shift in terms. Micio's appeal to fairness as a self-conscious tactic is worth noting; see section 3 of this chapter.

8 The cousins in Ter. *Ph.* so readily supply defenses for one another that Demipho says of them: *hic in noxast, ille ad defendundam causam adest; / quom illest, hic praestost: tradunt operas mutuas* ("the one gets in trouble, the other is there to plead his case; this other gets in trouble – his pal is there to bail him out: they run a mutual defense racket," 266–67). The reciprocal interest of the cousins in one another's well-being is matched by that of their fathers: Chremes apparently feeds Demipho the arguments to support his position against Phormio (918–20).

9 Smikrines in Men. *Epitr.* repeatedly makes charges against his son-in-law Kharisios in an attempt to persuade his daughter to leave him (see chapter 7.2.b). Callicles, the future father-in-law in Pl. *Truc.* IV 3, institutes a mock trial of Diniarchus before he threatens to summon him to court for fathering his unmarried daughter's son (see chapter 6.3.b).

10 Parmeno in Men. *Samia* 641–57 carefully examines the reasons why he ran away from

their conduct or consciously select strategies of persuasion.[11] The forensic disposition is ever keen for persuasive argumentation – and it appears frequently on New Comedy's stage.[12] Silence before an adversary, on the other hand, is a humiliation fraught with the "defendant's" self-reproach – and the "plaintiff's" triumph.[13]

The characters of New Comedy, just as their counterparts in the courtrooms of Athens, rehearse their speeches to be more persuasive when performance is required.[14] Moskhion in *Perikeiromene* rehearsed a speech inside his house, apparently to win Glukera's affection (550). Moskhion in *Samia* intended to practice a speech designed to win his father's consent to a marriage, but his mind became distracted (120–26). Simo in the *Andria* (406–08) is suspected of

Demeas in an attempt to prove to the audience (dikasts?) that he is innocent in the matter of Moskhion's conduct. Geta, in the opening scene of *Phormio*, perceives that he has need of a *precator* to plead his case for allowing Antipho's marriage (140–43).

[11] Glukera in Men. *Perik.* (708–19) presents a lively argument to Pataikos to refute charges that she moved into the house of Moskhion's mother as an adventuress, seeking to become the young man's wife or mistress. Pamphile in Men. *Epitr.*, and the daughters in *Pap. Didot I* and Pl. *Stich.* all argue against their fathers' intention of removing them from their husbands. On the rhetorical skill of these arguments – which might nevertheless be "legally otiose" (N. Lewis 1982: 169) – see chapter 7.2.b. The direct speech of women is allegedly reported on occasion in the orators; see note 81 below).

[12] Persuasion as a strategy for effecting one's ends, for example, is prominently pitted against violence in Menander's *Perik.* – a play that begins with the consequences of the violent activity of Polemon, who has shorn off the hair of his concubine, Glukera. For the operation of persuasion in this play, see esp. 271–75, 327–34, 474, 498, 504–10, 1130–08. Moskhion plans a strategy of flattery in 312–15, and practises a speech at 550. But Glukera's persuasive abilities appear the most well-honed (see preceding note).

[13] Pamphilus despairingly reports his stupefaction to Mysis at Ter. *And.* 256–59; Davos comments on Simo's stupefaction at 421. In Ter. *Ph.* 2.1, Demipho angrily imputes his son's loss of a court case to his silence during the trial (237–38, 279–81); Phaedria tries to excuse his cousin's conduct with the explanation: *functus adulescentulist / officium liberali'; postquam ad iudices / ventumst, non potuit cogitata proloqui; / ita eum tum timidum ibi obstupefecit pudor* (281–84: "he acted as any well-brought up young man would: when the case came before the judges, he was unable to reproduce his studied arguments – so profoundly did modesty stupefy his timid soul at that time"). Donatus on *Ph.* 281. 3 ascribes the line to Apollodoros. In Dem. 21. 95, silence in the courtroom betokens the ultimate civic dishonor, *atimia*; see MacDowell 1990. For the notion that silence signifies defeat – and even guilt, cf. Soph. *Tr.* 813–14, the chorus' last words to the silently departing Deianeira: τί σῖγ' ἀφέρπεις; οὐ κάτοισθ' ὁθούνεκα / ξυνηγορεῖς σιγῶσα τῶι κατηγόρωι; ("Why do you steal away in silence? Do you not know that by your silence you become an advocate for your accuser?").

[14] Alkidamas *Peri Sophiston* 11, 18, and 21 suggests that speakers memorized written speeches by heart for delivery in court; see Dover 1968a: 150–51 who cites Alkidamas and Ar. *Knights* 347–50: "If, on some occasion, you succeeded in pleading a piddling lawsuit against a metic, talking away to yourself, on and on, in the streets at night, drinking (sc. only) water . . . , and boring your friends by trying your speech on them, you thought you were a real orator!" (trans. Dover). Cf. Dem. 21. 191–92 (Demosthenes treats his own rehearsals in a favorable light); and Dem. 19. 255 (he treats Aeschines' practice sessions with contempt). On the rehearsals and memorization of speeches, see further, section 3 of this chapter.

rehearsing a speech in some lonely spot to convince his son to marry a neighbor's daughter. Habrotonon in *Epitrepontes* practices a speech intended for Kharisios (517–18, 526–29); her preparatory session has the veneer of an actor's rehearsal since she plays the role of infant's mother – but the goal of her performance is to acquire Kharisios' acceptance of a carefully worked out proof that he is the father of the infant she holds in her arms. Her rehearsal therefore has the same general goal as the rehearsals of the Moskhions or the one that Simo is envisioned as acting out in the *Andria:* to be persuasive in supporting or assailing a position. Attack and defense – and not only for Habrotonon – is the playing of a role, a performance.

The forensic disposition creates a lively, rhetoricized comedy – lively because its argumentation represents the habits of a living culture, rhetoricized because its discourse is shaped by courtroom strategies of attack and defense. It is no surprise that ancient critics thought that Menander himself may have penned the now lost speeches of the orator Kharisios.[15] Nor is it surprising that the courtesan in *Epitrepontes* should call upon the deity *Peitho* (Persuasion) as she essays a proof of paternity, nor that *Elenkhos* (Refutation) should be the prologue deity of one of the lost comedies of Menander.[16] Arcturus, prologue speaker of Plautus' *Rudens*, gazes down on earth from his heavenly seat and focuses upon the activities of litigants in court as he introduces a play that is filled with litigious characters.[17] Terence's "external prologues" to his plays, adversarial in nature and fully rhetorical, while not components of the Greek

[15] Quint. 10. 1. 69–70. A few fragments of Kharisios (in Latin translation) are embedded in the rhetorical handbook of P. Rutilius Lupus (*Schemata Lexeos* 1. 10 and 2. 6 and 16).

[16] *Peitho*: *Epitr.* 555. For *Peitho* both as the goddess of rhetorical persuasion and as the companion of Eros and Aphrodite, see Gomme and Sandbach 1973; connections between Peitho and Aphrodite in cult, literature, and visual arts are traced by Buxton 1982: 29–48. *Elenkhos*: fr. 717 K.–T., from an unknown play. Webster 1974: 50 thinks the deity may have appeared in *Sikyonios*, but the *Andria* is a likely candidate, too.

[17] The prologue falls into two halves (1–31 and 32–82); in the first part, Arcturus presents his "cosmic view," in the second, he provides expository information. The first part contains the references to lawcourts mentioned above. There is no way to determine with certainty whether any part of the prologue is traceable to the Diphilan original. Marx (1928: 52–62), who has a penchant for literally re-writing the Greek original, thinks that, while Plautus translated the entire prologue *nach dem griechischen Vorbild*, later interpolations mar the first part; he retains, however, the references to litigants in 17–18 as part of Plautus' translation. Arcturus' heavenly focus upon courtroom litigants suggests the same *Weltanschauung* as Strepsiades' observation of an important omission from the *ges periodos* (map of the world) he is shown at *Clouds* 206–08: Student: "And this is a map of the entire world. See? Here's Athens!" Strepsiades: "Nonsense – can't be – for I don't see any dikasts sitting around."

originals, nevertheless blend in tone with the essential forensic quality of the comedies themselves.[18]

What unites many of these exhibitions of the forensic disposition is their emergence in situations of dispute: a situation arises or is foreseeable in which the proper course of action is a matter of dispute between individuals. Such disputes are not usually equivalent to what we think of as the plot of a play; but they fuel its action – and perhaps much of the Athenian audience's interest. For them, "situational disputes" would be easily recognizable – and enjoyable. They encapsulate a code of conduct that was usual and ubiquitous – and often overlooked by modern readers. In tragedy and Old Comedy, disputes are often resolved by recourse to legal argument and technicalities – even though the details of these are less obvious to us than to the original audience; nevertheless, agonistic debate and actual trial scenes are hallmarks of fifth-century drama.[19] The issues of tragedy are, of course, weighty and touch the entire community: the unwritten laws or customs of a *polis* may be pitted against a tyrant's decrees; or a trial may determine the end or continuation of a murder-in-revenge cycle that threatens the demise of a ruling family. In Old Comedy, disputes likewise have a decidedly political focus: a radical change of government may be the solution, or a private settlement with another *polis*. In the late fourth and early third centuries, the stakes set in comedy are smaller and belong to an infinitely more private sphere: disputed ownership of a trunk

18 It is conceivable that Greek writers of New Comedy may have used their prologues to criticize the practice of their contemporaries; certainly that is the impression given by a fragmentary prologue, *Pap. Argent. Graeca* 53 (= Schroeder no. 7; Page 1941: 274–76). Terence may therefore have derived the notion of using the prologue as a vehicle of criticism from earlier writers, but he will have recast the criticism and aimed it against his own contemporaries. He twice uses his producer and star actor as prologue speaker, explicitly in the guise of an *orator* who pleads the playwright's case against his detractors; the *orator* treats the audience as a court of judges who will give a verdict on Terence (*HT prol.* 11–15 and *Hec. prol.* II. 9, 28, 52–55). It is interesting that one of the points for which Terence criticizes his rival in *Eunuchus* 10–13 is his misrepresentation of courtroom procedure – for the fact that he has a defendant give his defense before the plaintiff presents the case. For a close examination of the rhetorical shape of Terence's prologues, see Gelhaus 1972.

19 The trial in *Eumenides* and the mock trial in *Wasps* are of course well known and well treated in modern literature. Garvie 1969: 204–12 casts doubt upon the view that a trial took place in Aiskh. *Danaides*. While there has been considerable study of the legal language and scenarios in Aiskhylos and Aristophanes, there appears to have been less study of these elements in Sophokles and Euripides. For Sophokles in particular, such study would be worthwhile. For an introduction to the possibilities of such a project, see, in his grand style, Daube 1980, and for more detailed studies of *OT*, R. G. Lewis 1989 and Greiffenhagen 1966.

discovered by a fisherman, recovery of trinkets or of a small sum of money, compensation for a destitute victim of rape. The playwrights envision situations that any man might find himself in, or might know of from someone else – normal (sometimes not so normal) everyday life.

The code of conduct which is dramatized in the situational disputes of New Comedy is a reflection of the way the Athenian legal system has touched the lives of the inhabitants of the *polis*, on-stage and off. In assessing the way that code operates in New Comedy, I note three broad features of the system:

(1) the manifold options, formal and informal, for dispute settlement, which might allow one the opportunity to initiate proceedings of one sort or another;
(2) a prevalence of conduct undertaken with a view to foreseeable legal consequences; and
(3) a widespread appearance in courtroom speeches of arguments that are not based on legal technicalities.

I OPTIONS OF DISPUTE SETTLEMENT

The most well-known (and notorious) statement of the manifold options of dispute settlement appears in Dem. 22 *Andr.* 25–27:

> Moreover, you should be aware of this as well: Solon, who made these laws and many others . . . provided not only one procedure for each and every offense for those who wanted to obtain justice from wrong-doers, but many . . . He thought that no individual should be barred from obtaining justice in the way that was most suitable for him. How then would this come about? If he were to provide many legal procedures against wrong-doers, as in the case of theft. Suppose you are strong and self-confident – arrest the man (*apage*); you risk a thousand drakhmai. Suppose you are weaker – lead the way (*ephegou*) to the officials; they will take care of the arrest. Suppose you fear even to do this – indict him (*graphou*). You lack confidence in yourself and as a poor man would be unable to pay out a thousand – sue him (*dikazou*) for theft before an arbitrator and you will risk nothing. Not a one of these procedures is the same. Likewise in the case of impiety, it is possible to arrest (*apagein*), to indict (*graphesthai*), to sue (*dikazesthai*) before the Eumolpidai, to give information (*phrazein*) to the arkhon-basileus. About all the other cases, almost the same [multiplicity of procedure] holds. (25–27)

The passage has rightly been subjected to criticism, particularly for its lumping together of all cases of theft, as if every incident allowed the victim unrestricted choice from the smorgasbord of legal procedures.[20] Against this view, we know, for example, that *apagoge* (arrest), the procedure by which alleged *kakourgoi* (malefactors of specific type, including thieves, kidnappers, and clothes-stealers) were haled before the Eleven, could only be used if the *kakourgos* had been caught in the act; *ephegesis*, on the other hand, required that the *kakourgoi* be restrained until the officials could be fetched to execute the arrest.[21] The passage from Demosthenes is not, then, an accurate account of legal options for all victims of theft; nevertheless, it still sheds light on the social and economic concerns that might influence a person in cases where choice was permissible – for it certainly is true that numerous offenses could be redressed by multiple legal remedies in Athens.[22] As Demosthenes points out, a potential prosecutor would consider his own material risks when making his decision: risks to his person if he is too weak to effect the arrest by himself and not lucky enough to have friends at hand for assistance; and risks to his financial resources if he must pay 1,000 drakhmai for not garnering a fifth of the votes at a trial that would be the result of a *graphe* (an indictment for a public offense).[23] While Demosthenes has focused only upon the potential prosecutor's concern for himself, we can safely assume that he would deliberate just as carefully over what penalty might be exacted from the defendant.[24] Except in cases of *apagoge* and perhaps in some cases of *ephegesis* which called for immediate action upon catching a culprit on the spot, potential litigants would proceed slowly and with deliberation before settling upon the best (i.e., most expeditious, most rewarding, most certain to win) procedure to win redress.

Going to trial, however, was usually a last resort. Disputes were settled in a variety of more or less informal ways, determined both

[20] See D. Cohen 1983: 38–40 who views the passage as worthless for its information on laws about theft, and Lipsius 438 and n. 70.

[21] D. Cohen 1983: 38–40; Lipsius 438. *Apagoge* and related procedures are discussed in c. 2.1. For different interpretations of "being caught in the act," see c. 2, n. 33.

[22] Osborne 1985: 42–43, arguing against D. Cohen's view that the passage is worthless, stresses the social implications of the passage and the availability of varied remedies for similar offenses in Athens: "most offenses for which the law specified procedure by *graphe* could be redefined to fall within the scope of a law specifying procedure by *dike*." While that claim is somewhat exaggerated, the flexibility of Athenian procedures, abetted by the vagueness of substantive law, is not to be denied. Scholars have frequently pointed out, e.g., the overlap of the *graphe hubreos* with *dikai* for assault, violence, and slander (see chapter 5 at n. 52).

[23] For the penalty exacted of an unsuccessful prosecutor, see n. 66 below.

[24] This is pointed out by Osborne 1985: 43.

by the subject of dispute and by the relative strengths and weaknesses of the disputants.[25] In private disputes that arose over *oikos*-related issues – for example, when the estate of a deceased relative or a guardian's management of his ward's property came into question – relatives often intervened, gave advice, and sometimes furnished a solution.[26] If the opportunity for an advantageous *post mortem* adoption arose, relatives would be expected to unite together and agree upon a suitable candidate.[27] According to the speaker of [Dem.] 44 *Leokh.*, when Arkhiades died childless and his brother Meidulides was out of the country, his sister's son was adopted into the *oikos* of the deceased and so entered into possession of the estate; when Meidulides returned, although he was "vexed at the situation and disposed to bring a suit," his relatives persuaded him to leave the adoption undisturbed (44.19).[28] Friends and relatives would intervene on other occasions as well, especially when the injured party suffered a serious financial setback. Apollodoros' father-in-law Deinias, together with the pentecontarch, tried to convince a recalcitrant and dilatory trierarch to relieve Apollodoros of his expensive and extended tour of duty ([Dem.] 50 *Polykl.* 24); when these two failed, Apollodoros' friends and intimates approached the truant, offering to draw up an agreement and to act as sureties for their friend (50. 27–28). Epikrates summoned friends and relatives to read over the contract he had signed (to his great misfortune) with

[25] Extra-judicial methods of settling disputes have been relatively unnoticed in recent treatments of Attic law. It is remarkable, for example, that there has been no extensive study of private arbitration since Steinwenter's monograph in 1925. Harrison died before completing that section of his work (see Harrison 2: preface and 64–66); discussions by MacDowell 1978: 203–06 and Todd 1993: 123–25 are summary. V. J. Hunter 1994: 55–62 and 205–08 now provides the most detailed treatment of the topic in English; see further chapter 3, nn. 5–6 below. Recent studies that take into account extra-judicial procedures and more informal channels of settlement include Thür 1975 and 1977; D. Cohen 1991a: 155–64 and 1995.

[26] See V. J. Hunter 1994: 43–69.

[27] Rubinstein 1993: 33–55 argues persuasively that "the only persons who could legally be posthumously adopted were those who already had the inheritance of the deceased awarded to them by the People's Court. The procedure of posthumous adoption consisted in the heir being enrolled in the phratry (and deme if he was an adult) of the deceased" (55). It is during the candidate's admission to a phratry or deme that a disgruntled family member might exert influence on *phrateres* or demesmen to thwart the adoption.

[28] Cf. Is. 1. 2, 16, 28, 35, 51: a kinsman and friends are said to have offered a compromise for the sharing of Kleonymos' estate between his alleged testamentary and intestate heirs. Relatives are sometimes accused of having entered into "conspiracies" in order to wrest an estate from the hands of other kin; see [Dem.] 43. 4–8; Is. 10. 19. The speaker of [Dem.] 48 admits to making such an arrangement with another relative (7–8).

Athenogenes; the men then accompanied him for a confrontation with the shrewd Egyptian businessman (Hyp. 5 *Athen.* 10–12).

Frequently mutual agreements and third-party interventions have a more formal cast. In disputes over money, a creditor or other potential plaintiff might grant a release (*aphesis*) to the debtor or potential defendant upon payment of an agreed upon sum of money; a mutual settlement, i.e., a meeting of the terms demanded by the creditor or potential plaintiff (*apallage*), might also end the dispute. Such agreements were *kuriai* (authoritative) and would serve as grounds for barring action (by way of a *paragraphe*) if the dispute ever came to court.[29] In some cases, a formal challenge (*proklesis*) from one disputant to another may have included a provision that the dispute would end (and an *aphesis* be granted) if particular facts were established by the examination of a slave under torture.[30] Contractual agreements (*homologiai*), whether orally made or committed to writing, were also *kuriai* although the juridical basis of these agreements and the particular remedies available for their protection or enforceability are debated by scholars.[31] Disputants might also seek out a third party (*diaitetes hairetos*, literally, "chosen arbitrator") to end their dispute either by giving a verdict in an arbitration (*diaita* in a strict sense) or by assisting in arranging an acceptable reconciliation (*dialusis* or *diallage*).[32] Friends and relatives would often be chosen as *diaitetai* in *oikos*-related quarrels, while business associates would be likely choices in extra-*oikos* disputes.[33] Agreements arising from such interventions were also *kuriai*; the addition of an *aphesis* and / or *apallage* would serve to bar future legal action.[34]

If arrangements such as these failed and a disputant lodged a suit with the appropriate magistrate, both extra-judicial and official

[29] Ancient sources for the law that made *aphesis* and *apallage* authoritative are cited in chapter 3, n. 33. For discussion of these terms, see Isager in Isager and Hansen 1975: 228–37; Steinwenter 1925: 128–30. The meaning of the adjective *kurios* is discussed in chapter 3.1.a.

[30] See Thür 1977: 214–32.

[31] Ancient sources for the law rendering such agreements authoritative are cited in chapter 3, n. 34. For discussion of problems related to *homologia*, see Pringsheim 1950: 26–54; Wolff 1957; Todd 1993: 265–67; further discussion in chapter 3.1.a apud fin.

[32] For the differences between *diaita* in the strict sense as "arbitration" and *dialusis* and *diallage* as "reconciliation," see chapter 3.1.a.

[33] On the three occasions when precise relationships are specified (Is. 2. 29–30; 5. 33; Dem. 36. 17), brothers-in-law appear twice as *diaitetai*, and a husband of a wife's sister once. All three of these arbitrations deal with estates or family property and suggest a concern for a sister's material welfare, directly in Is. 5 and Dem. 36, indirectly in Is. 2.

[34] The evidence is discussed in chapter 3.1.a.

opportunities for reconciliation or arbitration still remained. Private suits (*dikai*) could be dropped without penalty, except perhaps for the loss of the court fee.[35] Between the time that a suit was filed and the day appointed for the court hearing, the disputants might come to an agreement or seek a third party to reconcile them or decide the case. Moreover, an official arbitrator (*diaitetes klērōtos*) was required to hear private suits which fell under the jurisdiction of the Forty whenever more than ten drakhmai were at stake. Official arbitrators were laymen; all citizens were compelled to serve in this capacity during their sixtieth year (*AP* 53.4). The official arbitrator's first task was to reconcile (*dialusai*) the disputants; only if such a reconciliation failed, was he to proceed to give a verdict (*gignōskein*).[36] If the verdict was unacceptable, then the official arbitrator would return the case to the four tribal judges (members of the Forty) who would preside over the courtroom trial.[37] Once in court, a litigant might still beseech the dikasts to reconcile him with his opponent ([Dem.] 48 *Olymp.* 3 and 58). While the protocols of such a reconciliation are unknown, we have evidence that one did in fact take place – after the dikasts had cast their votes but before those votes were counted (Is. 5 *Dik.* 17–18).[38]

The incorporation of the official arbitrator's functions of reconciliation and arbitration into the formal sequence of legal procedures demonstrates the significant role played by these methods of dispute settlement.[39] One could almost call it a habit, a first reflex. Private arbitration played a slightly different role, precisely because it was

[35] Lipsius 842 provides no sources for the litigant's loss of the court fee upon dropping a *dike*, nor do the lexicographers (Pollux 8. 38 and Harp. s.v. *prutaneia*) provide any evidence for the view. Possibly the inference can be drawn from Dem. 37 *Pant.* 41. Court fees are listed in n. 66 below. For *dikai* commenced and then dropped, see App. 2.d.

[36] *AP* 53. 2: οἱ δὲ παραλαβόντες [sc. διαιτηταί], [ἐ]ὰν μὴ δύνωνται διαλῦσαι, γιγνώσκουσι ("And [the arbitrators], upon getting a case, if they are not able to reconcile [the disputants], give a verdict"). For the jurisdiction of official arbitrators, see App. 1.a. It has become conventional to translate *diaitetes klērōtos* as "public arbitrator," which provides a neat antiphony with "private arbitrator." But both are laymen rather than magistrates, both act in public (often executing their arbitrations in temples), and both treat private cases. A more precise translation of *diaitetes klērōtos* is "officially allotted arbitrator", and of *diaitetes hairetos*, "chosen arbitrator."

[37] On the procedure by which a case that is not settled by an official arbitrator ends up in court: *AP* 53. 2.

[38] Steinwenter 1925: 123–24 considers Dem. 41. 4, [Dem.] 59. 53, and Isokr. 18. 3 (*sic*? 39), in addition to Is. 5. 17–18 and [Dem.] 48. 3 and 58, "als Material für den Vergleich im Zuge eines Gerichtshofprozesses"; he is tentative about excluding Dem. 38. 8–9 from this group. The evidence, however, is insufficient to support the claim in regard to Dem. 41. 4 and [Dem.] 59. 53. See further, App. 2.b.

[39] For the dating of the institution of official arbitration, see chapter 3 n. 27 and App. 1.e.

not incorporated in any streamlined way into Athens' system of law; it might take place at any time – i.e., before or after a suit was initiated. Both modes of arbitration – private and official – may have been more successful in ending disputes than is sometimes conceded by modern authorities.[40] Statistics from the orators are difficult to assess both because the orations obviously do not furnish us with a full record of all arbitrations (private and official) in Athens and because the evidence that is found there is likely to be skewed in favor of reporting unsuccessful hearings: all cases that were heard before an official arbitrator and which later came into court would necessarily have evolved from an abortive reconciliation and an unacceptable verdict in the preliminary hearing; and while a failed private arbitration as a preliminary to a trial would be likely to become a part of the oratorical record, a successful arbitration, agreed to and adhered to by both parties, as a final solvent of the dispute would presumably disappear from the record along with the trial that never materialized.[41] With these caveats in mind, we can nonetheless make some limited observations:

(1) The verdicts of official arbitrators appear to be important to litigants.[42] We should keep in mind that a verdict had already been given by an official arbitrator in all cases that came into court under the jurisdiction of the Forty. *AP* 53. 2 informs us that in cases that were appealed, the two jars or *ekhinoi* (one for the plaintiff, one for the defendant) which held the testimonies, challenges, and laws used during the hearings were sealed "with the verdict of the arbitrator, written on a tablet, fastened to them, and handed over to the four members of the Forty who act for the tribe of the defendant." It is conceivable (but not demonstrable) that the presiding tribal judges would have read the verdict aloud when the case was announced to the court. But even if the verdict were not read at that time, dikasts would know that one of the litigants had been condemned by the official arbitrator. Speakers allude to the hearing before the official

[40] Low evaluations of the success of the official arbitrator: Harrell 1936: 35; Gernet 1939: 408–12; E. Cohen 1973: 150, n. 116; Aicher-Hadler 1989. High evaluations: Hitzig 1899: 9–10; Hansen 1991: 179; Ruschenbusch 1989: 36–37.

[41] On the hazards of using statistics from the orators, see E. Cohen 1992: 26–40.

[42] *Pace* Gernet 1939: 411–12 and Aicher-Hadler 1989: 63–64; the latter has not taken into account that less than half (approx. 37 per cent) of the trials in private cases represented by the extant forensic speeches would have come under the jurisdiction of the Forty (see App. 1.b).

arbitrator frequently (and sometimes rather extensively) – in perhaps two-thirds of the trials belonging to the Forty that are represented by the extant private orations.[43] The particular attention given by speakers to the earlier hearings becomes explicable if we view the verdicts of official arbitrators as more than a *pro forma* activity.[44] It is a reasonable inference that such verdicts were respected and valued by dikasts;[45] that inference is bolstered by the consideration that official arbitrators were awarded crowns at the end of their year of service.[46]

(2) Official arbitrators may have been successful in many cases. Speakers report the verdicts of ten cases in the orators; in two or three, the disputants were reconciled or acquiesced to the decision.[47] While these figures cannot be used to calculate the percentage of reconciliations or accepted verdicts, nevertheless, they should give us pause before relegating the role of the official arbitrator to an almost purely bureaucratic one.

(3) Private arbitrations and reconciliations may have had a fairly high rate of success. Ancient and modern commentators often designate as a rhetorical topos the characterization of an opponent as litigious; the topos frequently includes the description of the opponent as being unwilling to enter into private arbitration or to abide by its verdict.[48] While not denying that such characterizations are topoi, we should not underestimate the valid content of the charges. The orators furnish us with many instances of private arbitrations and reconciliations which involve issues of law. While a mere handful of these

[43] This calculation is based on an examination of types of *dikai* and their presiding magistrates in the private speeches. See App. 1.b.

[44] See, e.g., the apologetic argument of Konon in Dem. 54. 26–33, and commentary of Carey and Reid 1985, ad loc.

[45] An objection to the view presented in the text: speakers will get mileage out of any available argument; a litigant who won the verdict in the official arbitration will therefore not refrain from mentioning his earlier success; conversely, the losing party will have to counter that embarrassing reminder in his speech. My response: the loser of the earlier hearing would not waste valuable time in explaining away his loss if the verdict of the official arbitrator were considered insignificant.

[46] Crowns: see Ruschenbusch 1989: 36–37. Official arbitrators were also liable to *eisangeliai* by litigants who claimed they had been wronged by them: *AP* 53. 6.

[47] See App. 1.c.

[48] For discussion of the topos and relevant citations from the orators, see n. 1 above. The best evidence for the codification of the topos in rhetorical handbooks is D. H. *Lys.* 24. The topos also demands that litigants should explain why they have refused to enter into private arbitration: e.g., [Dem.] 40. 39–40. D. Cohen 1995: 103–04 treats the topos of settlement in nugatory fashion.

instances appear never to have passed beyond the stage of a rejected offer "to refer the matter to arbitration," twenty-two negotiations materialized (apparently at least as far as the stage of offering a compromise or giving a verdict); moreover, eight or nine of the arbitrations or reconciliations appear to have been successful.[49] For such a small and haphazard sampling (i.e., considering the extant forensic speeches as a mere fraction of the entire pool of speeches presented to *dikasteria* in the fourth century), and for such a "hostile source" for information concerning successful arbitrations, this figure suggests that private arbitration may have played a significant and reliable role in the dispute settlement process.

Winning agreement to a private arbitration, however, would be no easy task. Built into the system of this most informal method of settlement is an almost paradoxical incentive for coercion, for one party to nudge the other to accept the method, agree to one or several private arbitrators, and abide by the judgment. The incentive for coercion is evident in the pre-trial activities that are portrayed by the orators in their (highly tendentious) recreations of the preliminaries to trial (one of which will be described at the end of the next section). The players in these scenes, the potential plaintiffs and defendants, neither speak nor act in any straightforward manner. Upon close inspection, however, definite patterns of pre-trial conduct emerge. Most remarkably, the orators provide numerous instances of private arbitrations initiated after a *dike* (private lawsuit) is lodged.[50] Moreover, the real or potential plaintiff appears to be the initiator of the proposal for arbitration twice as often as the accused party.[51] This evidence suggests that lodging a *dike* may have been regarded as a strategy to settle a dispute in private:[52] the

49 A list of 24 arbitrations and reconciliations appears in App. 2.a, list B. The figure of 22 negotiations given in the text above excludes those recorded in Hyp. 5. 1–5 (on the grounds that it does not refer to a legal issue) and Lys. fr. xix B–S (on the grounds that it is uncertain whether the proposed arbitration materialized). For the number of successful arbitrations, see App. 2.c.

50 The evidence (the 24 cases of private arbitrations and reconciliations) is set out in App. 2.d; 18 cases from list B supply pertinent information: in 16 of them, the offer of arbitration is made after a legal action has been initiated or after a legitimate self-help remedy has been applied.

51 See App. 2.d: 19 cases from lists B and C provide the requisite information: in 6 cases, the accused makes the offer; in 13, the accuser does.

52 Coercive and manipulative conduct is particularly evident in sequences in which agreements or arbitrations follow counter actions; two such sequences are described in chapter 2.1.

motive for bringing the suit may well have been to intimidate the adversary into accepting the verdict of a private arbitration – and possibly, too, the selection of the arbitrator(s).[53] Entering into private arbitration once a case has been initiated puts the plaintiff in a superior position both because he can use the material threat of the trial as leverage for gaining his ends and because he can use his opponent's refusal to submit to arbitration or to abide by its judgment as circumstantial character evidence against him if the case should ever come to court.

While the plaintiff appears to have had the upper hand in controlling the opportunities for out-of-court settlement, the defendant had means of his own to resist his adversary's coercive pre-trial activity.[54] Family members might intervene and pressure an accuser to drop his action; but if the latter had already gone so far as to initiate his case, he would probably retain superior bargaining power in reaching any agreement.[55] The defendant himself might seek arbitration; in such a case, the plaintiff in the original suit may have foreseen that option and welcomed its execution (if he had not orchestrated it in the first place) as the only possible means of

[53] This appears to be the case, for example, in the series of suits between Pittalakos and Hegesandros which are finally handed over to an arbitrator who is alleged to act in Hegesandros' behalf by putting off his decision (Aiskhin. 1. 63). Kallippos challenged Pasion to enter private arbitration and selected the arbitrator after he had initiated a *dike blabes* against him; he later challenged Pasion's son Apollodoros to a private arbitration with the same arbitrator after having initiated a *dike arguriou* against him [Dem.] 52. 14–15 and 30); while the arbitrator apparently gave no verdict in the dispute with Pasion, he appears to have decided against Apollodoros.

[54] Succumbing to an accuser's request for money or some other personal favor may not have been unusual. In Isokr. 18. 9–10 (a *paragraphe* in response to a *dike blabes*), the defendant claims that when Kallimakhos had initiated a suit on an earlier occasion, some of the latter's friends "visited and advised me to give up the dispute and not to allow myself to be talked about maliciously in public or to risk the loss of a great deal of money, however much confidence I had in my cause; they justified themselves by saying that courtroom decisions often turn out counter to one's expectation and that your decisions are made arbitrarily rather than justly, so that it was to my advantage to be rid of serious charges by paying a small sum rather than to risk great penalties by paying nothing. Why should I tell you the whole story? For they omitted none of the usual arguments employed in such cases. And at last, then, I was persuaded – for I will tell you the whole truth: I paid the man two hundred drakhmai." It is sometimes difficult to tell whether allegations or insinuations of bribery represent any grain of truth; it is likewise difficult to distinguish some accounts of bribery from "legitimate" settlements. Cf. Osborne 1990: 88–89; Dorjahn 1946: 27–28.

[55] Dem. 45. 4–5: Apollodoros allegedly had brought an indictment for *hubris* against Phormion, who had married his mother after the death of Apollodoros' father, Pasion; Apollodoros' mother made many tender-hearted speeches and entreaties in Phormion's behalf and Phormion himself presented himself with humility and moderation; an agreement was reached – but here the out-of-court settlement was probably necessitated by the abeyance of the courts during the 360s.

achieving an effective resolution of the dispute.[56] Defendants who did enter into private negotiations might try to prolong them as long as possible.[57] Or they might fend off the impending suit by issuing an objection to procedure, a *paragraphe.*[58] Challenges (*prokleseis*) could be made – and confounded.[59] The initiation of a cross-action or an unrelated suit could act as intimidating leverage on the plaintiff or prosecutor to drop his case or simply to sap his time and energy.[60] Other less wholesome means might be devised to stop the prosecutor or plaintiff. Meidias' brother initiated an *antidosis* (a challenge for an exchange of property) against Demosthenes only a few days before the latter was to begin the prosecution of his guardians.[61] Nikostratos apparently turned to physical violence after Apollodoros brought an indictment against his brother; Apollodoros, however, was not daunted and carried out the prosecution.[62]

The threat of legal action nonetheless stands out as the most effective and consistently used strategy for gaining a superior position in achieving an extra-judicial settlement. Gaps in the legal system allowed free play for such manipulative activity. We have already mentioned the fact that a plaintiff who dropped a *dike* suffered no penalty, except perhaps for the loss of his court fee. And while there was a law that penalized a prosecutor who dropped a *graphe* with a 1,000 drakhmai fine and partial *atimia* (disfranchisement), many *graphai* are alleged to have been dropped after an agreement was made between the disputants.[63] While most of these allegations are unprovable – especially when they are concomitant with allegations

56 Defendants request private arbitration in the following cases: Lys. fr. XIX B–S; Is. 5. 31–33; Dem. 29. 58 (cf. 27. 1); 34. 18–24; [Dem.] 40. 39 (request rejected); 59. 65–71. Only the last case ends with a successful reconciliation; see chapters 3.1.b; 5.1.c; 8.1.a; and App. 7.b.

57 E.g., [Dem.] 40. 16; Aiskhin. 1. 63–64.

58 The speaker's protest that postponement was not the motive for the present *paragraphe* brought by Phormion (Dem. 36. 2) suggests that *paragraphai* might frequently have been viewed as a tactic for delay.

59 Plaintiffs and prosecutors seem to tender challenges more often than defendants, but the evidence is difficult to assess; e.g., in [Dem.] 47. 5–10, the initiator of the challenge is in dispute; in [Dem.] 40. 9–11 (and cf. 39. 3–5) the "challenger" would have been the defendant had the case gone to court – but the challenge was allegedly formulated in accordance with the plaintiff 's wishes. See Thür 1975 and 1977.

60 For a scenario of a counter-action, see [Dem.] 47. 45–65 and for discussion of the procedure (*antigraphe*), see Harrison 2. 131–33; Lipsius 860–65; and Hitzig 1899: 21 for objections to Lipsius' view. For series of rather manipulative suits and counter-suits, see Aiskhin. 1. 58–66; [Dem.] 53. 14–17; 59. 51–54 (discussed in chapter 2.1) and 65–71.

61 Dem. 21. 78–79.

62 [Dem.] 53. 17.

63 The best evidence for penalties for dropping a public action: Lys. fr. x. 1 B–S; [Dem.] 58. 56; *Lex. Cant.* s.v. *prostimon.* Hansen 1976: 59–60 n. 23 lists instances of dropped *graphai.*

of bribery – they nevertheless iterate the pattern observed in the case of dropped *dikai*: indictment followed by private agreement.[64] The options of dispute settlement, therefore, left plenty of room for manipulation. Court actions might be threatened or in fact initiated – in cases where the accuser may have had as his goal an out-of-court settlement. In view of the penalties that were attached to losing a *graphe*, or in view of the alleged finality of a trial,[65] plaintiffs and prosecutors who were uncertain of their abilities to persuade a dikasterion of their side of the case would be well-motivated to seek private arbitration. The threat of a suit might easily persuade the defendant to accept arbitrators of his choosing (at least in part) rather than to undergo the uncertainties and publicity of a trial. For many, the opportunity to prolong their disputes, possibly indefinitely, may have been a major source of appeal (see chapter 3.1). For both parties, arbitration would avoid the costs of bringing the case and possibly losing it.[66] Additional costs would accrue if the litigant must hire a

[64] The speaker of [Dem.] 58, for example, makes the following allegations: Theokrines brought a *graphe paranomon* against Demosthenes, but the two men came to an agreement before trial; the defendant claimed illness and did not appear in court. An affidavit for postponement was filed and the case apparently forgotten; in permitting this, Theokrines "did nothing extraordinary, but the very thing that others of the same character have done" ([Dem.] 58. 43). Most speakers who insinuate that *graphai* were dropped as a result of a bribe provide no witnesses to the indictment or the bribe (see, e.g., Lys. 6. 12; Dem. 20. 145; [Dem.] 25. 47; Aiskhin. 2. 148; 3. 52).

[65] For reference to a general law that retrial was forbidden: Dem. 20. 147; 24. 54; 36. 25. Retrial, however, may have been permitted in some types of case following a successful prosecution for false witnessing committed during the original trial; see Behrend 1975; Scafuro 1994: 174 with nn. 98–102; and App. 5, add. 12 below (retrial in cases of *epikleroi*). A trial for false witnessing was itself a means of keeping a dispute active.

[66] The financial risk of litigation for the majority of potential litigants should not be minimized (pace D. Cohen 1995: 167–68). Fees: (1) In *dikai*, both plaintiff and defendant paid a fee called *prutaneia* (3 dr. if the sum claimed was between 100 and 1,000 dr., but 30 dr. if the sum claimed was over 1,000 dr.); the successful litigant would be reimbursed by his opponent: Pollux 8. 38. (2) In many *graphai*, prosecutors paid a fee called *parastasis* (Pollux 8. 39 and *AP* 59. 3) of unknown amount. (3) A fee of one dr. (likewise called *parastasis*) was paid by the plaintiff to the official arbitrator: Pollux 8. 39. (4) In inheritance hearings, claimants deposited a *parakatabole*, one-tenth the value of the estate and (5) in claims of property wrongfully confiscated by the state, the prosecutor deposited a sum (also called *parakatabole*) of one-fifth the value of the property; if in either case the claimant lost the case, he forfeited the deposit to the state; see Harrison 2. 179–83 and Lipsius 933–41 for references. Penalties: (1) For not garnering a fifth of the vote in *graphai*, the loser would have to pay a 1,000 dr. fine and suffer partial *atimia* (see n. 63). (2) Certain *dikai* which are difficult to categorize as a group (and perhaps a very small group), did carry a penalty; the losers in these cases were required to pay a fine called *epobelia* which was one-sixth the amount of the claim. The penalty is only confirmed for the *dike epitropes* (Dem. 27. 67, 69; 28. 18–19; 31. 14) and possibly the *dike khreos* ([Dem.] 35. 46; 56. 4). (3) *Epobelia* appears to be applied in *paragraphai* and *antigraphai*; see Harrison 2. 183–85; Lipsius 933–41. The *epobelia* and *parakatabole* may have encouraged many possible litigants to settle their disputes in private; indeed, many

logographos (speechwriter) to compose his speech; moreover, financial loss might be incurred by a litigant who takes time off from his daily work in order to gather witness statements and to appear at the preliminary hearing and at the trial itself.[67] Finally, private arbitration would be the most accessible and least fearful procedure for the poorer inhabitants of Attika, those who could not afford to pay *logographoi* to write a courtroom speech, for whom the stakes were higher than ten drakhmai but much less than the sums at stake in the trials we read about in the orators. Arbitration would be familiar to them: it would be the way that family disputes were often decided.

Dispute settlement options in Athens were numerous. While not every option would be available to a potential litigant in a particular instance of an alleged offense, nevertheless, he would frequently have available a number of different remedies from which to make a choice. His announced decision, however, would not always be straightforward: initiating a suit might in fact be intended as a preliminary step to out-of-court settlement. Private arbitration, though subject to manipulative strategies and often seemingly doomed to failure, would remain an attractive mode of settlement. While many Athenians may have deserved the epithet "litigious," their brand of litigiousness did not necessarily entail resolving their disputes in court.

2 ACTING BEFORE WITNESSES

The plaintiff of Isaios 3 *Pyrrhos* (a suit for false witnessing) categorizes three scenarios of witnessing as he attacks the defendant for his failure to execute properly and paradigmatically the third one:

For you all know that whenever we enter upon any course of action that we foresee might require the use of witnesses (*marturoi*), we customarily round up our closest friends and relatives as witnesses for such actions; but of unforeseen and sudden events, each of us uses any chance person. In the case of such depositions in court (*marturiai*) we must employ as witnesses those who were present – whoever they might be; but whenever anyone obtains a written deposition (*ekmarturia*) from witnesses who are ill or about to go abroad, each of us is careful to summon the most reputable citizens and those best known to us, and not in the presence of just one or two witnesses but with as many in attendance as possible do we all obtain

private arbitrations mentioned by the orators arise out of disputes that would be subject to such penalties in the dikasteria.

67 Preliminary hearings might be extensive and last over several days: e.g. [Dem.] 40. 10.

written depositions (*ekmarturiai*); we do this both in order to prevent a subsequent denial of the testimony by the person who made the out-of-court deposition (*ekmarturesas*) and to ensure that you put more credence in the many respectable men (*kaloi kagathoi*) who testify to the same effect. (19–21)

The first scenario sketched here undoubtedly occurred most frequently; its witnesses comprise all those persons – intimate friends and relatives – who are asked to attend an event of potential legal significance in order (1) to confer on it, by their presence, a special legitimacy and aura of more than everyday importance and (2) to testify subsequently, if necessary, before a court or official, to what they had observed.[68] Such witnesses (*Solemnitätszeuge*) would usually be summoned to attend three broad types of event:

(a) Acts that were important preliminaries to a court hearing: e.g., a plaintiff's summoning of the defendant to appear before a magistrate, challenges, tenderings of oaths, proceedings before a private arbitrator.

(b) Events of legal import to families: e.g., the name-day celebration of an infant on the tenth day after his birth (the *dekate*); the introduction of boys to phratry and deme; betrothal (*engue*); the wedding sacrifice (*gamelia*) offered by recent grooms to their *phrateres*; the writing of a will (although the witnesses would not usually know the contents of the document).[69]

(c) The conclusions of business agreements: e.g., contracts and financial agreements, whether composed orally or in writing would be concluded in the presence of witnesses.[70] A written agreement, moreover, would usually be deposited with a third party, who would then become an important witness for the genuineness of the document. Witnesses would also be used to testify to the transfer of the document to the third party.[71] The documents inserted in [Dem.] 35 *Lakr.* 10–14 exemplify the

[68] This roughly translates Leisi's (1908: 142) definition of what he aptly calls *Solemnitätszeuge*. Humphreys 1985c and Todd 1990 discuss the role of witnesses in court and see it as that of supporter and partisan of the litigant. *Solemnitätszeuge* in particular play this role, which Todd (27) characterizes as "a ritualised socio-political act of support." D. Cohen 1995: 110, taking topoi at face-value, offers a different and untenable generalization about witnesses, that they appear in court in order to exact personal vengeance on their enemies.

[69] On these sorts of witnesses, with references to the orators, see Leisi 1908: 143–46 and Scafuro 1994: 156–98. On witnesses to wills, see further Gneist 1845: 449–50.

[70] It seems to have been unusual to conclude transactions with bankers in the presence of witnesses; repayments of loans, however, would be witnessed; see Leisi 1908: 148; Carey and Reid 1985: 200–01; E. Cohen 1992: 117–18 and 205–06.

[71] Humphreys 1985c: 324.

procedure: the contract for a loan ending with the names of three witnesses; a deposition by the man with whom the contract was deposited; and a deposition by five men who witnessed the loan and testify to their knowledge of the depositing of the contract.[72]

The second scenario depicted by the speaker of Isaios 3 comes into play, in direct contrast with the first, when unforeseen events of legal consequence befall someone and by-standers must be called upon to act as witnesses. While such witnesses in the extant orations are most often called upon in cases of assault, they are occasionally called upon to testify to facts or events that only at a later time took on a legal significance – e.g., the witnesses who testify in [Dem.] 58 *Theokr.* 9 (and cf. 26) that a denunciation (which was later "struck out") had been posted in front of the office of the port overseers.[73] Humphreys has observed that "the speaker presents his witnesses as if they were picked at random, but actually he can have had no difficulty in calling on persons known to him."[74] When a potential litigant has the time available to choose such witnesses, he will certainly choose his friends (e.g., Lysias 1. 23–24). The relative scarcity of bystanders as witnesses in comparison with *Solemnitätszeuge* might in part be due to the character of the orations that have come down to us (i.e., the limited number of cases dealing with violence); moreover, a timely appeal to bystanders to witness a violent act may frequently have averted the commission of the crime or have sent the assailant or thief flying, leaving no trace in any court record – indeed, the scenario is common in Old and New Comedy alike.[75] Nevertheless, the circumscribed use of bystanders as witnesses, restricted to chance events – for bystanders could easily have been asked to witness the formal events of the first scenario – attests to the fact that Athenians preferred to select witnesses from amongst friends and relatives and were in the habit of doing so.

The third scenario depicted by the speaker of Isaios 3 rarely appears in the orators, but is nevertheless indicative of the same wariness toward written documentation that is evident in the widespread use of *Solemnitätszeuge.*[76] A witness who cannot appear in

[72] On the authenticity of these documents, see Drerup 1898: 317–18. For the combination of written documents and oral testimony as evidence in trials, and for the preference for the latter, see Harvey 1966: 585–635, esp. 610; Thomas 1989: 29 and *passim.*

[73] Bystanders as witnesses to assaults: e.g., Lys. 3.14; Dem. 54. 9 and 32; [Dem.] 47. 36, 38, 60, 67; 53.16.

[74] Humphreys 1985: 333.

[75] See chapter 2, nn. 106–07.

[76] The law regulating testimony from absent witnesses is paraphrased in [Dem.] 46. 7; specific

court gives his testimony, which is written down, in the presence of a set of witnesses; the latter will subsequently confirm in court that they were present when the absent witness gave his testimony and that the deposition read to the court is identical with the one given by that witness. Speakers use specific terms to distinguish the testimony of the absent witness from that of the witnesses present in court: the absent witness is said "to bear witness outside" (*ekmarturein*) when he gives his testimony outside of court and his testimony is called an *ekmarturia*; the witnesses in court are simply said "to bear witness" (*marturein*).[77] The terminological distinction, which is evident in the law paraphrased in [Dem.] 46. 7, underscores the carefulness with which Athenians secured testimony – without the aid of court-appointed officials.

The protocols by which out-of-court depositions (as in Is. 3. 20–21) and contracts (as in [Dem.] 35. 10–14) were concluded have an obvious "staged" quality. The witnesses are gathered purposefully, in the one case to witness a deposition and to testify later that it was the same as the one they originally witnessed, in the other, to witness both the contract and its deposit with a third party. Such an agenda demands direction, staging, and the assumption of specific roles: certain men must be chosen and asked to be witnesses, must be told where to meet to witness the deposition or contract – and in the latter case, must be directed to the house or building where the contract is to be deposited; the witnesses must also be advised of their future role when the deposition will be read in court or if the contract is ever disputed and so ends up in arbitration or before a dikasterion. The same staged quality is evident in all the various acts observed by *Solemnitätszeuge*, whether it be the celebration of an infant's name-day, an eighteen-year-old's deme enrolment, a young man's betrothal or *gamelia*, the summoning of an alleged criminal to court, an elderly man's sealing of a will. The assumption of the role of witness for a specific act ("step one witnessing") entails the possible resumption of that role at a later time ("step two witnessing"). Indeed, step one witnessing is designed with step two witnessing in mind: step one aims at providing the means for a

instances of such testimony (*ekmarturia*) appear in Is. 3. 18–27 and Aiskhin. 2. 19. Two documents inserted in [Dem.] 35. 20 and 34 have been interpreted as providing *ekmarturiai* (Drerup 1898: 318–20, followed by Leisi 1908: 99 and n.1).

77 The distinction is not always preserved: sometimes the *ekmarturesas* is designated a *martus* and he is said to *marturein*. For the terminology, see the passages cited in the preceding note and Leisi 1908: 99 and Schodorf 1904: 80–81.

quasi-permanent live reconstruction of the past in step two, as if a particular moment could be recaptured at any later time and recreated as a kind of tableau-image of the past in the present. The focus here on the use of the witness as a kind of human camera of the present should not blind us to the quality of the snapshot itself: its artistic composition of human conduct. Once the photographer-witness becomes a regular observer of certain aspects of daily life, then we might expect those aspects of daily life to become more formalized, more self-consciously arranged for the camera's ready and mindful eye.

The (failed) family council scene in Lysias 32 *Diog.* 11–18 illustrates the staged quality of *Solemnitätszeuge* (scenario 1a, above) and at the same time depicts the mechanics of dispute settlement (or rather, an editorialized version of those mechanics) on the *oikos*-level. Some of the background details (from Dionysios of Halikarnassos who has preserved the fragmentary speech and from the opening chapters of the speech itself) are the following: Diogeiton's daughter had married, with a dowry of 6,000 drakhmai, her father's brother, Diodotos, and had children by him. The latter, before sailing away to Asia to serve under Thrasullos in the Peloponnesian War, left Diogeiton as guardian of the children. Diodotos was killed in battle at Ephesos. Diogeiton thereupon took charge of the orphans' estate and, at least a year later, gave his daughter in marriage to another husband (Hegemon) with a dowry of five thousand drakhmai. Seven years later, when her eldest son (by Diodotos) came of age, Diogeiton claimed to have exhausted Diodotos' estate. The family council took place shortly after the announcement. It is narrated by the husband of Diogeiton's grand-daughter (son-in-law of the deceased Diodotos), the speaker of the oration. I have provided here a full translation of this section of the speech, an artistic tableau of *oikos* history:

It would be a long story to tell how much suffering there was at that time in my house. At last, their mother entreated and implored me to assemble her father and friends (*philoi*), saying that, although before this she had not been accustomed to speak in the presence of men, the weightiness of their misfortunes would compel her to reveal to us the full extent of their plight. Utterly vexed I went to Hegemon, the husband of Diogeiton's daughter, and I talked matters over with other intimate friends (*epitedeioi*), and I kept demanding that he be put to the proof concerning the disputed items. While at first Diogeiton refused his consent, at last friends (*philoi*) compelled him. When we assembled, the woman asked him what kind of man was he, to think it right to treat her children in this way, "seeing that you are the brother of their father, and my father, and their uncle and grandfather. Even if you felt no shame before men, you ought," she said, "to have feared the gods. For you received from Diodotos, when he was sailing away, five talents as a deposit. And about this matter, I am willing to stand over my children, both these and those born later, and to swear an oath wherever you yourself may name. And yet I am not so wretched, nor do I set such high value on money, that I would depart this life with a false oath upon my children and appropriate my father's estate unjustly." And she demonstrated, moreover, that he had recovered seven talents and four thousand drakhmai from bottomry loans, and she produced the records for them; for she explained that during the move he made from Kollutos to Phaidros' house, the children happened upon the account book that had been cast aside and brought it to her. And she proved that he had recovered a hundred *mnai* which had been lent at interest on land mortgages, and another two thousand drakhmai and furniture of great value; and she showed that corn came in each year from the Khersonesos. "And after this," she said, "you dared to say – although you were in possession of so much money – that their father left behind two thousand drakhmai and thirty staters – the very sum which, after it had been left to me upon his death, I handed over to you! Indeed, you thought it right to cast out your daughter's children from their own house – in threadbare garments, shoeless, without an attendant, without bedding, without cloaks, without the furniture which their father left them, and without the money which he had deposited with you. And now you are bringing up my stepmother's children amidst the comforts of wealth. While you are right to do this, nevertheless, you treat my children unjustly: you have cast them out of the house in dishonor, readily putting them on display as beggars rather than as persons of wealth. And for such deeds as these, neither do you fear the gods, nor feel shame before me – for I know the truth – nor are you mindful of your brother, but you value money ahead of all of us." Thereupon, oh dikasts, after the woman had made her shocking complaint at length, all of us who were present were so affected by Diogeiton's conduct and by his daughter's statements that when we saw the children – how they had suffered – and when we recalled their dead father – how unworthy a guardian for his estate he had left behind – and when we reflected – how difficult it was to find anyone who could be trusted with one's own affairs – oh men of the dikasterion! – no one among us was able to utter a word, but weeping no less than the sufferers we went away and departed in silence.

Now, first, witnesses to my statements, come forward.

The family council scene in Lysias 32 contains numerous elements that we find in other private arbitrations and reconciliations. The speaker, who has taken the role of advocate in behalf of Diogeiton's daughter and her children, visits family members and friends, canvasses their opinions, and rallies their support for a meeting with the adversary. The latter at first refuses to meet with them – until friends (*philoi*) pressure him to change his mind. The incentive to coerce is in operation, even though the arguments that effected it are not mentioned. Cogent inducements were certainly at hand: the council provided Diogeiton the opportunity either to clear himself and so be rid of the threat of legal action or else to learn in advance the arguments that might be used against him in the looming suit. (The speaker does not inform us whether the council took place before or after the suit was lodged.) The meeting takes place, attended by family members and friends: Hegemon, who is now married to Diogeiton's daughter, her children (by Hegemon and the deceased Diodotos), at least one son-in-law (the present speaker, husband of one of her children by Diodotos), "the friends" (*philoi*) – those who are mentioned when Diogeiton's daughter first requested the council (c. 11) and "the friends" (*philoi*) who are able to compel Diogeiton's attendance (c. 12). If the last are indeed separate from the first group mentioned, then Diogeiton may have had his own set of supporters at the meeting; if not, then "the friends" may be a group who try to represent the interests of both sides and claim to be friendly to each. Whether one group or two, then, "the friends" (*philoi*) might be seen as acting as an arbitration panel (cf. c. 2: "after many entreaties, I at first persuaded both parties to refer the dispute to the arbitration of *philoi*").[78] The speaker, however, reports only the complaints of Diogeiton's daughter and the sympathetic response of her supporters; later, he alludes to a concession made by Diogeiton (c. 20). Presumably, the defense will have its own description and witness testimonies of Diogeiton's conduct at the council. Since a suit followed (for which Lysias' speech represents the plaintiff's

[78] The wording of c. 2 of the speech is ambiguous concerning whether the family council described in cc. 12–18 was an informal interview or was actually arranged as an opportunity for reconciliation with the *philoi* acting as mediating party. Carey 1989: 209 and 219 apud cc. 2 and 20 takes the former view. But the latter view is probably correct; cf. c. 2, "after many entreaties, I at first persuaded both parties to refer the dispute to the arbitration of friends, believing it important that no others learn of these matters; but Diogeiton, after he was shown up (ἐξηλέγχετο) as being in clear possession of the disputed items, did not venture to heed any of his friends . . ." and c. 12, "and I kept demanding the man to be put to the proof about the disputed items (ἠξίουν δὲ τοῦτον εἰς ἔλεγχον ἰέναι περὶ τῶν χρημάτων); while at first he did not consent, at last he was compelled by friends." C. 2 is then a summary of the failure of the meeting depicted in detail in cc. 12–18 to bring about an acceptable reconciliation.

side in the *dike epitropes*, "private suit for the maladministration of guardianship"), it is obvious that the arbitration failed.[79]

Nevertheless, the family council served an important purpose: witnesses (*Solemnitätszeuge*) were present who would be able to testify to the meeting, to Diogeiton's appearance there, to his daughter's presentation of the evidence, to Diogeiton's apparent inflexibility.[80] It may even be the case that the meeting had been contrived with this end in view: to allow Diogeiton's daughter the opportunity to testify against her father, since she would be unable – or at least would not desire – to give evidence in court.[81] We may even go a step further and imagine that the council was rehearsed in advance; that Diogeiton's daughter and her daughter's husband planned the scene and studied their parts (and account books) carefully; that witnesses were asked to be present so as to testify later to its details in court. The family council, then, provides us with no bird's eye view of spontaneous life in the *oikos*, as if the family members had been caught unawares by a camera; rather, we see that at times – and particularly at times of conflict, family members act – or at least are represented as acting – in formalized ways. Diogeiton's daughter could or would not speak in court and so she asked that a family meeting be summoned, with all the hallmarks of an arbitration procedure; what she wanted, of course, was to win a suit against her father. She and her daughter's husband engineered the photography session from which the latter brought the edited film to court. The dispute settlement apparatus is finely manipulated. The stage is not limited to the courtroom itself; we might expand Osborne's state-

79 On the identification of the suit as a *dike epitropes*, see Lipsius 345 n. 22.

80 Todd 1993: 203 n. 2 is right to remind readers that the daughter's speech reported by the speaker is a "literary construct." While we cannot know to what extent it resembles what the woman might actually have said before the family council, we ought not to doubt that she spoke. The appearance of witness testimony directly after the depiction of her speech renders wholesale fabrication unlikely.

81 Whether there was a legal proscription against women appearing in court to confirm depositions, or whether women's absence there was a matter of social mores (esp. in force for the upper echelons of Athenian society represented by the orators) is not known for certain. Women neither appear as witnesses in the orations, confirming their own deposed statements, nor is there any explicit evidence that a woman's testimony was the subject of an *ekmarturia* (Leisi 1908: 17). Usually, a woman's *kurios* or other male relative presents her "evidence" (e.g., Lys. 31. 20–23; 32. 12–18; [Dem.] 47. 61; 55. 24–25); see Leisi 1908: 14–16 on *Fraueneid* as *Beweismittel*. Todd 1990: 26, n. 12, sums up the controversy concerning a woman's appearance as a witness for the prosecution in homicide cases; he argues that women and slaves were excluded from giving testimony altogether: "it is not that women and slaves cannot be trusted to tell the truth; but that they cannot sustain the privilege of witnessing because they do not have the capacity to be sued by *dike pseudomarturion*" (p. 28).

ment quoted in the introduction and say, "Athenian law courts were a public stage upon which private stagings could have a larger, more effective audience."

If we recognize the staged quality inherent in the protocols of step one and step two witnessing as exemplified in such orations as Lysias 32 *Diog.* and [Dem.] 35 *Lakr.*, we shall be more attuned to perceiving the same staged quality elsewhere in Attic oratory – and, as we shall see, in the conduct of characters in New Comedy.

3 ARGUING A CASE: LAW, FAIR PLAY, AND THE PRESENTATION OF CHARACTER

Every year, 6,000 male citizens over the age of thirty were selected by lot to serve on dikastic panels for the ensuing twelve months. At some time before assuming their duties, the dikasts swore an oath on the Hill of Ardettos. The oath, as reconstructed on the basis of citations in the orators by M. Fraenkel and as translated by J. F. Cronin, is as follows:

> I shall vote according to the laws and the decrees of the Athenian people and the Council of the Five Hundred, but concerning things about which there are no laws, I shall decide to the best of my judgment, neither with favor nor enmity (περὶ δ' ὧν ἂν νόμοι μὴ ὦσι γνώμηι τῆι δικαιοτάτηι καὶ οὔτε χάριτος ἕνεκ' οὔτ' ἔχθρας). I shall judge concerning those things which are at issue and shall listen impartially to both the accusation and defense. I swear these things by Zeus, by Apollo, by Demeter. May there be many blessings on me if I keep my oath, but if I break it may there be destruction on me and my family.[82]

While it is by no means certain that the oath had this form as it was first instituted or even in its developed stage, nevertheless, an oath was certainly in existence in the mid fourth century and probably contained the clause about deciding according to one's "best judgment" in the absence of laws.[83] In modern times, the oath

[82] M. Fraenkel 1878; Cronin 1936: 18. The fullest "citation" of the oath appears in Dem. 24. 149–51; most scholars, including Fraenkel, have rejected the greater part of this oath as the work of later writers and lexicographers. The clause "but concerning things about which there are no laws [I shall decide] to the best of my judgment" (περὶ δ' ὧν ἂν νόμοι μὴ ὦσι γνώμηι τῆι δικαιοτάτηι) does not appear in Dem. 24 but appears elsewhere in his corpus as part of the oath (20. 118; 23. 96; 39. 40). For a brief account of different views about the authenticity of the oath, see Bonner and Smith 1938:153–55; for more recent bibliography, consult Biscardi 1970: 222 n. 20.

[83] On the inclusion of this clause, see the preceding note. There is no direct evidence for the date of the oath's initiation. On modifications in the oath over time, see Biscardi 1970: 220.

has provoked much debate over the role played by the *gnome dikaiotate* ("the best of my judgment," in Cronin's translation above); that debate is part of a larger controversy which pits "the sovereignty of the law" against "the wilfulness of mass laymen juries." Concerning the *gnome dikaiotate*, two views have evolved.[84] According to the first, the *gnome dikaiotate* had played a triple role even before the fifth and fourth centuries: in cases (1) where the law needed interpretation, (2) where there were gaps in the law, and (3) where there were conflicts between law and fairness, in which case the *gnome dikaiotate* resolved the issue by favoring the cause of the latter.[85] For supporters of this position, the law is a kind of guideline which allows litigants to appeal to notions of fairness which extend beyond the strict letter of the law. The second view maintains to the contrary that the *gnome dikaiotate* was only a subsidiary means for establishing the law, limited to cases in which no legislation existed to cover the particular instance.[86] Whereas supporters of the first view see the legal basis of dikastic decision-making as something flexible (and sometimes as non-existent), supporters of the second view see it as rigorous adherence to the laws.[87]

Clearly we cannot know what the dikasts themselves thought the questionable clause meant; nor can we know what it meant for them "to vote in accordance with the laws and decrees."[88] A consideration of several features of Athenian law and procedure, however, shows that the second view presented above is difficult to maintain. Most importantly, the laws of the Athenians are notorious for their lack of technical definition of offenses.[89] Problems might arise, even before

[84] I am following here the account provided by Biscardi 1970: 219–20; for recent accounts of the controversy, see Meinecke 1971: 278–79; Hillgruber 1988: 105–06; and Lawless 1991: 65–80.

[85] Supporters of this position include Paoli, Hirzel, Vinogradoff, Gernet; bibliographic references cited in Biscardi 1970: 219 nn. 1–6, to which may be added Humphreys 1983b: 248; Hillgruber 1988:105–20; Todd 1993: 54–55; D. Cohen 1995.

[86] This position is taken by Wolff esp. 1962: 18; 1969: 2; Meyer-Laurin 1965; Meinecke 1971.

[87] The major point of difference between Meyer-Laurin and representatives of the opposing interpretation is the final evaluation of the way arguments of fairness functioned in the dikasteria. Thus Meyer-Laurin 1965: 2: "Rhetorische Berufungen auf Billigkeit und die häufige Argumentation *ad personam* hingegen haben . . . nichts mit juristischen Grundsätzen zu tun, nach denen die Dikasten zu entscheiden hatten. Es ist sicher nicht auszuschliessen, dass in der Rechtswirklichkeit alle möglichen Dinge und somit auch derartige Argumente mitunter emotional berücksichtigt worden sind und die Heliasten unbewusst gegen ihren Richtereid verstossen haben. Solche Umstände sind jedoch der Natur der Sache nach unwägbar und entziehen sich jeder systematischen Erforschung."

[88] Biscardi 1970: 221–25 is surely correct in seeing the two clauses as inseparable.

[89] D. Cohen 1995 rightly emphasizes (e.g., 152–53, 178, 180) the lack of legal definition of

the dikasts heard their cases. The yearly magistrates who allotted hearings to litigants had no special training in law; unlike their Roman layman counterpart (the praetor) in the last centuries of the Republic, they never developed the custom of consulting experts for advice.[90] Indeed, there existed no broadly versed body of legal experts whom Athenian magistrates might consult.[91] Yet the laws were often vague enough to render advice before trial desirable – e.g., were the circumstances alleged by prosecutor *X* appropriate for allotting a public trial for *hubris* (outrage)? Could an *eisangelia* (impeachment) for subverting the democracy be brought on the specific charge that the defendant was seducing the wives of citizens? These are questions not easily answerable on the basis of the laws as we know them. Nonetheless, non-expert Athenian magistrates regularly received requests for trial and were held accountable for their year-long stints in office; faced with the prospect of paying penalties for failure to carry out their duties, they were unlikely to have refused hearings to potential litigants for alleged offenses that fell within their jurisdictions.[92] An important component of Athenian democracy, the accountability of magistrates, will have fostered a judiciary environment receptive to a broad interpretation of offenses for allotment to trial. Legal issues, ideally reserved for judges or judicial experts in modern common and civil law systems, were thus thrown into the lap of dikastic panels in Athens.[93] Issues of law and issues of fact were inextricably mixed together for their non-expert deliberation.

Nor did presiding magistrates suddenly take juristic initiative in the course of their trials. They neither offered advice on points of

offenses (such as impiety and *hubris*): " . . . Athenian law left the task of deciding whether or not particular conduct fell within the statute solely to the mass courts of untrained lay judges assigned by lot to particular cases" (152 with n. 27). See also Todd 1996: 120–31.

90 For the *consilium* of the Roman praetor, see Kaser 1966: 31 with n. 51 for relevant modern bibliography; Behrends 1969: 192–93 for sources representing the late Republic.

91 See esp. Wolff 1964 (= 1974) who, after describing some figures (e.g., official arbitrators, *exegetai*) who may have developed a limited expertise, explores why the Greeks did not develop a systematic study of jurisprudence. The *exegetai*, it should be noted, only appear in our sources as advising potential litigants in two cases of homicide (Plato *Euthyphro*, Dem. 47. 68–70).

92 See *AP* 48. 4–5 for the procedure of *euthunai*, by which anyone might bring a charge against an official and recommend an appropriate penalty. For an example of magistrates going the extra mile to allow a case to be brought, see Lys. 13. 85–87.

93 For discussion of the treatment of questions of law and questions of fact in modern legal systems, see Stein 1984: 39–44 and 101–02; Hazard, Jr. and Taruffo 1993: 71–85; the latter two authors describe how, in American civil procedure, issues of law can be resolved before trial (p. 108).

law nor summed up the arguments of each side; after hearing speeches of plaintiff and defendant, dikasts immediately proceeded to vote.[94] Assistance in interpreting the laws and advice on the verdict were provided by the litigants themselves. Plaintiffs and defendants in private suits (*dikai*) often present a battery of laws for discussion and not simply the law that provided the remedy by which they entered court. They treat the laws – some relevant, many not – as evidence, as parts of the proof that their side of the case is the stronger one.[95] Plaintiffs not infrequently argue that the law does cover, or at least intended to cover, the particular case for which they have brought their opponents into court (and conversely, defendants argue that the law did not intend to cover the particular instance in which it is being applied to them).[96] Such arguments as these, which depend on the "spirit" rather than on "the letter" of the law – by furnishing interpretations (often by adverting to "the lawgiver's intentions"), or by attempting to adapt particular actions to ambiguous legal terminology, or by allowing arguments of fairness to compete with arguments of strict law – fall under the general rubric of arguments of *epieikeia* ("fair play," "fairness," "reasonableness").[97] An abstract juristic principle of adherence to the laws, as articulated, for example, in the dikastic oath, thus existed side by side with the practice (and in many cases, the necessity) of posing alternative interpretations of the law for dikasts to choose between. An assessment of the evidence concluding that litigants often argued in such ways and that dikasts may have formed their decisions accordingly

94 MacDowell 1978: 251–52; Humphreys 1983c: 7. A presiding magistrate might, however, take the initiative in overseeing compromises on penalties or claims; for brief consideration of the scanty evidence, see App. 2.b.

95 For the important notion of the use of laws as evidence in trials, see Todd 1993: 59–60; there, acknowledging Harrison 1955: 31, n. 42, he argues that "statute law has only persuasive and not binding force on an Athenian court."

96 Hillgruber 1988: 105–20 (with examples) argues that interpretation of laws was a general feature of forensic oratory, executed to harmonize individual interests with the laws.

97 *Epieikeia*, often translated by the ambiguous English term "equity," is perhaps better conveyed by the terms given above (*Billigkeit* in German). See Aristotle's discussion of the need for unambiguous laws in *Rhet.* 1.1354a26–b1, and his discussion of *to epieikes* at 1.1374 a26–b23, where the latter term, defined as "justice that goes beyond the written law" (τὸ παρὰ τὸν γεγραμμένον νόμον δίκαιον) is conceived of as a remedy for gaps in the written law, left unfilled by lawmakers either unintentionally (because the gap escaped their notice) or intentionally (because a law, being general, can cover most cases but not all). For a discussion of gaps in the laws, see Ruschenbusch 1957. Concerning obscurities or ambiguities in the law, see *AP* 9. 2 and 35. 2; one ambiguous clause mentioned in 35. 2 (concerning the testator's freedom to bequeath his property "except when he is insane or senile, or under the influence of a woman") was still in effect in the fourth century (cf. [Dem.] 46. 14).

(and may have understood it as their duty to do so), does not mean that the law in Athens was disregarded or was not "sovereign" (at least as an abstraction), or that litigants always misled dikasts, or that dikasts were easily swayed by their persiflage. Rather, such an assessment recognizes that litigants and dikasts operated within a system entirely different from our own, a system that made use of laws that often lacked technical precision, and that valued the common man's opinion (and bias) over the expert's ratiocination. Discussion of law and its application to individual cases was not eschewed in democratic Athens. To the contrary, such discussion appears to have been its very fiber.[98]

There is one area of the Athenian legal system where dikasts were regularly compelled to resort to the *gnome dikaiotate*; here, arguments of *epieikeia*, in the absence of law, might frequently have guided their decisions. Athenian court trials can be divided into those in which the penalty or monetary claim was fixed by law (*agones atimetoi*) and those in which the penalty or claim was assessed at trial (*agones timetoi*).[99] Such a division is not peculiar to the Athenian legal system; similar division appears in Rome and in modern systems as well. What distinguishes the Athenian one, however, is the manner in which the penalties or claims for damages were assessed. In *agones timetoi*, accuser and accused each gave two sets of speeches. After the first set, the dikasts voted on the offense, to convict or to acquit. In the second set, accuser and accused proposed opposing penalties or monetary claims – the litigants themselves thus performed the role of assessor, not according to statute, but according to the merits of their individual cases.[100] The dikasts then voted a second time, choosing the sum or

98 The dialectical tension between law and its application is nowhere more demonstrable than in the existence of *graphai paranomōn* (indictments against proposers of illegal decrees) and *graphai nomon me epitedeion theinai* (indictments against proposers of improper laws); adherence to the letter of the law might be required in theory – but that letter was not impermeable. The Athenian democracy thrived on its capacity to discuss law. It was the Thirty who "annulled the laws of Solon which provided scope for disagreement and [who annulled] the discretionary power which was left to jurors" (*AP* 35. 2, trans. Rhodes); and it was Demetrios of Phaleron who probably eliminated the two *graphai* named above (see Ruschenbusch 1957: 272–74).

99 Harrison 2. 80 supports Gernet's view that "any suit concerning a contractual obligation must have been τιμητός." For a convenient listing of (probable) *agones timetoi*, see pp. 81–82 of the same work.

100 The best evidence for penalty speeches is found in (1) *AP* 67. 5 (supplemented text) where we are told that the time allotted to speeches was extended in trials with additional penalties (imprisonment, death, exile, *atimia*, confiscation of property) or where "an assessment has to be made of what the offender should suffer or pay" (trans. Rhodes); and

penalty which seemed best according to the *gnome dikaiotate.* Rome during its formulary period of law developed special remedies for some of the types of trial that were *timetoi* in Athens; in the *bonae fidei iudicia* ("actions of good faith"), for example, a layman judge is to condemn the defendant to pay "whatever he ought to give or do in accordance with good faith (*ex fide bona*)."[101] The judge, sometimes referred to as an *arbiter* in these cases, performed both assessing and judging roles.[102] Not so in Athens. The peculiarity is obviously an essential (and not necessarily primitive) ingredient of Athenian democratic ideology: where priority is placed upon the availability of a large panel of dikasts, the notion of a regular dikastic conference dedicated to the formulation of penalties or claims in individual cases cannot be entertained.[103]

While no speeches survive from the second set in which the litigants argue for a penalty or a monetary claim, some speakers anticipate their proposals in the first round of speeches.[104] Here we can glimpse a wide spectrum of cases in which arguments of *epieikeia*

(2) *AP* 69. 2 which provides a brief description of procedure for the second vote; see Rhodes 1981 and MacDowell 1985 on the timing of penalty speeches. For the possibility of compromise between the litigants at this point in the trial, see App. 2.b.

[101] These *iudicia*, together with *actiones in bonum et aequum conceptae* ("actions framed on considerations of what is right and fair," are discussed in chapter 3.2; they are more extensive and developed than Athenian remedies. The formula cited above appears in the *actio iniuriarum* (*EP* 399). Stein 1984: 42 calls attention to the suitability of the Roman *iudices* (who are laymen rather than professionals) for deciding cases such as these which involve "a moral rather than a legal judgment on conduct. They call not for technical knowledge exactly applied but for common sense about everyday matters." Pringsheim 1961 (= 1932) examines the possibility of the influence of Greek assessment charges on Roman evaluative clauses (see esp. pp. 179–81).

[102] For the difficulties that a novice (layman) *iudex* might experience, see Aul. Gel. *N.A.* 14. 2. 1–26, where the author recounts his own experience.

[103] Aristotle thought the law should be written so clearly and unambiguously that there would never be any need for conference; hence his criticism of Hippodamos' ideal constitution in *Pol.* 2. 1268b 4–11: "And furthermore, even the law about rendering verdicts is a bad one, i.e., that [dikasts] should judge with qualifications, even when the suit has been entered in simple terms, and [in effect] that the dikast should be a *diaitetes.* But while this is permissible when there is an arbitration and a number of men [acting as *diaitetai*] (for they deliberate with one another about the verdict), it is not [permissible] in the dikasteria, but rather do many lawgivers provide for the very opposite so that the dikasts may not communicate with one another." Boegehold 1995: 39 points out that dikasts serving on large panels in Athens would have time to discuss matters amongst themselves during the time they waited to cast their vote individually into the appropriate urn.

[104] The only extant "penalty speech" is the fictive one in Plato's *Apology. Rhet. pros Alex.* 4. 1427 a1 ff. gives separate instructions for accuser and accused concerning arguments to use in penalty speeches. For examples of penalty arguments in the course of the first set of speeches, see Dover 1974: 292–95 (who, however, does not separate *agones timetoi* from *atimetoi*) and n. 107 below. Deinarkhos included the penalty in his written charge (*graphe*) against Proxenos in a case of damages (fr. XLII. 1 B–S).

might be applied. At one end, we might place guardianship cases in which the plaintiffs assess the amount of money or property which the allegedly wayward guardians owe their former wards. In the course of his first speech against Aphobos, Demosthenes makes a number of "fair play" adjustments in favor of his former guardians, sometimes decreasing the amount of interest owed to him on various sums, at other times increasing the amounts to be deducted as his guardians' legitimate expenses; similar, ostensibly straightforward adjustments are made by the speaker of Lys. 32 *Diogeiton*, another guardianship case.[105] At the other end of the spectrum, we might place cases in which life or continued residence in Athens might be at stake. In cases of *hubris*, for example, the court is to decide "whatever seems right for the convicted man to suffer or pay" (ὅτου ἂν δοκῆι ἄξιος εἶναι παθεῖν ἢ ἀποτεῖσαι.)[106] The penalty is a common one and, once again, prosecutor and defendant in such cases will make their own proposals for dikasts to choose between. If death or exile was proposed by the prosecutor, we might well expect his speech to be filled with depictions of the lawgiver's intentions and attacks upon the defendant's character; the latter's speech might be filled with emotional appeals and extra-judicial considerations (e.g., his record of public service).[107] No laws set down guidelines for litigants to follow in proposing penalties; none were at hand to direct dikasts in their decisions. In the area of deciding between proposed penalties in cases such as *hubris*, or of deciding between competing monetary claims in cases such as guardianship, dikasts regularly (possibly daily) adverted to "the best of their judgment." Arguments of fair play will have frequently guided their decisions.

How do such arguments fare when litigants address the offense rather than the penalty – when plaintiffs argue that the defendant is guilty and the defendant argues his innocence? To be sure, only a handful of the extant forensic orations rest entirely or almost entirely on arguments that are not strictly related to the law that is allegedly broken;[108] yet numerous speeches rely on a combination of arguments of law with arguments of fairness; and numerous other speeches argue their evidence by appeals to probability which often

[105] Dem. 27. 17, 23, 35–37; cf. also cc. 59–61; Lys. 32. 28.

[106] *Lex apud* Dem. 21. 47; see chapter 5 n. 50.

[107] For arguments in favor of a death penalty, see Lykourg. 1 (an impeachment for treason), 27, 45, 78, 91, 121, 131, 150. For discussion of the range of arguments that are used to support a mitigated or more severe penalty, see Saunders 1991: 104–22.

[108] E.g., Lys. 14 and 15; Dem. 39; Lykourg. 1; Hyp. 5; Is. 1.

owe more to the representation of character and to a common consensus of what is fair and just in human conduct than to any commitment to articulate the technicalities of law. While it is certainly true, then, that infringements of law are at issue in the courtrooms of Athens, it is equally true that *logographoi* (speech-writers) – especially in private suits – did not always hone their skills in order to present and explain the details of the law clearly for the mass consumption of large dikasteria. *Logographoi* may have taken a rather broad view of their task; Humphreys has argued that it was:

> in many cases at least, not to present a sophisticated argument about the interpretation of the law but to portray the litigant and the background to the case in such a way that the jury will feel that, in the circumstances, he has the right on his side. The jurors are invited to behave as if they were members of the local community, deciding on the fairest solution for each particular case, rather than specialists applying written law to cases . . . , and the speech-writer, like a playwright or a post-classical novelist, constructs a social milieu in which the audience can believe.[109]

By re-creating his "social milieu," the *logographos* strives to let the dikasts become familiar with the character (*ethos*) of the litigant and the special circumstances of the alleged offense. Humphreys' description suggests that our readings of orations suffer from one of the same deficiencies we have begun to correct in our readings of ancient drama: we forget that the (original) orations were, in a very real sense, performance texts, punctuated with entrances and exits, marked for the display of laws and contracts, witnesses and suppliants, and not infrequently, the speaker's own theatrical gesture.[110]

[109] Humphreys 1983b: 248, with acknowledgement made to Biscardi 1970; Humphreys' views are expanded in her 1985 article on witnesses in Athens. The particular view quoted in the text might more appropriately (as a generalization with exceptions) be limited to private suits. Types of argument, the deployment of topoi, and the use of witnesses differ, depending on whether a speech is part of a private lawsuit or public prosecution, and whether it is spoken by plaintiff, prosecutor, *sunegoros*, or defendant (see Rubinstein forthcoming). Todd 1990: 31–32, with charts on p. 39, notes the much greater frequency of witnesses in private procedures.

[110] On gestures as a feature of Greek and Roman rhetorical delivery, see Graf 1992; Katsouris 1989 and Boegehold's (1991) review; Hall 1995: 39–52. Boegehold 1986 explores the possibility that certain "non-sentences" in literary texts "can be explained as requiring merely an appropriate gesture on the part of the reader." Bers 1985: 1–15 treats another aspect of performance (or response to performance) – "dikastic *thorubos*" – the shouting that erupted during trials.

An anecdote reported in Dem. fr. XIII B–S depicts Demosthenes' theatricality: the orator, having perceived in the course of a defense that the dikasts were growing impatient, interrupted with a fable; when he reached the climax of the tale (two men come to court in a dispute over the shadow of a rented ass), he left the *bema*; when the dikasts then demanded to know the outcome of the trial, he returned to the *bema* and reproached them

The spectacle of witnesses in the course of an oration – the brothers, aged fathers and uncles, in-laws, *phrateres*, and friends so often called to the *bema* – might have spoken far more persuasively than the written depositions they confirmed.[111]

Clearly arguments on points of law, at least in private suits, were not considered sufficient to convince a dikasterion of the litigant's position. Let us take as an example a defense against a charge of premeditated wounding (*traumatos ek pronoias*), Lysias 3 *Simon*. The unnamed speaker sets out to prove that, while a fight did take place four years ago between himself and the plaintiff over rival claims for the affections of a Plataean youth, he neither started the fight nor had any premeditated intention of engaging in it.[112] All that would appear necessary to prove the defendant's case is the presentation of bystanders' testimony, to the effect that Simon (the plaintiff in the case) was not wounded in the way he said he was. The use of bystanders as witnesses, however, is a precarious prop in the Athenian court: in the first place, they were easy bait for allegations of bribery; secondly, they did not carry the same measure of respectability as a bevy of relatives who might rush to the support of their mistreated brother, cousin, or father-in-law.[113] Presumably, too, the plaintiff in Lysias 3 had provided his own set of witnesses. How then are the dikasts to decide between the witnesses for the defense and those for the prosecution? Faced with the problem of the weak evidence of his witnesses, the speaker of Lysias 3 produces an argument of probability (*eikos*) that is closely associated with the depiction of character (*ethopoiia*). *Eikos* arguments, popularized by the sophists in the late fifth century and of great longevity thereafter, can be intimately associated with *ethos*: a defendant can argue, by

for showing more concern for an ass's shadow than for the life of the man who was on trial.

[111] For a similar view, see Todd 1990. The display of witnesses as objects of evidence (rather than as personal supporters) was on occasion quite sensational: Isokr. 18. 52–54: the slave woman whom the plaintiff has alleged to be dead; [Dem.] 25. 60–62: the man whose nose Aristogeiton is alleged to have bitten off; Dem. 37. 44: the feeble slave who had been demanded for torture. Occasionally, the spectacle of defendants may have been even more sensational: Hyp. fr. LX *Phrynes* (Jensen) 178: Hypereides secured the acquittal of Phrune on a capital charge by displaying her "topless." For speculation on what Apollodoros meant when he said, "And when you have seen her face (*opsis*), reflect only on this, that she – Neaira! – has done what I have recounted," see Dover 1968a: 35–36.

[112] On the slave status of the Plataean youth, which is disputed, see Carey 1989: 87 and bibliography cited in Gagarin 1989: 59 n. 4. D. Cohen 1995: 131–35 treats the same speech in his discussion of cases involving assaults and wounding.

[113] Humphreys 1985c: 331–33.

first creating a portrait of his character, that it is entirely improbable that a man such as he could have committed the crime that has been imputed to him.[114] Aristotle in the *Rhetorike* describes this kind of argument as a means to assail atechnic proofs – i.e., proofs that rely on laws, witnesses, contracts, torture, and oaths:

When it comes to the confirmations of testimony in the case of a man who has no witnesses, [he can argue] that [the dikasts] must decide on the basis of probabilities, and that this is the meaning of "[making a decision] in accordance with the best judgment" (*to gnomei tei aristei*), and that probabilities cannot deceive upon payment of a sum of money, and that probabilities are not convicted of giving false testimony . . . Evidence sometimes concerns the litigant himself, sometimes his opponent, and sometimes it concerns the fact itself, sometimes character, so that it is never possible to be at a loss for useful evidence. For if there is no evidence about the fact – neither in confirmation of the litigant's story nor in refutation of his opponent's – still there will be evidence about character – either to support the fairness (*epieikeia*) of the one litigant or the foulness (*phaulotes*) of his opponent. (1.15.1376 a17–29)[115]

This is precisely the kind of argument that the speaker of Lysias 3 produces as he provides character portrayals of both himself and Simon – a proof, as it were, that it is not at all probable to suppose that he rather than Simon started the fight. The speaker throughout presents himself as a man who feels shame, who is in a state of great vexation upon being compelled to make public statements about his private life, especially since feelings of shame have, until now, caused him to conceal Simon's abuses rather than to air them abroad (3). He describes an earlier occasion when he was dining at home with

[114] Cf. Arist. *Rhet.* 2.19.1392b15–33, where he discusses the topic of "whether a thing has happened or not," which calls forth arguments of probability. Interestingly, he only conjoins these with arguments of *ethos* coincidentally.

[115] Cf. the opening of [Dem.] 52: "There is nothing more trying, Athenian dikasts, than when a man of repute and ability in speaking is bold at lying and well-furnished with witnesses. For the defendant is then no longer obliged to speak only about the facts of the case, but also about the *persona* of the speaker, to show that it is not reasonable (*eikos*) to believe him on account of his reputation." See also Dem. 54. 28–29, 37, 39–40. For examples of different arguments of probability to be used in cases of assault, see Arist. *Rhet.* 2.1402 a18–20 (Korax).

The sorry plight of defendants who lacked witnesses is highlighted by Sokrates' conundrum, posed to Strepsiades, in *Clouds* (Dover 1968b): ὅπως ἀποστρέψαις ἂν ἀντιδικῶν δίκην, / μέλλων ὀφλήσειν, μὴ παρόντων μαρτύρων; (776–77: "How would you, as defendant, rebut the case in a situation where you were sure to lose if no witnesses were present?") Strepsiades' reply shows the peril of the hypothetical situation: εἰ πρόσθεν ἔτι μιᾶς ἐνεστώσης δίκης / πρὶν τὴν ἐμὴν καλεῖσθ' ἀπαγξαίμην τρέχων. (779–80: "Supposing that one case was still to be heard before you called mine, I would run off and hang myself.")

the Plataean boy: a drunken Simon had broken into the house, entered the women's quarters, called him out, and tried to strike him; when the speaker resisted, Simon pelted him and a companion with stones and hit the latter (6–8). Thereupon the speaker decided to take the boy away and reside with him abroad; but when they returned to Athens, he was attacked by Simon once again (9–20). After this narration of "facts" in which the speaker has amply demonstrated his feelings of shame and those of his female kin and the shameless conduct of Simon, he presents an extended argument of probability (cc. 28–39) based upon the character portraits he has built up so far. In c. 32 he argues:

> So who among you can believe that I, who before this sailed away from the city with the youth in order to avoid a fight with Simon, upon my return took the boy to Simon's house, where I most of all would experience abuse? And who can believe that while I "plotted" against him, yet I arrived so ill-prepared, without friends or servants or any other man – except for this boy who, though unable to render aid, was capable of giving information under torture if I committed any crime? Who then can believe that I had sunk to such a depth of stupidity that when I "plotted" against Simon I did not keep a look-out for where I might catch him alone, by night or by day, but that I instead went immediately where I would be seen by the greatest crowd – as if I were contriving a premeditated act against myself – that I might suffer the greatest outrage at the hands of my foes? (32–34)

The *eikos* argument has become intimately associated with character portrayal: the speaker is simply not the sort of man who would ever pick a fight with anyone; thin-skinned and full of shame, he would rather leave the city than have a show-down with a proven lout like Simon. Not only, however, has the speaker carefully drawn his own character, Simon's character is also sharply contoured: such a scoundrel has he become, that even had the speaker ambushed him in the dead of night, the dikasts would have to commend him for having taken the initiative. Of course the speaker makes no such explicit statement,[116] but the vilification of Simon functions to turn the dikasts' feelings against him, to view him as an unjust man. The artful composition of character depends on its accurate calculation of the dikasts' sentiments about what is fair and just, a calculation of their shared social values and aversions.

[116] The speaker of Lys. 1 is more shameless: "I, gentlemen, thought my conduct would be just, if I were to seize, by any means whatsoever, the scoundrel who corrupted my wife" (37).

The most commonly adduced speech based on extensive argumentation of *epieikeia* is Hypereides 5 *Athenogenes.*[117] Yet the winning point in that oration is surely the creation of the speaker's *ethos*. On what charge the plaintiff (who speaks the case) has sued the defendant is not known for certain; a suit for damages (*dike blabes*) is the likeliest conjecture.[118] The plaintiff, a man of no trade but rather a farmer who cultivated his father's land (26), paints himself as the victim of a fraud perpetrated by Athenogenes who appears triply bad: "a speech-writer and low sort, and worst of all, an Egyptian" (ἄνθρωπον λογογράφον τε καὶ ἀγοραῖον, τὸ δὲ μέγιστον, Αἰγύπτιον, 3). At first the plaintiff had merely been cajoled by Athenogenes' accomplice, the bawd Antigone (formerly a celebrated courtesan) to pay forty *mnai* to purchase the freedom not only of the slave boy of whom he was enamored, but also of his brother and father, Midas, who managed a perfume store (4); next, Athenogenes induced him to purchase the men as slaves and to free them himself and to buy, at no extra cost, the perfumery's supplies (5); Athenogenes' only condition for the bargain was that the speaker become liable for the slaves' debts – which, he assured him, were trifling sums and would be amply recovered from the stocks in the shop (7); the speaker agreed to the proposal, admits to listening to the contract being read aloud to him – but strongly qualifies that he was in haste to complete the agreement (8). In three months' time, when all the debts had been declared, it turned out that he owed five talents. The speaker then rounded up relatives and friends for a serious reading of the contract: inaeed, it revealed that some small sums were owed to the two creditors who were specifically named, but the largest debts had not been specified – except for one possible allusion to them, which ran, "by way of appendage, 'and if Midas owes anything to any other person'" (9–10). Finding himself indebted beyond his means in, as he alleges, so unjust a way, the speaker decided to sue Athenogenes.

By the time the speaker has finished his narration of the "facts," the audience is undoubtedly convinced, if of nothing else, at least of the speaker's naïveté – his innocence in the business ways of the

117 While scholars disagree on the juridical quality of this argument, they generally agree that it is an argument based on analogy, designed to fill a gap in the law: see Lipsius 685; Meyer-Laurin 1965: 15–19 and 35; Biscardi 1970: 232; Meinecke 1971: 347–52; Hillgruber 1988: 111–12.

118 For a discussion of some issues of the disputed contract, see Pringsheim 1950: 191–92.

world, his honesty – after all, the "farmer's son" (26) admits that the contract had been read aloud to him but that he simply had not given it much attention. There had been a contract; he had agreed to it. How then will he move the dikasts to overturn it? He will present an argument of fairness, an argument that looks to the spirit rather than to the letter of the law. Hypereides' ingenuity continues to shine; if the dikasts thought the speaker the quintessence of naïveté before, they will surely think him its divine embodiment as he proceeds: he will argue that only just agreements are valid, and he will present a number of laws to prove it:

> For you [Athenogenes] have put me in such utter fear lest I be undone by you and your cleverness, that I have spent my days and nights scrutinizing and studying the laws, considering everything else as secondary to this pursuit. (13)

Claims of autodidactism and prolonged study of the law are of course topoi in the orators;[119] but here the claim is injected with fresh vitality as the speaker proceeds to list the laws that he has discovered, one after the other, expanding his argument as he proceeds (14–22). None of the laws cited by the speaker precisely fits his case; but in each instance, he looks to the spirit or intent of the law rather than its letter: had the lawgiver directed his attention to this particular case, he surely would have invalidated Athenogenes' contract.

Aristotle includes a discussion of this type of argument in the same chapter of the *Rhetorike* in which he outlines strategies for a litigant who lacks substantial witness testimony. He suggests that the validity of a contract can be assailed in a number of ways:

> And [these arguments are appropriate, that] while it is not possible to overturn fairness (*to dikaion*) either by deceit or by compulsion – for fairness is rooted in nature – yet contracts are made by men who have been deceived and who act under compulsion. Moreover, we must consider whether the contract opposes any written or universal laws – and in the case of written laws, whether the contract opposes laws of our own land or those of foreigners . . . (1. 15. 1376 b21–26)

Two of Aristotle's recommendations have been fulfilled in Hypereides' oration. Already in the opening narrative, the speaker had suggested that he had acted under the compulsion of love and the

[119] E.g., Dem. 54. 17–18; [Dem.] 58. 19 (the plaintiff's filial loyalty adds a flavor of credibility); [Dem.] 59. 15. Cf. Lys. 19. 45, where the young defendant claims to have learned his examples of analogous financial *peripeteiai* from his father and older men.

deceiving influence of a woman when he entered into the arrangements for the sale ("thus does love, I suppose, utterly derange a man's natural capacities, when it takes a woman as its accomplice": οὕτως, ὡς ἔοικεν, ἐξίστησιν [ἀνθρώπου] φύσιν ἔρως, προσλαβὼν γυναι[κὸς συνεργ]ίαν 2). Then, in the lengthy argument which takes up at least the second half of the extant speech, he had pointed to numerous written laws according to which his contract (by analogy) appears to be invalid. Isolated in this way, the arguments have the look of a "handbook speech" – but the oration is much more than that. The relentless energy of the young man who has spent his nights and days studying the law and who now presents the fruits of his labor in the cornucopia of analogous statutes to support his claim contrasts sharply with the young man who had once been carried away by love to such a degree that he had been duped by a bawd and caught out as inattentive to the fine print of a contract. How he has changed! Surely he has learned the lesson of youthful folly; must he pay for it, too? The speaker presents himself as a man who is now only interested in the just thing, a man to be sympathized with. The argument of fair play has become the argument of a fair-minded fellow.[120]

These arguments, both the *eikos*/ethopoiic argument of Lysias 3 *Simon* and the argument of fair play in Hypereides 5 *Athenogenes*, rely upon their authors' consensus of what the dikasts would view as just conduct. And what the dikasts would view as just conduct appears to be based on such intangibles as their view of what the laws mean in particular instances, sentiments arising out of kinship ties, and shared feelings about what is shameful and what is honorable.[121] The Athenian dikasts who listened to Lysias 3 would

[120] Among Demosthenes' speeches, only 54 and 55 have a similar ethical patina. For the former, see Carey and Reid 1985: 73–74 who comment: "The success of the characterization of Ariston in this speech may be judged from the fact that without ever offering a shred of solid evidence to his own good character Ariston emerges as an excellent young man" (74). As for Dem. 55, see Schaefer's (1858: 3. 2, 256–57) fine appreciation of Demosthenes' Lysianic skill. Lysias' own achievement in this realm is neatly summed up by Dionysios of Halikarnassos as he compares it with Isaios', and casts, over the centuries, a nettling barb at skeptical Wysian readers of the younger speechwriter: "Thus even a mendacious client of Lysias might be believed, whereas Isaios' client, even if he speaks the truth, will not be heard without suspicion" (*Isaios* 16).

[121] This triad is articulated by the speaker of Is. 1. 39 as he hypothesizes a situation in which his maternal uncle dies and leaves behind daughters; he and his brother(s) would then be compelled to support their grandfather and to marry the daughters or to provide dowries and find other husbands for them, "and kinship, the laws and your sensibility regarding shame would compel us to act thus, or else to become liable to the greatest penalties and

be attentive to the speaker's description of Simon's shameless conduct as exemplified, for instance, by his intrusion into the kinswomen's quarters (6–7, 23), and they would be attentive, too, to the speaker's avowals of shame for making his private life public.[122] The dikasts who listened to Athenogenes' accuser might be swayed by empathy or humor. Those who had sons of their own and who may have tried to keep them out in the country away from the allurements of city life might have reflected upon their possible reactions had their sons been caught in the same predicament. Others – probably the majority – who had neither farms in the country nor sons with forty *mnai* in their wallets, may have sat back and enjoyed the comedy. Hypereides apparently counted on their good will – or at least a token acknowledgement in return for the show.

The creation of *ethos* is the staging of a recognizable *persona*. And integral to the creation of a *persona* is the homogeneity of the audience's expected response. Presumably, the live performances of the ashamed speaker of Lysias 3 and of the fair-minded fellow of Hypereides 5 would not go unappreciated on the forensic stage. While undoubtedly such low-key masterpieces as the two orations under discussion here were not the daily fare of Athenian dikasts, surely the occasional stand-out would become celebrated – a subject for lively discussion if not outright mimicry in anyone's household. Aiskhines' less subtle theatrical triumphs, so evident, for example, in his seemingly ad hoc depictions of scandalous hypothetical trials with ready-made truncated speeches for not so imaginary prosecutors, would quickly find imitators, even among those infinitely less skilled.[123] Phaidros' attempt to memorize Lysias' epideiktic speech of a non-lover's attempt to persuade a youth to become his partner is probably not an isolated case of mimicry.[124] Nor should we expect that Aristotle himself as a first-hand witness had listened to – or bought – all the speeches he refers to in his rhetorical works. Surely he must have heard some of them, at least, from men who had

extreme censure" (καὶ ταῦθ' ἡμᾶς καὶ ἡ συγγένεια καὶ οἱ νόμοι καὶ ἡ παρ' ὑμῶν αἰσχύνη ποιεῖν ἠνάγκαζεν ἄν, ἢ ταῖς μεγίσταις ζημίαις καὶ τοῖς ἐσχάτοις ὀνείδεσι περιπεσεῖν).

122 Intruding into kinswomen's quarters, without doubt a heinous transgression, appears rather frequently in the orators, often as a topos that ensures vilification: cf. Lys. 12. 19; fr. CXIX 2.5 B–S; Dem. 21. 79; 37. 45–46; [Dem.] 47. 53 and 60.

123 See, e.g., Aiskhin. 1. 162–64.

124 Plato *Phaidros* 230e6–234c5. Note the resemblance between the two pairs: the non-lover (or at least non-violent lover) and the unruly lover of the epideiktic speech and the defendant and plaintiff (Simon) in Lys. 3.

served as dikasts, or even from second- and third-hand reporters. It is not difficult to imagine the effects of mimicry on less exalted men: the livelier common man would surely ham it up now and then, assuming the mask of plaintiff in his dealings with friends and associates; the livelier serious man would imitate courtroom arguments as he plotted out his rationale for some course of action that might have legal consequences in the future – even if he had never attended the schools of *rhetores* to learn how to construct his arguments.[125]

The infiltration of the formality of courtroom conduct into the daily activities of the inhabitants of Athens is illustrated by an episode in Xenophon's *Oikonomikos*. Iskhomakhos, having explained to Sokrates how he has arranged his life to be prosperous, honorable, and healthy, confesses that he is nonetheless beset by sykophants; he must practice defending himself (*apologeisthai*) and accusing others (*kategorein*) all the time – by wronging no one and treating many well, and by observing the unjust acts of others (11. 21–22). Asked by Sokrates whether he practiced the art of expounding (*hermeneuein*) these matters as well, he replies:

> "There is not a moment, Sokrates, . . . when I'm not practicing speaking. For when I hear one of the household slaves making an accusation or defense, I try to refute him or else I praise or blame someone before his friends, or I reconcile close friends and try to teach them that it is in their interest to be friends rather than enemies. I assist others in censuring a soldier, for instance, at a hearing – or I take turns in defending a man who is unjustly accused, or in accusing a man who is unjustly honored. Often we sit in council and recommend whatever course of action pleases us and censure whatever does not. Many times already, Sokrates, have I been singled out and condemned to suffer punishment and pay damages."
> "By whom, Iskhomakhos?" I asked. "I did not know this!"
> "By my wife," he answered (11. 23–25).

Courtroom arguments – whether in mimicry or in earnest – are the arguments used by *politai* (citizens) in the whole spectrum of their daily lives – in their own *oikoi* and in the agora, with their slaves, wives, neighbors, friends, fellow demesmen and councillors.[126] What

[125] Speakers sometimes claim that they have acted courageously and generously in the past in order to present this conduct as a defense if ever they are involved in an unjust prosecution: Lys. 16. 17; 20. 33–34; 25. 12–13; cf. Xen. *Oik.* 11. 21–22, cited in the text above. Conversely, the speaker of Isokr. 21. 17 claims that it is a commonplace that "all men whenever they set about committing a crime, at the same time are thinking up their defense."

[126] Cf. Alexis fr. 264 K–A: married men must undergo daily *euthunai* (official auditings) by their wives.

courtroom trials uniquely provided, however, was a public paradigm of formality and adversarial role-playing.[127] Part of the humor of the idiosyncratic arbitration scene in Menander's *Epitrepontes* may very well lie in the fact that it is two slaves who have taken on the roles of plaintiff and defendant with long expansive arguments of fair play – a gentle satire, perhaps, of the Athenian habit of creating and formalizing *personae* when entering the stage of dispute settlement.[128]

The creation of *ethos* in combination with arguments of probability and fair play is frequently found in New Comedy. Like the arguments of *logographoi*, they are often created for the situation, i.e., with a view to achieving an end, to providing a defense or justification, to winning an argument, to getting the better of someone else. Spectators attending performances of New Comedy, many of whom will have served as dikasts, will have been better attuned to the play-acting of the courtroom-on-stage than modern readers who frequently envision the creation of *ethos* without beholding its forensic staginess.

CONCLUSIONS

The manipulation of dispute settlement options, the avid recruitment of witnesses for the future, the use of arguments that demand the presentation of a credible *persona* – a focus on these features of the Athenian dispute settlement process demonstrates an interesting aspect of the normal intercourse of *polis* inhabitants: staginess. By this I mean that much of what is said and done in public – and in the *oikos* – is premeditated, an artifice of display rather than a spontaneous reflexion of present circumstances. Staginess is in evidence in the manipulation of settlement options: the lodging of a suit may have as its goal not a courtroom trial but a private settlement; the act might be understood as a stylized gesture to those who know the code, a means of communicating something other than its literal message. Staginess is likewise in evidence when witnesses are

[127] The popularity of forensic speeches is attested by the creation of a genre of "fictitious trial speeches"; the best known are the numerous defenses (and accusations) of Sokrates that began appearing in the beginning of the fourth century; Isokrates' *Antidosis*, a defense composed after he lost his case in court, belongs to the same genre.

[128] Ferguson 1911: 41 n. 2 seems to have missed the point when he adduces this scene to typify the impertinence of slaves in the late fourth century: "Two slaves might stop a citizen and solicit, almost as a right, his decision in a matter of dispute between them." See chapter 4. 1. a.

gathered for a will, an adoption, a wedding, a deme or phratry registration, a business contract. The scene is set for the transaction – with a view to questions of the legitimacy of that transaction in the future. Private arbitrations are stagings, too – as, of course, the presentation of cases in court are. The outstanding difference is the intimacy of the performance; in a private arbitration, the past is presented, staged, as it were, among a smaller group of friends and acquaintances. Discourse is formalized – i.e., not necessarily spoken "from the heart," but with an eye to the camera of witnesses who might bring the edited film to court at some later date. Arguments of probability and fair play are often constructed on the basis of a person's past conduct – but there can be different constructions; the particular construction one chooses to use will often suit one's self-interested ends for the present and future and will above all be aimed at the presentation of a particular staged *persona*. What I have termed "staginess," then, is the notion that conduct is designed to achieve a certain effect, even among close friends and kin, especially at critical moments when the apparatus of dispute settlement is called into operation.

The formalization of dispute settlement is evident in numerous distinctive scenarios that appear both in the speeches of Attic orators and in the dramas of New Comedy. In the following chapters of this study, I shall identify some of these scenarios. By locating and identifying them in both genres, we shall begin to envision the web of forensic discourse that unites them, the extension of the courtroom's stage to the proscenium of the *oikos*.

CHAPTER 2

Initiating justice: threat, summons, and arrest

Characters in New Comedy often engage in conduct that appears to be a prelude to a courtroom trial or that is a substitute for its formal apparatus: they warn friends of potentially indictable behavior and recommend legal action when their interests are infringed; they threaten their enemies with lawsuits and self-help remedies; they issue summonses and make arrests. Yet for all this pre-trial activity, only one character appears on stage who has clearly undergone a prosecution during the course of the play, and only one character actually suffers a self-help punishment endorsed by law. What, then, are we to make of all the summonses, arrests, and threats of legal action that do not end up in court? Or of the threats of self-help remedies that are not carried out?

It is the specific argument of this chapter that such activities are often strategies – pervasive in fourth-century Athens and so reflected in New Comedy – designed to coerce opponents to accept out-of-court settlements. In the last chapter, we noted how frequently the orators give reports of plaintiffs who try to induce their opponents to enter into private arbitration after a suit has been lodged. The pattern harmonized well with the Athenian system of justice: a plaintiff who dropped a *dike* would not be penalized. Threatening court action while intending to settle in private also provides, as we shall see, ready-made scripts: it ensures that certain roles will be played – plaintiff and defendant, accuser and accused – and it delineates, even as it attempts to control, the avenues of settlement. The argument presented here is part of the larger argument of this book: that dispute settlement is central to New Comedy (as it is to Attic life) and that staginess is an essential ingredient.

The specific argument about the use of threats in New Comedy to coerce private agreements requires some preliminary spadework. In the first place, my argument is based upon a view of the practical functioning of the system of justice in Athens: that intimidation and manipulative behavior was indeed characteristic of *polis* inhabitants in their pre-trial interactions. I therefore begin this chapter by augmenting the evidence presented in the last chapter (1). My next task is to demonstrate that similar conduct is reflected in New Comedy. Threats of legal action and of self-help measures must therefore be identified. Toward this end, I focus narrowly on the procedures of initiating court action in Athens and Rome and I point out similarities and differences with a view to identifying them in both Greek and Roman plays (2). The raw material for this discussion appears in Appendix 5, a catalogue of the summonses, arrests, threats, warnings, and recommendations of these procedures and self-help remedies in New Comedy. In section 3 of this chapter, I provide a brief general analysis of the catalogue that demonstrates the prevalence of pre-trial conduct ending in private agreements. In the final section (4), I focus upon a scenario of pre-trial intimidation in Terence's *Adelphoe.*

1 THREATENING LAWSUITS: A MEANS TO SETTLEMENT IN THE ORATORS

A detailed examination of two series of litigation can serve as examples of pre-trial manipulation and at the same time introduce us to phenomena that become the subject of dispute in a number of comedies, namely, the adjudication of *epikleroi* (heiresses without fathers and brothers) and the acquisition and recovery of dowries. Our first series of litigation appears in And. 1 *Mysteries* 117–23, in that part of the speech where Andokides describes the events which led to the trial in which he is now defending himself against a charge of impiety; the specific charges which have been brought before the court by Kephisios (allegedly under Kallias' direction) are that he infringed the decree of Isotimides by attending the Mysteries in 400 after committing impiety in 415 and that he had placed a suppliant-branch on the Eleusinion altar.[1] The dispute with Kallias, Andokides claims in his defense, arose over the adjudication of an *epikleros.* His uncle, Epilukos, had died in Sicily without male issue and had left behind two daughters. Andokides maintains that the man had died in debt: his tangible property was worth less than two talents, while

[1] For discussion of these charges, see MacDowell 1962: 13–14.

his debts amounted to more than five. Andokides and his cousin Leagros were nearest kin, both paternal cousins of the poor *epikleroi*. Andokides describes a meeting with his kinsman in the presence of *philoi* (friends); the situation of the fatherless girls was discussed:

> . . . I summoned Leagros before friends and I said that it was the duty of good men, in circumstances such as these, to point out to one another the proper course of action for family members. "For it is not just for us, by preferring [alliances with] someone else's estate or a prosperous man, to hold Epilukos' daughters in contempt. For after all, if Epilukos were alive or had he died a rich man, we would have claimed his daughters in marriage, as being their nearest kin. Whereas under either of those circumstances we would have acted readily, whether urged on by Epilukos himself or induced by his wealth, now we shall act out of virtue. You make a claim for the one, and I shall do the same for the other." (118–19)

The "staginess" of the meeting between the cousins may well remind us of the family council in Lys. 32 *Diog.* 11–18 (chapter 1. 2); just as the meeting described there had been staged so that Diogeiton's daughter might have an audience of witnesses to record in living memory her speech to her father, so too Andokides invites friends to hear his no doubt well-rehearsed remarks on the virtue of his decision to marry an allegedly poor *epikleros*; presumably, the *philoi* appeared in court to provide testimony after Andokides has finished relating the pre-history of the trial (123). One scholar has rightly asked what was so virtuous about Andokides' decision to marry his cousin – after all, according to the law that protected poor *epikleroi*, nearest kin would be obliged either to marry them or to provide dowries in accordance with their own census ranking.[2] Another scholar has suggested, moreover, that Epilukos' estate may have been in much better condition than Andokides' depiction might lead us to believe: "presumably as much was owed to the estate as by it, and possibly much more."[3] Nonetheless, marrying a poor *epikleros* was considered an honorable course of action, and the

[2] MacDowell 1962: 147. The law is cited at [Dem.] 43. 54.

[3] Schaps 1979: 31. The eagerness with which Kallias pursues a claim in his son's behalf for the other daughter suggests that there was something very attractive about marriage into Epilukos' family. Schaps sees the dispute that developed between Andokides and Kallias over the *epikleros* as an indication of the wealth involved in Epilukos' estate and plausibly suggests a motive for Kallias: "Callias, a man of fantastic wealth who was in the process of losing it, was casting about for a way to regain his fortune; he was willing to gamble on his ability to collect the outstanding wealth of the estate" (31, with n. 43, citing Davies 1971: 261–65).

astute Andokides has decided to get the most mileage out of broadcasting his "generosity."[4]

Andokides' good and well-publicized intentions, however, came to naught: the girl for whom he had initiated a claim fell ill and died. A dispute then arose among potential claimants for the other daughter. Andokides alleges that Kallias tried to bribe Leagros to withdraw his claim so that his son (who appears to have been a more distant relation to the *epikleros*) could marry the girl.[5] Andokides then tried to block Kallias' plans: first he announced to Leagros that if he did not pursue his claim for the girl, he would initiate one; then he paid the court fee to do so (120).[6] When Kallias discovered what Andokides had done, he likewise initiated a claim for the girl.

The precise actions of the different claimants at this point are left a bit vague: probably Leagros agreed to drop his claim, so that when Andokides paid the court fee to initiate proceedings, there was no rival as yet.[7] But when Kallias initiated his claim, he entered into competition with Andokides. The issue would have to be decided at a hearing (called a *diadikasia*) before a jury presided over by the arkhon.[8] Apparently, Kallias feared the outcome of the trial – and

[4] MacDowell 1962: 147 supposes that marrying the poor *epikleros* would be cheaper than dowering her. But obviously marrying her would prevent the relative from marrying a rich wife and acquiring the use of her dowry.

[5] Following the traditional stemma (see e.g., Cox 1989: 35, 41, n. 25 and MacDowell 1962: 207 and n. 2), Kallias' son was half-brother to the girl's mother. MacDowell 1962: 150 thinks that the law excluded a man related on the female side from putting in a claim for an *epikleros*. That is unlikely. The possible claimants for an *epikleros* are the same as the male claimants for an intestate inheritance (the law is cited at [Dem.] 43. 51 and is paraphrased at Is. 7. 20–22, on which see Wyse 1904 ad loc.). Relationship on the female side puts the claimant's chances behind a relation to the girl's father; it does not exclude the claim.

[6] I am following MacDowell's (1962) emended text here.

[7] The procedure for claiming an *epikleros* was as follows: (1) any man who wished to lay claim to her in marriage by virtue of his relation to her father made a declaration to the appropriate arkhon, to the eponymous arkhon if her father had been a citizen, to the polemarkhos if he had been a metic ([Dem.] 46. 22–23; *AP* 56. 6 and 58. 3); the grounds for the claim would be stated in writing, at least in the fourth century, λῆξιν λαγχάνειν τῆς ἐπικλήρου ("to have one's claim for an *epikleros* entered"; cf. [Dem.] 46. 23 and Is. 3. 30); (2) the arkhon published the *lēxis* and read it out at the next meeting of the *ekklesia* (*AP* 43. 4); (3) at some point, a herald invited anyone who wished to put in a claim ([Dem.] 43. 5); and (4) if only one claimant appeared, then the arkhon adjudged the *epikleros* (who is called an *epidikos* during this procedure) to the claimant. If there were more than one claimant, then the issue was decided by a *diadikasia* before a court with the arkhon presiding. The outline of procedure provided here follows Harrison 1. 10–11. For more detailed explication with review of earlier scholarship, see Karabelias 1979.

[8] *AP* 56.6; [Dem.] 46. 22. There is some debate concerning the nature of the arkhon's award of the *epikleros* (step 4 in preceding note): Wolff 1946: 70–71 thinks that the arkhon's award was a purely administrative act; other scholars (cited by Harrison 1. 159 n. 5) argue that the award was a formal act of the court and not merely of the arkhon himself.

with good reason: Andokides, as nearer relative, would be awarded the *epikleros*. The unfolding sequence of events now becomes more disastrous for Andokides. He maintains that Kallias, in order to prevent him from obtaining the heiress, paid Kephisios a thousand drakhmai to lodge the information against him which initiated the present prosecution for impiety; when Kallias saw that Andokides remained steadfast in his claim, he then framed him for the religious offense of putting a suppliant-branch on the Eleusinion altar at the time of the Mysteries (121). Apparently, Kallias hoped that Andokides would either be penalized with death or else go voluntarily into exile; either alternative would mean the surrender of his claim for the heiress. Andokides, however, still did not budge. Kallias' next move was to approach three of Andokides' close friends as intermediaries: if Andokides would give up his claim, he would put an end to Kephisios' action and offer compensation for his treatment, with the friends overseeing the agreement. Andokides told him to go ahead with the prosecution and to procure the help of other men to do it (122–23). Kallias apparently did so and now the case is being heard before the *dikasterion*.

Andokides has presented all of Kallias' actions as intimidating counter-measures against his claim for the heiress. Fearful of defeat in the *diadikasia* or aiming to nullify its consequences (we do not know whether the *diadikasia* in fact took place), Kallias paid Kephisios to initiate the prosecution for impiety; when the case had not yet come to trial, Kallias attempted to come to a private agreement with the rival claimant for the *epikleros*; since no agreement could be reached, Andokides appears in court to defend himself. Kallias' attempts to manipulate Andokides' withdrawal of a legitimate claim to the heiress have failed; the courtroom of initiates presided over by the arkhon-basileus becomes the final stage for dramatizing the domestic dispute; its preliminary scenes had been acted in the *oikos*.

Our next series of litigation occurs in [Dem.] 59 *Neaira*, in that portion of the speech (49–87) in which Apollodoros as *sunegoros* (advocate) offers the rather circular argument that Neaira's status as a *xene* (foreigner) can be proven by the problems that beset her alleged daughter Phano who, as the offspring of a *xene*, is herself a *xene* and in fact has been treated as one on a number of witnessed or documented occasions.[9] Apollodoros is at this point discussing the

[9] Two series of litigation are reported in this section: one arising from Phano's divorce, discussed above (49–63), and the other arising from Stephanos' alleged taking of Epainetos

aftermath of Phrastor's divorce from Phano; the girl had been given to him with a dowry of thirty *mnai* by Stephanos (49–63). Apollodoros claims that Phrastor divorced Phano because he had become disenchanted with her licentious conduct and because he had learned that she was not the daughter of Stephanos by a former *aste* (Athenian) wife – as he had been led to believe at the time of betrothal – but was instead the daughter of Neaira (50–51). A series of court actions terminated by an out-of-court agreement follows. According to Apollodoros: (1) when Phrastor refused to return the dowry, Stephanos brought a *dike sitou* (suit for alimony) against him; (2) Phrastor countered with a *graphe*, charging that Stephanos had betrothed to him the daughter of a *xene* as if she were his kinswoman (52); (3) Stephanos made the next move and came to terms with Phrastor, abandoning his claim to the dowry and withdrawing the suit for alimony; Phrastor for his part withdrew his indictment from the thesmothetai (53).[10] Apollodoros' narrative gives a clear picture of manipulative conduct. That picture, however, soon becomes distorted. In the witness deposition that follows Apollodoros' narrative (54), Phrastor presents the first two actions in the reverse sequence: (1) he brought the indictment for illegal betrothal at the same time that he repudiated his wife; (2) then Stephanos sued him for alimony; (3) at this point, an agreement between the two men was reached and both dropped their litigation; no mention is made of the financial arrangement – an embarrassing detail, no doubt.

Arguments for preferring one sequence or the other can easily be furnished; certainty is out of the question.[11] Nevertheless, the general

as a *moikhos* (64–71). In the latter episode, Epainetos supplies sureties for the demanded compensation (thirty *mnai*), then counters with a *graphe* for illegal detainment as a *moikhos*; a private reconciliation then takes place between the men overseen by two mediators, and Epainetos agrees to pay 1,000 dr. as a contribution to Phano's dowry (see chapters 3.1.c; 5.1.c; 8.1.a; and App. 7.1).

[10] Steinwenter 1925: 125–26 points out the imbalance in the agreement between the two men: Stephanos withdraws a *dike* which was in the power of none but himself to bring (as *kurios* of Phano); but Phrastor withdraws a *graphe* – which was in the power of any competent Athenian to bring, even after Phrastor's withdrawal. Steinwenter thinks that Stephanos' agreement to withdraw the *dike* would be legally binding (and hence bar the same action from entering court) by virtue of his "release of the dowry" (ἄφεσις τῆς προικός) and "removal of the *dike*" (ἀναιρεῖσθαι δίκης τοῦ σίτου). Phrastor merely renounces his purpose to proceed with the *graphe* against Stephanos. Phrastor is clearly the winner in this game.

[11] Drerup 1898: 347 argues that the testimony is authentic and offers an explanation of the discrepancy; cf. Humphreys 1985c: 361–62 n. 73 and Carey 1992: 114–15. The last author casts doubt on the veracity of Phrastor's account on the grounds that Apollodoros has provided witnesses neither for Phrastor's marriage nor for the legal actions between Stephanos and Phrastor. Perhaps unjustifiably: (1) Witnesses to the marriage may have

trend is clear: the second action, whichever it was, was initiated to forestall the first; undoubtedly, it was an invitation to settle out of court. A private arrangement would be attractive to both parties. If convicted by the *dike sitou*, Phrastor risked the eventual loss of the entire 3000 drakhmai dowry – and conviction was certain.[12] Stephanos, however, risked far more. The penalties for giving away in marriage a *xene* as if she were an *aste* were severe; Apollodoros recorded the law in c. 52:[13]

> And if any person give in marriage a *xene* to an Athenian man on the pretence that she is related to him, let him be *atimos* (disfranchised), and let his property belong to the state, and a third part of it to the man who secured his conviction. And let him be indicted before the thesmothetai by any person who is permitted to make indictments, just as in the case [of indictments] for *xenia*.

Stephanos, then, stood to lose not only his property, but also the alleged means of his livelihood: disfranchised, the *sukophantes* would be unable to bring cases into court.[14] And Phrastor, upon a successful prosecution of Stephanos, would appear in a position to gain a substantial award – one third of Stephanos' property. Why then would he agree to drop the indictment? Three reasons suggest themselves. First, Stephanos' estate may not have been worth much.[15] Secondly, even if Stephanos' estate had been substantial, it

elicited pre-trial testimony (whether true or false) that Phano was the daughter of an *enguete gamete kata tous nomous* (for that is what Phrastor allegedly believed at the time of marriage). (2) Witnesses that a *graphe* for unlawful betrothal had been initiated against Stephanos and then withdrawn may have been impossible to find. There was not likely to be any record of the two cases; moreover, the litigants' witnesses to their respective summonses, if they were known, would probably not have agreed to testify to the disadvantage of the summoners (presumably their friends) – and there would be no way to subpoena them (Todd 1990: 24–27).

12 A law is paraphrased at [Dem.] 59. 52 that directs that "if a man sends his wife away, he is to pay back the dowry, and if he does not, he is to pay interest at the rate of nine obols, and in behalf of the woman, her *kurios* may sue him for alimony (*sitos*) in the Odeion." Cf. Dem. 27. 17 and 30. 7, 9, 22; on the latter speech, see Wyse 1904: 296–97.

13 On the authenticity of this law, see Carey 1992: 113 and, more generally, see chapter 5, nn. 47 and 50.

14 For different views of the meaning of sykophancy in Athens, see Osborne 1990: 83–102 and Harvey 1990: 103–38, and summary by Todd 1993: 92–94. Carey 1992: 106–07 offers this definition: "The sycophant is basically someone who exploits the law for unfair or illegal gain. The activities covered by the term are very wide, including prosecution for profit in cases where the law allowed rewards to encourage volunteer prosecutors, prosecution for payment from people wishing to embarrass a personal or political enemy or to harass an opponent-at-law, extortion of money by means of the threat of prosecution, and more generally using legal and rhetorical expertise to pursue unjust prosecutions or to escape punishment when prosecuted." See further, n. 105 below.

15 Stephanos' estate, in order to produce the equivalent of the retained dowry for Phrastor,

would have been no easy task for Phrastor to prove that Phano was a *xene*; Apollodoros, after all, gives no positive evidence which proves that Neaira is Phano's mother. And thirdly, three thousand drakhmai was a considerable sum; evidently, Phrastor was satisfied with it. Court action countered by court action thus ends with a mutually agreed upon out-of-court settlement. Apollodoros gives us no glimpse of moral hyperbole from these actors; financial calculations are behind and on the surface of every action.

The strategies used by the potential litigants in these episodes demonstrate how the court system is manipulated in order to achieve one's ends in private. Actions are threatened and initiated – not necessarily with the intention of executing them in court. In the first series of litigation considered here, Kallias had underestimated his opponent's resistance to intimidation – or so the skilful orator leads us to believe; Andokides refused the invitation to settle, went to trial, and was successful. In the second, both disputants find it more rewarding to settle out of court. Scenarios of pre-trial manipulation hardly exhibit any straightforward mode of social intercourse, but they are a part of the forensic theatrics of potential Athenian litigants.

2 INITIAL STAGES[16]

2(a) Summons and arrest in Athens

So far we have discussed going to trial or threatening to do so in vague terms such as "lodging a suit." Here the mechanics of the

would have to be worth at least 9,000 drakhmai; that would make Stephanos a fairly rich man. Yet in c. 9 of the oration, it is reported that Stephanos sold his "small house" for (only) seven *mnai*, and in c. 39, it is alleged that Stephanos claimed before mediators that he had no money with which to dower Phano for another marriage. The mediators appear to believe him (70–71). While Stephanos may have had more assets than he disclosed, Phrastor may have been in possession of the greatest portion of his tangible property; if so, a successful prosecution of Stephanos may not have brought him much more than 1,000 drakhmai. For a different view, see Carey 1992: 106.

16 In formulating the material that pertains to summonses and arrests in this section, I have benefited much from Witt's important study (1971: 217–60) which treats in detail many of the issues discussed here. My disagreement with some of Witt's conclusions and some aspects of his method are not a mark of disesteem for the work. I have also made much use of Hansen 1976; his collection of references to court procedures is invaluable. Hansen's method of source citation, however, is somewhat confusing; I note particularly his habit of piling up references in one note to testify to several different aspects (*a, b, c*) of one procedure (*x*) as if that justified the conclusion that because (*x*) is associated with (*a*) in instance (1) and with (*b*) in instance (2) and with (*c*) in instance (3), therefore (*x*) consists of (*a, b,* and *c*) even when (*a*) is usually found without (*b*) and all this without due consideration to the possible equations of $x' = a$, $x^2 = b$, $x^3 = c$, and without differentiating *a, b,* and *c* in the reference.

scenario will be presented. A summons was the first step in initiating both *graphai* (public indictments brought by *ho boulomenos* – i.e., any person qualified to plead) and *dikai* (private suits brought by the wronged person or by his or her *kurios*).[17] *Apagoge* (arrest) could only be used against certain categories of offenders and under certain specified conditions. Arrests and summonses appear frequently in New Comedy and so these initiatory procedures are considered in some detail below.

In order to issue a summons, the accuser (potential plaintiff or prosecutor) must know in advance which magistrate handled the particular offense, and on which day that magistrate accepted charges.[18] Armed with this information, the accuser then issues an oral summons; he does this in the company of witnesses who could testify later, if necessary, that the summons had been issued.[19] The accuser would say to his opponent, "I summon you to appear before magistrate A on day B for the offense C." Lipsius has hypothesized the existence of a general rule that required a four-day interval (*propempta*) between the summons and the day assigned for appearance before the appropriate magistrate; while the evidence for the precise extent of the interval is weak, we can safely assume that an interval was required by law: without one, the requirement that witnesses be present for the summons and the existence of a *graphe pseudoklēteias* (indictment for falsely testifying that a summons had been issued) would be inexplicable.[20] On the appointed day, the accuser who had issued the summons submits his charge to the magistrate. At first, this was done orally and an official wrote down the charge, but by the mid fourth century, charges (for both *graphai* and *dikai*) were submitted in writing.[21] If the magistrate accepts

[17] Different procedures would be followed in *eisangeliai* (impeachments) and in homicide cases before the *basileus*; for *eisangeliai*: see MacDowell 1978: 238–39, Harrison 2. 87, and Hansen 1975: 26 (summary statement); for homicide: MacDowell 1963: 22ff. For discussion of "possible distinctions" between *dikai* and *graphai*, see Todd 1993: 109–12.

[18] The portrait of procedure that is given here pertains to the mid-fourth century (see Introduction); for an account of court procedure in three more or less distinct periods (between *c.* 460 and 410 BC, 410 and *c.* 340 BC, and 340 and 322 BC), see Boegehold 1995: 21–42.

[19] Two witnesses seem to be required in the late fifth century and in the fourth; the inference is based on [Dem.] 40. 28; 53. 14; *IG* I^3 236. 5 (a much supplemented text); and *Poletai Records P.* 5. 15 (= *SEG* XII, 100) where *klētēr* likely refers to the two named men and may be an abbreviation for the plural.

[20] Lipsius 809 and n. 22 infers the general rule from [Dem.] 43. 75 and Ar. *Clouds* 1131 with 1221–22.

[21] Calhoun 1919b collects the evidence for pleadings (both for *dikai* and *graphai*) in the last quarter of the fifth century and in the fourth; while there is some evidence that complaints

responsibility for the case, he determines a date for the *anakrisis* (interrogation).[22] After this first meeting, the magistrate posts a public notice of the charge (to which the accused's denial may be added) on the railings that ran around the statues of the Eponymous Heroes.[23] Later, at the *anakrisis*, the magistrate interrogates accuser and accused; the latter two could interrogate each other at this meeting.[24] Presumably, the purpose of interrogation was to determine the issues of the case, to collect the witness testimony that would be used at trial, and to provide litigants the opportunity to assess what lines of attack and defense would be necessary at that time. At the end of the *anakrisis*, a date for trial would be set.

Procedure would be slightly different in cases which fell to the jurisdiction of the Forty, four of whom were assigned to each tribe.[25] To initiate such a case, the plaintiff would have to know the tribal affiliation of the defendant and then would summon him to meet before his (i.e., the defendant's) tribal judges on a specific day.[26] If a sum of less than ten drakhmai were involved, the four tribal judges would decide the case; if more than ten drakhmai were involved, they would pass the case on to an official arbitrator chosen by lot (*AP* 53. 1–2).[27] The official arbitrator would then meet with plaintiff and defendant, and if he could not reconcile them, he would give a verdict (see chapter 1.1). If either party disagreed with the verdict, he could "appeal" the case. In that event, he would immediately inform the arbitrator and the latter would seal up the evidence and bring it forthwith to the four tribal judges; these magistrates would then bring the case into their own court (*AP* 53. 2–3). There are two major procedural differences between a case heard before an official arbitrator and one heard before another magistrate. First, there was

for public actions may have been written even before 425, no evidence suggests that any complaints were written by the litigants themselves (as opposed to court officials) until Dem. (e.g., 29. 30; 32. 4, 27; 36. 20; 37. 23; 38. 14). Calhoun suggests that (1) a law requiring litigants to present written charges may have been enacted at the same time as the law that required witnesses to give written testimony, and (2) there may have been a general revision of the judicial system in the arkhonship of Nausinikos in 378/77.

22 The plaintiff at this time is said "to get a hearing (by lot?)" (*langkhanein diken*); this is generally thought to mean that the magistrate allocated a date for the *anakrisis*. The manner of "allocation" is not clear; see Lipsius 817 f.; Harrison 2. 89.

23 Posting of public notices: Dem. 21. 103; examples of pleas: Dem. 37. 22, 25, 26, 28, 29; Dem. 45. 46; D. H. *Dein.* 3.

24 See, e.g., Is. 6. 12–13; for a discussion of the sorts of issues that might arise at the *anakrisis*, see MacDowell 1978: 240–42 and Todd 1993: 126–29.

25 For the jurisdiction of the Forty, see App.1.a.

26 Lys. 23. 2.

27 Probably the arbitrator was chosen from among those who were assigned to the defendant's tribe: see [Dem.] 47. 12 and Rhodes 1981 on *AP* 53. 5.

no *anakrisis* in an official arbitration; the arbitration itself served that end.[28] Secondly, official arbitration provided opportunity for settling the case before trial.

There were other procedures available, however, which sometimes rendered a summons unnecessary. *Apagoge*, *endeixis*, and *ephegesis* are procedures of arrest or procedures that could lead to the arrest and subsequent trial of *kakourgoi* (malefactors), *atimoi* (disfranchised citizens), and *pheugontes* (exiles). Only the way these procedures affected *kakourgoi* – the most frequently attested of these categories in New Comedy – needs concern us here.[29] *Kakourgoi*, in a technical sense, are alleged malefactors who are liable to the procedures listed above;[30] they include certain kinds of *kleptai* (thieves who steal at night, or from a gymnasium, or more than ten drakhmai from a harbor, or more than fifty drakhmai from anywhere else), *andrapodistai* (kidnappers – both enslavers of free men and slave-stealers), and *lōpodutai* (cloak-stealers).[31] The three procedures used against *kakourgoi* differ from one another most of all in the degree of the accuser's direct involvement in the arrest:[32] in *apagoge*, the accuser himself arrests the alleged *kakourgos* upon catching him *ep' autophōrōi* ("in the act" or "red-handed") and he hales him before the Eleven; in *endeixis*, the accuser denounces the alleged *kakourgos* to the Eleven, and then, if he so desires, arrests him by *apagoge*; in *ephegesis*, the accuser fetches the Eleven to carry out the arrest of the alleged *kakourgos* who is locked up until their arrival.[33] Once the alleged *kakourgos* has been arrested and put into the hands of the Eleven,

28 Harrell 1936: 21; Gernet 1939. Possibly *anakrisis* rather than official arbitration was regular in false witnessing cases which emerged from trials which fell to the Forty; see App. 1, n. 6.

29 For *apagoge* against *atimoi*, *androphonoi*, and *pheugontes*, see Hansen 1976: 54–107.

30 *Apagoge* against malefactors described as *kakourgoi* is frequently attested; see Hansen 1976: 38–40 for classical references. *Endeixis* against *kakourgoi* (as opposed to other classes of offender) appears once: Ant. 5. 9–10, and see Hansen 1976: 13–14. In App. 4.1.b, I argue that an *endeixis* followed by an *apagoge* appeared in the Greek original of *Rudens*. *Ephegesis* is rarely explicitly alluded to in our sources – only at Dem. 22. 26 and 26. 9; see Hansen 1976: 24–25.

31 *AP* 52. 1 mentions the three categories cited here; on the possible inclusion of other offenders (e.g., *moikhoi*, homicides, and temple robbers) see Hansen 1976: 39–48 and chapter 5.1.b. On the meaning of *andrapodistes*, an important character in New Comedy, see App. 3.1.

32 Hansen 1976: 26 sees the three procedures not as "three different types of process, but merely. . . three variants of one and the same type of public action."

33 Cf. Hansen 1976: 22–25. Hansen's developmental and elastic interpretation of "catching in the act" (48–53), which is followed most recently by Todd 1993: 80 and n. 5, is criticized in detail by D. Cohen (1983: 52–57). The latter supports a more literal interpretation, leaving enough slack for catching a thief who still had the goods on him but not the full rope for an arrest after a house search. In my view, Cohen is closer to the mark.

there are two possible courses of action: (1) if he admits the offense, the Eleven execute him;[34] (2) if he denies it, he is imprisoned until trial; the Eleven then bring the case before the dikasterion and preside over the trial; if he is convicted, the penalty of death was fixed by law.[35] Probably before the trial, imprisonment without bail was compulsory for an alleged *kakourgos* arrested by *apagoge*; bail, however, may have been allowed for an alleged *kakourgos* who had been denounced by *endeixis* before his arrest.[36] Presumably, before the case came to trial, the original accuser first presented to the Eleven a written indictment, called an *apagoge* or *endeixis*, depending on which procedure had been used.[37]

While the degree of the accuser's involvement in the arrest has been pointed out as the major difference among the three procedures (*apagoge*, *endeixis*, *ephegesis*), a number of other differences between *endeixis* and *apagoge* are evident: (1) *apagoge* can only be undertaken in cases where the *kakourgos* is taken in the act (*ep' autophōrōi*) whereas that is not a requirement for *endeixis*;[38] (2) arrest by the accuser is always a component of *apagoge* whereas it is optional in *endeixis*; (3) *apagoge* always precludes a court summons whereas in *endeixis*, if arrest does not follow denunciation, then a summons is necessary for a court trial. Why an accuser would choose one procedure rather than another will depend on his own specific circumstances (e.g., whether he is strong enough to effect the arrest

[34] Lipsius 318 n. 4 and Harrison 2. 222–23 in part distinguish *apagoge* from *endeixis* by claiming that *apagoge* resulted in summary execution upon admission of guilt whereas jury trial was obligatory in *endeixis*. Hansen 1976:17f. attempts to refute this, but the evidence is not decisive.

[35] Classical references in Hansen 1976: 21 n. 25; most of these references are to the general rule, and sometimes they are rhetorical, used in the course of *a fortiori* arguments. References to actual trials against *kakourgoi*, *atimoi*, and *pheugontes* appear in Hansen's catalogue on pp. 122–143; there are 33 all together (including trials that are apparently abandoned or dismissed). There are only 10 instances of trials against *kakourgoi*; 7 of these are against *androphonoi*, 3 are against such *kakourgoi* as thieves, temple robbers, and clothes-stealers (nos. 6, 18, and 30).

[36] This is the view of Hansen 1976: 23–24 who provides an interpretation of Dem. 24. 144 (*contra* Lipsius 317 and Harrison 2. 221) and supports it with reference to Ant. 5. 17.

[37] *Apagoge*: Lys. 13. 85; *Lex. Seg.* 6. 414. 19–26; Suda s.v. *apagoge* (references cited in Harrison 2. 223 and n.1). *Endeixis*: [Dem.] 58. 1 probably signifies a written complaint (so Harrison 2. 229).

[38] Hansen 1976: 22 and 48–52; in the latter pages, Hansen has collected all references to *ep' autophōrōi* and concludes that it is "characteristic of ἀπαγωγὴ κακούργων in contrast to other forms of *apagoge* and to all forms of *endeixis*." He does not think that "being caught in the act" was a requirement for *ephegesis* (25), but there is not enough evidence for a definite assessment.

himself) and the circumstances of the alleged offense (e.g., whether the offender was caught in the act).[39]

Was a summons or an arrest ever negotiable on the spot? The answer appears to be "yes." The utterance of one or the other is not necessarily a performative statement in which the words indicate that a summons or an arrest is underway; such utterances may on many occasions have been no different from a threat. No magistrate such as a modern-day "process server" is present to prohibit instant negotiation if, e.g., a summoned individual were to offer compensation or restitution to the summoner immediately. Unfortunately, the orators provide us with few glimpses of actual summonses taking place. One case, however, preserves the significant detail. The plaintiffs (Khrusippos and an anonymous partner) in a *dike emporike* (maritime suit) were trying to recover a penalty for non-fulfillment of the terms of a maritime contract; Phormion, they claimed, had not repaid their loan and so was subject to the penalty stipulated by the contract. Phormion, however, objected to the suit with a *paragraphe* (a hearing to bar action); the extant oration ([Dem.] 34 *Phorm.*, delivered by Khrusippos) belongs to this trial. In the course of the speech, Khrusippos alludes to Phormion's defense: the man claimed that the contract allowed him, while still in the Bosporos, to repay the loan to the shipowner, Lampis; moreover, he had done precisely that – he had paid the sum to Lampis while in the Bosporos.[40] Khrusippos counters the defense, claiming that Phormion never made any payment at all; the story of the payment to Lampis was fabricated after the summons for the maritime suit was issued. He reports what did not happen when he summoned Phormion to court:

And I, having witnesses with me, summoned Phormion. And although Lampis, men of Athens, was nearby when I uttered the summons, he did not once dare to say that he had received the money from Phormion. No! Nor did he dare to say – which would have been reasonable – "Khrusippos, you're crazy! Why are you summoning this man? No need for that – for he has paid the money to me." Well, not only did Lampis not utter a word, neither did Phormion himself think it worthwhile to say anything, although Lampis was standing next to him – the man to whom he now claims to

39 For the choice of procedure depending on the accuser's confidence and strength, see Dem. 22. 25–26, discussed in chapter 1.1. Hansen 1976: 16 and 26 argues that *endeixis* permitted the accuser to obtain the sanction of the magistrates through the denunciation, and supports this by adducing Dem. 23. 51.

40 For commentary on this complicated speech, see Isager and Hansen 1975: 156–69.

have paid the money! And yet, men of Athens, it would have been reasonable for him to have said, "Why, my good man, are you summoning me? For I have paid the money to this fellow standing next to me!" – and at the same time he could have furnished Lampis to corroborate the story. But as it was, neither of them, at that critical moment, uttered any word whatsoever. (14–15)

Khrusippos clearly thinks that either Lampis or Phormion could have responded to the summons on the spot – that neither did so can only be a sign that their current version of the repayment is false. Had it been true, and had they corroborated one another's story at the time of the summons, Khrusippos presumably would have revoked the summons then and there. The scenario shows that a summons was perceived – at least by the summoner – as a negotiable act.

Further illustration is provided by Aristophanes *Clouds* 1214 ff.: the first creditor, accompanied by a witness, enters the stage to summon Strepsiades to court for failure to repay a loan; he states the day on which the debtor is to appear before a magistrate (1221–22) and describes the offense (1224–27). While the summons has thus been issued, the creditor nevertheless offers – though indirectly – the option of immediate repayment: he will go away, once Strepsiades has told him whether he will pay or not (1243–44). Strepsiades leaves the stage for a moment; in the interval, the creditor turns to the witness and asks, "What do you think he will do? Pay the sum?" (1246).[41] Strepsiades, it turns out, does not return to the stage with a purse full of money; the negotiation is at an end and the case will presumably go to court.

Neither of the plaintiffs mentioned here – that is, neither Khrusippos in [Dem.] 34 nor the first creditor in *Clouds* – has directly asked to be repaid at the moment of summons; nonetheless, each foresees the possibility that his debtor might repay him on the spot – or at least offer some explanation. The two episodes suggest that the citation, "I summon you to appear before magistrate A on day B for the offense C," may often have entailed the coda, implicitly or explicitly, "unless you choose to settle this instant."

Similarly, with utterances of arrest: some may have had as their goal not the imprisonment and subsequent execution of the *kakourgos* caught in the act but rather the immediate cessation of his offending conduct – e.g., the instant return of a stolen cloak. Aiskhin. 1 *Tim.*

[41] See Dover 1968b ad loc. for the attribution of the whole line to the creditor.

provides an illustrative example this time. Among the events of Timarkhos' reputedly sordid life, Aiskhines reports one that occurred when the alleged citizen-prostitute was cohabiting with Misgolas. The elder man, unable to find his beloved on the morning of the procession of the City Dionysia, made a search with his friend Phaidros and the two of them, upon hearing a report of the young man's whereabouts, found him breakfasting with foreigners in a lodging house. The orator focuses on the conduct of the pursuers: "When Misgolas and Phaidros threatened the foreigners and were ordering them to follow immediately to prison, on the grounds that they had corrupted a free youth, the foreigners in fear abandoned their preparations and took to their heels" (43). Undoubtedly no criminal conduct deserving arrest can be imputed to the foreigners on the basis of this account; Aiskhines has recounted the story to demonstrate the ludicrous conduct of a man who was so bent on finding his darling and so jealous of his keeping company with others that he threatened foreigners with arrest during festival time for an alleged offense that in no way matched the procedure.[42] Certainly any utterance of arrest in this case (if there is any truth to it at all) sent the message that was evident to its recipients: "Leave Timarkhos alone and depart at once!"[43]

The data collected in the first chapter and in App. 2.d demonstrate that plaintiffs often tried to induce their opponents to enter into private arbitration after a suit was lodged with a magistrate. Now we can push the bargaining period back even earlier: the utterance of a summons or an arrest may have been perceived as

[42] The details, that the episode took place during the procession of the City Dionysia, that Misgolas and Phaidros were planning to march in the procession, and that Timarkhos had agreed to march with them, may have signalled to the dikasts that the departure of the two men on their "man-hunt" was a serious lapse of civic duty. Misgolas' threat of arrest will have appeared sorely out of place: a law quoted at Dem. 21. 10 makes it unlawful "to distrain or seize another thing from another person" during the procession; Demosthenes interprets the forbidden acts to include the use of violence (21. 11). While his interpretation is tendentious (see MacDowell 1990 ad loc.), such acts as Misgolas' may have been frowned upon during the celebration. Misgolas, for his part, may have viewed the foreigners' detainment of Timarkhos as their act of "corruption" – they had prevented the youth from carrying out his civic duty.

[43] Isokr. 21. 14 provides an example of a threatened arrest, but the threat does not (precisely) belong to the scenario described above. Timodemos, we are told, exacted thirty *mnai* from Nikias, "not by demanding repayment of a debt, but by threatening to arrest him" (οὐ χρέος ἐγκαλῶν ἀλλ' ἀπάξειν ἀπειλῶν). Here, the threatened arrest does not pertain to the alleged debt (i.e., arrest is not a remedy for the debt); rather, arrest is threatened (according to the speaker) as part of the political and self-interested plots rampant under the Thirty; the claim of the creditor is fraudulent and this is a case of extortion.

sending out two messages to recipients: either comply and follow along to the magistrate (four days after a summons, immediately upon an arrest) or find a means to settle right now (or at some point before the meeting with the magistrate). The discovery of the negotiable summons and arrest underscores a significant and well-known feature of the Athenian system of justice: summonses and arrests are self-help procedures. The laymen accusers who initiate them, however, do not automatically set in motion an unalterable sequence of events. The disputants have time to maneuver even before they arrive at the magistrate's gate.

"Bluffing," then, would appear to be an inherent part of the dynamics of the dispute settlement process. But if uttering a summons in a private case were regularly perceived as being potentially negotiable rather than absolutely performative, then it makes no sense to call a summons a "bluff" simply because the summoner intends to pursue the extra-judicial course of settlement. In such a context, "bluff" loses efficacy. If the accused offers to settle on the spot – for example, to repay an overdue debt – probably the summoner will revoke his action; witnesses will be on hand for the *aphesis* (release) and/or *apallage* (mutually agreed upon settlement). The summons in such a case has achieved its end – the settlement of a dispute over a financial obligation. But if instead the accused responds with a bold nod, "Go ahead – take the case to court," then the summoner either will do precisely that, or he might back down. Only in the latter case is the summons a genuine bluff. Summonses and arrests are stylized linguistic gestures; potential litigants in Athens know the code.

To sum up: two methods of initiating court action in Athens have been described. One way was to summon the alleged offender to court and thus set in motion a procedure that might end in a court trial or possibly a hearing before an official arbitrator. The other was to arrest the alleged offender or to have him arrested – procedures which might end in a court trial if the accused did not confess to committing the alleged offense. Evidence has also been presented, suggesting that summonses and arrests were perceived as negotiable utterances. Private settlements might be made at the time of an arrest or summons. If that did not happen in the case of a summons, arbitration or reconciliation might still take place before the disputants entered the courtroom – or even during the course of a trial (App. 2.b). The arrest of a *kakourgos*, on the other hand, was more perilous: the arrested man risked death both if he confessed the crime and if he were convicted in court. Immediate settlement would be the safest course of action. A focus upon the negotiable aspect of these pre-trial procedures strengthens our awareness of the contours of private initiatives in settling disputes extra-judicially.

2(b) Summons in Rome

Three systems of procedure are found in the history of Roman law – the *legis actiones*, the formulary system, and *cognitio extraordinaria*. The periods during which these systems were in use overlapped. The *legis actiones* (literally, "actions based on the law") was the dominant system during the time of Plautus and Terence.[44] The praetor was the most important jurisdictional magistrate in this period; elected for a term of one year, he would usually have no special training in the law. The praetor would pass on cases to a layman, also a non-expert in the law; acting as *iudex* or *arbiter*, he would give a verdict. The praetor, *iudex*, and *arbiter* appear frequently in Plautus, and their activities will be discussed in more detail here and in chapter 3.2. The jurisdiction of the (curule) aediles in private law at this time was nugatory if it existed at all.[45] Their criminal jurisdiction was not extensive: it appears to have been limited, for the most part, to imposing fines in cases concerning the occupation of public lands, the grain supply, and usury.[46] The basis of the aediles' capacity to invoke comitial trials for more severe penalties, for instance in cases of "public immorality," is debated; likewise debated is the role played by their assistants, the *tresviri*.[47] On a number of occasions in

[44] It is generally agreed that *formulae* were allowed under the *lex Aebutia* and that the *legis actiones* were all but entirely eliminated by two Julian laws (Gaius 4. 30); it is also generally agreed that the procedure by *formulae* did not appear as a fully developed system upon the promulgation of the *lex Aebutia* – some written *formulae* were in existence before that *lex*. Unfortunately, the *lex Aebutia* can only be vaguely dated to "the second century," to a period before the passage of the Julian laws mentioned above. For a concise discussion of the origin of the formulary system, see Kaser 1966: 107–16; Jolowicz and Nicholas 1972: 218–25. For our purposes, we shall follow the general view that the *legis actiones* prevailed alongside some formulary actions until the passing of the *lex Aebutia*, perhaps in the second half of the second century BC (cf., e.g., Arangio-Ruiz 1968: 121–23; Kaser 1966: 109–12; Watson 1971: 127 n. 3 and 162). Some formulary actions that were in existence in the Plautine era are discussed in chapters 3.2 and 5.2.b.

[45] Watson 1974b: 82–87.

[46] For references, see Mommsen 1887. 2: 492–99; recent discussion in Nippel 1995.

[47] Curule aediles have *iurisdictio* but no *imperium*; hence their capacity to convoke the *comitia* is anomalous; on trials for "public immorality," see chapter 5.2, nn. 84–85 with bibliographical references. On the *tresviri*, see App. 5, add. 2.

Plautus where the aediles are mentioned, their functions might be summed up as "policing" or as "overseeing the care of the city."[48] In one passage, they appear as jurisdictional figures – but the allusion is not specific enough to pin down.[49] Lesser magistrates with limited jurisdictions were the *centumviri* (literally, "one-hundred men"), the *decemviri stlitibus iudicandis* (literally, "ten men for trying cases"), and possibly the *recuperatores* ("recoverers"). The earliest known trial before the *centumviri* dates from *c.* 145 BC, that of Cn. Hostilius Mancinus (Cic. *de Or.* 1. 181); most scholars believe the court is at least a century older.[50] On the basis of limited evidence for the Principate, it has been hypothesized that the *centumviri* dealt with claims of inheritance.[51] Little is known of the *decemviri stlitibus iudicandis* during the Republic, except that at some point they began hearing cases concerning status (*vindicatio in libertatem* or *in servitutem*, the judicial procedure by which an individual living in slavery is claimed to be free or by which an individual living in freedom is claimed to be a slave).[52] Neither *centumviri* nor *decemviri* are mentioned in the plays of Plautus and Terence. *Recuperatores*, on the other hand, make their first appearance in Latin literature in the older playwright.[53] While under the later formulary system of law they formed a bench of several jurors hearing various suits, e.g., for extortion and acts of violence, it has usually been assumed that they

48 *Amph.* 72; *Pers.* 160; *Poen.* 1012; *St.* 353; *Trin.* 990. The first three are references to the aediles in their roles as overseers of the festivals at which comedies are presented. The aedile is often interchangeable in Latin for Greek *astunomos* or *agoranomos*, as at *Capt.* 823–24: *eugepae! edictiones aedilicias hicquidem habet, / mirumque adeost ni hunc fecere sibi Aetoli agoranomum* ("Good grief! The man is pronouncing aedilician edicts – it's a wonder if the Aetolians haven't made him their *agoranomos*!"); see Fredershausen 1906: 65–68.

49 *Men.* 587 (the reading of *Ambrosianus* is *apud aedilem*; that of the Palatine recension is *ad iudicem*) and 590. Fraenkel 1960: 152–54 contrasts the Roman coloring of this passage (571–601) with a similar passage in *Cas.* (563–75) where he thinks the Greek original is more in evidence; see chapter 1, n. 5.

50 Kelly 1976: 1–39 argues that the court is archaic in origin; he presents views of earlier scholars concerning the date of origin, jurisdiction, and size of the centumviral court. Festus s.v. *centumviralia iudicia* reports that the 105 members were made up of three men from each tribe; the number of tribes did not reach 35 until 241 BC.

51 See Kelly 1976: 9–17 for views of earlier scholars.

52 Cic. *pro Caec.* 33, 97; *de domo* 29, 78. Under Augustus, the *decemviri* were made into presidents of the centumviral courts (Suet. *Aug.* 36; Dio 54. 26. 6; *D.* [Pomp.] 1. 2. 2. 29); later evidence of their function in status cases is therefore not available to supplement the scanty evidence of the Republican period. On the date of origin of the *decemviri*, scholars are divided: e.g., Nicolau 1933: 16–34 argues for an early date (449) at the time of the *lex Valeria Horatia* (Livy 3. 55, 7); Franciosi 1961b: 18–28 argues for a date after the second half of the fourth century, when slavery was extensive; neither Kaser 1966: 40 nor Watson 1975: 96 n. 72 offer a date of origin. For speculations on the early form *stlis* (= *lis*), see Kelly 1976: 67.

53 *Bacch.* 270 and in *Rud.* 1282; see App. 4.1 at n. 68.

originally functioned as arbitrators in international disputes.[54] Precise demarcation of the jurisdiction of *recuperatores* in the early second century is, however, impossible.

In order to initiate a hearing under the *legis actiones* system, the plaintiff issued an oral summons to his opponent, bidding him to go to court. The well-known procedure is called *in ius vocatio* ("summons to court"). The opening sentences of the first of the *XII Tables* provide rules for it, and these rules appear to have remained in force throughout the early and classical periods of Roman law.[55] While neither the text of the *XII Tables* nor its meaning is absolutely secure, the general outlines of the procedure are clear enough: "1. A man summoned to court must go there. If he does not go, [the summoner] is to call for witnesses. Then [before the witnesses], he is to take hold of him. 2. If [the man so summoned] hesitates or tries to flee, [the summoner] is to lay hands on him [formally]. 3. If [the summoned man] is sick or old, [the summoner] is to provide a yoked animal. There is no need for a carriage."[56] A plaintiff can issue his oral summons to the accused anywhere, but he apparently was not permitted to enter the house of the accused.[57] There is no evidence

[54] Kelly 1976: 40–70 argues that *recuperatores* originated "within the domestic judicial sphere" (53) and had a dual competency, both to pronounce judgments and to execute them. Kelly's view has not won acceptance. The traditional view rests in part on an explanation given by Festus (Paul ex Fest.: p. 342. 9–13 Lindsay), relying on a jurist (Gallus Aelius) of the first century BC. Kaser 1966: 113 and n. 51, e.g., assumes that the early competency of *recuperatores* was limited to the recovery of property seized in war (e.g., the *lex Antonia de Termessibus* in Bruns[7] 94: no. 14. 2. 1–5). For the activity of the *recuperatores* in Cicero's era, see Frier 1985: 197–234.

[55] *In ius vocatio* was replaced (but not wholly eliminated) towards the end of the Republic by *vadimonium*, whereby the summoned man bound himself to appear *in iure* on a specified day instead of relying upon a *vindex* to stand surety for him (cf. n. 59 below). While the new procedure is found in Cicero's speeches, *in ius vocatio* remained an alternative where the defendant refused *vadimonium* (see Steinwenter *RE* 7A, 2054, s.v. *vadimonium*; Kelly 1966: 6–7; Kaser 1966: 52).

[56] Standard texts are Bruns[7] 17–18 and *FIRA*[2] 1. 26. I am following the text and translation of Kaser 1966: 48, who supplies full notes for his readings: *1. Si in ius vocat (ito). Ni it, antestamino: Igitur em capito. 2. Si calvitur pedemve struit manum endo iacito. 3. Si morbus aevitasve escit iumentum dato. Si nolet arceram ne sternito.* For a slightly different text and a discussion of its problems, see Daube 1956: 28 ff. The main difficulties are *antestamino* (i.e., what function the witnesses served) and the difference between *capito* and *manum endo iacito*. Kaser 1966: 48 suggests that the witnesses are to follow the summoner to the praetor and to inform him of the summoned man's refusal, in order to attest to the legality of forceful measures. Kaser treats the second "laying on of hands" as a sort of ritual act, a "formal intensification" of the summoner's first response to the accused's resistance, after which more forceful measures may be taken to bring the accused to the praetor. For a summary of other views, see Wesener *RE* 9A1. 686 s.v. *vocatio in ius*. The procedure is the subject of *D.* 2. 4–7.

[57] *D.* 2. 4. 18 Gaius I *ad leg. XII tab.* A summons was probably permitted as far as the house door and at every other opportunity, including the baths and theater (*D.* 2. 4. 20 Gaius I *ad*

that a plaintiff could expect assistance from any magistrate against a stronger defendant, even though a defendant's retaliatory use of force was at some point made illegal.[58] The defendant could, however, lawfully decline to follow the plaintiff to the magistrate by supplying a *vindex*, someone who would guarantee his appearance before the magistrate when required.[59] Early illustrations of summonses appear in Plautus and Terence. Usually the prepositional phrase *in ius* stands next to one of a number of verbs, e.g., *ambula in ius, eamus in ius, in ius te voco* ("go to court," "let's go to court," "I summon you to court").[60] Witnesses are sometimes summoned or else their absence may be observed in these comic scenes.[61] Force is specifically mentioned as being applied to the neck of the summoned person on a number of these occasions.[62] While such phrases may indicate that the procedure of summons or forced summons is underway, the variation in their phrasing renders them inappropriate as evidence for set formulae.[63]

Procedure might differ somewhat according to the type of action the plaintiff uses to open his lawsuit. Gaius names five *legis actiones*, three of which were used to establish a legal right for proceeding and to obtain a judgment; two were used to execute judgment.[64] The

leg. XII tab.). Wesener *RE* 9A1. 687 s.v. *vocatio in ius* assigns these strictures to the period of the *XII Tables*.

58 Gaius 4. 46 speaks of the praetorian edict containing *formulae in factum conceptae* for actions "against an individual who, upon being summoned to court, neither comes nor supplies a guarantor" and "against an individual who uses force against a summoned person." For discussion of the inadequacies of such sanctions, see Kelly 1966: 7ff., with references to earlier literature.

59 The specific role played by the *vindex* in a summons is not known. *XII Tables* 1. 4 prescribe that where the defendant was a member of the wealthier class (*adsiduus*), the *vindex* must be one also; on problems of text and meaning, see Kaser 1966: 49–51, Watson 1975: 181 and n. 19, and App. 5, cat. nos. I. 1 and x. 5.

60 Summonses in Plautus and Terence (one asterisk = corrupt text; two asterisks = emended text; square brackets = probable interpolation): (1) *Ambula*: *Curc.* 621 and 624; *Pers.* 745, 750; *Rud.* 860; *Ph.* 936. (2) *Ire*: *Poen.* 1229; [1342]; [1349]; *Truc.* 840*; *Ph.* 981. Cf. Martial *Epigr.* 1. 103, 12. 97. (3) *Vocare*: *Asin.* 480; *Curc.* 683; *Poen.* 1225** ; [1343]; *Rud.* 608. (4) *Sequi*: *Asin.* 490; *Curc.* 721. The procedure in Plautus and Terence is studied in detail by Witt 1971.

61 *Antestari* (to call as witness): *Curc.* 621–23; *Pers.* 747; *Poen.* 1230. On the *Curc.* and *Poen.* passages, see Zwierlein 1990: 281–83 and Tandoi 1961; on the *Pers.* passage, see App. 4.2.

62 *Poen.* 790: *optorto collo ad praetorem trahor* ("I am dragged to the praetor with my neck in a collar"); cf. *Curc.* 693; *Rud.* 853 and 868.

63 This is the view of Witt 1971: 233–50, who has examined most of the passages in which such phrasing occurs, and of Kelly 1966: 6 and n. 3, and certainly it is correct.

64 Gaius 4. 12 lists five *actiones*, "*sacramento, per iudicis postulationem, per condictionem, per manus iniectionem, per pignoris capionem*," and he describes them in the following chapters (4.13–29). The *legis actio per iudicis arbitrive postulationem* (= *p. i. a. ve p.*) could be used only where a statute had authorized the procedure (see chapter 3.2 at nn. 64–65). The *actio per condictionem*, the latest of the *legis actiones*, appears to differ from the *p. i. a. ve p.* in that "the

actiones of the first type were *sacramento* (literally "by oath"), *per iudicis arbitrive postulationem* ("by application for a *iudex* or *arbiter*"), and *per condictionem* ("by giving notice"). The *legis actio sacramento* was of a general nature and employed in all cases for which a statute did not make provision;[65] claims under this *actio* were of two types: *in rem* (a *vindicatio* or claim of ownership) and *in personam* (a claim to enforce an obligation).[66] While claims *in personam* were set in motion by *in ius vocatio*, it is a matter of scholarly dispute whether claims *in rem* were. Kaser, for instance, argues that the latter were not initiated by *in ius vocatio*; the *actio in rem* was merely an action "*auf die Sache*" and did not entail a right against the person of the possessor.[67] This somewhat arcane scholarly debate has some relevance for Roman Comedy in scenarios that are thought by some scholars to depict status suits (*vindicationes in libertatem* or *in servitutem*): according to Kaser's view, because such suits belonged to the general category of *actiones in rem*, they, too, would not be initiated by *in ius vocatio*. Nonetheless, summonses do appear in the Plautine scenarios under discussion.[68] Is Kaser's thesis wrong? Or has Plautus bungled? Unfortunately, certainty is impossible to establish: no ancient evidence reliably attests whether all or only some Roman claims were initiated by *in ius vocatio*; the *XII Tables* report only how a summons operated, not the conditions under which it was operable. In the absence of evidence, it is too speculative a method to use Kaser's thesis to explicate Plautine scenes and their Greek originals. Plautus may yet have "bungled" – he is no jurist – but not because he has failed to present status scenarios in accordance with Kaser's theory.[69]

ground or reason of the obligation, more particularly the type of contract which led to the obligation now sought to be enforced, need not be mentioned" (Schiller 1978: 201, reporting Baron's view). *Manus iniectio* and *pignoris capio* are chiefly methods of execution. For discussion of the five *actiones*, see Kaser 1966: 60–82 and 94–106, with references to scholarly literature.

65 Gaius 4.13.

66 Gaius 4.15: *in personam* (the ms. is defective and less informative here); 4.16–17: *in rem*.

67 Kaser 1966: 48–49, 67–69, 75; similarly, Arangio-Ruiz 1968: 116, 1. Kaser hypothesizes how these cases entered court in various publications (1943: 70–72; 1949: 201, 38; 1962: 85–88). A significant implication of Kaser's view ("that the proprietary remedy was originally connected with a suspicion of theft on the part of the person in possession") is indirectly attacked by Watson 1975: 128–29 and nn. 12–13.

68 E.g., *Curc.* V 2 and *Pers.* IV 9: scholars, however, dispute the type of the offense for which the summonses are issued; on *Curc.* V 2, see App. 5, cat. no. III. 11 and add. 3; on *Pers.* IV 9, see App. 4.2.

69 Witt 1971 uses Kaser's thesis to explicate the Greek originals; Paoli 1976 (= 1951) arrived at similar conclusions about the Greek originals without adverting to Kaser's view.

Our account of *in ius vocatio* – at least in the abstract – is complete. A compliant defendant follows his summoner to court; a resisting defendant is compelled to follow. Since little is known in this period about procedure before magistrates other than the praetor, we shall focus on cases brought before him. After the summons, procedure falls into two distinct parts: *in iure* ("in court") and *apud iudicem* ("before the judge"). The first part (*in iure*) took place before the magistrate (the praetor) who oversaw the preliminaries before the hearing; in the second part (*apud iudicem*), the issue was decided by a layman called a *iudex* or *arbiter*. Two important ends are achieved during a successful procedure *in iure*: (1) the complaint is determined, formulated, and formally entered (*litis contestatio*) and (2) the *iudex*, *arbiter*, or judging panel is selected. If the accused admits his guilt during the *in iure* procedure, the consequence depends on the type of *actio* in which he has become involved. If it is an *actio in rem* in which the possession of an object has been disputed, the object is awarded by *addictio* to the plaintiff. If it is an *actio in personam*, then, according to the *XII Tables* (3.1), the confessed offender has thirty days in which to make the payment to the plaintiff. If, however, the accused disputes the claim (whether *in rem* or *in personam*), and the praetor decides that the prerequisites for admitting the procedure have been met, he "gives the action" (*actionem dare*) to the plaintiff and permits the formal entrance of the claim. The entrance of the claim is effected by a series of solemn statements which characterize the *legis actiones* and provide the basis for the *lis*, the disputed claim.[70] The interchange of assertion and denial was called the *litis contestatio*, so named because witnesses were summoned at this juncture; the two parties are now bound to settle their dispute by law.[71] This was an important moment; as the authors of one study of Roman law have put it, "the plaintiff's right was held to have been 'consumed,' that is, even if judgment was not reached, no fresh action could be brought on the same claim."[72] If the complaint was not determined on the day of the summons, the defendant would have to provide

[70] See Gaius 4.16 for an example of the interchange of *formulae*.

[71] Kaser 1966: 57 and n. 34, citing Festus p. 50. 14–15 Lindsay: *Contestari litem dicuntur duo aut plures adversarii, quod ordinato iudicio utraque pars dicere solet "testes estote"*; p. 34. 18 Lindsay: *Contestari est, cum uterque reus dicit "testes estote"* (50. 14–15: "two or more disputants are said to attest the initiation of the complaint, since each party, when the procedure has been arranged, is accustomed to say, 'let there be witnesses' "; 34. 18: "Attestation occurs when each disputant says, 'let there be witnesses' ").

[72] Jolowicz and Nicholas 1972: 184. On the binding effect of the formal act, see Kaser 1966: 57–58.

sureties (who would be personally liable to the plaintiff) to guarantee his appearance for the continuation of the proceedings the next day; in this way, the defendant avoided being summoned a second time.[73]

The final proceeding *in iure* was the appointment of the *iudex* or *arbiter*. The appointment would be made at the end of the first (and only) pre-trial meeting for the *actio per iudicis arbitrive postulationem*, but at a second pre-trial meeting, thirty days later, for *actiones sacramento* and *per condictionem*;[74] after appointment, the hearing before the *iudex* or *arbiter* would take place after a day's interval.[75] While the choice of judge lay with the praetor, it is probable that he listened to the suggestions of the two parties and especially to their expressed disinclinations for one or another from the list of potential judges.[76] If the two parties could not agree to any name on the list, the praetor could then draw a name by lot.[77] Up until the time of the Gracchi only senators could be assigned as judge.[78] It is a matter of dispute whether and in what way the original roles of *arbiter* and *iudex* may have been distinguished;[79] they are mentioned together in the

[73] For details, see Kaser 1966: 51–52.

[74] The *arbiter* or *iudex* in *sacramentum* was originally appointed at the first (and only) meeting; but this was changed by the *lex Pinaria* (Gaius 4. 15) which is dated to 472 BC (see Schiller 1978: 192, n. 7). For the thirty-day period before the appointment of the *iudex* in *per condictionem*, see Gaius 4. 17b-18. For immediate appointment in the *actio p. i. a.ve p.*, see Gaius 4. 17a.

[75] Gaius 4.15 (speaking of claims *in personam*, but probably true of claims in the other *actiones*).

[76] Whether the litigants participated in the choice of *arbiter* or *iudex* has been a matter of debate; while the language of the *legis actio per iudicis arbitrive postulationem* suggests that the praetor made the appointment, it might not exclude either a custom or requirement of the litigants' agreement: *actor dicebat: QUANDO TU NEGAS, TE PRAETOR IUDICEM SIVE ARBITRUM POSTULO UTI DES* (Gaius 4. 17a: "the plaintiff said: 'Since you deny, I ask you, Praetor, to grant a *iudex* or *arbiter*' "). Cicero claims in *pro Cluent.* 120–21 that *maiores nostri* desired that no judgment be rendered even about the most trifling case "unless there was agreement between the disputants" and cf. Festus, s.v. *procum patricium* (p. 290. 21–27 Lindsay). Those who accept Wlassak's theory that private litigation was based on contract support the view that the litigants' agreement was essential in the selection of *iudex* or *arbiter*. For an attack on that view, see Broggini 1957: 9–11; for a recent vigorous restatement of the litigants' consent, see esp. Kelly 1976: 125–28; similarly Frier 1985: 244. Kaser 1966: 43 with nn. 25–27 will have it both ways, as I have presented the practice in the text above.

[77] Kaser 1966: 43, explaining Pliny *NH praef.* 8: *plurimum refert sortiatur aliquis iudicem an eligat* ("it is important whether one obtains a *iudex* by lot or whether one selects him").

[78] Polybios 6. 17. 7; according to tradition, this senatorial privilege went back to Servius Tullius (D. H. 4. 36. 2).

[79] Wlassak *RE* 2. 410 *s.v. arbiter* provides the most concise statement of the identification of the two. Broggini 1957 attempts a vigorous refutation of Wlassak's thesis of identification. Unfortunately, arguments about these matters as they pertain to early Roman law are largely speculative; for a review of Broggini's work that specifies the parameters of the evidence, see especially Wieacker 1959: 582–92 and chapter 3. 2, n. 75 below.

XII Tables.[80] The judge decides the case between two disputants, each of whom maintains a statement contrary to the other; in cases brought by *sacramentum*, he decides which statement is correct. There appear to have been few restrictions regarding the form of the proceedings *apud iudicem*, although a "customary etiquette" appears to have regulated the speeches of advocates and the presentation of witnesses in the late Republic.[81] While in the *XII Tables* (1. 9) sunset is given as the time limit of the proceedings, in later times (certainly in the late Republic) meetings might adjourn on following days. The *iudex* or *arbiter* usually sat in a public place in the city agreed upon by the two parties.[82] The presence of both parties was required when the verdict was handed down.

The actual dynamics of the proceedings from summons to court verdict were much less cut and dried, much less straightforward than the textbook presentation offered so far. The summons itself, a self-help procedure which resembles more an Athenian arrest than a summons, would often require for its successful execution a plaintiff's show of force or credible display of superior status.[83] As in an Athenian summons or arrest, negotiation might take place on the spot: Gaius, in his commentary on the *XII Tables*, noted that it was grounds for discharging a case "if, while the case is being brought to court, the affair is settled" (*si, dum in ius venitur, de re transactum fuerit*).[84] Negotiation seems to have been embedded in the judicial process from the outset. In the statute on *iniuria* in the *XII Tables*, "maiming" (*membrum rumpere*) allows for retaliation in kind, "unless the doer makes a composition with the victim" (*ni cum eo pacit*, 8. 2).[85] The *XII Tables* also seem to foresee the possibility that disputants, in general, might come to an agreement during the *in iure* procedure, before the *iudex* or *arbiter* heard their case (1. 6–7).[86] The praetor might in many such cases have overseen agreements

80 *XII Tables* 2. 2 and 9. 3. See chapter 3, nn. 64–65 for other collocations of *iudex* and *arbiter*.

81 Frier 1985: 203–10.

82 Behrends 1977: 450–53 with ancient references, contra Kelly 1976: 103–11.

83 Kelly 1966: 6–30.

84 *D.* 2. 4. 22.

85 *Furtum* might also have allowed for settlement – if the statute referred to by Ulpian goes back to the *XII Tables*: *nam et de furto pacisci lex permittit* ("For the statute [*Twelve Tables*] permits a pact to be made about theft," *D.* 2. 14. 7. 14).

86 *XII Tables* 1. 6–7: *6. Rem ubi pacunt, orato. 7. Ni pacunt, in comitio aut in Foro ante meridiem caussam coiciunto* (6. "If they compromise, [the judge] is to announce it." 7. "If they do not compromise, they are to put the arguments together in summary form in the comitium or forum before noon"). The meaning of 1. 6 is disputed; see Kaser 1966: 84, n. 6. Gaius 4. 15 glosses *causae coniectio* as *causae suae in breve coactio* ("a gathering up of their case into an epitome").

(called *transactiones* by classical jurists) between litigants (*D.* 2. 15); their successful execution would excuse the latter from appearing before the judge (*D.* 2. 11. 2 pr. Ulp.). The role of the praetor in such cases bears some resemblance to the Athenian official *diaitetes* who tries to reconcile the litigants before a dikastic trial takes place.[87] While the evidence just cited comes from the period of formulary law, the thirty-day interval between the first and final meeting with the praetor in *legis actiones sacramento* and *per condictionem* would allow plenty of time for mediation and agreement. *Iudex* or *arbiter* might also have played a mediating role during the second part of the judicial proceeding (*apud iudicem*). Valerius Maximus (8. 2. 3) and Plutarch (*Marius* 38. 5) report a story of Marius during his sixth consulship (100 BC). At that time he acted as judge in a case where a divorced woman (Fannia) was seeking the return of her dowry (*actio rei uxoriae*); her husband Titinius was trying to retain it by pleading the immoral conduct of his former wife (*retentio propter mores*).[88] Marius, apparently aware of Titinius' own scandalous conduct, met with him frequently in private, urging him to desist from the defense and to return the dowry. Only when the informal meetings came to nought did he hand down a verdict.

Cicero, in a much disputed passage in *pro Caecina*, observed that all trials (*omnia iudicia*) are established to serve "either to settle disputes or to punish misdeeds" (6: *aut distrahendarum controversiarum, aut puniendorum maleficiorum caussa*). Frier has commented elegantly on the passage:

> Cicero's dichotomy between dispute settlement and punishment of wrong-doing seems rather forced, but probably can be understood as describing a spectrum along which most private actions are to be arrayed: from those that are highly arbitrational (such as the action for dividing an inheritance, *actio familiae erciscundae*) to those that have a quasi-penal character (such as the action on theft, *actio furti*). Yet even in the most purely arbitrational suits the state retains some interest in the quieting of disputes, although it may be rather indifferent as to the outcome . . .

Although most Romans doubtless recognized the existence of this spectrum, the late Republican judicial system is strongly characterized by its effort to handle almost all private lawsuits through a consensual model of procedure akin to domestic arbitration. The consensual model may have

[87] Düll 1931: 124–50 examines evidence for mediation *in iure*; he compares the procedure *apud iudicem* to Athenian procedure "als eine Art Provokationsverfahren (ἔφεσις), das subsidär eintreten kann, wenn das Gütverfahren erfolgos war" (146 with n. 67).

[88] For details on the substantive law involved, see Watson 1967: 68–70.

little or nothing to do with the institutional origin of the formulary procedure, or with its "real nature"; but it is crucially relevant to the perceived ethos of late Republican civil procedure, which is dominated by the notion that the parties themselves, with the aid and assistance of the Praetor, define the issue between them, select a judge to determine the issue, submit their respective cases for the judge's unappealable determination, and then themselves supervise the verdict's enforcement.[89]

While the judicial process itself, then, might be viewed at aiming at negotiation – at least in its opening efforts, and more consistently so in arbitrational suits – litigants themselves cannot be expected to conform to that ideal. A litigant, for his part, will use his resources to swing the system to conform to his own needs and impulses. In the end, he might heed the mediating voice, or hear a verdict rendered by a judge. In the crevice between the ideal and the real, between mediation and assertion, resides the litigants' tactics. Roman litigants, we shall see, exhibit conduct similar to their Athenian counterparts: a reluctance to become involved in lawsuits and a concomitant proclivity to act as if lawsuits were underway.[90]

2(c) *Synthesis*

In very broad terms, the Athenian and Roman initial procedures for bringing an alleged offender to justice through the court system are similar. Under both systems of law, procedure falls into two parts: in Athens, summons is followed by at least two preliminary meetings before a magistrate or official arbitrator and then a hearing before a dikasterion; in Rome, summons is followed by the meeting(s) with the praetor (*in iure*) and then the hearing before the *iudex* or *arbiter* (*apud iudicem*).[91] It will be useful to point out more precise points of proximity and difference.

(1) In Athens, the accuser's summons to the accused was always oral; in this initial aspect, it resembles the Roman procedure of *in ius vocatio*.

[89] Frier 1985: 243–44, with nn. 26–28.

[90] Frier 1980: 48–50 lists ten reasons why a potential plaintiff might not press a claim; all of them can be duplicated from Athenian evidence. Whether all these reasons would be equally operative in the Plautine era is difficult to say; cf. "Introduction" at nn. 23–27. Frier 1985: 20–41 reconstructs, with fascinating detail, the pre-trial background of Cic. *pro Caec.* and examines "the problem of litigiousness."

[91] Legal historians have often pointed out the similarity and are usually careful to point out the differences as well; see, e.g. Pernard 1900: 185; Steinwenter 1925: 5; Wolff 1946: 68–69; Witt 1971: 228; Harrison 2. 95.

(2) During the first decades of the fourth-century in Athens, possibly in 378/7, oral complaints before the magistrate gave way to written ones – the accuser handed in a written charge. In Rome, the pleadings in the *in iure* procedure under the *legis actiones* were always oral.[92]

(3) In Athens of the late fifth century and in the fourth, the summoner was required to have two witnesses. In the initial summons by *in ius vocatio* in Rome, witnesses were required only if the accused refused to obey the summons; in that case, the summoner called bystanders or friends as witnesses and then proceeded to use force against the accused.

(4) In Athens, there seems to have been a general rule that there should be a four-day interval between the summons and the first required appearance before the magistrate. In Rome, the summoner brought the accused immediately before the praetor (*in iure*).

(5) In Athens, there were two preliminary meetings (presentation of the complaint to the magistrate and the *anakrisis*) before a trial that did not involve the Forty; in cases that fell to the latter's jurisdiction, an official arbitration (which might extend over several meetings) took the place of the *anakrisis*. In Rome, if the plaintiff proceeded by the *actio per iudicis arbitrive postulationem*; there was "one meeting" (even if it lasted longer than one day: *in iure*) before the hearing (*apud iudicem*); if the plaintiff proceeded by the *actio sacramento* or *per condictionem*, a second meeting (on the thirtieth day after the first) was required for the appointment of the judge.

(6) In Athens, the special procedure (*apagoge*) for the arrest of *kakourgoi* who are caught in the act renders a summons unnecessary. There is no equivalent procedure in Roman law. The offenses committed by *kakourgoi* comprise a limited category which is not coextensive with the wider range of offenses permitted to be brought by an Athenian or Roman summons. Moreover, *apagoge* sets in motion a different procedure (trial presided over by the Eleven) than a summons and provides a

[92] It is true that under the formulary system of law (and some *formulae* were in use during our period – see n. 44) complaints would be written out; but the praetor, not the accuser, would write the particular *formulae*. The phrase *dicam scribere* appears in Cicero in *Verr.* 2.14. 37; 15. 37; and 17. 42. All three instances concern procedure under the *Lex Rupelia* (homonymous with the cos. of 131 BC) in Sicily; the phrase may have entered Roman law through association with the native legal systems of Greek provinces.

mandatory death penalty if the *kakourgos* confesses before trial or is convicted by the dikasts. In a Roman summons executed by force, subsequent procedure is no different than if force had not been used (except, perhaps, for the evidence of witnesses that force had been applied), and there is no statutory penalty designed for offenders who have been convicted after a forced summons.

(7) Court verdicts in Athens are given by panels of 200 or 400 dikasts for private cases, depending on the amount of the sum involved (*AP* 53.3), and by panels of 500 dikasts (and sometimes of 1,000 or 1,500) for public cases.[93] Civil cases in Rome are heard by one *iudex* or one *arbiter*, sometimes a panel of three is used. While the centumviral and decemviral courts were probably in existence at this time, they are not mentioned in Roman Comedy. One point of certainty here: while Athenian *dikastai* and Roman *iudices* or *arbitri* are all laymen judges, their *personae* are not equivalent. A Greek playwright's address to his audience as *andres* (men) might carry overtones of "men of the dikasterion" (e.g., *Samia* 269), but for the Romans, there would be no such egalitarian echo.[94] On the other hand, the Roman judge bears some resemblance to the Athenian private *diaitetes*.[95]

On the basis of this sketch of procedures used in Athens and in Rome for initiating cases, it is easy to see that a Roman playwright who attempted to render a Greek scene entailing a summons or arrest would encounter problems. We can logically deduce and illustrate two:

(1) There is no equivalent in Roman procedure for a written indictment or complaint such as would be presented by a "summoner" (a potential plaintiff or prosecutor) to a magistrate in mid fourth-century Athens. Plautus and Terence refer to written complaints with variants of the phrase *dicam scribere* (literally, "to write out an action," i.e., "to sue") on six occasions.[96] *Dica* is clearly a Greek borrowing (= *dike*) and forms

93 See Todd 1993: 83 and nn. 9 and 10.

94 Wiles 1991: 30 and 231 n. 62 correctly observes, "A convention of direct address allowed the actor in a monologue formally to interpellate the audience as *andres* (sirs!) – implicitly, the group of adult males who formed the political community."

95 See chapter 4.4.

96 Pl. *Aul.* 759–60; *Poen.* 800 (see App. 5, cat. nos. III. 8 and 14, respectively). Ter. *Ph.* 127; 329; 438–39; 668 (App. 5, cat. nos. I. 3; VII. 3; III. 26; VI. 6, respectively). Probably the Plautine verses (less certainly *Aul.* 759–60) are modelled on the Greek original; likewise the

of *dicam scribere* suggest that the Roman playwrights (or the original inventors of the Latin phrase) may have had in mind *diken graphesthai* (literally, "to have a private suit written down," i.e., "to sue"), without due concern for the peculiar development of the middle voice in the Attic phrase[97] and probably without any concern at all to distinguish a private action (*dike*) from a public one (*graphe*).[98] While the phrase *dicam scribere*, then, alludes to Greek procedure, its occurrence in Plautus or Terence is by no means an ironclad proof that the Roman author is translating the Greek original at that particular point; the allusion might be no more than savvy Greek flavoring, added from the Roman author's knowledge of Greeks living in Italy. Only where an indictment is essential to the plot or staging of the play or where we have independent testimony (e.g., Donatus on *Ph.* 668) can we have confidence that the Roman author is translating the Greek procedure of the original (see App. 5).

(2) It will sometimes be difficult to determine whether a Roman summons is meant to render an Athenian summons or arrest. A Roman summons will always superficially resemble an Athenian arrest in which conveyance to the Eleven is immediate. The accompaniment of force in a Roman summons may be an indication that an arrest appeared in the original – not because we must assume that in Athens an arrested person always resisted, but because "to resist a summons" would have no meaning there. (An alleged offender in Athens might choose to ignore a summons by not appearing before the magistrate four days later – and he will suffer legal consequences for that absence; but "to resist a summons" would be tantamount to

Terentian verses, with the exception of *Ph.* 329, which might be the Roman playwright's addition; see the relevant discussions in App. 5.

97 For the "causative" middle, see K–G II. 108: "γράψασθαί τινα, einen anklagen (eigtl. den Namen des Angeklagten für sich niederschreiben lassen)." See further Calhoun 1919b: 178–79 for discussion of the development of the phrase. The phrase *diken graphesthai* is not common in the Attic orators (Isokr. 18. 12). Aristophanes uses forms of the phrase *graphesthai diken* at *Clouds* 758 (passive) and 770 (middle). *Dike* in the Attic phrase can refer to the document itself, the written complaint presented to the magistrate in a private suit (Lipsius 264 n. 1; cf. 240 for different meanings of *dike*). Written complaints for private suits are referred to elsewhere in Ant. 1. 2 (*graphe*); Dem. 27. 12 (*graphai*). See Hansen 1983: 309.

98 When public as opposed to private actions are designated by the Attic orators, usually (1) the verb *graphesthai* governs *graphen* (literally, "to have a public action written down," i.e., "to bring a public action" or "to indict"); or (2) *graphen* is omitted and the genitive of the charge is attached to the verb, as in *graphesthai hubreos* (literally, "to have a public action for *hubris* written down," i.e., "to indict for *hubris*"); or (3) *graphesthai* appears by itself and refers to the bringing of a public action. For full references, see Hansen 1976: 109 and n. 11.

sticking one's fingers in his ears.) The greatest difficulty in deciding whether a Roman summons represents an arrest or summons will arise when the summons takes place without violence, as appears to be the case in *Persa* IV 9.

Since there is no Roman equivalent to an Athenian *apagoge*, the Roman playwrights have two logical options, one from each end of the wide spectrum represented by *vortere*: (a) to translate Greek procedure with Roman legal terminology so the audience can form an idea of what is happening, but without scrupulous concern about resulting inconsistencies with Roman procedure or (b) to adapt the scenario considerably so that it conforms to Roman procedure. Since we do not possess the Greek originals, it is often difficult to decide which option Plautus has chosen. The easier method would be the first, to translate *apagoge* as a forced summons. Translation would only become successful adaptation (from a juristic perspective) if the playwright then resolved resulting inconsistencies and smoothed away the wrinkles so that the entire fabric might have the appearance of a seamless legal scenario (e.g., by transforming the Athenian offense into an appropriate Roman one and by ensuring that the envisioned penalty is congruent with the offense in the Roman system). Problems occasionally arise from what I would call "incomplete adaptations"; some of these problems are taken up in the detailed discussion of the summonses in *Rudens* and *Persa* in Appendix 4.

3 THREATENING LAWSUITS IN NEW COMEDY

In Appendix 5, I have catalogued scenarios which pertain to threatening, initiating, or carrying out lawsuits or lawfully endorsed self-help remedies in Graeco-Roman New Comedy. Roman plays yield far the greater number of scenarios in the catalogue; many of these, however, depend on Greek originals. In the Appendix, I explain the criteria I have used for assigning particular passages to Greek originals. My ultimate aim in creating the catalogue is to demonstrate the pervasiveness of intimidating pre-trial tactics in Athens; similar scenarios in the Attic orators confirm that the scenarios of New Comedy are not simply fictive and comic depictions of pre-trial conduct without any basis in social reality.

The 85 scenarios involving threats have been categorized in the appendix according to the proximity of the literal threat to its execution. To the first category belong threats of lawsuits or self-help remedies that were carried out before the play begins; to the tenth and final one belong threats of trials that occur in dreams or wishes. The organizational principle might therefore be described as "grammatic" – that is, according to whether the threat was made and executed in the past, or whether its execution is pending in the present, so as to be "future most vivid" (a threat made on-stage), "more vivid" (recommendations and warnings of lawsuits), and "least vivid" (dreams and wishes). The ten rubrics are as follows:[99]

I. A character appears on-stage after undergoing a prosecution or after trying to initiate one before the action of the play begins. (3 instances)

II. A character returns to the stage after being arrested or summoned to court during the play; he may have undergone prosecution or arbitration. (3 instances)

III. A character is arrested or summoned to court or is threatened with these procedures during the course of the play. The accuser either drops his charge or comes to an agreement with the accused; in some cases the outcome cannot be determined. (31 instances)

IV. A character, depicted as a sexual offender, is threatened with self-help remedies that are permitted by law or custom. In some cases, he undergoes physical punishment; in others, a private agreement is reached. (7 instances)

V. A character begins an examination of slaves under torture as a preliminary to trial – but with the aim of settling in private. (1 instance)

VI. One character challenges another to sue him in court. (7 instances)

VII. A character warns a friend that he is likely to be sued by an adversary. (3 instances)

VIII. One character suggests to another (usually a friend) that the arrest or prosecution of a third party is an appropriate response to a situation. (9 instances)

IX. A character fears that he will wind up in prison or be involved

[99] Five (cat. III. 3, 11, 21, 27 and IV. 3) of the 80 passages cited in App. 5 contain both a threat and counter-threat; each threat is counted as a separate "scenario" since threat and counter-threat advert to different remedies and might, in the Roman plays, have different origins.

in a future court action or subjected to a self-help remedy. (13 instances)

x. A character dreams, wishes for, or invents a story about a summons, a trial, or a self-help remedy. (8 instances)

In all, 15 scenarios appear in Greek plays and 70 in Roman plays. In App. 5, I assign 29 of the latter to Greek models ("probably Greek"); these are Roman adaptations of threats that are likely to have appeared in the Greek originals. Additionally, 19 scenarios are likely to be Roman additions and are not substitutes for Greek threats; the remaining 22 are of indeterminable provenance. In the following discussion, I allude to threats in all four categories of origin: Greek, probably Greek, Roman, indeterminable; I keep the categories distinct and give more attention to the first two.

Almost all of the 15 Greek and 29 probably Greek scenarios involve threats that correspond to charges for identifiable offenses in Athenian law. This does not mean, of course, that an Athenian magistrate would admit the charge under the given circumstances – some are splendidly misapplied – Nikeratos' recommendation of a prosecution for homicide against a young man who has allegedly cuckolded his adoptive father is a clear example (*Sam.* 512–13). Most frequently, characters fear, threaten, or recommend charges for kidnapping or enslavement (9 times) and assault (8 times). The remaining alleged offenses are: rape, 3 times; homicide, twice; maltreatment of an *epikleros*, thrice; undifferentiated maltreatment, once; theft, 5 times; adultery or seduction, 4 times; false witnessing, perhaps once (cat. III. 25); finally, there are 8 disputes over estates or money (e.g., return of a dowry or deposit). While it is possible to dispute the precise identification of offenses in some of these cases – and many could enter an Athenian court in various ways – the general trend is clear: charges for violent acts prevail, with a smattering of charges for domestic and financial wrongs. Scenarios of indeterminable origin display, for the most part, the same range of charges.[100] In the scenarios which are Roman additions, however, only a few of these offenses are replicated. Two striking (but not surprising) differences appear: instances of specifically Roman offenses for which there are no comparable Athenian remedies, and

[100] Two additional charges are added from this group: denunciations against prostitutes (III. 5 and III. 19), and one imaginary case – a summons by a monkey for refusal to loan a ladder (x. 6). See the discussion under individual entries and addenda.

a number of charges against laws or edicts invented by characters in the plays.[101]

Scenarios of pre-trial intimidation (of Greek or probably Greek origin) carry varying dramatic weight within the different plays. Sometimes, a threat of arrest or its execution is the cumulative point to which at least one strand of the plot has been explicitly directed. This is the case in those comedies in which a character is enticed to commit a crime or is framed for one for which he was not responsible. In *Poenulus*, a plot is devised to entice the pimp to commit a theft which will ensure his condemnation at a trial – a condemnation which will entail that the pimp's entire household be adjudged to his adversary (cat. III. 14). In *Persa*, another plot is devised, this time to trick the pimp into buying a citizen girl; the goal of this plot is to ensure the condemnation of the pimp once again at a trial (cat. II. 2 and App. 4.2). In *Miles Gloriosus*, the boastful soldier is enticed to commit adultery with a next-door neighbor – in fact, he has been framed since his new "love-interest" is a courtesan who has been cast for the role of divorcee only temporarily (cat. IV. 5). The sham preparations for an investigation of slaves under torture is a less extensive staging of another pre-trial scenario in *Mostellaria* IV 4 and V 1 (cat. V. 1).

Overt allusions to the staging of legal plots are less in evidence in other scenarios of Greek or probably Greek origin. A threat of court action looms ominously over the strand of plot in *Adelphoe* that concerns Aeschinus' rape of a destitute girl (cat. III. 23). The intimidating conduct that pervades *Phormio* originates in a trial that took place before the play begins: Phormio had orchestrated a prosecution against Antipho (127) that resulted in the latter's marriage to a sham *epikleros* (cat. I. 3);[102] thereafter, numerous threats appear to be made on the spur of the moment rather than after any extensive deliberation (cat. III. 25–27; VI. 5–7); nevertheless, these threats, and the fears that potential prosecutions inspire, mark all the significant action of the play. In many other scenarios belonging to categories III and IV, threats appear with similar spontaneity, but consume less dramatic time than those in *Phormio* and in the rape

101 Roman offenses: for fraudulent sale: cat. VIII. 3; infraction of the *lex Laetoria*: cat. VI. 4 and IX. 8; use of the remedy *in integrum restitutio*: cat. VIII. 9. Threats evolving from laws or edicts invented by characters: cat. III. 9, 13, and 18; cf. discussion under cat. III. 9, VIII. 1, and add. 2 ad init. (*Pers.* 53–80).

102 For the procedure for claiming an *epikleros*, see n. 7 above. For explication of the prosecution before the dramatic action of *Ph.* begins, see chapter 7, n. 45.

strand of *Adelphoe*. Most of the threats mentioned in this paragraph, however, are no different in effect from the summonses of *Poenulus* and *Persa*; whether or not a summons is planned, rehearsed in advance, and then "staged" as in those two plays, it still notifies the recipient, through more or less scripted language, that his action is now being regarded through the lens of the law; however else he may have regarded his conduct before this moment, he must now see it as the law sees it. An accuser's threat of a summons always initiates a staging or a performance insofar as his utterance conforms to a legal script and compels subsequent conduct to conform to one likewise.

A scenario from *Samia* will demonstrate how recourse to the language of law, even in the midst of blows, leads the disputants to pinpoint their quarrel and specify their options. The same Nikeratos who advises Demeas to prosecute his son for homicide, later, in a fit of rage upon discovering that his unmarried daughter has given birth and that Demeas' son is the father, runs outside his house, threatening murder, in pursuit of the infant who has been carried off by the *pallake* Khrusis. As he attempts to lay hold of the infant, he is blocked by Demeas. He warns the latter not to strike, but Demeas holds his ground – he will strike; Nikeratos responds that he will return like for like (574–75). The two men come to blows. Nikeratos cries out:

(NI.) πρότερος ἅπτει μου σὺ νυνί· ταῦτ' ἐγὼ μαρτύρομαι.
ΔΗ. σὺ δ' ἐπ' ἐλευθέραν γυναῖκα λαμβάνεις βακτηρίαν
καὶ διώκεις. (NI.) συκοφαντεῖς. (ΔΗ.) καὶ σὺ γάρ. (NI.) τὸ παιδίον
ἐξένεγκέ μοι. (ΔΗ.) γελοῖον. τοὐμόν. (NI.) ἀλλ' οὐκ ἔστι σόν.
(ΔΗ.) ἐμόν. (NI.) ἰὼ 'νθρωποι. (ΔΗ.) κέκραχθι. (576–80)

(NI.) You are the one who strikes first – I call on witnesses to this fact.
DE. But it is against a free woman that you are bringing a stick
and making pursuit! (NI.) You're playing the part of a sykophant!
(DE.) Tit for tat. (NI.) The baby –
hand it over! (DE.) Absurd – it's mine. (NI.) No, it's not yours.
(DE.) It's mine. (NI.) Help! Men! (DE.) Go ahead and shout!

A fast-paced legal duel takes place amidst the actual blows. Nikeratos' claim (576) that Demeas is the first to strike and his call to bystanders to witness that fact is quasi-formulaic procedure in scenarios of assault – i.e., the stage is being set for a suit as witnesses are sought to confirm that the opponent struck first.[103] Demeas

[103] On the importance of establishing that one has been struck first in an assault (*aikeia*), see:

counters Nikeratos' intimation of a looming suit with a description of Nikeratos' present conduct that conforms to *hubris* (577–78); the detail of Khrusis' status is the giveaway: although she is not an Athenian citizen, Demeas can seek redress for her as *ho boulomenos* with a *graphe hubreos.*[104] Nikeratos' retort (578) shows his awareness of Demeas' tactic of counter-incrimination: he charges him with "playing the part of a sykophant." The term – whether verb (as here) or noun – is always difficult to define; in v. 578, its texture is dense, combining generalized opprobrium, "you are being a litigious nuisance" with undertones of, "you are blackmailing me with an absurd threat (a prosecution for *hubris*) in the hope that I'll give up my threat (a suit for assault) against you" and "you are sykophanting me – and that's an indictable charge."[105] Demeas' response (578) is quick-witted: he is only doing what Nikeratos is doing (literally, "Yes [I am being a sykophant], for you are [acting like one], too." When Nikeratos then demands the infant and Demeas refuses to hand it over, Nikeratos' call for help, ἰώ 'νθρωποι ("Help! Men to the rescue!" 580) is a quasi-formulaic utterance (a "*Notruf*") that is both a summons for assistance and a notification to witnesses that a wrong has been committed.[106] The evidence for the scenario (assault and call to witnesses) in New Comedy is reinforced by evidence in the orators, tragedy, and Old Comedy.[107]

Lys. 4. 11; Isokr. 20. 1; Dem. 23. 50; 54. 28; [Dem.] 47. 47; and cf. 53. 17 where Apollodoros carefully presents the scenario of an assault. For discussion of the offense, see Hitzig 1899: 3–22; for a more elastic view, see Maschke 1926: 113. Our sources often make it difficult for us to distinguish assault (*aikeia*) from *hubris* (cf., e.g., Arist. *Rhet.* 1402a and 1374a).

104 A law on *hubris* is cited in Dem. 21. 47; see chapter 5, n. 51.

105 Charges of sykophancy could be brought by *graphe* or a *probole*: see Lipsius 448–51; MacDowell 1978: 64–68; D. Harvey 1990: 107. The best commentary on Nikeratos' charge of Demeas' sykophancy is perhaps Menander fr. 545 (K–T = Kock 635): . . . ὁ δ' ὁρῶν τοὺς νόμους / λίαν ἀκριβῶς, συκοφάντης φαίνεται (" . . . but if a man has an overly precise eye for the laws, he appears to be a sykophant." Cf. n. 14 above.)

106 This was pointed out by Bain (1981: 170), who recognizes it as a "Notruf" and calls attention to its Indo-European background which was studied in an important essay by Wilhelm Schulze (1933: 160–89 [= 1918: 418–51]). Gomme and Sandbach 1973 on 572–76 observe that ταῦτ' ἐγὼ μαρτύρομαι is "standard formula to call bystanders to witness wrongful treatment, above all an assault" and cite Ar. *Clouds* 1297, *Frogs* 528, *Birds* 1031, *Wealth* 932. *Notrufe* appear regularly in New Comedy; most frequently they are made by victims of assault (*Amph.* 376; *Aul.* 406–07; *Curc.* 620–26; *Men.* 999–1000); elsewhere by a cuckolded husband (*Amph.* fr. XVI [x]) and by defenders of young women whose asylum has been infringed (*Rud.* 620–26).

107 For the orators, see Lys. 3. 15 and [Dem.] 53.17. For Old Comedy, see preceding note. Cf. Lukian *Timon* 46 (which may have a source – though not necessarily first-hand – in Antiphanes, a poet of Middle Comedy to whom a play with the title *Timon* has been attributed). For tragedy, see Schulze 1933: 179–85 and Fraenkel 1950: 614 apud *Agam.* 1317 (noted by Bain 1981).

The scene from *Samia* not only illustrates the characters' knowledge of the law, it also shows their agility in using that knowledge as a manipulative tool. Demeas is the master here: when Nikeratos erroneously characterizes Demeas' attempts to protect infant and *pallake* as unlawful, Demeas counters by showing that Nikeratos is out of control; precise legal definition marks the boundary of acceptable conduct. Finally calmed and aware of the futility of his conduct, Nikeratos confesses his real source of anger: Moskhion has cozened him (585–86). Conciliation can now take place: Demeas offers mythic exempla (divine impregnations of women 589–602) framed by the promise that his son will marry Nikeratos' daughter (586 and 610). The specific pattern of conciliation here – violent conduct, threats of prosecution, conciliation through *muthoi* – has comic and forensic predecessors. In Aristophanes' *Wasps*, Bdelukleon, the son who is knowledgable in the ways of the law, tells how to avoid cash settlements for drunken assaults: either a company of gentlemen make an appeal to the victim, "or you yourself tell him some witty story, something funny from Aesop's tales or the Sybaritic jokes, one you learned at a drinking party; and then, with the whole mess turned into a gag – he releases you and goes away!" (1258–61).[108]

A brief survey of the Greek or probably Greek scenarios in categories II–V will show that persons who are threatened with court action or self-help remedies most often, like Nikeratos in *Samia*, choose the script for agreement. Only in two plays (cat. II. 2 and 3: *Persa* and *Rudens*) are characters haled off-stage to the magistrate; both reappear later in the play. While in *Persa* the action intervening between summons and reappearance is unclear, in *Rudens*, the alleged culprit has presumably – in one of those temporal brachyologies acceptable to drama – appeared before the praetor, been assigned to a panel of *recuperatores*, suffered condemnation, and paid the penalty. In the Greek originals of these plays, however, it is likely that the culprits came to private agreements with their accusers before they ever reached their fearful destinations (see App. 4); in the original of *Persa*, moreover, we can be sure that the accusers had no intention of bringing the suit before a magistrate. In another case (cat. II. 1: *Curc.*),

108 Bdelukleon's father later takes the advice to heart: summoned to appear before the market commissioners for damaging a bread-seller's stock, he responds with a story (1406–11) – comically, to no avail; summoned by another accuser, this time for *hubris*, Bdelukleon offers a private settlement – cash and gratitude, but his father intervenes with another (futile) story (1417–41).

the pimp had been summoned to court for a bankruptcy proceeding, but friends oversaw an amicable arrangement.

Well over a third of the total number of scenarios (regardless of origin) belong to the third category; it includes not only utterances of summonses or arrests, but also threats of these actions. As we saw earlier in this chapter, the utterance of a summons or an arrest in Athens is not necessarily a performative statement; on many occasions, an arrest or summons may have been perceived as a negotiable act, the equivalent of a threat: e.g., "I arrest you for kidnapping" might convey, "Return the woman you kidnapped or I'll arrest you and bring you to the Eleven." All the summonses and arrests in the third category, regardless of origin, are negotiable.[109] Few of the Greek or probably Greek scenarios are genuine bluffs – i.e., threats which do not aim at negotiation or execution in a court of law.[110] In most scenarios, it is clear that the person who makes the threat prefers, from the outset, to settle in private. When the blustering soldier in the famous siege scene of *Eunuchus* (cat. III. 24) is told that the girl whom he has come to seize is Chremes' sister, and when he is thereupon threatened with a suit for violence, he is immediately cowed and leaves the stage. A threat such as this one might be a bluff (one can hardly imagine the timorous Chremes haling the rival to the appropriate magistrate), but it can be extraordinarily effective. So effective, in fact, is the threat in *Eun.* IV 7, that it may well be that – in Terence's play – the soldier's cowed reaction, his resourcelessness that emerges in the ensuing dialogue with the parasite, was meant as a parody of law's efficacy in Greek New Comedy rather than as a contribution to the convention.[111] Threats of Roman origin in this category show a distinctive disproportion: they are all bluffs. Sometimes they serve as non-negotiable aggressive intimidation or bluster (especially against slaves), sometimes as vents for anger or righteous indignation, sometimes merely as jokes or clever exhibitions of Roman legal (especially edictal) terminology.[112]

109 Only two summonses, one in *Persa* and the other in *Rudens*, are performative (cat. II) – or at least appear so in the Roman adaptations; in the Greek originals, they may have been negotiable arrests (see App. 4).

110 Three of the Greek scenarios are too fragmentary to yield information (App. 5, cat. III. 1, 2, and 4). Four of the remaining fifteen Greek or probably Greek scenarios are genuine bluffs: *Curc.* 619–21; *Ad.* 248–49; *Ph.* 408; 935–36 and 981.

111 The parasite probably did not appear in the Menandrian *Eun.*; see App. 5, add. 9.

112 Intimidation or bluster: *Aul.* 415–17. Righteous indignation (combined with clever legal

In the Greek or probably Greek scenarios belonging to category IV, private agreements are reached after a character is threatened (or thought to be threatened) with a self-help remedy permitted by law or custom against rapists and adulterers. In two of these plays (*Sam.* and *Bacch.*, and cf. *Fab. Inc.* and *Eun.* in cat. X), a father is led to believe that his son is about to suffer a physical punishment for committing a sexual offense; in *Samia*, the father hastens his son's marriage to the girl he has violated and in *Bacchides*, he agrees to pay a sum of money as compensation for the alleged adultery. In neither play is there any danger that the physical punishment will be carried out. In category V, the pretence of a pre-trial procedure (examination of slaves under torture) ends with a reconciliation overseen by a friend of the profligate son.

That private agreement rather than the execution of a court case is the script chosen most often in the scenarios of categories II–V is undeniable. That in most cases the agent of the threat appears to desire a private settlement rather than a judicial one invites further reflection. To attribute this phenomenon to the nature of the comic genre itself – to maintain that agreement rather than the compulsion of the law is more suitable to comedy – would be to neglect the cultural context of these plays and to set aside the evidence for pre-trial intimidation adduced from the orators. The data presented in chapter I and in the first section of this chapter showed the frequency with which *graphai* and *dikai* were dropped and detailed particular cases where threats of litigation were used to compel an adversary to come to agreement outside of court. Evidence of negotiable summonses and arrests has also been gleaned from the orators. When dramatists present similar situations, they are not creating them in a vacuum. They are staging scenarios before an audience who will recognize the scripts and be amused by particularly clever riffs.

4 THREATS OF LEGAL ACTION AGAINST A RAPIST: *ADELPHOE* III 2 AND 4 AND IV 3

Strategies of pre-trial intimidation play an important role in *Adelphoe*, particularly in the strand of plot, certainly part of the Greek original, that concerns Aeschinus' rape of the poor and fatherless Pamphila.

terminology): *Capt.* 492–95. Joke: *Poen.* 1225. Edictal terminology: *Capt.* 791–826; *Poen. prol.* 16–45; *Pseud.* 143, 148, 172.

When Geta, a slave belonging to the girl's mother Sostrata, reports that he had seen Aeschinus abduct a girl from a brothel, both are convinced that Aeschinus has deserted Pamphila and that he no longer intends to carry out his promise of marriage (III 2, 324–34). Together with Sostrata's maid Canthara, they debate what course of action they should follow. "Should we endure it or tell someone?" Geta asks (336). In the end, Sostrata decides that the case must go to court – she has evidence against Aeschinus; moreover, neither she nor her daughter have done anything shameful (344–50):

> *peiore res loco non potis est esse quam in quo nunc sitast.*
> *primum indotatast; tum praeterea, quae secunda ei dos erat,*
> *periit: pro virgini dari nuptum non potest. hoc relicuomst:*
> *si infitias ibit, testi' mecum est anulus quem amiserat.*
> *postremo, quando ego conscia mihi sum a me culpam esse hanc procul*
> *neque pretium neque rem ullam intercessisse illa aut me indignam, Geta,*
> *experiar.* (344–50)[113]

Circumstances could not be worse than what they are now:
first, she is undowered; second, the dowry which would have been next best has been lost – she cannot be given in marriage as a virgin. This remains:
if he denies it, I have a witness with me – the ring he lost.
Finally, since I know that I have done no wrong –
that neither money nor any gift unworthy of me or my daughter has changed hands, Geta,
I shall go to court.

To initiate her bold plan of action, Hegio, a friend and relative, must be summoned (350–52). What Hegio's relationship is to Sostrata in Terence's play is not made precisely clear; she calls him his daughter's relative (351: *cognato huius*), a man highly esteemed by

[113] Among modern editors, Kauer-Lindsay (OCT) follows *A* (*Bembinus*) at 347: *si infitias ibit, testi' mecum est anulus quem miserat*; Marouzeau (Budé) and Gratwick 1987 follow S (the Calliopian recension), reading *amiserat*. Rieth 1964: 74, arguing in favor of *miserat*, produced evidence that it was a Roman custom for the future bridegroom to present a ring of betrothal and hence this detail (*anulus quem miserat* "the ring which he *sent*") is a Terentian addition. Most critics have followed Rieth (Arnott 1965: 259; Fantham 1975; Martin 1976). However, if Aeschinus lost the ring (*anulus quem amiserat*), then, according to the conventions of New Comedy (e.g., *Epitr. and Hec.*), it implies a ring lost during a rape by which the rapist might later be identified. That the ring is not mentioned later in the play (Rieth 74, Fantham 1975: 55, n. 29) does not amount to much of an argument against a Menandrian "lost" ring. The ring serves its purpose in the scene with Sostrata: she is prepared to go to court (for rape – not "breach of promise" which is not an offense) and she naïvely thinks that a ring lost in a rape ten months ago will be good evidence. Sostrata is not a "woman of the world"; she does not know that good and innocent people sometimes lose their cases – but Hegio does, and Hegio is eager to avoid trial and has no need to make any mention to Demea of the ring with its disputable tale.

her husband and a guardian of the family (352: *nam is nostro Simulo fuit summus et nos coluit maxume*, and cf. 457). Later in the play, Hegio will recall his relationship to Simulus: he was *cognatus* to him, they were brought up together from boyhood and shared the experiences of war, peace, and poverty (III 4, 494–96). Donatus reports that in Menander's play, "Hegio" was brother of "Sostrata."[114] If Donatus has represented the relationship correctly, then he had a more formal role to play as *kurios* of Sostrata and perhaps as *epitropos* (guardian) of her daughter – and potential (if distant) claimant for the hand of the *epikleros*; why he has not participated actively in the arrangements for his niece until she is on the verge of bearing a child out of wedlock could have been explained in a prologue – perhaps a long business trip to Byzantium, such as Nikeratos' in *Samia*. Terence's change reflects Roman law and social *mores*: Sostrata is *sui iuris*; Hegio appears to be her and her daughter's guardian (*tutor*), the person who would represent them in litigation, but without the power of a *paterfamilias* to make decisions for her.[115]

Hegio, informed of the case by Geta, gladly takes it up at the end of the third act (III 4). Described by Demea as "a man of old-fashioned morality and loyalty" (*homo antiqua virtute ac fide*, 442), Hegio turns out to be a shrewd forensic strategist – more knowledgeable than Sostrata of the informal channels of power, more keenly sensitive to the dangers incumbent upon a destitute woman who sets out to have a rich young man prosecuted for rape. When Demea, who has overheard some of Hegio's conversation with Geta, greets him, Hegio responds, "Ah! The very man I was looking for" (461). Hegio's presentation of the case against Aeschinus is a model of forensic expertise. He begins with a moral indictment of the youth (462–64), that he is neither a good nor decent man (*neque boni / neque liberalis functus officiumst viri*). He proceeds to a simple statement of facts, making sure first of all that the name of the girl's father is known to Demea (465–66) and next stating, simply and baldly of Aeschinus, "He raped his virgin daughter" (*filiam eius virginem / vitiavit* 466–67). He then produces a suspenseful *narratio*, informing Demea that he hasn't heard the worst yet (467–68), and goes on to detail Aeschinus' conduct, beginning with the rape, purposefully and explicitly deflating the young man's culpability for that action in

[114] Donatus on 351: *apud Menandrum Sostratae frater inducitur*; see App. 5, add. 8.

[115] For thoughts about the reasons for Terence's change, see Gratwick 1987: 36–38; R. H. Martin 1976: 351; Rieth 1964: 72–77.

order to make his later exploits appear all the more villainous by comparison. Speaking of the rape, he begins:

> . . . *nam hoc quidem ferundum aliquo modost:*
> *persuasit nox amor vinum adulescentia:*
> *humanumst. ubi scit factum, ad matrem virginis*
> *venit ipsus ultro lacrumans orans obsecrans*
> *fidem dans, iurans se illam ducturum domum.*
> *ignotumst tacitumst creditumst. virgo ex eo*
> *compressu gravida factast (mensi' [hic] decumus est);*
> *ill' bonu' vir nobis psaltriam, si dis placet,*
> *paravit quicum vivat, illam deserit.* (469–77)

> . . . for this could be borne somehow or other –
> night love wine youth impelled him –
> it's human. When he knew what happened, to the girl's mother
> he himself of his own accord went, crying praying beseeching
> promising swearing that he would marry her.
> There was forgiveness, there was a hush-up, there was trust. The girl
> became pregnant as a result of that rape – it is the tenth month.
> That splendid man of ours – a *harpiste* – would you believe it –
> he has acquired for a housemate – he has deserted the girl.

While our interest here is mainly in the function of the speech as executing a forensic strategy – to persuade Demea of Aeschinus' guilt and to acquire him as an ally to influence Micio's response to settle out of court – it is difficult to pass by the particular rhetorical flourishes that Terence has allowed the potential plaintiff: most notable are the repeated asyndeta, the accumulation of unconnected words (the nouns in 470, the participles in 472–73, the predicate phrases in 474 and 477) that drive home Hegio's point.[116] In the first asyndeton (470–71), he covers up the young man's guilt in the rape: "Night passion wine youth impelled him – it is human" – indeed,

[116] Hegio's language is characterized by asyndeta, not only in this passage, but also at 478–79, 482, 497, 502. While the stylistic feature may be Roman – particularly when coupled with the homoeoptoton of 472–74, it is an observable feature of Menander; see Handley 1990: 136, citing Men. *Dusk.* 19–20, Ter. *Ad.* 867, and Dem. *de eloc.* 193–94 (cf. Arist. *Rhet.* 3.12.1413b where the use of asyndeta is likewise said to lend itself to acting or delivery); Ferrero 1976 provides a detailed study of asyndeta in Menander. Gomme and Sandbach 1973 frequently note the scribal habit of interpolating particles (esp. δέ) into Menander's text; see their *Index*, s.v. "asyndeton." *Rhet. ad Her.* 4.41 describes asyndetic style briefly: . . . *et acrimoniam habet in se et vehementissimum est et ad brevitatem adcommodatum* ("it has pungency in itself and utmost forcefulness and is suitable for brevity"). At 4.18, the author uses an asyndetic example to illustrate a stylistic device that should not be used if *conpositio* is to be artistic: *flentes plorantes lacrimantes obtestantes* ("wailing, imploring, weeping, protesting"). O. Skutsch 1985 includes the spondaic hexameter among the *sedis incertae fragmenta* (F498) of Ennius' *Annales*. Cf. *Ad.* 472–73, *lacrumans orans obsecrans / fidem dans.*

how could anyone stand up to such an onslaught of external and internal forces? Next (471–73): "When he knew what happened, he himself, of his own accord, to the girl's mother went, crying praying beseeching promising swearing that he would marry her." The impressive accumulation of present active participles, climaxing in the explicit contents of the oath made even more distinct by the repetition of d-sounds, stress both the importance of the oath and the young man's eager and active sincerity. Sostrata's reception of his conduct is then swaddled in a blanket of kindness, which Hegio distances from himself by his use of impersonal constructions (474): "There was forgiveness, there was a hush-up, there was trust."[117] The consequences of the rape are now brought to the fore (475): "the girl became pregnant as a result of the rape – it is the tenth month" – an implicit reminder of a marriage promise left unfulfilled for too long and, as Donatus points out (apud 474. 3), an absolute assertion of Aeschinus' paternity – there is to be no question of any other lover. Finally the charge comes (476–77): "That splendid man of ours – a *harpiste* – would you believe it – he has acquired for a housemate – he has deserted the girl." *Ill' bonu' vir nobis* is thick with irony, conjoined, as it is, with the *psaltria* whom Aeschinus has carried off. The final words come abruptly, in asyndeton, encapsulating Aeschinus' villainy: *illam deserit.*

Demea, in the face of such a charge, has a proper forensic response: he asks for proof (478). And he quickly obtains it:

HE. mater virginis
in mediost, ipsa virgo, res ipsa, hic Geta
praeterea, ut captus [es]t servolorum, non malus
neque iners: alit illas, solus omnem familiam
sustentat: hunc abduce vinci, quaere rem. (478–82)

HE. The mother of the girl
is out in the open, so is the girl herself, so the pregnancy itself, Geta here
moreover, as slaves go, is neither bad
nor lacking know-how: he feeds them, the entire household
he alone keeps alive: lead him away, fetter him, investigate the matter.

Hegio's proofs are all, in Aristotelian terms, *atekhnoi* ("inartistic"): they are the eyewitnesses to the rape or its consequences. Geta is generously offered for interrogation under torture – no testimony

117 Gratwick 1987: 246: "Terence neatly dissociates Hegio from any part in the arrangement between Sostrata and Aeschinus by using impersonal constructions . . ."

will be withheld. The detail is significant as a pointer to Hegio's willingness to settle out of court. The description of the slave is not extraneous here – it is part of the forensic design – the creation of a credible witness (cf. Donatus apud 481. 2). The description at the same time provides testimony of Sostrata's household – Geta alone supports it, there is no outside assistance (e.g., from young men bringing gifts as if to a courtesan) – it is an honest household (cf. Donatus apud 481. 5).

Demea responds, perhaps ingenuously, that he is at a loss what to do (485–86). Precisely at this moment, Pamphila, off-stage, cries out her labor shrieks, almost as if to confirm Hegio's case against Aeschinus. Hegio takes advantage of the moment to make his final petition (488–93), imploring Demea to do voluntarily what the force of the law compels him and his brother to do (*quod vos vis cogit id voluntate impetret*, 490).[118] Most significantly for our understanding of Hegio's strategy, the petition contains an explicit threat; after explaining to Demea the basis of his connection with Sostrata's family – his long-time friendship with her now deceased husband, he ends:

> *quapropter nitar faciam experiar, denique*
> *animam relinquam potiu' quam illas deseram.*
> *quid mihi respondes?* (497–99)

> Therefore I shall make every effort I shall act I shall go to court, in the end
> I would sooner die than desert them.
> What response do you have for me?

Hegio's future course of action is clear. Aeschinus must marry the girl without putting her family through the ordeal of a court trial (490); but if Hegio's persuasion of Demea and Micio will not effect this, then he will take the case to court himself. The final words of Hegio's threat (*animam relinquam potiu' quam illas deseram*) are stinging; the rhetorically effective position of *illas deseram* at the end of the comparative clauses that follow the climactic tricolon crescendo (*nitar faciam experiar*) recall his earlier description of Aeschinus' behavior: *illam deserit* (477).

Hegio has put Aeschinus' conduct in its legal context. The young man has three options: to come to an agreement (by marrying the girl), to defend himself in court, or, most fearful for Hegio and so kept silent – to make a counter-charge. Hegio has designed his

[118] On the confusion in the mss. at 490, see chapter 6, n. 16.

strategy to prevent the third option from being chosen, and he makes his threat of court action at the same time as he indicates his preference for settling out of court. But why does he present his argument to Demea rather than to Micio? The latter, after all, has legal authority over his adopted son; the natural father had conceded that position. Within the dramatic context of the play, a meeting between Demea and Hegio that anticipates the meeting between the latter and Micio provides Demea with ammunition to support his view of child-raising over Micio's; he may now approach his brother fully armed with a vindication of his position – only, of course, to be overthrown by Micio's equanimity. But there may well be another reason for a prior meeting between Demea and Hegio, a reason emanating from Hegio's forensic plan: he may suspect that Demea, a man reputedly of a strict moral character, may be more easily won over to his side than Micio, a reputedly more liberal man who has allowed his adopted son free rein to indulgences. Hegio, then, may have purposefully sought support from Demea (recall 461: "Ah! The very man I was looking for") before confronting Micio: though no longer legally responsible for Aeschinus, Demea can be used to exert moral pressure on his brother (recall 462, an explicit reminder of Demea's blood relationship: "Your elder son, Aeschinus . . . "). But Hegio's expectations are baffled, and the defeat creates suspense over the plight of Sostrata's daughter. While Demea is ready to go to his brother (499), he does not offer to support Hegio's remedy. The disappointed advocate now gives a final peroration (500–04): wealthy and fortunate men such as Demea and his brother must judge with fairness if they want to be counted among the morally upright. The meaning is clear: they should choose a fair settlement, one that will take place outside the courtroom.

Hegio later appears with Micio on stage (IV 3) after the two men have already come to an agreement. Apparently, Hegio had no need for long persuasive speeches with Micio – the latter readily agreed to the marriage. But Micio shows his awareness of the grounds for Hegio's concern as he turns away the latter's praise for his easy compliance:

> *Ego in hac re nil reperio quam ob rem lauder tanto opere, Hegio:*
> *meum officium facio, quod peccatum a nobis ortumst corrigo.*
> *nisi si me in illo credidisti esse hominum numero qui ita putant,*
> *sibi fieri iniuriam ultro si quam fecere ipsi expostules,*
> *et ultro accusant . . .* (592–96)

I find no reason in this affair why I should be praised so highly, Hegio:
I am doing my duty when I correct an offense that originated on our side –
unless you thought that I was one of those men who think
they are being wronged without cause if they hear their own actions protested,
and then without cause bring counter-accusations.[119]

There are men, Micio realizes, who, when a charge is brought against them, will react by making a counter-charge. It was precisely this fear – that Micio might select such a script – that produced Hegio's forensic strategy. If Micio had refused the marriage, the case might have entered court; the risk of a trial lay in the possibility that the defendant might have turned the charge against the victim: not only was she a willing partner in seduction, she was a prostitute.[120] Sostrata had foreseen that maneuver – hence her claim that no material rewards had been passed on to her or her daughter (349).[121] But Sostrata's claim might not have held up in court; surely the young man, it could be argued, had visited her daughter during her pregnancy, surely he had given her something that could be construed as a gift or payment. This is the very claim that Epainetos allegedly made against Phano in [Dem.] 59 *Neaira* 67. Hegio's arguments before Demea were aimed at rendering such a counter-charge untenable – hence his production of "proofs," and, most importantly, his offer of Geta for torture. But Demea had been unreceptive. Luckily, and contrary to Hegio's expectations (514–16, 592), Micio proved to be a *probus vir* and opted for the script of private agreement.

The strand of plot concerning Aeschinus' rape in *Adelphoe* illustrates the forensic disposition of its various characters. Sostrata and her household debated openly whether to seek redress in court; Hegio took up the women's cause and devised a strategy to accomplish a marriage without going to court – although he would threaten a suit against Aeschinus; he first put his strategy into effect with Demea but failed to win him whole-heartedly to his remedy; finally, his strategy worked with Micio – the court battle is averted

119 Part of the translation of lines 595–96 is indebted to R. H. Martin 1976 ad loc.

120 Rieth 1964: 63–64 has compared the situation of Sostrata and her daughter to that of Neaira and Phano in [Dem.] 59. The claim that one is not a *moikhos* because one has been with a prostitute may have been a common counter-charge to complaints of seduction and adultery.

121 Rieth 1964: 63–64.

and the marriage will take place. Hegio's strategy, working through informal channels to avoid the damaging publicity of a court trial, is common in New Comedy – especially in those plays in which a rapist is brought to account for his offense.[122] As Aristotle recognized – or at least codified as a believable argument – the families of such victims are not likely to go to court when "the wrongs are such that men, when subjected to them, are ashamed to speak, as in the case of outrages committed against the women of their household or against themselves or against their sons" (*Rhet.* 1.12. 1373 a34–35).

It has sometimes been observed that the multiplicity of plots in New Comedy that have to do with rape betokens some strange preoccupation of the composers of these plays.[123] Such critiques reveal modern biases; they reveal especially how our attention has shifted from observing rhetorical and forensic strategies – even to the point of blotting them out entirely so that we are left with the sensational alone. But rape offered more than a sensational focus of interest for the composers of New Comedy. It is very likely that rape was not often prosecuted in the courts; informal arbitration – the goal of which might be to obtain the victim a dowry without the damaging publicity attendant on a trial – was probably the usual mode of settlement.[124] As in other cases, a potential litigant might use either the threat of a suit or the actual lodging of one as a lever by which to obtain some advantage from the defendant before going to trial; sometimes the advantage will be a financial settlement that may be less than what the prosecutor or plaintiff originally hoped to obtain in court, but it avoids the vagaries – and exposure – of a court action. Pre-trial forensic strategies are an important part of the court system; they foster types of communication that are not straightforward: threats and bullying, the preparation of witnesses and their accounts, the playing of roles, the perfection of persuasion. Rape cases above all allow for the demonstration of these strategies, for displaying informal channels of power, for showing how persuasion is effected outside the court. This, I think, is the attraction that a rape plot held for the writers of New Comedy: it allowed them to

[122] See chapter 6.2.

[123] Fantham 1975: 56 attributes these "strange intrigues" and "such tortuous, and in some ways shocking" plots to "the romantic ideal of a love sealed by marriage, in a society which all but excluded the combination of the two elements in everyday circumstances."

[124] See chapter 5.1.c.

explore forensic strategies in an area where, above all, men and women had exerted great ingenuity in concealing the truth in order to obtain justice. If we look only at the offense and not at the strategies used to resolve it, then we miss, I think, a central feature of New Comedy's representation of Athenian activity and culture.

PART II

Reconciliation and its rhetoric

CHAPTER 3

Arbitration and reconciliation in Athens and Rome

Arbitration and reconciliation are the most common procedural scenarios of dispute settlement in the comic genre. Sometimes they have a decidedly formal legal cast; more often, they appear as informal reconciliations between friends or adversaries. But formal or informal as they may be, the characters who take part in them have roles that would be recognizable to an Athenian audience. Except perhaps for the rather grand arbitration of *Epitrepontes* (literally "men who refer their dispute to arbitration") and the preparations for one in *Rudens* ("Rope," based on a Diphilan original, the title of which is unknown),[1] scenarios of arbitration and reconciliation have not usually been noticed by interpreters of New Comedy. Moreover, legal historians have devoted little attention to these procedures in the last fifty years. The aims of this chapter are to create an Attic typology for them and to trace out what can be known about private arbitration in Rome of the middle Republic. In the next chapter, I examine arbitration in New Comedy. I have reserved the reconciliations of rape and adultery as the subject of chapters 5 and 6, and a consideration of the arguments used during reconciliations as the subject of chapter 7.

I PRIVATE ARBITRATION IN ATHENS

1(a) Differences between arbitration and reconciliation in the orators: a traditional and untraditional view

Private arbitration and reconciliation were probably means of settling disputes in Athens long before we have any written record of their existence.[2] Aristophanes' *Wasps*, produced at the Lenaia in 422

[1] See chapter 4 n. 1 below.

[2] For a succinct account of early methods of dispute settlement, see Gagarin 1986: 19–50; for the use of oaths in archaic times, see Thür 1996.

BC, provides the first traces of the technical terminology that becomes associated with the procedures as we know them on the basis of more fully attested instances in the fourth century.[3] Private arbitration appears to have been "institutionalized" in Athens at some point in the fifth century – i.e., the law recognized it as "authoritative" or "decisive" (*kuria*) in ways that are defined below. Some scholars think we have a genuine piece of that legislation, mistakenly inserted into Dem. 21 *Meid.* 94.[4] Unfortunately, both the date of the "institutionalization" of private arbitration and its precise requirements for legal standing are controversial issues. Moreover, the general picture of private arbitration and reconciliation that we obtain from fourth-century orations is somewhat confusing because of the fluctuating terminology that is used of these procedures and because depictions of them are editorialized by speakers who choose to tell their audiences what will be to their own best interests. English treatments of this topic have simplified the picture by focusing on arbitration and excluding reconciliation from consideration. That tendency, perhaps inherited from Lipsius, is justifiable to the extent that writers of legal handbooks traditionally occupy themselves with procedures that are recognized by law. But Lipsius had himself inherited at least a century of detailed German scholarship on both arbitration and reconciliation; moreover, the blossom of that yoked tradition arrived later, in 1925, with Steinwenter's important monograph which set arbitration and reconciliation within the full context of methods of dispute settlement.[5] A conse-

[3] See App. 2.e for terminology of arbitration in Old Comedy and tragedy.

[4] Text of MacDowell 1990 with modified trans.: Ἐὰν δέ τινες περὶ συμβολαίων ἰδίων πρὸς ἀλλήλους ἀμφισβητῶσιν καὶ βούλωνται διαιτητὴν ἑλέσθαι ὁντινοῦν, ἐξέστω αὐτοῖς αἱρεῖσθαι ὃν ἂν βούλωνται {διαιτητὴν ἑλέσθαι}. ἐπειδὰν δ' ἕλωνται κατὰ κοινόν, μενέτωσαν ἐν τοῖς ὑπὸ τούτου διαγνωσθεῖσι, καὶ μηκέτι μεταφερέτωσαν ἀπὸ τούτου ἐφ' ἕτερον δικαστήριον ταὐτὰ ἐγκλήματα, ἀλλ' ἔστω τὰ κριθέντα ὑπὸ τοῦ διαιτητοῦ κύρια ("If any men dispute with each other about private contracts and wish to choose anyone as arbitrator, let them be permitted to choose whomever they wish. When they have made an agreed choice, let them abide by the decisions of that man, and let them not thereafter remit the same charges from him to another place of judgment, but let the judgments of the arbitrator be authoritative"). For different views on the authenticity of this law, see n. 23 below.

[5] Hudtwalcker 1812; Meier 1846; Hubert 1885; Matthiass 1892. Huwardas 1938 is a critique of Steinwenter 1925. Most of these authors focused upon the following inter-related questions: (1) how is private arbitration distinguished from reconciliation? (2) what are the legal effects of the two procedures? (3) if the verdicts given in arbitrations are legally binding and likewise any of the agreements resulting from reconciliations, what effected that binding quality? The last question has been the most controversial and has involved three issues: (i) the oath of the arbitrator; (ii) the agreement of the disputants; and (iii) the evaluative basis of the arbitrator's verdict.

quence of what might be termed the "legal handbook approach to law" (i.e., the focus on procedures recognized by law) is the exclusion of the long-lasting debate concerning the definitions of arbitration and reconciliation – as if the case had been decided once and for all – and, more lamentably, the disappearance of reconciliation from scholarly discussion.

According to the view transmitted by Lipsius and represented (in general) by scholars writing in English, private arbitration can be typified as follows:[6] two opposing parties agree upon one or more arbitrators (*diaitetai hairetoi*); conditions upon which the decision is to be based are agreed upon in advance and may be set down in writing; the arbitrator gives his verdict under oath. The verdict is legally binding upon the two parties in the same way as a verdict given in a courtroom: (i) the same issue could not be subjected to another hearing – and if it were, a plea to bar action (a *diamarturia* in the late fifth century, a *paragraphe* in the fourth century) could be made, claiming that the suit was not admissible (*eisagōgimos*); (ii) moreover, if the verdict or settlement involved the surrender of money or property, it was (indirectly) enforceable by the *dike exoules* (suit for ejectment).

There are two flaws in such a presentation. First, it conceals the controversy mentioned earlier concerning the criteria for distinguishing arbitration from reconciliation. Secondly, it accepts certain century-long entrenched views, even though some of the evidence for those views has been called into question. To present a thorough re-examination of the evidence here, with all the detailed argumentation it requires, is beyond the scope of this chapter. Nevertheless, I

The legal historians who accepted the law cited in Dem. 21. 94 as genuine also accepted the binding quality of arbitration (see n. 23); most accepted the oath as a requirement for binding arbitration (Hudtwalcker 1812, Thalheim 1906, and Steinwenter 1925 dissenting) and thought that the disputants were required to accept the verdict before it was announced (Huwardas 1938 dissenting). No *opinio communis* ever emerged from the final issue concerning evaluative criteria.

6 Lipsius 220–26; Harrison 2. 64–66; Isager in Isager and Hansen 1975: 107–08; MacDowell 1978: 203–06; Todd 1993: 123–25; V. J. Hunter 1994: 55–62 and 205–08. Citations of ancient sources to support the contentions of this paragraph can be found in the first four authors and the last. All the authors claim that arbitration was legally binding; only Lipsius, Harrison, and Hunter specify the *dike exoules* as a remedy. Neither Isager nor Todd make the arbitrator's oath a prerequisite for a binding arbitration. Hunter now provides the most detailed English treatment of the topic. While focusing on arbitration between kin, she has taken into account the entire pool of arbitrations presented in the orators. Hunter's is a valuable contribution to the sociological context of arbitration. Unlike the legal historians mentioned here, she appears to recognize a difference between arbitration and reconciliation, but seems to limit it to a friend's reconciliation of personal enemies (pp. 205–06, n. 14).

shall present a synopsis of my analysis of the differences between arbitration and reconciliation and then I shall outline a new interpretation of the evidence concerning the binding quality (*Verbindlichkeit*) of arbitration.

The essential difference between arbitration and reconciliation is the method of ending the dispute: in the former, the arbitrator (*diaitetes*) decides the case and gives a verdict; in the latter, the opposing parties agree to accept a compromise that has been suggested by a mediator (*diallaktes*, *dialutes*).[7] The distinction is clear from [Dem.] 33 *Apat.* 17: the speaker claims that an earlier arbitration had broken down because of a disagreement over the preliminary procedural arrangements; whereas he had been assigned to act as one of three *diaitetai* who were to give a decision that was to be authoritative (*kuria*, 15), his current opponent "contended that Aristokles was his *diaitetes* and said that Phokritos and I were authorized to do nothing (*oudenos kurious*) except to bring about a reconciliation (*tou dialusai*)." Similar conceptual and terminological distinction appears elsewhere, e.g., in Dem. 55 *Kall.* 32 and in *AP* 53. 2. The latter passage depicts the two different procedures followed by the official arbitrator: οἱ δὲ παραλαβόντες, [ἐ]ὰν μὴ δύνωνται διαλῦσαι, γιγνώσκουσι, κἂν μὲν ἀμφοτέροις ἀρέσκηι τὰ γνωσθέν[τ]α καὶ ἐμμένωσιν, ἔχει τέλος ἡ δίκη ("after they receive the case, if they are unable *to reconcile* the parties, they *give a verdict*, and if the decision is satisfactory to both parties and if they agree to abide by it, the suit is finished").[8]

The orators and lexicographers, however, do not always maintain a strict terminological distinction between the two procedures.[9] A survey of the evidence shows that *diaitetes* (the third party agent), *diaita* (the procedure), and *diaitan* (the verb) have both a general and a strict usage which is determinable by context: a *diaitetes* in the general sense can be either an arbitrator or mediator but, in the strict sense, he is an arbitrator who gives a verdict. *Diaitan* is sometimes used of the activity of arbitators who give a verdict, but sometimes of mediators who propose a settlement. The verb *epitrepein*, with or without *diaita* ("arbitration") as object, means "to refer

[7] Steinwenter 1925: 105. *Dialutes* only appears in *Agora* i. 3394. 6.

[8] Matthiass 1892: 10 n. 1, whose work appeared in the year following the first publications of *AP*, was the first to note the significance of this chapter of *AP* for distinguishing the procedure of arbitration from that of reconciliation.

[9] This observation was made by Steinwenter 1925: 97–99. For examples of *diait*-words used to refer to reconciliations, see e.g., Is. 2. 30 and [Dem.] 59. 45–47 and 68–71.

a dispute to arbitration," whether the procedure envisioned is reconciliation or arbitration in the strict sense.[10] Moreover, while certain verbs indicate or imply a verdict (*katadiaitan*, *katagignoskein*, *apogignōskein*, *diagignōskein*, *proskatagignōskein*) and others designate reconciliation (*diallattein*, *dialuein*), yet the verbs *apophanesthai* and *gignōskein* are sometimes used to designate verdicts and sometimes the proposals of mediators.[11]

While *diaitetes*, *diaita*, and *diaitan* can be used of either arbitration in the strict sense or of reconciliation, there is no palmary classical example of a term of reconciliation (*dialusis* and *diallage* "reconciliation," *dialuein* and *diallattein* "to reconcile," *diallaktes* and *dialutes* "mediator") used for arbitration in the strict sense; such terms always refer to reconciliation when used in descriptions of third-party procedures.[12] It is notable, in this respect, that the agreement made between the Athenians in the Peiraieus and those in the city in 403/02 was brought to conclusion by Pausanias the Lacedaimonian king together with ten *diallaktai* (*AP* 38. 4, cf. Xen. *Hell.* 2. 4. 38); it is notable, furthermore, that that agreement is always referred to as *dialuseis* (e.g., *AP* 38. 4) or as *diallagai* (e.g., And. 1 *Myst.* 90, Isokr. 18. 25).[13] No verdict was imposed upon the Athenians – whether propaganda or reality, the terminology was pure reconciliation. And notable for us among the features of that reconciliation is the "amnesia clause": "Otherwise no one was to recall the past misdeeds of anyone (μηδενί πρὸς μηδένα μνησικακεῖν ἐξεῖναι) except for those of the Thirty, the Ten, the Eleven, and the governors of Peiraieus, and not even of these if they successfully submitted to examination" (*AP* 39. 6, trans. Rhodes, and cf. And. 1 *Myst.* 90). Similar formulae also appear in private *diallagai* reported by the orators. In Apollodoros' narrative of the terms of agreement between Stephanos and Phrunion in [Dem.] 59 *Neaira* 46, the speaker reports, as the last item, that "for the future the men are to be friends (*philoi*) to one another and are not to recall past misdeeds (μὴ μνησικακεῖν)." Later in the same speech, Apollodoros cites the terms of reconciliation between Stephanos and Epainetos, the first of which is "they are to have no recollection (μηδεμίαν μνείαν ἔχειν) of what took place in regard to the imprison-

[10] *Epitrepein* of reconciliation: e.g., Dem. 41. 1 and [Dem.] 59. 45. *Epitrepein* of arbitration in the strict sense: e.g., [Dem.] 33. 14; 34. 18; Is. 2. 30.

[11] *Apophanesthai* and *gignōskein* in a reconciliation (*diallage* specified): [Dem.] 59 *Neaira* 46–47. *Gignōskein* in a reconciliation: Dem. 41. 14 (with *dialuein*); *Agora* i. 3244. 5 (of *diallagai*).

[12] See App. 2. f., "Technical Terminology of Arbitration in *Agora* i. 3244 = Sokolowski 19."

[13] See Rhodes 1981: 463 for full references.

ment" (71).[14] The "amnesia clause," both in the reconciliation of the "political parties" in 403/02 and in the private reconciliations in the orators, proscribes any kind of vindictive action (judicial and extra-judicial) for past conduct.[15] The dispute is at an end.

The best way to distinguish between arbitration and reconciliation is to determine whether a verdict has been given or a compromise has been proposed and accepted. Terminology, for all its difficulties, remains the best aid. The presence or absence of a third party's oath, on the other hand, is an unreliable criterion;[16] no passage shows indisputably that an oath was required by law and it seems more likely that the decision whether an arbitrator or mediator was to take an oath would be part of the preliminary agreement between him and the disputants.[17] Sometimes, classification as one or the other procedure is impossible; Dem. 36. 14–16, e.g., is one such problematic case. In my view, classification matters little. Why it mattered, however, to German legal historians, and why reconciliations have dropped out of the accounts of legal handbooks, will soon become clear.

Was either arbitration in the strict sense or reconciliation binding in the fourth century – i.e., did one or the other allow a *dike exoules* to enforce execution and was a *paragraphe* available to bar action on the same issue in a court of law? German scholars who had drawn a

[14] For discussion of the authenticity of the documents preserved in the text (deposition of the *diallaktai* and copy of the *diallagai*), see Drerup 1898: 349–50 and Carey 1992: 121. Steinwenter 1925: 126 finds the terms (Stephanos' renunciation of the 3,000 dr. *moikhargia* and Epainetos' payment of 1,000 dr. toward Phano's dowry) "*juristisch fassbar.*"

[15] Rhodes 1981: 468–69 points out that μὴ μνησικακεῖν ("not to recall past misdeeds") is standard formula for an amnesty. On the broad interpretation of the phrase in the Amnesty agreement, see Ostwald 1986: 499; Carawan 1998 chapter 3.3 stresses its proscription of retributive self-help remedies. Context must determine meaning; certainly the phrase cannot mean "not to bring suit" when Andokides (1. 91) cites the phrase as part of the dikastic oath – surely the dikasts do not swear "not to bring suits" against the men they are judging! In the reconciliations of private disputes (having nothing to do with the Amnesty), the phrase will proscribe both judicial and extra-judicial retaliation.

[16] See the arguments of Thalheim 1906: 156 and Steinwenter 1925: 96–97. Huwardas 1938: 304–10 attempted a vigorous refutation of Steinwenter. In my view, the issue of the binding quality of arbitration takes precedence over the issue of an oath. For a brief sketch of my interpretation of one of the most controversial "oath passages," see n. 25 below.

[17] *IG* II^{2}1196, an inscription of 326/5 (Whitehead 1982: 38–39) from the deme Aixone, appears to provide general directions for debtors (in regard to pasturage dues) who choose to undergo arbitration by the demesmen. Face A of the inscription can serve as a sample "preliminary agreement" to an arbitration: " . . . the demesmen (i.e., the arbitrators) having sworn, before introducing (the case) to the dikasterion, [to execute?] the arbitration in the most just way (ὡς δικαιοτάτε), (the debtors) are to [put off business?] until the demesmen give judgment. And also (the debtors) are to swear [when they refer the matter to arbitration] to abide by whatever the demesmen vote and . . ." (9–12). Interpretation of the demarkh's (?) oath in Face B is difficult.

rather strict line between the two procedures answered: whereas private arbitration in the strict sense was fully binding under the law (provided, according to most, that it was accompanied by the arbitrator's oath and the disputants' agreement to abide by the verdict), only reconciliations that included an *aphesis* and/or *apallage* were binding, and these were binding in a limited way – they barred further action on the same issue, but the *dike exoules* was not available for execution.[18] This is the view that legal historians writing in English generally follow, except that they have omitted discussion of reconciliation and therefore, for the most part, of *aphesis* and *apallage*.[19] After citing the evidence that scholars have garnered to support their contentions, I offer below a brief reassessment of it.

The evidence:

(1) The law concerning private arbitration inserted in Dem. 21. 94 (quoted in n. 4) which prescribes that the disputing parties in a private arbitration are to abide by the arbitrator's verdict and are not "to remit the same charges from him to another place of judgment."

(2) Pollux 8. 57: "*paragraphe* is the same procedure as *diamarturia* [reading B], whenever a person says that a *dike* is not *eisagōgimos* on the grounds that he has already been brought to trial (*kekrimenos*) or because a *diaita* has taken place, or that a release has been given (*apheimenos*), or that [the particular *dike* must not be heard] since the time has lapsed in which it should have been heard."

(3) Isokr. 18 *Kall.* 11–12: the speaker reports that he had used a *diamarturia* in an earlier suit brought against him by Kallimakhos; the basis of the *diamarturia* was that the dispute had been settled by a private arbitration. If we follow MacDowell's dating, Kallimakhos' earlier suit was brought in 401/0 (other scholars have dated it to 403 or 402) and the current *paragraphe* trial takes place in 400/399.[20]

[18] See n. 5. *Aphesis* and *apallage* seem only to have become important in discussions of arbitration and reconciliation after Schwarz's publication of documents from Roman Egypt in 1920; thus Steinwenter 1925: 128–40; Huwardas 1938: 325–32. Since German legal historians had created the dichotomous distinction between arbitrations that were binding and reconciliations that were not, the attribution of negotiations winding up with *apheseis* and/or *apallagai* to the category of reconciliation was easy: this was the only way that reconciliations could be binding.

[19] Isager in Isager and Hansen 1975: 228–37 is exceptional and supplies an important appendix on these terms.

[20] MacDowell 1971a. Loening 1987: 124 with n. 71 (citing earlier discussions) dates the current *paragraphe* trial to 402/1. The later dating is significant; see n. 28.

(4) An *aphesis* and/or *apallage* that was the result of an arbitration or reconciliation is used as grounds for a *paragraphe* twice: Dem. 36 *Phorm.* 23–25 (the *aphesis* emerges from an arbitration or reconciliation, 14–17) and Dem. 38 *Naus.* 5 (the *aphesis* and *apallage* emerge from a reconciliation, 6, 10, 13). The first speech has been dated between 352/1 and 350/49; the second cannot be dated.[21]

(5) [Dem.] 52 *Kall.* 16: "But that I am speaking the truth and these men are lying, let this in itself be a clear proof (*tekmerion*) to you: that [if what they say about my father's refusal of an oath is true,] Lysitheides would have condemned (*kategnōkei*) him and I would now be defending myself in a *dike exoules* – not a *dike arguriou*!" The speech has been dated to 369/68.[22]

The reassessment:

(1) The law cited in Dem. 21. 94 has no claim to authenticity and must be rejected on the grounds of its use of imprecise terminology.[23]

(2) Pollux's report is useless: *diaita* is ambiguous and might refer to either official or private arbitration; furthermore, the report might not rely on the testimony of a law but rather on the interpretation of an oration (such as Isokr. 18. 11!) by Pollux or his source.[24]

(3) There are no grounds for believing that *paragraphai* in the fourth century were used to bar actions under precisely the same circumstances that had permitted *diamarturiai* in the fifth century. The speaker of Isokr. 18 *Kall.* had used a *diamarturia* in 401/0 to protest a suit on a matter that had previously been settled by a private arbitration. When the same plaintiff (Kallimakhos)

[21] Dem. 36 is dated 352/51 by Schaefer iii, 168–69; 351/0 by Isager and Hansen 1975: 177; and 350/49 by Trevett 1992: 48 n. 28.

[22] Trevett 1992: 31–32, n. 15.

[23] The view that the text is genuine and was inserted by a later editor is argued by Hudtwalcker 1812: 61 n. 2 and 177, n. 24; Meier 1846: 6–7; and Drerup 1898: 304; that view is accepted by Matthiass 1892: 41–43; Lipsius 222 n. 6; and Steinwenter 1925: 60–61. It is rejected by Hubert 1885: 23 on linguistic grounds; by Latte 1926: 211, mostly on the grounds of the imprecision of technical terminology in the law; he is followed by Huwardas 1938: 305 and Gernet 1939: 391 n. 3 (= 1955: 104 n. 7); additional arguments against the terminology used in the law are presented by MacDowell 1990: 317–18 (who also dismisses the law on the grounds that it lacks what he thinks a "binding arbitration" should require).

[24] Wolff 1966: 91–93 thought the binding quality of arbitration was beyond doubt and accepted Dem. 21. 94 as evidence for it; however, he called into question Pollux's report on the grounds I have presented above. Pollux's text here is not sound; consult Bethe's *app. crit.* for supplement.

brought the same suit in 400/399, the speaker of Isokr. 18 once again made a plea to bar action, but this time he followed the procedure of *paragraphe* (Isokr. 18. 1–3). At its initiation (or re-initiation) under the law of Arkhinos, *paragraphe* was limited to cases which infringed the Amnesty (Isokr. 18. 2), and this is the grounds for the present *paragraphe.* No fourth-century evidence demonstrates that a *paragraphe* could serve to bar action in a dispute previously settled by private arbitration.

(4) While an *aphesis* and/or *apallage* that was the result of an arbitration or reconciliation is used as grounds for a *paragraphe* twice, the arbitration or reconciliation itself is not presented as the legal basis for the objection.

(5) [Dem.] 52. 16, the only "evidence" for the *dike exoules*, can prove nothing: the speaker's statement about the *dike exoules* is couched inside a triple hypothesis and is part of an argumentative strategy designed to show the opponent's inappropriate and exploitative use of legal procedures.[25]

There is not, then, a shred of reliable evidence that demonstrates the binding quality of private arbitration in the fourth century: no trustworthy evidence explicitly connects arbitration with the *dike exoules*; none connects it with *paragraphe.* The necessary conclusion to be drawn is that we do not know whether it was binding or not; the view that it was so is only an hypothesis. A different hypothesis might explain the evidence more cogently, one that requires us to examine private arbitration in conjunction with its younger sibling, official arbitration. The new hypothesis is this: while a *diamarturia* could be used to bar a trial on the grounds of a successfully executed private arbitration at the end of the fifth century, *diamarturia* may

[25] Scholars who have uncritically accepted the evidence of [Dem.] 52. 16 were forced to explain why Kallippos, who had won a verdict against Apollodoros, did not use a *dike exoules* to enforce judgment but instead brought the same case to court as a *dike arguriou.* The explanation required the creation (or confirmation) of the arbitrator's oath as a requirement for a binding arbitration: since the arbitrator gave his verdict unsworn, therefore it was not binding. But the scenario can be interpreted differently (especially once one has rejected the notion that the *dike exoules* was available) and should be compared with [Dem.] 33. 19. In the course of both arbitrations, one party objects to the procedure of the other party on the grounds that it contravenes the preliminary procedural agreement; the protesting party has witnesses to his objection. The speakers in both cases are trying to show that the arbitrations were not "authoritative" (*kuriai*), presumably against the opponent's arguments that they were. [Dem.] 52. 16 does not demonstrate that oath was a requirement for a binding arbitration; it shows that, in this case, oath was a prerequisite for an authoritative arbitration executed in accordance with the preliminary procedural agreement among the participants. On the meaning of "authoritative" (*kurios*), see text above. For a sample "preliminary agreement," see n. 17.

have fallen out of use in such cases (if it was not explicitly disallowed) after official arbitration was instituted, probably in 400/399 (according to MacDowell's dating).[26] Thereafter, private arbitration may simply have been perceived as a method for arriving at non-binding decisions. *Paragraphe* may never have become a remedy to protest suits on issues that had previously been decided by the private procedure. Official arbitration, limited to hearing a large sub-set of all private *dikai*, became the formalized mechanism by which the administrative task of collecting evidence for dikastic presentation was executed and by which a binding quality might now be conferred upon reconciliations that were agreed upon by the disputants or upon arbitral verdicts that were accepted by them.[27] It also provided a mechanism by which arbitrators (the official ones) could now be held responsible for their decisions (*AP* 53. 6). This important feature may even have been the impulse for the institution of the new procedure: during the years preceding and following the Amnesty (404/03–401/0), private suits had probably been suspended; private arbitrations would have had to fill the gap.[28] Many disputants (such as Kallimakhos, in his first suit against the speaker of Isokr. 18) may have been dissatisfied with the decisions of private arbitrators who could not be held accountable for their decisions. The institution of official arbitration may thus have been, at least in part, a response to perceived inequities.

According to this hypothesis, the legislation concerning arbitrators (τὸν νόμον τὸν περὶ τῶν διαιτητῶν, Lys. fr. xix B–S) will have concerned both private and official arbitrators. It will certainly have detailed the new procedure, and it is likely to have furnished an administrative mechanism for the transfer of cases between the

26 A law concerning official arbitration is thought to be alluded to in Lys. fr. xix B–S with the words τὸν νόμον τὸν περὶ τῶν διαιτητῶν ("the law about arbitrators") and is cited but not included in the text of Dem. 21. 94 (Λέγε δὴ καὶ τὸν τῶν διαιτητῶν νόμον: "Read out now also the law about arbitrators"). Most scholars have dated the law to the late fifth century, between 403 and 400: Bonner and Smith 1930: 348; Harrell 1936: 1–3; Gernet 1939: 389–414; Harrison 1971: 65; MacDowell 1971a: 267–73 plausibly argues, however, that the law was passed in 400/399 and that the first official arbitrators took office in 399/8. Humphreys 1983b: 240–42 is exceptional in ascribing the introduction of official arbitrators to Kleisthenes; Lipsius 220–21 and Steinwenter 1925: 61–62 support an undefined early date.

27 See App. 1.d for the evidence for the binding quality of official arbitration.

28 MacDowell 1971a: 267 argues on the basis of Isokr. 21. 7 and Lys. 17. 3 that private cases were not heard from 404/403 until the arkhonship of Xenainetos in 401/400. Some scholars have disagreed about the extent of the duration of the abeyance (whether it did last until 401/400), but not about the abeyance itself (see App. 1.e, "The Introduction of Official Arbitration").

newly appointed official arbitrators and the privately selected arbitrators and mediators.[29] The legislation might also have provided guidelines for private arbitrations in the future: possibly a preliminary agreement between the disputants concerning procedural arrangements became a requirement (whether it was to be a reconciliation or arbitration, who the arbitrators or mediators were to be, whether they were to take an oath, what the subject of dispute was); arbitrators and mediators may even have been required to render decisions or to offer proposals "in accordance with the laws" (see 1.c below). These matters, however, are quite uncertain.

The institution of official arbitration was not death to private arbitration – far from it. The law never stripped the latter of "authority."[30] Arbitral verdicts and terms of reconciliations remained *kuriai* in the fourth century. The adjective *kurios* does not in itself mean "binding"; it means "authoritative" or "decisive." There is, in fact, no technical word or phrase in Greek that means "legally binding." In practice, a directive to magistrates and a legal remedy (e.g., *paragraphe*, a *dike exoules*) are required to turn what is "authoritative" (*massgeblich*) into something that is "binding" (*verbindlich*).[31] In the general sphere of private agreements to which we might subsume private arbitral decisions, Athenians appear to have had only a rudimentary juridical notion of "binding." In a word, agreements were expected to be kept; the law itself had not provided a specific remedy against broken agreements or contracts.[32] The "authority" of private arbitration is thus an ethical, not a legal, imperative; the "risk" involved in entering private arbitration is that a party's failure to accept or abide by the verdict is suspect, prima facie.

29 See [Dem.] 40. 16 and 52. 14; also Harrell 1936: 29 and MacDowell 1978: 204.

30 Wolff 1957: 37, n. 29; Pringsheim 1950: 138, n. 5.

31 Dikastic decisions, for example, are "binding" both for litigants and magistrates by the following mechanisms. For litigants, monetary penalties to the state must be paid under threat of becoming a state debtor; penalties in private cases can be sought by the plaintiff (indirectly) through a *dike exoules* (see Todd 1993: 144–45). Litigants are protected from further litigation on the same issue by a law that directs magistrates "not to introduce into the (heliastic) court" *dikai* that have been decided. That law, quoted in Dem. 24. 54 (and in App. 1.d), is itself "binding" upon magistrates because they can be penalized for infringing it if anyone brings a charge against them at their *euthunai* (*AP* 48. 4–5, see chapter 1 at n. 92).

32 Pollux 8. 13 cites a δίκη συνθηκῶν παραβάσεως (lawsuit for breach of contract), which Lipsius 663 appears ready to accept as a legal remedy, adducing Plato *Laws* 11. 920 D; but it is more credible that Pollux has his reference from Plato (see Pringsheim 1950: 50–51 and Wolff 1957: 34–35).

Nonetheless, legal remedies were used to turn authoritative arrangements into binding ones; the remedies, however, had not been designed for this specific application. *Diamarturia* had become such a remedy for private arbitral decisions in the late fifth century, but on my hypothesis, the application of that remedy to arbitration had fallen by the wayside after official arbitration was instituted. At some point in the fourth century, *paragraphe* became the remedy by which agreements concluded with an *aphesis* and/or *apallage* might be protected.[33] Since *aphesis* or *apallage* might come about between two disputants without the aid of any third party's intervention (Isokr. 17. 19–31; Dem. 37. 11–17; [Dem.] 33. 14), the remedy cannot have been specifically designed for arbitration; but the availability of the remedy would encourage participants who sought a conclusive ending to their disputes through private arbitration to finalize them in this way.

Was there any legal remedy by which the decision itself might be enforced or its neglect be penalized? Here we might seek an analogy in the way the law appears to have treated *homologiai*, agreements that created contractual obligations between individuals. *Homologiai* were considered *kuriai* by law and we have numerous instances of paraphrases of that law or laws.[34] We do not know how or if the law enforced the authority of *homologiai*. Probably there was no specific *dike* by which violators of *homologiai* could be brought to court. Wolff argued, however, that the *dike blabes* (suit for damages) became a remedy for such cases – not because one party had failed to carry out a contractual obligation, but because his failure to do so caused material damage to the other party – i.e., the remedy was delictal.[35] Recently, Todd has suggested in regard to contracts "that it may be misleading to attempt to isolate from the generality of agreements

[33] The law apud Dem. 24. 54 (see n. 31) is incomplete and probably contained the provision, paraphrased in Dem. 36. 25, 37. 19, 38. 5, and mentioned in [Dem.] 33. 3, that there can be no *dikai* in disputes where an *aphesis* or *apallage* has been issued (Isager and Hansen 1975: 228–29). If a plaintiff denies the defendant's claim that an *aphesis* or *apallage* has been issued, the magistrate still accepts the case – he of course would have no record of the private transaction; but the defendant can bar the trial (at least temporarily) by presenting a formal objection, a *paragraphe*, by which the question of the existence of the *apallage* or *aphesis* is decided. This is the "legal remedy" that protects those agreements and makes them "binding."

[34] A law (or laws) that bid *homologiai* to be *kuriai* is paraphrased at [Dem.] 42. 12; 47. 77; 56. 2; Hyp. 5. 13; it is to be read to the court (but is not preserved in our texts) at [Dem.] 47. 77 and 48. 11. The earliest of these orations was delivered in the mid 350s ([Dem.] 47), the latest in the 320s ([Dem.] 56 and Hyp. 5). See Pringsheim 1950: 35 for full references.

[35] Wolff 1957: 61–72.

that particular sub-group of agreements which are legally binding and which form the basis for legal action." He continues:

> At Athens, except perhaps in one particular type of case . . . [*dikai emporikai*] . . . an agreement seems to become actionable when and only when an Athenian court grants a successful action on the basis of that agreement. To that extent, a contract cannot be binding in the same way that a law cannot be binding: there is no way in which an Athenian jury can be forced to be so bound. On the other hand an agreement, like a law, can furnish very useful persuasive evidence. It is notable that the rhetorical theorists classified them both as forms of *pistis*, a term which is perhaps better translated as "supporting argument" rather than as "proof" . . .[36]

I suggest that arbitrations and reconciliations that had been successfully completed, i.e., with the agreement of both parties and in accordance with the preliminary arrangement, may have been *kuriai* in ways suggested by Wolff and Todd in regard to *homologiai*. If a litigant could demonstrate that he had suffered material loss from the violation of an arbitral agreement, he might be able to persuade a magistrate to grant him a *dike blabes*; this might explain the grounds for the series of *dikai blabes* granted to Nausimakhos and Xenopeithes against their former guardians (Dem. 38). On the other hand, if a litigant could argue that the terms of an arbitration or reconciliation had been violated and if a rubric could be found, he might be able to persuade a magistrate to allot a *dike*; possibly this can explain why the plaintiff of Isaios 5 *Dik.* was able to bring a *dike engues* (suit over suretyship) and why Apatourios had been granted the same kind of suit against the anonymous speaker of [Dem.] 33. While the law did not furnish any specific remedy to ensure the binding quality of the decisions of private arbitrators, there were more general remedies available by which the authority of private arbitral decisions might be upheld and enforced. The decisions of private arbitrators were thus *kuriai* – even though they were not in themselves binding.

Private arbitrations and reconciliations were undoubtedly popular mechanisms of dispute settlement in the fourth century (see chapter 1.1); during periods when the courts were closed, they would be the only means to settle disputes.[37] That they need not be final, but would last as long as the parties to such agreements would abide by

[36] Todd 1993: 267, with reference to Todd 1990: 32.

[37] Private suits were suspended for several years in the 360s (Dem. 45. 4) and for a shorter period in 348 (Dem. 39. 17); Antipater is said to have closed the dikasteria in 322, but the duration of that period is not known (see Introduction, n. 34). For a suspension of private suits at the end of the fifth century, see n. 28 above.

them, tells us something interesting about dispute settlement in Athens: though the lawcourts were available to them, though in many cases the opportunity for a legally binding end to their disputes was available through an official arbitrator's reconciliation or decision, and, failing that, through a hearing before a dikasterion, still, Athenians promoted the notion that settling in private without the intervention of the courts (but not without using the threat of the courts as intimidating leverage) was the proper way to go about ending their disputes. What made such tenuous settlements so attractive? In chapter 1.1, immediate economic concerns were seen as an important impetus for adverting to these private procedures. Now a more deeply-rooted impetus can be suggested. The success of non-binding out-of-court settlements would depend on the preservation of goodwill between the participants. As an example, imagine a boundary dispute settled through a private arbitration. The non-binding quality of the settlement might encourage the neighbors to be more attentive to their treatment of one another: ties between the neighbors might be strengthened so as to shore up the settlement – or they might be weakened. The settlement might create a sense of gratitude on the part of one neighbor, a readiness to complain on the part of the other. The non-finality of the settlement would offer opportunity for favors to be asked and new obligations to be created, a score-keeping of checks and balances. The memory of the settlement might last and linger, perhaps rankle, for years to come – until finally, goodwill (or account books) might be stretched too far.[38] Legal historians have recently pointed out the tendency of courtroom litigants to perpetuate legal conflict, to re-open disputes that had, in theory, been concluded by courtroom verdicts.[39] That

[38] The scenario I envision here may well underly the "corporate disputes" between two branches of a *genos*, the Salaminioi "of the seven *phulai*" and the Salaminioi "from Sounion"; the settlements are witnessed by two inscriptions, separated by a century or more (Ferguson 1938; see App. 2. f). Cf. also the complicated series of suits described in [Dem.] 40. 14–18: the needle that is lost in this haystack of litigation is the original agreement by which the estate was divided between Mantitheos and his two half-brothers (14–15). Mantitheos has preferred for a decade to abide by an agreement according to which he has always retained the right to sue and claim 1 T. Why did he wait? Possibly because by postponing the suit indefinitely he maintained significant leverage for obtaining favors from the half-brothers.

[39] Osborne 1985; D. Cohen 1991a and 1995; Todd 1993: 160–63. The view of these scholars might be typified by Todd's iteration of Osborne: "The purpose of litigation at Athens, Osborne argues, was not so much to secure justice in the modern, objective sense, but rather to reassess the relative social position of the two litigants. This in his view is why, even though in theory the decision of the *dikastai* was final, nevertheless there were in practice ways of reopening the dispute" (161); Todd then develops the same explanation on

tendency might not have been reserved for courtroom displays; it might have been the impetus, even the satisfaction, that many non-binding, non-final arbitrations and reconciliations provided.

1(b) The ideology of friendship

A closer look at particular arbitrations and reconciliations in the orators will identify certain characteristic features (choice and type of arbitrator, the "ideology of friendship," and criteria of evaluation) which in turn help to identify scenarios of arbitration and reconciliation in New Comedy. In this and the following section, I use the terms arbitrator and arbitration (*diaitetes* and *diaita*) in general references to both arbitration and reconciliation; I use a more particular terminology, namely, "arbitration in the strict sense" and "reconciliation," when I differentiate those procedures.

First, to examine who the arbitrators are. There is no set number of arbitrators in a given case. The *sine qua non* of arbitration appears to be the agreement of the disputants both to the procedure and to the *personae* involved – however much intimidation might induce that "agreement." Sometimes we find four arbitrators, in cases where each side has chosen two; sometimes three, where each side has chosen one and agreed in common upon the third; sometimes two or one; in the last category, the selection usually appears (at least at the outset) to have been agreeable to both.[40] Where the choice of arbitrator is left entirely to one party, the party who offers this option is likely to be in a particularly tight spot, under indictment or even on the verge of being meted out a courtroom penalty.[41] Usually the arbitrators are friends or relatives of the disputants; occasionally, the

"a more theoretical level." While the phenomenon itself (the reopening of disputes) is certain, its explanation by these scholars is not. The topic, nothing less than "the purpose of litigation in Athens" cannot be addressed in a footnote. The reader is advised that the topic is a fertile field for discussion. That litigants often use arguments of probability and character does not mean that their "social position" rather than probity is undergoing assessment; that they plead their past benefactions to the *polis* often signals a last ditch effort to save their lives (rather than social position) in public cases. There is need to keep in mind the differences between public and private litigation in treating the issue.

40 In 14 of 24 arbitrations described in the orators (list B in App. 2.a), the speaker specifies the number of arbitrators: a panel of four appears twice (Is. 5. 32–33; Dem. 36. 17); a panel of three appears thrice (Dem. 29. 23; [Dem.] 33. 14–15; 59. 45–48); a panel of two appears once ([Dem.] 59. 68–71). One arbitrator is used on eight occasions ([Dem.] 34. 18–21; 40. 16; 40. 44; 52. 14–15; 52. 21; 52. 31; Aiskhin. 1. 63; Hyp. 5. 5). In the remaining 10 instances, the number is always an unspecified plural.

41 Under indictment: [Dem.] 59. 68; about to be penalized (in an impeachment trial before the *boule*): [Dem.] 47. 43.

sharing of tribal or deme membership is mentioned in addition to a tie of close friendship.[42] Friends (*philoi*) predominate. Indeed, the notion that arbitrators should be friends of the disputants is so pervasive that Apollodoros seeks to prove that Kallippos was not a friend (*philos*) of Lukon by virtue of the fact that the latter chose someone else to mediate in a dispute over a loan ([Dem.] 52 *Kall.* 20–21). An interesting aspect of such an arrangement in which arbitrators are preferred who are either kin or close friends of the disputants is that the procedure appears to favor an arbitrator with intimate knowledge of disputants and their disputes over an arbitrator who might be viewed as impartial. From the fact that in a number of cases an equal number of arbitrators represents each side and that in other cases an additional member is added to the panel by the common choice of the disputants, we can infer that balance rather than strict impartiality was the goal of representation, that is, a balance in favor of both sides alike at the outset rather than a balance with favor to neither.[43] The same inference can be drawn from cases in which one arbitrator is chosen in common.[44] While it may be difficult to perceive how such panels could ever reach a decision without becoming hopelessly deadlocked, decisions once reached and accepted would appear to have a reasonable claim to having worked out a representative solution.[45]

[42] Fellow demesman: Aiskhin. 1. 63; fellow tribesmen: Dem. 29. 23. Relatives are specified in Is. 1. 28; 2. 29–30; 5. 32–33; Dem. 36. 17.

[43] The view of the ideal choice of private arbitrators presented here, that they should be "balanced" by virtue of their familiarity with the disputants rather than by an impartiality derived from non-participation in their daily lives, is similar to Humphreys' (1985c) assessment of witness selection in Athens (see esp. 322 and 353–54).

[44] One configuration that might be alluded to in [Dem.] 59. 45 is a panel of three arbitrators, one chosen by each of the disputing parties, and the third chosen by the other two arbitrators in common. The configuration is well-attested in other societies (see, e.g., Ulpian in the next note) – and our own. Consider the codicil to George Washington's will, in which the testator provides for such an arrangement in the event that any part of his will is disputed: " . . . My Will and direction expressly is, that all disputes (if unhappily any should arise) shall be decided by three impartial and intelligent men, known for their probity and good understanding; two to be chosen by the disputants – each having the choice of one – and the third by those two. Which three men thus chosen, shall, unfettered by Law, or legal constructions, declare their sense of the Testators intention; – and such decision is, to all intents and purposes to be as binding on the Parties as if it had been given in the Supreme Court of the United States" (ed. Fitzpatrick 1939: 28). The editor of the document notes (p. 41): "There were no disputes over the provisions of the Will. A minor controversy was carried into court, but this was unconnected with the direct bequests." So much for *Verbindlichkeit*.

[45] Cf. Ulpian (*D.* 4. 8. 17. 6) as he ponders the problem that beset Roman arbitrations (*ex compromisso*) that have been referred to two persons: " . . . if an arbitration has been referred to two persons, ought the praetor to compel them to make an award because, considering

The adjectives that are sometimes used to describe arbitrators, *isoi* and *koinoi*, are probably best understood along lines suggested by these observations.[46] The speaker of Dem. 41 *Spoud.* 14 says that "when friends wanted to reconcile us (*dialuein*) and after many discussions took place, he [Spoudias] was unable to abide (*emmenein*) by whatever they proposed. And yet who could have refuted our claims better than those who had been present at all these transactions, who knew no less than ourselves what happened, who were chosen in common (*koinoi*) and were friends of ours?" Similar remarks are made by the speaker of Dem. 55 *Kall.* as he defends himself against Kallikles' charge of damaging his property; a wall built by the defendant's father had allegedly dammed up a water-course and so was responsible for the flooding of Kallikles' land. The speaker claims in c. 8 that if the dikasts themselves could see the property they would know that Kallikles' charge was groundless. He continues, "for this reason I wanted to refer the case to those who know the place and who would be balanced in their judgment (*isoi*)" (9, and cf. 35). The speakers of both Dem. 41 and 55 stress that the sought-after quality in the ideal arbitrator is the first-hand knowledge of a friend, relative, or neighbor who is familiar with the question at issue and the history of the dispute. The dikasts in a courtroom can at best have only second-hand information, and unless it chance that any of them know the disputants personally, they are not likely to be *isoi* and *koinoi.*[47]

how prone by nature men are to disagree (*propter naturalem hominum ad dissentiendum facilitatem*), the matter is never likely to come to an end? . . . But it is common for an arbitration also to be referred to two persons and the praetor ought to compel the *arbitri*, if they do not agree, to select a particular third person whose authority may be obeyed." Trans. Watson.

46 *Isos*: [Dem.] 40. 39; Dem. 55. 9. *Koinos*: Dem. 41.14. *Isos* and *koinos* together: Dem. 55.35. In both [Dem.] 33. 14 and 59. 45, one of three *diaitetai* is said to be *koinos*. Cf. Theophr. *Char.* 5.3.

47 Cf. [Dem.] 56. 18, where the speaker imputes to his opponent a reason for refusing to enter arbitration and preferring a courtroom verdict: " . . . he said that we were utter simpletons if we supposed him to be so foolish as to go before a *diaitetes*, who would surely condemn him to pay the money, when it was possible for him to go before the dikasterion, carrying the money, and then, if he were able to bamboozle you, to depart with it – though it belonged to someone else, and if he failed, only then to surrender the sum, just like a man who does not trust in *to dikaion*, but who prefers to make trial of you." The remark is biased, of course: while *to dikaion* here might be firmly planted in arbitration, it has a weaker setting before the dikasts; the speaker colors the past and throws the gauntlet to the dikasts to shore up their standards (cf. Is. 2 *Men.* 30 and see n. 57). Nevertheless, the remark pinpoints an important difference between dikastic and diaitetic hearings: in the informal hearings of the latter, it might be easier for *diaitetai*, with their more particular knowledge of the disputants and their dispute, to cut through the webs of subterfuge woven for dikastic consumption.

That a "balanced" arbitrator or arbitrating panel was expected can readily be seen from certain logographic distortions. The one which appears most frequently is that of a speaker who, in presenting evidence from an earlier arbitration, provides the names of all the arbitrators, specifies the relationship between his opponent and the arbitrators chosen by him, but omits these details in regard to his own. Consequently, the panel appears lopsided, unfairly weighted in the opponent's favor. The speaker can use this kind of presentation to best effect if it also happens that his opponent refused the decision of the arbitrators – "even though some of them were close friends or relatives" (as if that were not usually the case and as if half the arbitrating panel were not composed of the speaker's own friends or relatives).[48] Likewise a speaker can create sympathy for his case when he describes an unfavorable decision which he (or the person he advocates) nevertheless abided by – "even though the arbitrators included his opponent's friends and relatives."[49] In cases where one arbitrator has been chosen in common, it is not unusual for a speaker who received an adverse decision to claim that the arbitrator had a particularly close relationship to the opposing party, certainly closer than his own.[50]

A private arbitrator, then, should have a friend's knowledge of the two disputants and be well-disposed to each – so much is clear, even from the biased portrayals of arbitration in the orators. Indeed, what might be called an "ideology of friendship" not only guides the relationship between arbitrator and disputant, it also pervades many of the decisions and terms of compromise reported in the orators. Documents purporting to be the terms of reconciliation and the narratives that paraphrase either those terms or the awards of arbitral verdicts are cast in language that pays heed to the values of friendship, to mending disturbed relationships and to maintaining restored ones, to the giving of gifts rather than the paying of forced penalties. The "amnesia clauses" of reconciliations have already been described in the last section. Akin to the notion of "forgetting past injuries" is the proposal of future good relations between the two disputants. In Dem. 36 *Phorm.* 15, for example, one of the terms of the (paraphrased) award is that "Phormion was to have Apollodoros as a friend (*philos*) rather than an enemy because of this . . . " Similarly, in Apollodoros' narrative of the terms of reconciliation

[48] Is. 5. 31–33; cf. Dem. 29. 58.
[49] Dem. 36. 14–15 and Is. 2. 29–30, 33.
[50] [Dem.] 34. 18; 52. 31; and Isokr. 18. 13–14.

between Stephanos and Phrunion in [Dem.] 59 *Neaira* 46, the speaker reports that "for the future the men should be friends (*philoi*) to one another." The proposal is iterated in other accounts as well.[51]

Another aspect of the "friendship ideology" is the occasional expression of the compensation as a "gift": "*A* is to give *X* (money, property, etc.) to *B* as a gift." In a reconciliation, the giving of a gift can signal the concession of *A* of his own claims in a compromising spirit and thus removes his acceptance of the proposal from being considered the imposition of a verdict; in an arbitration in the strict sense, the giving of a gift as part of the verdict might signal the arbitrators' sensitivity to the feelings of the "loser" and might in fact represent a compromise among the members of an arbitrating panel evenly divided between representatives of both parties. The speaker in Dem. 36 *Phorm.* 15, for example, reported that the arbitrators persuaded Phormion "to give as a gift (δοῦναι δωρεάν) the 3,000 drakhmai and the additional items" to Apollodoros. Identical "gift-giving language" appears in Is. 2 *Men.* 31, where the speaker reports the mediators' proposal "that we [i.e., Menekles' side] should give up those things he disputed and give them as a gift (δοῦναι δωρεάν); for they said there was no other relief unless they obtained a share of his [i.e., Menekles'] property."

A final aspect relevant to the ideology of friendship might be added. In some disputes, restitution or compensation may not have been so important as the rehabilitation of one's honor before a small gathering of friends. This may very well have been the impetus for reconciliations between parties who had been involved in assaults. Reconciliation offered an intimate but formal stage for restoring relations and displaying magnanimity – or for bullying one's opponent. The presence of friends as arbitrators guaranteed a sympathetic audience. A similar impetus may have driven those reconciliations that followed upon one party's dropping of allegations or even of formal charges against the other. These could be quite solemn occasions – especially if the dropped charge had been homicide.[52] One such reconciliation took place on the Akropolis near the temple of Athene (Ant. 6 *Khor.* 37–39).

[51] Dem. 41. 4; Is. 2. 32; Hyp. 5. 5.

[52] And. 1. 122 and Dem. 21. 104, 110, 116–17, 119, 122. In the first, a reconciliation was allegedly suggested by Kallias if conditions for his dropping a *graphe asebeias* were fulfilled (see chapter 2. 1). In the second, the reconciliation was allegedly envisioned after Meidias dropped charges of homicide against Demosthenes; see n. 55 below, for another possible motive for reconciliations following accusations of murder.

1(c) Criteria of arbitral assessment

Most disputes, not surprisingly, involve issues of law. If we create a pool consisting of 32 arbitrations and reconciliations (including rejected offers; see App. 2.a., lists B–D), we can break down the pool into three groups on the basis of the subject of dispute:

A. The majority (21) concern money (e.g., contracts, loans, deposits) or property (e.g., exchanges of property) or a combination of the two (e.g., inheritance, guardianship, and dowry disputes).[53]

B. Of the remaining, some (6) concern a variety of more or less identifiable offenses such as assault, *moikheia*, property damage, and status.[54]

C. A few (5) are more difficult to classify: one concerns the use of a name (which was later brought into court, probably as a *dike blabes*); one concerns compensation, allegedly for trumping up a *graphe asebeias*; two possibly concern slander; one was probably without legal implications – simply a matter of restoring relations between a businessman and client.[55]

The designations I have used for the subjects of some of these disputes are necessarily oversimplified here. It is enough to observe that most of these cases could have been brought into court as *dikai* – many, in fact, were initiated as *dikai* before being handed over to private arbitrators, and many, in the end, had to be resolved in court (App. 2.d).

[53] Loans and contracts: Lys. 8. 9–13; fr. xix B–S; [Dem.] 34. 18–21; 52. 20–21; 56. 11–18. Deposits and recovery of money: Isokr. 17. 17–19; 18. 9–13; Dem. 41. 4 and 28; [Dem.] 52. 15–16; 52. 30–31. Suretyship: Is. 5. 31–33. Dowry: [Dem.] 40. 16; 40. 39; Dem. 41. 1, 14, 28. Guardianship: Lys. 32. 11–18; Dem. 29. 58; 38. 3–9. Exchange of property: Lys. 4. 4. Property claim: Is. 2. 28–30 and 38. Inheritance: Is. 1. 2, 16, 28, 35, 51; Dem. 36. 14–17.

[54] Assault: [Dem.] 33. 14–17 (the dispute might also include an alleged violation of contract); [Dem.] 47. 43 and 45. *Moikheia*: [Dem.] 59. 65–71. Property damage: Dem. 55. 9, 32, 35. Status: Aiskhin. 1. 62–64 (possibly concerns assault as well); [Dem.] 59. 45–48.

[55] Concerning a name: [Dem.] 40. 44; trumping up a *graphe asebeias*: And. 1. 122; slander (?): Ant. 6. 37–39; Dem. 21. 104–19 and 122; no legal implications: Hyp. 5. 1–5. Designation of two of the disputes as "slander" is hypothetical: in both cases, one party had accused the other of murder; in the first, the accusing party had tried (but failed) to bring a charge of homicide against his opponent; in the second, the accusing party is alleged to have brought a charge of homicide (Dem. 21. 110). The substance of the offense of slander is highly controversial (for recent discussion and citation of relevant bibliography, see Wallace 1994 and Hillgruber 1988); if, as seems likely, one type consisted in *X* alleging falsely that *Y* was a murderer (*androphonos*, see Lys. 10), then in both cases mentioned here, the party accused of murder might be able to sue the accuser for slander. If so, then the reconciliation mentioned in Ant. 6. 37–39 and the one envisioned in Dem. 21. 110, might have been initiated with a view to securing the accused party's goodwill and so (with the aid of an *aphesis*) to ensure that no suit for slander would be brought.

One of the aspects of Athenian forensic practice that was discussed in chapter 1. 3 should be recalled here: most litigants do not base their entire argument on legal issues and technicalities; often they combine arguments of fairness with arguments of strict law, and dikasts probably formed their decisions accordingly. Moreover, dikasts who voted on monetary claims and penalties in *agones timetoi* (trials in which the penalties were not fixed by statute) would regularly resort to the *gnome dikaiotate* ("the best of their judgment"). If we accept such a view, then we are not likely to insist that arbitral procedures required a stricter adherence to lawful criteria than cases presented before a dikasterion,[56] nor will we need to invent a special procedure for disputants who wished to introduce criteria of fair play as the standard of judgment into arbitrations.[57]

Indeed, the scope for arguments of fairness may have been rather limited in many of the cases concerning money (e.g., contracts, deposits) and property. In disputes of the latter sort, evidence for settlements or attempts at settlements based on such arguments is difficult to accept at face value.[58] Concessions allegedly made in one dispute over an estate (Is. 5. 29) nevertheless seem relatively straightforward: payments for liturgies and repairs to buildings are balanced off against the value of revenues produced by the estate in question.

56 The eclectic view that I am developing here is similar both to Meyer-Laurin's (1965: 41–45) and Steinwenter's (1925) in that I agree that the *diaitetes*, like the dikast, made decisions in accordance with the laws; but I differ from them in placing emphasis on the lack of definition of Athenian laws. Arguments of fairness, in my view, regularly entered into dikastic decision-making.

57 Steinwenter 1925: 95–96, 106–07 thought that the private arbitrator, if his decision was to be binding in a court of law, must offer a verdict in accordance with *ta dikaia* (here = "lawful criteria"); therefore the decision to adjudicate according to fair play must be specified by an explicit agreement made by both parties as an additional basis of judgment. To support this view, Is. 2. 30 is called into action: certain individuals are said to have refused to act as arbitrators if the case were entrusted to them to judge *ta dikaia*, since they did not wish to quarrel with either side; but if they were permitted to judge *ta sumpheronta pasin*, then they would arbitrate. There is no need, however, to treat this passage as evidence for a special arbitral procedure rather than as an example of a rhetorical topos. The speaker here is giving a biased view: by announcing at the outset that the arbitrators were to decide *ta sumpheronta* rather than *ta dikaia*, he colors the audience's reception of the terms of the agreement which were so unfavorable to his own party (note that the speaker does not expect the arbitrators to consent to testify, c. 33). The skepticism of Wyse 1904: 256–57 and 260 on Is. 2. 27–37 and 29. 6 respectively is well warranted. A similar distortion, in my view, occurs in Is. 5. 31–32.

58 Evidence for an attempted settlement based on fair play comes from Is. 1. 2, 16, 28, 35 and 51; see Wyse 1904: 176 who is skeptical of the speaker's use of this evidence. I agree with Wyse's interpretation except on one point: I doubt very much that the reported offer of a settlement was anything more than a suggestion by one or two friends or relatives; no technical language of arbitration is used at all.

On another occasion, we are given a glimpse of a failed arbitration concerning a father's abuse of the guardianship of his daughter's children (Lys. 32 *Diog.* 11–18). Little pertaining to arguments of fair play can be gleaned from the narrative: Diogeiton's daughter is depicted as having presented a precise account of her father's maladministration; apparently, at some point during the meeting, Diogeiton changed his story and admitted part of the claim – but only to deduct it from his allegedly inflated expenses (20).[59] A settlement made by Leokrates with Polueuktos and Spoudias (Dem. 41 *Spoud.* 3–4) reveals no greater scope for the maneuverability of fair play. Polueuktos adopted Leokrates, the brother of his wife, and gave him his daughter to marry; the two men subsequently quarrelled, and Polueuktos "removed his daughter" and gave her to Spoudias as wife. Leokrates brought suit, but in the end the men were reconciled, on the terms that "Leokrates, upon receiving back everything he had brought into the estate, was not to be ill-disposed to Polueuktos and releases were to be given of all claims made by each upon the other." We do not know what caused the quarrel between the two men, nor do we know what kind of suit Leokrates brought against Polueuktos – possibly it was for the recovery of money (a *dike arguriou*), possibly it was for damages (a *dike blabes*). The dissolution of the marriage, however, appears to have entailed the dissolution of the adoption as well: Leokrates lost not only a wife, but a portion of a future inheritance. Yet the terms of the reconciliation suggest no nicety of concern for Leokrates' loss of expectation.

Two categories of dispute, by their nature, will have regularly given wider scope to arguments of fair play. To the first belong disputes which, in a court of law, would have required a dikastic vote on a penalty or claim not easily evaluated on the basis of objective criteria and which, additionally, would create unwanted publicity of private life – e.g., cases of assault and of sexual violations against children and women. It is precisely in this area of assessing compensatory "penalties" – and of proving (or disproving) intention in alleged cases of *hubris* and rape – that we might expect arguments of fairness to have played a significant role in arbitration – in the same way that such arguments would have played a role in dikasteria when litigants made penalty speeches after the verdict had been given.[60]

[59] The arbitration is discussed in chapter 1.2.

[60] Arbitration in such cases is discussed in chapters 5.1.c and 6.2. The role of "intention" in relation to assault and rape is discussed in those chapters.

But there would be one significant difference: there would be no time limit on the "speeches" of disputants in an arbitration. To the degree that an arbitrator in a case involving compensation rather than strict restitution might be called upon to listen to extended arguments of fair play, that arbitrator might be described, in Aristotle's phrase, as "one who looks to fairness" (*Rhet.* 1.13.1374b 21). As an example, consider [Dem.] 59 *Neaira* 69–70: here Apollodoros is describing the arguments which Stephanos had used during his reconciliation with Epainetos; the dispute concerned the latter's alleged commission of *moikheia* and its aftermath, namely, Stephanos' detainment of Epainetos:

Stephanos was unable to say anything in accordance with the law (*dikaion*), but he requested Epainetos to contribute toward the dowry [*ekdosis*, lit., "giving away"] of Neaira's daughter, mentioning his own lack of means and the misfortune that had earlier befallen the girl in her relations with Phrastor, and that he had lost her dowry and could not give her away dowered again. "But you in fact have used the girl," he said, "and it is right (δίκαιος εἶ) for you to do something good for her," and he used other appealing arguments such as anyone else might who is begging in sorry plight.

On the basis of the witness depositions in the next chapter of the oration, the one statement in Apollodoros' description of Stephanos' arguments that can be relied upon with some confidence is that Stephanos did request a "dowry contribution." Apollodoros' paraphrase and quotation of Stephanos' appeal may not be totally fallacious – at any rate, he expects the dikasts to believe that Stephanos made an appeal to considerations of fair play, and he suggests that his appeal was of the usual sort for a person caught in this kind of bind.[61] Moreover, it worked – Phano was "dowered."

The second category of disputes where fair play had a more extensive role are those in which the law offered no precise provisions to protect alleged victims from what they perceived as wrongs. In some disputes, the issues are not quite so clearly defined as the oversimplified list, presented at the opening of this section,

[61] The prosecutor in the case, Theomnestos, for whom Apollodoros takes over as *sunegoros* in cc.16ff., justifies Apollodoros' participation in the case on the grounds of Stephanos' abusive treatment of him; included under this rubric is Stephanos' procuring of a large fine against Apollodoros which would have made him a state debtor and reduced his family to dire straits (c. 8): "And furthermore his other daughter was likely to be unmarriageable – for who would ever marry a dowerless girl whose father was in debt to the state and without means?"

might suggest; an appropriate rubric by which to bring such cases into a court of law might have been difficult to find. And. 1 *Myst.* 122–23 (see chapter 2.1) offers illustration: Kallias allegedly had offered to have the indictment for impiety withdrawn in return for Andokides' dropping of his claim to an *epikleros*; friends are to be asked to decide what compensation Andokides should exact from Kallias – whether for putting him through the ordeal of facing a trumped up charge of impiety or for depriving him of an epiklerate marriage is unclear. Even in other cases where there are more self-evident charges by which one or both parties could be brought into court, it is difficult to see exactly how some of the significant internal issues could ever be resolved as issues of law. As a matter of speculation, we might wonder, what goods should Neaira be allowed to keep after she left the house of Phrunion – the same goods as a departing wife ([Dem.] 59. 45–48)? This is not an issue the law – so far as we know it – has determined in advance; considerations of fair play in the course of an arbitration would lead to a solution. The *diaitetes* would have to arbitrate "in accordance with his best judgment" – the very standard that dikasts in the same situation would have to apply.

Earlier I suggested that the law may have offered guidelines for authoritative arbitrations and that these may have included a provision that lawful criteria of judgment be used. That view is tempered by the belief that considerations of fair play would nonetheless enter the picture. Whether there were such a provision or not, however, is not so important as seeing that such considerations would regularly play a role in disputes where one party sought compensation above restitution and where the law offered no provisions – it was probably easier to have disputes of this latter sort settled before an arbitrator rather than attempting to have them brought before a court.

1 (d) Conclusions

Private arbitrations and reconciliations in fourth-century Athens were formalized procedures. They were not, on my hypothesis, legally binding; nevertheless, they carried an ethical imperative that held them authoritative. The procedures were popular and used in a wide variety of disputes; while most of those reported in the orators concern money or property – and sometimes substantial estates –

others, such as rival claims to a courtesan or disputes arising from an assault, suggest that private settlements may sometimes have been sought less for financial remuneration than for the rehabilitation of one's honor among friends. Their popularity might have several sources: (1) they involved less financial risk than going into court; (2) they provided private forums for extensive arguments of fair play when compensation above restitution was sought; (3) they provided "places of judgment" for cases that had no neat rubric for entrance into court; and (4) arbitrators who were friends of the disputants and acquainted with the history of the dispute would decide the cases and promote friendly relations; they could establish a new status quo which would, in some cases, create fresh opportunities for subsequent favors and obligations – an altogether fertile ground for the renewal of conflict between parties who might not be displeased at such prospects.

2 ROMAN ARBITRATION

Before embarking on a brief survey of Roman arbitration, a few words must be said about the sources. These can be divided into two groups. The first are legal writings: the *XII Tables* (preserved in citations from later authors), Gaius' *Institutes* (written in the second century AD), and Justinian's sixth-century AD collection of Roman law known as the *Corpus Iuris Civilis* (consisting of the *Digest*, *Code*, *Institutes*, and *Novels*). While the procedure that we are examining is not – by its nature – one that we should necessarily expect to find encoded in such sources, nevertheless, because of the peculiar ways in which categories of private and official practice can overlap, it is useful to examine them. But for a sense of "law-in-action" in the mid-Republic, a sense of how private arbitration might actually have operated at that time, there are no contemporary legal sources (cf. Introduction 1). Nevertheless, there is some non-legal literature that might tell us something – the second group alluded to above: literary sources of the late third and early second centuries BC, namely, Plautus, Terence, and Cato the Elder. Additionally, Cicero's writings allow us to see some of the more fully developed institutions in operation at the end of the Republic. Among these authors, the use of Plautus and Terence is fraught with problems: scenarios of private arbitration usually depend on Greek models. In view of the special problems involved in using the comic evidence, I have reserved detailed treatment of it for the next chapter; some of those problems, however, will be anticipated here.

Legal sources unfortunately do not define differences between *arbiter* and *iudex*; nor do they provide an account of the historical development of arbitral figures in different procedures and actions. Although they record numerous procedures in which *arbitri* are involved, their introduction usually cannot be dated except in vague ways (e.g., if they are reported as belonging to the period of the *XII Tables* or to the period of the *legis actiones* system, or if the jurist whose extract appears in the *Digest* refers to the work of a pre-classical jurist or is himself one). Many legal historians of the nineteenth and twentieth centuries have devoted their energies to reconstructing what the sources have not provided: schemata of the historical development of Roman legal procedures in which the *arbiter* and his relationship to *iudex* play an important role. Such schemata are necessarily hypothetical – especially for the pre-classical period of Roman law – and often very complicated. It is entirely beyond the scope of this chapter to engage in detailed discussion of these matters. An architecture of presentation must nevertheless be established. I have presented below arbitral procedures which can be at least vaguely dated to the middle Republic, beginning with judicial procedures and following them with private ones. While I point out similarities and connections between some and while I occasionally advert to developmental schemata and do not eschew chronology, I have not tried to see these procedures as part of an evolutionary picture of Roman law. My goal is to identify situations in which arbiters and mediators were used and to employ these as a basis for comparison with scenarios and terminology of arbitration in Roman Comedy.

Arbitri participated in the second half of the bipartite procedure (*in iure* and *apud iudicem*) under the *legis actiones* system that was operative in Rome in the early and middle Republic. At the end of the *in iure* proceeding, the magistrate, with the agreement of the litigants, selected a single *iudex* or *arbiter* (but three *arbitri* in some cases) who would hear the opposing parties at a subsequent meeting (*apud iudicem*). *Iudex* and *arbiter* are mentioned in conjunction with claims that could be brought by the *legis actio per iudicis arbitrive postulationem* (an action "by application for *iudex* or *arbiter*").[62] The

[62] See chapter 2. 2. b. and n. 76.

actio could only be used for claims that were specifically authorized by statute. The *XII Tables* authorized its use in cases (1) where a plaintiff sued on a stipulation (the formal verbal contract of the Romans) and (2) where a dispute arose over an inheritance; a later statute authorized its use in actions for dividing property.[63] Other early claims that involved *arbitri* are the *actiones finium regundorum* (boundary disputes: three *arbitri* required), *pluviae arcendae* (disputes over property damage caused by rain water), and claims against a defendant who has apparently been convicted of using property under a false claim (three *arbitri*).[64] Some scholars have argued, on the basis of the specification that *arbitri* be used in making assessments of property values and boundary lines, that *arbitri* had to draw upon greater technical expertise than *iudices*; moreover, *arbitri* involved in these cases would have considerable discretionary power.[65]

The Plautine era, however, might be considered as the beginning of the long tail's end of the *legis actiones* system; some formulary actions were already in existence around 200 BC. Scholars have produced cogent arguments that certain of the *bonae fidei iudicia* ("actions of good faith") and *actiones in bonum et aequum conceptae* ("actions framed on considerations of what is right and fair") were now available.[66] In the former type, a judge is to condemn the defendant to pay whatever "he ought to give or do in accordance with good faith (*ex fide bona*)"; in the latter type, the defendant is condemned to pay "whatever amount of money seems right and fair (*bonum aequum*)" or some variant, such as "whatever is better and more fair (*quod eius melius aequius*)."[67] The

[63] Stipulation, inheritance, and dividing property: Gaius 4.17a, which mentions the *iudex* without the *arbiter* in the title of the *actio*, but provides both terms in the formula *ex sponsione*; likewise Probus 4. 8. *XII Tables* 5. 10 mentions only the *actio* for inheritance.

[64] Penalty for use of property under false claim: *XII Tables* 12. 3. Boundary disputes: *XII Tables* 7. 5 (= Cic. *de leg.* 1. 21. 55). *Actiones finium regundorum* and *pluviae arcendae*: references to legal sources in Düll 1931: 3–5; also Broggini 1957: 162–69 and Kaser 1966: 79, both of whom discuss whether these *actiones* should be subsumed under the *legis actio p. i. a.ve p.*

[65] E.g., Kaser 1966: 42–43; Watson 1971: 72–73 and 97; Jolowicz and Nicholas 1972: 178 and n. 9. For a review of scholarly literature hypothesizing differences between *iudex* and *arbiter* in the *legis actio p. i. a.ve p.*, see Schiller 1978: 199.

[66] For the overlapping of the *legis actiones* and formulary systems of law, see chapter 2, n. 44. Watson has argued in various publications (specified in Watson 1971: 129, n. 2) that the following *bonae fidei iudicia* were in existence at this time: the *actiones tutelae* ("actions regarding guardianship"), *empti venditi* ("purchase and sale"), *locati conducti* ("lease and hire"), and *pro socio* ("partnership"). Among *actiones in bonum et aequum conceptae*, the edict for *iniuriai* and (less certainly) the *actio rei uxoriae* ("action for return of dowry") have been assigned to the late third century: for the former, see chapter 5. 2. b and n. 108; for the latter (dated after 230 BC), see Watson 1967: 66 n. 3 and 1974b: 43, n. 2.

[67] For concise discussion of the formulae for these actions, see Watson 1971: 129–30 and Jolowicz and Nicholas 1972: 211–13, with references to earlier literature.

formulae (such as those cited here) have been reconstructed on the basis of information from juristic literature of the classical period.[68] While the origin of the phrase *bonum aequum* is controversial, its use as an evaluative standard can be accepted as being in existence during the Plautine era.[69] The appearance of the phrase at Plautus *Men.* 580 and Terence *HT* 642 at least indicates that the spheres of strict law (*ius*) and fairness (*bonum aequum*) were recognized as distinct in the early second century.[70]

Who gave the decisions in these formulary actions in the Plautine era? Is the judicial *arbiter* to be particularly associated with the *bonum aequum* at this time? Or did the *iudex* hear these cases? While in most of the classical formulae for the actions presented here, it is the *iudex* (*unus*) who is to make the condemnation, Cicero and classical jurists occasionally refer to the judge as *arbiter*.[71] For modern non-jurists, inquiry into the fluctuation of terminology might be considered foolhardy hair-splitting; Cicero's well-known statement in *pro Murena* 12. 27 might aid the protest: "Now this indeed seems remarkable, that so many men – so shrewd, too – after so many years, remain even now undecided as to whether one should say, 'two days hence' or 'the day after tomorrow' (*diem tertium an perendinum*), 'judge' or 'arbitrator' (*iudicem an arbitrum*), 'cause' or 'case' (*rem an litem*)."[72] Nonetheless, inquiry into terminology by modern jurists has elicited provocative and detailed hypotheses concerning the development of Roman legal

68 The formulae were reconstructed by Lenel and published in 1883 (*Das Edictum Perpetuum*, commonly cited as *EP*); the standard edition is the third, published in 1927. Of the two examples I have given in the text above of the latter sort of formula, the first is found in the *actio iniuriarum* (*EP* 399), the second in the *actio rei uxoriae* (*EP* 305).

69 As an evaluative standard, the *bonum aequum* is integral to the late third and early second century *iudicia* and *actiones* mentioned in n. 68. The development of the legal concept of *bonum aequum* is documented by Pringsheim 1961 (= 1932); a brief account of *aequitas* appears in Watson 1974b: 173–78. As a slogan that is part of the *Umgangssprache* of that era, see Plautus, most commonly in the superlative, in the phrase *optumum atque aequissumum orare*: *Capt.* 333; *Epid.* 725; *Men.* 1147; *Pseud.* 389; *Rud.* 1029; *St.* 728; in the simplex (*bonum aequomque oras*): *Most.* 682; *Pers.* 399; *Rud.* 184; elsewhere the collocation of adjectives appears at *Cas.* 375; *Curc.* 65; *Men.* 580. Plautus' use of the phrase is studied by Ahrens 1970: 28–34.

70 *Men.* 580: *qui nec leges neque aequom bonum usquam colunt* ("men who have never cherished either the laws or the *bonum aequom*"); see Fraenkel 1960: 152–53 for Plautine elaboration in this passage. *HT* 642: *quid cum illis agas qui neque ius neque bonum atque aequom sciunt?* ("what can a man do with people who know neither law nor the *bonum atque aequom*?").

71 *Actio rei uxoriae*: Cic. *de off.* 3. 15. 61; *D.* 23. 4. 1. 1 (Jav. from Cas.); 46. 3. 48 (Marcellus). *Actio tutelae*: *D.* 49. 1. 28. 2 (Scaev.); but cf. 46. 6. 12 (Pap.) apud fin.; 27. 3. 1. 3. (Ulp.); and *h. t.* 21 (Pap.). *Actio pro socio*: *D.* 17. 2. 38 pr. (Paul. from Sab.).

72 See Broggini 1957: 199–273 and Kelly 1976: 118–19 for different interpretations of the passage.

procedure. The prevailing one is as follows.[73] Originally, private arbitrators operated entirely extra-judicially in disputes, for instance, over boundaries and the division of estates. Their role, in the main, was an assessing one. These *arbitri* were incorporated into the the pre-formulary system of law (e.g., in *actiones finium regundorum* and *familiae erciscundae*) and later into the first *actiones bonum et aequum conceptae* and *bonae fidei iudicia*. Gradually, however, the *iudex* appropriated the (substantially) assessing role of the *arbiter*. His dual role (as judge and assessor) is already evident, for example, when he both gives a judgment and assesses the monetary value of a disputed object during an *actio in rem*;[74] likewise is it evident when he condemns a defendant to pay "whatever amount of money seems right and fair" in *actiones in bonum et aequum conceptae*. At what point the change of designation occurred, it is impossible to say; nonetheless, *iudex* does not appear to eclipse *arbiter* totally – hence the latter term is applied in juristic literature to cases traditionally associated with the *arbiter*.

The strength of the hypothesis lies in its identification of an assessing role for the judicial *arbiter*: the firmly established designation of *arbiter* in pre-formulary actions renders it plausible that *arbitri* might have been the designated judges in the early actions that required assessments based on *bonum aequum* or *bona fides*. Nevertheless, the fact remains that no contemporary evidence exists for the designation of the judge in these early formulary actions. Some of the references to the judicial *arbiter* in the late Republic might well be explained as references to the *iudex* when he is acting in a specifically arbitral (assessing) capacity.[75] The same rationale might

[73] Broggini 1957 is the main proponent of the view; in essence, his formulation is an attack on Wlassak's theory that formulary procedure was contractual in origin and ultimately was rooted in the voluntary submission of disputants to an extra-judicial arbiter. Wlassak had erased the differences between *iudex* and *arbiter* in the *legis actiones* and thereafter; Broggini carefully reintroduced them. While Kaser remained skeptical of the origins of formulary procedure (1966: 19–21, 109–14), he is equivocal in regard to the arbiter's role in *bonae fidei iudicia* (1966: 138–39 and cf. 42–43). Behrends 1970: 99–175 and n. 42 opposes Broggini's hypothesis of the origin of the *arbiter* in *bonae fidei iudicia* and offers a different rationale for the use of the term in these cases.

[74] Gaius 4. 48 (corrupt) appears to say that *condemnationes* in *actiones in rem* were formerly given *in ipsam rem*, i.e., the disputed object was to be returned. If this is so, then at the time when the decision was expressed in monetary terms, the *iudex* had appropriated the traditional arbitral role of assessing; see Düll 1931: 15–16; Zulueta 1953: 239–40 and 264; Broggini 1957: 145–47; Kelly 1966: 69–71.

[75] Cicero *de off.* 3. 16. 66 refers to a case against a certain Claudius concerning a sale heard by an *arbiter*; the latter was to decide *quicquid sibi dare, facere oporteret ex fide bona* ("what he [the owner] should pay or do in good faith"); Cicero then reports that M. Cato was the *iudex*

explain references to the *arbiter* in the jurists, although here it is also possible that some might be shorthand references to the *arbiter ex compromisso* (described below); as one scholar has pointed out, *arbiter* and *arbitrium* are rarely qualified in the *Digest*.[76] Perhaps all that can be said with some certainty is that the *arbiter* acts as an assessor in his first appearances in the judicial system; the association of *arbiter* with assessment is maintained in later (scattered) uses of the term *arbiter* in actions of good faith and in references to the procedure of *arbitrium* in subsequent *clausulae arbitrariae*; however, the history of the technical terminology used in these remedies is not available to us.

If we omit international arbitrators entirely from our account and turn to the extra-judicial sphere as represented in prose literature, the first arbitral figures we meet are called *viri boni* ("good men").[77] Cases treated by them were perhaps too insignificant to belong to the judiciary.[78] Cato in *de agri cultura* recommends that various kinds of contract should include a clause by which a *vir bonus* is to settle foreseeable points at issue:

(1) In contractual arrangements for harvesting olives (144.1):

144. 2: Ladders are to be returned in the condition in which they were given, unless any shall have been broken because of age; if they are not returned, a fair deduction (*aequom*) will be made by the arbitration of a *vir bonus*.[79] (3) Whatever damage is done the owner through the fault of the

and he quotes his verdict. Cicero's usage here has a parallel in Gaius *Inst.* 4. 163 which provides an example of a *clausula arbitraria*; here it is clear that while the *iudex* acts as an *arbiter* when he appropriates an arbitral function, it is as *iudex* that he gives his decision: "For if the defendant has demanded an *arbiter*, he receives a *formula* known as *arbitraria*; and if in obedience to the arbitral pronouncement of the *iudex* (*iudicis arbitrio*) he produces or restores anything, he produces or restores it without penalty, and is then absolved" (trans. Zulueta). The bare references to an *arbitrium* for the *actio rei uxoriae* (*top.* 17. 66 and *de off.* 3. 15. 61) and the later juristic references to *arbitri* in the context of the *actiones* cited in n. 66 might also be allusions to the arbitral role of the *iudex* rather than to the person of an *arbiter*. In support of this interpretation, see Wenger 1940: 149 (sect. 14), n. 32 and Zulueta 1953: 225.

76 Kelly 1976: 119.

77 For Roman activity in international arbitration, see esp. Gruen 1984: 96–101. Summary statement on p. 101, with nn. 22–23: "The practice of arbitration simply did not form part of Rome's diplomatic arsenal in the third century. When, for the first time in our records, the senate actually sent an arbiter to rule on a territorial dispute between two Italian cities, in the early second century, the setting was Greek Campania, the contest between Naples and Nola. The Hellenic character of the institution plainly predominates." For a slight modification of Gruen's views (but not of the thesis of the Hellenic character of international arbitration), see Scafuro 1987.

78 Broggini 1957: 122.

79 *de agri cult.* 144. 2 is corrupt (Teubner text of Mazzarino 1982; app. crit. ad loc.): *scalae ita uti datae erunt, ita reddito, nisi quae vetustate fractae erunt: si non erunt †reddet, eaeque arbitratu reduceretur†.* My translation is based on Mommsen's commonly accepted emendation: *si non erunt redditae, aequom <viri boni> arbitratu deducetur.*

contractor is to be made good; this will be deducted by the arbitration of a *vir bonus*.

(2) In contractual arrangements for pressing olives (145. 1):

145. 3: Whatever damage is done the owner through the fault of the contractor is to be made good; this will be deducted by the arbitration of a *vir bonus*.

(3) In contractual arrangements for selling wine in jars (148. 1)

148. 1: Only wine that is neither sour nor musty (*neque aceat neque muceat*) is to be sold. Within three days it is to be tasted, under the arbitration of a *vir bonus*. If he [the purchaser] does not do this, the wine shall be considered "tasted." As many days as the seller causes delay for the tasting, so many days will accrue to the purchaser.

(4) In contractual arrangements for pasturage (149.1):

149. 2: If the renter or herdmen or renter's cattle do any damage to the owner, it is to be settled by the arbitration of a *vir bonus*. If the owner or any member of his household or his cattle do any damage to the renter, it is to be settled by the arbitration of a *vir bonus*. Until he has paid the sum or given security or transferred the sum [as a debt], all the cattle and household slaves on the premises are to be held in pledge. If there are any disputes over these matters, a decision (*iudicium*) is to be made at Rome.

The Catonian *vir bonus* is the morally upright man, best represented, perhaps, by the sturdy farmer in the fields (cf. *de agri cult.* 2); his general quality of "goodness" renders him a good *arbiter*. The multiple passages in which he appears in this role in *de agri cultura* – together with his *Nachleben* in the jurists, suggests that *vir bonus* at some point – perhaps even before Cato – acquired a technical significance.[80] We should note that the arbitral task of *vir bonus* in Cato is limited to deciding a specific and foreseeable issue in a contract: he does not decide whether a wrong has been committed; he only determines the value of property damage or the marketability of wine. The limited role of *vir bonus* is likewise in evidence in his later appearances in the *Digest*.[81] Even more so: while he often is

[80] The only (vague) reference to *vir bonus* as arbitrator during this early period, aside from Cato, is cited by Broggini 1957: 118 from *D.* 18. 1. 7 pr. (Ulp.): *placuit itaque veteribus magis in viri boni arbitrium id collatum videri quam in domini* ("Accordingly, it was settled by the earlier jurists that one looks to the judgment of an honorable man and not to that of the master himself"). Cf. Gaius 3. 140 citing Cassius and Labeo. On (the different) *vir bonus dicendi peritus*, see Winterbottom 1964.

[81] E.g., *D.* 18. 1. 7 *pr.* (Ulp.): *vir bonus* in a conditional contract of sale determines whether or not the condition is satisfied before the execution of the sale (see preceding note). Elsewhere of the decision of a *vir bonus* in regard to contracts: *D.* 50. 8. 3. 2 (Ulp.); 45. 1. 137. 2 (Ven.: a full description of all the considerations *vir bonus* should take into account in measuring the

presented in the *persona* of a third party, *vir bonus* also appears there as an abstract standard of judgment.[82]

The extra-judicial "assessing" role of *vir bonus* conforms to the assessing role which the judicial *arbiter* played in cases, e.g., of inheritance and boundary disputes. As in the case of the judicial *arbiter*, it has been hypothesized that Cato's *vir bonus* used a more discretionary but nonetheless objective criterion in rendering a decision, *viz.*, the *bonum aequum*.[83] This seeming paradox can be explained by pointing out that the law has not determined, e.g., how much it costs to replace a ladder. Presumably, the cost of a ladder might vary in different times and places, and not all ladders will be of the same quality. It is the task of *vir bonus*, then, to establish the cost of replacing a particular ladder in a particular time and locale. Not even the wine-tasting assessments of *vir bonus* can be qualified as "subjective": as Watson has pointed out, "in all of the texts, even of the classical period, the right of rejection is considered only in connexion with *acor* and *mucor* which suggests that the buyer can only reject if the wine has gone sour or musty, not if he merely dislikes the flavour, and this is an objective test."[84] These reflections upon the "objective criterion" of *vir bonus* ought not, however, to overwhelm the broader umbrella of *aequitas* under which he made his decisions. An example from Labeo, the preeminent early classical jurist, will clarify. First he poses a question about the size of a dowry, apparently to be measured by a *tutor* for the daughter of a deceased man, "How can you tell how much dowry ought to be provided for the daughter of this person or that, at the discretion of an upright man (*boni viri arbitratu*)?" Celsus cites his answer, "He says it is not difficult to estimate from the rank, means, and number of children of the person making the will."[85] The

length of time it should take to arrive at Ephesos from Rome – worthwhile reading!). Other examples: *D.* 17. 2. 6 (Pomp.): *vir bonus* determines respective shares in a partnership (similarly *h. t.* 78 and 80); *D.* 39. 5. 31. 1 (Pap.): a *iudex* is to make a valuation of a gift and render a decision (under a very specific set of circumstances) "appropriate to the respect properly to be felt toward a mother (*verecundiae maternae congruam*) and in accordance with the judgment of a *bonus vir.*"

82 E.g., *D.* 19. 2. 24 *pr.* (Paul.): leasing; 32. 43 (Cels., citing Tub. and Lab.): a *tutor* decides the amount of dowry for the daughter of a deceased man *ac si viri boni arbitratu* (Tub.) and this can be estimated "from the rank, means, and number of the children of the person making the will" (Lab.); *D.* 47. 10. 17. 5 (Ulp.): in determining the extent of a slave's thrashing "by the judge's ruling" (*arbitratu iudicis*), the praetor means "by the ruling of a good man" (*quasi viri boni*). Cf. also *D.* 7. 1. 9. 2 (Ulp. citing Sab.): the usufructuary may hew stones or quarry chalk or sand *quasi bonum patrem familias.*

83 Broggini 1957: 116 with n. 15.

84 Watson 1965: 97.

85 *D.* 32. 43. Trans. Watson.

criteria are objective, no doubt; rank can be ascertained, resources can be tallied, children can be counted. But the fact that these criteria are used at all – the fact that the material well-being of brothers and sisters, for example, is not to be neglected – demonstrates that the umbrella of *aequitas* is protective of special interests and values. Denomination of the standard of judgment as "objective" is misleading if divorced from consideration of its inspiration.[86]

We hear of various sorts of more and less formalized private arbitral figures in Cicero's writings. Surprisingly, while *vir bonus* as exemplar of superior moral character appears frequently, his technical persona (*vir bonus* as *arbiter*) is difficult to identify.[87] Even the most promising candidates remain dubious. Cicero in *pro Cluentia* 36. 101 claims that in a former trial Staienus denied having taken money from Oppianicus to bribe the court; instead, he had taken it "to effect a reconciliation" (*conciliandae gratiae causa*). Cicero continues, "the court laughed at his 'reconciliation' and at his playing the role of *vir bonus* (*persona viri boni suscepta*) – just as in the episode about the gilded statues – the ones he set up at the Temple of Juturna with the inscription that kings had been reconciled to Rome by him." Staienus was shown up and found guilty; his role as "paid negotiator of peace and concord" (*nummarius interpres pacis et concordiae*) was not believed.[88] The rare appearance of technical *vir bonus* in Cicero can, in good measure, be explained by the crowning importance he maintains as the morally superior man throughout the orator's works; but it might also be due to the narrow role which technical *vir bonus* played in extra-judicial dispute settlement – unlikely to be

86 Cf. Watson 1974b: 174: ". . . many legal developments, especially those resulting from distinctions drawn by jurists, are based on the notion of what is just or fair, though this basis is left unexpressed."

87 For Cicero's philosophical notion of *vir bonus*, see Pohlenz 1934: 16 and n. 1.

88 Another promising Ciceronian passage is *pro Cluent.* 63. 176–65. 182: at Sassia's inquiry into the death of Oppianicus, a torture of slaves takes place in the presence of *amici et hospites Oppianici et ipsius mulieris multi, homines honesti atque omnibus rebus ornati* (176). The inquiry was abandoned *de amicorum sententia*. On the second day, *quidam ex advocatis, homo et honoribus populi ornatus et summa virtute praeditus*, caused the inquiry to come to an end (177). When another inquiry took place three years later, none of the *honestissimi viri* were present; in fact, it was undertaken *nullo adhibito . . . bono viro* (182). The duties of the respectable men at the inquiry are to ensure that the torture is not excessive and that the questions are put fairly to the slave victim; cf. the duty of *vir bonus* in *D.* 47. 10. 17. 5 Ulp. (n. 82). Cicero's bloated phrases depicting the respectable men might very well have been perceived by his expert audience as rhetorical superlatives for *viri boni* in the "technical" (i.e., arbitral) sense. *De off.* 2. 12. 41–42 and *pro Caec.* 2. 6 are also promising for the technical figure, but will not endure critical scrutiny.

mentioned in a speech *apud iudicem*, yet utterly familiar to a small audience of expert peers.

Disceptatores and *arbitri* also appear here and there in Cicero's works. *Disceptator* is a general term for a judge or arbitrator of a dispute; context provides more particular shadings. The praetor himself might be so designated (*iuris disceptator* at *de leg.* 3. 3. 8 and 9) – likewise *populus Romanus* (*de leg. agr.* 1. 7. 23 and *pro Fl.* 38. 97), likewise *iudex* and *senatus* (*de part. orat.* 3. 10). On one occasion, Cicero asks a friend, Serv. Sulpicius Rufus, current proconsul in Akhaia, to act as *arbiter* and *disceptator* in settling disputes arising from an estate left by a Roman in Elis (*ep. ad fam.* 13. 26. 2); the private nature of the envisioned settlement is underscored by Cicero's directives concerning the possibility that the case might subsequently enter court. Rufus' official position, however, is expected to aid the matter.[89] The most controversial use of the term occurs in *pro Caec.* 2. 6, in the phrase *disceptator domesticus*: while some have interpreted it to refer to *iudex* in a private case (*apud iudicem*), others have identified it as a reference to a private arbitrator.[90]

In a passage of *pro Rosc. Com.* notorious for its difficulties, Cicero, with carefully contrived astonishment, asks his client's opponent a question: why, concerning the very sum of money at stake in the present trial, did he enter into an agreement (*compromissum feceris*), accept an arbitrator (*arbitrum sumpseris*), and make a claim thus, "however much was fair and just should be given or promised (*quantum aequius et melius sit dari repromittique*)?" (4.12). The procedure to which Cicero refers with these last words is debated; while their affinity with formulae in *actiones in bonum et aequum conceptae* is evident, the modern *opinio communis* maintains that the words refer to an *arbitrium ex compromisso* (arbitration based on an agreement to abide by the award).[91] The procedure is attested elsewhere in Cicero as well, but its outlines are barely visible.[92]

Extensive regulations appear in the jurists, however, some of

[89] Cicero when proconsul in Cilicia took upon himself a similar role (without giving it any specific designation), assisting in the settlement of debts of the Cyprian Salaminioi with Brutus (*ep. ad Att.* 5. *ep.* 21, 12–13; 6. *epp.* 1, 7; 2, 7; and 3, 5); see Düll 1931: 128–29. A *disceptator* appears as a third party in a dispute over a political office in *Tab. Herc.* 84. 1. 3–5 (AD69/70); according to Arangio-Ruiz and Pugliese Carratelli (1955: 465), he is a mediator rather than arbiter.

[90] A judicial *arbiter* or *iudex*: Düll 1931: 126; Kelly 1976: 119–21. Private (extra-judicial) *arbiter*: Broggini 1957: 212, 216; Behrends 1970: 123 n. 28; Ziegler 1971: 20: n. 80; Frier 1985: 242.

[91] Broggini 1957: 201–03 (201, n. 6 for earlier literature); Ziegler 1971: 18–20.

[92] Cic. *Verr.* 2.2.27.66; *ad Q. fr.* 2.14.4; *ad Att.* 4.15.7; *ad Fam.* 12.30.5; see Ziegler 1971: 16–23.

whom belong to the era of the late Republic or early classical era.[93] The two most important features of an *arbitrium ex compromisso* are (1) the *compromissum*, which refers to the preliminary agreement between the disputants to pay a specified penalty if one or the other fails to carry out the arbitrator's verdict, and (2) the *receptum arbitri*, the arbitrator's agreement to undertake the arbitration. The *arbiter ex compromisso* of the jurists is a "quasi-judicial" figure; while he is chosen in common by the disputants rather than with the assistance of a magistrate, once he has undertaken the arbitration he can be compelled by the praetor to render a decision.[94] Moreover, while the decision of the *arbiter* is not equivalent to a court verdict (*res adiudicata*), it is indirectly enforceable: the penalty agreed upon by the disputants (*poena compromissa*) can be collected under the stipulation by suing in court.[95] The praetor's compulsion is set forth in a simply worded edict: *QUI ARBITRIUM PECUNIA COMPROMISSA RECEPERIT, EUM SENTENTIAM DICERE COGAM.* (*EP* 131: "Whoever has accepted an arbitration when a penalty has been agreed upon, I shall force him to give a verdict.") The precise date of the edict is not known; Ziegler, who has examined the wording carefully, assigns it to an indefinite date in the second century; the introduction of the formulary system is a probable *terminus post quem*.[96] While *arbitri* are mentioned in Roman Comedy, there is not a single reference to the penalty in the arbitral scenarios portrayed there – a detail that might confirm Ziegler's *terminus post quem* for the procedure.

The sphere of activity of the *arbiter ex compromisso* appears to

[93] Ziegler 1971: 28–43 for references. The most important are: *D.* 44. 7. 23 (Afr. citing Serv., possibly interpolated): the excerpt mentions the penalty in an *arbitrium ex compromissum*. *D.* 4. 8. 15 and *h. t.* 17. 1 (Ulp. citing Lab.) and *h. t.* 19 *pr.* (Paul. citing Lab.): all treat the limits of praetorian compulsion. *D.* 4. 8. 25 *pr.* and 2, *h. t.* 27.1, and 44. 4. 4. 3 (Ulp. citing Lab.): various questions are posed, e.g., extension of time for the *arbiter's* award, later additions to the original *compromissa*.

[94] Various regulations for compulsion are set out in the *Digest* article on arbitration (4. 8). The extent of the law is especially clear in 4. 8. 32. 12 (Paul.): "If an *arbiter* has tried to conceal himself, the praetor ought to track him down, and if for a long time he has not appeared, a fine is to be imposed on him" (trans. Watson). Many of the excerpts in *D.* 4. 8 define categories of individuals who cannot be compelled, such as women, lunatics, and slaves (*h. t.* 4; 7; 9; 11; 13; 16; 17; 32; 35; 41; 48; 49).

[95] Paul. *Sent.* 5. 5a. 1; *D.* 4. 8. 2 (Ulp.).

[96] Ziegler 1971: 24–25, with additional arguments from commercial, social, and political circumstances; Broggini 1957: 125–26 argues for a similar date on the grounds that the stipulation for penalty in an *arbitrium ex compromisso* required the more fully developed system of formulary law before it could come into existence. Matthiass 1888: 29 doubts edictal compulsion in Cicero's time, but those doubts are put to rest in view of Ziegler's careful treatment of the juristic extracts.

overlap with that of *vir bonus*; it is not identical. While the former might conceivably both give a judgment (e.g., decide whether a former *tutor* is in the wrong) and assess the amount of the penalty, *vir bonus* appears to be limited to performing tasks of assessment. The *arbiter's* sphere of activity was extensive – but in the classical period he was excluded from making decisions on delicts involving *infamia* and in public actions such as those for adultery and murder (*D.* 4. 8. 32. 6 Paul. citing Jul.); moreover, he was not compelled to make an award in a *causa liberalis* (*h. t.* 32. 7). The classical private *arbiter* and *vir bonus* nevertheless share the same criterion of judgment, *aequitas* – even if the *sententia* (decision) of the *arbiter* might, on occasion, appear *iniqua* to the disputing parties.[97]

Our search for private arbitral figures outside of Roman Comedy has so far turned up the *disceptator*, *vir bonus*, and *arbiter ex compromisso*. The first is a general term for mediator or judge but does not appear to have a specific technical meaning. *Vir bonus* makes his first appearance in Cato, shows up dubiously in Cicero, teases us in Horace, and subsequently appears in the *Digest* giving decisions (or is made the paradigm for the decisions of others) in infinite matters of quite finite concern – he is the umpire of contractual conditions, shares in a partnership, the size of a dowry, the monetary value of a gift, the extent of a slave's thrashing, the amount of time it takes to arrive in Ephesos from Rome.[98] He is the equivalent of Chancery's "special master" – hardly the equal of the Athenian private *diaitetes*. The elusive figure of the *arbiter ex compromisso* does not appear in our sources until the late Republic – and there on rare occasions only. It is impossible even to sketch a typical scenario of private arbitration before the *arbiter ex compromisso* arrives on the scene – and then documents of the first century AD (e.g., Bruns[7] 404) and excerpts from early jurists must be used to paint the canvas.

The final point is the most important one: while we can hardly doubt that third parties privately intervened in disputes in the Plautine era, Cato's allusions to *vir bonus* provide the only contem-

97 *D.* 4. 8. 3. 1 (Ulp., interpolated), *h. t.* 27. 2 and *D.* 17. 2. 76 (Proc.); cf. *D.* 8. 4. 19. *pr.* (Paul. citing Labeo).

98 For examples of *vir bonus* in the *Digest*, see nn. 81–82 above. In Horace, he is depicted in *Ep.* 16. 41–43, in answer to the question, *vir bonus est quis?* ("who is the good man?"): "*qui consulta patrum, qui leges iuraque servat, / quo multae magnaeque secantur iudice lites, / quo res sponsore et quo causae teste tenentur*" ("He is the man who preserves the decrees of our fathers, who guards statutes and laws, the judge who makes an end of many terrible suits, the guarantor of property, the witness at our hearings"). Horace's *vir bonus* turns out to fit the mold of Cicero's dubious Staienus in *pro Cl.* 36. 101 (*persona viri boni suscepta*).

porary prose evidence.[99] The gap in our sources is self-evident. Should Roman Comedy be used to fill it? This is a question to which we shall return in the next chapter.

[99] A boundary dispute is settled by the Minucii between the Genuans and Veturians in 117 BC – hardly a private dispute; the two men have no technical designation (Bruns[7] 401–03).

CHAPTER 4

Scenarios of arbitration and reconciliation in New Comedy

I THE ARBITRATIONS OF *EPITREPONTES* AND *RUDENS*

1(a) A comparison of procedure

The most celebrated scenes of arbitration in New Comedy appear in Act II of Menander's *Epitrepontes* and in Act IV 3 and 4 of Plautus' *Rudens*, which is based on an unidentifiable play by Diphilos.[1] What is immediately striking about these scenes is their elaborate parody of dispute settlement: in both, the disputants are slaves, and here they display well-honed forensic skills which would rarely be theirs to exhibit in a court of law – with remarkable eloquence on the part of one disputant in *Epitrepontes* and with savvy urbanity on the part of another in *Rudens*.[2]

[1] *Rud. prol.* 32–33: *primumdum huic esse nomen urbi Diphilus / Cyrenas voluit* (32–33: "First of all, Diphilos wanted the name of this city to be Cyrene"). The title of the original is not attested; the most frequently suggested candidate has been *Epitrope*. See Marx 1928: 273–74, *passim*, and 1926: 482 for a vigorous circular argument that Diphilos' *Epitrope* is the original. One word (ἐξιδιάσασθαι) survives from Diphilos' play; Marx fleshes it out to accord with *Rudens* 989. The hypothesis has sometimes been uncritically accepted. *Epitrope* is not limited to meaning "referal to arbitration"; it can also mean "stewardship" or "guardianship". Friedrich 1953: 171 denies the plausibility of Diphilos' *Epitrope* as the model for *Rudens* on the grounds of the title's ambiguity.

All is speculation: a Diphilan play with the title of *Epitrope* could conceivably have a plot entirely different from *Rudens*; other Diphilan titles have just as much (and therefore just as little) support – e.g., 'Εγκαλοῦντες (fr. 25 K–A) and 'Ελλεβοριζόμενοι (fr. 30 K–A and cf. *Rudens* 1006). Moreover, we do not possess a complete list of titles for Diphilan comedies. When I advert to the Greek model in my discussion of Plautus' play, I have assumed that the playwright was Diphilos and that the title of his play is still unknown.

[2] Slaves had no legal capacity in Rome and probably that was the case for the majority of slaves in Athens (for Rome: Kaser 1966: 45–47 and Watson 1967: 173–84; for Athens: Lipsius 793–800 and MacDowell 1978: 79–83). While slaves in Athens might be prosecuted for committing offenses, a slave belonging to an individual could only, it appears, take independent legal action in mercantile cases (E. Cohen 1992: 96–97). Since private arbitration in Athens was not, in my view, binding (e.g., execution of an award was not protected by the *dike exoules*), there is no reason why slaves might not find a third party to mediate a dispute. For aspects of slave life in *Epitr.* (e.g., their capacity for ownership and the status of an exposed infant brought up by slaves), see esp. Taubenschlag 1926.

In *Epitrepontes*, Suros, a charcoal burner and slave of Kharisios, quarrels with the shepherd Daos over the ownership of trinkets which the latter had found together with a new-born infant; Daos had handed the infant over to Suros, but had kept the trinkets for himself.[3] The dispute is decided by Smikrines who unwittingly arbitrates the fate of his own grandson. In *Rudens* IV 4, Trachalio, slave of Plesidippus, and Gripus, fisherman and slave of Daemones, dispute the ownership of a trunk which the latter has fished out of the sea. Trachalio suspects that the trunk belongs to the pimp Labrax and that it contains the birth tokens of his master's sweetheart Palaestra. Daemones is called upon to arbitrate the dispute and so ends up, unwittingly, the *arbiter* of his long-lost daughter's identity. The similarities between the arbitration scenes in *Rudens* and *Epitrepontes* have been noted before and have led one scholar to posit a tragic archetype for both scenes and other scholars to identify the ur-tragedy with Euripides' lost *Alope*.[4] We shall not concern ourselves here with creating a stemma of the relationships among these plays; instead, we shall consider the dramatizations of procedure in *Epitrepontes* and *Rudens*, focusing on the issues in dispute, the manner of settlement, and the choice of arbitrator. At the end of this comparison, we shall consider whether *Rudens* contributes to our knowledge of arbitration in Rome of the middle Republic.

3 The name Suros appears on the Mytilene mosaic. For arguments concerning whether the slave should be called Suros or Suriskos, see Gomme and Sandbach 1973: 303 and 309–11.

4 Friedrich 1953: 194–99 does not specify Euripides' *Alope* as the model for the arbitration scene. MacCary 1973: 25–44, esp. n. 30, sees a dual heritage for Diphilos' arbitration scene: (1) from Eur. *Alope* through Men. *Epitr.* and (2) from various mythological tragedies about Danae, Tyro, Alope, etc. through satyr plays and plays of Middle Comedy which parody the mythical material of tragedy. While Menander, according to MacCary, "draws directly on tragedy – exact parallels with, and actual quotations from, famous scenes – Diphilos depends on comic adaptations of originally tragic situations" (p. 203).

While some of MacCary's parallels with fragmentary comedies strain the evidence, the connection between *Rud.* and Aiskh. *Diktyoulkoi* may be closer than he suggests. When the fisherman hauls the casket from the sea, he calls upon neighbors for help:]ἔστι τοὔργον οὐ χωρ|εῖ πρόσω / β]οὴν ἵστημι τοῖσδ' ἰύγ|μασιν /]πάντες γεωργοὶ δεῦτε | κἀμπελοσκάφοι /]ε ποιμήν τ' εἴ τίς ἐστ| [' ἐ]γχώριος /]οι τε καὶ μα| [ρ]{ε}[ιλ]ευτῶν ἔθνος / |]ἐναντιωτάτης (*TrGF* 3 F 46a, 16–21: "This work isn't going forward. I'll raise a noisy shout: Help! All farmers and vine-diggers, hither! . . . and any shepherd in the neighborhood! The whole tribe of . . . and . . ."). Cf. *Rud.* 615–17: *Pro Cyrenenses populares! vostram ego imploro fidem, / agricolae, accolae propinqui qui estis his regionibus, / ferte opem* . . . (615–17: "Help! citizens of Cyrene, I implore you by your faith! Farmers, neighbors who dwell near these regions, bring help . . . "). While such *Notrufe* are not infrequent in Greek and Roman Comedy (see chapter 2, nn. 106–07), the one in *Rudens* 615 ff. is distinguished by its length and specificity of addressee (note particularly *agricolae*); those features (cf. Ar. *Pax* 296–336), together with the verbal similarity of *Rud.* 616 and *Dikt.* 46a 18–19 and the sharing of a common motif, suggest that the reminiscence might be intended.

The arbitration scene in the second act of *Epitrepontes* is compact and formal: the two slaves enter the stage (218), disputing the ownership of the trinkets, and almost immediately agree to find an arbitrator to settle the dispute (219–20). Smikrines happens by and is pounced upon to assume that role (224); one disputant readily agrees to abide by his decision (237–38) – the singularity of that agreement may be a legal joke. Daos speaks first (249–69, 274–92), then Suros (293–352); Smikrines gives his decision (353–54), ensures that it will be carried out (366, 367), and leaves the stage (370). The catch-words of arbitration are present: the case must be referred to an arbitrator (*epitrepteon*, 219), Suros says; a judge is called for (*krites*, 223 and 226) who will be "balanced" (*isos*, 227) and who will reconcile the men (*dialuein*, 228); Smikrines asks if the disputants will abide by his decision (ἐμμενεῖτ' οὖν, εἰπέ μοι, / οἷς ἂν δικάσω; 237–38). The arbitration scene in *Rudens* is less formalized and more discursive: the pre-arbitration dispute between Gripus and Trachalio goes on at great length (IV 3); Gripus does not immediately yield to Trachalio's suggestion that they should seek an *arbiter*; the latter must repeat his suggestion several times before gaining the fisherman's assent (1002, 1004–05, 1017–18, 1035, 1038). There are no long "set" speeches in the following scene of arbitration (IV 4); in fact, Gripus asserts his claim to the disputed trunk in one verse:

si in mari retia prehendi, qui tuom potiust quam meum? (1071)

If my net snatched it in the sea, how is it yours rather than mine?

Soon thereafter Trachalio deflects the subject matter of the original dispute; Daemones gives no arbitral verdict about the trunk.

The basis for the claims to ownership is similar in the two plays: one party claims the disputed object through the unwritten law of "finders-keepers";[5] the other party offers an argument, favoring or rejecting an alternative of "going shares."[6] In *Epitrepontes*, Daos argues the case for "finders-keepers": since he found both infant and tokens, both are his possessions; if he then gave away infant

[5] For a summary of ancient and modern sources pertaining to "finders-keepers," see Konstan 1983: 76, n. 7 and Marx 1928: 265–67. The concept has a bearing on two related issues in *Rudens*: one is ownership (or possession) of an object that is found, the other is the commonality of what is found in the sea.

[6] Taubenschlag 1926: 76–79 traces the remnants of this "law" in Greek and Latin authors; it is defined by Hesykhios s.v. κοινὸς Ἑρμῆς, παροιμία ἐπὶ τῶν κοινῇ τι εὑρισκόντων (literally: " 'Common Hermes': proverbial for those who, together, find an object."

without tokens, it was his right to do so. To support his case, he argues that if the two men together had found infant and tokens, then it would be incumbent upon them "to go shares" (κοινὸς Ἑρμῆς 284); since that did not happen, it is surely wrong for him to have nothing at all (283–86). In *Rudens*, Gripus, like Daos, insists that his find belongs to him alone; Trachalio tries to convince the fisherman "to go shares" in the preliminaries to the arbitration (IV 3), but he changes his argument when he presents the case before Daemones (IV 4).

In both plays, claims upon the unwritten law of "finders keepers" fail. In *Epitrepontes*, Suros presents an opposing argument that combines considerations of law and fairness. As for the former, he maintains that he is guardian (*kurios*) of the infant (306–07); as for the latter, he argues that the infant ought not to be deprived of birth tokens that could be used to identify his parents (309–11, 320–45); he brilliantly deflects the argument of "finders-keepers" by an emphatic denial of the moral applicability of "going shares" (317–19) – even though Daos had already pointed out that "going shares" did not fit the circumstances.[7] Smikrines' verdict, which recognizes the inseparability of infant and tokens, is offered succinctly and without explanation:

> ἀλλ' εὔκριτ' ἐστί . πάντα τὰ συνεκκείμενα
> τοῦ παιδίου 'στί. τοῦτο γινώσκω. (353–54)

> An easy matter to judge: everything left together with the infant
> belongs to him. This is my judgment.

In *Rudens* IV 4, Trachalio foregoes his earlier claim to half the trunk and only now reveals that it contains a casket belonging to Palaestra; the casket is full of tokens which might assist in identifying her parents (1078–84). When the tokens of identification become the new subject of dispute, Daemones announces his intention to take control of the trunk, *faciam ut det* (1084: "I'll see that he hands it over"); Gripus eventually agrees to surrender it, provided that it be returned (1127–28). At the end of the scene, Daemones bids the trunk be brought into the house; no explanation is given for the

[7] . . . κοινὸς Ἑρμῆς; μηδὲ ἓν / εὕρισχ', ὅπου πρόσεστι σῶμ' ἀδικούμενον. / οὐχ εὕρεσις τοῦτ' ἔστιν ἀλλ' ἀφαίρεσις ("'Go shares' – you say? Not one thing does he find, when the person who is being wronged is present; this is not a finding but an act of removal"). Gomme and Sandbach ad loc. call this "a fine piece of rhetorical effrontery." Wilamowitz 1925: 157–58 comments on the unusualness of such a rhetorical antithesis in Menander.

appropriation. The real adjudication of the trunk is postponed until the final scene of the play.[8]

While the arguments of the disputants are presented briefly in *Rudens* (and punctuated with a good deal of comic horseplay), no opportunity for the display of theatric oratory (or forensic theatrics) is wasted in Menander's arbitration scene.[9] Quasi-formulaic phrases of procedure had announced the new roles to the spectators at its beginning. Thereafter, Menander plays upon the shifting boundary between oratory and theater. Suros' speech is the high mixing point: the physical recruitment of the infant to support his rebuttal of Daos' position transports the audience temporarily from the theater to the courtroom (302–05); his references to tragedy – to dramatizations of Tyro (325) and to the general use of birth tokens (341–43) – underscore the concatenation.[10] While these references are instances of Menander's "metatheatricality," they also mimic rhetorical devices of courtroom speeches. Allusion to tragedy in forensic oratory increased markedly in the course of the fourth century; Suros' speech, chock full of tragedy, mimics its grand heights.[11] At the end of the act in which the scene of arbitration takes place, the happy orator comments on his success:

> . . . οὐδὲ νῦν κακῶς ἀπήλλαχα.
> πάντων δ' ἀμελήσανθ', ὡς ἔοικε, δεῖ δίκας
> μελετᾶν. διὰ τουτὶ πάντα νυνὶ σώιζεται. (416–18)

[8] Daemones appears to appropriate the trunk by virtue of being owner of his slave's possessions. As is clear from IV 7, 1230–31, he has no intention of claiming it as his own, but awaits the discovery of its owner. In V 2, Labrax promises on oath to give Gripus a *talentum argenti magnum* (1344) if the trunk is found; in V 3, Daemones hands over the trunk to Labrax, but the latter refuses to hand over the talent to Gripus. When Daemones hears that Labrax had promised the money on oath (1376–1380), Labrax claims the agreement with the slave was not valid, and challenges Gripus to find someone to represent him in court (1380–82); see App. 5, cat. VI. 4 for the Roman remedy envisioned here. Rather than go to court, Daemones cuts a deal with the pimp and splits the money owed Gripus: the pimp retains half for the purchase of Ampelisca; Daemones pockets the other half as payment for Gripus' freedom.

[9] For discussion of the rhetoric of the two speeches in *Epitr.*, see Cohoon 1915: 157–230.

[10] Tragedies about Tyro had been written by Sophokles, Karkinos, and Astydamos: see Gomme and Sandbach 1973 apud 326.

[11] Aiskhin.: 1. 128 (one line from Euripides), 151 (two lines from Eur. *Stheneboia* = Nauck^2 672), 152 (9 lines from Eur. *Phoinix* = Nauck^2 812, followed by interpretation in c. 153); 190 (general reference); Dem. 18. 267 (one line from Eur. *Hek.* and another line and half line from unidentified tragedies), 180, 242 (general references); 19. 245 (three lines from Eur. *Phoinix* = Nauck^2 812.7–9), 247 (Soph. *Ant.* 175–90); Lycourg. 1. 92 and 132 (four and two lines respectively from an unidentified poet), 100 (55 lines from Eur. *Erekhtheus* = Nauck^2 360) followed in c. 101 with interpretation. Demosthenes' references are usually less sophisticated than Aiskhines' or Lykourgos'; they are often references to Aiskhines' failures in acting.

. . . I've not come off badly, now, either!
It's clear I must ignore all else and practice law.
That's how everything is protected nowadays.

Suros has been playing a role, and it is one that he would find attractive to play again in the future. Role-playing is underscored by status transformation: the slave playing the role of disputant before an arbitrator envisions himself as a citizen pleading before a dikastic audience.

Menander's play is named after the scene of arbitration. The characters who refer their dispute to arbitration appear in one scene only and the arbitration occurs in that scene. While the arbitration is not mentioned later in the play, nevertheless, the result of its decision (that infant and tokens remain together) is the springboard for subsequent events. Stage action – the humble spectacle of Habrotonon carrying infant with tokens in her arms – is the visual result of the arbitral verdict. The role played by infants in drama has often been neglected; nevertheless, the infant as stage-prop was an important and traditional component of drama's repertoire: an infant dressed in funeral garb, another rushed outside a house after grandfather's threat to burn it up, another one set on a doorstep and threatened with a roll in the mud – each infant is just as powerful and meaningful an image as Elektra's urn and the putative ashes of Orestes.[12] The infant who had been hoisted upon Suros' shoulders in Act II of *Epitrepontes* – *sans* tokens – in a gesture of supplication is now, in Acts III and IV, carried about with the paraphernalia of identity. That spectacle, moreover, becomes just as forensically theatrical as the arbitration itself: Habrotonon has rehearsed a new role (III. 513 ff.); she will play-act the mother of Kharisios' infant in order to dramatize a proof of the infant's paternity (Act III) and she will entice the real mother to unmistakable maternal curiosity shortly thereafter (Act IV). One extra-judicial scenario leads to another.

While the presence of Habrotonon carrying infant and tokens in Acts III and IV may have impressed the audience, it is the formality of the arbitration scene that has left its mark on legal historians. So formal, indeed, is its presentation of arbitration that one legal historian has used the opening of the scene (218–39) to illustrate the

[12] The infants belong to the following plays, in order: Eur. *Melanippe the Wise* (Nauck[2] pp. 509–10); Men. *Samia* 553–69; Ter. *Andr.* 775–77. For a discussion of "dramatic infants," see Post 1939: 193–208.

procedure followed in a private arbitration and another has used it to suggest the success and popularity of such settlements.[13] And yet in one important respect the arbitration in *Epitrepontes* is strikingly different from the private arbitrations and reconciliations attested in fourth-century orators: in none of them do we find an example of a bystander, unknown to both disputants, who is asked to settle their dispute. When there is only one arbitrator, he is always a friend or relative of at least one of the parties, and we may suspect that he was usually an acquaintance of the other as well. Such an arbitrator would be thought *isos* – that is, balanced in his view of both parties by virtue of interest in each rather than equally indifferent to the lot of the two.[14] Smikrines, however, is entirely unknown to the two disputants – and yet Suros has called for an arbitrator who will be *isos* (227). The inconcinnity will be explained shortly. The following verses spoken by Suros should be interpreted as Menander's attempt to smooth over the procedural oddity rather than as a more or less standard justification for the participation of a bystander in arbitration:

μὴ καταφρονήσῃς, πρὸς θεῶν. ἐν παντὶ δεῖ
καιρῶι τὸ δίκαιον ἐπικρατεῖν ἁπανταχοῦ,
καὶ τὸν παρατυγχάνοντα τούτου τοῦ μέρους
ἔχειν πρόνοιαν. κοινόν ἐστι τῶι βίωι
πάντων. (232–36)

Don't despise us, by the gods! Whenever conflict
arises, justice should prevail everywhere,
and any chance person on the spot should feel
compunction for this – it's a universal in the life
of all.

That Menander should use a "bystander" as arbitrator in *Epitrepontes* may strengthen the position of those scholars who think that he has borrowed the dramatic situation from Euripides' *Alope*. While the fragments of that play do not preserve such a scene, the story given in Hyginus *fabula* 187 is thought to represent, in broad outline, Euripides' version. Alope, the daughter of Kerkyon, is violated by Poseidon; without her father's knowledge, she gives birth and surrenders the infant to her nurse. She exposes him; a mare nurtures him; a shepherd then finds him. He gives him to another shepherd – but keeps the infant's royal clothing. A quarrel ensues: second

[13] MacDowell 1978: 203–04; Todd 1993: 124.

[14] See chapter 3, at nn. 40–43.

shepherd demands birth tokens from the first. The two men bring their dispute to the king; he recognizes the tokens as his daughter's possessions.[15] If in fact Menander has borrowed some such skeletal plot from Euripides, then he is constrained to use the infant's grandfather as arbitrator, regardless of his unfamiliarity with the disputants. Mythic paradigm thus conflicts with legal convention here as elsewhere in Menander.[16] The significant feature for Menander is the working of *tukhe* ("fortune," "luck").

1(b) A Greek or Roman scenario in Rudens?

Rudens IV 4 contrasts sharply with the compactness and formality of Menander's scene of arbitration. Nevertheless, the abortive arbitration of *Rudens* is essential to the plot of the comedy: it introduces the mechanism by which the young woman is identified and so was certainly a component of the Greek original.[17] Analytic critics have pointed out extended Plautine additions and alterations in IV 4; Jachmann, for example, cogently argued that Plautus has united two Diphilan scenes into what has become the rather long scene of identification (IV 4) in *Rudens*.[18] The alterations are characteristic: slave roles are enlarged. And the result is self-evident: slapstick humor and wit – but the structure of the proceeding as an arbitration is hardly visible at all. After an entire scene devoted to the preliminaries of an arbitration (IV 3), after all the hustle and bustle on the part of Trachalio to win Gripus' agreement to an arbitration presided over by Daemones, the latter is never even formally asked to perform that role; he never gives a verdict that bears upon the

15 Wilamowitz 1925: 127–32 dissents from the general view that Hyginus *fabula* 187 represents Euripides' version and that Euripides is therefore the model for Menander; Wilamowitz thinks that the story found in Hyginus belongs to a post-Menandrian mythographer. See Wehrli 1936: 119 for arguments against this view.

16 See chapter 6. 4.

17 Leo 1912: 159; Jachmann 1931: 67–68. Contra Lefèvre 1984a: 18–21: he extirpates the arbitration from the Greek original; this is, I think, impossible.

18 Friedrich 1953: 182–94 takes a somewhat middle position between Marx's (1928) tendency to view Plautus as almost a literal translation of Diphilos and Jachmann's (1931) virtuoso assertions of Plautine addition and alteration. Conservative critics will find no difficulty in assigning to Plautus the joking in 1064, 1073, 1075, 115–16, 1125 (which depends on the homosexual connotation of *comprimere*). The repetitions in 1078–84 and 1104–11 have elicited varied critical treatment; Jachmann 1931: 53 thinks the entire passage from 1085 to 1118 is Plautine addition; for other views, see Monaco 1947: 325–34 and Friedrich 1953: 191–92. Jachmann's most significant contribution is his analysis (pp. 44–47) of the staging in IV 4 and consequent hypothesis that Plautus has sutured two Diphilan scenes; the break in the original would have occurred at 1129.

ownership of the trunk; he simply bids the trunk be carried into the house. If we are looking for an arbitration, Greek or Roman, it is clear that we do not find one in *Rudens* IV 4.

The preceding scene, the preliminaries to the arbitration, is more promising. Here, too, analytic critics have found fertile ground for hypothesizing Plautine creativity. Many of their attributions are compelling, especially in regard to verses which are pointlessly repetitious or which involve word-play and jokes; some of their attributions are more disputable.[19] On the other hand, details which conform to Athenian practice in a very particular way point to the Diphilan original and these will be the focus of our attention. Especially on the basis of the latter set of observations, it is clear that we encounter, at least in *Rudens* IV 3, an essentially Athenian scenario.

The manner of choosing an arbitrator in *Rudens* conforms to what we know of fourth-century Athenian practice. In IV 3, Trachalio asks Gripus to choose an arbitrator (1002) and later asks whether he knows anyone in the neighborhood (1032); upon Gripus' vague acknowledgement of his familiarity with the district (1032 and 1033), Trachalio points to the house belonging to Daemones and asks if he would allow the man who lives "*in hac villa*" to act as arbitrator (1035). Trachalio is, of course, a city-slick slave from Athens and his pretence of generosity in allowing Gripus the choice of arbitrator is precisely that – pretence. He has recently made Daemones' acquaintance (III 2) and has informed him of Palaestra's situation as a free-born Athenian who is being kept by a pimp (III 4. 738 and 741); Daemones had indicated his sympathy by acknowledging that he, too, is Athenian (740–42). Trachalio, moreover, knows that Daemones is the owner of the house to which he points in IV 3: already in III 2, when both Daemones and Trachalio were on stage, the former had called his slave overseers to come out from it (656); the house is contiguous with the temple of Venus. Trachalio, who has spent the duration of III 2–III 4 outside of that temple, is familiar with the neighborhood. But in IV 3, he conceals his acquaintance with Daemones and acts as if Gripus is to have sole choice, a clear

[19] Jachmann 1931: 82–87 ascribes 986, 989–90, 993–1000, 1004–12, 1016–18 to Plautus. See Friedrich 1953: 184–85 for arguments against some of these ascriptions. For our purposes, the most important verses in contention are 1004 and 1018. Jachmann had complained that the repetition of Trachalio's request that Gripus enter into arbitration served no purpose; for my answer to that objection, see n. 27 below, apud fin.

advantage – so he leads him to think. Gripus, local Cyrenian fisherman and unaware of Trachalio's forensic tactics, feigns ignorance of Daemones (1043–44): he'll pull one over on the foreigner (1037–40).[20]

This is one-upmanship of a particularly Athenian cast. The scenario is, above all, spoof of the manipulative activities of potential litigants who engage in private arbitration. It is a common ploy of Athenian forensic speakers to conceal from dikastic audiences their relationship to arbitrators and to mention only their opponents' (chapter 3.1.b). One speaker, a former (and disgruntled) party in an arbitration, complained that he had only learned subsequently – after the verdict! – of the close relationship between his opponent and the sole arbitrator.[21] The ploy of concealment – whether before a dikastic audience or in the actual act of selecting an arbitrator with an opponent – distorts the friendship ideology ingrained in Athenian arbitral practice. In *Rudens*, the success of the ploy relies on the particular casting of roles: city-slick slave is portrayed as trying to bamboozle country-bumpkin counter-part. Opposition of city-slick character and country-bumpkin not only runs through Aristophanic comedy but is portrayed rather consistently in the Attic orators: Apollodoros' portrayal of Stephanos and Theogenes in [Dem.] 59 *Neaira* 72–84 is one example; Hypereides' depiction of shrewd Egyptian businessman taking unfair advantage of farmer's son (Hyp. 5 *Athen.*, see chapter 1.3) is another. That slaves should duplicate foibles of their masters is part of the humor of the Diphilan scenario; that country-bumpkin should (at least momentarily) even the score, is Aristophanic legacy of the underdog's appeal.

The Attic origin of the scenario is likewise evident in the city slave's initial strategy of negotiation with Gripus. As soon as Trachalio espies the fisherman with his catch at the opening of IV 3, he picks up the rope dangling from the trunk (an important bit of

20 The scene ends with typical Plautine wordplay, but the verses do not undermine the essentially Athenian notions of the scene: *quamquam ad ignotum arbitrum me appellis, si adhibebit fidem, / etsi ignotust, notus: si non, notus ignotissumust* (1043–44: "You are leading me to an unknown arbitrator. However, if he'll credit my story, although unknown, he'll be known; but if not – though known, he'll be most unknown"). Marx 1928 ad loc, depicting the verses as "eine in eine zierliche Antithese gekleidete Gnome," compares *Aul.* 260 and *Cas.* 512–13; the latter verses end a scene, as in *Rud.* 1043–44. I doubt very much a technical significance for *fides* in 1043; Gripus' thought is very similar to Tranio's at *Most.* 557–58: *cape, opsecro hercle, cum eo una iudicem, / (sed eum videto ut capias, qui credat mihi)* . . . ("I beseech you, get a *iudex* along with him, – but make sure you get one who will believe me").

21 [Dem.] 34. 18.

stage action which we will consider below). He will try to persuade him "to go shares." His strategy is the offering of a tale (an *ainos*) in the form of a riddle (954–61): once he had watched a thief steal the property of a person whom he knew; he threatened the thief with informing the owner and then proposed going shares with the thief's stolen goods; what should be his fair share, he asks Gripus, a half? Having won the ready answer, "Even more!" (961), Trachalio informs the fisherman that the story applies to him; the "riddle" is solved (962–64). Fraenkel has maintained the Diphilan origin of the tale on formal grounds: the narrative anapaests (a rather low register for a canticum) faithfully preserve the riddle of the original; the shape of the "tale as riddle with solution provided" is a traditional form with exemplars in Soph. *Ajax* 1142–58 and the *apologus* of *Stichus* 539–69.[22]

Fraenkel's formal argument can be strengthened in two ways. First, the tale is attached to the underlying structure of the play. Gripus in IV 7 seeks out Daemones and raises the issue once again of his right to possess the trunk. Daemones responds in high moral tones and informs the slave that he has neither the intention of keeping the trunk for himself nor of splitting the find with Gripus; wise masters do not collude with slaves in the interest of profit (1235–48). After Gripus departs, Daemones has a short monologue:

> *illuc est quod nos nequam servis utimur.*
> *nam illic cum servo si quo congressus foret,*
> *et ipsum sese et illum furti astringeret;*
> *dum praedam habere se censeret, interim*
> *praeda ipsus esset, praeda praedam duceret.* (1258–62)

> This explains the worthlessness of our slaves!
> Why, if he had met up with some other slave,
> he would have implicated both himself and that other in theft;
> while he might think that he himself possessed the loot, meanwhile
> he would himself become loot, loot would have led off loot![23]

Daemones' remarks are self-congratulatory: thank heavens Gripus has a master of my ilk – unlike those masters who don't keep a watch on their slaves' activities; now no harm will befall Gripus for encountering this windfall of treasure – had a villainous slave (and not I) met up with him and his treasure chest, who knows what

[22] Fraenkel 1960: 329–30, n. 3; further examples in 1920: 366–70.
[23] "Loot" has been filched from Nixon's translation.

would have happened to him, let alone the treasure! While the final two verses (1261–62) are a typical Plautine coda,[24] Daemones' imaginary scenario is precisely what Trachalio had portrayed in his tale, and is precisely what he tried to enact in the course of IV 3: to loot Gripus of his loot.[25] The interplay of Trachalio's tale and Daemones' reflections suggest a careful patterning that may be attributed to the original.

Now, the second argument that supports Fraenkel's thesis of the Diphilan origin of the tale: the city slave makes use of it in a way that is fully in accord with Athenian dispute settlement strategies (chapters 1.1 and 2.1). The tale thinly conceals a threat to have Gripus prosecuted for theft – even though Trachalio has no intention of carrying out that threat. The dispute between the two slaves could only enter the judicial realm under two circumstances: if Trachalio notified the owner of the trunk (Labrax) and if the owner then sued Gripus (or Gripus' owner). But Trachalio is in a hurry and knows he cannot wander off and fetch Labrax who has just been haled to court at the end of Act III (see App. 4.1.b). There can be no question, then, of a prosecution for theft; if there is to be an end to the dispute over the possession of the trunk, it will have to be decided out of court. *Rudens* IV 3 dramatizes pre-trial intimidation aimed at private settlement.

The preliminaries to arbitration in *Rudens* IV 3, then, bear significant and quite particular Athenian coloring: Trachalio attempts to induce Gripus' agreement to arbitration by insinuating that a prosecution hovers in the near future and he tries to bamboozle him into accepting Daemones as arbitrator without admitting his own acquaintance with the man. The most significant element of intimidation, however, has yet to be examined: the rope. We do not know the title of the Diphilan original (see n. 1), but Plautus' play is called *Rudens* ("Rope"). The title calls attention not to the scene of arbitration, but to its preliminaries, and not to any legal or quasi-legal procedure, but to the tangible instrument of intimidation that Trachalio uses to compel his adversary to extra-judicial settlement. The audience first encounters the rope visually in

[24] See n. 20 above, for other examples of Plautine wordplay at the end of a scene. The particular wordplay here occurs in 1242, and again in *Pseud.* 1029 (cf. *Epid.* 359). While Plautus thus appears to be rather fond of the expression, "looting the looter," it might also have been gnomic in Greek; cf. Aiskh. *Ag.* 1562 and *Sept.* 352.

[25] Contra Jachmann 1931: 41–43.

IV 2 when Gripus, alone on stage except for Trachalio who lies hidden from his view, drags his netted catch before the audience; a rope is attached to the net. The rope operates as a "drawstring," running around the edge of the circular net that encloses the trunk. An Attic red-figured pyxis by the Wedding Painter (*c.* 450 BC) depicts such a net (encircling a casket) with a rope attached to it; one end of the rope is visible, the other is not.[26] While the following details of the rope's operation in *Rudens* are my own (imaginative) reconstruction, the red-figured pyxis offers some basis for comparison. The two ends of the rope emerge from different openings in the "waist-band" of the net; the openings are close to each other. If the ends of the rope are drawn tightly together, the trunk will be entirely enclosed, and the person drawing the ends together will be able to drag the net behind him. Two persons might each hold one end of the rope; if they walk in the same direction, the trunk will follow; if they walk in opposite directions and are of equal strength, the result will be a "tug-of-war" and they will go nowhere. In order to make progress, the two must walk in the same direction.

Apparently, in the course of his monologue (IV 2), as he boasts of his piscatory triumph and dreams aloud of its worth, the fisherman drops one end of the rope to the ground. A good director would not fail to see the value of that prop; the text provides some hints in the next scene. Trachalio emerges from his hiding-place; he has heard enough of the fisherman's monologue to deduce that the netted trunk belongs to the shipwrecked pimp and that it might contain Palaestra's birth tokens; he wants very much to lay hold of it. He immediately asks the fisherman to remain where he is; he then quickly picks up the rope and begins to coil it:

TR. Heus, mane. GR. quid maneam? TR. dum hanc tibi quam trahi' rudentem complico. (938)

TR.: You there – wait. GR.: What am I to wait for? TR.: Until I wind up this rope you're trailing.

As he winds the rope, he steps closer to both fisherman and trunk. Stage action will reinforce the gradients of verbal intimidation throughout the scene as Trachalio sometimes allows the rope to slacken and at other times gives it a forceful yank.[27] The rope,

[26] See Trendall and Webster 1971: 30, plate II 3 and Clairmont 1953: 92–94 with plates 50–52.

[27] Trachalio uses the greatest force at the beginning and end of the scene (938–1044). Gripus' comments often furnish the best idea of the stage action, since he is reacting to Trachalio's

however, has two ends, and the fisherman can answer Trachalio's yank by giving his end a forceful pull. At verse 1013, Gripus announces his departure (*abeo ego hinc*), turns away from Trachalio, and tugs:

> . . . *TR. at ego hinc offlectam navem, ne quo abeas. mane.*
> *sei tu proreta isti navi es, ego gubernator ero.*
> *GR. mitte rudentem, sceleste. TR. mittam: omitte vidulum.* (1013–15)[28]

TR.: But I'll have the ship go backwards – you won't be going anywhere. Stop. If you're the look-out man at the prow – I'll be the pilot!
GR.: Let go of the rope, villain. TR.: Sure. You let go of the trunk.

Trachalio's retaliatory tug in 1013 is futile; when he circuitously proposes that the two of them go in the same direction, he insists on being pilot. Neither he nor his adversary relents; each now pulls the rope in his own direction. The message of this tug-of-war is clear and simple: two equally-matched adversaries cannot come to agreement by arguing their own cases ad infinitum; if neither party will relinquish his position, then only a third party can save the day. When Gripus is offered the opportunity of having his own master arbitrate the dispute, he shows signs of yielding and Trachalio slackens the rope:

> *TR. vin qui in hac villa habitat, eiius arbitratu fieri?*
> *GR. paullisper remitte restem dum concedo et consulo.*
> *TR. fiat.* (1035–37)

TR.: Will you have the arbitration decided by the man who lives in that house?
GR.: Let the rope go for a moment while I withdraw and think about it.
TR.: It's done.

pulling on the rope; his exclamations, e.g., that he will not let go, are responses to Trachalio's tightening grip; thus at 945: *quid tu, malum, nam me retrahis?* ("What are you dragging me back for, wretch?"); 1006: *hunc non amittam tamen* ("nevertheless, I shall not let go"); 1015–17: *GR. mitte rudentem, sceleste. TR. mittam: omitte vidulum. / GR. numquam hercle hinc hodie ramenta fies fortunatior. / TR. non probare pernegando mihi potes* (GR.: "Let go of the rope, villain." TR.: "Sure. You let go of the trunk." GR.: "I swear you'll never be a whit bit richer because of this scrappy find." TR.: "You can't win with all your nayings"); 1030–32: *GR. iam dudum fero: / ut abeas, rudentem amittas, mihi molestus ne sies. / TR. mane dum refero condicionem. GR. te, opsecro hercle, aufer modo* (GR.: "My offer's been made: that you go away, let go of the rope, and stop being a nuisance." TR.: "Stay while I make a counter-offer." GR.: "By god – why don't you just go!"); 1035–37: see text above. Each indication of tugging is either preceded or followed by Trachalio's invitation to enter arbitration. Jachmann paid no attention to the crucial staging of the scene when he determined that the repetitions were meaningless.

[28] I am following Marx's (1928: 186) attribution of lines and interpretation. On verse 1015 he comments, "erreicht der Kampf seinen Höhepunkt, dieser Vers gab dem lateinischen Lustspiel seinen Namen."

The fisherman now quickly agrees to Trachalio's choice of *arbiter*; the notions of arbitration which are a part of that agreement have already been discussed. Here we should observe how stage action reinforces our analysis of Athenian arbitration: that winning agreement to an arbitrator is the most difficult aspect of the procedure and that intimidation may play an important role in achieving that agreement (chapters 1.1 and 2.1). That *Rudens* IV 3 should dramatize this feat of intimidation so well, that its author should choose almost to allegorize the intimidating aspect of arbitration through the stage action of a rope, shows how theatrical the settlement of disputes could be – even without adverting to any explicit language of rehearsal and staging.

2 ARBITRAL FIGURES IN ROMAN COMEDY

Plautus in his portrayal of the preliminaries to arbitration in *Rudens* has translated a scenario that is both integral to the plot of the Greek original and consonant with certain ideological notions that belong peculiarly to Athenian arbitral practice. The discovery is of some importance: *Rudens* is the only play in which it is certain that Plautus uses the term *arbiter* of a private arbitrator. Some legal historians, however, have claimed that Plautus uses the term of a Roman private arbitrator not only in *Rudens* but twice elsewhere as well (*Cas.* 966 and *Truc.* 629); on the latter two occasions the adjective *aequus* modifies the noun.[29] The Plautine passages, in conjunction with two Terentian passages (*Ad.* 123–24 and *HT* 498–508), are then used not only as evidence for the existence and frequency of private arbitration in the early to mid-second century, but also as components in evolutionary schemata of Roman legal procedures. Proponents of such schemata have hypothesized the existence of an obscurely dated primeval private *arbiter* whose criterion of judgment was the *bonum aequum*; not only did this *arbiter* become the model for the judicial *arbiter* who presided over "actions of good faith" and "actions framed on considerations of what is right and fair," he also is the forebear of Plautus' private *aequus arbiter*, who is allegedly called *aequus* because he bases his decisions on the *bonum aequum*.[30] Moreover, the private *arbitri* of Plautus and Terence in turn become

[29] Broggini 1957: 119, n. 19; Ahrens 1970: 26–27.
[30] See chapter 3.2 at nn. 66–76.

the fathers (grandfathers?) of the *arbitri ex compromisso* who appeared at some point in the second century.[31]

Legal historians have treated the comic evidence too optimistically. Alliterative effect rather than precision of meaningful referent might be the decisive factor for Plautus' choice of the epithet *aequus*. Only one passage (Ter. *HT* 498–508) aside from *Rudens* IV 3 depicts an individual who is a technical *arbiter* – and the passage owes its origin to Menander; in the Terentian version, it is impossible to discern whether the *arbiter* is private or judicial. In App. 6, I present a survey of Plautus' and Terence's use of the terms *arbiter* and *iudex* in technical, non-technical (e.g., a "judge of a good piece of cake"), and metaphorical contexts. What can be said about the *arbiter* of Roman Comedy who has a definitely private arbitral function is quite limited: he appears in one play only and the scenario is dependent on a Greek original.

Characters in Roman Comedy, however, sometimes have an arbitral or mediating role without being explicitly designated as *arbitri*; usually an Attic scenario of arbitration can be reconstructed in the episodes in which these undesignated figures appear. Five will be discussed here, one each from *Adelphoe* II 2, *Phormio* IV 3 and V 9, and two from *Curculio* V 3. Most Terentian scholars would find little difficulty in accepting the hypothesis that the action of *Adelphoe* II 2 is closely modelled on Menander's play; some details will have been different, especially in the opening of the scene where Terence has sutured the Menandrian original with the Diphilan scene that precedes (App. 5, cat. III, nos. 21 and 22). Attribution of *Phormio* IV 3 to the Greek original (Apollodoros' *Epidikazomenos*) is certain on the basis of Donatus' references to Apollodoros' play;[32] some scholars

31 Broggini 1957: 119–20, n. 19; Ziegler 1971: 6, n. 4; Schmidlin 1974: 437; Behrends 1976: 680.

32 Donatus quotes or paraphrases words from the original corresponding to IV 3 at *Phormio* 647 and 668. Lefèvre 1978a: 24–27 argues that the *senex*, not the slave, conducted the interview with the parasite: (1) Donatus on 647 reports that the *senex* in the original spoke that line; and (2) all instances (at least those cited from Arnott 1970) of reported speech in a Greek playwright are speeches that could not be dramatized on stage, whereas the speeches reported by Geta could be dramatized. Against (1): Donatus only attributes a line or two to the *senex* (which could easily be mere interjection). (2) Three reported speeches in *Epitr.* (890–91 and 895–90, in which Onesimos quotes Kharisios' response to Pamphile's speech to her father, and 920–22 in which Kharisios quotes some of her speech) not only could have been dramatized on-stage, we now know that the last speech was (Sandbach App. p. 349, verse 820). More significantly, as Fantham 1982: 368 points out, Phormio's words "are 'quoted' by Geta because the conversation is not a real event . . . but a fiction" and have a parallel in "Syrus' reported excerpts from Ctesipho in *Adelphoe* 405–10 [which] allow the audience to enjoy the old man's deception."

think that Terence has introduced Antipho as eavesdropper into the scene, but that problem is not relevant to our discussion.[33] Attribution of *Phormio* v 9 and *Curculio* v 3 is more controversial; the final scenes of plays are notorious locations for free adaptation and invention. Some scholars have seen considerable Terentian rewriting and addition in the last two scenes of *Phormio*; their views have not won universal acceptance; the explication presented below may be considered as additional support for Terence's dependence on his Greek model.[34] An hypothesis of close agreement between Plautus and the Greek original of *Curculio* – which does not survive in any fragmentary shape – is, however, precarious.[35] Zwierlein has nonetheless cogently demonstrated that the pimp's monologue at the opening of v 3 provides a motive for his entrance which had been anticipated earlier in the play. Such structural patterning suggests dependence on a Greek model. Moreover, the features of arbitration in the dialogue following the pimp's entrance conform to what we know of Athenian practice – and suggest a further patterning which will be identified shortly. While Plautus has treated the Greek original of *Curculio* freely and added much of his own material (some of which will be pointed out below), we can be reasonably certain that its skeleton is Greek.[36]

[33] The scene demands four speaking parts, and Antipho's eavesdropping role would be the easiest to eliminate; but if Antipho is not present in IV 3, then, it is claimed, he could hardly know in the very next scene that Geta has apparently betrayed him (Arnott 1970: 44 and n. 3; Fantham 1982: 369). The problem is not insurmountable; Fantham adduces *Andria* III 5 as a parallel to *Phormio* IV 4, but discounts it as possibly "self-imitation by Terence from *Andria* to *Phormio*"; alternatively, she suggests, Apollodoros may have written a scene for the slave and young man after the Greek equivalent of 681.

[34] For arguments against the views of Büchner 1974: 356–60 and 479–81 and Lefèvre 1978a, see App. 5, add. 10.

[35] For the abbreviated nature of this play, see Webster 1953: 196–204; Fraenkel 1960: 145–46; Fantham 1965: 84–100. Against Zwierlein's view (1990) that Plautus' play was even more abbreviated than the play transmitted to us with the anonymous Bearbeiter's additions, see Jocelyn 1993: 134–37.

[36] For Plautus' enlargement of the role of the parasite in this play, see Lowe 1989: 165–66, with references to earlier literature. Lefèvre 1991: 71–105 argues that *Curc.* has only a distant relationship to a Greek model: Plautus has invented the play out of his *Pseud.*, which was based on a Greek model (pp. 91–93). Impromptu-style characterizes Plautus' invention, which is most notable in the structure of the play: "Das Unorganische ist ein Kriterium der Mündlichkeit, das Organische ein Kriterium der Schriftlichkeit – jedenfalls der griechischen Schriftlichkeit. Hieraus folgt, dass eine römische Komödie, die nicht einem griechischen Original folgt, eine besonders unorganische Handlung hat" (p. 98). Roman (as opposed to Greek) motivation for stage entry depends on an "Erwartungs-Dramaturgie" (p. 75) – whomever the on-stage character or audience expects to appear, appears. Mere "expectancy," however, does not explain the pimp's entrance at IV 4. 557 ff.; for Lefèvre (p. 80), there is no logical motivation involved here (a component of the "organic"), but

2(a) Adelphoe II I

In *Adelphoe* II I (Diphilos), Aeschinus had mercilessly pummelled the pimp Sannio and carried off a courtesan. The pimp had threatened the young man with a suit – perhaps for hubristic assault (163). Aeschinus ended up offering the alternative: accept the original price for the courtesan, twenty minae, or start rehearsing a courtroom plea (191, 195: App. 5, add. 6 and 7). The comic upheaval of the Diphilan scene – the pimp is clearly victim rather than predator – is maintained in the Menandrian scene that follows. As Syrus enters the stage to open negotiations with the pimp, he calls back to Aeschinus inside of Micio's house:

> *Tace, egomet conveniam iam ipsum: cupide accipiat faxo atque etiam*
> *bene dicat secum esse actum. – . . .* (209–10)
>
> Quiet – I'll meet the man now. I'll make sure he eagerly agrees –
> he'll even say that he's been well-treated – . . .

With the announcement of a plan to win the pimp's agreement, Syrus appropriates the role of *diallaktes*, a third party who will bring the disputants to an end of their quarrel. While no one in the audience will think he has the best interests of the pimp at heart, he will pretend he does throughout the scene (217–19, 240–42, 251–52). He holds one trump card in hand: he knows the pimp must leave for Cyprus soon; a time-consuming prosecution is out of the question. Upon dealing this card at 224, Sannio has a long aside (228–35): should he sue and lose his chance for profit-making in Cyprus, or abandon his claim to the courtesan? The latter alternative seems best. Syrus, however, is ready with a compromise: accept ten minae for the woman – half her cost-price (241–42). Sannio weakly bluffs his final reply:

> *utut haec sunt acta, potiu' quam litis sequar,*
> *meum mihi reddatur saltem quanti emptast, Syre.*
> *scio te non usum ante(h)ac amicitia mea:*
> *memorem me dices esse et gratum . . .* (248–51)

rather psychological (apparently a component of the "expected"). In Act V, even Lefèvre (p. 80) has to admit the entrances are well-motivated; but this is conditioned by the subsequent *anagnorisis*. It is hard to swallow all of this. I am reluctant to give up an immediate Greek model for the play, am willing to see plenty of Plautine expansion (and omission), am happy to see a theory of Roman dramaturgy, but prefer Zwierlein's explanation of logically structured motivation for the pimp's entrance at IV 4, which connects backwards to IV 2 and forward to V 3. See nn. 45, 46, and 49 below.

However the situation has evolved, rather than my pursuing him with suits,
at least, Syrus, let her cost-price be returned to me.
I know that up to now you've not experienced my friendship,
but in the future you'll say that I am mindful of your kindness.

The pimp has been defeated. He requests the kidnapper's slave to negotiate the sale; the pimp himself is not in command of the price of his courtesan – comic upheaval, certainly. His allusion to suits foregone in the interest of friendly settlement verges on parody of the Athenian "litigious code": private negotiation must be preceded by legal threat.[37] Syrus has been an exemplary mediator *poseur.* He has an analogue in Hyp. 5 *Athen.* 1–5: the bawd Antigone reconciled two men to smooth the way for the sale of three slaves – and was in cahoots with the seller all the time.

2(b) Phormio IV *3*

Another slave mediator appears in *Phormio* IV 3. Demipho, at this point in the play, is extremely anxious to dissolve his son's marriage to Phanium. In II 3, he had tried to convince Phormio to accept a dowry of five *minae* for the girl; Phormio himself should marry her. The gambit failed. Now, in IV 3, Demipho's slave Geta advances the much desired private settlement (Phormio's acceptance of the dowry) when he accidentally comes upon Demipho and his brother Chremes and fabricates a story for them. Geta's aim is a bit complicated: it is not to part Antipho and Phanium, but rather to acquire thirty *minae* so that Chremes' son Phaedria can purchase a mistress. A problem will arise if Demipho in fact pays the dowry and if Phormio accepts it; Phormio will then be obliged to marry Antipho's wife. But Geta (as we learn later in IV 4) has a remedy (slipshod though it be): Phormio will postpone the marriage and if Demipho should demand repayment of the "dowry," the young men can find funds elsewhere and so preserve Antipho's marriage.[38]

Geta's story consists of an alleged conversation with Phormio which he reports to the two *senes* in lengthy *oratio recta.*[39] The form is

[37] Rieth 1964: 47 thought 248–51 was an allusion to the friendship terminology of reconciliation; but the friendship terms are between mediator and one party rather than between the two disputants.

[38] Clever slaves produce slipshod plans elsewhere in New Comedy; see chapter 8.3 at n. 12.

[39] Geta's reported speeches: 620–25, 626–31; 633–35; 636–39; 645–47; Phormio's reported responses: 650–58; 661–62; 663; 665–67; 674–76.

worth noting. Swatches of reported dialogue appear frequently in New Comedy: e.g., in *Samia*, Demea quotes a conversation he overheard between an old freedwoman and slave of his household (242–61); the "messenger" in *Sikyonios* IV quotes numerous speeches from the deme meeting at Eleusis – both shorter and longer samples; and in *Eunuchus* II 2 (236–53), in a passage that indubitably derives from Menander's *Kolax*, the parasite Gnatho recites his own conversation with a down-and-outer whom he had encountered just moments ago.[40] Extended reports of dialogue, then, can be considered features of New Comedy. In *Phormio*, however, the dialogue is all a fabrication.[41] It is Geta's masterpiece, an improvised drama in which he takes the self-appointed role of mediator between Phormio and his master Demipho.

The mechanics of settlement follow the Athenian "litigious code": suits are threatened and then an agreement is made. Geta begins his improvisation by reporting his advice to Phormio: he should settle the dispute in a friendly rather than ill-spirited manner (*"quor non," inquam, "Phormio, / vides inter nos sic haec potiu' cum bona / ut componamu' gratia quam cum mala?"* 620–22). Demipho, he said, preferred to avoid lawsuits (*fugitans litium*, 623), even though all his friends recommended that he expel the woman (624–25). The compromise eventually overseen by the slave is perverse: the "intimidated party" (Geta as Phormio) sets the price and the master is bamboozled into paying a sum – six times the amount he would have been compelled to pay had he lost the case in court. Like Syrus in *Adelphoe* II 2, a slave mediator pretends to represent both parties, but in fact is in cahoots with one.

2(c) *Phormio* V 9

The penultimate scene of the play had ended in an impasse. The *senes* who had succeeded in dowering the parasite threaten to sue him for the return of the dowry (935–36, 981); Phormio responds

[40] On the derivation of *Eun.* 232–64 from Menander's *Kolax*, see Gomme and Sandbach 1973: 420. Reported dialogue also appears at *Misoumenos* A 53–56 (Sandbach App.), but the dramatic situation is unclear; part of the conversation might be fantasy.

[41] As emphasized by Fantham 1982: 368 who notes a parallel with the way Syrus invents for Demea's satisfaction speeches for his son at *Ad.* 407–09 and 410. In *Epid.* 243–44 and 250–53, Epidicus fabricates a conversation which he pretends to have heard between two women as part of a strategy to bamboozle his master in behalf of his son. The dynamics are similar to those in *Ph.* IV 3.

with a movement toward the house: *in ius? huc, siquid lubet!* (981: "To court? Court is in this direction, please!"). When Demipho and Chremes, one after the other, lay hands on Phormio, he responds with charges of assault (983–84). In v 9, the courtroom trial is replaced by a meeting with the household's mistress. Phormio lays his information against Chremes: he had married a woman in Lemnos (1004–05). Demipho, advocate for his brother, attempts to give a less lurid account of his offenses (1014–20). Nausistrata, on the point of forgiving her husband, is derailed by Phormio. Mindful of the thirty *minae* "dowry" he has collected from Demipho and certain of its loss should Nausistrata be won over to her husband's side (1036–37), he confesses: he tricked the old man out of the money and gave it to her son Phaedria to purchase a slave-girl from a pimp. The words are well-calculated to set off a chain reaction: first Chremes' indignant interjection and then Nausistrata's indignation that her husband – a man with two wives – should be angry at a son with one girlfriend (1040–41).[42] The indignant wife postpones forgiveness; her son will be *iudex*: *ei(u)s iudicio permitto omnia: / quod is iubebit faciam* ("I refer everything to his judgment: I shall do as he enjoins" 1045–46); her final words in the scene are: *sed ubist Phaedria / iudex noster?* ("But where is Phaedria, our judge?" 1054–55). The dispute has broadened; its pregnant contours had been signalled in the course of the play. No longer is it a dispute over the "dowry" of thirty *minae*, but over Chremes' abuse of the Lemnian property that had belonged to his rich wife's father (1012–13, and compare 679–81 and 786–93); the abuse entails the diminution of their son's inheritance.[43] Nausistrata's choice of *iudex* is well integrated with the economic concerns of the play. The comedy concludes as the apparatus for dispute settlement has been firmly set into place – a family arbitration to settle what is indubitably a family matter of utmost importance, the son's inheritance and the stability of the household. Lys. 32 *Diog.* (see chapter 1. 2) shows that a request for the adjudication of a family dispute about inheritance can be depicted as emerging from a woman – who might look for assistance from a sympathetic kinsman (a son-in-law in Lys. 32) to carry out the

[42] For the Roman flavor of this sentiment, see chapter 6, n. 63.

[43] In App. 5, add. 10, I present the hypothesis that in the Greek original, "Nausistrata" may have been an *epikleros*; if so, then the structure of the original is even more tightly patterned, and the son is even more appropriate as arbitrator of the dispute – the Lemnian property will be his shortly, when he is two years past puberty; he need not wait for his mother's death to inherit it.

task. Terence's *iudex*, then, represents a private arbitral character who is envisioned as acting in a way consonant with Athenian practice. Menander's use of *krites* at *Epitr.* 223 and 226 and Euripides' use of the same word in *Phoinix* fr. 812 Nauck² illustrate that Greek dramatists, at any rate, did not restrict themselves to one word (*diaitetes*) when denoting an arbitral figure.

2(d) *Curculio* V 3, 679–86

A private arbitration that was the sequel to a court summons is reported by the pimp Cappadox as he enters the stage in the final scene of *Curculio* (V 3, 679–86).[44] The subject of dispute between Cappadox and the banker Lyco was a sum of ten minae (525); the banker owed the pimp. Determination of the debt's origin need not detain us, but the manner of its repayment is pertinent.[45] Upon the pimp's first demand for the sum, the banker had promised payment the next day (IV 2, 526–27). In IV 4, before the pimp encounters Therapontigonus who is already on stage, the pimp reveals in an entrance monologue his current worry: Lyco might leave town before returning the sum; his motive for entering the stage is to find the banker – not Therapontigonus (557–60).[46] Thereafter, in the interval of the pimp's absence from the stage (he exits at IV 4, 590 and returns at V 3, 679ff.), he has sought out the banker once again. In the monologue that opens V 3, Cappadox begins with a few general remarks on the character of bankers, and then uses his recent experience with Lyco to exemplify them:

[44] For a discussion of some of the legal issues in this play, see App. 5, add. 3.

[45] From verses 492, 535, and 666, it is clear that Therapontigonus, the soldier who had arranged to purchase the courtesan, had paid out thirty *minae* to the banker, and from verses 348, 433–35, it is clear that the girl's jewelry and clothing were to be delivered together with her; only at 344 is the price of the jewelry and clothing said to have cost an additional ten *minae*. Zwierlein 1990: 236–39 argues convincingly that 344 is spurious. The ten *minae* which Cappadox demands from the banker at 525 has nothing to do with the transaction with the soldier. Zwierlein 238 points out that the debt serves a useful dramatic purpose: it provides motivation for the stage entrances of Cappadox at 557ff. and 679ff.; were it not for this additional demand on the banker, the pimp would have no further role in the play after the girl is handed over. Pringsheim's proposal (1950: 423–24) misinterprets *Curc.* 612 out of context – the person addressed is not the receiver of *arra*; see Andreau 1968: 505 n. 5.

[46] Grounds for the pimp's anxiety are foreshadowed to the audience in the banker's monologue at 371–81. The authenticity of these lines (with the exception of the metrically deficient 374) has been cogently defended by Zwierlein 1990: 251–53. It is plausible that there was some such foreshadowing in the original in which the banker would have had a larger role.

vel ille decem minas dum solvit, omnis mensas transiit.
postquam nil fit, clamore hominem posco: ille in ius me vocat;
pessume metui ne mihi hodie apud praetorem solveret.
verum amici compulerunt: reddit argentum domo.
nunc domum properare certumst. (682–86)

682: vel ille: Leo

Lyco's the paradigm: while he was trying to pay the ten *minae*, he visited every bank.
When nothing came of it, I start shouting for the man. He summons me to court;
I was horrified to think that he would settle with me today before the praetor.
But friends coerced him: he paid out the money at home.
Now I must hurry home.

Careful motivation for stage entry points to the Greek original: the pimp had announced at the opening of IV 4 (557–60) his intention to visit the banker again, and now his return homeward (686) provides the motive for his reappearance on stage when he meets Therapontigonus and Phaedromus.

Plautus has adapted the original passage, using almost exclusively Roman banking and legal terminology: bankers are called *argentarii* in the first line of the monologue (679) rather than *trapezitae*;[47] Lyco had summoned the pimp to court with an *in ius vocatio* (683), and in conformance with that procedure, the pimp was to appear before the praetor (684). The precise legal action is not clear. Possibly we are to imagine a special action for bankers; the claims of the latter might be set-off by the claims of their creditors (Gaius 4. 64). Unexpectedly, by the coercion of friends, the banker settled in private and paid the debt (684–85). What Greek legal situation

[47] Andreau 1968: 469–77 examines all the instances of *argentarius* (10 in 5 plays) and *trapezita* (14 in 6 plays) in Plautus and concludes (477): "En définitive, sauf exception, Plaute semble avoir choisi le terme *argentarius* ou le terme *trapezita* en fonction de critères dramatiques. Le second désigne un banquier de la comédie, probablement hérité du modèle grec. Le premier désigne un banquier extérieur à l'action, dont on parle pour faire allusion aux banquiers de Rome (c'est-à-dire le plus souvent pour s'en moquer)." In *Curculio*, *argentarius* appears at 377 and 679; *trapezita* at 341, 345, 406, 420, 559, 618, 712, and 721. The use of the terms bears out Andreau's conclusions: *trapezita* in this comedy always refers to the banker Lyco, who of course figured in the Greek original (although the use of the term in verse 721 is probably Plautine addition – see text at n.54); *argentarius* is used in "satiric" passages referring to bankers in general. The opening of the pimp's monologue (679–81), with its mocking reference to *argentarii*, may have undergone some Plautine expansion; but that expansion does not affect the underlying legal situation in 683–85 which is required by the stage action.

might lie behind Plautus' adaptation? Witt tentatively proposed the following: the pimp feared a declaration of insolvency on the part of the banker; if that happened, the banker would have to surrender his property to creditors – and possibly would leave the pimp out of account.[48] While declarations of bankruptcy, bank failures, and consequent "surrenders of property" appear in Demosthenes, details of legal remedies for creditors are uncertain; Lipsius reasonably suggests that if no private arrangement could be made, then the case would be brought to court. That some such scenario lies behind the pimp's monologue at *Curculio* 682ff. is supported by the banker's earlier remarks at 371ff.; after declaring that he is a rich man if he does not pay his creditors (373), he says, "If they will press me further, I'll let [the case be taken] to the praetor" (376: *si magi' me instabunt, ad praetorem sufferam*). Whatever details of procedure are imagined, it is clear from the pimp's report that the two men were reconciled in private. The Roman dramatist has not given us much information and certainly no Roman technical terminology bearing upon the private arrangement. But the reconciliation in the Greek original may have been more detailed – and *amici* (685), if it translates *philoi*, is a pointer to the Attic scenario. The mediating "friends" may have been the banker's – creditors who feared the results of a bank failure – rather than "friends" of the pimp. A report in Demosthenes suggests that such private negotiations between failing bankers and creditors may not have been unusual: "And Sosinomos and Timodemos and the other bankers . . . , when they had to settle (*dialuein*) with their creditors, gave up possession of all their property" (Dem. 36 *Phorm.* 50). Moreover, the sequence of lawsuit followed by private agreement overseen by friends is, as we have seen, common Attic practice. And it ends happily for the pimp.

2(e) Curculio 686–729

The scenario of court summons followed by a private agreement which is implied by the monologue is enacted in the dialogue that follows – this time, with a reversal of the pimp's fortunes; the

[48] Witt 1971: 235 n. 50, citing Lipsius 734f. Persons who declare bankruptcy are said "to give up possession of all their property" (ἐξίστασθαι ἁπάντων τῶν ὄντων): Dem. 36. 50; 45. 63–64 (in both passages, bankers have become insolvent and have had "to give up possession of their property"); similarly: [Dem.] 33. 25 and Dem. 37. 49. Bank failures are mentioned in [Dem.] 33. 9 and 49. 68. For discussion of bank failures in Athens, see E. Cohen 1992: 215–24.

careful patterning suggests dependence on a Greek original.[49] Therapontigonus and Phaedromus have entered the stage and demand the return of the soldier's money: the soldier had never received the courtesan for whom he had paid the purchase price, and moreover, as the pimp will learn only later in the scene, the girl has turned out to be free-born and so must be returned under the terms of the contract (App. 5, add. 3). Upon the pimp's refusal, the two young men apply force and threats of legal action. The latter are not explicitly articulated. But that court action is implicitly threatened is clear from (1) the language of forceful summons (693, 707) that Plautus uses in other comedies where the same activity is explicitly labelled as *in ius vocatio*;[50] (2) the pimp's allusions to witnesses who are not present (695);[51] and (3) the girl's plea, in behalf of the pimp, that he not be condemned (697).[52] Throughout the episode, then, the threat of a forced court summons is thinly veiled. That threat – accompanied by a fair amount of physical intimidation – prompts the pimp to yield to Phaedromus' timely intervention as *arbiter*:

> *PH. animum advortite <hoc>, si possum hoc inter vos componere.*
> *mitte istunc. accede huc, leno. dicam meam sententiam,*
> *siquidem voltis quod decrero facere. TH. tibi permittimus:*
> *CA. dum quidem hercle ita iudices, ne quisquam a me argentum auferat.*
> (701–04)

[49] The artfulness of this sequence – narrative of a set scenario followed by the dramatization of the same scenario by a cast of characters including one or two who were involved in the first and who thus link the two scenarios together – strikes me as Greek. A parallel may be found in *Aspis*, where *Tukhe*, in the prologue, describes a scenario involving the false identification of a corpse; a similar scenario is acted out by the characters later in the play, at the instigation of the character who had misidentified the corpse in the first place. See chapter 8.3.

[50] *Curc.* 693: *collum opstringe* . . . ("collar his neck"); 707: . . . *collum opstringe homini* (" . . . collar the man's neck"). Cf. *Rud.* 853 (Plesidippus to Labrax): *rapi te optorto collo mavis an trahi?* ("Do you prefer to be seized with your neck in a collar – or dragged?") The *in ius vocatio* is articulated at *Rud.* 860 and 882.

[51] *Curc.* 695: *hocine pacto indemnatum atque intestatum me abripi?* ("Am I to be whisked away thus – without verdict or witnesses?"); cf. 621: *PH. ambula in ius. TH. non eo. PH. licet te antestari? TH. non licet.* (621: PH.: "Go to court." TH.: "No." PH.: "Can I call on you to be a witness?" TH.: "No, impossible." On these verses, cf. Tandoi 1961 and Zwierlein 1990: 283–84. Also *Persa* 746–47: *SAT . . . sed ego in ius voco. / DO. nonne antestaris?* (SAT.: "But I am summoning you to court." Do.: "Aren't you going to summon witnesses?").

[52] *Curc.* 697: *frater, opsecro te, noli hunc condemnatum perdere.* ("Brother, I beseech you, don't let him be condemned and ruined!"). Cf. *Poen.* 1405–1406: *ADE. mi pater, ne quid tibi cum istoc rei siet † acmassum † opsecro. ANTE. ausculta sorori. abi, diiunge inimicitias cum inprobo* (ADE.: "Father, I beseech you, don't have any trouble with that man!" ANTE.: "Listen to my sister. Go away, drop the dispute with the rogue").

PH. Give your attention here, and see whether I can compose the dispute between you,
Let go of him. Come here, pimp. I shall give my verdict,
if indeed you consent to do what I shall have decreed. TH. We entrust it to you –
CA. Provided, by Hercules, that you do not judge in such a way that anyone carries off my money.

A threat of court action ends with an arbitration.

The scene is cleverly contrived: not until 716 – after Phaedromus' intervention as arbitrator and during the delivery of his verdict – does the pimp learn the basis of the demand for payment: Planesium is of free birth and has been recognized by her brother; the condition that had been attached to her sale (490–91, 709) must now be carried out. Had the information been announced at the outset of the meeting, the pimp may have yielded his claim more quickly. In the Greek original, the dynamics of the scene may have been similar: the pimp will be threatened with a suit for the recovery of money (a *dike arguriou* or possibly, a *dike blabes*) unless he hands over the sum. Physical intimidation, even of the gratuitous brand, cannot be ruled out in the ending of a Greek play; the treatment of Knemon at the end of *Duskolos* is palmary example. "Phaedromus" will then have intervened as *diaitetes* and given his verdict against the pimp. Hallmarks of Athenian procedure are present in the Roman scene: Phaedromus will give a verdict if the disputants agree to abide by its terms (702–03); he gives the verdict later in the scene (715–17). The arbitration, moreover, arises out of a typically Athenian sequence amply attested in the orators, the threat of a suit precedes the offer of arbitration. If the Greek playwright adhered to the "Menandrian three-actor rule," then the girl would not have spoken and may not have appeared in the scene.[53] In that case, the pimp would call only on "Phaedromus" for assistance at the Greek equivalent of 696, and would himself mention the crucially important extenuating circumstance that might invite fair play rather than a stricter decision, the fact that the girl's virginity had been preserved (cf. 698: *bene et pudice me domi habuit*). "Phaedromus" could confirm the fact – he is *isos* and *koinos*, with expert knowledge of recent events. "Phaedromus" need

[53] Young women in Greek plays who have been identified on-stage as being of free or citizen birth usually do not appear again on-stage (or at least do not speak) once that identification has been made. While this "rule" may have been invented in order to conform to the "three actor rule," it does make it unlikely that the girl appeared in the last scene of the Greek original of *Curculio*.

not have been designated formally as *diaitetes*; his role would be obvious to the Athenian audience.

While the dynamics of the Greek original may have been similar, Plautine expansion is probable. Three points are worth observing:

(1) Physical intimidation continues during the arbitration (707, 713); even the arbitrator threatens violence (707); moreover, intimidation continues after the verdict is announced (718, 723, 725–27). In fact, the pimp does not concede to the verdict until he is threatened with a beating by the soldier:

> *TH. novi ego hos pugnos meos.*
> *CA. quid tum? TH. "quid tum" rogitas? hisce ego, si tu me inritaveris,*
> *placidum te hodie reddam. CA. age ergo, recipe . . .* (725–27)

> TH.: I know these fists of mine.
> CA.: What then? TH.: "What then," you ask? If you provoke me, they'll reconcile you in a flash. CA.: Come on, then, take your money. . .

(2) The pimp's joke, that his banker is his praetor, which follows upon his command, "follow me" (721: *tu me sequere*), uses Plautine language of *in ius vocatio*.[54] The "summons" is humorous because it is so out of place: it follows the arbitral verdict; it makes the pimp a plaintiff rather than defeated defendant. It also conflicts with the presentation of a bankrupt Lyco (the pimp's banker) just moments ago.

(3) Instead of a promise of future friendship between the two disputants after the arbitral verdict, the pimp prays for the soldier's death and destruction (720 and 724).

The Greek arbitration of the ending has been subverted: the simultaneity of arbitration with physical intimidation and the appearance of post-arbitral threats of lawsuit and violence shatter any notion of strict dependence on the original. On stage, physical intimidation may have played a much larger role – and reduced the language of arbitration to mere parody, a verbal accompaniment for blows showered upon the pimp. Arbitration has become a foreign element, marginalized by violence, attenuated by further legal threat. Plautine joking is the finale, and it is unmistakably Roman.

[54] *Curc.* 721–23: *CA. tu me sequere. TH. quo sequar te? CA. ad tarpezitam meum / ad praetorem. nam inde rem solvo omnibus quibu' debeo. / TH. ego te in nervom, haud ad praetorem hinc rapiam, ni argentum refers* (CA.: Follow me. TH.: Where am I to follow you? CA.: To my banker, to the praetor. For that's where I settle business with all my creditors! TH.: I shall drag you to prison, not to the praetor, unless you pay back my money). Cf. *sequere* in context of *in ius vocatio* at *Asin.* 490: *sequere hac ergo* ("then follow in this direction").

3 RECONCILIATION AS THE END OF NEW COMEDY

The end of a play is an appropriate point for the characters to become reconciled with one another – even in cases where the "real dénouement" takes place in the fourth act. Sometimes these final reconciliations are more or less organically connected with one major plot strand of the comedy – as in the case of *Curculio* v 3; sometimes they are resolutions of rather tangential matters: e.g., a dispute left suspended while the major issues of the comedy were worked out (the dispute over the trunk in *Rudens*) or else a dispute that flares up at the very end as the result of the comedy's real dénouement earlier on (*Samia*). So frequent, indeed, are such endings, that they perhaps need no pointing out at all. We might borrow Aristotle's notion and say, "the complications of the play, major and minor, are dissolved." Yet, upon closer inspection, the "dissolution" almost always involves the conclusion of a dispute, as if "reconciliation" is the harmonious note on which the playwright must have his players leave the stage: Aristotelian *lusis* becomes *dialusis*.[55]

There are numerous ways in which these conclusions evolve. Occasionally, one character's threat to go to court motivates the (allegedly) offending character to settle with his accuser, as happens at the end of *Rudens* (and as might have happened at the end of *Poenulus*).[56] Sometimes the inflicting of physical violence or its threat as a self-help remedy solves the problem. This happens in *Samia* and *Miles Gloriosus*. In the latter, Pyrgopolynices has been caught in the act as a *moechus* as part of a plot devised by the characters in the play. In the former, Moskhion feigns a readiness to become a mercenary soldier and is brought to heel by Nikeratos' threat to treat him as a *moikhos*. In *Amphitruo*, a potentially disastrous family council presided over by the cuckolded husband and a relative of the alleged adulteress is only circumvented by the timely appearance of Jupiter as *deus ex machina*. A more common conclusion to a dispute, however,

[55] The proximity of *lusis* and *dialusis* can be seen in the very example which Aristotle in the *Poetics* (1455b29–32) adduces to illustrate it: ὥσπερ ἐν τῶι Λυγκεῖ τῶι Θεοδέκτου δέσις μὲν τά τε προπεπραγμένα καὶ ἡ τοῦ παιδίου λῆψις καὶ πάλιν ἡ αὐτῶν * * λύσις δ' ἡ ἀπὸ τῆς αἰτιάσεως τοῦ θανάτου μέχρι τοῦ τέλους. "Thus, in the *Lynkeus* of Theodektes, the complication (*desis*) consists of the earlier events and the seizure of the child, and again the . . . [gap in text]. And the dissolution (*lusis*) extends from the accusation of murder to the end." For *lusis* in later comic theory, see Prescott 1929.

[56] On the ending of *Rudens*, see n. 8 above; on the ending of *Poen.*, see App. 5, add. 5.

involves a human character who acts as a third-party mediator. In examining some of these conclusions, we must keep in mind once again that the finale of a Roman play may have undergone considerable transformation from its Greek original.

We have already considered the ending of *Curculio* where Phaedromus assumed the role of arbitrator (701–03) and intervened in a dispute about a sum of money. Most of the final reconciliations which use a mediating figure, however, end domestic disputes; many have legal ramifications – especially when they concern the abuse of money. We begin with *Mostellaria*, which depends on a Greek play called *Phasma*.[57] At the end of the fourth act, the *senex* Theopropides learns the extent to which his son Philolaches, under the guidance of his slave Tranio and with the assistance of his friend Callidamates, has consumed his estate; in v 1, he begins to bring his slave Tranio to account. In the next and final scene of the play, Callidamates enters the stage, announcing his new role: *nunc ego de sodalitate solus sum orator datus / qui a patre eiius conciliarem pacem* . . . (1126–27: "Now I've been selected as lone speaker from the fraternity to negotiate a peace with his father"). He immediately meets up with Theopropides and Tranio, the latter of whom takes refuge at an altar as he addresses the *senex*: *nunc utrisque disceptator eccum adest, age disputa* (1137: "Now here's a mediator for both parties; come, present your case!"). After Theopropides and Tranio begin their pleas, Callidamates asserts his role: *sine me dum istuc iudicare* (1143: "Allow me to offer a decision here") and then comically appropriates Tranio's seat at the altar as his place of judgment; the mediator is himself implicated. The appropriation of the altar both as asylum and seat of judgment points to the Greek original.[58] In *Most.* v 2, the irate father calms down when Callidamates offers the terms of compromise between father and son: Philolaches and his friends will collect money to pay for the girl whom Philolaches bought, and Theopropides will forgive his son (1153–61). By the end of the scene, Theopropides is reluctantly persuaded to forgive Tranio as well. Callidamates has proposed the solution, the disputants have accepted it. This is not a formal reconciliation, but it follows the general shape of one.[59]

[57] For a recent review of the evidence for the title and author of the Greek original, see Stärk 1991: 109–11.

[58] Private arbitrations in sanctuaries: [Dem.] 33. 18; Dem. 36. 15–16; Is. 2. 31; official arbitrations: [Dem.] 40. 11; Is. 12. 9–10.

[59] Stärk 1991: 131–34 argues for extensive Plautine invention in this scene, corresponding "mit der Lazzi-Technik des nichtliterarischen Theaters" (133). The arguments are not compel-

Terence uses a mediating figure in the final acts of three plays (*Phormio*, *Heauton Timorumenos*, and *Andria*) to bring about reconciliations in family disputes which have legal ramifications. In the final scene of *Phormio*, a son replaces his father in the role of arbitrator of conduct – in the important matters of Chremes' abuse of his wife's dowry and Phaedria's inheritance. Family property is again at stake at the end of *Heauton Timorumenos*. Chremes had threatened to disinherit his son Clitipho by dowering his newly-discovered daughter (who is to marry Menedemus' son) with all his property. In the final scene, Menedemus enters the stage, concerned about Chremes' severe treatment of his son. He will negotiate peace, he says (*exeo ergo ut pacem conciliem*, 1046). Chremes, who remains adamant in his decision to disinherit, is appealed to twice by each of the characters on stage – by his wife (1048–49, 1052), son (1049 and 1051–52), and Menedemus (1047–48 and 1049–50: *da veniam, Chreme: / sine te exorem*: "Be forgiving, Chremes; allow my plea").[60] Under this barrage of mediators, Chremes finally gives in and alters his terms (1054–55): he will not disinherit his son, and Clitipho will marry a neighbor's daughter. Menedemus clears the path for the son's agreement (1058–59).[61] In the Greek original of the scene, Menedemus'

ling. I mention two of his examples of the psychological absurdity of the scene. First, (a) Callidamates enters the stage, commissioned by the *sodalitas* to negotiate a peace (1126–27) – and yet, as far as the *sodalitas* knew, Theopropides had not yet discovered anything which might require pardon; moreover, (b) Callidamates says that Philolaches knows that his father knows what he has done (1156) – and yet Philolaches could not know that yet. Response: no rational son on-stage or off could expect father to remain ignorant of his massive debt or pretended purchase of next door neighbor's house; better to bite the bullet and negotiate in the belief that father knows. A second absurdity noted by Stärk: no master would put himself on the level of his slave and enter a "complaint" against him before a *disceptator* who has himself, in accepting that role, forgotten that he himself is a defendant. Response: this is not a real legal scenario; the characters are not appearing before a courtroom judge; this is comic mis-appropriation of arbitral language which is evident, e.g., in Ar. *Wasps* 1417–26 (cited in App. 2.e).

60 Maltby 1983: 27–41 argues that Terence added material in the final scenes. He finds suggestive of such addition (pp. 38–39) that Menedemus' appeals (1049–50: *da veniam, Chreme: / sine te exorem*, "be forgiving, Chremes – allow my plea") duplicate Demea's in *Adelphoe* (937: *age, da veniam filio*; 942: *da veniam*; and 936: *sine te exorem*) in precisely that part of the play where Donatus' remarks suggest Terentian expansion (Donatus *apud Ad.* 938). But the evidence of *Ad.* cannot strengthen Maltby's argument for expansion (consisting of Menedemus' appeals) in *HT*; Chremes' role as mediator in *Andria* (which must be a part of the Menandrian original) and his and Pamphilus' appeals there (*And.* 901) suggest equally well, that Menedemus' expressions could belong to the Menandrian original of that play. What we see is Terence's consistency of language in scenarios of reconciliation.

61 *HT* 1058–59: *haec dum incipias, gravia sunt, / dumque ignores; ubi cognori', facilia.* ("It's a difficult thing, while you're just beginning and while you're inexperienced; when you get the hang of it, it's easy").

role may have been larger. Since the Latin scene has four speaking parts and the Menandrian original presumably had three, Terence probably added a character to his finale; the most likely addition is Sostrata.[62] A transferral of roles between the old men may have been more apparent in Menander: "Chremes" the *diaitetes* at the end of III I is replaced by "Menedemus" the *diallaktes* at the end of the play.

The last act of Terence's *Andria* consists of five scenes; in v 3 and 4, Chremes acts as mediator between father (Simo) and son (Pamphilus).[63] While none of the characters use any technical language of mediation, Chremes' control of the interview between father and son and between Crito and Simo – his tempering of Simo's outbursts and his judgments of requests and character mark him as a mediating figure. In v 3, Pamphilus enters the stage; his father has just now learned not only that he is still involved with Glycerium, but also that a witness has opportunely arrived who will attest that she is an Athenian citizen. Chremes repeatedly steps in, checks Simo's castigations (873), and intervenes in Pamphilus' behalf (893–95, 901–03). In v 4, when Crito appears on stage, Chremes more actively interrupts and even directs the situation in his self-imposed role as mediator.[64] He testifies to Crito's character (914–15) against Simo's revilings, silences the latter's objections to and interruptions of Crito's testimony (919, 925, 926), takes over the examination of the witness (928, 931–32, 940–42) and acts as final judge of the witness' evidence about the Attic origin of Glycerium (945, 947). Chremes, like Daemones in *Rudens*, shifts his role from *arbiter* of dispute between two opposing parties and becomes, in the end, *arbiter* of the identification of his own long-lost daughter. Simo accepts the outcome: *iamdudum res redduxit me ipsa in gratiam* (948: "The whole turn of affairs has reconciled me"). Nor has the scene been without legal implications: Simo has suspected his son of attempting to falsify Glycerium's status. This is the real issue of the dispute between father and son in which Chremes has intervened.[65]

[62] Mette 1962: 403; Sandbach 1975: 200–01; Maltby 1983: 38.

[63] Chremes' role as "mediator" begins in v 2, when he asks Simo to treat Davos less severely: *ah ne saevi tanto opere* (868).

[64] There are four speaking roles in this last scene; as Sandbach 1975: 199 has observed, "none of them can be easily eliminated." He follows Webster's suggestion (1960: 81), that in the Menandrian original, "Pamphilus" did not return to the stage with "Crito" at 904; "Crito" left after identifying "Glycerium" as "Phanium's niece" and "Pamphilus" then returned to the stage.

[65] For discussion of analytic treatments of the *Andria*, see chapter 8, nn. 30–33, with particular reference to the citizenship scenario depicted in this play.

In other plays, the domestic disputes resolved at the end do not have legal ramifications; nevertheless, mediators appear. This happens in *Trinummus*, based on Philemon's *Thesauros* (*Trin.* 18–19, *prol.*) and in *Mercator*, based on the same playwright's *Emporos* (*Merc.* 9, *prol.*). At the end of the first play, after the dispute about the dowry is settled, Lysiteles takes upon himself the role of peacemaker between father and son (1167 and 1168); instead of an angry outburst, Charmides offers gentle terms to Lesbonicus (that he marry Callicles' daughter). More interesting and more complicated is the final scene of *Mercator*.[66] There Eutychus announces to his father Lysimachus that his mother Dorippa has been pacified (965). Dorippa had been under the false impression that her husband had brought a courtesan into their house to be his mistress; she had already sent a messenger to her father – apparently to start negotiating a divorce (IV 4. 787–88). In fact, Lysimachus' next-door neighbor Demipho had been the culprit who bought the girl – away from his son Charinus – for his own enjoyment. Demipho will have his comeuppance now: Eutychus exacts repentance and is aided by his father in a *flagitatio* (977–1006), a form of "Italic folk justice" consisting in the public shaming of a wrong-doer: the wronged man summons his friends, who then surround the wrong-doer in a public place and take turns loudly castigating him.[67] In the course of the *flagitatio*, Demipho concedes: he will relinquish Pasicompsa to his son (989); he asks Eutychus to act as peace-maker between them (992: *modo pacem faciatis oro, ut ne mihi iratus siet*); he will become Eutychus' *cliens* and predicts that "you'll say I am mindful of your kindness"

[66] See Braun (1980: 59–65), who argues that Plautus, unwilling to protract the conclusion with unnecessary formalities, has abbreviated the play, omitting details that would tell the audience how Eutychus learned that his father had installed Pasicompsa in their house as a favor to Lysimachus; Plautus returns to his Greek model at verse 964. I am in accord with Braun's reconstruction and ascription of motive; I think, however, there is further abbreviation in the final scene.

[67] Usener 1901: 1–28 is the best treatment of the subject. Usener not only points out instances in Roman Comedy, but also cites one in Cato (fr. 157 *ORF*^{3} = Gellius 17. 6) and sees its features in *XII Tables* 2.3 (Usener: pp. 11, 20, 22). Usener found no evidence for this remedy in Greece, but did not exclude the possibility of a similar folk remedy there (20). West 1974: 27 has identified what appears to be a kindred form of abuse in a report of archaic Naxos (Arist. fr. 558) and finds "something of a parallel in one of the stories about the beginnings of Attic comedy. It was said that some farmers, done down by certain men of the city, went in at night-time and proclaimed their injustices in the streets: 'Here abides so-and-so who has done as follows to so-and-so the farmer'. Those who had done this were sought out and made to do it in the theatre, where however they disguised themselves with wine-lees. (Schol. Dion. Thr. p. 18. 15 Hilgard.)"

(*memorem dices benefici*, 996, cf. *Ad.* 251). The *flagitatio* finally ends when Eutychus remarks:

> *eamus intro, non utibilest hic locus, factis tuis,*
> *dum memoramus, arbitri ut sint qui praetereant per vias.* (1005–06)

> Let's go indoors – this is not an appropriate place to recall
> your conduct – for *arbitri* to hear as they pass by through the streets.

And Lysimachus agrees:

> *hercle qui tu recte dicis: eadem brevior fabula*
> *erit. eamus.* (1007–08)

> Well said, I swear: by the same token, the play
> will be shorter – let's go!

The *flagitatio* has replaced the mechanism of reconciliation that probably belonged to the Greek original. Only a faint trace of the mediator's role remains. Here we have another instance of the parody of Attic social practice and theatric convention (cf. *Curc.* v 3). Demipho's request that Eutychus reconcile him with his son is mere lip-service to the Hellenic creed, a tag-on to the raucous Roman inflicting of shame and exacting of repentance. There is to be no scene of arbitral intervention – the pun in 1006 clarifies that – *arbitri* can be "onlookers" or "arbitrators," and both are to be excluded. The appearance of mediating *arbitri* would lengthen the play – why add a tiresome scene for a tired audience? An ending through reconciliation would be tame by comparison, would lack the cultural vibrancy of *flagitatio*. Rather than being merely associated with genre, reconciliation has become generic.

The attenuation of convention is evident in other plays as well. At the end of *Casina*, Cleustrata heeds Myrrhina's advice to forgive her husband (*dare veniam*); Cleustrata agrees – more speedily than might be expected, she says, *hanc ex longa longiorem ne faciamus fabulam* (1004–06: "so that we may not lengthen a lengthy play"). The reconciliation at the end of *Epidicus*, on the other hand, is teasingly extended but no less diluted. The homonymous slave has his hands bound by his master Periphanes as he undergoes an examination that reveals his role in restoring a long lost daughter. When Periphanes is finally convinced of the truth and desires to unbind Epidicus, the slave refuses: he must have recompense (722–24). Periphanes offers shoes, tunic, and a cloak (725) – not enough; he offers freedom (726) – still not enough; he offers food (727) – the slave is still unsatisfied; he must be "beseeched". The master obeys – he begs the slave to pardon his offenses and informally frees him (*oro te, Epidice, / mihi ut ignoscas siquid inprudens culpa peccavi mea. / at ob eam rem liber esto*, 728–30). The slave's response is neither gracious nor Greek: *invitus do hanc veniam tibi, / nisi necessitate cogar. solve sane si lubet* ("I don't want to forgive you, but necessity impels me. Go ahead and free me if that's your pleasure," 730–31). The wordplay is Roman: the rope is loosened, the slave is freed, the play is concluded. Forgiveness is not in itself desirable, but it has the virtue of ending a play.

4 ROMAN COMEDY AND ARBITRATION

Is there a Roman private arbitrator in Roman Comedy?

We saw in the last chapter that Athenian private arbitration was a highly formalized procedure, even if, as I have argued, it may not have been legally binding in the fourth century. It had its own set of technical terms and developed a particular ideology of friendship so pervasive and so conducive to forensic distortion that clever playwrights could exploit it for its humor. When we turned to the evidence for Roman private arbitral practice in the late third and early second centuries BC, we found only the Catonian *vir bonus* and the arbitral figures of Roman Comedy. It is time to review the latter evidence and to assess what it might tell us about Roman arbitral practice. I begin with the most important interpretive observations made in the course of this chapter and I add pertinent conclusions from the appendices:

(1) Where arbitral figures are designated in Roman Comedy and are recognizable as private arbitrators, the scenarios are dependent upon Greek originals: *Rudens* IV 3 (*arbiter*: 5 times) and *Phormio* V 9 (*iudex*: once).

(2) It is sometimes difficult to discern whether *arbiter* is meant to represent or allude to a private or judicial figure of Rome: e.g., the (Greek) technical *arbiter* of *HT* 498–500 (for other dubious *arbitri*, see App. 6).

(3) The mediating or arbitral figure who often appears in the final scene of a Roman comedy (section 3) may be called *orator* (*Most.* 1126), *disceptator* (*Most.* 1137), or *iudex* (*Ph.* 1055), but often he has no specific designation at all; e.g., the markedly arbitral figures in *Curculio* V 3 (two episodes) are undesignated (section 2). The

mediator's activity is called "judging" (*iudicare*: *Curc.* 719, *Most.* 1143) or "making peace" (*conciliare pacem*: *Most.* 1127, *HT* 1046) or "settling differences" (*haec componere*: *Ph.* 621–22). These scenarios are attributable to Greek originals.

(4) Plautus parodies the position of Greek arbitral practice in New Comedy at the end of *Casina*, *Curculio*, *Epidicus*, and *Mercator*; he minimalizes and objectifies it, overwhelms it with Plautine and Italic folk justice.

(5) Plautus on occasion may have altered the arbitrations or private agreements of his Greek originals. In the scenes depicting the aftermath of the arrests of Labrax and Dordalus in *Rudens* and *Persa* (App. 4), the Roman playwright may have changed the private agreements between accuser and accused of the Greek originals into a courtroom verdict in *Rudens* and into ambiguous persiflage in *Persa*.

Roman private arbitration no doubt existed in the middle Republic. Roman Comedy, however, has not transmitted to us any notion of its peculiar protocols or ideology. In part, the view I have offered might appear to contradict a widespread notion that private arbitration played a significant role in the early period of Roman law. I am not objecting to that view; I am simply not concerned with it. I am, however, concerned with the middle Republic, and this era, so mistily represented in our legal sources, is so confounded with the "early period" by some legal historians, that at times the private arbitrator of the second century BC appears as ubiquitous as the hypothetical self-helping Wlassakian *arbiter* of the pre-law era, while at other times, he is made so much a part of the evolution of the *actiones bonae fidei* and *actiones in bonum et aequum conceptae*, that he is furnished with his own evaluative criterion of the *bonum aequum* and is made the lurking precursor of the *arbiter ex compromisso*. On what evidence other than the alliterative genius of Plautus?

At this point, it will be useful to consider an important difference in the texture of legal proceedings in Rome and Athens: pleading a case before a *iudex unus* or judicial *arbiter* is a much different affair from pleading a similar case before, at a minimum, two hundred dikasts. J. M. Kelly has called attention to the rare appearance of the phrase *arbiter ex compromisso* and the relative frequency of *arbiter* or *arbitrium* without qualification in the *Digest*. Kelly is referring to a later age, when we know the *arbiter ex compromisso* was in full-fledged existence; nevertheless, we may apply his further observation about the *arbiter ex compromisso* to any private *arbiter* who operated in the middle Republic when the judicial *arbiter* and *iudex unus* were likewise available:

it is evident that the technical distinction between an *arbiter*. . . [belonging to the judiciary] and an *arbiter* [*ex compromisso*, i.e., a private *arbiter*] . . . did not seem important. It was a distinction which the circumstances of the parties might find serviceable, but which was altogether subordinate to the essential privacy of choice, where such details were concerned, in any matter falling generally outside the public-interest-oriented jurisdictions of *centumviri* and *recuperatores*.[68]

For Kelly, the private arbitrator and the *iudex unus* function in similar ways. One distinctive feature they share is that they are chosen by the disputants. Another is that their tasks could be carried out in private: "single-judge litigation could be conducted away from the public view, in private, or, to use a modern expression conveying the nearest judicial equivalent, 'in camera'."[69]

While Kelly's view of the privacy of single-judge litigation must be rejected, a modification of that view might help explain the ambiguity of some of the scenarios of Roman Comedy in which an arbitral figure is designated *arbiter* (App. 6).[70] In these cases, the distinction between private arbitration and court settlement would make little difference to the Roman playwrights and their audiences; what is uppermost is the notion of intimacy. Hearings before a *iudex unus* or judicial *arbiter* might have much the same resonance as the hearings before a private *diaitetes* in Athens. While hearings before the latter might often have taken place in a sanctuary and hearings before the former in a public place in the forum, there is no need to imagine that crowds of idle bystanders in fourth-century Athens or in early second-century Rome would regularly rush to hear a vast majority of these cases. Intimacy might often have been guaranteed by the insignificance of the disputes, notwithstanding the public character of the place of judgment. But the most significant features of the intimacy of the meetings – with private *diaitetai* in Athens and with *iudex unus* in Rome – are the consensual

68 Kelly 1976: 119. Kelly's observation rests on the thesis that disputants had a say in the choice of the judicial *arbiter*.

69 Kelly 1976: 121.

70 Kelly's view (1976: 103–11) has been vigorously attacked by Behrends 1977: 450–53. While the evidence supports Behrends' view (to which C. Titius fr. 2 *ORF*[3] might be added for the mid-second century), Kelly's view can, I think, be modified in the way presented above (i.e., intimacy can be achieved in a public place of judgment).

foundation of the disputants' agreement in selecting arbitrator or judge and the comfort afforded by the presentation of a case before one's friends or kinsmen in Athens and before a single judge in Rome.[71]

Nevertheless, the threat of litigation before a *iudex unus* or judicial *arbiter* remains intimidating in much of Roman Comedy – as Tranio says to Theopropides in *Mostellaria* v 1, *nescis quam metuculosa res sit ire ad iudicem?* (1101: "Don't you know how fearful a thing it is to go before a *iudex*?"). Tranio's sentiment may well derive from the Athenian original: the Athenian brand of litigiousness did not necessarily entail resolving disputes in court; while threatening suits was a common phenomenon, the risks of trial inspired many potential litigants to settle in private (chapter 1.1). But it is difficult to imagine that Tranio's remark and such sentiment elsewhere in Roman Comedy is mere translation of Athenian response to forensic intimidation. Here, another important difference in the texture of legal proceedings in Rome and Athens must be considered: in Athens, any citizen over the age of thirty who wanted to be a dikast could put his name into the pool from which 6,000 (in the fourth century) would be chosen by lot to serve for the year; in Rome of the middle Republic, a *iudex* or judicial *arbiter* would be selected from the senatorial class for each individual case. For the masses in Rome, appearance before *iudex* or *arbiter* – even if the disputants were given a say in his selection – would be an unequal experience. Hence the intimidation – and the triumph of folk justice in Plautine comedy. Contradictory notions about the dispute settlement process thus coexist in Roman Comedy – both fear of the single judge and a comfort in his intimacy; the contradiction is symptomatic of status disparities in the middle Republic.

"Parody" has been used to describe a number of the arbitral scenarios presented in this chapter. At the opening, the two celebrated scenarios in *Rudens* and *Epitrepontes* were called parodies of dispute settlement. It is time to pick that statement apart. Menander's parody is one that will invite the Athenians in his audience (the largest component, by conjecture) to a feeling of communal cohesiveness. Seeing slaves ape their conduct in all earnestness objectifies their own conduct, refocuses it: "We are silly, aren't we, with all our forensic gestures? Perhaps we are too earnest . . . " The parody in

[71] For the consensual basis in Athens, see chapter 3.1.b and for that basis in Rome, see chapter 2.2.b. at n. 76.

Rudens is played to a different audience; its contours are different from those in the original. The slapstick and homosexual humor of IV 4 perhaps renders the original parody of that scene irrecoverable. But what stands out in IV 3, in the preliminaries to arbitration, is the opposition of city slave to country bumpkin. Here, the Roman audience can respond communally, in a way similar to their Athenian counter-parts, "Aren't we silly to plume ourselves for being smart city folk?" The "near-parody" of the original of *Adelphoe* II 2 would center, for Athenians, on the pimp's tenacious adherence to the "litigious code": the gesture of threatening a lawsuit before entering private negotiation – even when the game is clearly lost. The pimp's feeble attempt to hold his ground before the wily slave may have been the major component of humor for the Romans. The parodies of *Curculio* and *Mercator* are notches grander, and were absent from the Greek originals: they nourish at once the commoner's and connoisseur's palate. For the commoners in the audiences of both plays, the parodies provide sheer holiday fun. For the connoisseurs of Greek and Roman drama in the audience of *Curculio*, the parody provides the triumph of Plautine violence: Phaedromus' arbitral verdict becomes mere background accompaniment to the foreground of physical intimidation; in *Mercator*, the parody provides the triumph of Italic folk justice and the relegation of Greek convention to a minimum. Reconciliation can be objectified, can be made into an ethnic ingredient in a recipe for drama, can be ladled generously or sprinkled lightly. The point is, Plautine reconciliation is foreign, and it is Greek. That Plautus disrupts scenarios of arbitration and reconciliation to the degree he does in *Curculio* V 3, *Mercator* V 4, and *Rudens* IV 4 suggests that his dramatic interest did not lie in mirroring procedures of settling disputes. Roman playwrights and actors have their own way of settling the score.

I conclude this chapter with a glance at *Perikeiromene* which ends with the settlement of the quasi-marital dispute between Polemon and Glukera with which the play had begun. Pataikos had played the role of "mediator."[72] As he enters the stage, leading out his recently identified grown-up daughter, he says to her:

> πάνυ σοῦ φιλῶ τὸ 'νῦν διαλλαχθήσομαι'·
> ὅτ' εὐτύχηκας, τότε δέχεσθαι τὴν δίκην
> τεκμήριον τοῦτ' ἐστὶν Ἕλληνος τρόπου. (1006–08)

[72] For Pataikos' promotion of persuasion in this play, see chapter 1, n. 12. For another play in which a father acts as reconciler of his daughter's marital disputes, see *Menaechmi* V 2.

Indeed, I admire your saying, "Now I shall be reconciled";
for a person who experiences good fortune to accept the proffered satisfaction –
this is proof of the Hellenic disposition.[73]

"Now I shall be reconciled": the words have a rich resonance in Greek culture; much of that resonance owed its origin – or at least its dissemination – to the forensic arena. That we perceive it in such a muted, dispersive, and diluted fashion in Roman Comedy attests not only to the difficulty of translating the day-to-day practices of one culture into those of another, but to the different artistic aspirations of Greek and Roman playwrights, and the different audiences for whom those playwrights composed.

We return to the question that initiated this chapter: is there a Roman private arbitrator in Roman Comedy?

Caveat lector!

[73] For the translation of δέχεσθαι τὴν δίκην, see Gomme and Sandbach 1973 on 1007.

CHAPTER 5

Redress for sexual offenses in Athenian and Roman law

Unlike arbitration, which has received relatively little scholarly attention in the last decades, sexual offenses in Athens and Rome have been subjected to prodigious scrutiny. In an area where ancient men and women were ashamed to speak, contemporary scholars have filled the gap. Modern treatments of the subject have tended to focus upon lawful sanctions against sexual offenders. Playwrights of New Comedy, however, in their frequent employment of plots touching upon sexual violations, dramatize extra-judicial settlements.[1] They present us with the interstices of the law rather than with episodes of courtroom drama. Their focus of attention is not surprising: the Athenian forensic record turns up only one reliable attestation of an offender who is brought to court for the sexual violation of a woman.[2] Athenians preferred to settle out of court. The scenarios dramatized by New Comedy playwrights might therefore contribute to our understanding of the ways in which sexual offenses were, in practice, redressed in Athens. Interpretation of these scenarios, however, requires familiarity with legal terrain.

While New Comedy's terminology of sexual violation and evidence for penalties are combined cautiously with evidence from the orators in this chapter, the more fully blown comic scenarios are reserved, in general, for treatment in chapter 6. A methodological issue that underlies the agenda of that chapter, however, must be

[1] The sexual violations and remedies discussed in this chapter and the next all pertain to heterosexual activity; some of the remedies, e.g., the *graphe hubreos* and *dike biaiōn*, might also be used in the case of homosexual rape – but this is not our concern here. While there are humorous allusions to homosexual activity in Plautus (and sometimes a fair amount of homosexual horseplay – as, e.g., in the last act of *Casina*), such activity is not made the subject of legal complaint: no young boy is raped by a man in New Comedy, whereas numerous girls are.

[2] See n. 31 below for discussion of Hyp. 2, in which the speaker defends himself in an impeachment trial (*eisangelia*) under the general charge of subverting the democracy; the specific charge, however, is *moikheia*. Less certain cases are cited in n. 66.

brought to the surface here: is it really possible to use New Comedy as a source for establishing the ways in which Athenians treated rape and seduction in their own society? How can we distinguish social realities from genre motifs? As in treating other substantive offenses and remedies, parallels must be sought from the orators. However, once the parameters of the law's operation have been established on the basis of a critical examination of our sources (chapter 5), New Comedy can be more fully exploited (chapter 6). The special value of the latter genre is its capacity for suggesting how the law operated in day-to-day life, not, indeed, for painting the entire canvas, but for animating the outlines provided by the orators. In the last two chapters, private arbitration and reconciliation were shown to be important components of dispute settlement in Athens; arbitral scenarios in the orators were shown to have counterparts in New Comedy. If we now observe in the orators that disputes about the violations of women are settled by family members in private (chapter 5) and we begin to discern the frequency with which such arrangements appear in New Comedy (chapter 6), we are justified in believing that the procedure at least is not simply a matter of genre convention. We shall never know how frequent an occurrence sexual offenses – or their private dénouement – were in Athens. The popularity of the rape plot in particular, as I suggested at the end of chapter 2, was not due to any pornographic instinct; rather, it allowed the composers of New Comedy to explore forensic strategies in an area where men and women had exerted great ingenuity in concealing the truth in order to obtain justice.

I SEXUAL OFFENSES IN ATHENIAN LAW[3]

Terminology for sexual offenses is problematic. Athenian writers do not always distinguish among what we think of as rape, adultery (consensual sexual relations between a man and woman, at least one of whom is married), and fornication (consensual sexual relations between an unmarried man and woman). Moreover, the act which Athenian writers call *moikheia* and the actor whom they designate

[3] In setting out the problematic contours of the evidence, I have found the following scholars helpful, even if I have disagreed with their views: Lipsius 429–35; Paoli 1976: 251–307 (= 1950); Harrison I. 32–37; Cole 1984; D. Cohen 1984, 1991b: 98–132, 1991c and 1995: 143–62; E. M. Harris 1990: 370–77; Cantarella 1976: 131–59 and 1991: 289–95. Cohen's stimulating re-evaluation of the evidence has induced me to reconsider the issues anew and in greater depth.

moikhos are not easily defined. Technical definitions of offenses, we have noted before, seem to be alien to the Athenian legal sensibility; dikasts would decide whether a litigant's depiction of an offense fits their notion of what that offense was.[4] Where the relevant terms appear in our texts, particular attention must be given to social code, genre, and genre conventions, to distinguishing among forensic distortion, philosophical ratiocination, and *Umgangssprache*. It will be convenient here to discuss sexual offenses according to procedures of redress; these may be broadly divided into self-help and judicial remedies. Definition of the type of offense is therefore subordinated to discussion of its remedy; in this way, ambiguities that are inherent in the law can best be demonstrated.

1(a) Self-help remedies

There was an early homicide law which is sometimes called "the Drakonian law." While we know a late fifth-century version (*IG* I[3] 104) which was inscribed at the time of the "recodification" of the laws in Athens (409/08), we do not know its precise relation to the original Drakonian legislation. The lacunose remains of the inscription do not contain the provision with which we are concerned; instead, it is found in a citation from Demosthenes (23.53) who attributes the law to Drakon. We shall refer to this as the law on justifiable homicide or simply, the law on homicide.[5] It runs as follows:

[4] On the difficulties involved in defining Athenian legal offenses in general, see chapter 1. 3 and n. 89. As for *moikheia*, the greatest areas of controversy among legal historians concern the extent of the offense: (1) whether it was an offense against the marital bond (and so equivalent to what we call "adultery") or was extended to include the seduction of unmarried women, and (2) whether it was limited to illicit consensual relations or was extended to include rape. Most legal historians think that *moikheia* did extend beyond the marital relationship; see, e.g., Lipsius 424 and n. 42; Harrison 1. 36; MacDowell 1978: 124–25; Cantarella 1976: 146; 1987: 40–41; 1991: 292–95; Carey 1995. D. Cohen 1991b: 98–132 and 1984: 147–65 has argued that *moikheia* was an offense against the marital bond; Todd 1993: 277 appears to have accepted this view. Harrison, ibid., thinks that *moikheia* may have included rape; cf. Cole 1984: 100–01.

[5] Ruschenbusch 1966 thinks the law is possibly Solonian (F 20**) and attributes a paraphrase of part of the law to Solon (F 28a = Plut. *Solon* 23. 1): . . . μοιχὸν . . .ἀνελεῖν τῶι λαβόντι δέδωκεν ("he allowed a man who took a *moikhos* to kill him"). If Plutarch is paraphrasing a later source that attributed the law (or one of its clauses) to Solon, then the attribution is riddled by the problem that besets all later attributions of laws to Solon: the tendency to ascribe laws to him indiscriminately and ahistorically; see Todd 1996. But even if Plutarch did have Solon's laws before him in some shape or form, his words might be an interpretive paraphrase, for instance, of the law allowing the detector "to treat the *moikhos* in any way he likes" (see n. 19).

If a man kills another unintentionally in athletic games, or in a fight on a highway, or in ignorance in war, or upon [or beside] his wife, mother, sister, daughter, or *pallake* [concubine] whom he keeps for the purpose of producing free children, he shall not go into exile for these reasons.

The law does not require the killing of the offender caught in the circumstances listed in the text above; a man who kills such an offender might still be prosecuted for homicide, but he can plead that the homicide was justifiable. If the dikasts (called *ephetai* in these cases) vote in his favor, then the killer suffers no penalty. The law does not mention the term *moikheia* or any of its cognates; nor does it specifically define the offense of the man.[6] Since, however, the offender is envisioned as "upon [or beside] wife, mother, sister, daughter, or *pallake*," his offense might be construed (by us) as adultery, fornication, or rape, depending on the status of the woman (married or unmarried) and the circumstances of the act (consensual or non-consensual).[7]

Fourth and early third-century authors who allude to this provision and to the other self-help remedies described in this section sometimes use *moikhos* as a kind of technical or quasi-technical term to designate the sexual offender.[8] In some of these passages, the *moikhos* is identifiable as an adulterer;[9] in others, he is a fornicator;[10] in one, he can be inferred to be the violator of a *pallake* in the context of the homicide law;[11] more commonly, his specific act cannot be discerned. While it is not implausible that the term may have been

For different interpretations of the law cited in Dem. 23.53, see Drerup 1898: 276–77 and Carawan 1998 chapter 3.

6 This is stressed both by Cole 1984: 100–03 and D. Cohen 1984: 151–52, both of whom go on to argue, in different ways, against the broad interpretation of *moikheia*.

7 The circumstances under which a sexual offender might be killed as preserved by Dem. 23. 53 are vague; the preposition *epi* with the dative might mean "on" (interestingly, LSJ reports that *eph' hippoi* is never found for *eph' hippou*, "on horseback"), "upon," "in," "over," but also "beside"; the phrase was probably open to some interpretation, both by the killer and by the dikasts.

8 In nn. 9–13, evidence is limited to fourth and early third-century texts in which the phrase *moikhon labein* or *moikhon katalabein* ("to take a *moikhos*" and "to detect a *moikhos*") appears. For a list of these instances, see App. 7.1, n. 99.

9 *Moikhos* as adulterer in the context of the law on justifiable homicide: Lys. 1. 30; in the context of other self-help remedies: Lys. 1. 29, 49.

10 *Moikhos* as fornicator in the context of homicide: Arist. fr. VIII. 611 paragr. 1 Rose (and cf. Aiskhin. 1. 182); the phrase is used anachronistically to describe a legendary father (the last of the Kodridai) who took a *moikhos* upon his daughter and killed him (see App. 7.1, n. 101). *Moikhos* as fornicator in the context of other self-help remedies: [Dem.] 59. 65 and 71 and possibly Men. *Samia* 717–18 (see n. 12 below). For argument against D. Cohen's (1991b: 108–09 and n. 32) rejection of the instances in [Dem.] 59, see App. 7.1.

11 Lys. 1. 30.

used of rapists in the context of self-help remedies,[12] and of violators of *pallakai* in self-help contexts in addition to that of the homicide law,[13] no reliable examples of such specific usage in legal or quasi-legal contexts turn up in fourth-century literature. Women, it should be noted, are usually represented as passive participants in *moikheia*. The active of *moikheuein* occurs with a female subject (a transvestite Athene?) on one occasion; it is allegedly an example of Demosthenic humor *ex tempore*.[14]

The intention of the provision of the homicide law under discussion here has been much debated. Paoli, for example, viewed it as aiming to protect men from the introduction of illegitimate offspring into their *oikoi*.[15] That view founders upon a detail, viz., that impunity could be granted by courtroom decision to men who killed the violators of their *pallakai*: while their children may have been legitimate members of the household in Drakon's time (insofar as they may have been allowed to inherit some part of their fathers' estates), their status diminished in the following centuries; by 403/02 if not earlier, *nothoi* ("bastards") could no longer inherit under the rules of intestate succession.[16] Why then should the law, as we find it expressed in Dem. 23. 53 (i.e., as a law in operation in the fourth century), extend protection to a man who killed an offender upon a "*pallake* whom he kept for the production of free children"? Cantarella has recently proposed a solution: "The women listed in the legitimate homicide law, whose lovers could be killed with impunity, lived in the house of the man who was allowed to kill their lovers,

12 *Moikhos* might be used of a rapist (?) at Men. *Samia* 717–18; an angry father (Nikeratos) threatens to fetter the *moikhos* of his unmarried daughter. But the instance probably should be discounted; see App. 5, cat. IV. 1.

13 *Moikhos* might be used of the violator of a *pallake* (?) at Men. *Perik.* 356–57 (*katalabein ton moikhon*), but the phrase is probably comic *katakhresis* here; see nn. 28 and 46 below and App. 5. cat. nos. vii. 1 and x. 3.

14 Demades fr. II. 31 B–S (Plut. *Dem.* 13); cf. the passive, used of a man, at Men. fr. 683.9 K–T.

15 Paoli 1976 (= 1950): 266.

16 *Nothoi* is traditionally translated as "bastards." The law that excluded *nothoi* from inheritance is cited in Dem. 43. 51 and paraphrased at Is. 6. 47. Patterson 1990 thinks that *nothoi* are usually children of *pallakai* (who, in her view, are foreign women); thus a *nothos* is usually "a child born of a mixed or unequal union . . . Typically, the *nothos/e* is the child of a concubine and is known and acknowledged as such by his/her father. Thus the *nothos* can have a patronymic but is not a 'legitimate (*gnesios*) offspring' " (41). For Patterson, *nothoi* are distinct from other non-legitimate children, viz., those whose fathers have not recognized them or whose fathers are unknown. The law excluding *nothoi* from inheritance focused on *nothoi* because they comprised the more problematic category insofar as their fathers had recognized them (pp. 69–70). For a different (and implausibly argued) view of the Athenian *nothos*, see Ogden 1996: 15.

whether or not these women were subject to his *kyrieia* [i.e., lawful authority]."[17] The violator's offense may thus have been envisioned as the intrusion into an *oikia* (house) and concomitantly as the violation of the *tīme* (honor) of the head of the household. Although these circumstances might have had different social reverberations in Drakon's age (if the provision of Dem. 23. 53 replicates Drakon's law), the urge to protect a man's *tīme* might nonetheless have been the impetus behind the exception granted men with *pallakai* in the late fifth and fourth centuries. In support of this view, Cantarella and other scholars have noted the frequency with which the intrusion of a *moikhos* into an *oikia* is depicted as an act of *hubris*.[18]

Aside from homicide, our sources report two other self-help remedies against *moikhoi*. In Lys. 1. 49, the laws are said to prescribe that "if anyone take a *moikhos*, he is to treat him in any way he likes."[19] The meaning of the apodosis is ambiguous.[20] Does the clause allow the "discoverer" to kill the *moikhos* – or only to beat and humiliate him?[21] If the wording of the law(s) was as bare as the paraphrase in the speaker's report, then the dikasts would have to decide the extent of injury permissible by law whenever the family of an alleged *moikhos* sought redress for injuries in court. Some scholars

[17] Cantarella 1991: 293. Cantarella's solution explains the inclusion of *pallakai* in the law; their "quasi-husbands" were not their *kurioi*. Note that the wording of Demosthenes' citation of the law allows for the killing to be executed by other non-*kurioi* as well – i.e., a brother or son who might be living in the same household where the *kurios* is the father or husband of the violated woman.

[18] Cantarella 1991: 293; Foxhall 1991: 300; Paoli 1976: 266–70 (= 1950). Ancient references: Lys. 1. 2, 4, 16, and 25; Dem. 23. 55–56; Men. *Samia* 507–08. For discussion of sexual acts and their connection with *hubris*, see Fisher 1992: 104–11 and D. Cohen 1991c and 1995: 143–62.

[19] Lys. 1. 49: . . . [οἱ νόμοι] οἷ κελεύουσι μέν, ἐάν τις μοιχὸν λάβηι, ὅ τι ἂν οὖν βούληται χρῆσθαι . . . ; cf. Is. 8. 44. Lipsius 429 and 431 with n. 45 supposes that the law which granted the right of physical abuse (but not death) was Solonian and that the abuse was limited to adulterers; Lys. 1. 49 represents the phrasing of the law and this law is read to the court in Lys. 1. 28; moreover, the *nomos moikheias* quoted at [Dem.] 59. 87 is part of the same Solonian law. Cf. the views of D. Cohen and Carey in n. 23 below.

[20] D. Cohen 1991b: 115–19 runs through three possibilities: that the clause permits death, that it does not, that ambiguity may be an inherent feature of the law. He concludes with a *non liquet*, but then speculates without warrant that "according to custom, aggrieved husbands normally abused and ransomed adulterers but did not kill them" (118).

[21] D. Cohen 1985: 385–87 argues against the widely accepted view "that adulterers in Athens were subjected to the painful and humiliating punishments of ῥαφανίδωσις and depillation." Carey 1993 reinserts the radish into the tradition: the reticence of the orators might be due to a standard of propriety in the dikasterion which differs from that of the stage of Old Comedy; the punishments of *moikhoi* (as represented in classical and post-classical literature), while varied and not restricted to a particular mode, usually involve humiliation. See further, Carey 1995: 414.

have proposed that *moikhoi* were *kakourgoi* and liable to arrest to the Eleven;[22] some have additionally proposed that the law regulating their arrest was read to the court in Lys. 1. 28 and that this law may have contained the provision allowing for the (ambiguous) abuse of *moikhoi* caught in the act (Lys. 1. 49).[23] These are attractive proposals (which have been offered in various shapes), but there is no clinching proof for them.[24]

The other self-help remedy that occasionally appears in our sources is the extortion of a monetary settlement; in such a case, the aggrieved party (*kurios*?) might hold the offender prisoner until sureties are supplied for the sum.[25] Laws are not directly mentioned as sanctioning this remedy and it is conceivable that it had no specific legal authority.[26] The remedy may simply have become socially acceptable practice, established over the centuries. Since there was a law against the procuring of free women (one may not,

22 Paoli 1976 (= 1950): 278–81 first made the argument that *moikhoi* were *kakourgoi*; Hansen 1976: 36–48, independently, made it again; D. Cohen 1984: 156–63 and 1991b: 110–22 "reconstructed" the law; Cantarella 1991: 291–92 has offered a refinement; Todd 1993: 276–78 is in general agreement with Cohen, save for the latter's optimistic reconstruction of the law.

23 D. Cohen, Todd, Cantarella: references in preceding note. Cohen offers the most detailed view. A new law which made adulterers into *kakourgoi* may have limited physical abuse: a husband might treat an adulterer "in any way he liked," but he might not kill him; this is the law referred to in Lys. 1. 49 and the one read to the court in Lys. 1. 28; [Dem.] 59. 87 provides the penalties for a wife whose adulterer has been caught as a *kakourgos*. Carey 1995 proposes, alternatively, that the law cited in Lys. 1. 28 was a Solonian self-help remedy (cf. Solon F 28a, quoted in n. 5 above) which permitted the aggrieved party to kill the *moikhos*. The foundation for Carey's view (its conferral of weight upon the "Solonian fragment") is weak (see n. 5); its logic, improbable (the trend in the development of archaic law is to take power away from family heads, not to augment it). Cf. Lipsius at n. 19 above. In my view, a law granting the right of physical abuse might very well have been read in Lys. 1. 28 (it is impossible to know its contours – a provision for arrest cannot be ruled out); the *nomoi* referred to in Lys. 1. 49 might represent a lumping together of the homicide law and the law allowing physical abuse – hence *nomoi*, and hence the wording of 1. 49 might not represent the precise wording of either law.

24 E. M. Harris 1990: 376–77 certainly shows the inadequacy of Aiskhin. 1. 91 as evidence for the technical definition of the *moikhos* as *kakourgos* – but the passage neither contradicts the notion nor disproves the hypothesis. The possibility that Zeus, in mimicry of a φῶς κακοῦργος, violated Antiope is derided at Eur. fr. 210 Nauck^2; this is not "technical usage" of the term *kakourgos*, but it is suggestive. The arrest of *moikhoi* as *kakourgoi* is a theoretical possibility – no less, no more.

25 Monetary agreement: Lys. 1. 25; [Dem.] 59. 41–42 and 64. Sureties: [Dem.] 59. 66.

26 If the controversial "missing law," read out to the court in Lys. 1. 28, allowed for the physical abuse of the *moikhos* caught in the act (n. 23), then the speaker's statements, following the reading of the law, might indicate that monetary compensation was not sanctioned by law. The speaker reports that the alleged *moikhos* begged him not to kill him, but to accept, instead, a payment in compensation; in response, the speaker replied that he would not consent to the payment; in his view, the *nomos* of the city was more authoritative.

e.g., prostitute one's wife), and another law against detaining a man unjustly as a *moikhos*,[27] the law protected alleged sexual offenders from fraudulent demands for monetary compensation – and thereby indirectly recognized the existence of that remedy. Both remedies, physical abuse and compensation, were probably available only to *kurioi* or other close male kinsmen living in the same *oikos* as the *moikheusamene* (a woman who has been made a partner in *moikheia*): their application depends upon immediate recognition that a woman is in the company of a man who is not her husband.[28]

It is not known for certain how women who were "taken in the act" were treated. Some scholars assume that the *nomos moikheias* ("the law regarding *moikheia*") quoted in [Dem.] 59 *Neaira* 87 is Drakonian or Solonian in origin and that it provides the penalty for a married woman: her husband must divorce her and she is forbidden entry into public sanctuaries.[29] A different interpretation will be argued in the next section of this chapter, viz., that the law cited in 59. 87 provides penalties for a woman whose *moikhos* has been convicted in court, not taken in the act. If this interpretation is accepted, then the laws that sanctioned self-help remedies against *moikhoi* may not have penalized women. Self-help remedies develop out of custom. Husbands presumably had murdered *moikhoi*, physically abused them, or made private arrangements long before laws regulated or sanctioned such conduct. A strong social subtext of unwritten norms (unavailable to us) may have guided the treatment of *moikheusamenai* who were taken in the act. Such norms may have remained in practice, even after laws, such as those on homicide, citizenship, and *moikheia*, were passed. What we might perceive as "gaps in the law" may not ever have been filled – nor even have been perceived in the fourth century. If a *moikhos* taken in the act was treated to physical abuse and if the incident was kept private, then a husband might choose to divorce his wife or not. The social norms that guided practice might have been consonant with the *nomos moikheias*; they might have required the divorce of married women and possibly, too, the exposure of infants born from illicit unions –

[27] Law against procuring of free women and children: Aiskhin. 1. 14 and 184; against unjust detainment: [Dem.] 59. 66; see chapter 8.1.a.

[28] It is uncertain whether these remedies were available to men with *pallakai*. It would be highly irrational to allow a "quasi-husband" to kill a *moikhos* caught upon his *pallake*, but not allow him to abuse or accept payment as a substitute for killing. There is no conclusive evidence on this point.

[29] Drakonian: Cantarella 1987: 41. Solonian: Lipsius (see n. 19 above); Gernet 1960: 97 n. 1.

indeed, this is common practice in tragedy and New Comedy for infants born of rapes. *Gennetai* and *phrateres* may not have required the publicity of a public conviction to learn that the circumstances of the birth of a particular child were suspect (cf. [Dem.] 59. 59–61).[30] On the other hand, such children may have (occasionally?) entered the legitimate family – provided no one found out otherwise or no personal or political enemy attempted to prove a suspicion or coax a wishful dream into reality. We have little evidence on these matters. What evidence there is allows no more than an amorphous view of the "penalties" imposed upon a woman whose *moikhos* has been taken in the act; the treatment of that evidence presented here differs from other treatments by leaving gaps unfilled by the creation of hypothetical laws.

1(b) Judicial remedies

The judicial system appears to have offered a number of different procedures and charges that might be used against sexual offenders: a *graphe moikheias*, *graphe hubreos*, and *dike biaiōn*. While the remedies themselves are sufficiently witnessed,[31] there is no absolutely certain attestation of their application against a sexual offender.[32]

[30] A *gennetes* is a member of a *genos*, which, in its technical usage, refers to a descent group united around a cult. A *phrater* is a member of a phratry, which is traditionally thought of as a kinship group. Fathers might introduce their sons to these groups, and they might accept or reject the children on the grounds of legitimacy; see Scafuro 1994: 158 and Lambert 1993: 64–74 who additionally discusses the relationship between the two groups.

[31] For attestation of the *graphe hubreos* and *dike biaiōn*, see nn. 53 and 60. The existence of the *graphe moikheias* has been called into question by D. Cohen 1991b: 122–25, unnecessarily. In *AP* 59. 3, the *graphe moikheias* appears in a list of *graphai* which fall under the jurisdiction of the thesmothetai. In Hyp. 2. 12, the speaker (Lukophron) charges his prosecutor with manipulating legal procedures for his own advantage: he has proceeded by *eisangelia* (impeachment) against him, accusing him of subverting the democracy by breaking the laws; yet the prosecutor himself has transgressed the laws by impeaching Lukophron on charges "for which *graphai* were available before the thesmothetai in accordance with the laws" (ὑπὲρ ὧν [γρα]φαὶ πρὸς τοὺς θεσ[μοθ]έτας ἐκ τῶν νό[μων] εἰσίν); he has proceeded thus, the speaker continues, "in order to be free from risk" (a prosecutor in an *eisangelia* did not risk a 1,000 dr. penalty whereas a prosecutor in a *graphe* did). No one has ever doubted that the specific charge for which Lukophron was impeached was *moikheia* (e.g., Harrison 1. 34–35 n. 2; MacDowell 1978: 186; Hansen 1975: 106–07). Cf. the charges addressed in the passage cited here and in c. 15 and in Lykourg. fr. x. 11 (Conomis). It follows, therefore, that the *graphe* which was available for charges of *moikheia* was the *graphe moikheias*. If we take seriously the plural of *graphe*, then we shall think of both the *graphe moikheias* and the *graphe hubreos*; but the latter is not the *graphe* which first comes to mind for the simple reason that, in the extant portions of the oration, Lukophron does not appear to be answering a charge of hubristic conduct (see esp. Hyp. 2. 6).

[32] See n. 66.

The *nomos moikheias* ("law regarding *moikheia*") quoted at [Dem.] 59 *Neaira* 87, provides some penalties. Unfortunately, the *nomos* does not specify the remedy to which the penalties belong. The wording of the *nomos* deserves careful attention:

Ἐπειδὰν δὲ ἕληι τὸν μοιχόν, μὴ ἐξέστω τῶι ἑλόντι συνοικεῖν τῆι γυναικί· ἐὰν δὲ συνοικῆι, ἄτιμος ἔστω. μηδὲ τῆι γυναικὶ ἐξέστω εἰσιέναι εἰς τὰ ἱερὰ τὰ δημοτελῆ, ἐφ' ἧι ἂν μοιχὸς ἁλῶι· ἐὰν δ' εἰσίηι, νηποινεὶ πασχέτω ὅ τι ἂν πάσχηι, πλὴν θανάτου.

After he *successfully prosecutes* (ἕληι) the moikhos, *the prosecutor* (τῶι ἑλόντι) is no longer to dwell in marriage with the woman. If he continues to dwell so, he is to be disfranchised. And the woman, in whose case a moikhos *has been convicted* (ἁλῶι), is not to enter into public sanctuaries. If she does so, she is to suffer any mistreatment with impunity, except for death.

Aiskhines appears to paraphrase a part of the same *nomos*, which he ascribes to Solon (1 *Tim.* 183); he adds an additional penalty for the woman: she is not permitted to adorn herself (*kosmeisthai*). Some scholars, as mentioned earlier, view the penalties as belonging to a Drakonian or Solonian self-help remedy;[33] some view them as belonging to a hypothesized law which made *apagoge* a remedy against *moikhoi* and think the penalties were imposed as soon as the *moikhos* was taken;[34] others have recognized an ambiguity in the law and have treated the penalties as if they might belong both to a self-help and judicial remedy for *moikheia*.[35] If, however, we treat the law as operative in the fourth century, that ambiguity disappears: the *nomos moikheias* provides some of the penalties that were imposed after the successful prosecution of a *moikhos*. The italicized words are decisive for the point at issue.[36] Whereas *labein* is the verb used in the fourth century to express "to take a *moikhos*", *helein* is the technical verb used in laws to denote "to convict" or "to prosecute

[33] See nn. 19 and 29.

[34] D. Cohen 1991b: 110–22, followed by Cantarella 1991: 291–92.

[35] Gernet 1960: 97 n. 1; Harrison 1. 36 and n. 1.

[36] Gernet 1960: 97 nn. 1 and 2 first maintained by comparison with the paraphrase of the law at Aiskhin. 1. 183 that the law was Solonian, and then made the observation, "[l]'emploi de ἕληι à l'époque classique pourrait faire penser à une condamnation en justice," but added, "mais ce que la législation solonienne a en vue, c'est le cas de flagrant délit." He translated accordingly. Harrison 1. 36 n. 1 cites Gernet's note and implies that the ambiguity between "procure the conviction of" and "take in the act" would be present in the fourth century ("[w]e should assume that in the classical period the woman was treated alike in both cases"). This is nonsense: we do not know whether the law is in fact Solonian; a fourth-century orator's attribution is not reliable (see n. 5). Moreover, regardless of the law's historical origin, a fourth-century audience will understand the law's language in accordance with contemporary usage.

successfully"; *halonai* is the passive, "to be convicted."[37] Apollodoros, for instance, uses *helein* in this technical sense when he quotes laws in cc. 16 and 52 and when he paraphrases another law in c. 66 . . . καὶ ἐὰν μὲν ἕληι τὸν εἵρξαντα καὶ δόξηι ἀδίκως ἐπιβεβουλεῦσθαι ("and if he *convicts* the detainer and is proven to have been plotted against unlawfully").[38] The type of prosecution envisioned by the law can only be conjectured. A *graphe moikheias* seems most likely, on the grounds that such a *graphe* is firmly attested (*AP* 59. 3 and see n. 31); a trial following the arrest of a *moikhos* as a *kakourgos* is less likely, on the grounds that the arrest of *moikhoi* is not attested.

The law appears to provide safeguards to the community. In the first place, it protects men: it guards their *oikoi* against the possible pollution of lineal descent in the important matter of inheritance. A wife whose *moikhos* has been publicly convicted and who herself is subsequently divorced will not easily be able to have her offspring acknowledged as the offspring of her former husband. Moreover, if citizenship was limited to the children of lawfully married *astoi* (i.e., marriage initiated by *engue*, "betrothal," or by *epidikasia*, "the judicial awarding" of an *epikleros*), then the law also protects the purity of the citizen pool.[39] The view that citizenship was so restricted cannot be conclusively proven but is consistent with the consequences of conviction for *moikheia*. The putative offspring of a father who had been convicted of *moikheia* would find admission into a phratry difficult: if we presume (for the sake of argument) that death was not the penalty for the *moikhos*, then the latter must agree to acknowledge the child and must, by chance, belong to a phratry which did not require birth from a woman who had been betrothed to him.[40] That

37 For *labein* in the expression "to take a *moikhos*," see App. 7.1, n. 99. *Labein* is the usual verb used with *ep' autophōrōi* in the expression "to take someone in the act" (Dem. 19. 133; 45. 59 and 70, 81; [Dem.] 26. 24); *halontes* appears once with *ep' autophōrōi* (Aiskhin. 1. 91), in the expression *hoi ep' autophōrōi halontes* ("men who are caught in the act") where the subject is generalized and includes *moikhoi*, but is not restricted to them. This last passage could provide grounds for objection to my thesis – but not serious ones: my claim is that, in the fourth century, *labein* is used regularly in the expression "to take a *moikhos*." Fourth century instances of *helein moikhon* are cited in the next note and examined in App. 7.2.

38 In addition to the phrases in the *nomos* cited in [Dem.] 59. 87, we find forms of ἑλεῖν μοιχόν in Ar. *Wealth* 168; Arist. frr. VIII. 611 paragr. 24 Rose; Aiskhin. 1. 183; and [Dem.] 59. 85, 86. See App. 7.2.

39 For earlier scholarship on this vexed question, see Patterson 1990.

40 The requirement of lawful marriage (via *engue*) is attested at Isaios 8. 19 (phratry); Dem. 57. 54 (phratry); [Dem.] 59. 60 (*gennetai*). In the decrees of the Demotionidai, the oath for phratry enrolment includes the requirement that the son is *gnesion eg gamet|es* (*IG* II^2 1237. 110–11; *gamete* here probably implies *engue* and *epidikasia*: a son who is *gnesios* is one whose parents have been joined by *engue* or in a marriage initiated by *epidikasia* (lex apud [Dem.]

combination of circumstances appears unlikely. Without phratry enrolment, deme enrolment might be difficult if not impossible.[41] One effect of the penalty imposed on the married woman in the *nomos moikheias*, therefore, is the virtual impossibility for a child of the illicit union to acquire citizenship – unless the parents marry one another; the law's effect squares with the notion that citizenship required the lawful marriage of the two *astoi* parents.

The law provides another safeguard as well: it protects men and women from abuse; by requiring that trial take place before penalties are imposed upon a forgiving husband or guilty wife, it ensures that untried allegations of a wife's *moikheia* cannot be used as a political weapon against a husband (e.g., "a man who is powerless in his household should be powerless in public") or as a pretext for thrashing or otherwise humiliating an innocent woman who enters a public sanctuary (e.g., "beat her, she's a whore"). A public trial for *moikheia* will make known to the community the husband who must divorce his wife under pain of losing his civic rights and the woman who must avoid public sacrifices in the future. If this were not the case, then we might expect to find another powerful and dirty political weapon in the orators' arsenal – why trouble to have one's enemy declared a state debtor when all one need do is cast aspersions upon his wife's reputation? But we find no calls for disfranchisement in the orators on these grounds.[42]

Before leaving the *nomos moikheias* in [Dem.] 59 *Neaira* 87, we should reflect that conclusions based upon it must be tentative. The advocate introduces the law *in medias res* – possibly, *apud finem*. Portions of the law, presumably of no concern to Apollodoros, have been omitted – the practice is not uncommon in the orators. Thus

46. 18); cf. Sealey 1990: 34. We do not know whether all phratries had similar requirements – but there is no evidence as yet to the contrary.

41 Scholars seem more and more ready to see phratry enrolment as a credential for citizenship; see Lambert 1993: 49–57 and 237–41; Ogden 1996: 152–53. Individual grants of citizenship in the fourth century always provide for membership in a phratry; "group" grants do not and are exceptional in this respect.

42 In Lys. fr. 1 B–S (= Athen. 13. 612 E), the speaker claims that his opponent (Aiskhines the Sokratic) in the suit for debt had seduced the seventy-year-old wife of one Hermaios; the speaker insinuates that the seduction was responsible for Aiskhines' acquisition of Hermaios' perfumery. In Dem. 45. 84, Apollodoros insinuates an illicit relationship between his mother Arkhippe and Phormion; at the time of the delivery of the speech (*c.* 350), both Arkhippe and Pasion are dead, the former for *c.* 10 years, the latter for *c.* 20 (see Trevett 1992: 8–15 for dates). In Aiskhin. 2. 149, Aiskhines alleges that Demosthenes' wife had children by one Knosion, implying that the orator was impotent (in keeping with his extended attack on Demosthenes' masculinity). The mudraking of none of these speakers is aimed at the disfranchisement of his opponent.

the procedure by which the charge of *moikheia* was brought is omitted.[43] Likewise omitted are the penalty for the convicted *moikhos* and the penalty attached to Aiskhines' paraphrase of the law, the restriction on the woman's adornment.[44] Abridgement is therefore certain. Moreover, the law only provides penalties under the circumstance that the successful prosecutor is the husband of the woman whose *moikhos* has been convicted. But if the penalties do belong to a *graphe*, then the *persona* of the prosecutor (*ho boulomenos*) might not have been restricted to the woman's husband; possibly the full law provided for that circumstance.[45] Possibly it had provisions for unmarried women and *pallakai* as well.[46] Alternatively, the law may have been restricted precisely in the way it has been transmitted to us – as a remedy for husbands. While sexual violators of unmarried women might suffer a self-help punishment if caught in the act (section a above), there may have been no judicial remedy – and no (lawfully sanctioned) penalty for either the male offender or his female partner – if they were not caught thus. The disparate treatment of unmarried and married women under the law might then be explained in this way: whereas the children of unmarried women are, in any event, unlikely to gain entry into phratries and to acquire thus a sure and easy stepping stone to paternal inheritance and citizenship, the children born from the illicit unions of married women might still creep in without observation – save for the law's requirement that their mothers be divorced. There was no need, then, for a law to ensure a disability for children of unmarried women – but there was a need in the case of illegitimate children borne by married women. Speculation on any of the issues addressed

43 Cf. the laws cited at Dem. 21. 47; [Dem.] 59. 16 and 52; *SEG* 26. 72 (the law on silver coinage of 375/74 BC). The procedure to be followed is specified in each of these laws.

44 There has been considerable speculation concerning the penalty for the *moikhos*. Less than death: Lipsius 432–33, n. 50, followed by Cole 1984: 104. Possibly death: Harrison I. 35; E. M. Harris 1990: 374. Certainly death: Carey 1995.

45 This problem could be partially resolved if *sunoikein* in the law means "dwell together" and not "dwell together in marriage." For doubts on the ubiquity of the latter meaning, see Gomme and Sandbach 1973: 392. To instances cited there, add Aiskh. *Kho.* 909, of a son "living together" with his mother.

46 Violators of unmarried women are occasionally designated *moikhoi* in literary texts in the context of self-help remedies (n. 10); it is not *prima facie* implausible that the law on *moikheia* covered this group of offenders. The situation in Men. *Perik.* might be relevant to *moikhoi* of *pallakai* in the context of judicial remedies; the alleged violator of Glukera is called a *moikhos* on four occasions (357, 370, 390, 986); see App. 5. cat. VII. 1 for discussion of 499–503 where legal retaliation against the *moikhos* might be implied – but the remedy might be a *graphe hubreos* rather than a *graphe moikheias*.

in this paragraph can be buttressed by speculative argument; there is no conclusive argument, and certainly no conclusive evidence.[47]

If, as the sources suggest (see section c), the remedy was infrequently applied, the law may have served an ideological rather than a practical function: it promoted the notion that a husband's and wife's capacity to participate in the civic community depended upon the regulation of their marital conduct. A non-compliant husband (i.e., one who does not divorce his wife) becomes *atimos* (disfranchised). A wife whose *moikhos* has been convicted is excluded from civic life in a different, but no less essential, way. A woman's participation in that life is exemplified above all by her attendance at public sacrifices and in the production of legitimate sons who will eventually become citizens. Exclusion from public sanctuaries and the sacrifices performed there deprives a woman of an important opportunity to be identified as a member of the community; loss of identity (as well as the practical concomitant – she is out of socially acceptable circulation), renders remarriage, and the opportunity to fulfill her function of producing legitimate children, unlikely.[48] Such a woman may be said to be *atimos*.[49]

The substance of *moikheia*, we have seen, is nowhere conclusively defined for us. We are no better informed concerning the legal definitions of *hubris* (commonly translated as "insolence" or "outrage") and *biaia* ("acts of violence"). Neither charge was restricted to sexual offenses. The *graphe hubreos* could be brought by any legally competent Athenian citizen "if anyone treats with *hubris* any

[47] The most exasperating issue of all is whether the law – even in this abbreviated form – is genuine at all. A long tradition of scholarly discussion has questioned the authenticity of laws and other documents inserted into Athenian orations. For summary of the general debate, see MacDowell 1990: 43–47; for a more skeptical view, see E. M. Harris 1992: 75–78 and Trevett 1992: 180–82. Most general arguments, for and against authenticity, are inconclusive. The shortcomings that I have adduced in the law cited at [Dem.] 59. 87 render conclusions based on it tentative; those shortcomings, however, can be explained as the result of abbreviation; the language itself is not suspect. Harris' (1994a: 22) reasons for doubting the law's authenticity impute an extraordinary degree of inventive ingenuity to the hypothesized forger.

[48] The speaker who defends himself against a charge of *moikheia* in the course of an impeachment trial reports that his prosecutor has alleged "that I am causing many women to grow old unmarried in their houses." The text is lacunose: Hyp. 2 fr. 4. 12: . . . ὅτι [πολλὰς μὲν γ]υνα[ῖκας ποιῶ] ἀγάμ[ους ἔνδον κα]ταγηρ[άσκειν . . .

[49] Concerning a woman's attendance at public sacrifices as testimony of her civic identity, see Scafuro 1994: 167–69. For a woman's *atimia* as a consequence of the penalties, see Paoli 1976 (= 1950): 292–93; Parker 1983: 94–96; Fisher 1992: 79. Aiskhin. 1. 183 depicts the intention of the lawgiver's penalties on the woman (prohibitions from public sacrifice and self-adornment) as aiming "to disgrace such a woman and to contrive that her life be not worth living" (ἀτιμῶν τὴν τοιαύτην γυναῖκα καὶ τὸν βίον ἀβίωτον αὐτῆι κατασκευάζων).

person, either child or woman or man, free or slave, or does anything unlawful against any of them."[50] Physical assault and sexual misconduct may have been most relevant to the law's purview.[51] Scholars have been troubled, however, by the apparent overlap of the *graphe hubreos* with the *dike aikeias* (private action for assault). Some have stressed the different consequences of the two procedures: the *hubristes* convicted by the *graphe* paid the penalty to the state whereas a losing defendant in the *dike aikeias* paid the penalty to the plaintiff. Moreover, the *graphe* allowed a harsher penalty: it was assessed by the dikasterion;[52] the successful prosecutor could propose any penalty – including death.[53] Other scholars have given their attention to the substance of the offense; some have proposed that *hubris* involved a subjective element. MacDowell describes the hubristic person in this way: "A person shows *hubris* by indulging in conduct which is bad, or at best useless, because it is what he wants to do, having no regard for the wishes or rights of other people."[54] Fisher emphasizes the victim's injury; *hubris* is "the deliberate attack

[50] Dem. 21. 47, from the law purporting to be the *nomos hubreos*; trans. MacDowell 1990: 117. A *nomos hubreos* is paraphrased and then cited in Aiskhin. 1. 15–16. The authenticity of the *nomos hubreos* cited in these passages has been the subject of much debate (cf. n. 47). The *opinio communis* now is that Demosthenes' law is essentially genuine and that the law inserted in Aiskhin. 1. 16 is not. Hitzig (1899), Lipsius (1. 421–29), Ruschenbusch (1965), Gagarin (1979), MacDowell (1990), and Fisher (1992) have treated Dem. 21. 47 as an (essentially) authentic law; Drerup (1898), perhaps the most commonly adduced authority for scholars in need of confirmation of forensic documents, thought neither the law cited in Dem. 21 or Aiskhin. 1 authentic – a judgment all the more remarkable in a scholar who was painfully aware of the *Unechtheitsfanatikern* among his contemporaries and predecessors. More recently, only E. M. Harris (1992), to my knowledge, has taken a stand with Drerup.

[51] D. Cohen 1991c: 173–74, on the basis of "approximately 500 occurrences of *hubris* and its cognates in the principal Athenian prose authors," finds that "73 passages, or about 15 per cent of all usages, explicitly characterize a physical assault against a free person as *hubris*. 82 passages, or about 18 per cent, refer to various kinds of sexual aggression, sexual misconduct, or violations of sexual honour." Wariness is required in interpreting this evidence – *hubris* is a term of broad usage and significance in Greek literature; it is difficult to discern whether any particular instance is pertinent to the Athenian law on *hubris*.

[52] Ruschenbusch 1965: 302–09 argues that the *graphe hubreos* was meant to replace earlier laws on assault and rape with more severe penalties, but fails to explain why the *dike aikeias* nonetheless survived. Gagarin 1979: 229–36 argues that the *graphe hubreos* was designed to offer an alternative procedure (a *graphe* not a *dike*) by which a more severe penalty could be imposed. See Fisher 1992: 53–62 for discussion of these and other views. See also chapter 2, n. 103 on *aikeia*.

[53] Lex apud Dem. 21. 47. For death as a penalty for *hubris*, see Lys. fr. LXIV (B–S) and Dein. *Dem.* 23 (ambiguous, see n. 55) and the discussions of E. M. Harris 1990: 373–74 and Brown 1991.

[54] MacDowell 1978: 129 with n. 280; 1976: 14–31; and 1990: 18–23 and 263–67. Cf. Dover 1978: 34–39 (esp. for the application of the *graphe* to sexual offenses).

on the *timē* (honour) of another."[55] If the law against *hubris* did entail (even implicitly) the evaluation of the alleged offender's intentions in addition to his objectively abusive conduct, then it might have been difficult to apply the *graphe* successfully to cases of the rape of women.[56] A defendant's plea that he lacked a "disposition to abuse power" may have won him acquittal. This view is endorsed here and in the next chapter (6.2.c), where defenses for *hubris* and assaults in the orators and for rape in New Comedy are examined.

While most scholars who have examined the heterosexual and homosexual component of *hubris* have focused upon coercive acts, D. Cohen has shown that, at least in common usage, *hubris* is used to depict consensual conduct as well:

> In short, *hubris* arises in heterosexual contexts through behaviour which damages the sexual honour or reputation of a person or family. Violence or coercion are not necessary components of *hubris* in ordinary usage, but most of the cases do involve conduct that enhances one's own position at the expense of another's honour and reputation.[57]

Whether such cases would in fact be brought before a dikasterion is another matter, about which we are, not surprisingly, ill-informed.[58] Cohen tentatively suggests that "the action for hubris may have served as a convenient 'catchall' category for prosecuting offenses against sexual honor."[59] The resemblance of *hubris* so defined to the

[55] Fisher 1990: 126; also 1992: 36–85. E. M. Harris 1992: 74 has pointed out that the two views are not contradictory: whereas Fisher "stresses the objective circumstances, *hybris* as an action that brings dishonor on the victim," MacDowell stresses "the mental element, *hybris* as a state of mind characterized by certain types of unrestrained behavior." Since *hubris* so broadly defined (whether by combining the definitions of MacDowell and Fisher or by applying one or the other separately) would appear to cover a wide range of conduct, it is overly restrictive to conclude that "when the subject of the verb *hubrizein* is an adult male and the object a woman or boy, *hubris* implies, unless the context gives a clear indication to the contrary, that the offense is the commission of sexual or homosexual assault" (Dover 1980: 36). Sometimes the context gives no clue whatsoever; thus, e.g., at Dein. *Dem.* 23, the speaker reminds the dikasts that they put Themistios of Aphidna to death "because he outraged (*hubrisen*) the Rhodian (female) kithara player at the Eleusinian festival." Inference of rape in this instance is possible, but other inferences are equally cogent; see, e.g., Cole 1984: 104, with nn. 31–32 and Worthington 1992: 169. On the other hand, *hubrizein*, as used in the contexts of Lys. 12. 98 and 14. 20, seems to imply rape as a physical act, but not as a technically designated offense brought before a dikasterion.

[56] So Harrison 1. 19 n. 2, and 34, followed by Dover 1978: 36.

[57] D. Cohen 1991c: 177.

[58] The case of *hubris* alluded to in Dem. 45. 4, an important piece of Cohen's evidence (1995: 149 and 154), never unfolded in a courtroom; Apollodoros alleges that he brought an indictment before the *thesmothetai*, the case was postponed, and the courts were shut down. See Bonner 1919, a repository of earlier views about this elusive case.

[59] D. Cohen 1995: 155, dropping the more explicit suggestion made in his earlier version of the

umbrella of Roman *iniuria* renders the suggestion at once attractive and (perhaps unwarrantably) suspect. Nevertheless, Cohen's discussion is a salutary reminder that the notion of *hubris* as an offense, determined by dikasts when confronted with such cases in court, will not have been restricted to physical acts of violence.

The *dike biaiōn*, on the other hand, was a "private suit against violent acts"; the penalty was monetary.[60] Since the suit was private, damages would be paid to the victim himself, if the victim were an adult male, but to a guardian (*kurios* – usually the father, or else a husband, in the case of a married woman), if the victim were a young boy or female. The remedy is not specifically designed for obtaining redress for rape; indeed, the Athenians appear to have had no specific word for designating that act. In prose works, it is often referred to with the more general verb *biazesthai* ("to use force")[61] and sometimes with the (slightly) euphemistic *aiskhunein biai* ("to shame by force"). It is alleged that in Solon's time, the fine was fixed at 100 *drakhmai* (Plut. *Solon* 23), but in the fourth century, "at double the damages" (Lys. 1. 32). MacDowell, noting that cases of violent theft also carried a double penalty, has proposed that the amount of the fine, assessed by the dikasterion, was paid to the victim or to the victim's *kurios*, and then paid over again to the state.[62] The similarity between the two offenses deserves further reflection. In Dem. 21. 42–46, the orator lays the ground for his citation of the *graphe hubreos* by asking the dikasts to "observe how much more severely the laws punish those who offend intentionally and from insolence than those who err in some other way" (42). Among the laws he marshals to support the argument, he includes some in which the penalty is doubled: thus it happens in the case of damage (*blabe*), if the offense was committed intentionally (43); so also, in the case of theft, if the act of appropriation was accompanied with violence (*bia*, 44). It is

essay (1991c: 181): "Over time, the action for *hubris* may have functionally replaced an earlier action for seduction."

60 For attestation of the *dike*, see Lipsius 637, n. 1.

61 *Biazesthai*: e.g., Lys. 1. 32; Plato *Laws* 874C (also *hubristhenai biai*); Xen. *Hell.* 6. 4. 7; Ar. *Wealth* 1092 (with female subject – an old woman!). *Aiskhunein biai*: Lys. 1. 32; *aiskhunein*: Men. *Heros* fr. θη *recto* 83; Paus. 1. 21. 4. *Kataiskh[unei*: Men. *Phasma* 93 (apparently of rape). See further nn. 67–68 below.

62 So MacDowell 1978: 124 (cf. Harp. s.v. βιαίων ὄνομα δίκης); see further chapter 6 at nn. 25–28. There have been numerous interpretations of what "double the damages" means. Glotz 1904: 393 suggested that Lysias has paraphrased only part of the law, and that in the full version, the penalty for assaulting a free person is double the penalty for assaulting a slave. For other views, see Lipsius 259 and n. 63, 435, 638–39.

conceivable that the penalty for "violent acts" (*biaia*) had been changed – or augmented – in the course of time to conform to laws which imposed "double penalties," depending on whether intention (as in the case of damage) or violence (as in the case of forceful theft) was present. Since "violence" is already an essential component of offenses traditionally designated as "violent acts" (in the remedy associated with Solon), then it may be that the presence of the doer's "intention" subsequently made acts of rape (as well as other "violent acts") more culpable and hence liable to the double penalty.

It will be useful to consider an argument made by Euphiletos, the speaker of Lys. 1, which is repeated by Plut. *Solon* 23 and by modern writers as well. Euphiletos compares the penalty for violent acts (apparently read out to the court in c. 31) with the consequences for the *moikhos* who is caught under the conditions of the homicide law (apparently read out in c. 30); he concludes: "[the lawgiver] thought that those who use force (*tous biazomenous*) deserve a lesser penalty than those who use persuasion" (*tous peithontas* 32). As some have pointed out, the analogy is falsely contrived: a rapist, if caught in the act, might very well be killed on the spot with justification according to the law on homicide – or he might be punished with a death penalty under the *graphe hubreos*.[63] On the other hand, a seducer, even if caught in the act, is not required by law to be put to death – there were alternatives. The injured husband might prosecute the alleged offender with a *graphe moikheias* (if it were available at this date); we cannot, as we have seen, be certain of the penalty.[64] Or he might demand a sum of money or physically abuse the offender – without killing him. Euphiletos' argument is trumped up: its goal is to highlight the punishment of the *moikhos* caught in the act, to demonstrate the desirability, even "necessity" of that punishment – which in fact has already been inflicted, which cannot be retracted (the alleged offender is dead), and so needs justification. What better way to achieve such justification than to take one law (the law on justifiable homicide), to present it as if it required the death of a *moikhos* (defined as "seducer") caught in the act, and then to contrast that punishment with the penalty of a related offense – when the real end of the latter was the acquisition of compensation for a victim of violence?

Compensation: herein lies a significant difference between the two

[63] See n. 53. [64] See n. 44.

graphai and the *dike* under discussion. The *graphe moikheias* is penal; it looks toward the punishment of the *moikhos* (which can only be conjectured) and also penalizes the woman after the trial; a married woman loses not only her husband, but also, by exclusion from public sanctuaries and the celebration of their rites, her civic identity. Remarriage, as suggested earlier, might be difficult (see nn. 48–49). The *graphe hubreos* is also penal; it looks toward the punishment of the *hubristes*, but offers no compensation to the victim. The *dike biaiōn* took care of that. It may have been the pay-off for a woman's innocence. And compensation would be useful. The husband of a raped woman might very well divorce her. The husband in *Epitrepontes* has left his raped wife; the husband of (raped) Philumena in *Hecyra* has been put in the awkward position of not wanting the wife back who has left their marital home. Remarriage for women in these circumstances might also be difficult; rumors of adultery might taint their reputation. A raped unmarried woman might likewise arouse suspicion. Those in her family's circle of kin and close friends who knew about a rape might always wonder, was it thus? Was she to be trusted? Yet these are the very folk from whom she might expect a husband to emerge. Rejection would be likely – unless perhaps a large enough dowry could be amassed to attract a husband willing to be blind to the past or one outside her family's circle of acquaintances and so unaware of her circumstances. Compensation would help her to subsist in her father's household, or to amass that dowry. Compensation, then, was (legally) at hand for the *kurios* of the victim of rape, not for the *kurios* of the woman who had been seduced.

1(c) The law and social practice

While the law treated sexual offenses as serious matters, we have no idea whether their commission – or prosecution – was a common occurrence. We can sum up the instances of judicial and extra-judicial redress in the orators as follows, limiting our evidence to statements which are witnessed (and which are not risk-free insinuations) except where a sexual offense is part of the prosecutor's main charge:[65]

[65] An unwitnessed instance of a self-help remedy appears in [Dem.] 59. 41: Stephanos is alleged to have extorted money from rich, inexperienced foreigners whom he caught committing *moikheia* with Neaira.

(1) Hyp. 2 *Lyk.* 12: the speaker is charged by the procedure of *eisangelia* (impeachment) with subverting the democracy on the specific grounds that he committed *moikheia* (see n. 31).
(2) Lys. 1 *Eratosth.*: the speaker is defending himself on a charge of homicide, alleging that he had applied a self-help remedy under circumstances permissible by law; witnesses are summoned to testify to the speaker's account of the detection of the *moikhos* (29).
(3) Lys. 13 *Agor.* 66: the defendant is said to have been taken (*elēphthē*) as a *moikhos* in the past and witnesses are called to testify to that fact.
(4) Is. 8 *Khiron* 44 and 46: Khiron's nephew is said to have been taken (*lēphtheis*) as a *moikhos* in the past and witnesses are called to testify to that fact.
(5) [Dem.] 59 *Neaira* 64–66: Stephanos allegedly caught Epainetos committing *moikheia* with Phano and tried to extort money from him. Witnesses testify to the private agreement presided over by mediators (71).

Only the first instance listed above falls into the category of judicial redress; the use of an *eisangelia* (impeachment) to bring the charge is undoubtedly an unusual stretch of that procedure. The other instances are extra-judicial. The first of these (no. 2) is the subject of the current trial; the other instances (nos. 3–5) are not directly related to the trial that is underway. The one judicial instance might, with reservation, be supplemented with four others: two *graphai* for *hubris*, one for *moikheia*, and one *dike biaiōn*. None of these is securely attested.[66]

While the paucity of evidence for trials might be explained by the accident of preservation, hints here and there in the orators suggest that sexual offenses were customarily settled in private:

(1) The defendant in Hyp. 2 *Lyk.* 12 suggests that the prosecutors brought the case by *eisangelia* in order to avoid the risk of a prosecution by *graphe.*

66 Dein. *Dem.* 23 mentions three offenders who were convicted and voted a death penalty by the court; it is conceivable but not certain that two of them had been charged with *hubris* for sexual assault. In one case, a Rhodian kithara player was the victim, see n. 55 apud fin. The charge against the man who had detained a free boy from the deme Pellene in a mill may have been the enslavement of a citizen (so Worthington 1992: 169), but possibly *hubris* (so Fisher 1992: 41 and Cohen 1995: 154, who depicts it as involving a sexual component). Lys. fr. xxv (B–S) furnishes a title of a lost speech (κατὰ Αὐτοκράτους μοιχείας) purporting to belong to a trial for *moikheia*; the exiguous fragments of the speech shed no light on the case. Lys. fr. cxxiv (B–S) κατὰ Φιλωνίδου βιαίων is tantalizing (esp. fr. 3) but too vague to identify the type of alleged violence.

(2) Aiskhines makes the following statement in 1 *Tim.* 107: "And so much licentiousness (*aselgeia*) did he show toward the wives of free men as no other man has yet done. I summon none of these men to bring testimony before the public of his own misfortune which he has chosen to keep silent, but I leave it to you to investigate these matters." The insinuation that men conceal sexual offenses committed against members of their own households is reinforced by a statement made by Aristotle in *Rhet.* 1.12.1373a34–35; there he includes among the criminal acts for which men are likely to escape punishment: "all those wrongs which are such that men, when subjected to them, are ashamed to speak, as in the case of outrages committed against the women of their household or against themselves or against their sons."

(3) There is a tendency in the orators to mention the grounds for a divorce when the divorce of a woman is mentioned: Lys. 14. *Alk.* 28; Is. 2 *Men.* 8; Dem. 57 *Eub.* 40–41.

That this collection of data does not amount to anything very solid is not surprising: these are offenses which men and women took pains to conceal. The first datum suggests one reason why prosecutors may have refrained from bringing indictments for *moikheia* or *hubris*, the risk of the 1,000 drakhmai fine if they failed to garner a fifth of the vote. *Hubris* and non-flagrant *moikheia* may have been difficult to prove; potential prosecutors may have feared to bring the charges. The second datum suggests another reason why such indictments may not have been brought: men preferred to conceal sexual transgressions committed in their households rather than to publicize them through court trials. Aristotle offers a motive for concealment: the shame of the head of household.[67] Women, too, whether raped or seduced, would find the dishonor intolerable and publicity unthinkable.[68] We might suggest still another motive for avoiding trial: in

[67] Gorgias, speaking of his half-sister at *Dusk.* 243–46, says: "For if [she] should fall into any shameful trouble (*aiskhunei tini*), this becomes a [rebuke] to me as well. For the outsider does not know the man responsible – [whoever] it was – only the consequence." For the phrase *aiskhunein biai* ("to shame by force") , see n. 61. According to a scholiast's paraphrase of the plot of a tragedy by Karkinos (*Alope* Nauck² p. 797), when Alope's father discovered the identity of the man who *emoikheuse* her, he was unable to bear life because of the pain (*lupe*) and committed suicide.

[68] Scafuro 1990: 136–51 discusses the shame-directed discourse of rape in Greek tragedy. The editors of a fragment of a speech by Lysias, ὑπὲρ Ἀχιλλείδου φόνου (Lys. fr. xxvi B–S, "concerning the murder of Akhilleides"), have conjectured that the case is similar to Lys. 1 (justifiable homicide); according to them, the speaker's sister, who "unable to control her pain (*lupe*), killed herself," had been found with a *moikhos*.

cases of adultery, divorce would be required and the husband would probably be compelled to return the dowry. The tenuous third datum suggests that private agreements between a husband and a guilty wife may not have been uncommon: why publicize grounds for divorce, which were not required by law, except to allay suspicions that such an agreement had been made, e.g., an agreement to divorce without an antecedent trial of a *moikhos*?[69]

How then were flagrant and non-flagrant sexual offenses treated? Most likely, *kurioi* came to terms privately with offenders. Husbands might decide to divorce guilty wives without pursuing a trial – if they could afford it (cf. Hyp. 2. 12). In the case of unmarried girls who had been raped or seduced, probably an inter-family meeting would convene. Its aim would be to induce the father of a young rapist or seducer to consent to a marriage between his son and the girl, or to pay a sum of money which could be applied to the girl's dowry and used to attract a husband outside the family's circle of friends and relations. Such arrangements are simply extensions of the practice of accepting monetary compensation in cases where offenders were caught in the act. This is necessarily a hypothetical reconstruction; there is hardly a shred of historical record here. But three factors support such a reconstruction. The first is least weighty but reassuring: comparative evidence from *Exodos* 22. 16, 17 (= *Coll.* 4. 1) provides a pattern of settlement very similar to the reconstruction offered here: "When a man seduces a virgin who is not yet betrothed and lies down with her, he shall pay the dowry (*pherne*) for her to be his wife. If her father refuses to give her to him, the seducer shall pay in silver a sum equal to the dowry for virgins."[70] The settlements

69 For the practice of divorce in Athens, see chapter 7.2.a.i. It has sometimes been thought that witnesses were required for a husband's divorcing of his wife on the basis of Lys. 14. 28 and *Epitr.* 659–60 (Beauchet 1. 381; Taubenschlag 1926: 75–76; Zucker 1944: 204). The evidence of these passages should probably be interpreted differently; on *Epitr.* 659–60, see Gomme and Sandbach 1973: 351. As for Lys. 14. 28 : "And Hipponikos, upon summoning many men, sent away his wife, saying that this man [Alkibiades] kept visiting his house not as her brother, but as her husband." When Hipponikos sends away his wife, he calls witnesses not merely to that act, but to his statement of the grounds; the latter can be interpreted as an allegation, not only of incest, but also of *moikheia*. Hipponikos thus calls upon witnesses to testify that he has acted in accordance with the law about *moikheia* – without any trial taking place. Since husbands may have chosen to divorce wives guilty of *moikheia* (or of *xenia*) before a trial (or even, as is likely, without prosecuting the alleged *moikhoi* or *xenai*), some procedure (declaration of grounds for divorce before witnesses) would be desirable to ensure an innocent wife's reputation against imputations of offense. Evidence from the orators (cited above) and New Comedy (*Epitr.*, *Fab. Inc.*, *Hec.*) suggests that husbands were heedful of their wives' reputations when divorcing them.

70 'Εὰν δὲ ἀπατήσῃ τις παρθένον ἀμνήστευτον, καὶ κοιμηθῇ μετ' αὐτῆς, φερνῇ φερνιεῖ

between father and seducer articulated here reflect Jewish law of the third century BC and demonstrate the influence of Hellenistic Egypt on the Jewish community; influence is confirmed by the use of *pherne* (dowry) rather than a translation of Hebrew *mohar* (bride-price).[71] The comparative evidence suggests that the reconstruction of Athenian practice offered here is not infeasible fantasy. The second supporting factor is one of the terms of the reconciliation between Stephanos and Epainetos in [Dem.] 59 *Neaira* 71. Stephanos is said to have taken Epainetos as a *moikhos*; the latter provided sureties for the demanded compensation and then indicted Stephanos for detaining him unlawfully. The two men were then reconciled in private:

> . . . and Epainetos shall give to Phano a thousand drakhmai toward her dowry [εἰς ἔκδοσιν, lit., toward her "giving away" or "transfer" into the *kurieia* of another], since he has used her often; and Stephanos shall provide Epainetos access to Phano whenever he comes to town and wishes to enjoy her.[72]

The terms appear to legitimize a relationship of *pallakia* (concubinage) or at least to put the relationship of the couple on a secure economic basis by the requirement that Epainetos "give a thousand drakhmai toward her dowry." Epainetos is not explicitly required to pay compensation to Stephanos for *moikheia*; instead, he must contribute toward the unfortunate girl's "giving away," a euphemism – as is the language of gift-giving elsewhere in reconciliations – but this time, for compelling a shot-gun quasi-marriage, concubinage. Epainetos is a foreigner; marriage is out of the question. While the mediators are not family members (again, we must recall that Epainetos is a foreigner in Athens), the provision of dowry and the regulation of the couple's relationship might serve as a model for the inter-family meetings that have been hypothesized here. In cases where rape was in question, there may have been no less interest in

αὐτὴν γυναῖκα. ἐὰν δὲ ἀνανεύων ἀνανεύσηι καὶ μὴ βούληται ὁ πατὴρ αὐτῆς δοῦναι αὐτὴν αὐτῶι γυναῖκα, ἀργύριον ἀποτείσει τῶι πατρὶ καθ' ὅσον ἐστὶν ἡ φερνὴ τῶν παρθένων.

71 Bickerman 1956: 91–92 says of the chapter: "Since the translation [i.e., Septuagint] was made under Ptolemy II, that is between 284–46 BC, the Septuagint offers the interpretation of Mosaic law current among the Alexandrian Jews in the second quarter of the third century BC. Now, the Alexandrian translators used the term *pherne* where the Hebrew text speaks of the *mohar*. It shows that before 250 BC, at least in Ptolemaic Egypt, dowry already supplanted the purchase in Jewish marriage settlements." Bickerman further discusses the process of reception of Greek law into Jewish, focusing on the transformation of bride-price into dowry.

72 See chapter 3, n. 14; on the authenticity of the scenario, see App. 7. 1, n. 103.

compensating the injured girl and her *kurios* by requiring a dowry payment or marriage from her assailant. The third factor is the way in which rape cases are regularly resolved in New Comedy: an agreement is made between two families concerning the marriage of the rapist and his victim, often under the threat of the law. We shall consider such episodes in the next chapter.

2 SEXUAL OFFENSES IN ROMAN LAW

Roman terminology referring to adultery, fornication, and rape reveals some of the same ambiguities as the Athenian. Words of special concern are *adulterium* and *stuprum* (along with cognate nouns and verbs). Scholars have frequently pointed out the observations of the jurists Papinian and Modestinus concerning the use of these terms in Augustus' famous legislation, the *lex Iulia* on sexual offenses, passed sometime between 18 and 16 BC. Papinian writes: "The law refers to *stuprum* and *adulterium* indiscriminately and with rather a misuse of terms. But properly speaking *adulterium* is committed with a married woman, the name being derived from children conceived by another (*alter*); *stuprum*, however, is committed against a virgin or widow or divorced woman; the Greeks call it *phthora* (corruption)."[73] The chastised authors of the *lex Iulia* were not the only ones who used these terms "indiscriminately"; *literati* show similar indifference to specifying the act and a marked preference for *stuprum* as the umbrella term. Plautus, for example, uses *stuprum* and cognate verb on twelve occasions to refer to adultery, fornication, and possibly rape; he uses *adulterium* only three times, apparently of adultery.[74] Terence uses neither *stuprum* nor *adulterium*. Livy, writing in the

[73] Trans. Watson, modified. *D.* 48. 5. 6. 1: *Lex stuprum et adulterium promiscue et καταχρηστικώτερον appellat. sed proprie adulterium in nupta committitur, propter partum ex altero conceptum composito nomine: stuprum vero in virginem viduamve committitur, quod Graeci φθοράν appellant.* Similarly Modestinus at *D.* 50. 16. 101; he gives a more troublesome definition at 48. 5. 35. pr.-1: *Stuprum committit, qui liberam mulierem consuetudinis causa, non matrimonii continet, excepta videlicet concubina. Adulterium in nupta admittitur: stuprum in vidua vel virgine vel puero committitur.* ("*Stuprum* is committed by someone who keeps a freewoman for the sake of sexual relations not marriage, unless indeed she is a concubine. Adultery is committed with a married woman; *stuprum* is committed with a widow or divorced woman, a virgin, or a boy." Trans. Watson, modified). The words *excepta videlicet concubina* have been considered an interpolation, but the case is not conclusive; for discussion of the jurists' problematic treatment of the question whether *concubinae* were subject to or protected by the law on adultery, see Treggiari 1981: 71–76. For discussion of the terminology of sexual offenses in general, see Treggiari 1991: 262–64.

[74] *Stuprare*: *Aul.* 36; *Truc.* 821. *Stuprum*: *Amph.* 488, 883, 898, 1016, fr. XVI (Lindsay); *Cas.* 82, 201, 887; *Merc.* 537; *Truc.* 263. *Adulterium*: *Cas.* 876; *Miles* 90, 802.

Augustan age, uses *stuprum* and cognate verb on twenty-four occasions of adultery, fornication, and rape; he uses *adulterium* only once.[75] None of these authors uses the term *adulter* for the male actor; both Plautus and Terence use the term *moechus* instead, usually without specific reference to the act (adultery, fornication, rape).[76] Context sometimes assists in identifying the act; often it does not.

It is likely that no specific judicial remedy existed for these different offenses before the first century BC. One jurist, however, reports that the Augustan legislation on *adulteria* abrogated earlier legislation.[77] Scholars have searched for traces of these statutes and their author. While Sulla has been a candidate for legislator on adultery, no substantial argument has been made for legislation of an earlier date.[78] A criminal prosecution for the rape of women and children could be brought under the *lex Iulia de vi*, a law passed by either Caesar or Augustus.[79] It was a capital offense.[80] The absence of reliable evidence for earlier, specific legislation on rape has been viewed as particularly troublesome by some scholars.[81] Those who argue that there were such statutes derive their position in large measure from a feeling of disbelief that there could not have been any.[82] Those who argue that the absence of evidence signifies the

[75] See citations in Packard's concordance. Livy occasionally distinguishes specific acts by adding words, e.g., *per vim* (by force) at 1. 57. 10 or *voluntarium* at 38. 24. 3. But simple *stuprum* can refer to rape (3. 44. 1) or adultery (10. 31. 9), or fornication (22. 57. 3). *Adulterium* only occurs at 1. 58. 5.

[76] Plautus: *Bacch.* 918; *Miles* 775, 921, 1131, 1390, 1398, 1436 (bis); *Poen.* 862; *Truc.* 610. Terence: *And.* 316; *Eun.* 957, 960, 992. In *Eun.*, the term refers to a rapist.

[77] *Coll.* 4. 2. 2 (Paul.): *et quidem primum caput legis [Iuliae de adulteris] prioribus obrogat* ("In fact, the first chapter of the Julian law [about sexual offenses] repeals a number of prior statutes").

[78] See Bauman 1993 for interesting argument on the nature and motivation of Sulla's hypothesized legislation. Robinson 1995: 58 suggests that the "abrogated legislation" of *Coll.* 4.2.2 "may refer to (non-domestic) masculine *stuprum*, as under the *lex Scantinia* . . . or to laws passed on specific occasions."

[79] Mommsen 1899: 655 assigns this law to the dictatorship of Julius Caesar rather than to the legislative activity of Augustus. For discussion with citation of relevant bibliography, see Bauman 1993: 556–63 and n. 16.

[80] Mommsen 1899: 665 and n. 1, citing Paul *Sent.* 2. 26. 12 = *Coll.* 5. 2. 1: *qui masculum liberum invitum stupraverit, capite punitur* ("anyone who has sexual relations with a free male against his will shall be punished with death") and *Sent.* 5. 4. 4: . . . *pulsatio pudoris poena capitis vindicetur* ("a forcible attack on a person's sexual integrity is punished with death").

[81] Occasionally, *Rhet. ad Her.* 4. 8. 12 is adduced: *In iis qui violassent ingenuum, matremfamilias constuprassent, vulnerassent aliquem aut postremo necassent, maxima supplicia maiores consumpserunt* . . . ("Against those who violated a free man, outraged the mother of a family, wounded a person, or, worst of all, killed him, our ancestors used the most severe penalties"). As Mommsen 1899: 664–65 n. 10 rightly saw, this piece of rhetoric cannot be used to formulate a legal definition.

[82] Kunkel 1962: 122–23 and n. 446 adduced the *ad Herennium* passage (see preceding n.), Livy 8. 22. 3 (see n. 84), and Coll. 4. 2. 2. (see n. 77 above), and remarked, "Dass es für den Fall

absence of statutes call attention to the persistence of self-help as a means of seeking justice in Roman society; criminal courts for other specific crimes of violence awaited the legislative activity of Sulla.[83]

There are some reports, mainly in Livy, that the aediles initiated actions against adulterers and *matronae* for *stuprum* and *probrum* (immoral conduct) in the late fourth and third centuries, and these resulted in *iudicia populi* (public trials before the people).[84] The aediles were, in general, responsible for the *cura urbis*, for ensuring the orderliness of inhabitants and the cleanliness of the city. Probably the men and women who were charged with *stuprum* and *probrum* had not broken any specific law – i.e., their offenses had not been defined as such in an edict; their conduct instead was viewed as creating public disorder.[85]

Judicious assessment of the evidence suggests, then, that there were no laws that specifically concerned sexual offenses of or against women before the first century BC. The major issues of legal controversy concern (a) the law's attitude toward self-help remedies, i. e., whether it explicitly sanctioned them in our period or whether the remedies developed as part of custom distinct from law and (b) the applicability of the *actio iniuriarum* to sexual offenses during this time.

der Notzucht bis zur *lex Julia de vi publica* keine Kriminalanklage gegeben habe (vgl. Mommsen *Strafr.* 664 f. u. 664 Anm. 10), ist noch unglaublicher als das Fehlen einer Anklage wegen Ehebruchs oder Verführung einer unverheirateten Frau."

[83] Gardner 1986: 119–20.

[84] Livy 8. 22. 3 reports under the year 328/27 that Marcus Flavius *ab aedilibus crimine stupratae matris familiae absolvisset* ("was acquitted by the aediles of the charge of having engaged in illicit sexual relations with a married woman"). Val. Max. 8. 1. *Absol.* 7 mentions the acquittal but omits the charge. Livy 10. 31. 8–9 (295 BC): Q. Fabius Gurges (possibly curule aedile in that year: Broughton 1951: 178) brought several *matronae* before the people for *stuprum.* Livy 25. 2. 9 (213 BC): the aediles of the plebs accused several *matronae* before the people of *probrum*; those condemned were exiled. Mommsen 1899: 690–91 treats these cases as exceptional; similarly, Nippel 1988: 33. For brief discussion with citation of relevant bibliography, see Treggiari 1991: 276. Garofalo 1986 collects the testimony of all *iudicia populi* in the third and second centuries BC; offenses committed by women appear to belong exclusively to the domain of the aediles.

[85] Bauman 1992: 16 with n. 15 interprets the episode of the women fined for *stuprum* in 295 BC (Livy 10. 31. 8–9) in this way, taking as his starting point the substantial fines which were subsequently used to build a temple to Venus Obsequens: "That the fines sufficed for a project of that size suggests that a large number of women were involved. As *stuprum* here means systematic fornication rather than occasional adulteries, the matrons were trading as prostitutes. That brought it within the jurisdiction of the curule aediles, for as market masters they were responsible for brothels." There is much speculation involved here, but it does provide a possible explanation of how *stuprum*, without being an offense defined by law, might come under the purview of the aediles.

2(a) *Self-help remedies*

Roman fathers possessed, at least in theory, extensive *potestas* (power) over their children. The *vitae necisque potestas* ("power over life and death") appears to have been conferred or confirmed by the *XII Tables*.[86] Historical instances of the application of the right in regard to adult sons and daughters are rare.[87] Valerius Maximus reports two instances of fathers who killed their unmarried daughters upon discovering their sexual activity; one father killed both daughter and lover.[88] A father who detected his married daughter in adultery might also kill her by virtue of the *vitae necisque potestas*; during our period, however, it is not certain whether that right was held by a father whose daughter was married *in manu* (i.e., a daughter who entered the family of her husband and became subordinate to the power of her husband or his *paterfamilias*). Papinian interpreted Augustus' legislation as granting that right to fathers of all daughters, both those who were married *in manu* and those who were not.[89] Whatever lawful or traditional right pertained to fathers in our period, however, we should observe that paternal *vitae necisque potestas* did not require the killing of any daughter – or son. Recent scholarship has drawn attention to ways in which legal and constitutional constraints, demographic considerations, and social and economic dynamics within the Roman family had a mitigating effect on the severity of *patria potestas* in general.[90] In regard to a father's right to kill his children, we should note the relevant fact that no literary source provides any instance of a father killing a married daughter for committing adultery. We shall take up the question of a father's

[86] *Coll.* 4. 8 (Pap.) attributes the conferral to a *lex regia*. There may have been a proviso in the *XII Tables* that a *paterfamilias* could only put a son to death *ex iusta causa*. Textual evidence for the proviso is supplied by a paraphrase of a fragmentary chapter of Gaius 4. 80 in *cod. Augustod.* 85–86. See Kunkel 1966: 241–46 for discussion.

[87] For a reassessment of the *vitae necisque potestas*, see W. Harris 1986.

[88] Val. Max. 6. 1. 3 and 6.

[89] *Coll.* 4. 7 (Pap.). The right to kill all daughters may have been a new permission granted by Augustus' legislation (i.e., the *ius occidendi iure patris* of Augustus was separate from the *vitae necisque potestas*) – or a confirmation of the traditional one; see the recent discussions of Lorenzi 1991 and Lambertini 1992. What Papinian seems to consider new in the law was the requirement that *paterfamilias* kill his daughter at the same time as he killed the adulterer (*Coll.* 8. 1 and cf. *Coll.* 2. 3 Paul.). The law contained the following further restrictions: the father who kills must be *paterfamilias* (*D.* 48. 5. 21, Ulp.); he must catch the adulterous couple in the act in his own house or in that of his son-in-law (*h. t.*, 24 Ulp.).

[90] Legal and constitutional constraints: Kaser 1938; Crook 1967. Demography: Saller 1986 and 1987. Social and economic dynamics within the Roman family: Kaser 1938; Saller 1988 and 1991. For a reassessment of the *vitae necisque potestas*, see n. 87.

right to kill a daughter married *in manu* once again when we discuss Roman family councils.

Whether the woman's husband had a similar right is controversial. Cato is quoted as saying in a speech "On dowry" that a husband who took his wife in adultery could kill her with impunity without a trial; a wife, however, would not dare to lay a finger on her spouse, whether he committed adultery or was adulterated, since she has no right (*in adulterio uxorem tuum si prehendisses, sine iudicio impune necares; illa te, si adulteres sive tu adulterare, digito non audet contingere, neque ius est*).[91] Some scholars have accepted the statement as evidence that husbands were legally entitled to kill wives who were apprehended in the act of intercourse.[92] Under the Augustan legislation, a husband's right to kill was a limited one: he had no right to kill his wife;[93] moreover, he was only permitted to kill adulterers of a certain status (e.g., pimps, actors, men condemned in public trials who had not been restored to their former status, freedmen belonging to members of the family, slaves), and only if he caught the offender *in ipsis rebus Veneris* in his own house.[94] Whether the prohibition against killing a wife was a new one or was a restatement of a traditional one is impossible to discern.[95] Uncertainty therefore remains about a husband's right to kill his wife in the earlier period; much depends on interpretation of Cato's "On dowry." Treggiari has recently argued that Cato's statements lack juristic content; a husband might plead before a tribunal that the homicide was justifiable under the circumstances, and the tribunal might often agree and let him off with impunity – but that is quite different from being granted in advance the right to kill a wife who was found *in flagrante delicto*.[96] As for the literary record, once again it provides no example of a husband killing a wife – or her adulterer – under such circumstances.

Elsewhere we find evidence that husbands participated in family councils to determine the fate of an allegedly errant wife. Family councils appear frequently in literary sources and they are by no

[91] Cato *de dote* fr. 221 *ORF*[3] (= Aulus Gellius *N.A.* 10. 23. 5).

[92] E.g., Cantarella 1976: 180–82; 1991: 231. Watson 1971: 23 and n. 3 (similarly 1967: 28) suggests that even husbands of wives in marriages without *manus* had this right; for support, he cites Plautus *Miles* 1164ff., 1276 ff., 1394 ff., *Bacch.* 851 ff., 917 ff. The passages do not support the contention.

[93] Paul. *Sent.* 2. 26. 4; *Coll.* 4. 3. 1 and 4. 12. 3 (Paul.); 4. 10. 1 (Pap.).

[94] *D.* 48. 5. 25 *pr.* (Macer); *Coll.* 4. 3. 1–5 and 4. 12. 3 (Paul.).

[95] Treggiari 1991: 274.

[96] Treggiari's view is rejected by Bauman 1993: 553, n. 7.

means limited to cases of adultery; often their task is to consider the punishment – which might include death – of a son or daughter.[97] Such councils were probably not required by law – *paterfamilias*, after all, possesses *vitae necisque potestas* – but developed, as Watson puts it, "as a social fact."[98] *Paterfamilias* retains control, but will be wise to listen to family members. Dionysios of Halikarnassos reports a tradition about such councils in early Rome. After depicting Romulus' establishment of marriage as "indissoluble relationship" (*oikeiotes adialutos*), he describes how a wife who drank wine or participated in adultery was to be treated: she was to be judged by a family council consisting of her husband and *sungeneis* (kinsmen); a death penalty was permitted.[99] It is a matter of dispute whether *sungeneis* refers to the woman's blood-relations or her husband's. Support for the view that the *sungeneis* are the *cognati* of the injured husband is based primarily on the character of the wife's marriage as *in manu*.[100] Support for the view that the woman's blood-relations are meant has been adduced from the appearance of both Lucretia's husband and father at her bedside before she kills herself, from reports about *cognati* and *propinqui* (usually "blood-relations") in the second century BC who decide the punishment of women who have been charged with serious offenses (the poisoning of their husbands), and from the Augustan legislation mentioned earlier which conferred power on *paterfamilias* even over a daughter married *in manu*.[101]

The marriages to which Dionysios refers in the passage under discussion are probably with *manus* – the woman is in the power of

[97] For detailed discussion, see Düll 1943: 54–69; Volterra 1948; Kunkel 1966.

[98] Watson 1975: 43; Volterra 1948 presents the argument (viz., that family councils had no lawful jurisdiction) in great detail, resuscitating Mommsen's succinct presentation (1899: 16–26). Watson, however, differentiates the character of family councils that meet to decide the fate of a woman married *in manu* who has committed a serious offense; these councils were required by law. See further, n. 102 below.

[99] D. H. *A.R.* 2. 25. 6. Dionysios' value as a source for the regal age is of course highly dubious, but he can at least tell us, as Treggiari (1991: 265 with n. 17) puts it, "what people in the Augustan age wanted to believe. He clings to the idea of the self-regulating family. Like Cicero, he deplores direct state interference. The principle that the *paterfamilias* should take no serious action without consulting a council (*consilium*) was well established in Roman practice, though not in law. Dionysius' reference to kinsmen (*syggeneis*) is therefore fairly convincing."

[100] E.g., Volterra 1948: 113 and n. 16 and Cantarella 1976: 177–79.

[101] The Lucretia episode (Livy 1. 58): see Watson 1975: 35 and Treggiari 1991: 265–66. Later episodes of family councils composed of *cognati* and *propinqui* deciding upon the fate of married women (Val. Max. 6. 3. 1 and Livy *Per.* 48 in 154 BC, both concerning the same two women): see Watson 1975: 44 and n. 23 and Treggiari 1991: 266–67 and n. 22.

her husband's family. Scholars who have interpreted the *sungeneis* of the family council as the woman's blood-relations then ask two questions: does the wife's father have *potestas* over his daughter married *in manu*, and does the family council have legal recognition? One solution is to give a positive answer to both questions: *paterfamilias* has a residual or resumed *potestas* over his daughter when she is married *in manu* and has committed a serious offense – the husband is not sole arbiter of his wife's fate; family councils in such cases were required by law.[102] An alternative solution is to point to a gap in the law: a husband will customarily convene a meeting with his wife's blood-relations; the law did not interfere.[103] Possibly future considerations are uppermost: the husband seeks assurance that, if a death penalty is decreed, his wife's family will not seek revenge. Family councils under these circumstances would aim, in part, to impede subsequent feuding.

Reports of the treatment of adultery and fornication in the early and middle Republic focus upon the treatment of the woman; there are no reports that the law during this period granted impunity to a husband or father who actually killed the male offender who was caught in the act. Such murders no doubt occurred (e.g., Val. Max. 6.1. 3). Alleged adulterers and fornicators are threatened with beatings and castration in Plautus; puns on *testis* ("witness" and "testicle") and later evidence suggest that the Plautine punishments are not mere translations of Greek practices.[104] Valerius Maximus names a number of cuckolded husbands and the various indignities they inflicted upon named adulterers caught in the act: floggings, castration, and slave-rape.[105] Presumably redress for offenders who had been maimed or killed might be sought through prosecutions for *iniuria* or murder (provided that private suits for murder were available). An offending *filiusfamilias* ("son in the power of his father or paternal grandfather") who was caught in the act and not

102 Watson 1975: 44 thinks that the family council had legal recognition in the case "where a woman who was no longer in the *potestas* of her *pater* had misbehaved." He goes on to add that "very reasonably the right of inflicting the supreme penalty was not simply entrusted to the husband even when the wife was in his *manus*."

103 Treggiari 1991: 264–68 doubts that such councils were prescribed by statute; instead, the evidence "supports the view that custom allowed a family council consisting of the woman's *propinqui* to take disciplinary action against her, even when she was *sui iuris*" (268).

104 *Curc.* 23–38 and *Poen.* 862–63 (castration hinted); *Miles* 1394–1426 (on-stage beating, castration hinted, monetary compensation demanded). On the Plautine puns in these passages, see Lowe 1985a.

105 Val. Max. 6. 1. 13. Some of these figures might be historical: see Treggiari 1991: 271, n. 46.

immediately killed or maimed might not escape with impunity: Mommsen supposes that such an offender would be tried by a council composed of members of his own family.[106]

2(b) *Iniuria*

Legal redress for rape, seduction, and related offenses might have been possible through an action for *iniuria*. The evolution of early *iniuria* into the classical delict of the jurists is difficult to discern and fraught with controversy. Rape may have been embraced under the rubric of *iniuria* long before seduction found a place beneath that expanding umbrella. The *XII Tables* 8. 2, 3, and 4 (cf. Gaius 3. 223 and *Coll.* 2. 5. 5, Paul.) contained three provisions concerning assaults: (1) a penalty of retaliation in kind or a private composition for the maiming of limbs (*membrum rumpere*); (2) a penalty of 300 *asses* for the breaking of bones (*os frangere*) of free men and a penalty of 150 *asses* for the bones of slaves; (3) the final provision is controversial (8. 4: *Si iniuriam faxsit, viginti quinque poenae sunto*). The *opinio communis* understands it to mean a penalty of 25 *asses* for all other assaults and views it as a general norm which included all types of personal injury – and which therefore might include rape.[107]

A praetorian edict (the *edictum generale*), which may have been introduced as early as the last quarter of the third century BC, made the earlier provisions obsolete.[108] The edict issued instructions on how to proceed when *iniuria* had been inflicted on a person; in its origin, it appears not to have altered the substance of the earlier law but rather to have created an estimatory machinery.[109] The penalty was now always pecuniary and determined at the discretion of the judge according to the seriousness of the offense (*quantum ob eam rem*

[106] Mommsen 1899: 689.

[107] So, e.g., Kaser 1971: 156–57. Birks 1969: 188–90 and 1974 offers a different interpretation and eliminates the *iniuria* of *XII Tables* 8. 4 as an independent delict.

[108] For the date of the edict, see *EP* 397f.; Watson 1971: 155 n. 6; 1970: 112–13, and 1965: 248. Lenel (*EP* 398 n. 7) had suggested that Plautus *Asin.* 371 (*pugno malam si tibi percussero*, "if I strike your cheek with my fist") might be a comic citation of a formula; the pattern for the formula was: *Quod Auli Agerii pugno mala percussa est* (e.g., *Coll.* 2. 6. 4). The late third-century date is generally accepted and the edict is frequently thought to be due to changes in monetary values which made the fine imposed by the *XII Tables* absurdly low in the mid-Republic: Watson 1971: 155–56, 1970: 112–13, 1965b: 250; Jolowicz and Nicholas 1972: 272–73; Thomas 1976: 369. Birks 1969: 195 accepts the Plautine date but suggests a different origin for the edict (199–201); Birks 1974 offers refinements of his earlier view.

[109] *Coll.* 2. 6. 1 (Paul.); *D.* 47. 10. 7 *pr.* (Ulp.).

aequum iudici videbatur).[110] It is generally thought that all types of physical assault were covered by the edict.[111] Indeed, the pattern for the formula, *Quod Auli Agerii pugno mala percussa est* (e.g., *Coll.* 2. 6. 4: "Whereas Aulus Agerius was struck on the cheek with a fist"), may have been chosen, as Watson has argued, "to show the extreme limit of the action, i.e., that minor physical assaults would also be covered."[112] *A fortiori*, rape would be covered by the *edictum generale.* If a distinction were drawn at the outset between aggravated (*atrox*) and lesser *iniuria*, then rape would have been considered the former; Ulpian cites "the rending of garments" as an obvious example of *atrox iniuria.*[113]

Praetors, however, also issued special edicts to cover related offenses where no blow had been struck, e.g., *convicium* ("publicly vociferated abuse against another"), *adtemptata pudicitia* ("attempts on chastity"), and *infamandi causa facta* ("defamation"). At some point, the *edictum generale* began to absorb the special edicts; indeed, *convicium* and other forms of verbal abuse are certainly witnessed in the late Republic as covered by the *edictum generale.*[114] Whenever this absorption first occurred (and possibly long before), the term *iniuria* might refer either to physical assault or to assault on an individual's personality. Translators of juristic extracts on *iniuria* commonly translate the term as "contumely," "insult," or "affront." The notional range of *iniuria* therefore covers a broad sweep; ancient and modern scholars have frequently compared it with *hubris.*[115]

In the classical delict which is a synthesis of the praetorian wrongs which had been grafted onto the general edict, "contumely" appears to be the common factor: "A component that is common to all *iniuriae* is that it offends against good morals and that it is to someone's interest that it not occur. This edict applies to that *iniuria* which is committed for the sake of contumely" (*Coll.* 2. 5. 2–3, Paul.).[116] To commit *iniuria* "for the sake of contumely" (*contumeliae*

110 *D.* 47. 10. 17.2 (Ulp.); Kaser 1971: 625. See chapter 3.2.

111 Daube 1939: 45–54 dissents and argues that serious injuries did not enter *iniuria* until a later date; against Daube's case, see Watson 1965b: 249–50 and Birks 1969: 202–05.

112 Watson 1965: 249.

113 *D.* 47. 10. 9 *pr.*

114 *Convicium*: *Rhet. ad Her.* 4. 25. 35; verbal abuse of poets onstage: *Rhet. ad Her.* 1. 14. 24; 2. 13. 19. For discussion, see Watson 1965b: 250–52.

115 Labeo cited by Paul. in *Coll.* 2. 5. 1; Hitzig 1899; Daube 1939: 50; Pringsheim 1961: 178–83; Kaser 1971: 624; Watson 1974b: 187 (denying Greek influence).

116 *commune omnibus iniuriis est, quod semper adversus bonos mores fit idque non fieri alicuius interest. hoc edictum ad eam iniuriam pertinet, quae contumeliae causa fit.*

causa) implies intention.[117] While the classical delict is usually thought to have been confined to intentional cases, it is not certain whether praetorian *iniuria* was so restricted at the outset, especially in regard to serious physical assaults.[118] Nonetheless, it is the contumelious and intentional aspects of *iniuria* that permitted seduction and related offenses to be brought beneath its umbrella.[119] Thus Ulpian, citing Labeo:

(1) Labeo says that contumely (*iniuria*) can be perpetrated by act or by words: by act, when an assault is made; by words, there is insult (*convicium*) whenever there is no physical attack.
(2) Every contumely (*iniuria*) is inflicted on the person or relates to one's dignity or involves disgrace. It is to the person when someone is struck; it pertains to dignity when a lady's companion is led astray (*abducitur*); and to disgrace when an attempt is made upon a person's chastity.[120]

Classical jurists do not specifically designate the actual seduction (whether *adulterium* or *stuprum*) of free women as *iniuria*.[121] They do, however, discuss an offense called an "attempt upon chastity" (*pudicitia adtemptata*). Paul defines it: "There is said to be an attempt upon chastity when it is sought to make the virtuous wanton."[122] Ulpian explicates the (same?) offense when he depicts the contumelious accosting of a woman:

[117] E.g., *D.* 47. 10. 3. 1–4 (Ulp.); 9. 2. 5. 3 (Ulp. citing Julian): "Julian therefore says that the action for *iniuriae* does not lie because he did not strike him with the intent to commit an *iniuria* (*quia non faciendae iniuriae causa percusserit*), but in order to correct and teach him"; *h. t.* 41 *pr.* (Ulp.): " . . . it is better to bring an action *in factum* or sue for *iniuria* if he published the secrets of one's legal affairs with the intent to commit an *iniuria (iniuriae faciendae causa)*"; trans. Watson.

[118] Confined to intentional cases: Daube 1939; Watson 1965: 250; possibly not so restricted at the outset: Birks 1969: 203–04.

[119] Treggiari 1991: 309 misleadingly suggests that plaintiffs could sue for damages due to seduction, attempted seduction, and rape under the *lex Aquilia*. That plebiscite, however, provided actions for "wrongful damage to property" (*damnum iniuria datum*), not actions for *iniuria*; see *D.* 9. 2. 5. 1. (Ulp.) for differences between the two. Occasionally, offenses might give rise to both actions. For the *stuprum* of a slave *virgo inmatura*, see n. 121 below.

[120] Trans. Watson. *D.* 47.10. 1. 1–2: *iniuriam autem fieri Labeo ait aut re aut verbis: re, quotiens manus inferuntur: verbis autem, quotiens non manus inferuntur, convicium fit: omnemque iniuriam aut in corpus inferri aut ad dignitatem aut ad infamiam pertinere: in corpus fit, cum quis pulsatur: ad dignitatem, cum comes matronae abducitur: ad infamiam, cum pudicitia adtemptatur.*

[121] *Stuprum* of a slave woman, however, is said to be covered by the *actio*; *D.* 47.10. 25 (Ulp.): "If a female slave be debauched (*stuprum*), the action for insult will lie; and if the wrongdoer conceal the slave or do something else with a view to theft, the action for theft also, or if it be an adolescent maiden (*virginem inmaturam*) who is debauched, there are those who think that an action under the *lex Aquilia* is also competent" (trans. Watson). For plausible if distasteful rationale for Aquilian liability in the case of the stupration of *virgo inmatura*, see Birks 1981: 160–63.

[122] Trans. Watson. *h. t.* 10: *Adtemptari pudicitia dicitur, cum id agitur, ut ex pudico inpudicus fiat.*

If someone accosts (*appellasset*) maidens, even those in slave's garb, his offense is regarded as venial, even more so if the women be in prostitute's dress and not that of a matron. Still if the woman be not in the dress of a matron and someone accost (*appellavit*) her or abduct (*abduxit*) her attendant, he will be liable to the action for insult.[123]

Later in the same chapter, Ulpian (if he has parted from Labeo at this point), defines "accosting" thus: "To accost is with smooth words (*blanda oratione*) to make an attempt upon another's virtue; this is not a shouting (*convicium*), but an attempt contrary to sound morals."[124] Mommsen explains the anomaly – that only attempts at seduction appear to be covered by classical *iniuria* but not their execution – in this way: the Augustan laws that had criminalized *adulterium* and *stuprum* put an end to their coverage under the *actio iniuriarum*; thereafter, only attempts at seduction and the actual *stuprum* of individuals who were not covered by the new legislation remained actionable as *iniuriae.*[125] Seduction and related offenses (e.g., *pudicitia adtemptata*), if committed against a married *filiafamilias* ("daughter-in-power"), might give rise to three separate actions: one brought by her husband, another brought by herself, and still another by her father (47. 10. 1. 9, Ulp. citing Ner.). Seduction is thus envisioned not only as an affront to a wife's *dignitas*, but also to that of her husband and father.

The date of the introduction of the offenses described in the last paragraph (whether as special edicts or as components of the *edictum generale*) cannot be determined; likewise uncertain, as mentioned earlier (n. 118), is whether the intention to insult was essential to the *Tatbestand* of praetorian *iniuria* for serious assaults. Relevant to both these questions is an episode in Terence's *Eunuchus*. Chairea rapes a girl in Thais' establishment before her brother has confirmed her family and Athenian identity. Since the girl's citizen status is not yet established, she has no one at hand to seek redress for her in court; it is left to Thais to represent the girl's interests in private or to find someone (a *patronus*) to represent them in court. The situation is resolved quickly enough between the courtesan and rapist in v 2. Thais remarks to the young man:

[123] Trans. Watson. *h. t.* 15.15: *Si quis virgines appellasset, si tamen ancillari veste vestitas, minus peccare videtur: multo minus, si meretricia veste feminae, non matrum familiarum vestitae fuissent. si igitur non matronali habitu femina fuerit et quis eam appellavit vel ei comitem abduxit, iniuriarum tenetur.*

[124] Trans. Watson. *h. t.*15. 20: *Appellare est blanda oratione alterius pudicitiam adtemptare: hoc enim non est convicium, sed adversus bonos mores adtemptare.*

[125] Mommsen 1899: 792 and 694, n. 1.

non te dignum, Chaerea,
fecisti; nam si ego digna hac contumelia
sum maxime, at tu indignu' qui faceres tamen. (864–66)

You acted unworthily of yourself,
Chaerea; for even if I were especially deserving of this insult,
you nonetheless were unworthy to commit it.

Shortly thereafter Chaerea assures Thais that his violence had not been malevolent:

unum hoc scito, contumeliae
me non fecisse causa, sed amoris. . . (877–78)

know this one thing: no insult
was intended – I acted out of love.

Thais' formulation of Chaerea's conduct as *contumelia*, as an "insult" or "affront," is not so surprising as her formulation that it is an insult to her (no matter that she might be "especially deserving"). Her high-mindedness (momentary – or complicated – as it might be) is indicated by the formulation of her injury as equal to or less than Chaerea's injury to himself: he has betrayed his own *dignitas* by his violent conduct. Equally interesting is Chaerea's response, that he did not act with the intention of insulting. Chaerea's admission of impaired mental state – he had not intended an insult but acted out of love – wins him immediate forgiveness (879). Significantly, he is pardoned before he offers to marry the girl (885–88).

Terence's scenario does not fit the usual one in New Comedy; a rapist's admission of his deed is usually followed by a demand that he marry his victim – unless the rapist makes the offer voluntarily at the moment of confession; certainly no young man is ever forgiven before he makes an offer of marriage (chapter 6. 2). The scenario depicted here, however, accords with Roman notions of (contumelious) *iniuria*. The rape itself is not the subject of Thais' pardon; what is pardoned is Chaerea's affront to Thais' *dignitas* which he has injured by raping her "attendant." Consider the courtesan's statements that immediately follow her formulation of Chaerea's conduct:

neque edepol quid nunc consili capiam scio
de virgine istac: ita conturbasti mihi
rationes omnis, ut eam non possim suis
ita ut aequom fuerat atque ut studui tradere,
ut solidum parerem hoc mi beneficium, Chaerea. (867–71)

By Pollux – now I don't even know what plan to choose
about that maiden – you've so confounded
all my strategies that it's not possible to hand her over to her kinsmen
as it was right and as I was eager to do
that I might win some advantage for myself, Chaerea.

Violation of the girl's virginity has made her unsuitable for identification by her kinsmen. Only Chaerea's ardent desire to marry the girl (885–88) – a surprise to Thais – subsequently resuscitates the courtesan's confidence; the "scene of identification" will go forward. But for the brief interval, from the moment of Thais' discovery of the girl's rape until Chaerea's offer to marry her, the girl's potential citizenship is not to be thought of – hence Thais' treatment of the girl as her "attendant" and of the offense as an affront to her own (Thais') *dignitas*.

In Athens, the rape of a woman, free or slave, could be treated as *hubris*; but a rapist's demonstration of the absence of an intention to outrage may have won him acquittal or a private settlement. In the Menandrian original of Terence's play, it is possible that "Thais" forgave the young man for the rape itself – he had not intended to insult the girl.[126] In Rome, on the other hand, it is possible that praetorian *iniuria* may not have provided that loophole (lack of intention) in the case of serious assaults. But the situation was different, at least in a later age, for a defendant charged with committing an outrage upon a slave that was directed toward the slave's owner: a defendant's demonstration that he had not intended to dishonor the owner may have got him off the hook.[127] Whether or not we think that such an instance of contumelious *iniuria* was a lawful offense at this date, Terence may still have tailored an Athenian defense for *hubris* based on mental disposition (the young man did not intend to outrage the girl) to fit the contours of a defense for conduct (insulting a slave's mistress) that might have been considered contumelious and morally reprehensible, even if not remediable by law.

[126] It is conceivable that the courtesan in the Greek play may have depicted the young man's rape as an act of *hubris* against her "household" (cf. Lys. 1. 25), but that sentiment may have evoked amusement there (cf. *Eun.* 960–61) rather than the (Roman) sympathy conjured here. Cf. Ulpian's expressions as he cites Labeo in *D.* 47. 10. 1. 1–2 (n. 120 above), for the sentiments and values which it projects.

[127] *D.* 47.10.15. 35 (Ulp.). *Stuprum* of a slave could be treated as *iniuria* under the classical delict (n. 121).

3 SYNTHESIS: JUDICIAL AND EXTRA-JUDICIAL REDRESS IN ATHENS AND ROME

There are some broad similarities but also significant differences between the ways in which Athenians of the fourth century and Romans of the middle Republic conceived of and redressed sexual offenses of and against women. We may summarize these as follows:

(1) Both societies consider fornication, adultery, and rape as wrongs.

(2) Athenian law of the fourth century offered more avenues of legal redress than Rome of the middle Republic.

(a) Athenian law provided a *graphe moikheias*. If the law cited in [Dem.] 59. 87 belongs to this *graphe*, then it only enforces penalties against violators of married women. The law, however, is abridged and may have enforced penalties against other offenders (e.g., seducers of *pallakai* and fornicators); there is no conclusive evidence. Athenian law also provided the less specific *graphe hubreos* and *dike biaiōn* which might be used against rapists; the former allowed a death penalty.

(b) Roman law during the middle Republic may only have offered redress for rape; this could be accomplished by a prosecution for *iniuria*. The remedy was not specifically designed against rape, and in this respect resembles the Athenian *graphe hubreos*. Unlike the latter, however, *iniuria* allowed only a monetary penalty. Moreover, praetorian *iniuria* for rape and other serious acts of violence might not have required the alleged offender's intention to insult his victim; there is no certain evidence about this issue. *Iniuria*, at some point, covered seduction and attempted seduction as contumelious offenses (i.e., these offenses will have required the intention to insult); there is no evidence that supplies a date for their introduction under the rubric of *iniuria*.

(3) (a) Athenian law sanctioned the killing of a male offender as justifiable when a man took that offender upon or beside a wife or kinswoman of his household or a *pallake* who was to produce free children.

(b) Roman law or custom in our period appears only to have given *paterfamilias* a right to kill, and that right was limited to the killing of his daughter, not the male offender, by virtue of *vitae necisque potestas*; whether *paterfamilias* was permitted to kill a daughter married *in manu* cannot be determined with certainty (see 5b). Husbands do not seem to have had a lawful right to kill their wives when apprehended *in flagrante delicto*, although they might have done so with *post facto* social approval. There is no evidence that a Roman father ever killed a married daughter or that a husband killed his wife for adultery.

(4) (a) Athenian law or custom allowed other self-help remedies against *moikhoi* as well: physical abuse and the acceptance of monetary compensation. Arrest of a *moikhos* caught in the act might also have been permitted, but there is no conclusive evidence.

(b) Roman custom appears to have allowed the same remedies (excluding arrest) against sexual offenders.

(5) (a) Athenian married women whose *moikhoi* were taken in the act and whose husbands settled privately with their *moikhoi* were left outside of the law's purview. Social norms, however, may have dictated the divorce of a married couple and the exposure of an infant born of the illicit union. There is no evidence beyond the patterns of conduct followed by raped wives and their husbands in New Comedy. The matter appears to have been a private one, determined by husband and wife.

(b) In Rome, a family council composed of husband and kinsmen decided upon the penalty for an adulterated wife. Since the council may have included the wife's father, it is possible that even a father whose daughter was married *in manu* took part in deciding his daughter's fate. Such councils may have evolved through custom. The remedy has no counterpart in Athenian sources.

(c) The singularity of the Roman remedy might stem from differences in divorce in Athenian and Roman law: in Athens, a husband needed no grounds to justify sending his wife away; in Rome of the mid-Republic, penalties may have been imposed upon spouses who divorced without showing due cause.[128] But the difference is undoubtedly more deeply rooted in the different ideological conceptions of women in Athens and Rome and in the different and more extensive

[128] See chapter 7.2.a.ii and n. 72.

power of *paterfamilias* in the Roman family. Symptomatic of these differences is the capacity of a Roman father to emancipate his daughter so that the latter becomes *sui iuris*. The opportunity to become independent *personae* under the law was at hand for Roman women. Possibly, potential for independence was concomitant with a greater recognition of personal responsibility for conduct. Athenian married women, on the other hand, always remained under the guardianship of a male; they remained children, in the eyes of the law.

(6) (a) In practice, rape and seduction of unmarried women may have been settled privately in Athens. Only the arbitration in [Dem.] 59. 71 gives us a glimpse of such an arrangement in the orators.

(b) Comparable reliable evidence is lacking for Rome of the middle Republic.

On the basis of this synthesis, we might expect that Roman playwrights, if called upon to translate scenarios of sexual offense in which the threat of legal redress appeared in the original, will have to summon their creative powers to find an appropriate adaptation. Translation might be easier in treating private remedies against adulterers – these appear to be similar in Athens and Rome; treatment of the adulterated woman, however, will have been different (see items 3 and 5 above). Our major focus in the next chapter, however, will not be so much on the ways that Romans adapted Athenian scenarios of sexual offense, but rather on establishing the pattern of family settlements in Athens, especially in cases of rape. At the end of chapter 3, we asked, was there a Roman *arbiter* in Roman Comedy? Our question for the next chapter has a different focus: by comparing Athenian plays with Roman ones, can we discern a pattern of settlement that is essentially Athenian? The lack of evidence from contemporary Roman sources dictates this decidedly Athenian perspective.

CHAPTER 6

The resolution of seduction and rape in New Comedy

Adultery scenarios appear in only three plays of extant New Comedy: *Amphitruo*, *Bacchides*, and *Miles Gloriosus*.[1] *Amphitruo* is a mythological comedy, the only extant example of an apparently extensive subgenre. It is also the only extant comedy in which an adultery actually takes place: Jupiter, as elsewhere, displays prerogative and prowess. The adulteries of the other two plays are staged affairs – courtesans play the role of seduced *matronae* and so no marital offenses in fact are committed. Adultery, it is clear, is not an activity for mortal citizens, not, as such, a subject to be dramatized on-stage, and not, even when sham, an offense that goes unpunished. Moral lessons are drawn in *Miles*; hear Pyrgopolynices, who never perceives the extent of the deception played upon him, as he makes his final exit:

> *si sic aliis moechis fiat, minus hic moechorum siet,*
> *magi' metuant, minus has res studeant. eamus ad me. plaudite.* (1436–37)

> If other *moechi* suffered this treatment, there would be fewer *moechi* here, they would have more to fear – and less enthusiasm for these affairs. To my place! Applaud!

While sham or divine adulteries can be staged, fornication (*stuprum* in the narrow, juristic sense) probably did not appear in Roman Comedy under any guise, and probably not in Greek New Comedy either.[2] Better to present stories of rape, where girls do not consent.

[1] Three plays were called *Moikhoi* (Ameipsias T 2 and p. 203 K–A; Antiphanes F 159 K–A; and Philemon F 45 K–A); another has the promising title *Adelphai Moikheuomenai* (Alkaios F 1 K–A). Unfortunately, titles and exiguous (if any) fragments of lost plays usually are of little assistance in indicating the type of plot.

[2] The only Roman comedy in which fornication rather than rape may have occurred is *Andria*; the text never specifies whether Pamphilus knew Glycerium's true status (as citizen or courtesan) when he impregnated her. I have chosen not to treat that play as a "rape plot." For explicit statements that refer to the "younger generation rapes" of Roman Comedy, see Plautus *Aul.* 28–30; *Truc.* 812–13; Ter. *Ad.* 308; *Eun.* 645–46, 820, 858; *Hec.* 383. On the

The consequences of the act may have been the same: a shot-gun marriage. Rape provides the more socially acceptable and palatable resolution for drama: it preserves the spiritual innocence of girls and does not provide happy endings for female licentiousness.[3]

This chapter begins with a brief discussion of adultery scenarios. The bulk of the chapter comprises an examination of rape in New Comedy. Issues relating to extra-judicial settlement are the focal point of the first section devoted to rape: (a) the so-called laws of rape and seduction that are occasionally mentioned in Roman plays; (b) the composition of inter-family meetings; and (c) defenses for rapists and seducers. The final two sections of the chapter address the dramatic treatment of rape, first by considering novelties of presentation, and then by setting the treatment of rape in New Comedy against the background of its treatment in tragedy.

I ADULTERY SCENARIOS

1 (a) Self-help remedies

Self-help remedies against the alleged adulterers of *Miles* and *Bacchides* share common ground with Athenian practice.[4] In the last scene of *Miles*, Pyrgopolynices is taken as an adulterer by Periplectomenus who pretends to be the cuckolded husband. Physical abuse is inflicted upon the soldier; a demand for money gives closure to the retribution. In *Bacchides* IV 8, Nicobulus, in the belief that he is rescuing his son from dalliance with death, agrees to pay the sham husband a substantial sum. Afterwards, alone on stage, Nicobulus thanks the slave who presided over the agreement:

nam ni illic hodie forte fortuna hic foret,
miles Mnesilochum cum uxore opprimeret sua
atque optruncaret moechum manufestarium. (916–18)

ambivalent language used in *Samia* and elsewhere in Greek scenarios of sexual violation, see n. 48.

[3] On the moral suitability of Menandrian plays ending in marriages for men returning home to their wives, see Plut. *Mor.* 712C; cf. Xen. *Symp.* 9. 7.

[4] Plautus has indeed Romanized the scenarios (e.g., the pun on *testes* at *Miles* at 1420 and cf. 1416; allusions to castration: see Lowe 1985a); but what he has chosen to represent does not conflict with the way adultery would have been settled in Athens. It might be objected that in *Bacch.*, the soldier's threat to kill both lovers (848–49, 859–60) represents a husband's self-help remedy that has sometimes been attributed to Roman law or custom; but when the soldier utters this threat, he is not yet acting the part designed for him by Chrysalus. He has directed his (lawless) threat against Bacchis as jilting courtesan, not as wayward wife.

> For if he had not by lucky chance been here today,
> the soldier would have taken Mnesilochus with his wife
> and killed the *moechus* in the very act.

A husband's killing of a *moechus manufestarius* was lawfully sanctioned conduct in Athens; it might not have been so in Rome (chapter 5. 2. a). In any event, there is no need to suppose that Nicobulus would ascribe only lawful conduct to the soldier, nor that the latter, in anger at a jilting prostitute (not a wife), would threaten only lawful retaliation.

Only in *Amphitruo* do we glimpse a detail that might suggest a peculiarly Roman treatment of a self-help remedy for adultery. Mercury provides the background for the on-stage action in the prologue (especially 97–115) and in I 2 (479–95): Alcumena is pregnant both by her husband Amphitruo and by Jupiter; the latter had assumed the guise of Amphitruo for his encounters with the faithful wife. When the play begins, Amphitruo has just returned from a long but victorious war against the Teloboeans; Jupiter, however, had arrived the day before in the guise of returning hero, dined with Alcumena, and then spent a pleasurable and extended night with her. When the real Amphitruo greets his wife in II 2 and is puzzled by an anti-climactic reception, she explains: she has just spent the night with him and knows all about his victory. Amphitruo suspects the worst: *perii miser, / quia pudicitiae huiius vitium me hinc apsente est additum* ("I'm a lost wretch! An encroachment upon her chastity has occurred in my absence!" 810–11); he himself had dined shipboard at Port Persicus (823). The case will have to be investigated: *mulier, istanc rem inquisitam certum est non amittere* ("Wife, my decision is made: the investigation of this affair is to go forward!" 847). Amphitruo then proposes to bring Naucrates, Alcumena's own relative (*tuom cognatum*, 849) to testify that the two men had been on ship together the preceding night; if he does so testify, Amphitruo asks, *numquid caussam dicis quin te hoc multem matrimonio*? ("you can't specify any reason, can you, why I shouldn't penalize you with divorce?" 852).

The summons to Alcumena's relative – rather than to any other fellow voyager – is important. A domestic tribunal is thus proposed, with divorce as the penalty upon Alcumena's "conviction." The remedy is Roman, not Greek. The search for the dinner companion provides dramatic motivation for Amphitruo's absence from the stage during Jupiter's return visit in III 1; accordingly, the search probably belonged to the Greek original. Details, however, may be Plautine adaptation or addition. In the Greek original, the husband's fellow diner might have been any boon companion; his identity or relationship would make no difference to the establishment of fact – nor to the husband's next move – if that were foreseen at this point: according to Athenian practice, he needs no kinsman present to effect a divorce (chapter 5, n. 69). The hypothesized changes need only have been slight: alteration from "any boon companion" to Alcumena's kinsman (unless a kinsman did appear in the Greek play), and the formulation of divorce as a penalty to be imposed after the tribunal has met and established the facts. The changes do not affect the plot: in IV 1, Amphitruo returns to the stage; his search has been futile; Naucrates was neither aboard ship nor anywhere in the city. Had not portions of Act IV been transmitted in tatters, we might better perceive a corresponding scene of redress against the adulterer: Jupiter pretending he is husband captures Amphitruo (with comic bluff) "in the act" at the same time as Amphitruo, the real but weaker husband, captures Jupiter "after the act."

1 (b) Adultery and fornication: the double standard for men and women

A double standard is evident in both the Athenian and Roman conceptions of adultery and fornication.[5] Even a brief examination demonstrates the difficulty of isolating Greek and Roman details when that dubious standard is articulated in Roman Comedy. In both societies, a man, whether married or unmarried, is penalized only if he engages in sexual relations with a woman who is a citizen and not a prostitute. Citizen women have no such institutionalized loophole for pleasure – apparently, a social rather than legal sanction: we hear of no Athenian or Roman brothels catering to a female clientele, no socially acceptable institution wherein a woman might hire a "*pallakos*" for any short or long period of time – in addition to or in lieu of a husband. Euripidean women sometimes complain of the inequity; hear Klytaimestra in *Elektra*, after recalling that Agamemnon brought a concubine into their house:

[5] Treggiari 1991: 199–200 briefly treats the appearance of the double standard in the Greek philosophical tradition, with due attention to the strand of thought that ran counter to it. She traces in more detail Roman expressions of the attitude in pp. 299–319.

μῶρον μὲν οὖν γυναῖκες, οὐκ ἄλλως λέγω·
ὅταν δ', ὑπόντος τοῦδ', ἁμαρτάνηι πόσις
τἄνδον παρώσας λέκτρα, μιμεῖσθαι θέλει
γυνὴ τὸν ἄνδρα χἄτερον κτᾶσθαι φίλον.
κἄπειτ' ἐν ἡμῖν ὁ ψόγος λαμπρύνεται,
οἱ δ' αἴτιοι τῶνδ' οὐ κλύουσ' ἄνδρες κακῶς. (1035–40)

Yes, women are a foolish lot; I don't deny it.
But when a spouse goes astray – for this is natural –
and spurns his own bed, a wife is quite ready
to mimic her husband and acquire another friend.
Then reproach puts us in the limelight
while guilty husbands keep their fair reputations.

Similar complaint is found in a fragment of Plautus' elder contemporary, Naevius: *desubito famam tollunt si quam solam videre in via* ("If men see some lone woman in the street, at once they destroy her reputation"). The fragment comes from a tragedy, *Danae* (F VI Ribbeck), based on a Greek original. The complaint is dressed up with a proposal for legal reform in *Mercator*. An old slave woman (Syra) addresses the audience after her mistress' husband (Lysimachus) has brought a slave courtesan home:

Ecastor lege dura vivont mulieres
multoque iniquiore miserae quam viri.
nam si vir scortum duxit clam uxorem suam,
id si rescivit uxor, inpunest viro;
uxor virum si clam domo egressa est foras,
viro fit caussa, exigitur matrumonio.
utinam lex esset eadem quae uxori est viro:
nam uxor contenta est quae bona est uno viro:
qui minu' vir una uxore contentus siet?
ecastor faxim, si itidem plectantur viri,
si quis clam uxorem duxerit scortum suam,
ut illae exiguntur quae in se culpam commerent,
plures viri sint vidui quam nunc mulieres. (817–29)

Women live under a harsh law and suffer far more inequity than men. For if a wife discovers that her husband has secretly enjoyed a whore, husband gets off scot-free; but if wife once sets foot outdoors without her husband's knowledge, husband has grounds for divorce. Would that the law ruling wife were the same for husband! For a good wife is content with one husband: why should a husband be less content with one wife? If husbands who secretly go whoring were punished in the same way as guilty wives, I'm sure there would be more ex-husbands than there are now ex-wives.

At the end of the play, after the *flagitatio* in which the guilty husband (Demipho) has been heaped with abuse for his lascivious conduct toward the courtesan (see chapter 4.3), Eutychus remains on stage to frame a law that would punish such culprits (1015–24). Another double standard is proposed: only men aged sixty and over are to be penalized; young men are to be permitted their whoring, provided that it be "in good measure" (*quod bono fiat modo*, 1022).

The "double standard," castigated in one passage (817–29) and redefined in the other (1015–24), is easily transferable from one society to the other; the texts might be based on the Greek original – or they might be Plautine elaborations.[6] Syra speaks of a woman's suspicious behavior as grounds for divorce (822). She may be speaking loosely: while grounds for divorce may not have been required in Rome at this time, penalties may have existed for "divorce without due cause."[7] In a Roman husband's mind, a wife's outdoor excursion is equivalent to adultery. In Athens, neither husband nor wife needs grounds for divorce – but a husband might very well divorce a wife on the suspicion of adultery (chapter 7, nn. 58–59). Husbands in either society, of course, may walk in daylight to a brothel.

So Syra complains. The acceptance of female prostitution as a legitimate activity creates an automatic imbalance: every extra-marital affair for a woman is adultery, but only one type of extra-marital affair is adulterous for a man. Two points are of interest in regard to New Comedy: first, the genre depicts only the legitimate extra-marital affairs of mortal men; secondly, it by and large treats the affairs of married men with prostitutes and courtesans in an unfavorable light.[8] Young married men who consort with prostitutes or courtesans bring disharmony and instability into their marital homes and the homes of their in-laws (e.g., *Epitr.*, *Hec.*); those on the

[6] Contra Leo 1912: 119–22. Leo argued that Plautus was working closely with his Greek model here (Philemon *Emporos*, cf. *Merc.* prol. 9) which in turn was heavily influenced by Euripides. None of his arguments is conclusive.

[7] The formulation is Watson's (1967: 55); see further, chapter 7.2.ii, at nn. 72–76. Syra's speech is usually treated from a legal viewpoint, with attention focused on verse 822 ("husbands have grounds for divorce"). The question is raised, is the divorce envisioned in accordance with Athenian or Roman law, and if the latter, is it in accord with marriages *in manu* or not *in manu*? For discussion and relevant bibliography, see Treggiari 1991: 462–63; McDonnell 1983: 57–59; Watson 1967: 54–55. The range of answers that have been given to these questions (esp. to the second one) suggests that the passage and its context are too vague for definitive answer.

[8] Similarly, Treggiari 1991: 463 on the second point.

verge of marriage who still consort thus imperil their betrothals (*Andria*).[9] Old men who play the part of young gallants are depicted as lascivious fools (*Asin.*, *Bacch.*, *Cas.*, *Merc.*, *Stich.*); even those merely suspected of such exploits might be treated to abuse (*Merc.* 784–802; 923–26, *Rud.* 1045–47).[10] Marriage is idealized as exclusive partnership; the double standard, once a marriage is planned or has taken place, is rarely maintained. Eutychus' proposal for reform in fact represents the status quo of New Comedy.

2 THE RESOLUTION OF RAPE IN NEW COMEDY

Rape plots were popular in New Comedy. They challenged playwrights to generate new riffs on a very old melody. Two limitations have been made on the type of rape plot considered here. First, discussion is limited to comedies in which recent rapes affect the current younger generation; comedies in which the dramatic background is shaped by a rape that occurred in an older woman's youth have been excluded.[11] Secondly, within the pool of "younger generation rapes," one type has been excluded: those in which the rapist is discovered to be the young man to whom the young woman is now

9 The response of the *senex* in *Men.* v 2 to his daughter's complaints about her husband's dalliance with a prostitute (787–806) is unusual: she should allow him free rein, provided he do no wrong (such as stealing her belongings to give to the prostitute). For discussion of the wide range of Greek and Roman comedies in which prostitutes play a role, see esp. Brown 1990.

10 Cf. Moskhion's reported advice to his adoptive father in *Samia* 19–28: he should withdraw from competition with younger rivals and establish his beloved *hetaira* in a stable relationship at home. For the depiction of the Plautine "lecherous old man," see chapter 7, n. 23.

11 E.g., in Men. *Heros*, *Sunaristōsai*, and possibly in *Hiereia* (Gomme and Sandbach 1973: 695), *Georgos* (Arnott 1979: 105), and *Phasma* (Gomme and Sandbach 1973: 683–75); Plautus *Cist.* and *Epid.*; Ter. *Ph.* In *Heros*, Myrrhine unwittingly is married to her rapist (*hypothesis* 3, cf. verse 79). At the end of *Hiereia*, the priestess marries the man who (presumably) raped her in her youth (supplemented summary, *POxy* 1235; Sandbach OCT p. 305). The remains of *Phasma* are too fragmentary to trace out the subsequent relationship of rapist and victim. In *Cist.* (based on Men. *Sunaristōsai*), the Lemnian merchant Demipho has returned to Sicyon and married the woman he had raped years ago (177–79, 620). In *Epid.*, there is no such subsequent marriage between Philippa and Periphanes – although the latter is contemplating one (167–73); the Greek original is unknown. If Demipho is to be believed in *Ph.* (1018–19), Chremes had raped a girl years ago in Lemnos and did not marry her; if Phormio is to be believed, he was married to the Lemnian and his Attic wife at the same time (1005). Usually the "older generation rapes" form the background to the plays in which they occur; had these rapes been compensated immediately in the form of a marriage between acknowledged rapist and victim, there would be no comedy: the children of uncertain origins – rather than their parents – suffer the complications of status which become the subject matter of these New Comedy plots.

married (i.e., she was raped before marriage: Menander *Epitrepontes* and Terence *Hecyra*). Once the discovery is made that rapist and victim are husband and wife, there is no demand for compensation – the couple are married already and will remain so (see chapter 7.2.b.ii). That leaves us with the comedies in which rapes are resolved by a special type of arbitration scenario, an informal meeting between members of the two families affected by the rape (Menander *Samia*, and *Fabula Incerta;* Plautus *Aulularia* and *Truculentus*; Terence *Eunuchus* and *Adelphoe*).[12] The "inter-family meetings" in these plays differ from the more formalized (Athenian) private arbitrations and reconciliations that were discussed in chapters 3 and 4: there is no agreed upon third party mediator or panel of mediators; there are no set formulae, e.g., of "referring the matter to arbitration" or for declaring a willingness "to abide by the terms." The opposing parties, members of rapist's family and victim's family, make the agreement between themselves: the young man will marry the girl. Lawsuits are explicitly presented as alternatives in *Adelphoe* and *Truculentus.*

The impulse for marriage, although in some cases intensified by avowals of the rapist's love and made critical by the birth of an infant, is the righting of a wrong. Consider Micio's words to the victim's guardian in *Adelphoe*, after he has agreed to the marriage of his adoptive son to the destitute girl: *meum officium facio, quod peccatum a nobis ortumst corrigo* (593: "I am doing my duty when I correct a wrong that originated on our side"). Or Lyconides' words to Euclio in *Aulularia*: *qui homo culpam admisit in se, nullust tam parvi preti / quin pudeat, quin purget sese* (790–91: "no man who has incurred blame on his side is so worthless that he will not feel shame, that he will not atone for it"). The compensatory aspect of the scenario differentiates it from a less complicated betrothal. The crux of the issue is the actual or potential birth of an illegitimate infant – birth is always foreseen as a consequence of the violation.[13] But the marriage is

12 Younger generation rapes also occur in Menander *Heros* and *Georgos*; in the former, an older woman had also been raped in her youth, and this may be true of the older woman in the latter play as well. Unfortunately, the plays are too fragmentary to allow for reconstruction of the rape scenarios.

13 The actual birth of the infant is not a prerequisite of the rape scenario. Moskhion in *Fab. Inc.* had married a girl "willingly, not by force"; rape can be inferred, but not a ten-month interval. (It is difficult to make sense of the scenario that opens the fragmentary play and to discern how much of the sham story pertains to events that actually took place.) Phaedria is forgiven his offense in *Eun.* on the same day he committed it. Aeschines in *Ad.* was forgiven by the girl's mother when he became sober and offered marriage. The birth of an infant,

required not only to legitimize the infant by providing it with identifiable and acknowledging parents, but also to rescue the imperilled reputation of the citizen girl and her family. One young man, worried about an intruder's interest in his half-sister, explains the grounds of his concern, "For if [she] should fall into any shameful trouble (*aiskhunei tini*), this becomes a [rebuke] to me as well. For the outsider does not know the man responsible – [whoever] it was – only the consequence" (*Dusk.* 243–46: ἂν γὰρ αἰσχύνηι τινὶ / αὕτη] περιπέσηι, τοῦτο κἀμοὶ γίνεται / ὄνειδο]ς. ὁ γὰρ ἔξωθεν οὐ τὸν αἴτιον / ὅστις] πότ' ἐστιν οἶδεν, ἀλλὰ τὸ γεγονός). One father sums up the wrong resulting from his daughter's rape as, "We were treated unjustly" (*Fab. Inc.* 28, ἠδικήμεθα). A young man in another play, slow to inform his father of his violation of the girl next door, is quickly reminded by his slave, "But what about the girl whom you've injured (ἠδίκηκας) – and her mother?" (*Samia* 67–68). Another young man confesses to the father of the raped girl in this way, "If I without thinking injured (*inprudens peccavi*) you or your daughter" (*Aul.* 792). Marriage, then, rectifies a wrong against a girl and her family, a wrong which, while committed in the past, has foreseeable and devastating consequences for the future. It makes no difference to the compensatory nature of the scenario that the young rapist might have been in love with the girl before he violated her, nor that he fell in love with her afterwards (as appears to be the case in *Adelphoe*). Nor does it make any difference that young rapists (with the possible exception of Diniarchus in *Truculentus*) show no reluctance to marry, even though "they have to."[14] Compulsion to carry out an act can coexist with ardent desire to do so. The young rapists, usually willingly, concede they have done wrong and then right that wrong by offering or agreeing to marry.

The scenario, as argued in the last chapter (5.1.c), is Athenian. Designation of the informal encounters as "inter-family meetings" is meant to distinguish them from the more formalized "family council" (*iudicium domesticum*) of Roman sources and Roman juristic

then, does not control the decision to marry; but the potential birth, and the feeling that a wrong was committed, do.

14 Cf. Brown 1993: 189, on *Aul.* and *Ad.*: "In both cases, the young man who deflowered the girl loves her and is keen to marry her; there is no suggestion that he agrees to marry her reluctantly because he has to."

scholarship.[15] While the mode of settlement might also have been used at Rome, there is no contemporary evidence to confirm that thesis – apart from Roman comedies based on Greek originals. On the other hand, the existence of a similar practice there might help to explain why adaptation of the rape scenario seems, for the most part, to occur with such fluidity.

2 (a) *Patterns of settlement: the "laws" of rape and seduction in New Comedy*

"Laws" that compel a man to marry a woman are cited in Roman Comedy at *Aulularia* 793 and *Andria* 780–81 and are implied at *Adelphoe* 490. In *Aulularia*, Lyconides, the young man who had raped the citizen girl, beseeches her father Euclio:

ut mi ignoscas eamque uxorem mihi des, ut leges iubent. (793)

forgive me and bestow her as my wife, as the laws bid.

In the *Andria*, Davos and Mysis have this exchange within the hearing of Chremes, the father of the girl who has just given birth (Chremes is still unaware that the new mother is his long-lost daughter):

DA. . . . *iam susurrari audio*
civem Atticam esse hanc. CH. hem. DA. "coactus legibus
eam uxorem ducet." (779–81)

DA. . . . Now I hear it being whispered about
that she is an Athenian citizen. CH. What! DA. "Compelled by the laws
he will take her as his wife."

In *Adelphoe*, Hegio, who is acting as protector of the poor fatherless girl whom Aeschinus has raped, says to the latter's natural father as the girl cries out labor shrieks from off-stage:

quod vos vis cogit id voluntate impetret. (490)[16]

Let her obtain by good will what force compels you to grant.

15 Cf., e.g., Düll 1943: 54: "Im neueren Schrifttum hat sich die technische Bezeichnung 'iudicium domesticum' eingebürgert zur Kennzeichnung des Richteramtes, das der pater familias über seine Gewaltunterworfenen, über sämtliche Angehörige seiner Familie, die Personen, welche in seiner manus und in seiner patria potestas standen, ausüben durfte." On the Roman family council, see chapter 5.2.a.

16 Confusion over the meaning of *vis* ("force") in v. 490 is evident in the codices (*Parisinus* = *P* and *Ambrosianus* = *F*) which have "corrected" original readings (*ius* from *vis* in *P* and *vis* from *ius* in *F*); Donatus comments that *vis* here means the "force of the laws" (*vis legum*). Fredershausen 1912: 211 n. 2, while favoring *ius*, compares Men. *Fab. Inc.* 47, discussed in the text above.

That a lawsuit (and not simply physical force) is implied is signalled by the legal language used in the speech (e.g. *experiar*, "I shall go to court," 497; cf. 350).[17]

The precise circumstances under which the "laws" compel marriage are not specified. In all three instances, however, an unmarried citizen girl has just given birth. Nothing is said or implied in the comic laws about the manner in which the girl conceived: rape and seduction equally fit the scenario. The "laws" appear to be concerned not with the penalizing of the doers of the deed but rather with providing a legitimate marriage for the unwed mother and identifiable paternity and legitimacy for the infant.

The "laws" cited by Plautus and Terence cannot be considered authentic: there is no earlier or contemporary evidence for such "laws" in Athens or Rome outside of these Roman plays.[18] Our task therefore is a speculative one, to consider why the marriage of violator and violated is viewed as "compelled by the laws." One explanation might be based on a comparison with a Menandrian fragment. In *Fabula Incerta*, Kleainetos (?) describes a young man's conduct after he allegedly had raped a citizen girl: [ἔλαβ]' ἐθελοντής, οὐ βίαι (47: "[He married the girl] willingly, not by compulsion"). What "compulsion" is envisioned? Athenian law did not compel marriage between rapist and victim; rather, the law might sanction a self-help remedy against the rapist who was caught in the act, or it might penalize a rapist if the girl's *kurios* brought a *dike biaiōn* or if *ho boulomenos* brought a *graphe hubreos* against him and won the case. Accordingly, the "compulsion" mentioned in the Menandrian verse might be understood in this way: the girl's father had no need to threaten the offender with lawful avenues of redress (i.e., he had no need to use "compulsion") in order to obtain a satisfactory settlement; the young man of his own accord offered to marry the girl.

17 See the detailed discussion of the passage in chapter 2.4.

18 There is no evidence of specific legal remedies for the non-flagrant fornication of unmarried women in Athens (chapter 5, n. 46) except for a law ascribed to Solon that was certainly not in operation in the fourth century (n. 67 below). Possibly such cases might be redressed by a *graphe hubreos* there or by an action for *iniuriae* in Rome (see text at chapter 5, nn. 57–59 and 119–25). In the case of rape, there is no evidence that any law compelled marriage between rapist and victim. "Laws" similar to the comic ones appear in Greek and Roman rhetorical exercises of the early empire and late antiquity. The historical basis of the cases elaborated by the rhetoricians is too difficult to discern given their remoteness from the fourth century BC and the possibility that the cases may evolve from earlier fictive treatments (e.g., from New Comedy) rather than from real legal and social circumstances. So Frederhausen 1912: 212 and Paoli 1976 (= 1950): 295–97.

Such an interpretation might explain the *vis* that appears in *Adelphoe* 490 and possibly the *leges* of *Andria* 780–81: the young man in Roman Comedy who is compelled by force (*vis*) or laws (*leges*) to marry a violated girl is compelled by his fear of undergoing trial and suffering a lawful penalty. Density of expression, however, becomes nonsense in *Aulularia*: Lyconides asks Euclio to obey these laws!

A different explanation emerges, however, from the evidence cited in chapter 5 (e.g., the terms of the reconciliation in [Dem.] 59 *Neaira* 71) as well as from the evidence discussed below (the regularity of the appearance of inter-family meetings in comedies of rape). On the basis of these sources, we can infer that there was a strong social requirement for bringing sexual offenders to account for their wrongs; courtroom trials could be replaced by informal meetings between the father of the rapist or seducer and the father or *kurios* of the girl; marriage or a monetary settlement might be the outcome of such family meetings. It is conceivable, then, that allusions to "laws" compelling marriage in Roman Comedy reflect the regularity of the outcome (marriage) of inter-family meetings portrayed in Athenian originals; the "laws" alluded to by the Roman playwrights will be the Roman perception of the customary way rape and the seduction of unmarried women were treated in fourth-century Athens (via New Comedy). Marriage may usually have been the consequence of inter-family meetings; to Roman eyes, "laws" must have been responsible for the regularity of this result.[19]

2 (b) *Participants in inter-family meetings*

The presence of the young man's father and the girl's father or *kurios* appears to be the norm for the scenario of settlement, but the plays demonstrate a variety of substitutes. Occasionally the rapist's father is replaced by the rapist himself, but when this happens, there is usually some excuse for the father's absence: e.g., in *Aulularia*, he is dead and in *Truculentus*, Diniarchus' father might be dead since he is nowhere mentioned.[20] Usually one or two meetings between family members precede the final agreement to a marriage or the confirmation of one already executed; often one father or *kurios* is absent from

[19] Similarly Fredershausen 1912: 212–13.

[20] Daube 1939: 35 n. 42 suggests that the sequence of *Truc.* 834–36 might indicate that Diniarchus is thought of as *sui iuris*; Diniarchus confesses that he is *obnoxius* ("legally liable"), whereupon Callicles summons him to court.

the earlier meetings and his presence is required for the final one.[21] In two plays, a mother first meets with the rapist and the latter promises marriage: in *Samia*, the girl's father is out of town; in *Adelphoe*, he is dead. The girl's father in the former play consents to the marriage upon his return and her guardian arranges for it in the latter – but only after meeting first with the rapist's natural father and then with his adoptive one. In *Eunuchus*, a mother-substitute (?), Thais, meets with the rapist first; he promises marriage before the final meeting between his father and the girl's brother. In two plays, an "injured" fiancé meets with the rapist or his father and withdraws from the intended marriage; then the victim's father meets with the offending party (*Fab. Inc.* and *Aul.*). The path to settlement thus operates, sometimes slowly, through secretive family networks and culminates in a final meeting that brings closure (marriage) to the scenario.

The participants in the meetings in our group of plays are as follows:

(1) *Samia*: (a) Girl's mother meets with rapist who promises marriage before the play's beginning; fathers are away on business (50–53). (b) Girl's father (Nikeratos) meets with rapist's adoptive father (Demeas) on-stage.

(2) *Fabula Incerta*: (a) Girl's father (? Kleainetos) met with rapist (Moskhion) in the past and the latter married his victim. (b) Girl's husband or fiancé (Khaireas) meets with rapist's father (Lakhes) on-stage (Khaireas is masquerading in order to win Lakhes' acceptance of his son's marriage).[22] (c) Girl's father meets with rapist's father to confirm the marriage.

(3) *Aulularia*: (a) Girl's fiancé (Megadorus) meets with rapist (Lyconides) and his mother off-stage. (b) Girl's father (Euclio) meets with rapist (Lyconides) on-stage.

(4) *Truculentus*: Girl's father (Callicles) meets with rapist (Diniarchus) on-stage.

(5) *Adelphoe*: (a) Girl's mother meets with rapist who promises

[21] On the need for parental consent for marriages in Athens and Rome, see chapter 8, n. 37.

[22] The text is ambiguous in regard to Khaireas' role. Possibly he pretends to be betrothed when he asks what excuse is he to give to those who gave her away (τοῖς δὲ δοῦσι τίνα λόγον / ἐρῶ, Λάχης; 18–19). Gomme and Sandbach 1973: 686 apud v. 18, however, think it more probable that Khaireas pretends to be married on the grounds that "a prospective husband would have every reason for repudiating a prospective bride on discovering that she was not a virgin and could bear a child that might or might not be his," whereas the rape of a married woman "would be a misfortune that they both must share." The rationale is not overly persuasive: a married man might still divorce a raped wife.

marriage before the play's beginning (334–35, 471–73). (b) Girl's indefinite *cognatus* (Hegio) meets with rapist's natural father (Demea) on-stage (in the Menandrian original, "Hegio" was maternal – possibly paternal – uncle, and probably *kurios* of the girl; see App. 5, add. 8). (c) Girl's indefinite *cognatus* meets with rapist's adoptive father (Micio) off-stage.

(6) *Eunuchus*: (a) Girl's unrelated friend (the courtesan Thais) meets with rapist (Chaerea) on-stage. (b) Girl's brother (Chremes) meets with rapist and his father off-stage.

Of interest is the participation of a girl's fiancé in the reconciliation of a rape. In *Aulularia* and possibly in *Fabula Incerta*, the young rapist or his father fears retaliatory measures from the fiancé (Megadorus in the former, Khaireas in the latter). Does a betrothed man have legal capacity to seek compensation in behalf of his fiancée in Athens?[23] Unfortunately, neither scenario provides an answer. Khaireas receives a new fiancée from the rapist's father and wins the latter's agreement to his son's marriage to the victim – but we do not know whether Khaireas pretends to be betrothed or married when he makes the arrangements. Megadorus withdraws from his betrothal, apparently without exacting any penalty at all – despite his nephew's fear for his life (*Aul.* 700). Probably Lyconides had imagined an illicit retaliatory action – a betrothed man in Rome would have no lawful right to exact a self-help remedy against the violator of his betrothed, and the *actio iniuriarum*, even if available to betrothed men, did not carry a death penalty.[24] If the young man

[23] It is difficult to determine at what point a man becomes *kurios* of his wife. While a husband is *kurios* of his wife when they cohabit after *engue* (betrothal or "pledging"), is he *kurios* in the interval between *engue* and *sunoikein* (marital cohabitation)? The cases of Demosthenes' mother and sister unfortunately do not supply answers: the orator's mother was "pledged" to Aphobos while her husband was still alive and his sister was "pledged" to Demophon for a marriage to take place in ten years' time (Dem. 27. 4–5; 28. 15–16; and 29. 43); in neither case did the fiancé carry out the marriage. Apparently, the two men, together with Therippides, acted as guardians (*epitropoi*) rather than *kurioi*, and neglectful ones at that. On the other hand, legal effects pertaining to dowry begin to operate as soon as the dowry is paid; the recipients of dowry must provide for the sustenance of the pledged women (Dem. 27. 17 and cf. 15). This suggests that the betrothed man is *kurios*. But whether such *kurieia* extended beyond obligations arising out of dowry, e.g., to acting as *kurios* in court to seek compensation for a sexual violation, remains obscure.

[24] *D.* 47. 10. 15. 24 (Ulp.): *Sponsum quoque ad iniuriarum actionem admittendum puto: etenim spectat ad contumeliam eius iniuria, quaecumque sponsae eius fiat* ("I think that a fiancé also should be able to bring the action for insult; for there is an outrage to him in any affront that his betrothed may suffer" trans. Watson). Of course, we do not know whether any fiancé ever tried to bring an action under these circumstances, nor whether a similar view about the correctness of such conduct would have been expressed by anyone in the second century BC; Ulpian's "*puto*" might in any case signify an idiosyncratic view.

had expressed a similar fear for his life in the Greek original, his uncle would not need to be *kurios* of the girl in order to bring a *graphe* for *hubris* against the rapist – and a death penalty might be sought. Eunomia's parting words to Lyconides might then have had a specific reference in the Greek original: *et caussa iusta est, siquidem ita est ut praedicas, / te eam compressisse vinolentum virginem* (*Aul.* 688–89: "moreover, your case is a just one, if indeed it is as you assert, that you violated the girl while drunk"). She might, in effect, be assuring her son that his uncle cannot (or will not) bring a charge of *hubris*. A defense based on the young offender's lack of intention to insult – he had been drunk when he raped the girl – will win him forgiveness.

2 (c) *Mental disposition and culpability in defenses for* hubris *and rape*

The young rapists of New Comedy frequently plead in their defense that they did not intend their deed; they acted out of love, or drunkenness, or youthful impetuosity. Their arguments have a definite forensic context: establishing the presence or absence of a defendant's intention to injure played an important role in a number of Athenian laws. The laws on homicide, for example, distinguished between homicides that were intentional (*hekon*) and those that were not (*akon*).[25] A person accused of intentional homicide was tried by the council on the Areopagos; the penalty upon conviction was death. A person accused of unintentional homicide was tried by the *ephetai* at the Palladion; if he was convicted, he was exiled.[26] A person who was sued for damage (*dike blabes*) was liable to pay simple compensation if the damage was unintentional, but double that amount if it were intentional.[27] A similar subjective requirement of "intentionality" was hypothesized as the basis for the double penalty for "violent acts" (*biaia*) in the last chapter (at n. 62). The *nomos hubreos* that has been transmitted to us does not define what *hubris* is;

25 *Hekon* and *akon* (often translated as "intentional" and "unintentional," or "deliberate" and "accidental," or "voluntary" and "involuntary," or "willing" and "unwilling") are slippery terms; for a thorough examination of pre-fourth-century *hekon* words, see Rickert 1989; for examination of the concept of intention in (mostly) Athenian law, see Maschke 1926; in the specific context of homicide, see Gagarin 1981: 30–37 with bibliographic references.

26 *IG* i^3 104; Dem. 21. 43; 23. 53 and 71; Arist. *M.M.* 1188b 29–38; MacDowell 1963: 117–25 and 1978: 113–18.

27 Dem. 21. 43 (paraphrase). MacDowell 1990: 253 thinks that in Dem. 23. 50, "a phrase quoted from a law evidently refers to this distinction" (i.e., between intentional and unintentional damage); the phrase in question is: ἄν τις καταβλάψηι τινὰ ἑκὼν ἀδίκως. For discussion of the double penalty for the *dike blabes*, see MacDowell 1978: 149–53.

the offense, however, is thought by many scholars to have included a subjective element; the *hubristes* was a person who not only attacked or abused another, he also aimed at dishonoring his victim (chapter 5.1.b). In *hubris*, the doer's intention may not have been an explicit part of the offense, but as a subjective criterion it may have become a means of denying culpability after the prosecution established that the objective elements of the offense had been fulfilled.[28]

The defenses reported in the orators of those accused of *hubris* resemble the defenses made by or in behalf of the rapists of New Comedy. Forensic speakers use various arguments such as intoxication to prove the absence of intention. When these are used to deny culpability (as in cases of *hubris*), we might call them "exculpatory arguments"; such arguments look to the verdict on the offense. The very same arguments, however, might be used by defendants who are seeking a mitigated penalty after they have been convicted; these might be called "arguments of mitigation."[29] Whereas, properly speaking, "exculpatory arguments" belong to the first round of speeches in *agones timetoi* (trials in which the penalty is determined by the dikasts) and "arguments of mitigation" belong to the second (i.e., the penalty speeches), both become entwined in the first round, i.e., in the type of speech we find in the extant forensic corpus.[30] Dem. 54 *Konon*, the plaintiff's speech in a trial for assault (*aikeia*), offers an example. So far as we know, *aikeia* required only the fulfillment of an objective criterion for conviction: the plaintiff must establish that the defendant was the first to strike.[31] The plaintiff of our speech claims that the defendant, together with his son and another young man, had beaten him one evening in the agora (7–9). As he proceeds, he anticipates his opponent's argument; Konon will say:

that there are many in the city, sons of decent men, who, in the sporting fashion of young men, give themselves nicknames such as the *Ithuphalloi* and the *Autolekuthoi*, and that some of these lust after courtesans, and, in particular, that his son is one of these, and that he has often given or received blows because of a courtesan, and that such conduct is to be expected of young men. (14)

[28] This formulation is borrowed from D. Cohen 1983: 86–91 who draws a distinction between liability and culpability in cases of theft.

[29] Dorjahn 1930 treats all excuses as "extenuating circumstances" under the following rubrics: "anger and various passions," "intoxication," "poverty and physical infirmity," "ignorance and blunder," "occasion of offense and status of offender," "relationship," "first offense and recidivism," "purpose or intent."

[30] See chapter 1, n. 100 for the two sets of speeches.

[31] See chapter 2, n. 103 for references.

While we do not have Konon's defense, it seems plausible, even on the basis of this tendentious abstract, that Konon may have tried to claim that it was not he who was responsible for the attack, but rather his son, that the fight was not in fact unprovoked, but was a mere tussle over a courtesan, and that all this sort of behavior is exactly what one expects of young men – too trivial, really, to warrant a hearing before a dikasterion.[32] Ariston's response to the alleged defense is full of indignation. Konon's conduct, so he claims, is inexcusable; had Konon been a young man, the situation would be different: his drunken attack could be considered grounds not for escaping punishment entirely, but for mitigating it (cc. 21–22). The speaker thus imputes to his adversary the use of an inappropriate defense: even if Konon's version of events were true, his excuses would not be exculpatory but only applicable to a request for a less severe penalty.

Another speech shows how similar pleas might be used as exculpatory arguments. In Dem. 21 *Meid.*, Demosthenes prosecutes Meidias for unjust treatment during a festival, on the specific grounds that Meidias struck him while he was *khoregos* ("chorus producer") attending a festival.[33] The orator, in his attempt to prove that Meidias' aggression was intentional, appears to have advance knowledge once again of the arguments that his opponent will use in his defense (25, 36). The alleged argument that concerns us is Meidias' use of precedents to justify his conduct (36–41). The defendant, Demosthenes claims, will furnish a list of victims of insolence who subsequently dropped their charges and settled in private with their attackers:

> for example, the proedros who is said to have been hit by Polyzelos at a meeting of the Ekklesia, and the thesmothetes who was hit recently when removing the woman piper, and some men of that sort. He assumes that, if he shows that many other men have been victims of many serious incidents, you will be less angry at what has been done to me. (36)[34]

To refute Meidias' alleged defense, Demosthenes first states a

[32] Cf. Carey and Reid 1985: 70–73.

[33] Whether the speech was actually delivered is a matter of debate. MacDowell 1990: 23–28 concludes that we do not possess enough evidence to answer the question. For vigorous objections to that view, see E. M. Harris 1989.

[34] Trans. MacDowell 1990. Cf. *Rhet. pros Alex.* 7.1429 a 11 ff.: "If you must admit [having done the deed], liken your action as best you can to the habits of the multitude of men, saying that most men, indeed all men, do this and such like even as it happens to have been done by you."

general reason why it is for the common good to punish offenders (an argument on the effectiveness of deterrence) and then points out that Meidias' case lacks the grounds for forbearance (*sungnōme*) that had been present in the other cases:

> First, the man who hit the thesmothetes had three excuses: drink, love, and inability to recognize him because the incident happened at night and in the dark. Secondly, Polyzelos, from anger and impetuosity of character, acted without thinking and struck by mistake; for he wasn't on hostile terms, and didn't intend his action to be insolent. But Meidias can't say any of these things. He was hostile; he acted insolently in daylight, knowing who I was; and it's clear that he was deliberately insolent to me not only on this but on all occasions. (38)[35]

While Demosthenes represents the private settlements of the earlier cases as flagrant breaches of the court system (indeed it suits his own case to do so) and insinuates that bribery was involved, yet he carefully demonstrates why those cases could be treated this way and why his case against Meidias should not: the distinguishing criterion is the presence of Meidias' intention.

On the basis of these and other examples from Demosthenes, we can make the following observations about the use of arguments concerning the absence of intention in cases of *hubris* and related charges such as *aikeia* (assault):

(1) Mitigating factors and subjective grounds for acquittal are, in practice, interchangeable in forensic argumentation, even if their juridical role in fact differs. Youthful folly, for example, might be pleaded to trivialize an offense in an attempt to win acquittal ("illicitly") in a case of *aikeia* where subjective criteria do not pertain to the verdict (Dem. 54. 14), or the same grounds might be used (more legitimately) in the same case to win a mitigated penalty (Dem. 54. 21–22).

(2) The absence of the intention to insult might be claimed on the basis of a disturbed state of mind brought about by love, drunkenness, anger, and ignorance arising out of external factors such as the darkness of night (Dem. 21. 38, 180).

(3) A defense based on the absence of intention must be persuasive; an assertion of intoxication will not automatically win acquittal (Dem. 21. 180); premeditation might have to be discounted – i.e., the alleged insult was not motivated by a long-standing relation-

[35] Trans. MacDowell 1990. Chapters 38–42 and 38–41 are obelized in two tenth-century mss. There is no reason, however, to doubt their authenticity; see MacDowell 1990: 47–48.

ship of hostility or rivalry but was a momentary eruption caused by intoxication or ignorance.[36]

(4) Absence of intention might be acceptable as the basis for a private agreement before a case came to court (Dem. 21. 39).

Designation of an act as intentional or unintentional is often accompanied by a classification of that act either as an injustice deserving punishment or as a mistake deserving pardon (e.g., Dem. 21. 38). Systematizations of injuries into a triad consisting of mishaps (*atukhemata*), mistakes (*hamartemata*), and injustices (*adikemata*) appear as early as the sophist Gorgias and are codified as forensic topoi in *Rhet. pros Alex.*[37] Demosthenes himself adduces the classification as one that is generally known in 18. 274–75:

Among all the rest of mankind I see that such matters are divided up and arranged in a certain way. Someone intentionally commits an unjust act (*adikei tis hekōn*); anger and punishment are his. Someone unintentionally has made a mistake (*exemarte tis akōn*); forbearance (*sungnōme*) instead of punishment is his. Someone neither commits an unjust act nor makes a mistake, but, having devoted himself to a course of action that everyone thinks is advantageous – he fails along with everyone else. It is not right to reproach such a man, nor even to rail at him, but to grieve along with him. All these matters are manifest thus not only in the laws (*en tois nomois*), but also nature herself has defined [them] in unwritten customs (*tois agraphois nomimois*) and in the morality of mankind (*tois anthropinois ethesin*).

The classification is not part of a lawcode, but is a commonplace of litigants and appears widely in other genres of Athenian literature. Litigants frequently plug their own offenses or those of their

36 In Dem. 21. 180, the orator instances one Ktesikles who had been convicted of committing an offense during a festival: "Why was this? Because he had a whip in the procession, and with this, being drunk, he struck a man who was on bad terms with him. It was thought that it was insolence, not wine, which prompted him to strike, and that he made the procession and his intoxication the excuse for his offense, treating free men as slaves" (trans. MacDowell 1990). Instances such as these have led some scholars to suppose that not only intention, but premeditation as well, was a requirement for *hubris* (see Maschke 1926: 113).

37 Gorgias *Helen* 15 and 19; *Rhet. pros Alex.* 1427 a1–1427 b1, 1428 b38 ff., 1429 a11 ff., 1444 a 7 ff. For discussion of the classification in fifth and fourth-century texts, see Bremer 1969: 40–64; for philosophic issues involved in the classification in a wide range of texts, see esp. Sorabji 1980. Daube 1969: 131–56 compares the Greek classification with Roman standards of liability: *dolus* ("evil intent"), *culpa* ("negligence"), and *casus* ("accident"). Daube thinks the Roman triad does not represent "a simple transfer into Roman law of a ready-made Greek classification" (156); while there may be some influence, the Roman classification is distinct from the Greek one: the root of the former is "in civil law, concerned with compensation, rather than in criminal law or, more narrowly, the law of homicide, concerned with retribution" (151).

opponents into the system, to their advantage. Philosophers use the classification as a device to define ethical conduct. Characters in tragedy and comedy apply it in ordinary usage to depict the rightness or wrongness of their conduct or that of others. The classification frequently appears in contexts descriptive of hubristic acts. In New Comedy, it is often adduced in contexts of sexual violation and assault. A plea of intoxication (usually) wins the young offender pardon or a mitigated penalty – the act was unintentional, a "mistake." Acceptance of such a defense endorses the same attitudes that appear operative in Demosthenes' orations concerning *hubris* and assault. Before we examine instances in New Comedy bearing upon sexual violations, it will be instructive to consider a few dissenting voices.

A fragment from Philippides (F 27 K-A), a poet of New Comedy who wrote in the late fourth and early third centuries, is of particular interest because it concerns the types of offense (assault and outrage) which have been the major subject of discussion so far:

> οὐκ ἔστιν 'ἐμεθύσθην, πάτερ' λεγοντα, _
> 'ἥμαρτον', †ὥστε πρὸς σέ μετ† συγγνώμης τυχεῖν.
> ὁ γὰρ εἰς τὸν ἀσθενῆ βίαι τι, Πάμφιλε,
> ποιῶν ὑβρίζειν, οὐχ ἁμαρτάνειν δοκεῖ.

> It is not a case of saying, "I was drunk, Father," _
> "I made a mistake," † . . . . † to win forbearance.
> For a person who offers violence of any kind to a defenseless man
> seems to commit an outrage, not a mistake.

Intoxication may be grounds for pardon in some types of assault, the speaker suggests, but not when the victim is without strength to fight back; that removes the offense from the realm of forgivable mistakes and defines it as an outrage (*hubris*), which we are to infer is an unforgivable act. The speaker of the fragment dissents from the hegemonic view that intoxication deprives an act of its intentional quality – even in a case where there may have been no premeditation.

The loudest voice of dissent is Aristotle's. The classification of injuries is a topic of much creative reflection in the philosopher's ethical works.[38] In *NE* 3. 1 and 5, Aristotle distinguishes between

[38] Esp. *NE* 3.1–5, 5.8, and *EE* 2. 6–11; also *Rhet.* 1.13.1374b4–10. The development of Aristotle's thought on the matter is beyond the scope of this chapter. For important discussions of the place of negligence in Aristotle's theory, see Daube 1969: 131–56; Schofield 1973: 66–70; Sorabji 1980: 278–81 and 292–93, following the work of Maschke 1926. Barigazzi 1965: 135–60 attempts to show Peripatetic influence on Menander by an

acts committed through ignorance (δι' ἄγνοιαν πράττειν) and acts committed while a man is in a condition of ignorance (τὸ ἀγνοοῦντα ποιεῖν). The difference lies in the responsibility of the actor: if the cause of his ignorance lies outside himself (e.g., he kills a man by administering a drug, intending to save his life), the act is not intentional and the actor has committed a pardonable mistake; but if the actor is responsible for his own ignorance, then the act is an intentional one.[39] His conclusions, Aristotle says, are attested by private individuals and lawgivers: "For they punish and exact redress from those doing wicked acts, except those who act through force or through ignorance for which they are not the cause (ὅσοι μὴ βίαι ἢ δι' ἄγνοιαν ἧς μὴ αὐτοὶ αἴτιοι), and they honor those who act nobly, to encourage the latter and deter the former . . . " (*NE* 3. 5. 1113b 23–26). He then cites particular instances from penal law codes:

> For in fact they [the law-givers] provide punishment for the individual [committing offenses] in a condition of ignorance (ἐπ' αὐτῶι τῶι ἀγνοεῖν); for example, the punishment is doubled in the case of men who are drunk, for the origin [of the cause of ignorance] is in the man himself since it is within his power to avoid drunkenness and this is the cause of his ignorance . . . And similarly, too, in other cases where men seem to be ignorant because of negligence (δι' ἀμέλειαν), on the ground that their not being ignorant was dependent on them – for they are in control of their heedfulness. (*NE* 3.5. 1113b 30–33; 1114a 1–3)[40]

Since a man could avoid intoxication and therefore avoid the condition of ignorance that might attend his drunkenness (e.g., he might "forget" that it is not right to fulfill a desire for sexual intercourse with any woman whom he sees and finds appealing), he is doubly penalized for offenses he might commit in this condition. He is the cause of his own drunkenness. In the case of offenses committed while drunk, Aristotle, it seems, would favor little – if any – forbearance.

Aristotle's view is at odds with the usual treatment of intoxication in New Comedy – and possibly with tragedy as well. In a fragment of a drama that has been attributed to Euripides' *Auge*, the speaker says:

analysis of the classification in Aristotle and comparison with *agnoia*, *hekousion*, *prohairesis*, and *sungnōme* in the playwright.

39 *NE* 3. 1.1110b 24–25; 3.5.1113b 19–21.

40 We know from *Rhet.* 2.1402b, *Pol.* 2.1274b 19, and Diog. Laert. 1. 76 that the lawgiver to whom Aristotle refers is Pittakos, the tyrant of Mytilene – i.e., his example is not Athenian.

νοῦ δ' οἶνος ἐξέστησέ μ'· ὁμολογῶ δέ σε
ἀδικεῖν, τὸ δ' ἀδίκημ' ἐγένετ' οὐχ ἑκούσιον (fr. 265 Nauck[2])

Wine drove me out of my senses; I admit that my offense to you
is unjust, but the injustice was not intentional.

The speaker is probably Herakles and the offense is rape. If we follow Webster's reconstruction of the plot (which follows the hypothesis of Moses Chorenensis), then Herakles' admission is made to Auge's father. What Herakles appears to achieve is not only pardon for himself (which might be taken for granted), but a mitigation of Auge's punishment: "instead of death Auge was now to be cast adrift with Telephos in a chest."[41]

When an inter-family meeting determines the fate of a young man who has raped a virgin in New Comedy, drunkenness and sometimes love are offered as excuses; they will win the young man forgiveness and an extra-judicial settlement (a compensatory marriage rather than a dikastic penalty). We have already discussed the surprising formulation of Chaerea's rape in *Eunuchus* as an act of contumely against the courtesan in whose house the victim lives; Thais had pardoned the young man upon being assured that he had intended no insult (*contumelia*) but had acted out of love (877–88; see chapter 5.2.b). Eunomia tells her rapist son in *Aulularia* IV 7:

et caussa iusta est, siquidem ita est ut praedicas,
te eam compressisse vinolentum virginem. (688–89)

moreover, your case is a just one, if indeed it is as you assert,
that you violated the girl while drunk.

Lyconides will escape punishment at the hands of the girl's fiancé because he had been drunk when he raped her; his offense was not intentional and so is pardonable. The scenario is played again in *Adelphoe.* Hegio, protector of the impoverished family of the raped girl, tries to obtain the support of the rapist's (natural) father before he takes the case to court:

persuasit nox amor vinum adulescentia:
humanumst. ubi scit factum, ad matrem virginis
venit ipsus ultro lacrumans orans obsecrans
fidem dans, iurans se illam ducturum domum.
ignotumst tacitumst creditumst . . . (470–74)

41 Webster 1967: 240. Wilamowitz 1875: 189, while attributing the fragment to Euripides, thought it might possibly be the "fourth play" in a tetralogy.

night love wine youth impelled him –
it's human. When he knew what happened, to the girl's mother
he himself of his own accord went, crying praying beseeching
promising swearing that he would marry her.
There was forgiveness, there was a hush-up, there was trust . . .

The rape itself was understandable, Hegio argues, because of the conditions under which it took place; Aeschinus promised marriage and pardon followed. What is not excusable is that Aeschinus has now carried off a kithara player and abandoned the violated girl. The law's compulsion will have to be applied unless some pressure can be brought to bear upon the young man to execute his former promise voluntarily (490, see section a above and chapter 2.4).

In the three Roman plays, the young men are pardoned (or will be) because they intended no injury. Lack of intention in *Adelphoe*, for example, clears the young man's character and makes possible the particular form of "mitigated compensation." Had the young man been sober and cool-headed at the time of the rape, had he been a ruthless and plotting rapist, there would have been no pardon, certainly no marriage, surely a lawsuit – or private financial arrangements. The inter-family meeting is simultaneously a resolution of rape and a betrothal; marriage is the compensation designed to right a wrong.

A common thread that unites these passages from comedy is that the young man's sexual conduct must be viewed as aberrant behavior – it was usually caused by *vinum* or *amor* or by *vinum* in conjunction with the additional factors *amor*, *nox*, and *adulescentia*. Violence, however, is not a regular feature of the young man's character. The rape is thus an admitted fact, but the young man is not a "rapist".[42] The character of these young men is, in general,

[42] The ethical position adumbrated here is similar to (but not identical with) Aristotle's at *NE* 5. 5.1134a 1ff.; after he has argued that "justice is the quality according to which the just man is said to bring about by deliberate choice (*kata prohairesin*) the just thing," Aristotle poses a question, the point of which is to indicate that an unjust act must be a consequence of the doer's deliberate choice if it is to render the doer, and not simply the act, unjust: "Since it is possible for a man who is not yet unjust to do injustice, what are the unjust actions the doing of which makes a person *eo ipso* unjust in respect to each sort of injustice, as in the case of a *moikhos* or a thief? Or will he not differ in the sorts of act? For in fact a man could have intercourse with a woman, knowing who she is, but not from the rule of deliberate choice (*dia prohaireseos arkhen*) but because of passion (*dia pathos*). True, he acts unjustly, but is not unjust; e.g., he is not a thief, though he committed theft, not a *moikhos*, though *emoikheuse*." Aristotle appears to have replaced the more common exculpatory factor, intoxication – which, in his view, is unpardonable – with the plea of passion, which, under some circumstances, is.

preserved; they will be fit husbands for their wives.[43] Even in comedies in which the dramatic situation does not involve the rapist defending himself or an advocate who pleads for him during an inter-family meeting, the playwright usually lets the audience know that the rape occurred when the young man was drunk.[44] Onesimos in *Epitrepontes* mentions Kharisios' drunken state twice (first to Suros at 407, and then to Habrotonon at 472). Bacchis in *Hecyra* informs the audience in a monologue that Pamphilus was *vini plenus* ("full of wine," 823) when he raped the girl who later married him. Demipho in *Phormio* explains to Nausistrata that her husband had been drunk when he raped a girl in Lemnos fifteen years ago (1017); no need that we believe him – only that we see him as trying to make his brother's offense an excusable one. The prologue speaker (*Auxilium*) of *Cistellaria* informs the audience that Demipho had been *vinulentus* (159) when he raped Phanostrata many years ago. The plea of drunkenness in all these cases except *Phormio* is aimed at no one but the audience: it, too, must be assured that the rapist, now married to his victim, is essentially a good person worthy of his wife; he had acted out of character when he committed the offense. The acceptance of drunkenness as a plea worthy of pardon in cases of rape is thoroughly engrained in the society inhabited by fourth-century theater-goers. The habit of forgiving an unintentional, unpremeditated offense which was committed while intoxicated explains the brevity for the defense in New Comedy; what might appear to us as a mechanical lifesaver is the enucleation of socially sanctioned conduct. There is no need to pipe the whole tune when the melody is so well known.

Plautus, not surprisingly, disrupts that melody twice. Lyconides had exited with his mother's assurance in *Aul.* IV 7 that his uncle (the girl's fiancé) would pardon him since he had acted while drunk (688–89). Successful in his off-stage meeting with Megadorus, the young man now meets with the girl's father (IV 10) and presumably applies the same arguments that had been efficacious just moments

[43] The exception is Diniarchus; see section 3.b of this chapter.

[44] Exceptional is *Samia*: Moskhion in his opening monologue mentions the circumstances of the impregnation of Plangon (38–51) and makes no mention of any inducement from wine – although the circumstances of the women's night-time dancing during the celebration of Adonis and the noise that kept him sleepless are duly recorded. Odd, too, is *Epidicus* IV 1, the scene in which Philippa and Periphanes encounter each other for the first time since the former was raped (540: *comprimere*) by the latter many years ago; but Periphanes evinces a poverty of memory here, and possibly he has forgotten the circumstances (see Scafuro 1990: 150 and n. 49).

before. Lyconides confesses: he is the author of the outrage (*istuc facinus . . . id ego feci et fateor*, 733–34); a god impelled him (*deu' mihi impulsor fuit*, 737); he admits the wrong and knows he merits blame (*fateor peccavisse <me> et me culpam commeritum scio*, 738); he begs forgiveness (739); he had acted under the influence of drink and love (*vini vitio atque amoris feci*, 745). All the while, Euclio has remained under the false impression that the young man's *facinus* is the theft of his pot of gold. On the admission of intoxication, he erupts with rage, "Boldest man of all, daring to come to me with such a plea, scoundrel!" (745–46). He continues:

nam si istuc ius est ut tu istuc excusare possies,
luci claro deripiamus aurum matronis palam,
postid si prehensi simus, excusemus ebrios
nos fecisse amoris caussa. nimi' vilest vinum atque amor,
si ebrio atque amanti inpune facere quod lubeat licet. (747–51)

For if the law is such that you can excuse yourself this way,
we could snatch a woman's golden jewelry openly in broad daylight;
upon apprehension, we could say by way of excuse, "we were drunk,
we acted out of love." Wine and love are far too cheap
if it's permissible for drunken lovers to do what pleases with impunity.

Later the young man will realize Euclio's source of error and specify his offense. Again he begs forgiveness; he asks to marry the girl "as the laws bid" and confesses outright:

ego me iniuriam fecisse filiae fateor tuae
Cereris vigiliis per vinum atque impulsu adulescentiae. (794–95)

I admit that I injured your daughter during the night time
celebration of Ceres –
wine and the impulse of youth drove me.

Euclio is not entirely won over by Lyconides; he delays pardon until he can confirm the young man's story (800–02); indeed, this is the first time he has heard of his daughter's violation – and the birth of a grandson. Unfortunately, the play's ending is fragmentary and we do not know precisely how Euclio articulated his consent to the marriage. But the prologue, in any case, had assured the audience at the outset that the marriage between rapist and victim would take place (33). In the meantime, at the end of Act IV, Lyconides sighs with relief, safe shores are at hand (803).

Euclio's diatribe against wine and love as excuses is probably Plautine addition. It overthrows the expectations created by Eunomia's assurances (688–89) and by her brother's pardon – and it plays with the conventions of the genre. The diatribe is the lengthiest speech in a scene of very short speeches – and the text shows clear signs of Plautus' insertion. Lyconides' response at 754–55 connects backwards to 740 or 744; thus:

> *EUC. qur id ausu's facere ut id quod non tuom esset tangeres?* (740)
> . . . *EUC. quid tibi ergo meam me invito tactiost?* (744)
> *LY. ergo quia sum tangere ausus, hau causificor quin eam*
> *ego habeam potissumum.* (755–56)

> EUC.: Why did you dare to touch what was not yours?
> . . . EUC.: Why then did you touch what was mine without my permission?
> LY.: Well, then, since I dared to touch, I make no objection to keeping it for good.

The interplay of theft and rape, the mistaking of one offense for the other, the dialogue at cross-purposes, underpins the humor of most of the scene and can be ascribed to the Greek model. The highpoint, however, is reached in Euclio's diatribe (745–54) – and this unfolds in the interval between the question (740, 744) and retort (755–56) quoted directly above. Plautus has extended the transmitted motif (the equation of theft and rape) and here depicts a miser so miserly that he can imagine (even as an absurdity) a thief trying to exonerate himself by offering the excuse, "I acted out of love" (cf. 750). Euclio's hypothetical juristic scenario in 747–50 is, in a word, brilliant – and in keeping with other examples of his aptitude for (somewhat absurd) legal reasoning in passages that are arguably Plautus' invention.[45] His rationale is analogical: acceptance of the young man's excuses (for the theft of his pot of gold, so Euclio thinks) would be equivalent to accepting the same excuses for "snatching a woman's golden jewelry in broad daylight." The analogy, if interpreted metaphorically, precisely describes Lyconides' deed – save for the circumstance of broad daylight: the young man has indeed "snatched a woman's golden jewelry."[46] Euclio thus rejects excuses in the case of literal theft or metaphorical rape which he will (presumably) end up accepting in a specific case of actual rape. We might conjecture that, at play's conclusion, the miser becomes more humane – or in any case, more Greek.

[45] *Aul.* 318–19, 415–17, 457–58, 465–69 (see App. 5, cat. nos. I. 1, III. 7, and VI. 1).
[46] Cf. *Ad.* 345–46: Sostrata metaphorically depicts her daughter's loss of virginity as the loss of her only dowry.

In *Truculentus* IV 3, another angry father has a similar angry response. In 826ff, Diniarchus asks forgiveness from the father of the girl he had raped – a girl to whom he had formerly been betrothed, but for whom, for reasons never told us in the comedy, the wedding had been cancelled:

> *CA. ubi is homost quem dicis? DI. adsum, Callicles. per te opsecro*
> *genua ut tu istuc insipienter factum sapienter feras*
> *mihique ignoscas quod animi inpos vini vitio fecerim.*
> *CA. non placet: in mutum culpam confers <qui non> quit loqui.*
> *nam vinum si fabulari possit se defenderet.*
> *non vinum <viris> moderari, sed viri vino solent,*
> *qui quidem probi sunt; verum qui inprobust si quasi bibit*
> *sive adeo caret temeto, tamen ab ingenio inprobust.*
> *DI. scio equidem quae nolo multa mi audienda ob noxiam.*
> *ego tibi me obnoxium esse fateor culpae compotem.* (826–35)

CA.: Where is the man whom you name? DI.: I am here, Callicles. I beseech you by your knees, that you bear wisely what was done foolishly and forgive me what I did bereft of reason through the fault of wine. CA.: It is not right to confer blame on a mute thing that cannot speak. For if wine could tell stories, it would defend itself. Wine ought not to control men, but men wine – at least, respectable men. But a worthless man – whether drinker or teetotaler – nevertheless is worthless by nature. DI.: I know I must hear a great many things I don't want to, because of my guilt. I confess that I am liable to you, the party at fault.

While Euclio's response had played with the conventions of New Comedy, Callicles' disrupts it entirely. There may be a legal pun in 834–35: *noxia* in 834 may carry overtones of "liability," as *obnoxium* in 835 seems to suggest. If so, then Diniarchus' response is also exceptional: he attributes his act to drunkenness just as rapists do in other comedies; but he not only admits the commission of the offense, he also accepts liability (*ob noxiam* and *obnoxium*, 834–35). Drunkenness does not pardon him. Callicles follows up the admission with a summons to court (840). Diniarchus responds with a request that Callicles be praetor – he will marry the girl (840–41). The angry father exacts a penalty: "But I shall fine you this choice chunk of fortune: / I shall subtract six hefty talents from her dowry because of that stupidity of yours" (*pro ista inscitia*, 844–45). True, Callicles will give his daughter to Diniarchus and not charge him in court; but the penalty he exacts is a severe one – presumably, the subtracted six talents had been part of the dowry he had promised Diniarchus before the earlier engagement had been broken. The exaction of a penalty sets Callicles apart from other fathers and guardians of New Comedy. That he explicitly exacts it *pro ista inscitia* (Aristotle's "acting in a condition of ignorance" for which the agent is responsible?) might suggest an Aristotelian context; but the punitive measure might also be perceived as mimicry of an injured (Roman) husband who retains fractions of a dowry for his wife's adultery upon divorce.[47]

The two Plautine passages thus run counter to the general pattern observable in New Comedy. Possibly Euclio's and Callicles' responses typify a Roman and less indulgent attitude toward drinking wine; possibly they point toward a Roman intolerance of "lack of intention" as an exculpatory plea in serious offenses. But they are also flagrant flauntings of New Comedy convention, the introduction of the unexpected.

3 NEW RIFFS ON OLD MELODIES: DRAMATIZING THE RESOLUTION OF RAPE AND SEDUCTION

While the pattern of settlement and cast of characters are broadly similar in the group of plays under discussion here, playwrights vary the scenario, especially in regard to the position it holds in the overall structure of the play. Here our attention will be not so much on the mechanics of settlement as on the playwright's dramatic treatment of the scenario. Two will be discussed, one in *Samia*, the other in *Truculentus*.

3 (a) Samia

Samia dramatizes responses to two sexual acts, one which is mistakenly thought to have occurred (Moskhion's seduction of his adoptive father's Samian *pallake*, Khrusis), another which in fact took place (Moskhion's violation of Nikeratos' daughter, Plangon). The alleged offense plays as much a dramatic role in the comedy as the real one; Demeas must come to terms with the former just as Nikeratos subsequently must come to terms with the latter. The dramatic action of the play is accordingly structured to present the fathers' parallel responses to the "offenses" of one man's son. Interpretation of Menander's treatment of the actual offense there-

[47] See chapter 7, nn. 75–76.

fore requires interpretation of its parallel, the alleged seduction. Before we examine these, it should be pointed out that Moskhion's violation of Plangon is always spoken of in a neutral way: it is designated neither as rape (there is no talk of violence) nor as seduction (there is no mention of persuasion).[48] A stronger case can perhaps be made for rape: first, rape rather than seduction is conventional in New Comedy; secondly, in this play, it is most often Moskhion who speaks of his act, and he, like Kharisios in *Epitrepontes* (891, 895–899, 915), is circumspect in reporting its details. Nonetheless, other characters in the latter play had filled in the picture. We shall return to this point after our examination of the "offenses."

In Act III, Demeas has seen Khrusis lift a new-born infant to her breast. He has been told that the infant is his. But moments before seeing her take up the infant, he overheard Moskhion's childhood nurse address it as Moskhion's. His slave Parmenon then admits the infant's paternity as a fact – it is Moskhion's. Demeas is now under the mistaken impression that his son has cuckolded him and that his *pallake* has produced a *nothos*. Whether Moskhion's alleged offense could be characterized as *moikheia* and lawfully redressed as such is impossible to say;[49] Demeas seems ready to view the wrong as an act of *hubris* against himself and Nikeratos certainly treats it this way in the next act.[50] Demeas' dilemma is not an easy one to solve: whom should he blame – Khrusis, Moskhion, both? The playwright has sharpened the intellectual contours of the dilemma by the nature of the relationships of the alleged offenders to Demeas: Khrusis is not a wife, but a foreign *pallake*, not a woman whom Demeas has chosen to marry in order to produce legitimate children for his *oikos*, but a woman he has chosen as a companion for his exclusive pleasure (25–26); moreover, Moskhion is not a natural son, but an adopted one, not a son whom social norms might have constrained Demeas

[48] See esp. 3 (cf. 646), 47–48, 68 (mother and daughter both included as victims of wrong), 477–79, 485–87 (where the reference might be to the consequences of the sexual act, the production of an infant outside of wedlock, rather than to the act itself, rape or seduction), 528–29, 590–91, 601–08 (cf. 485–87). Menander and his characters do not make the nature of the act explicit in this play; the phenomenon is not uncommon elsewhere in Greek literature. The ambiguity of articulation suggests that the nature of the act (consensual or forced) was often not so significant (from the perspective of Greek writers at least) as were the consequences of the deed, the production of an infant outside of marriage.

[49] See chapter 5.1.b and n. 46.

[50] (NI.) ἀνδράποδ[ον εἶ, Δημέα./ εἰ γὰρ ἐμὸν ἤι[σχυνε λέ]κτρον, οὐκ ἂν εἰς ἄλλον ποτὲ/ ὕβρισ' οὐδ' ἡ συγ[κλ]ιθεῖσα· (506–08: NI.: You're a slave, Demeas. For if he shamed my bed, he would never outrage another – nor would his bedmate.)

to bring up, but one he has chosen of his own will to integrate into his *oikos*.[51] Has Demeas made two bad choices? His solution to the dilemma, we can be sure, will be a highly rationalized one, befitting a man accustomed to making distinctive decisions.

Demeas sides with his son:

> οὐδὲν γὰρ ἀδικεῖ Μοσχίων σε. παράβολος
> ὁ λάγος ἴσως ἐστ', ἄνδρες, ἀλλ' ἀληθινός. (329–30)
>
> For Moskhion does you no injustice. An extraordinary argument, gentlemen, but nevertheless true.

The words are part of a monologue; the address to "gentlemen" (*andres*), directed to the audience of spectators, carries overtones of an address to dikasts. The speaker proceeds to exonerate Moskhion of any guilt: "if he had acted willingly (*boulomenos*), or from lust, or in hatred of me, he would still be bold and ready to battle me. But as it is, his defense holds up (*apolelogetai*) – he happily accepted the marriage I suggested to him" (330–35). Moskhion, of course, has not offered any defense for his activity; it is Demeas who is creating it now, interpreting his son's motives for accepting without complaint the marriage arranged for him with a neighbor's daughter: "For it wasn't out of love [*sc.* "for Plangon"], as I thought then, that he was keen for it [i.e., the marriage with Plangon], but because he wants to flee at last that Helen of mine from within my house. For she is responsible for what has happened. Obviously she caught him when he was drinking, when he wasn't in control of himself. Strong wine and youth work much foolishness when a man finds himself near someone who has contrived a plot with these accomplices" (335–42).[52] Demeas thus attributes the greater part of the blame to Khrusis – and a lesser part to Moskhion's intoxication and youthful age. Demeas' leniency toward his son is based on a belief in his character: "For in no way can I be persuaded that he who is so well-behaved and temperate toward everyone could behave in such a way to me . . ." (342–45). Of course Demeas' interpretation of Moskhion's motives is all wrong – he was never intimate with Khrusis; the infant's mother is the girl whom Moskhion is now engaged to marry. But the forensically disposed characters of New Comedy often

[51] For other views concerning Menander's decision to make Moskhion an adopted son, see Gomme and Sandbach 1973: 544.

[52] I follow Gomme and Sandbach 1973 on 340–42 for the interpretation and translation of 340–42.

err in their rational inferences (compare, e.g., Simo in *Andria* I I), in their stitching pieces of evidence together without looking at the whole fabric, without cross-examining that most important witness, the alleged criminal, the son – in Demeas' case – an ideal son who slips once when tipsy and is then forced into intimacy by a Helen-like concubine. Moskhion's conduct was a temporary aberrance; his character remains blameless. The Aristotelian program of *epieikeia* appears to be in operation – even though Aristotle would not have permitted its application in this particular case: "And [it is *epieikes*] to have regard not for . . . the deed but for the moral choice and not for the part but for the whole, and not for what sort a person is now, but for what sort he always or usually was" (*Rhet.* 1374b and cf. n. 42).

Demeas' anger is directed elsewhere: he sees conspiracy in his household (308, 317, 456); he threatens to whip and brand one slave (321, 323) and to beat another to tears (440); he rushes into his house like a madman, shouting (361–64, 415). The major target of his anger, however, is Khrusis – he sends her from the house and essentially "divorces" her.[53] Moskhion's subsequent confession to his father paves the way toward restoration of that relationship:

> οὐχ ἑκὼν λέγω μέν, ἀλλὰ μείζον' αἰτίαν φυγὼν
> λαμβάνω μικράν, ἐὰν σὺ τὸ γεγονὸς πύθηι σαφῶς. (526–27)

> I don't want to speak out, but I shall avoid the greater blame
> and accept the lesser one, if you learn what happened clearly.

Moskhion's violation of Plangon is less blameable than violation of

[53] Insofar as there exists a "technical terminology" for the informal act of divorce in Athens (chapter 7.2.a.i), Demeas does not use it during the scene in which he expels Khrusis from his house (369–98). Nor should we expect him to follow a "script" for divorce when he is expelling a *pallake*. Nevertheless, it is of interest that Khrusis (408) uses the verb *ekballein* (literally, "to cast out"), which is commonly used when a man initiates the divorce of his wife, to describe what Demeas has done. Moreover, Demeas as he expels her, tells her to keep her own things and an old woman (373); she has her own possessions, he says, and he'll give her some slave women in addition (381–82). Gomme and Sandbach 1973 ad loc. comment that "her own possessions" will mean "any clothes and jewelry that she had brought with her and gifts she had received from Demeas"; such items belonging to a bride are "often enumerated alongside her dowry, e.g. Dem. 17. 13 (*sic*: 27. 13?), 41. 27 and would be taken away by her if she were later divorced." The lot of a free woman in an informal relationship undergoing a "divorce" may in fact have been much better than that of a slave *pallake* in similar circumstances: cf. the treatment allegedly accorded the *pallake* of Philoneos in Ant. I. 14: he planned to place her in a brothel. Possibly a *graphe hubreos* was brought against the man who put a free Olynthian woman in a brothel (Dein. *Dem.* 23) – but we do not know whether she had been his *pallake*. For different interpretation of the Menandrian scene, see Konstan 1993: 142.

his father's *pallake* would be – not because it was less grievous in and of itself, but because it was remediable: while the former can be righted by a marriage that is about to take place, the alleged intimacy with Khrusis can cause only irreparable rupture to the relationship between Khrusis and Demeas and acute difficulty between Demeas and the young man. Moskhion's confession of paternity is thus articulated at a critical juncture in the relationship between father and son. The confession has immediate effects: Demeas will be able to accept Khrusis into his household once again, and Moskhion will have his father's assistance in reconciling Nikeratos. Upon Demeas' subsequent success in stifling Nikeratos' anger and in ensuring that the marriage between Moskhion and Plangon will go forward, he sighs with relief:

. . . . - - -χάριν δὲ πολλὴν πᾶσι τοῖς θεοῖς ἔχω
οὐθὲν εὑρηκὼς ἀληθὲς ὧν τότ' ᾤιμην γεγονέναι. (614–15)

. . . . - - - I heartily thank all the gods
since I have discovered that nothing I thought had happened is true.

Demeas' efforts in his son's behalf have stemmed less from a concern to right the wrong to the violated girl than from a concern to right the wrong to the son he has violated by misconstruing his conduct (cf. 537–38: οὐδὲν ἀδικεῖς Μοσχίων <μ'>· ἐγὼ δέ σε/ ὑπονοῶν τοιαῦτα, "Moskhion, it's not at all you who injure me, but I injured you by suspecting such offenses").

Nikeratos' reaction to Moskhion's alleged offense is also violent. He tells Demeas what he would do if he were the "cuckolded husband": he would sell his *pallake*, disown his son, and prosecute him for murder (507–13). When Nikeratos learns the true situation, that Moskhion has fathered the infant upon Plangon, his reaction is even more violent – he protests the complicity of neighbors and household (556–62, 583–84); he threatens to burn the baby (553–54), to kill his wife (561, 580), to strike Demeas (575), and to beat Khrusis with a stick (577). Since Moskhion left the stage before Nikeratos' outburst, it is left to Demeas to calm the irate father; this he does by repeatedly assuring him that Moskhion will marry the girl (586, 599, 610) and by interspersing promises with stories of the divine impregnations of mortals. The encounter between the two men, violator's father and *kurios* of the violated girl, constitutes the inter-family meeting. The coincidence that a wedding between the young couple had been planned for that day adds irony to the scene:

the decision that is made now is one that had already been agreed upon and cancelled. But Nikeratos clearly feels the injury: even after Demeas' third assurance that his son will marry Plangon, he asks, "What if he'd been taken then (εἰ δ' ἐλήφθη τότε – 612)?" Nikeratos' reaction to Moskhion's subsequent feigned departure from Athens (Act v, 717–18) suggests that a violent self-help remedy would have been his solution.

The motif of sexual violation in the play has been subsumed to a plot in which the fundamental dramatic concern is the exploration of a father-son relationship. The son's sexual offenses, alleged and real, have provided fertile ground for that venture. Attention is thus focused, necessarily, on the young offender rather than on his alleged partner (Khrusis) and actual victim (Plangon). It was remarked earlier that none of the speakers characterized Moskhion's violation of Plangon as either rape or seduction. A reason can now be suggested for that ambivalence: the nature of Moskhion's violation makes no difference to the major dramatic concern of the play, the father-son relationship. That dramatic concern shifts, however, during the two sensational acts (III and IV) in which the stability of the father-son relationship is made to depend on the identification of the mother of the infant. The rich oddity and wit of these central acts derive from two sources. First, they present a fundamental subversion of social and biological expectation, that whereas paternity is usually an inference, maternity is an infallibly knowable thing.[54] In this play, however, maternity is fallibly inferred; hence the parallel accounts of mother (?) giving breast to infant (first Khrusis at 265–66 and then Plangon at 535–36) are offered up for scrutiny, confoundment, and comedy. Secondly, the two acts present a perversion of the rape scenario. Of particular interest is Demeas' request to his son at 487–88, at a time when he is still under the impression that Khrusis is the infant's mother:

ὦ Ζεῦ, τοῦ θράσους. ἐναντίον
δή σ' ἐρωτῶ τῶν παρόντων· ἐκ τίνος τὸ παιδίον
ἐστί σοι; . . .

[54] Versions of the statement that a woman with milk has born a child was a stock example of a *tekmerion* ("necessary sign"); see, e.g., Plato *Men.* 237 E; Arist. *Rhet.* 1.2.18,1357b14–17; *A. Pr.* 2.27.70 a 9–12; Sex. Emp. (reporting on the Stoics) *P. H.* 2.104–106; *Rhet. ad Her.* 2.25.39. Demeas' and Nikeratos' inferences (265–66 and 535–36) of maternity in *Samia* are articulated as altered *tekmeria* from the philosophic and rhetorical tradition.

Good god! What boldness! I ask you
now before witnesses: by whom was the infant
born to you?

The request has an interesting pedigree – or rather, none at all: in conventional presentations of the rape scenario, the dénouement of the offense is usually presented from the perspective of the girl's family alone; they ask, "who is the father?" and seek acknowledgement of paternity (e.g., *Adelphoe*, *Aulularia*, *Truculentus*).[55] In *Samia*, the rape is presented predominantly from the perspective of the violator's family. Paradoxically, in this androcentric play, the violator's father must ask the question, "who is the mother?"

3 (b) Truculentus IV *3*

Truculentus differs from all other plays of younger generation rape in that so little attention is given to the plight of the violated girl. Indeed, there is no hint that such a victim exists until IV 2 and 3, when Diniarchus watches Callicles, who was once to be his father-in-law, haul two fettered slaves on-stage. Even in *Aulularia*, a play in which the young rapist does not confess (and at first, only to his mother) until the fourth act, the playwright has introduced the girl's plight both in the prologue and in the first scene; the audience is at least somewhat prepared for the eventual identification and confession of a culprit. When Callicles enters the stage at the end of *Truculentus* IV 2, he apparently has just discovered that his daughter has given birth to a son and that the new-born infant is no longer at home. In the next scene (775–853), he seeks information from the two slaves, one a servant in his own household, the other, the hairdresser of Diniarchus' beloved prostitute, Phronesium (772). Meanwhile, Diniarchus, who overhears the entire conversation from a concealed position on-stage, is overcome with fear:

lapideus sum, commovere me miser non audeo.
res palam omnis est, meo illic nunc sunt capiti comitia.
meum illuc facinus, mea stultitia est. timeo quam mox nominer. (818–20)

I've turned into stone – I dare not make a move in my wretched condition.
Everything is out in the open, now the court is deciding my fate.

[55] In mythic versions of girls raped by gods as presented in tragedy, irate fathers demand to know the father's identity; see Scafuro 1990. *Epitrepontes* demonstrates originality in this respect, too; in that play, the identities of both mother and father are put to the proof.

That's my crime, my stupidity. I fear my name will be mentioned any minute.

Diniarchus envisions the proceedings as if a trial were unfolding before his eyes. The presence of irate father presiding over slaves' inquisition gives more vivid context for the metaphor than the empty stage had provided for Lyconides' similar utterance at *Aulularia* 700.

Still Diniarchus does not come forward; instead, he waits until he is named by Callicles' slave (825). Then he emerges from his hiding-place, begging forgiveness, pleading that he had been overcome by wine (826–28), putting himself at Callicles' mercy and confessing his guilt (835). The courtroom language continues as Callicles' servant warns her master:

Callicles, vide quaeso magnam ne facias iniuriam:
reu' solutus caussam dicit, testis vinctos attines. (836–37)

Callicles, please be careful that you don't commit a great wrong:
the defendant pleads his case unfettered while you keep your witnesses bound.

Callicles heeds the warning and dismisses the women (838–39); he then bids Diniarchus to go to court with him (*eamus tu in ius*, 840) – to which the offender replies:

quid vis in ius me ire? tu es praetor mihi.
verum te opsecro ut tuam gnatam des mi uxorem, Callicles. (840–41)

Why do you want me to go to court? You're my magistrate.
Yes, I beseech you, give me your daughter as wife, Callicles.

The scene is full of Roman legal terminology. Does it represent an Athenian or Roman legal situation? Before we can address that particular question, we must address a more fundamental one: was the scene necessarily part of a Greek original? The question is a vexed one. Nineteenth-century scholars thought that theories of contamination could explain the disjunctions and inconsistencies in Plautus' play; twentieth-century scholars who have treated individual passages often assumed adherence to a Greek original; occasional voices from the past and present have argued that the play is the independent creation of Plautus.[56] Adherents of the last view

[56] For a brief survey of nineteenth and twentieth-century tendencies in the criticism of *Truculentus*, see Lefèvre 1991: 176–77. Lefèvre vigorously argues that *Truculentus* is the independent creation of Plautus; the argument deserves serious consideration.

admit that a Greek kernel may hover in the background, if only as a mere trace of a play once read and recalled dimly as Plautus wrote his comedy "from scratch."

IV 3 depicts, in outline, at least, a conventional scenario of New Comedy, the inter-family meeting that convenes to settle a rape; we have seen several different versions of the scenario in the course of this chapter and in the discussion of *Adelphoe* in chapter 2. Plautus' treatment of it here, however, is anything but conventional. While his spectators might recognize it as belonging to a type of New Comedy scenario, they would also be struck by its remoteness from that type. We shall discuss IV 3 against the background of conventional motifs and dramaturgy; this theoretical construction will be arbitrarily designated as the "model." No particular rape scenario, of course, exactly replicates another and the notion of a generic type is somewhat false. Therefore, to aid in identifying the particular departures from the norms of New Comedy in Plautus' scene, we shall imagine our model as having a shape similar to Plautus': father initiates investigation; violator eavesdrops, then confesses, and finally is betrothed. Moreover, we shall imagine that our Greek playwright adheres to certain conventions of New Comedy dramaturgy and replicates the social norms of his society. While I think that such a reconstructed Greek scene could have been a model for Plautus, it matters little; Plautus' changes are so substantial that the scene would have to be designated "Plautine." Our imaginary model is simply a heuristic device.

Four speaking characters appear in Plautus' scene: Callicles, the slave servant (*ancilla*) of his wife and daughter, the hair-dresser of Phronesium (Syra), and Diniarchus. Callicles announces that the slaves have already been tortured; now he wants to see if they will give the same information without torture (777–79). The preliminary torture of both women and their haling on stage will be Plautine alteration of our imaginary model for three reasons. First, our model adheres to the three-actor rule; one of the four characters must have been added by Plautus.[57] Secondly, the irate father has no right to torture the prostitute's slave without her permission. In *Mostellaria* IV 3, 1038, Theopropides had asked his neighbor's permission when he envisaged a scenario of slave torture. Plautus, who adheres to the

[57] For the view that the three-actor rule was applied generally in New Comedy, see Gaiser 1972: 1038, 1078; Sandbach 1975; Frost 1988: 2–3 (in regard to Menander); Lowe 1991: 39 and n. 28.

lawful scenario (and arguably the Greek original) there, departs from it here.[58] Thirdly, Callicles says that he has been unable to extract the name of the violator so far (816); now his household slave readily supplies it (825); torture has been made superfluous. In the hypothetical Greek model for the scene, the father will have entered with the announcement that he had tortured his own slave, but still lacked a vital piece of information, the all-important name of the violator. He will now meet the prostitute's slave on-stage, and intimidate or entice her to identify his daughter's violator; she might be tipsy and so more likely to relent and supply the name.[59] The major portion of the Plautine scene, the dialogue of Callicles with his household slave and Syra, is the Roman poet's invention. It could not have stood, except in abbreviated and much different form, in our Greek model.

Hallmarks of Plautine dramaturgy are evident. The entrance of Callicles, accompanied by the fettered women and slaves with whips in hand is the sort of spectacle beloved by Plautus.[60] Clearly the comic poet wanted both women in *Truculentus* on-stage at the same time. Spectacle is not gratuitous, but impelled by dramatic instinct and motif: in the course of the scene, the slave-witnesses become slave-criminals, complicit co-conspirators with the women in the households they represent. Callicles gives stage directions for the inquisition soon after arrival on-stage:

> *omnium primum divorsae state – em sic, istuc volo;*
> *neve inter vos significetis, ego ero paries. loquere tu.* (787–88)

> First of all, stand apart – yes, like this, I want you there.
> And so you don't send signals to one another, I'll be a wall. You, talk.

Callicles then begins the examination, first questioning his household slave on one side, then Phronesium's slave on the other. The careful demarcation of stage space is similar to that in *Persa* IV 4, where Toxilus divides the stage geopolitically between representa-

[58] Langen 1886: 232 suggests that anger might be viewed as a motivation for Callicles' unlawful behavior, but finds it odd that Phronesium does not seem to complain about this breach of the law in the next scene.

[59] In the opening lines of the next scene of *Truc.*, Phronesium seems to complain about her hairdresser's inability to hold her liquor and look to her own interest simultaneously (854–55); the verses, however, are poorly transmitted.

[60] Compare, for example, the extensive Plautine additions that have been hypothesized for *Rudens* III 4 and 5, where Daemones leads Labrax out of the temple and *lorarii* (floggers) hold him at bay throughout the two scenes. See Jachmann 1931: 91–96 and Drexler 1934: 50–60; more recently, Lowe 1991: 39–44. Lefèvre 1978b argues that Plautus introduced Artamo and the on-stage binding of Chrysalus in *Bacch.* 794ff.

tives of east and west.[61] The demarcation in *Truculentus* IV 3 has its own distinctive markings: the representative of female aristocrats on one side, the representative of female prostitute household on the other, each representative fettered and threatened with a whip (782–83, 793); Callicles stands in the middle, a wall of separation rather than a "go-between."

The doubling of slave parts in the scene replicates the doubling of mistresses: each represents two: Callicles' slave serves both his wife (*era maior mea*, "my elder mistress," 796) and daughter; the hairdresser serves both Phronesium and her mother (*duae sunt istae*, "those are two different mistresses," 801). Callicles' questioning discovers a chiastic chain of complicity between the two households: his daughter who bore the infant; her mother, the *maior era* of the household who had given the infant to her slave and ordered her to hand it over to the slave of the other household; that slave who then gave it to her *maior era* who passed it on to her daughter (798–805). The report confirms Phronesium's earlier account to Diniarchus in II 4, 401–09; that account, however, had omitted the identities of the infant's parents – Diniarchus was ignorant that Phronesium's "adopted" son was his own. The responses of the two men differ not so much in substance as in tone. Whereas Diniarchus had prefaced his comments about the doubling of mothers with sardonic and alliterative admiration, *o mercis malae* (409: "ah, mischievous merchandising!"), Callicles explodes with an oath, *di, opsecro vostram fidem!* ("may the gods help us!"); he then comments on the ease with which one woman can bear another woman's son (806–07, cf. 410–11); he ends with provocative computation:

> *puer quidem beatust: matres duas habet et avias duas:*
> *iam metuo patres quot fuerint. vide sis facinus muliebre.* (808–09)

> The boy is indeed blessed: he has two mothers and two grandmothers:
> now I fear how many fathers there may have been. Behold the crime of women!

The particular depiction of anger resembles, in some respects, Nikeratos' in *Samia* IV, 553–85: he, too, is angry upon discovering that his unmarried daughter has given birth; he, too, is angry at numerous individuals and perceives a plot to keep him in the dark (562, 571–72, 584). But Nikeratos' anger is directed not only at the

[61] Scafuro 1993.

women, but at Demeas (575, 584) and the infant as well (553–54, 568–69). Callicles' anger has a specific object, the chain of complicit women summed up in *facinus muliebre* (809) and visualized on-stage by the two fettered women, the links between two households, now divided by a "wall."

The complicity between aristocratic and meretricious households had been initiated by mothers in the economic interest of daughters: Callicles' wife, no doubt interested in concealing the birth of an unwanted infant and in preserving her daughter's reputation for advancement to the next upward stage of life, marriage with a kinsman (848–49); Phronesium's mother, interested in cementing a mercenary soldier's lifelong support for her daughter (397–400, 401–04). Mothers and daughters are complicit elsewhere in New Comedy. Such complicity may be embedded in nature or society; but in Greek New Comedy, it does not usually extend to transactions between prostitutes and married aristocratic women.[62] The children of New Comedy who end up in brothels or in a prostitute's establishment have not been put there by their mothers or grandmothers; they are either abducted by pirates (*Curculio*, *Poenulus*, and, in a more round-about way, *Andria* and *Eunuchus*), or simply abandoned (*Cistellaria*). Even Khrusis in *Samia* (84–85) does not envision a brothel as alternative to her caring for Plangon's infant. Plautus' scenario is a radical departure from the norms of New Comedy. Nevertheless, the playwright has carefully prepared his audience for the reconstruction of the infant's past (II 4, 407–09): he has emphasized the doubling of mothers and the duet of households. His goal is achieved as Callicles' angry arithmetic leads to the crude and unequivocal equation of verse 809: "now I fear how many fathers there may have been! behold the crime of women!" Our imaginary Greek model has been derailed. Cato the Elder might be speaker.[63]

62 Plangon in *Samia* put her infant in Khrusis' care, perhaps with her mother's knowledge – but Khrusis is hardly a prostitute, at least not so long as she is Demeas' *pallake*. Myrrina in *Hecyra* had planned to expose her daughter's unwanted infant in the interest of preserving her daughter's reputation and future prospects – but she had not entered into negotiations with the prostitute's underworld. That channel of exchange is limited to men – and it is the men in *Hecyra* who impel Bacchis' entrance into Myrrina's house.

63 Cf. the sentiment and language of *Truc.* 808–09 and Cato fr. 172 *ORF*^{3} (= Gellius *N.A.* 1. 23); the Catonian fragment is (explicitly) Gellius' paraphrase of a portion of a Catonian speech. It is a story about Papirius Praetextatus, an *aition* that explains the prohibition of boys from attendance at meetings of the *curia* with their fathers. One particular meeting, attended by Papirius and his father, concerned an important matter of state and had to be continued the next day; those present were asked not to reveal anything until a decree had been passed. Papirius' mother, curious to know what was being discussed, and persistently

Callicles' slave restores order with a reminder of who the criminal is:

> *magi' pol haec malitia pertinet ad viros quam ad mulieres:*
> *vir illam, non mulier praegnatem fecit.* (810–11)

> The villainy is more a man's than a woman's:
> a man, not a woman, made her pregnant.

The women are still united; Callicles' further provocation will put an end to that and at the same time elicit his slave's identification of the violator:

> *CA. idem ego istuc scio.*
> *tu bona ei custos fuisti. AN. plus potest qui plus valet.*
> *vir erat, plus valebat: vicit, quod petebat apstulit.* (811–13)

> CA.: Yes, I know that.
> You were an excellent guardian. SLAVE: The more powerful person is the one who has more muscle.
> He was a man, he had more muscle: he conquered, what he sought, he carried off.

Daughters of aristocrats do not consent to sexual relations, they are raped. With aristocratic women distinguished from prostitutes, with class demarcations re-established, the drama appears to shift to the conventional dénouement, a return to our imaginary model. But Plautus keeps veering from the trodden route. The rapist is named and summoned into the open; he confesses, admits that he was drunk (conventional). He is refused pardon for drunkenness (unconventional); he concedes liability but does not accompany the concession with an offer to marry the girl (unconventional). Father threatens lawsuit (conventional – probably a suit for *iniuria*). Rapist now offers to marry the girl and father contracts for marriage – but

urging her son to reveal the secret, was told the senate was debating *utrum videretur utilius exque re publica esse, unusne ut duas uxores haberet, an ut una apud duos nupta esset* ("whether it was more useful and to the advantage of the state for a husband to have two wives or for one woman to be married to two men"). Papirius' mother grew fearful and went to the senate the next day "with a throng of *matresfamilias*". The women expressed their point of view clearly: *lacrimantes atque obsecrantes orant, una potius ut duobus nupta fieret, quam ut uni duae* ("amidst tears and prayers they begged that a woman be married to two husbands rather than that two women should be married to one man"). Papirius was rewarded for not revealing state secrets; he alone was exempted from the prohibition of boys from the senate. Cato's story and Callicles' calculations suggest a similar perspective about women: they are likely to desire two husbands (or two fathers for their children – or numerous lovers, one of whom might turn into a father). Both also suggest a traditional play upon numbers when calculating couples and their coupling. Cf. Ter. *Ph.* 1041–42.

not without deducting from the dowry a substantial sum which the rapist would have been offered had he married the girl without violating her (unconventional: section 2.c, apud fin.). Father then exits to cancel his daughter's betrothal to a kinsman (a final and remarkable unconventional doubling).

Plautus' alterations to the rape scenario of New Comedy are considerable. The inter-family meeting has been deprived of family quality: violator has no visible family, nor visible attachment to family sentiment – and certainly no trace of passion for his victim. The latter's father is neither poor nor miserly; acquisition of alternative son-in-law is guaranteed – kinsman-fiancé, after all, is waiting in the wings. There is not so much an inner core of New Comedy in this scene as there is an empty shell.[64] To imagine a New Comedy equivalent, re-write Menander's *Aspis* and have the elderly Smikrines marry Kleostratos' sister. That script would accord with law, possibly life, but not New Comedy: a Plautine message? Overriding all in *Truculentus* IV 3 is superb dramaturgy, the Roman father-praetor-director who controls the scene, positions his actors, directs the discourse, extracts confessions, obtains a son-in-law, deducts a price. The power and poverty of wealth are on display, the Plautine city of theatrical Rome pitted mercilessly against New Comedy's subtle and sentimentalized Athens.

4 DEMYTHIFYING THE "GIRL'S TRAGEDY": *TACE OBSECRO, MEA GNATA!* (*HECYRA* 318)

We have considered the ways in which sexual offenses against unmarried girls are settled in six plays: *Samia*, *Fabula Incerta*, *Aulularia*, *Truculentus*, *Adelphoe*, and *Eunuchus*. The central feature of the scenario is the meeting between the members of the families of rapist and victim; the settlement which ends in marriage is a family affair. The inter-family meetings in all these plays take up a very small part of the dramatic action; but they occur regularly, whether on stage or off. That the scenario leaves traces at all is significant and marks a radical departure from the presentation of mythic rapes in fifth-century tragedies. In this concluding section, I shall turn briefly to the wider range of rape plots in New Comedy and to some of the mythic plots of tragedy in order to suggest the contours of the

[64] See Konstan 1983: 142–64 for interpretation of this play as "satiric comedy."

change; full-scale treatment of the process of demythification is beyond the scope of this chapter.[65]

The rape plots of New Comedy can be divided into those in which the rapist's identity is known to the victim and those in which it is not. So long as the rapist is unknown, there is no chance for recourse to the law since the victim's *kurios* has no one to prosecute. In the comedies in which this situation arises (*Epitrepontes*, *Hecyra*, and *Aulularia*), the young woman or her mother or maid exposes the infant or plans to do so. The only apparent exception is *Aulularia*; but even there the old nurse Staphyla is concerned to keep the birth a secret (74–76, 274–77) and merely appears resourceless (or perhaps never sober enough) to contrive any sort of plan. The young girls of these comedies thus conceal their rapes and try to get rid of their infants. The same pattern is evident in a number of other comedies in which the dramatic background is formed by women who were raped almost twenty years ago by unidentified assailants ("older generation rapes": Menander *Heros*, possibly his *Phasma* and *Hiereia*, and Plautus *Cistellaria* based on Menander's *Sunaristōsai*).[66] In none of these plays does the woman keep the infant as her own; even in *Phasma*, where the offspring is housed next door, the mother keeps the birth and "abandonment" a secret.

A secret pregnancy and parturition, usually followed by exposure or concealment of the infant, is thus the conventional pattern of behavior for women who are raped by unidentifiable assailants. The fathers or *kurioi* of the raped girls are not taken into the secret – Smikrines in *Epitrepontes*, Phidippus in *Hecyra*, Euclio in *Aulularia* – not one has been informed of his daughter's plight. Why not? Does such hesitation reflect any social reality? A law attributed to Solon had allowed men to sell daughters and sisters who were discovered to have had sexual relations with a man outside of marriage (Plut. *Solon* 23. 2); while the authenticity of that law is questionable and while it certainly was not in operation in the fourth century, it does suggest a tradition of paternal rejection of unwed, pregnant

65 I have treated the mythic pattern in more detail in 1990: 126–59.

66 In *Heros*, Myrrhine gave birth to twins as the result of a rape; the twins were handed over to a freedman shepherd who brought them up as his own children. The Sicyonian Phanostrata in *Cistellaria* had been raped by Demipho, a Lemnian merchant, while the latter was visiting Sicyon; he fled back to Lemnos and she abandoned the infant. In *Phasma*, a woman who had borne a daughter, probably as the result of a rape, brought her up secretly (see Gomme and Sandbach 1973: 673–75). In *Hiereia*, a priestess who had borne a son, probably as the result of a rape, gave him to a married woman who passed the boy off as her own (see Gomme and Sandbach 1973: 694).

daughters.[67] Rape or seduction might have made no difference – how could a daughter prove she had been raped by an unidentified assailant? Possibly a fear of some sort of paternal sanction, then, motivates the silence of the daughters of New Comedy. Yet bits and pieces of evidence from the fourth century suggest that fathers may have been more compassionate – even to their seduced daughters. Stephanos, portrayed by Apollodoros as unlawfully detaining Epainetos as a *moikhos* with his alleged daughter Phano in [Dem.] 59 *Neaira*, nevertheless won that daughter a "dowry" in a private reconciliation. A speaker who defends himself against a charge of *moikheia* in the course of an impeachment trial (Hyp. 2 *Lyk.* 12) reports that his prosecutor has alleged that he is "causing many women to grow old unmarried in their houses and causing many others to live together [i.e., in marriage] with men with whom it is not appropriate, against the laws."[68] While the papyrus text is lacunose, the prosecutor's alleged charges appear to assume that women who had been involved in illicit sexual relations might find themselves living unmarried in their natal *oikoi* – there is no indication of worse treatment at the hands of angry kin. And the story of the maiden and the horse, abbreviated in Aiskhin. 1 *Tim.*, has a sequel in the Atthidographic tradition: the Kodrid king who had imprisoned his violated daughter with a horse was in turn the victim of his subjects' wrath on account of that very cruelty.[69]

If, as I think, the social realities suggested by this evidence do not accord with the representation of rapes in New Comedy, what then

[67] Plut. *Solon* 23. 2 (= F 31a Ruschenbusch, with Hartman's deletion): ἔτι δ' οὔτε θυγατέρας πωλεῖν οὔτ' ἀδελφὰς δίδωσι, πλὴν ἂν [μὴ] λάβηι παρθένον ἀνδρὶ συγγεγενημένην.

[68] Hyp. 2. 12: . . . ἔπε[ιτ]α ἐξ[ῆι σοι τραγ]ωιδίας γρ[άψαι εἰς τὴ]ν εἰσαγγελ[ίαν οἵασ]περ νῦν γέγρ[αφας, ὅς μ' α]ἰτιᾶι ὅτι [πολλὰς μὲν γ[υνα[ῖκας ποιῶ] ἀγάμ[ους ἔνδον κα]ταγηρ[άσκειν, πολλ]ὰς δὲ σ[υνοικεῖν ο]ἷς οὐ προσήκει παρὰ τοὺς νόμους.

[69] The story of the last king of the Kodridai is recorded in the fragmentary opening of Herakleides' epitome of the *AP* (Arist. fr. VIII. 611 paragr. 1 Rose); see App. 7.1, n. 101. The ending of the politicized story is missing in the Aristotelian fragment, but is hinted at in the opening statement that kings were no longer chosen from the Kodridai – the story of Hippomenes' punishment of his daughter and her *moikhos* is presumably offered as explanation of the family's political eclipse. The ending can be somewhat filled out by the report in Nikolaos of Damaskos *FGrHist* 90 F 49 who depended on a source (Ephoros: *FGrHist* III b II, p. 54 n. 29 and p. 55 n. 34) who had available to him the same materials as the Atthidographers (probably Kleidemos: his *Atthis* appeared "not earlier than 354 BC, and hardly much later" [Jacoby 1949: 74]). Nikolaos reports that after the deaths of the maiden and the horse, the dwelling place was razed. Jacoby has interpreted the statement in this way: "the Athenians . . . are so disgusted with his [sc. Hippomenes'] brutality that they now finally remove the unpopular *genos*, inflicting a kind of *damnatio memoriae* by destroying the palace" (*FGrHist* III b II, p. 54 n. 29).

explains the silence of the victims? A mythic rather than socially realistic paradigm controls the plotting of these plays. The paradigm is evident in a number of Greek myths about virgins who have premarital sexual relations with gods. Walter Burkert has called the pattern "the girl's tragedy." A modified version of that paradigm is the following: (1) a daughter has sexual relations with a god or hero; (2) she conceals the deed and her subsequent pregnancy and exposes the new-born infant; (3) her father discovers his daughter's sexual activity, or her pregnancy, or her infant; (4) he disbelieves her story of divine impregnation and punishes the girl – together with her infant if she has already given birth.[70] The heroines of these myths appeared in numerous productions on the Attic tragic and comic stage in the fifth and fourth centuries BC. A mere selection from the three major fifth-century tragedians will give an idea of the popularity of these heroines: Io plays an important role in Aiskhylos' *Prometheus Bound*, Sophokles produced a *Danae* and two versions of *Tyro*, while Auge may have played a role in *Aleadai* and perhaps a larger one in *Mysoi*; Euripides produced an *Alope*, *Antiope*, *Auge*, *Danae*, *Melanippe Bound*, and *Melanippe the Wise*.

Later dramatic productions attest to continued interest in these myths. Perhaps as a result of Euripides' play *Auge*, there was an upsurge of interest in the Auge strand of the Telephos legend in the fourth century. The tragic poet Aphareos produced an *Auge* at the City Dionysia of 341; two poets of Middle Comedy, Euboulos and Philyllios, each composed an *Auge*.[71] Menander explicitly alludes to Euripides' play in *Epitrepontes* (1123–24): first Onesimos cites a verse and a half to assist Smikrines in comprehending his daughter's plight (i.e., that she had been raped before marriage, concealed her pregnancy, and exposed her infant) and then he threatens to recite a whole speech if Smikrines still remains in the dark. The story of Danae, not infrequently alluded to by epic and archaic poets,[72] was popular on the Attic stage throughout the fifth century, in tragedy,

[70] Burkert 1979: 6–7 adduces seven myths (Kallisto, Auge, Danae, Io, Tyro, Melanippe, and Antiope) that conform to the pattern (which he describes slightly differently) to show "how a set of unrelated myths can be analyzed as covering the same basic structure" which he sees as "a prelude to the emergence of the hero." Burkert points out that, while the tale type has been treated as part of the hero pattern for over a century, "it is a detachable unit in itself, following the sequence Interdiction – violation – consequence – (attempted) escape . . . " (147, n. 19).

[71] Amphareos: *TrGF* I DID A 2a, 15; Euboulos: F 14 K–A; Philyllios: FF3–5 K–A.

[72] *E.g.*, Homer *Il.* 14. 319; Hes. *Aspis* 216; Pindar *P.* 10. 45, 12. 17, *N.* 10. 11.

satyr plays, and comedy.[73] Sophokles' and Euripides' tragedies have already been mentioned. Two fifth-century comic poets, Apollophanes and Sannyrion, also composed plays about Danae; so did Euboulos in the next century.[74] In Menander's *Samia,* Demeas tries to assuage Nikeratos' anger by suggesting that his daughter's violator had been Zeus: "Tell me, Nikeratos," Demeas says, "haven't you heard the tragic actors tell how Zeus turned himself into gold and flowed through the roof and then *emoikheusen* the girl who had been confined there?" (589–91).The reference may be topical, to a recent revival of Euripides' play – or to some other production.[75] The *Samia* itself follows the same broad outlines of the mythic paradigm: unmarried girl is violated, gives away her infant, is discovered by her father who reacts in anger (he threatens to kill his wife, burn the infant, club the *pallake*, etc.). The myths of unmarried girls raped by gods and heroes used by fifth-century comic and tragic poets are readily available for transformation into the heroines of New Comedy.

In the mythic paradigm represented here by Auge and Danae, the girls fear to tell their fathers about their rapes and child-bearing. Why? The answer is simple: they fear harsh punishment. Their stories are not believable because they cannot be proven. The fathers of myth cannot track down a Zeus or Poseidon as if he were a Moskhion who lived next door; how, in any event, are these girls to be "married" to gods? Divine and human institutions do not so easily blend. The girls are resourceless; their rapes, pregnancies, and parturitions are kept secret and their infants abandoned or concealed. The girls raped by unidentifiable assailants in New Comedy are similarly resourceless. Their stories will be disbelieved and are unprovable: how can one track down a man whose identity is unknown? New Comedy has substituted the unidentifiable assailant for the rapist gods of the mythic paradigm.

But the innovation of New Comedy is the identifiable human assailant. Where the latter is known, the *kurios* of the violated girl

[73] Epikharmos wrote a comedy called *Diktyes* (*CGFP* 81,17), to which Aiskhylos may be indebted for his satyr play *Diktyoulkoi* (*TrGF* III FF46–47); the latter appears to treat that part of the myth in which the chest containing Danae and Perseus is fished out of the sea. Sophokles' tragedy *Danae* may have formed part of a trilogy with *Akrisios* and *Larisaioi* as its two other members (for this and other views, see *TrGF* IV p. 136; Carden 1974: 244–50). And Euripides wrote an *Akrisios, Danae,* and *Diktyes* (Nauck^2 pp. 453–64).

[74] Apollophanes p. 520 K-A; Sannyrion FF 8–10 K–A; Euboulos F 22 K–A. In Sannyrion F 8, Zeus appears to be on stage, attempting to devise a way to penetrate Danae's chamber.

[75] This suggestion was made by Gomme and Sandbach 1973: 611–12.

does have recourse to the law – even if he settles in private. First and foremost, then, these plots (as in *Fabula Incerta*, *Samia*, *Adelphoe*, *Truculentus*, and *Eunuchus*) are innovative by virtue of the fact that the "law" – or social practice – has been integrated with them. No raped girl's story is disbelieved, no punishment imposed on her. Her *kurios*, once he learns the assailant's identity, tracks him down and comes to terms with him or his father – so Hegio in *Adelphoe*, Callicles in *Truculentus*, Nikeratos in *Samia*. In plays in which the assailant confesses to the *kurios* or a substitute, a marital arrangement immediately follows: so it happens in *Fabula Incerta*, *Aulularia*, and *Eunuchus*. Such plots may reflect contemporary social values – with some speculative transmutations: possibly fathers compelled rapists to pay "dowries" without compelling subsequent marriage; possibly the compelled marriages of New Comedy represent the usual solution for young couples whose secret and consensual intimacies had been discovered; possibly the nature of the violation, whether seduction or rape, made no difference to concerned fathers. The most significant factor, however, of the rape scenarios of New Comedy is that redress is sought for the victim in private. Precisely when such values – the impulse to bring rapists to justice and the desire to provide *oikoi* for unmarriageable girls – were first embraced by Athenian society is impossible to gauge; certainly Ion in Euripides' homonymous play had shown his discomfort with the mythic paradigm (*Ion* 442–51). The innovative rape plots of New Comedy – those with identifiable assailants – have adopted a social rather than mythic paradigm. Bringing the rapist to justice, rather than inflicting a penalty on the daughter, is emblematic of the former rather than the latter. The mechanism of the administration of justice is thus integrated with these plots, and so we see in them, even fleetingly, the threat of lawsuits and inter-family meetings about rape. Myth is subverted; tragedy becomes comedy.

Nevertheless, even the innovative plots have left traces of the mythic paradigm. In some of the plays with identifiable assailants, the daughters still do not confide in their *kurioi*: in *Samia*, Plangon gives away her son, even if only temporarily, to Khrusis; in *Truculentus*, the daughter abandons her infant; in *Adelphoe*, Sostrata only informs Hegio of her daughter's rape when Aeschinus seems to have retracted his promise of marriage. Why are these women silent – women who could tell their *kurioi* whom to prosecute? Is their silence a vestige of the mythic paradigm? A consideration of the particular situation in each play reveals that it is in the interest of the plot that the *kurios* discover neither the violation nor the infant until a particular dramatic moment. In *Samia*, the dramatic tensions of the play focus predominantly on the father-son relationship which demands that the infant's mother (rather than father) remain unidentified until the climax of the play. In *Truculentus*, delayed discovery of the infant's birth and paternity in the fourth act provides audacious means for a brief reunion of the currently shut-out lover with the conniving prostitute in the next (and penultimate) scene of the play. In *Adelphoe*, a play in which the dramatic tensions focus upon the relationship between two brothers with competing pedagogies, Micio must be the last to know of his adoptive son's offense so as to provide Demea with a chance to score against him. The mythic paradigm is thus exploited in each instance for a particular dramatic purpose. The effect is one of inconcinnity. This is especially so in *Samia*, where the mythic paradigm is explicitly alluded to in the course of the play (589–91). The mythic paradigm leads us to expect the punishment of the daughter, the social paradigm, the punishment of the son. The intersection of myth and social reality, the uncomfortable juncture of two quite different conceptions of sexual violation, the competing claims on the audience's attention of maternity and paternity, mark *Samia* as one of the most interesting documents of literary and social history.

CHAPTER 7

Arguing behind closed doors

Characters in New Comedy sometimes convene to discuss epiklerate marriages and to argue over the necessity of divorce. Smikrines in Act I of *Aspis* reports the advice of friends that he should marry an *epikleros* (184–86); in Act II, he discusses the issue with his brother. Another Smikrines, this one appearing in a lacunose scene of *Epitrepontes*, discusses divorce with his son-in-law (637–99); in the following act, father and daughter take up the issue. In the opening scene of *Stichus*, Antipho reports that friends have advised him to dissolve his daughters' marriages (128); he relays this information to his children while urging them to divorce. The characters in these scenes typically dispute the competing claims of law and fairness. Do their arguments reflect those used "behind closed doors" in Athens – or are they dramatically idiosyncratic and distortions of social and legal realities?

In an earlier chapter we examined arguments used in private arbitrations and reconciliations in Athens. We concluded that disputants may have used arguments of fairness more frequently in cases where they sought compensation above restitution and where the law did not seem to cover an alleged offense (chapter 3.1.c). Not all out-of-court settlements in the orators, however, carry along with them the paraphernalia of arbitration; frequently settlements are alluded to without mentioning the presence of a mediating figure. Often they are presented as bribery; occasionally a different basis for agreement can be glimpsed. By incorporating such instances as these into our quarry of evidence, we enlarge our material for comparison with the private arrangements made by the disputants of New Comedy. We have already engaged in this kind of comparative inquiry in the last chapter (6.2.c). There we found an overlap of courtroom and out-of-court argumentation in cases of *hubris* and assault: men who pleaded the absence of intention might win acquittal or a mitigated penalty in the courtroom, or pardon in a private settlement. When we turned to New Comedy, we saw characters using the same arguments once again, when offering defenses for rape during inter-family meetings.

Some of the private arrangements described in the orators emerge from disputes not over alleged infringements of the law but rather over alternative methods for carrying out legal or moral obligations. In the case of epiklerate marriages (section 1 below), it was legally incumbent upon nearest kin to marry or dower a poor *epikleros*. Andokides has already provided us a glimpse of the arguments used by one individual to compass that obligation (chapter 2.1 on *Myst.* 119). Andokides described how he met with his cousin Leagros before an audience of *philoi* (an account now being iterated before a much larger audience of Athenian dikasts) to discuss the plight of their allegedly poor cousins. He urged no lawful compulsion to support his recommendation of marriage to the girls who had now become *epikleroi*; instead, he appealed to sentiment: the two men should act in accordance with *arete* ("virtue"). Other hints here and there in the oratorical record which will be discussed below allow us to formulate a more varied notion of the arguments used by kin in their deliberations over *epikleroi* and so provide material for comparison with the arguments in New Comedy. Modern scholars have called attention to forensic speakers who sometimes use arguments of fairness to oppose epiklerate marriages; some have further maintained that the epiklerate system was deteriorating in the fourth century. Our examination will show that arguments of fairness which oppose adherence to the laws regarding *epikleroi* are given no privileged position in the orators; our conclusions require us to re-examine instances of the same type of dispute in New Comedy where modern critics have almost unanimously identified the endorsement of fair play.

We have no forensic material, however, when we turn to a daughter's arguments to dissuade her father from dissolving her marriage (section 2). The daughter's argument appears to be a stock motif in a number of comedies; lawful or traditional authority is pitted against arguments of fairness in highly rhetoricized fashion. Since there is no way to hold up these arguments even to the distorted prism of the orators, they are treated below in their dramatic contexts; how and why they are so rhetoricized are the questions that are posed there.

It may seem odd that I have chosen to treat "arguments behind closed doors" on the same level as the other scenarios examined so far. But certainly the repetition of such arguments under set circumstances in New Comedy justifies such treatment. Recognizing the encounters between family members and friends at critical junctures as fixed components of dispute settlement explains the formality of the arguments used by the participants. And formal modes of dispute settlement, even within the family, involve the deployment of forensic strategies. Lysias 22 *Diog.* 12–18 is the *locus classicus* in the oratorical record for depiction (albeit editorialized) of dispute settlement on the *oikos* level. As I argued in the first chapter, the formality of scenario and discourse is symptomatic of the extension of the courtroom stage to the proscenium of the *oikos*.

I DISPUTES ABOUT *EPIKLEROI*

1(a) The evidence of the orators

Recent scholarly literature has portrayed fourth-century Athens as a period of transition during which traditional family values underwent considerable change; collective values of the fifth century gave way to more individualistic values in the next century.[1] Within the larger picture, the epiklerate system is viewed as protector of the solidarity of the family in its early (Solonian) period and as slowly disintegrating in the fourth century. New Comedy, with its dramatizations of conflict between legal regulations regarding *epikleroi* on the one hand and individual preferences on the other, marks a shift downward, to the advanced stages of deterioration. In the Hellenistic Age, the epiklerate system finally disappears.[2]

Enticing as the larger view may be, the appropriation of an evolutionary framework to describe the epiklerate system in Athens is unjustifiable. Characterization of change within it as "deterioration" is misleading when so little of that system's beginnings is known and when no significant statistical pool of epiklerate marriages can be created for any historical period in Athens; moreover, inference of its disappearance in the Hellenistic Age, when the record of forensic speeches is all but lost, is foolish; and finally,

[1] For brief bibliographic survey, see Rubinstein 1993: 7–9; she traces the view back to the beginning of this century.

[2] Disintegration during the fourth century: Humphreys 1978: 199–200; Cox 1983: 528; Mossé 1989. Disintegration and disappearance: Karabelias 1979.

dependence on Greek papyri from Egypt (*e silentio*!) for Athenian law is a dubious venture. An Attic inscription dated between 300 and 250 BC records a decree of the Erekhtheid tribe conferring honors upon Antisthenes son of Nikandros and his daughter, the *epikleros* Aristomakhe; the yearly *epimeletai* are "to be responsible for the *epikleros*, if she needs anything, and are to report to the tribe whenever they hold assembly, so that she may not [be treated unjustly by anyone]."[3] If the dating of the decree is correct, then the inference of the disappearance of the *epikleros* cannot be maintained. The sheer number of New Comedy plays preserved with the title, *Epikleros*, moreover, suggests that dramatists were not beating a dead horse (see n. 33).

The laws regulating *epikleroi*, as they are transmitted in the orators, appear vague enough to allow a certain degree of flexibility in their application – and combination with or exclusion by other methods of inheritance. In fact, the epiklerate system belongs to a larger structure of inheritance strategies (e.g., adoption *inter vivos* and adoption *post mortem*) that existed simultaneously in fourth-century Athens – and earlier.[4] Ar. *Wasps* 583–86 (quoted below) illustrates that *epikleroi* and wills were "in competition" as early as 422 BC when the play was performed. In the fourth century, evidence for the competition is more ample – not because the competition grew more fierce but because the forensic record is more extensive in this period. Rubinstein sums up three ways in which adoption might serve as an alternative to the *epikleros* system:

[3] *IG* II² 1165. 30–38: ἐπειδὴ δὲ συμβαίνει Ἀντισθένει θυγατέρα εἶ̓ναι ἐπίκληρον ἐκ τῶν νόμων γεγενημένην, τοὺς ἐπιμελητὰ|ς τοὺς ἀεὶ καθισταμένους κατ' ἐνιαυτὸν ἐπιμελεῖσθαι Ἀριστομ|άχης τῆς Ἀντισθένου θυγατρός, ἐάν τινος δέηται ἐμφανίζοντ|ας τεῖ φυλεῖ ὅταν ἀγορὰν ποιῶσιν, ὅπως ἂν μη[δ' ὑφ' ἑ]νὸ[ς ἀδικῆτ]|αι. τὴν δ' εὔνοιαν τὴν παρ' ἑκά[σ]τ[ου τῶν φυλετῶν καὶ ἰδίαι καὶ κ|οινῆι ὑπάρχειν τῆι θυγατ[ρὶ τῆι Ἀντισθένους Ἀριστομάχηι δ|ιὰ τὴν τοῦ πατρὸς ἀ[νδραγαθίαν καὶ φιλοτιμίαν ἣν ἔχων περὶ τ]|ὴν Ἐρεχθ[ηῖδα φυλὴν διατετέλεκεν - - - - - - - - -]. The inscription is dated to the first half of the third century by Wilhelm 1905 solely on the basis of its lettering. If this Antisthenes (*PA* 1198) is the son of Nikandros who was *tamias* (steward) in 343/42 (*PA* 10688, citing *IG* II² 1443.6), then the general date is likely to be correct.

[4] Todd 1993: 228–31; Rubinstein 1993: 87–104. Authenticating dates for laws attributed to Solon regarding wills, *epikleroi*, and adoption is difficult. Some fifth-century dates, however, are reasonably secure. Ar. *Wasps* 583–86 is mentioned in the text above. Dikaiogenes son of Menexenos adopted a son by testament (Is. 5. 6, 14–15); Dikaiogenes died in 411 BC Themistokles' son, Diokles, was adopted by Lysander (Plut. *Them.* 32); the adopter was Diokles' maternal grandfather; the adoption is probably fifth century, since Themistokles himself died in 459 BC. See Rubinstein 1993: 97–98 for the argument that adoptions such as this one (by a maternal grandfather) may have been carried out to prevent an only daughter from becoming *epidikos* upon the grandfather's death.

a father could safeguard an already existing marriage by adopting his daughter's husband *inter vivos* or by will, or he could adopt a prospective husband for her (e.g., in case he died while she was still too young to marry), or thirdly, he could prevent her from becoming ἐπίδικος [an *epikleros* who is the subject of rival claims] simply by adopting a son *inter vivos*, no matter whether the adoptee was to marry her or not.[5]

The last option mentioned by Rubinstein is controversial, as we shall see shortly (n. 15). The important point to notice now is that the frequency of these practices cannot be calculated; nonetheless, as they are (with the possible exception of the third) legitimate options within the structure of inheritance strategies even in the fifth century, it is arbitrary to identify and isolate the epiklerate system as the particular victim in a stepped-up competition in the next century. A father's *inter vivos* or testamentary adoption of an heir – whether or not he has an *epikleros* daughter – serves the same end: it prevents his nearest kinsmen from acquiring his estate. On the other hand, Athenians still attached practical significance to family estates and their acquisition by kindred young men in the last decades of the fourth century: the *AP*, composed between 333 and 322 BC, reports that ephebes were not allowed to appear in lawsuits – "except in cases concerning an inheritance or *epikleros*" (42.5); the two exceptions permitted ephebes are probably not mere props for dying institutions. Viewed from the perspective of the larger structure of inheritance strategies, tensions among proponents of the individual competing ones are to be expected; personal discomfort was bound to be felt – and there are no grounds for claiming that such sensitivities were fourth-century developments.

More to the point, conflicts between the laws regulating *epikleroi* and individual preferences are already demonstrable in the orators; such conflicts do not make their first appearance in New Comedy. The speaker of Isaios 3 *Pyrrhos* claims: "The law has a provision concerning women who have been given in marriage by their fathers and who are living together in marriage with their husbands (and who could counsel better in these matters than a father?); if their father dies without leaving them legitimate brothers, even though these women have been thus married, they are to be claimed in an

[5] Rubinstein 1993: 96–97. The orators provide only one instance of a father adopting his daughter's husband: Dem. 41. 3–5; they provide possibly three instances of a father's adoption of a daughter's son: [Dem.] 42. 21, 23, 27; 43. 37, 45; Is. 10, 4, 7, 8; see Rubinstein 1993: 97–104.

epidikasia by their nearest relatives; many husbands, moreover, have already been deprived of their wives" (64). Another speaker claims that his mother, although an *epikleros*, had been defrauded of her rights; her next-of-kin had threatened to claim her in marriage if her husband claimed her paternal estate. The speaker comments, "my father, so as not to be deprived of my mother, would have allowed them to enjoy an estate twice as large – and this is the reason why he brought no suit for the estate" (Is. 10. 19–20). One scholar who has recently called attention to both these passages as depictions of the opposition of "law" and "the individual," says of the first, "Here we find the speaker contrasting the rigidity of the legislation on *epikleroi* to the individual father and his capacity to arrange the most suitable marriage for his daughter."[6] In the second passage, that generalized opposition unfolds as one husband's personal experience.

Unfortunately, examination of epiklerate scenarios presented in the orators is of little assistance in gauging the level of social approbation of the system. Exogamous marriages of *epikleroi* are occasionally mentioned without wincing or whining.[7] Egregious violations are sometimes alleged with indignation.[8] Disputes between rival kin claimants were played out in the procedure called *diadikasia*; bargains "behind closed doors" may often have preceded the final act in the courtroom (cf. And. 1. 119; Is. 10. 19–20).[9] No extant oration, however, belongs to a *diadikasia* in which an *epikleros* is currently under dispute. Presumably, issues of fact would be of the utmost importance: the degree of the claimant's relationship to the father of the *epidikos* would have to be determined. The nearest relative would obtain both her and the estate; the eldest of kin in same proximity to the *epikleros* probably had the right to marry her over younger relations of the same degree – but it is not certain whether such a "right" was conferred by law or simply honored by custom.[10] In cases where a father had assigned his daughter by written will to a husband, the husband-elect (whether kin or non-kin)

6 Rubinstein 1993: 94.

7 The elder daughter of Polueuktos was married by *engue* to the speaker of Dem. 41. 3–4; the two daughters of Gulon, Demosthenes' maternal grandfather, were married by *engue* (Dem. 28. 1–7, and see Rubinstein 1993: 101–02).

8 E.g., Is. 8. 40; 10. 19–20; *POxy.* 2464 (Hyp.?).

9 On the procedure for claiming an *epikleros*, see chapter 2, n. 7.

10 The existence of such a law is hypothesized on the basis of *Aspis* 142–43 and 255; see MacDowell 1982: 47 and Karabelias 1975: 232–33. Brown 1983: 418 points out, "*Aspis* may reflect practices which many Athenians would have found acceptable rather than behaviour which was explicitly sanctioned by the laws."

would also have to appear before the magistrate to legitimize the will (and possibly to compete against other rivals in a *diadikasia*).[11] While the lawful grounds for claiming an *epikleros* seem fairly straightforward (i.e., the claimant must establish his relationship or authenticate a will), kindred claimants may sometimes have appealed to fairness in their attempts to prevail over competitors. Ar. *Wasps* 583–86 no doubt comically exaggerates; nonetheless, Philokleon's boast suggests that dikasts were not consigned to hear only verbal diagrams of family stemmata or testimony of a will's authenticity: "And if a father leaves behind an *epikleros* and in his last gasps gives her away to anyone, we bid his testament to bawl its head off – likewise the shell that solemnly accompanies its seals; then we give the *epikleros* to the rival who persuades us with his appeals (*antibolesas*)."

Only the merest hint of the application of such an "appeal" appears in the orators. Sositheos, speaker of [Dem.] 43 *Makar.*, after citing the law requiring kin to marry or dower poor *epikleroi*, describes his conduct when Phulomakhe became an *epikleros* (c. 55): ". . . and when it was requisite for me to claim the hand of the *epikleros* Phulomakhe . . . I came forward out of respect for the law and claimed her as being nearest kin; but Theopompos the father of Makartatos neither came forward nor disputed the claim at all, since it was in no way relevant for him to do so – and he acted in this way even though he was in the same age bracket [*sc.* as I am] (διὰ τὸ μηδ' ὁτιοῦν αὐτῶι προσήκειν, καὶ ταῦτ' ἐν τῆι ἡλικίαι ὢν τῆι αὐτῆι)." The clause that purports to explain Theopompos' acquiescence to Sositheos' claim (διὰ τὸ μηδ' ὁτιοῦν αὐτῶι προσήκειν) insinuates the former's lack of a lawful right to the *epikleros* – Theopompos was clearly outside the *ankhisteia* in this particular dispute.[12] The concessive clause (καὶ ταῦτ' ἐν τῆι ἡλικίαι ὢν τῆι

[11] The law is paraphrased and then read to the court (but omitted from our texts) in [Dem.] 46. 22: "Read in addition the law, please, which bids that an *epidikasia* take place for all *epikleroi*, both *xenoi* and *astai*, and that in the case of *politai*, the arkhon is to introduce and oversee it, and in the case of *metoikoi*, the polemarkhos, and that it is not permissible to possess either an estate or an *epikleros* without being subjected to an adjudication (*anepidikon*)." After the law is read, the speaker says, "Therefore, if Phormion wanted to proceed correctly, it was incumbent on him to have a claim entered for the *epikleros*, whether it was right for him by virtue of a gift or by virtue of his family relationship (εἶτα κατὰ δόσιν αὐτῶι προσῆκεν εἴτε κατὰ γένος) . . . , and then, if he had any just claim to present, when he had persuaded those of you who were allotted dikastic duty, he ought to have obtained the *epikleros* with the aid of the laws and your verdict . . . ". The phrase "by virtue of a gift" (κατὰ δόσιν) refers to a will, implying that the father had bequeathed his estate to an individual whom he had also designated as son-in-law. See Karabelias 1979: 207.

[12] The *ankhisteia* is the legally defined group of kin who have the rights, in hierarchical order

αὐτῆι), however, insinuates that Theopompos might have made an appeal to fair play if he had initiated a rival claim – he was of the same age as Sositheos.[13] The neglect of that appeal is made to sound surprising. Sositheos' tendentious point appears to be that Theopompos' son, by actively seeking the estate of Hagnias at the present time and by trying to establish his close relationship to Hagnias' family, is shown to be acting quite differently from the way his father had acted years ago when a relative of Hagnias had become an *epikleros*: at that time he did not even try to support a claim with an appeal to fair play, by adducing proximity of age – to a rival!

Sositheos' comment might allow the inference that discussion of age was a catalyst for arguments of fairness in disputes over *epikleroi*; seniority and prestige of rivals rather than disparity with the age of an *epikleros* may have been the crucial issue. But Sositheos gives no endorsement to such an argument here. The dikasts might have understood him to mean, "Theopompos lost a good chance at a marriage by not using a claim that has often been successful before"; but they might also have understood him to mean, "If Theopompos really desired a connection with Hagnias' family, we might at least have expected him to use the argument about age – it would have been grasping at straws, but nevertheless, it would have shown that he was interested."[14]

of degree of kinship, to an intestate inheritance and to marriage with an *epikleros*; the law is quoted at [Dem.] 43. 51 and discussed at Is. 11. 11–12. Sositheos' relationship to Phulomakhe was closer by virtue of his relationship to her father, Euboulides II: Sositheos is (maternal) grandson of Euboulides' (paternal) uncle, whereas Theopompos is (paternal) grandson of the brother of Euboulides' (maternal and paternal) grandfathers. The clause under discussion can also be translated, "since he had no relationship at all."

13 The words themselves do not specify whether the neglected claim is viewed as being based on Theopompos' proximity of age to his rival Sositheos or to the *epikleros* Phulomakhe. The second alternative, however, must be disqualified on external grounds; Theopompos was not an agemate of the *epikleros*. Chronological precision is out of the question; there are no hard and fast dates in the oration. An arkhon date in witness testimony provides a year (361 / 60) for Phulomakhe's success in her claim for Hagnias' estate (43. 31); those who accept that date infer that her marriage with Sositheos took place before that hearing, since he had acted as her representative ([Dem.] 43. 9, Is. 11. 9 and 16). Among those daring historical reconstructions, some hypothesize Theopompos' birth between 420 and 410 (Davies 1971: 84–86; Thompson 1976: 93); Sositheos' birth around 400 (Thompson 1976: 93); Phulomakhe's birth around 385 (Thompson 1976: 69–70) or 375 (Humphreys 1983: 223–24). According to Thompson's reconstruction, Sositheos married Phulomakhe in 370; accordingly, Theopompos will be 45 (if he was born *c.* 415), Sositheos 30, and Phulomakhe 15. All these relative dates are slippery; it may very well be that Theopompos and Sositheos are closer in age than Thompson has supposed; there is no way to know for certain.

14 The speaker's tendentious agenda renders inference specious: it is in his interest to present Theopompos as if he had been in a good position to claim the *epikleros*, even if that were patently untrue.

There are no hints in the orators that disparity between the ages of *epikleros* and kinsmen was ever an issue in courtroom decisions – but we are not well-informed about these matters. Age disparity and a backroom bargain, however, have been proposed to explain away one puzzling case. In Isaios 3 *Pyrrhos*, the speaker allegedly quotes the words of a law: "a man can dispose of his property however he like, provided that he leave behind no legitimate sons; but if he leave behind female children, [the estate goes] with them" (68). He next interprets: "thus a man can bequeath and dispose of his property with his daughters; but he can neither adopt nor bequeath any of his property to anyone without [disposing of] his legitimate daughters" (68). Most scholars have accepted the speaker's interpretation of the law; they believe that the father of an *epikleros* who adopts a son must arrange for the adopted son to marry the daughter.[15] The speaker in Isaios 3, after maintaining this interpretation, logically argues against accepting the following depiction of events that had allegedly been posited by his opponents, one of whom is now on trial for false witnessing: that Phile, a legitimate daughter of Pyrrhos, upon becoming an *epikleros* when her father died, was permitted to marry outside her kin group while an adoptive son enjoyed the deceased's estate (69, cf. 50–51). Such a state of affairs, according to the speaker, would indeed be deplorable – but the defendant is lying. Phile was no *epikleros* he explains; she was illegitimate and thus incapable of transmitting her father's estate – hence her exogamous marriage.

The arguments of the defense are not preserved; modern historians have been ready with their speculative ones: while the fact that the adoptive son Endios did not marry Phile is suspicious, nevertheless, Phile may have been an infant at the time of her father's death; moreover, a bargain may have been struck between Phile's eventual husband and the adoptive son who entered into the estate: the former might have agreed "not to contest the estate until the

[15] E.g., Lipsius 511–12; Gernet 1920 (= 1955: 136):154; Harrison 1. 83. MacDowell 1978: 100 and n. 221 (citing Men. *Dusk.* 729–39), however, proposes that the adopted son might also "give her in marriage to another man with half her father's property as dowry, and when she eventually had children they could claim the whole of her deceased father's property." MacDowell 1982: 46 suggests that this option was a legal requirement when a man adopted his stepson. The alternatives proposed by MacDowell are plausible, but we should not expect a precise replica of the law in Menander. For discussion of the differences between the scenarios portrayed in Is. 3 and in Menander's play, see Paoli 1976 (= 1961): 559–70. Rubinstein 1993: 95–96 (and text above) plausibly argues against the speaker's interpretation of the law cited at Is. 3. 68.

latter's death."[16] Out-of-court bargains might indeed have been made – and they might have been fair.[17] Or the speaker may have distorted the law – or at least have presented only one interpretation of it: possibly a father might adopt a son without requiring him to marry his daughter; the alleged wording of the law and the speaker's interpretation of it, as Rubinstein has argued, are vague enough to support the hypothesis.[18] If so, then a bargain of another sort can be supposed: a promise from Endios to dower Phile handsomely – and within the boundaries of the law. Or Phile may in fact have been illegitimate.

In the eyes of the law, respective ages of kinsman and *epikleros* made no difference; but practicalities (e.g., long engagements for infants) would have to be worked out. A law ascribed to Solon (Plut. *Solon* 20. 2–3) provided that the husband of an *epikleros* should have sexual intercourse with her thrice a month; the wife of a husband who was unable to perform was to be given to next nearest kinsman.[19] Plutarch is not an exceptionally good source for sixth-century Athenian law and there is no certain reference to the law elsewhere; nonetheless, it is not implausible in itself and legal historians have generally accepted it: the functioning of the epiklerate system depends, after all, upon the production of male heirs.[20] Of interest is the lawgiver's focus of attention: he (apparently) has not designated any specific age to mark the extinction of sexual capacity; instead, he has formulated a rule by which sexual incapacity can be legally defined. No doubt an older man's sexual capacity

16 Schaps 1979: 30; similarly, Wyse 1904: 333–34. Details of the allegedly unlawful bargain are sketched further: there may have been enough wealth in the family to make an agreement palatable; Endios may have dowered Phile generously – even if the sum did not amount to one-tenth of the estate (on textual difficulties in the report of the amount of the dowry, see Wyse 1904 apud Is. 3. 49. 5); Endios himself remained childless and so was no threat to Phile's children.

17 Another "bargain" has been posited to explain some of the family history that lies buried in Is. 10 – different from the one alluded to by the speaker; see Wyse 1904: 649–51.

18 Rubinstein 1993: 95–96: see also MacDowell's view in n. 15.

19 Solon ff 51 a and 52 a Ruschenbusch. Cf. Todd 1993: 230: "perhaps the only example of a statute at Athens ordering specific performance."

20 A fragment of Demosthenes (VII. 1 B–S = Pollux 8. 53) refers to the availability of *eisangeliai*, either "against non-kinsmen who marry an *epikleros*" or "against men who live together with the *epikleros* in a manner that is inappropriate [i.e., by failing to have intercourse with her]" – depending on whether Meier's emendation is accepted in the latter case: Δημοσθένης δὲ ἐν τῶι κατὰ Μέδοντος καὶ κατὰ τῶν μὴ προσηκόντων [codd.: προσηκόντως Meier] τῆι ἐπικλήρωι συνοικοῦντων γίνεσθαι τὰς εἰσαγγελίας λέγει. The reading of the codices makes no sense (non-kinsmen may be married to *epikleroi* – e.g., in instances where there are no available kinsmen or when a poor *epikleros* has been dowered by a kinsman for marriage to a non-kinsman). Meier's emendation is to be preferred.

is, for the most part, less than a younger man's. But the lawgiver is generous to older men: he gives them a chance. Thrice a month, after all, is not thrice a night.[21] A man's unsuitability, then, is not to be determined by publicly identifiable criteria prior to marriage – age, a head of white hair, a brilliant set of wrinkles make no difference. A society for which the typical age for first marriage is thirty or thirty-five years for the husband and fifteen for the wife might not have winced at even larger age gaps (if they were larger!) between uncle and young niece, the *epikleros*.[22]

The phenomenon of marital age difference in Athenian society has been frequently noticed by social and legal historians; its implications for New Comedy, however, have not been fully appreciated.[23] A brief digression is in order. In *Misoumenos*, a slave sees an elderly man embracing the young sweetheart of his master. A similar scenario is dramatized at *Poenulus* v 5, 1296–1327 – another elderly man is viewed embracing a young woman. In *Georgos*, a slave reports that an elderly (*gerōn*, 51, 66, 73) farmer plans to marry a destitute girl, in gratitude to her brother who has nursed him through an injury (71–84). In *Aulularia*, Eunomia proposes to her elderly brother Megadorus that he marry a woman *grandior natu: media est mulieris*

[21] In Ar. *Ekkl.* 619–20, Blepuros worries how Praxagoras' plan for the new government will affect old men (*tous presbutas*); according to the plan, a man must consort with an ugly woman before he lies down with a fair one. Note that Blepuros only worries about the elderly man's stamina in regard to the second go-around.

[22] For collection of ancient evidence (mostly generalizations) on age at first marriage, see M. Golden 1990: 212 n. 82. There was undoubtedly greater variety than Golden's evidence suggests. Mantitheos, e.g., reports that his father persuaded him to marry when he was "about 18 years old" because he wanted to see children born from him ([Dem.] 40. 12; his description of the circumstances suggests that such a youthful marriage was unusual and this may well be an instance of Mantitheos trying to make himself older than he is (and older than his half-brother). For instances of "cross-generation marriage" (e.g., between uncle and niece) at Athens, see Thompson 1976: 102 and n. 70. As he points out, there is no full study of such marriages.

[23] My remarks here are limited to Athenian views of marital age difference. In Plautus, the "lecherous old man" is a favorite character; while his amorous instincts are directed toward young women (and not infrequently toward his son's beloved – e.g., *Asin.*, *Bacch.*, *Cas.*, *Merc.*), the young women are always prostitutes. A strong strand of disapproval is voiced against these *senes amatores* (cf. ch. 6.1.b); sometimes the protest focuses on the old man's hypocrisy and squandering of his (or his wife's) estate (*Asin.* v 2); sometimes the man's age is viewed as being unsuitable for amorous avocation (*Cas.* 518, *Merc.* 972–73, 982–87, 1015–20) and more particularly for the prerequisite exertion (*Stich.* 571–73). Barsby 1986: 185 (with citation of relevant bibliography) discusses possible Plautine divergences from Menandrian models in depictions of such *senes*. Note that Aristophanes in *Ekkl.* only ridicules the old hags who hanker longingly after a young lad; but the comic poet probably could not have staged, with the same effect, old men in hot pursuit of young citizen girls; decorum (stage and social) may have guided the playwright's decision: App. 7.1. See Henderson 1987 on the presentation of "older women" in Old Comedy.

aetas ("a bit older – she's middle-aged," 159); Megadorus proposes a younger candidate in response. Modern conventional notions of acceptable age differences between men and women ought not to color our reception of these scenes. What might appear to some contemporary readers of our era and western culture as a marker of an "odd couple" may not have been marked at all to a fourth-century audience. The slave in *Misoumenos*, for example, assumes the elderly man is a rival lover, "caught in the act" (*ep' autophōrōi* 218). The man is the girl's father – his manifest age (sixty, 220) and grey head of hair (219) had not been a tip-off.[24] The elderly Carthaginian's appearance in *Poenulus* is no hindrance to Antamoenides' suspicion that he has come upon a rival *amator.* The slave in *Georgos* gives no intimation that the disparity in the ages of potential bride and groom might cause any hesitation in the acceptance of so advantageous a union; the mother's only concern is that her daughter (a victim of a rape, it seems, 30) is about to give birth (87). Eunomia's guiding concern in her choice of the middle-aged (but nonetheless capable of child-bearing – 148, 163–64) bride in *Aulularia* is the size of the woman's dowry (158); when Megadorus rejects that candidate and suggests another, the young daughter of his neighbor, the only objection he foresees is the girl's poverty (173–74); the girl's age does not enter the discussion at all. Only in *Aspis* is an age disparity noted with disapproval (Act II, 255–67); the argument offered by Khairestratos there, however, might be no more than special pleading – and a red herring for modern commentators. As we shall see shortly, Khairestratos is apt to try anything (including the offer of a slippery – if not unlawful – bargain and the faking of his own death) in order to prevent his older brother from marrying the alleged *epikleros.*

Since nearly a generation separates the "normal" married couple in Athens, the young lovers of New Comedy, or the young men on the brink of marriage, are themselves likely to be twenty-five to thirty-five year olds. They are not, as commentators sometimes seem to envision, a uniform cadre of like-aged youth.[25] Pollux in his

[24] Gomme and Sandbach's (1973) comment apud *Mis.* 223 demonstrates how presuppositions about age might color interpretation and restoration of texts: "Does Geta suspect that he has made a ridiculous mistake in taking Krateia's father for a lover (e.g. [ἦν ἐγὼ] οὕτω γελοῖος) or protest that he has never heard such an absurd story (e.g. [τίς λόγος] οὕτω γελοοῖς;)?"

[25] Probably no precise age or technical meaning should be attached to *ephebus* in Latin texts. Phaidria's younger brother is disparagingly depicted as *ephebus* at *Eun.* 824 after raping a

taxonomy of masks lists eleven types for young men, and the first four are presented in descending order of age.[26] Pollux also presents parasites as wearing the masks of "young men"; yet the parasite in *Menaechmi* gives his age as over thirty (*Men.* 446). If we are hesitant to apply this later evidence to fourth and third-century Athenian stage practice, a text of Greek New Comedy offers persuasive demonstration of variety. Moskhion, the "young lover" of *Samia*, remarks in the opening monologue of that play, "I excelled when I was *khoregos* / and in displays of generosity; . . . / . . I was brilliant as commander of my tribe's regiment of cavalry" (τῶι χορηγεῖν διέφερον / [καὶ τῆι] φιλοτιμίαι· . . . / . . ἐφυλάρχησα λαμπρῶς, 13–15). Neither of the positions which Moskhion claims to have filled belongs to twenty-year-olds. While the minimum age of thirty for the tribal cavalry commander is only attested by *AP* 30. 2 for the constitution of the Five Thousand, yet the age of thirty did remain the minimum for most offices in Athens under the democracy – unless a higher minimum was stipulated.[27] And as for being *khoregos*, while Demetrios of Phalerum had abolished festival liturgies *c.* 316–15, still, there is no reason to believe that the traditional "older age" associated with carrying out liturgies immediately gave way to a rush of rich and generous twenty-year-olds in performing local ones that still survived.[28] A comparable scenario appears in an indubitably Plautine passage of *Captivi* (see App. 5, cat. no. iii. 9): the parasite alludes to *iuventus* (470) and *adulescentes* (478) as the same men who give guilty verdicts in court (476) – even "young men," then, are envisioned as belonging to the senatorial class. These dribbles of

girl. Charinus reports sowing wild oats for an undefined period after he left *ephebi* (*Merc.* 40, emended text); he then left Athens for two years (10). Pamphilus after leaving *ephebi* has raised horses, hunted, and studied with philosophers (*And.* 51–57). Donatus (apud *And.* 51.3) interprets *ephebia* correctly as *prima aetas adulescentiae*; the phrase *postquam excessit ex ephebis* will mean "after he left his early teens" (rather than, "after he left the ephebes" i.e., military service," à la *AP* 42. 2–5); the phrase is syntactically similar to *ek paidōn* in Greek, (e.g., Dem. 21. 154) and just as vague. Menander only uses *ephebos* in fr. 724 K–T: παῖς γέγον', ἔφηβος, μειράκιον, ἀνήρ, γέρων ("he has been a boy, a teen-ager, a youth, a man, an old man"); the term is obviously neither technical nor precise; see M. Golden 1990: 14–15.

26 Pollux 4. 146–48. On Pollux's catalogue in comparison with the terracottas at Lipari, see Brown's review (1984: 111–12) of Brea 1981. Brown 1987: 194–95 appears to allow a certain fluidity to the ages of men in New Comedy: "In the world of Greek and Latin Comedy a man is old if he is old enough to have a marriageable son or daughter. If he is old enough to consider marrying, or recently married, he belongs to the younger generation. Married men with young children do not exist" (194, n. 44).

27 Rhodes 1981: 390.

28 See Pickard-Cambridge² 1988: 91–92 for the dating of Demetrios' change. *AP* 56. 3 informs us that forty was the minimum age for the *khoregos* of a boys' chorus.

detail are cited here not to suggest that the "young men" or *adulescentes* of New Comedy are all aging Lotharios, but rather to show that they are not all the same age (see nn. 25–26), and to urge that our own cultural preconceptions about age and about what is "young" and what is "old" not be pasted onto our reading of ancient texts. To a fourteen or fifteen-year-old *epikleros*, a thirty, forty, and fifty-year-old man (without a mask) might all appear fairly the same; whether adults thought that one age category rather than another was more suitable for the *epikleros*, and whether such thoughts had consolidated into a social consensus, is information unavailable to us.

Ostensible motives for marriage to a kinswoman who is an *epikleros* are occasionally adduced in the orators; notable for its absence is that of age similarity:

(1) Such marriages fulfill a lawful obligation (And. 1. 119; [Dem.] 43. 54).
(2) Such marriages provide sons, who, if they are adopted into the *oikos* of the deceased, become heirs for *oikoi* that are all but extinct and allow family members to carry out duties of kinship for the tomb-cults of the dead ([Dem.] 43. 12–13).
(3) Marrying a poor *epikleros* is virtuous (And. 1. 119).
(4) Marrying a rich *epikleros* is materially advantageous (Dem. 57. 41; Is. 6. 47).
(5) The property of a rich *epikleros* ought not to pass outside of family (Is. 3. 45–53).

It is difficult to measure the amount of social approval accorded some of these alleged motives. Forensic context colors depiction. The speaker of Dem. 57 *Eub.* explains the grounds of his mother's divorce (motive no. 4): her first husband, Protomakhos, was a poor man; when he had the opportunity to marry a rich *epikleros*, he persuaded a friend to marry his wife and he himself married his kinswoman (41). The motive of material advantage is not always described so compassionately. A claimant who ascribes the motive to a rival might depict it as robbery (e.g., Is. 6. *Phil.* 47).

Only one ostensible motive is found for the exogamous marriage of an *epikleros*: the refusal of an endogamous partner allows an existing marriage to be maintained (Is. 10. 19–20). The speaker who claimed that his father allowed his mother to be defrauded of her lawful estate "so as not to be deprived of her" may or may not be telling the truth – Isaios exerts little effort to expatiate. Some historians have used the speaker's explanation as an example of an "emotional argument" and one uses it as evidence that "the court was expected to understand a man's affection for the woman he had taken in marriage."[29] But it may be that such an alleged marriage of sentiment in this case would be in bad odor with the majority of dikasts – not because marital affection was a rare commodity in Athens – that certainly is not so.[30] Rather, the notion of the inviolability of property appears so firmly implanted in kin that a marriage of sentiment which destroys that inviolability – when kin had been ready to prevent it by marriage – might reasonably seem little else than foolish and transient self-indulgence. Isaios, at any rate, wastes no words on his client's sentimental appeal.[31]

When so little is known for certain, it is difficult to maintain that the epiklerate system was both deteriorating and subject to social disapprobation in the fourth century. We cannot calculate the rate of approval accorded actual and hypothesized manipulations of inheritance strategies. Arguments of fair play may sometimes have prevailed over strictures of law; affection or greed may have been the impetus. It does not seem odd to find similar arguments and motives in New Comedy. What is clear is negative: social approval for lawful practice versus individual manipulation cannot be measured from the evidence of the orators. Can it be measured in New Comedy?

1(b) The comedies

Plays presumably about *epikleroi* were popular among writers of New Comedy. We have titles but few fragments of three comedies called *Epidikazomenos* ("The man to whom an estate [and *epikleros*] is adjudged").[32] Seven comedies were called *Epikleros*; two Roman comedies bore the transliterated title.[33] Only one Greek play

[29] Just 1989: 102.

[30] For a strongly expressed notion of marital love, see Eur. *Tr.* 661–68; for erotic love in marriage, see Xen. *Symp.* 9. Brown 1993: 191 argues that even "the notion of marrying for love was not seen as a comic absurdity in the time of Menander."

[31] See Wyse 1904: 649–51 for plausible discussion of the opponents' case.

[32] Diphilos, Philemon, and Apollodoros of Karystos are the authors; Apollodoros' play was the model for Terence's *Phormio*.

[33] Alexis, Antiphanes, Diodoros, Diphilos, Euetes, Heniokhos, and Menander (who appears to have written two plays with this title). Another play may have been called *Diadikazomenoi* and so might be pertinent (by Dioxippos: *IG* ii^2 2323, 169 Διαδικ]αζομένοις supplied by Koehler, but 'Αγο]ραζομένοις read and supplied by Ruck). *Epicleros* is the title of lost plays by the Roman poets Caecilius and Turpilius.

survives, however, in which an alleged *epikleros* is subject to dispute – and that play bears the curious but uninformative title, *Aspis* ("Shield"). Two Roman plays also survive in which an alleged *epikleros* figures and is subject to dispute: *Phormio*, based on Apollodoros' *Epidikazomenos*, and *Adelphoe*, based on Menander's homonymous play. The scenarios of epiklerate marriages in both Roman plays probably follow closely their Greek originals since there is no corresponding Roman institution; Roman sentiments about marriage, however, might occasionally color their depiction.[34] On the other hand, the *epikleros* of a Greek original can sometimes be transformed into an *uxor dotata* ("richly dowered wife"); Caecilius certainly adapted the *epikleros* of Menander's *Plokion* in this way.[35] Other *uxores dotatae* who appear in Roman Comedy may also have been *epikleroi* in the Greek originals: e.g., Nausistrata in *Phormio*, *Matrona* in *Menaechmi*.[36] These women are not subject to dispute and the plots of these plays do not hinge upon the peculiar marital arrangements of *epikleroi* – the women need only be rich by virtue of a handsome dowry, not married to a relative in fulfillment of a lawful claim.

In three extant plays (*Aspis*, *Phormio*, *Adelphoe*), the epiklerate laws seemingly come up for scrutiny as some characters hold that an *epikleros* should be married to kin or remain in such a marriage and others maintain in opposition that such a marriage should not take place or, if it has already, that it should be dissolved. In *Aspis*, a rich putative *epikleros* is subject to dispute between an elderly kinsman and a younger non-kindred rival. In *Phormio*, a poor girl pretending to be an heiress has married an alleged kinsman; she is now on the verge of being divorced and dowered off to a non-kindred husband. In *Adelphoe*, a poor heiress is said to be sought after by a kinsman – against the wishes of a non-kindred rival. The easiest arguments for the disputants to make are those in support of marrying the *epikleros* endogamously: the claimant can simply adduce or allude to the law (as Smikrines does in *Aspis* I and Micio in his fictive *ludus* in *Adelphoe* IV 5); he can also add a sentimental interpretation of the lawgiver's intentions to support that position (as Phormio does in II 3 of the homonymous play). Disputants who oppose the endogamous marriages of *epikleroi* offer

34 See n. 46 below.
35 Williams 1968: 363–66 on Caecilius' *Plocion*; Schuhmann 1977 treats the *uxor dotata* in the Plautine corpus.
36 For argument about Nausistrata's status, see App. 5, add. 10; for Matrona's status, see Gratwick 1993: 29–30.

bargains to their supporters (as Demipho does in *Phormio* II 3), or arguments of sentiment (as Aeschinus does in *Adelphoe* IV 5), or combinations of the two (as Khairestratos does in *Aspis* II). Examination of these scenarios will show these arguments in operation.

Before the staged action of *Aspis* begins, the fatherless Kleostratos had gone off to enrich the family's ebbing fortune by fighting in Lykia; apparently, he left his father's brother, Khairestratos, as *kurios* of his sister (127–37). Kleostratos' slave, Daos, returns to Athens in Act I, bringing home his master's shield and a large quantity of money, slaves, and other booty captured in the campaign. He also reports (erroneously, it will turn out) to Smikrines, another paternal uncle, that his young master died in battle. The conjunction of the booty's arrival and the report of Kleostratos' death provoke Smikrines' cupidity: he will marry the young *epikleros* as her closest and eldest relative and take control of the property.[37] His resolution ruins the plans of his brother Khairestratos; he had hoped that Khaireas (his wife's son from an earlier marriage) would marry Kleostratos' sister; indeed, the young man (Khaireas) was already engaged to the girl (284–98) and was to have married her that very day (136–37). Smikrines, however, as oldest paternal uncle appears to have either a legal or customary right to abrogate that agreement.[38] Pretending to resent his younger brother's decision to hand over the girl to Khaireas without having consulted him, he says to Daos:

τὴν οὐσίαν
οὐχὶ καταλείψω τὴν ἐμὴν διαρπάσαι
τούτοις, ὅπερ δὲ καὶ παραινοῦσίν τινες
τῶν γνωρίμων μοι λήψομαι τὴν παρθένον
γυναῖκα ταύτην· καὶ γὰρ ὁ νόμος μοι δοκεῖ
οὕτω λέγειν πως, Δᾶε . . . (182–87)

This property
of mine shall not be left behind for them
to plunder, and the very thing some of my acquaintances
advise me to do, I'll do: I'll marry the girl – for really the law, in my opinion,
means something like that, Daos . . .

[37] Whether Kleostratos' sister has become her brother's *epikleros* upon his alleged death or whether she inherits his booty (separately from the paternal estate) in her own right as "intestate heiress" is a question that has exercised scholars. MacDowell 1982: 48 and Karabelias 1975: 231–32 take the first position; Brown 1983: 419 takes the second. Wyse 1904: 651 on Isaios 10 had suggested a similar situation for the daughter of Aristarkhos I, i.e., she might not have been an *epikleros* but rather the heiress of her brother Demokhares.

[38] See n. 10 above.

As Gomme and Sandbach point out, "Smikrines is justified in not making an absolute statement that the law said he should marry her."[39] His relationship to the girl must first be established by an *epidikasia*; given the fact that he is the nearest and eldest relative, the *epidikasia* can be expected to establish his right – which is not an obligation – to marry her. Smikrines' (or his acquaintances') careful interpretation of his legal right is then correct – and in accordance with Smikrines' own "law-abiding" urges.[40] But the elderly uncle's meanness resonates far more than his concern for the law here. The character type is familiar from the orations of Isaios and would be easily recognized by the Athenian audience: the disgruntled wealthy relative who plans an inheritance strategy (e.g., a will which cuts out nearest kin) as the result of a long-lasting family feud or recent familial quarrel.[41] In *Aspis*, the hitherto childless Smikrines now plans to disrupt his own intestate line of inheritance by marrying the *epikleros*; presumably, he has in mind the production of children to inherit his estate. While the motive that Smikrines expresses in 182–83 (the spoiling of his kinsmen's alleged expectations of inheritance) may only have been fabricated on the spur of the moment to conceal his own cupidinous impulse (to acquire – if only temporarily – the estate of the *epikleros*), the spitefulness of the articulated motive puts Smikrines' character on full display.

In the next act, Khairestratos tries to persuade his brother to withdraw his claim. His appeals are sentimental: Smikrines should act with moderation; he should heed his age:

(ΧΑ.) ὢν τηλικοῦτος παῖδα μέλλεις λαμβάνειν;
(ΣΜ.) πηλίκος; (ΧΑ.) ἐμοὶ μὲν παντελῶς δοκεῖς γέρων.
(ΣΜ.) μόνος γεγάμηκα πρεσβύτερος; (258–60)

(KHA.) Old as you are, you would marry a girl?
(SM.) Old as I am? (KHA.) In my opinion, you're quite an old man.
(SM.) Am I the only elderly man to enter the marital state?

Khairestratos' appeal to age persists as he reminds his brother that

[39] Gomme and Sandbach 1973: 78.

[40] These were made evident earlier in the act, when the war-booty had been conveyed to Khairestratos' house. Smikrines had explained why he had not counted the items; he did not want to be called a "money-lover" (149–51). He then justified his neglectful conduct: slaves could be counted upon for accuracy, and Khairestratos' household would willingly abide by law and justice (οἶμαι μὲν οὖν ἑκόντας αὐτοὺς τοῖς νόμοις / καὶ τοῖς δικαίοις ἐμμενεῖν . . . 156–57).

[41] E.g., Is. 1. 9–15.

Khaireas had been planning to marry the girl; after all, Khaireas had been brought up together with her (*suntrophos*, 263). Khairestratos is even ready to make a deal – and once again, he alludes to age:

τί οὖν
λέγω; σὺ μηδὲν ζημιοῦ· τὰ μὲν ὄντα γὰρ
ταῦθ' ὅσαπέρ ἐστι λαβὲ σὺ πάντα, κύριος
γενοῦ, δίδομέν σοι. τὴν δὲ παιδίσκην τυχεῖν
καθ' ἡλικίαν ἔασον αὐτὴν νυμφίου.
ἐκ τῶν ἰδίων ἐγὼ γὰρ ἐπιδώσω δύο
τάλαντα προῖκα. (263–69)

What then
do I suggest? Suffer no financial loss – for the property,
as much as there is, take all of it, be its master,
we give it to you. But as for the girl –
let her have a bridegroom her own age.
Out of my own estate I'll add
a dowry of two talents.

Smikrines, however, guided by materialistic concerns, wastes no words on the appeal to "age-mates"; indeed, there is no further mention of that argument in the remainder of the play. Khaireas himself, when he hears the news in the next scene, accepts what he perceives is the law's verdict: "the law that judges my case worthless for good assigns another to be her *kurios*" (297–98: ἕτερον κύριον δ' αὐτῆς ποεῖ / ὁ νόμος ὁ τοὐμὸν οὐδαμοῦ κρίνων ἔτι). Smikrines, for his part, had been quick to point out the legal weakness in Khairestratos' offer: if Khaireas and the girl produce a son, then a claim might be made, in behalf of the son, for possession of the property:

πρὸς θεῶν, Μελιτίδηι
λαλεῖν ὑπείληφας; τί φῄς; ἐγὼ λάβω
τὴν οὐσίαν, τούτωι δὲ τὴν κόρην ἀφῶ
ἵν', ἂν γένηται παιδίον, φεύγω δίκην
ἔχων τὰ τούτου; (269–73)

By the gods – have you supposed
you were talking to Melitides? What are you suggesting? I should take
the estate, but let him have the girl
so that, if a son is born, I'll be brought to court
for holding on to his property?

Interpretations of Isaios 3 *Pyrrhos* and 10 *Aristarkhos* suggest that such claims may indeed have been brought before the courts of Athens; in *Aspis*, Khairestratos' offer is a bargain of the sort which the speaker of Isaios 10 had depicted.[42] The bargain in *Aspis*, if executed, will endanger the prosperity of the children born of Khaireas and Kleostratos' sister – so long as the children arrive at majority and Smikrines (a) lives to a very ripe old age, or (b) marries elsewhere and produces an heir, or (c) adopts an heir. The Athenian audience need not be composed of astute legal experts to recognize that separation of *epikleros* and estate is egregious violation of law or that separation of lawful heiress from intestate inheritance is tricky business. In either case, Khairestratos is skating on rather thin ice.[43] Smikrines' concern about the bargain is therefore not unjustified – not because he is truly and selflessly concerned lest the girl's future children be deprived of their rightful estate, but because he foresees that their potential claims on the estate might endanger his continued peaceful possession of it. Smikrines will have the estate, and he will obtain it in a legally airtight way – by claiming the *epikleros*. Smikrines exploits legal argument without sentimentalizing it.[44]

In *Phormio*, Demipho offers the parasite a different sort of bargain: Phormio (a non-kinsman) should accept five *mnai* as dowry and marry the poor "heiress" whom Demipho's son (allegedly a kinsman) had recently married as the result of a prosecution.[45] In response, Phormio produces an argument in favor of the law:

[42] Schaps 1979: 30 points out the similarities between Khairestratos' offer and the alleged and hypothesized bargains of Is. 10 and 3.

[43] If Kleostratos' sister "possesses" her brother's booty by virtue of being his *epikleros* rather than by virtue of being an intestate heiress, then Khairestratos' proposal is illegal. If she possesses it as intestate heiress and Khairestratos makes the bargain for her by virtue of being her *kurios*, the deal is still fishy. See n. 37 above.

[44] See chapter 8.3 for a more detailed discussion of Smikrines' role in this play.

[45] Lefèvre 1978a: 12–15 and 23–27 implausibly argues that Terence's references to a courtroom decision as the basis of the award of Phanium show that the Roman playwright has changed what had been a pretended, not actual, *epidikasia* in Apollodoros' play into a *diadikasia*. Brown 1980: 195 shows there is no discrepancy between the Greek original and Terence's account of the events that led to the marriage: "there is no question of a *diadikasia* at any stage." Kinsmen of a poor heiress are compelled by law either to marry her or dower her ([Dem.] 43. 54); *ho boulomenos* can remedy neglect of this duty by denouncing the neglectful kinsman to the arkhon ([Dem.] 43. 54) who might bring the case before the Eliaia ([Dem.] 43. 75); the procedure might be the one mentioned at *AP* 56.6, a *graphe* (or *eisangelia*) for maltreatment of an *epikleros* (see Rhodes ad loc.). As Brown maintains, Phormio has acted as *ho boulomenos* and "we may assume that the arkhon referred the matter to a court after the usual preliminary hearing (*anakrisis*)." Brown's interpretation best suits the language of 127 and 135–36 (127: *ego te cognatum dicam et tibi scribam dicam* and 135–36: *persuasit homini: factumst: ventumst: vincimur: / duxit*). The *scribere dicam* of 127 is a Latin rendering of *graphesthai diken*, i.e., a written indictment brought before the arkhon by *ho boulomenos* (see

itan tandem, quaeso, itidem ut meretricem ubi abusu' sis,
mercedem dare lex iubet ei atque amittere?
an, ut nequid turpe civis in se admitteret
propter egestatem, proxumo iussast dari,
ut cum uno aetatem degeret? quod tu vetas. (ii 3, 413–17)

So then, really, in the very way that you might use a prostitute –
does the law bid you to pay her price and then dismiss her?
Or was it so that a citizen might not suffer any immoral treatment
on account of poverty, that she was to be given to her nearest kin,
that she might spend her life with one man? The very thing you forbid![46]

Later, when the situation has changed – when Phormio has accepted the sum and Demipho now wishes to preserve his son's marriage to the "heiress," Demipho relies on a similar argument; he claims that he has been persuaded by his brother Chremes not to hand the girl over:

"nam qui erit rumor populi" inquit "si id feceris?
olim quom honeste potuit, tum non est data:
eam nunc extrudi turpest." ferme eadem omnia
quae tute dudum coram me incusaveras. (v 8, 911–14)

"For what will be the talk of the town," he asks, "if you should do this?
Before, when she could have been married off with honor, she wasn't;
now it is immoral for her to be turned away." These are almost the same
arguments which you used against me a little while ago.

Phormio's argument in ii 3 had been based on his interpretation of "what the law bids"; Demipho's new argument (or his brother's) in v 8 is based on "the talk of the town." The gist of both is the same: the "heiress" should not be subjected to immoral treatment (cf. 415–16 and 913). Demipho's offer to bargain in the earlier scene is, by his own admission, immoral. The law itself has been sentimentalized and is envisioned as the protector of the weak and impoverished rather than as a stern, dehumanized regulator of conduct. The arguments in both scenes have, of course, been tailored for the

chapter 2.2.c at nn. 96–98). Since there was no rival claimant, the only point in saying "we lost" (135) is that a trial had taken place.

46 No law that we possess stipulates that a poor young heiress cannot be divorced by the relative who marries her; indeed, the laws regulating the marriage of *epikleroi* show no concern at all for the *matrona uni nupta*; the emphasis in 417 may be Terence's: see Arnott 1970: 41–42. On the other hand, it is conceivable that an *eisangelia* for maltreatment of an *epikleros* might be brought in behalf of such a woman who was divorced by her husband; for a highly speculative scenario of an epiklerate divorce, see the editor's interpretation of *POxy.* 2464.

moment; both men are experts in such manipulation. Phormio had orchestrated the prosecution which took place before the comedy began and which had resulted in Antipho's marriage to the alleged *epikleros*; he thus arranged a marriage of sentiment. Demipho had argued against that marriage (II 3) and later argued in its favor (V 8) in order to ensure a marriage that would have one end in common with an epiklerate marriage, a union of close kinsman and kinswoman – the two are in fact first cousins.

The epiklerate laws are once again the subject of dispute in Terence's *Adelphoe*. Here we must focus upon the strand of plot concerning Aeschinus' rape of Pamphila and a dialogue that takes place between the young man and his adoptive father Micio in IV 2. After Micio has cleared the way for Aeschinus' marriage, he catches sight of him at the very moment when he has finally gathered the courage to go to the girl's mother and explain his delay in carrying out his promise. Aeschinus is unaware at this point that Micio knows all about the affair. As soon as Micio sees him at the door of the house, he decides to have some fun at Aeschinus' expense:

MI. tune has pepulisti fores?
(tacet. quor non ludo hunc aliquantisper? melius est,
quandoquidem hoc numquam mihi ipse voluit credere.)
nil mihi respondes? AE. non equidem istas, quod sciam.
MI. ita? nam mirabar quid hic negoti esset tibi.
(erubuit: salva res est.) (638–43)

MI. Have you been knocking at these doors?
(He is silent. Why not play a little trick on him? A rather good idea,
since he himself would never trust me in this affair.)
Why do you say nothing to me? AE. What – me knocking? No, not on those doors, so far as I know.
MI. Really? For I was wondering what business you might have here.
(He has blushed – all is well.)

Aeschinus will not, of course, admit the real reason for his appearance at Sostrata's house. But he blushes. For Micio, this is a sign that his adopted son has some vestige of integrity that assures his salvation.[47] Aeschinus, for his part, is also interested in why Micio should be at Sostrata's house. Micio's explanation is his *ludus*, a complicated story (644–777) that leads Aeschinus to think not only

[47] *Cf.* 821–825. Simo at *And.* 878 is irked when his son shows no such *signum* : *vide num ei(u)s color pudori' signum usquam indicat* ("look at him – does his coloring show any sign of shame?")

that he is about to lose his Pamphila, but that Micio has been instrumental in effecting that loss.

The *ludus* is a fiction, involving – as in the *Phormio* – a marriage compelled by the law concerning *epikleroi.* Micio begins by telling Aeschinus that he had been called in by a friend as *advocatus* (646). He continues: a fatherless girl lives with her mother in the very house where Aeschinus appeared to be knocking; Aeschinus surely does not know them since they have only moved in recently; Micio's friend, as the girl's nearest relative, is compelled by law to marry her (645–52). Aeschinus, who has interrupted Micio's story thus far with impatient directions to "go on," now interrupts "I am destroyed!" (652). Micio mercilessly continues the fabrication: his friend has come to take the girl away with him to Miletos. Aeschinus interrupts in disbelief, "to take the girl away with him?" "Even so," Micio replies. "All the way to Miletos?" "Even so." To Aeschinus' eager question, "What do the women say?", Micio tells him that the mother has contrived a story that a son has been born from some other man; he was first, she says, and the girl ought not to be married to Micio's friend (656–59). Aeschinus can hardly contain himself – "Will he take her away?" Micio, apparently with nonchalance, responds, "Why not?" The young man now lets loose his pent-up anger and reproaches his adoptive father, "You acted cruelly and without pity, and if the truth must be known, unworthily of a gentleman!" Father and son now passionately take up opposing positions, with Micio defending his "friend" and Aeschinus that "miserable first lover" (665–79).[48] Finally, when Aeschinus, in tears, is about to confess everything, Micio reveals that he knows already. In the remainder of the scene, Micio will reproach Aeschinus for violating the girl and hesitating to do anything about it. The scene will end with Micio's assurance that the marriage will take place and with Aeschinus' exuberant appreciation of Micio's activity in his behalf.

Micio's *ludus* is a strategy designed to elicit an admission from Aeschinus of his wrongdoing (640: *quandoquidem hoc numquam mihi ipse voluit credere*); it replaces direct communication and is a substitute for more explicit cross-questioning. It is essentially a trap. Yet Micio

[48] Aeschinus defends his personal position, but presents it as if it were someone else's case. Menander may have borrowed the strategy from Euripides; cf. *Melanippe Sophe*, Nauck² fr. 485 and *Ion* 330–91. Antipho uses the narrative strategy in his *apologus* at *Stichus* iv 1. 538ff., another play with a Menandrian model.

knows his son is guilty, and he also knows he is redeemable – Aeschinus' significant blush had indicated that before Micio staged the *ludus*. Why then does he devise the circuitous strategy? In the course of the *ludus*, Micio taunts Aeschinus, cruelly plays with his emotions as he sharpens his own arguments in behalf of the fictive friend and incites Aeschinus to come more and more passionately – and ever more helplessly – to the defense of that "miserable first lover" – and Micio does not relent until Aeschinus breaks down in tears. One critic has observed in this scene "the practical joker's streak of cruelty."[49] It perhaps seems so – in isolation; but is it?

Surely not. The dynamics of the scene are similar to those in the general plot of *Andria* (see especially I 1, 155–70).[50] In both instances, fathers test their sons and the results of the "tests" are significant: in the *Andria*, a son's compliance with his father's wishes regarding marriage is at stake – and the same is true of *Adelphoe*. Recognition of the pivotal moment in the "test" in the latter play makes this clear. At this point (657–59), Micio informs Aeschinus that the girl's mother has contrived a story about a son born from another man. The precise significance of the detail is controversial; many legal historians, however, have argued that a woman who was already married when she became an *epikleros* could maintain that marriage against the claims of kinsmen under one condition – if she had already produced a son. Whether the loophole was provided by law or honored by custom, Micio's remark helps Aeschinus.[51] If the loophole is lawful and Aeschinus admits paternity, then the "friend" of Micio will no longer be able to claim the *epikleros*. If the loophole is honored by custom and Aeschinus confesses, he might still be able to block the alleged kinsman's claim. And Micio has pointedly left Aeschinus the chance to name the father: Sostrata, he says, would not do so (*neque enim nominat*, 658). Aeschinus, however, still flees confession. Only now does Micio let go a barrage of questions (670–72) – "who betrothed the girl? who gave her away? to whom and when was she married? the man responsible for these events – who is he? why did he take another's bride?" Ostensibly, Micio aims at upholding his friend's claim to marriage with an heiress; in reality, he aims at eliciting a confession of rape from a young man whose

[49] Grant 1975: 48.

[50] The "tests" in *Poen.* v 4, 1224–57 and *Stichus* i 2, 103–27 are different and are probably Plautine invention; on the former, see App. 5, cat. no. iii. 15; on the latter, see n. 98 below.

[51] For summary of this debate with relevant bibliography, see Harrison I. 309–11.

hesitation to confess has become pitifully hopeless; seen in either light, it is difficult to see cruel joking rather than a father's foiled expectations. Some in the audience of the original Greek play may have sympathized with the young man, but Athenian fathers may have been even more indignant and outraged than that paragon of emotional and rhetorical control, "Micio." A young man, an "outsider," had come along and taken advantage of a poor *epikleros* without protection; timely marriage to her kinsman would have prevented that calamity.[52] In the dispute between law and sentiment, the sentimental aspect of law itself, law as the guardian not only of property rights but of the weak and unprotected, surfaces once again.

Smikrines in *Aspis*, the brilliant parasite and later the *senex* Demipho in *Phormio*, and Micio in *Adelphoe* all argue for adherence to law: nearest kinsman should be allowed to carry out his right to marry an *epikleros*. Smikrines argues that he should thus marry his niece, Phormio in ii 3 and Demipho in v 8 argue that Antipho should thus remain married to his kinswoman, and Micio argues that his "friend" should marry his relative. Interestingly, in none of these plays does the adverting to the epiklerate laws effect an "unwanted marriage." Smikrines' rigorous adherence to the laws, guided by materialistic instincts, will lead him into a trap, a sham epiklerate marriage, which will ensure that he renounce his plans to marry Kleostratos' sister; she will thus be able to carry out her prior engagement. Phormio supports the epiklerate laws as part of a trick which allowed Antipho to marry the girl he loves; Demipho later adds his endorsement to maintain the marriage between the kindred couple. And Micio uses the story of a kinsman's attempt to marry an *epikleros* in order to extract a confession from his son of his passion for the very same girl – with a view to cementing in marriage the relationship between the latter two. In each play, then, the situation of an *epikleros* is faked in order to ensure the initiation of a marriage of sentiment. The epiklerate system, which might be viewed as an obstruction to marriages of sentiment, becomes a vehicle for executing marriages of that very sort.

It is sometimes thought that plays such as these involve the playwright's social commentary, his criticism of the epiklerate system. This notion has played a particular part in recent discussions

[52] For the role of Hegio in the Greek original, see App. 5, add.8.

of *Aspis*, where the play is seen to be a debate between love and the law with the playwright supporting the position of the former.[53] In Act II of the play, the bargain to separate *epikleros* (or intestate heiress) and estate was offered by a sympathetic character (Khairestratos) rather than by a roguish fiend. Tukhe herself, prologue speaker for the play, had tipped the audience off that Khairestratos was deserving of good will (125) – and that his brother, Smikrines, deserved quite the opposite (116–21). But the sympathetic brother, upon the rejection of his slippery bargain, will go on to fake his death and offer up his own daughter on the altar of sham *epikleroi*. Khairestratos is good-hearted, no doubt; we like him – even without Tukhe's directive. But the extensive buffoonery of the "play within the play," the production of Khairestratos' own death, stretching as it does over the course of three acts (chapter 8.3), hardly provides a venue for serious criticism. Smikrines himself is an unsympathetic character not because he upholds the law but because he has chosen to apply it for materialistic and mean motives.[54] Other elderly uncles in Athens might also have chosen to apply the law in their favor when younger rivals were yet available – we have seen no evidence that age disparity in and of itself would have been considered opprobrious. But not all uncles will have acted from motives of greed and spite. An uncle, for example, might have felt a powerful bond of affection for a dead brother; marriage to his brother's daughter may have been particularly meaningful to such a man – especially if he himself were unmarried and had no son of his own to carry out the "duty." A personal desire to take charge of the yearly rites in his brother's behalf – a duty that may not have extended to collateral kin – might have loomed large in that decision.[55] Smikrines, however, has displayed none of these impulses. His plan to make the son (Kleostratos) of his dead brother the heir to his wealth materializes rather late in the day (168–71) – after the alleged death of the young man. And Smikrines' reactions to the (sham) fatal illness of his brother Khairestratos dramatize only the absence of brotherly affection (433–35, 465–67). It is not the law that is scrutinized in this play, but rather the character of two brothers –

[53] MacDowell 1982: 42–52 has used these terms; cf. Turner 1979: 120: ". . . it is hard to imagine that the institution of the epiclerate emerged in good standing from this derisory treatment." Cf. Karabelias 1975 and Mossé 1989. Brown 1983 argues specifically against MacDowell's position; the argument presented here is generally in accord with Brown's.

[54] Similarly Brown 1983: 413–14.

[55] Rubinstein 1993: 71–75.

both of whom manipulate inheritance strategies from entirely different motives.

The sentimental presentation of the epiklerate laws in *Phormio* and *Adelphoe*, the former based on an Apollodoran original, the latter on a Menandrian, should at least commend the view that the notion of these laws as guardian of the weak and unprotected was still afloat in Hellenistic Athens. Law itself is static; men give it sinews and suppleness – or stiffness – in accordance with their character or whim. In *Aspis*, the epiklerate system is subverted, but the playwright himself is not thereby suggesting that the world would be better off if that system were dismantled for good. The system is subverted when Menander paradoxically creates the situation of a sham *epikleros* to effect a marriage of sentiment. But "paradoxical subversion" rather than social commentary may be the goal in and of itself. Similarly in *Andria*, Simo creates a sham marriage (*falsae nuptiae*) undesired by his son in order to promote his acceptance of a real marriage (*verae nuptiae*). Social commentary on marriage – or a game with *falsae nuptiae* and *verae nuptiae*? The crucial issue of comedies with *epikleroi* motifs may have been formulated by their composers in this way: how can the epiklerate laws, which usually compel marriages in which financial and family considerations play the greatest role, be exploited to effect marriages of sentiment? The issue, so formulated, becomes a legal puzzle – of the sort we might well expect the Athenian audience to enjoy. The spectators envisioned here do not depart the theater saying, "Yes, there are serious flaws in the epiklerate system," but rather, "Wasn't it funny – the way Daos figured out how to use the epiklerate laws to obtain for Khaireas the wife he wanted?" In earlier chapters I argued that the resolutions of rapes offered the writers of New Comedy the opportunity to exploit dramatically the channels of extra-legal dispute settlement; similarly, plots that dealt with the epiklerate laws offered them the opportunity to dramatize some rather astute manipulation of lawful institutions outside the court system – and, in the process, to focus upon the motives and characters of the men who performed those manipulations. To mistake the interest in the operation of extra-legal dispute settlement for social commentary is, I think, to incorporate without warrant modern sentiment into our reading of ancient texts.

2 DISPUTES ABOUT THE DISSOLUTION OF MARRIAGES

So far we have examined arguments of law *versus* arguments of sentiment in *Aspis*, *Phormio*, and *Adelphoe*. These were all arguments produced by men who were interested in initiating, preserving, or dissolving marriages. Now we shall examine the arguments of a number of young women who protest their fathers' explicit desire to end their marriages. A brief discussion of divorce, with attention to the role played by a wife's father, must precede discussion of the plays.

2(a) The mechanics of divorce

2(a)i Athens

In Athens, a husband could divorce his wife by sending her away (an act usually referred to by the verbs *apopempein*, *ekballein*, and *ekpempein*) or a wife could divorce her husband by leaving him (*apoleipein*).[56] Procedure seems to have been relatively informal. A woman who left her husband on her own initiative apparently had to give a written notice to the arkhon; presumably she would need the support of her natal *kurios* to ensure her future maintenance.[57] Such notification, however, was apparently unnecessary when a husband sent away his wife. Why notification was required in the one case (*apoleipsis*) and not in the other (*apopempsis*) is a matter of speculation.[58] No evidence suggests that specific grounds for divorce were required by law. Dowry would have to be returned to the wife's natal *kurios*, regardless of the "grounds" for the divorce and the person who initiated it; a *dike sitou* (suit for alimony) was available against former husbands who ignored this obligation. Summoning witnesses may have been customary practice rather than legal requirement when effecting a divorce.[59]

56 *Apopempein*: [Dem.] 59. 52, 59, 82; *ekballein*: [Dem.] 59. 51; *ekpempein*: Is. 3. 35; [Dem.] 59. 55, 56; Lys. 14. 28. *Apoleipein*: Is. 3. 8, 35, 78; Dem. 30 *passim*; [And.] 4. 14; *apoleipsis*: *Lex. Seg.* 201, 22.

57 [And.] 4. 14; Dem. 30. 17, 26; Is. 3. 78; Photios s.v. *sitou dike*. For discussion, see Rosivach 1984.

58 For discussion of this question with citation of relevant bibliography, see Harrison 1. 40–43.

59 It would be in a women's interest (esp. an innocent woman's) if her husband summoned witnesses and declared his grounds for the divorce; it is easy enough to believe that some such statement in any event would be made to relatives. Nonetheless, witnesses do not appear to be required by law (see chapter 5, n. 69).

A brief account of a husband desirous of divorcing his wife in Isaios 2 *Men.* suggests the (idealized) amicable character of the procedure. The woman who is to be divorced is the speaker's sister, and the speaker wants to show that the husband, Menekles, had been on good terms with her (and more particularly, that the marriage had been a legitimate one). Regardless of whether we think the following account of Menekles' conduct is the truth or not (it is not substantiated by any witness's report), it nevertheless shows what the speaker thought was ideal conduct under the circumstances, and it is precisely "ideal conduct" that we are interested in at this moment:

And he (Menekles), in the second or third month thereafter, offered many praises of my sister and entered into discussion with us, saying that he viewed his age and childlessness with suspicion. He said that she ought not therefore to enjoy this as the fruit of her goodness – to remain childless while growing old together with him; for it was enough, he said, for him to be unfortunate. [And his words show that he was in love when he cast her off; for no one is solicitous for a person whom he hates.] Accordingly, he requested us to do him this favor, to give her to another man with his consent. And we bid him to persuade her of this – for of whatever she would be persuaded, we said we would carry that out. And at first she would not even suffer him to speak, but, with the passage of time, she was with difficulty persuaded. (6–9)

In this idealized vignette of a divorce, the husband first discusses the necessity of divorce with his wife's male kin and then he tries to persuade her to accept it; initially, she will have nothing to do with it, but, after a while, she agrees. Had Menekles' wife steadfastly refused, Menekles certainly was under no obligation to heed her sentiments; he could simply send her away. But the point of interest for us is that the speaker should casually introduce the element of persuasion into his story, as if it were a normal feature of domestic life for a husband to obtain his wife's consent before he actually divorced her.

Whether fathers had the legal right to compel their daughters to divorce their husbands is a debated question.[60] Modern scholars have bestowed the technical term *aphairesis* upon this procedure,

[60] For a review of scholarly opinion on this issue from the turn of the century up to the forties, see Wolff 1944: 47 n. 23; Wolff thought the evidence was inconclusive but nevertheless entertained the possibility that "if an Athenian father did have the right to dissolve his daughter's marriage at his discretion, it certainly would fit into the general marriage system." Recently published papyri from *Epitrepontes* have not advanced our knowledge on this question.

although there is no ancient authority for this usage of the noun.[61] Troublesome for the resolution of the debate is the absence of any text which unequivocally asserts that fathers had this right by law. While some scholars claim that certain texts are better understood if fathers did in fact have it,[62] other scholars have argued that a strongly traditional moral obligation to obey fathers in marital matters may also explain them.[63] The texts in question are one report in the orators (Dem. 41. 4) and four dramatic treatments which depict a father who has asked his unwilling daughter to leave her husband: (1) Smikrines makes the request of Pamphile in *Epitrepontes*; (2) a daughter argues against such a request in a 44-line speech known as the Didot *rhesis* (or "Didot papyrus 1") from a play of uncertain authorship and genre;[64] (3) Antipho's daughters argue against their father's request in the opening scenes of Plautus *Stichus*, a play based on a Menandrian original (probably the so-called *Adelphoi a'*)[65] and (4) four verses (without attribution to author or genre), spoken by Cresphontes' wife in opposition to her father's request are cited in *Rhetorica ad Herennium* 2. 24. 38.[66] Passages from two other Plautine plays (*Men.* 782ff. and *Merc.* 784ff.) have also been brought into this debate, but these have more pertinence for a different question, namely, whether a daughter needed her father's permission to leave her husband.[67] The passage from Demosthenes is an abbreviated account of a father who "removes" his daughter from a marriage and does not explicitly say that he does this "in accordance with the law."[68] Some of the dramatic passages speak of

61 Rosivach 1984: 229–30.

62 N. Lewis 1982; Gatti 1957: 62–65; Paoli 1976: 161–73 (= 1956), 385–91 (= 1953a).

63 So Brown 1983: 420 who thinks the evidence inconclusive, following Turner 1979: 120–22; similarly and independently Rosivach 1984.

64 A majority of scholars are of the opinion that the *rhesis* belongs to New Comedy; and many ascribe it to Menander; for bibliography of these and other views, see Page 1962: 181–84 and Gomme and Sandbach 1973: 723–24. The fragment is included in Sandbach's OCT of Menander (*Pap. Didot 1*) among the papyrus fragments of uncertain authorship. A number of scholars hypothesized that the *rhesis* was spoken by Pamphile in *Epitr.* iv; that hypothesis has been made obsolete by the discovery of new fragments from *Epitr.* iv in *POxy.* 50. 3532 and 3533 (= Sandbach *App.* 1990). See further n. 90.

65 The didascalic notice to *Stichus* names Menander's *Adelphoi* as the Greek original, probably the *Adelphoi* α' of *POxy.* 2462.

66 Jocelyn 1967 attributes both the four verses and the three that follow it in the same chapter to Ennius' *Cresphontes* (F 53); detailed discussion of earlier views and relevant bibliography appear on pp. 272–77. In my opinion, neither of the replies to Cresphontes' wife can be ascribed to Ennius' play. For restatement of Wilamowitz' view, that the verses are drawn from a comedy, see Rosivach 1984: 216–17 and n. 55.

67 See Gatti 1957: 62–65; Watson 1967: 50–52; Rosivach 1984: 207–10.

68 Dem. 41. 4: τούτων δ' οὕτως ἐχόντων, διαφορᾶς γενομένης τῶι Πολυεύκτωι πρὸς τὸν

the father's authority as compulsory, but again, none of them explicitly say that the compulsion derives from law.[69] In my discussion of the dramatic texts (section 2.b), I have assumed that the fathers have a great deal of moral authority to enforce their wishes; whether that authority is based in law makes no difference to my interpretation. My focus is upon the type of arguments used by daughters against their fathers; these are always arguments of fair play (*epieikeia*). If fathers did have a lawful right to dissolve the marriages, then we would expect the daughters to use such arguments as these against their fathers; but even if fathers had no such right by law, we might still expect them to use the very same type of argument rather than an argument that the absence of a legal right on their father's side conferred justice on their own.[70]

2(a)ii Rome

As is usual in discussions of Roman law and institutions of the mid-Republic, we are hampered by the sketchy nature of our sources. For the regal period, Plutarch (*Rom.* 22. 3) reports that a husband could initiate a divorce but a wife could not. According to the same author, grounds for divorce were limited at this time to poisoning a child, substituting keys, and adultery.[71] A woman divorced for any of these

Λεωκράτη, περὶ ἧς οὐκ οἶδ' ὅ τι δεῖ λέγειν, ἀφελόμενος ὁ Πολύευκτος τὴν θυγατέρα δίδωσι Σπουδίαι τουτωιί ("Since circumstances were thus, when a quarrel arose between Polueuktos and Leokrates – about which I see no need for me to speak – Polueuktos took away his daughter and bestowed her on this Spoudias"). The case is complicated by the fact that Polueuktos had adopted Leokrates when he married his daughter. It is the only passage where *aphairesthai* is used (as a middle) of divorce initiated by the father; the verb is used (passively) at Is. 3. 64 of husbands who are deprived of their wives when the latter become *epidikoi*: . . . καὶ πολλοὶ συνοικοῦντες ἤδη ἀφήιρηνται τὰς ἑαυτῶν γυναῖκας ("many husbands, moreover, have already been deprived of their wives"). The term does not seem technical here.

69 The only texts that can be adduced for one interpretation or the other are those mentioned above. The most convincing argument in support of the father's legal position is made by Taubenschlag 1926: 74–75; even so, the argument is inconclusive.

70 When Kharisios suffers his volte-face in *Epitr.*, he argues in a monologue against Smikrines' plan to remove his daughter but does not adduce any form of legal redress which he might have used against such conduct: "What business has her father with me? I'll speak to the point, 'Stop making trouble for me, Smikrines. My wife is not leaving me. Why do you keep disturbing Pamphile and pressuring her? Why do I see you here again?'" (928–32). Kharisios' speech shows that he does not adduce any lawful right against Smikrines, not that none exists. The passage is inconclusive.

71 Plut. *Rom.* 22. 3: ἔθηκε δὲ καὶ νόμους τινάς, ὧν σφοδρὸς μέν ἐστιν ὁ γυναικὶ μὴ διδοὺς ἀπολείπειν ἄνδρα, γυναῖκα δὲ διδοὺς ἐκβάλλειν ἐπὶ φαρμακείαι τέκνων ἢ κλειδῶν ὑποβολῆι καὶ μοιχευθεῖσαν· Reiske adds a καί after φαρμακείαι; if his supplement is accepted, then the grounds for divorce might also be translated as "poisoning, substitution of keys or of children, and adultery." Plutarch's statement on the availability of early

reasons could not demand the return of any property she may have brought into the marriage. Plutarch (*Rom.* 22. 3) also informs us that a husband who turned out a wife for any other reason faced a stern penalty (one-half of his property would go to his wife, the other half to Ceres or Tellus).

It is uncertain whether specific grounds for divorce were required in Plautus' time; in classical law, they were not. Watson has argued that the law, while not invalidating divorces where no due cause had been shown, might have imposed penalties for divorces without due cause.[72] A brief consideration of the role of matrimonial offenses in divorce settlements will illustrate the argument. According to a frequently iterated Roman tradition, the first divorce was that of Sp. Carvilius Ruga, the date for which is variously given as 604 BC, 524 BC, and *c.* 230 BC; the last date has won the widest acceptance – and likewise the view that Carvilius' divorce was not the first in Rome.[73] Watson has argued that the divorce became famous and so won its palmary position in the Roman tradition not only because neither husband nor wife was at fault (Carvilius claimed that his wife was sterile), but also because the case brought home the unfairness of divorce settlements: the law, up to this time, provided no mechanism by which a wife might obtain a share of the marital property or the return of her dowry in a case where neither she nor her husband was at fault.[74] Eventually, arrangements were institutionalized to fill in the legal gaps: parties to a marriage made their own agreements (*cautiones rei uxoriae*) for the division of property in the event of divorce, and an *actio rei uxoriae* was provided for the recovery of a wife's dowry. In classical law, fractions of a dowry might be retained for specified faults; a husband, for example, might retain one-sixth of the dowry if his wife was guilty of adultery.[75] The law's recognition of matrimonial offenses which might lead to a husband's retention of

divorce is (apparently) contradicted by D. H. *A.R.* 2. 25, who states that marriage was indissoluble under the law of Romulus; for proposed solutions, see Corbett 1930: 219–22.

72 Watson 1967: 54–55.

73 Gellius *N.A.* 4. 3. 2 (*c.* 230 BC); D. H. *A.R.* 2. 25 (*c.* 230 BC); Plut. *Lyk. and Num.* 3. 13 (524 BC); *Q. R.* 14 (no date); *Thes. and Rom.* 35 [6] 3–4 (no date); Val. Max. 2. 1. 4 (604 BC). For a brief survey of modern preferences, see McDonnell 1983: 70 n. 2. For detailed treatment of Carvilius' divorce (dated to 230 BC), see Watson 1965a. Another early divorce, that of L. Annius, can be dated to 307/06 (Val. Max. 2. 9. 2; the date is confirmed by Livy 9. 43. 25). Valerius Maximus (2. 9. 2) reports that the censors removed Annius from the Senate because he had divorced his wife without consulting friends.

74 Watson 1965a.

75 *Tit. Ulp.* 6. 9: fractions of dowry retained, inter alia, for bad morals; 12: husband retains a sixth of the dowry for major offense (adultery), an eighth for lesser offenses; 13: adultery of

a portion of his wife's dowry (and sometimes a reduction in the amount he was lawfully permitted to retain) demonstrates that the law did recognize certain types of misconduct as providing due cause (and, *a fortiori*, grounds for divorce) – without necessarily invalidating those divorces where no due cause had been shown. While it is not known whether fractions had been determined by law in the Republic, the right of retention is attested during this period. Cato's speech "On dowry" attests generally to a husband's right of retention in cases of a wife's wine-drinking in the second century.[76]

Legal historians usually point out that early divorces all proceed from the husband's initiative, and they often explain this inequality as peculiar to marriages *in manu* (i.e., marriages in which the woman passes into her husband's family and becomes subject to him or his *paterfamilias* if the latter is still alive).[77] The evolution of the extension of the capacity to divorce is then depicted as a consequence of the growing popularity of marriages without *manus* (wherein the woman remains *in patria potestate* rather than passes into her husband's family) during the middle and late Republic. In these marriages, divorces initiated by the wife's father were permissible; moreover, wives who were emancipated from their fathers' *potestas* and who thus became *sui iuris* could initiate divorces on their own behalf.[78]

While we can be certain that marriages *in manu* and not *in manu* were simultaneously in existence by the third century, other features of the evolutionary scheme are less reliably anchored in Plautus' time.[79] Attribution of a woman's capacity to initiate divorce to this

husband is penalized by requiring immediate return of dowry, lesser offenses by requiring dowry's return in six months. For discussion, see Treggiari 1991: 350–53.

76 The same right is attested for one case that might belong to the early second century (Pliny *NH* 14 [13]. 90); a woman was mulcted of her entire dowry for imbibing wine beyond the requirements of health and without her husband's knowledge. The right of retention is also attested in another case decided in 100 BC (Val. Max. 8. 2. 3 and Plut. *Marius* 38: see chapter 2 at n. 88). For discussion of these two cases, see Watson 1967: 68–70. For possible parody of the right of retention in Plautus *Truc.* 844–45, see chapter 6.2.c, at n. 47.

77 Corbett 1930: 222; Kaser 1971: 81. See Treggiari 1991: 442–46 for skeptical presentation of the view.

78 Corbett 1930: 222 and n. 5 and 242; Watson 1967: 48–56.

79 The best evidence for the existence of marriage not *in manu* during this period derives from the *lex Cincia* of 204 BC (Paul. in *FV* 302 = *FIRA*[2] 2. 531); see the argument of Corbett 1930: 91. On the other hand, the relative vigor of marriages *in manu* and those not *in manu* cannot be measured on the basis of Plautine texts; characterization of a marriage as one type or the other will depend somewhat on the contours of the Greek original. Greek plots requiring fathers to urge the dissolution of their daughters' marriages require depictions of marriages not *in manu*; likewise those plots requiring wives to summon their fathers to effect divorces for them.

period, for example, is highly debatable; the argument depends on a combination of Plautine evidence with later literary and legal sources – but the Plautine evidence is open to different interpretations.[80] The only feature of divorce that concerns us here, however, is the subordination of sons and daughters in marriages not *in manu* to their fathers' *potestas* after marriage; the *paterfamilias* had the right to dissolve a marriage, even against the wishes of his married son or daughter.[81] The evidence for this right comes from the late jurists who report a change in the time of Marcus Aurelius or Antoninus Pius: at that time, a *paterfamilias* was forbidden from dissolving a marriage that was *bene concordans* except perhaps in some instances for *magna et iusta causa*.[82] I assume, along with most legal historians, that the right of *paterfamilias* to dissolve a marriage extended back to the early Republic; that right is fully in accord with *patria potestas*.

2(a)iii Synkrisis: a father's right to dissolve his daughter's marriage

Athenian practice of the fourth century BC and Roman practice of the second century BC, in the matter of the father's right to dissolve his daughter's marriage would appear to be quite similar – at least if we limit the Roman practice here to cases where the married daughter remains in her father's *potestas* (i.e., in marriages not *in manu*). The only possible difference is a point which we cannot decide for certain – whether the Athenian father had this right by law. Because of the proximity of practice, it is impossible to decide whether Plautus, when he speaks of the father's *imperium* in *Stichus*, is translating or adapting his Menandrian model. The word appears three times in the play, the first time in an interpolated passage:[83]

(a) *verum postremo in patri' potestate est situm:*
faciendum id nobis quod parentes imperant. (53–54)

but, after all, our situation rests on paternal *potestas*:
we must obey parental commands.

[80] See especially McDonnell 1983 for a detailed study of the Plautine evidence. It is not known for certain how early a *filiafamilias* in a marriage without *manus* could divorce without the consent of her father. For different views, see Gardner 1986: 11 and n. 21; Corbett 1930: 242 and n. 5; Treggiari 1991: 445–46. It seems rash to ascribe this right (or practice) to Plautus' era.

[81] See Sachers *RE* s.v. *Potestas patria*, col. 1112; Corbett 1930: 122–24, 239–40.

[82] *C.* 5. 17. 5 attributes the regulation to Marcus Aurelius and provides the exception of *magna et iusta causa* to *filiafamilias*. Paul. *Sent.* 5. 6. 15, attributes the regulation to Antoninus Pius. See also *D.* 43. 30. 1. 5 (Ulp.) and *Nov.* 22. 19.

[83] For the interpolation, see Leo 1912: 378.

(b) *pati*
nos oportet quod ille faciat, quoius potestas plus potest. (68–69)

We must endure his course of action; his *potestas* is the more potent.

(c) *certumne est neutram vostrarum persequi imperium patris?* (141)

Have neither of you resolved to obey your father's command?

If Plautus is "translating" (we shall leave the interpolator's intention out of account), then by representing the father's right as his *imperium* he may be reproducing an Athenian legal notion that happens to be the equivalent of the Roman one. But if he is "adapting," then he may be changing what was a traditional moral right in Athens into the legal right that was operative in Rome. There is no way to distinguish which procedure (translation or adaptation) he has adopted here since, in this instance, we do not know what the Athenian law was.[84] In my treatment of the Roman texts below, whether Plautus has translated or adapted the legal situation makes no difference; my focus, as I have said, is upon the daughters' arguments, which are arguments of fair play; it is unlikely that Athenian daughters would have argued otherwise, even if they had the law on their side.

2(b) Dramatic treatments

The debate over divorce in *Epitrepontes* IV is lacunose; enough, however, remains to suggest its contours. We know from Smikrines' earlier remarks in the play that he was concerned that Kharisios, Pamphile's husband, was wasting her dowry on extravagant living and a courtesan (136–37, 680–82, 691–94); his concern appears to be financial and limited to the material well-being of his daughter.[85] At the beginning of what remains of Act IV, Pamphile makes a

[84] The view that I have expressed here differs from two sets of earlier views about *Stichus* I 1 and 2: (1) "the pure and simple Roman view": the scenes provide evidence that in Roman marriages not *in manu*, the father has the right to dissolve the marriage of his daughter; Athenian practice is irrelevant to the Roman legal situation (e.g., Watson 1967: 56 n.1; Sachers *RE* s.v. *Potestas patria*, col. 1112); and (2) "the pure and simple Attic view": the scenes provide evidence of the Attic practice of *aphairesis* without Plautine alteration (Paoli 1976: 161–73 [=1956, 233–47] followed by Gatti 1957 and N. Lewis 1977).

[85] Fr. 7, 793–96 (Sandbach OCT [1972], which now has a context in *POxy.* 50. 3533 and is reprinted in Sandbach *App.* [1990] p. 349) suggests that Smikrines might also be concerned for his daughter's psychological well-being; but I suspect that Smikrines' arguments about the courtesan's superior advantages in a battle over a husband are aimed at provoking Pamphile to leave her husband rather than at providing solace for her disadvantaged position.

request of her father, perhaps continuing a conversation that had commenced off-stage:

> ἀλλ' εἴ με σῴζων τοῦτο μὴ πείσαις ἐμέ,
> οὐκέτι πατὴρ κρίνοι' ἂν ἀλλὰ δεσπότης. (714–15)
>
> But if in saving me you do not persuade me of this,
> no longer will you appear a father but a tyrant.

Like Menekles' wife who allegedly required persuasion before agreeing to divorce (Is. 2. 9), Pamphile demands a cogent argument. The text at this point (716–835) is lacunose but not uninformative.[86] What appears as a scrappy exchange between father and daughter may originally have been a pair of well-ordered speeches – which, together with the slaves' speeches presented during the arbitration in Act II, would make *Epitrepontes* a rhetorical showpiece worthy of Quintilian's praise.[87]

At the outset of his response, Smikrines tells Pamphile that he will make three points (τρία δέ σοι προθήσομαι, 719). Precise discernment of this tripartite plan presses ingenuity beyond the boundaries of the preserved text. The Oxyrhynchus editor has nevertheless optimistically suggested, by comparing Pamphile's 24 half-lines (812–35, Sandbach *App.*) with her father's lacunose speech, the following triad: (1) the pain she will undergo (754) while Kharisios enjoys a care-free (721) and profligate (749–56) existence (compare Pamphile's response 812–20); (2) Kharisios is engaged in an affair with another woman (compare 792 and 821–28); and (3) divorce will be the end (compare 797–800 and 829–35).[88] This particular triad is not implausible, and we need not linger here by suggesting unprovable alternatives. What calls for our attention, however, is simply the fact that an order has been imposed on Smikrines' speech: it suggests a rhetorically con-

[86] Smikrines gives his response in 716–24 (the last four lines are very scrappy), after which there is a gap in the text of perhaps 24 verses; when the text resumes (749), Smikrines is speaking, but the text soon breaks off once again (758). After a gap of about 32 lines, Smikrines is speaking in 790–800 (Sandbach *App.*), and Pamphile responds at 801–35 (with at least a nine line gap after 802). Most of Pamphile's response is preserved in half-lines (812–35); the sense of some of these verses is suggested by comparison with subsequent speeches of Kharisios (919–22) who had eavesdropped on the scene and of Onesimos (883–93) who had heard his master's response to it. What is now 788–822 in Sandbach *App.* (1990 OCT) was first published in 1983 as *POxy.* 50. 3532; 790–810 Sandbach *App.* was first published as *POxy.* 3533 in the same volume. P. Mich. Inv. 4733 (see Gronewald 1986) can be used to correct portions of these verses.

[87] Quint. 10. 1. 69–70.

[88] *POxy.* 50: p. 40. Earlier scholars proposed different triads – without the advantage of possessing Pamphile's response; for summaries, see Gomme and Sandbach 1973: 355.

scious composition.[89] That, together with the lengthiness of the speeches (Pamphile's may have been as long as the daughter's speech in the Didot *rhesis*) and the repetition of the theme in the three other dramatic treatments, indicates that the issue involved, a father's persuading of a daughter to leave her husband (or the reverse: a daughter's persuasion of a father that she should not) is a set *topos* of drama. By *topos* I mean a clearly defined subject of debate which has well-known supporting or opposing arguments.

A comparison of the arguments used in the four dramatic treatments shows the commonality of positions and argumentation (i). Good dramatists, however, exploit *topoi* for their own particular purposes. This can only be shown where we possess enough text to establish what those purposes might be; I shall therefore limit my concluding observations to the way the *topos* is used in *Epitrepontes* and *Stichus* (ii).

2(b)i Antithetical arguments and paradoxical conundrums

To take up the so-called Didot *rhesis* first: we do not know its dramatic context; the mid-second-century BC papyrus fragment contains forty-four iambic trimeters – the continuous speech of a daughter who argues against her father's request that she should leave her husband.[90] The rhetorical character of the speech is striking. After a twelve-line proemium, the daughter makes a shrewd false start: she grants her father's case, ἔστω δ' ὃ βούλει τοῦτο (13, "let it be as you wish"), but immediately interrupts by questioning the basis of her father's judgment, τί μ' ἀδικεῖ λέγε (13, "tell me, what wrong does he do me?"). The question ushers in the lengthiest part of her refutation (14–26). After that, she hypothetically concedes

[89] Cf. Robert's (1915: 263) analysis of the style of Smikrines' speech: "er ist ein geschulter Rhetor."

[90] For arguments of attribution, see note 64 above. The proximity of sentiments in the fragment to sentiments expressed in Roman plays based on Menander might suggest a Menandrian origin or an author imitating that poet or borrowing from the same stockpile of sentiments as Menander. Cf. verses 1–2, ὦ πάτερ, ἐχρῆν μὲν οὓς ἐγὼ λόγους λέγω / τούτους λέγειν σέ and *Adelphoe* 674–75, . . . *haec, mi pater, / te dicere aequom fuit et id defendere.* Cf. verses 25–26 and *Epitr.* 818, Sandbach *App.* (both passages are quoted and discussed above) *Stichus* 133–34, *placet ille meus mihi mendicus: suo' rex reginae placet. / idem animust in paupertate qui olim in divitiis fuit.* Cf. verse 16, τῆι δ' ὅσ' ἂν ἀρέσκηι τἀνδρί, ταῦτ' αὐτὴν ποεῖν and (for the obverse) *Menaechmi* 111, *quod viro esse odio videas, tute tibi odio habeas.* The repetition of *dike*-derivatives in verses 1–12 might also be compared to the "clustering of value terminology" noted by Arnott 1972: 58 as an element of linguistic characterization in the opening scene of *Stichus*.

to her father's position once again, φέρ' ἐὰν ὁ νῦν με λαμβάνειν μέλλων ἀνήρ (27: "suppose this second man who is to take me as his wife – "), but immediately interrupts herself again, this time with a two line wish of quittance from such an ordeal, and then adds to the earlier refutation a hard-line logical rejoinder (30–33). She rounds off her speech with an eleven-line peroration (34–44), consisting of two final pleas to her father and a promise of compliance if her pleas are denied. The structure of the speech is thus skilfully contrived: a proemium (1–12), a brief false concession to her father's position and an interrupting question (13), the grounds of her refutation (14–26), a reversion to her father's position (27), an interrupting wish (28–29), the final and clinching refutation (30–33), a peroration (34–44).

The daughter begins the lengthy part of her refutation by referring to a law:

> ἔστ' ἀνδρὶ καὶ γυναικὶ κείμενος νόμος,
> τῶι μὲν διὰ τέλους ἣν ἔχει στέργειν ἀεί,
> τῆι δ' ὅσ' ἂν ἀρέσκηι τἀνδρί, ταῦτ' αὐτὴν ποεῖν (14–16)

> There is a law for husband and wife,
> for him to cherish forever the woman he marries,
> for her to do all that is pleasing to him.

The law is of course an unwritten one, and by adverting to it, she squarely sets herself in the sphere of *epieikeia*. What is remarkable about her extension of this argument is its rhetorically antithetical shape. After expressing satisfaction with her husband, she continues:

> ἀλλ' ἔστ' ἐμοὶ μὲν χρηστός, ἠπόρηκε δέ,
> σὺ δ' ἀνδρί μ', ὡς φήις, ἐκδίδως νῦν πλουσίωι,
> ἵνα μὴ καταζῶ τὸν βίον λυπουμένη.
> καὶ ποῦ τοσαῦτα χρήματ' ἐστίν, ὦ πάτερ,
> ἃ μᾶλλον ἀνδρὸς εὐφρανεῖ παρόντα με;
> ἢ πῶς δίκαιόν ἐστιν ἢ καλῶς ἔχον
> τῶν μὲν ἀγαθῶν με τὸ μέρος ὧν εἶχεν λαβεῖν,
> τοῦ συναπορηθῆναι δὲ μὴ λαβεῖν μέρος; (19–26)

Well, then, in my eyes, he is a good husband, but he has become poor, and you, as you say, are now going to betroth me to a wealthy man, that I may not live out my life in distress. Yet where is there so much money, father, which, by its presence, will cheer me more than my husband? Or how is it right or fair for me to take a portion of the good things he once had but of sharing in his poverty – to take no portion of that?

In the brief span of eight verses, three teasing antitheses are set up, and each one is implicitly or explicitly refuted. Her husband's goodness is contrasted with his poverty – but his goodness is a permanent quality while his poverty is a contingent condition (19). The intended husband is rich and so might be expected to provide her a comfortable life, but no amount of money can buy her the happiness which her husband provides (20–23). Prosperity and poverty are distinct as external conditions of life, but both are to be shared in, if one acts according to justice and fairness (24–26).

The ethical kernel of the daughter's position is thus established in the lengthy refutation of what had probably been her father's charge – that her husband treats her unjustly because he has become impoverished. She completes the argument in 30–33 with a logical conundrum: "If this second husband should in turn lose his property, / will you give me to another? And then if / this third husband [should lose his property], again to a fourth? Up to what number, / Father, will you make trial of accident (*tukhe*) in the course of my life?" The "trial of accident" and its consequences, the (infinite!) number of husbands she must inevitably endure, is flatly rejected (cf. 42–44); what is essential and permanent – the "law" of marriage, the character of a man, happiness, just conduct – is endorsed.

Artful structure and argumentation that verge on the sophistical characterize the fragment. Similarities are at hand in the three other dramatic treatments. In Pamphile's response to her father in *Epitrepontes* iv, it is possible that the distraught daughter had formulated an antithesis similar to the one that appears in the Didot *rhesis* at vv. 24–26:

διὰ τοῦτο πότερον η [
συνευτυχήσουσ' {ε} ἂν δ'
αὐτῶι προίδω; μὰ τόν [
κοινωνὸς ἦλθον τ[οῦ βίου (817–20)[91]

The following translation is based on restoration: "Therefore [did I come to my husband only] to share his good fortune but if [he suffered a reverse, was I then to withdraw] my concern for him? By [Hymenaeus (?)], at that moment I entered as partner of his

[91] I have followed Gronewald 1986: 6–7 for the readings in these verses; Sandbach *App.* prints συνευτυχήσασ' in verse 818 without explanation; Gronewald's reading is that of *P.Oxy.* 3532 fr. 2. 7 and is confirmed by P. Mich. Inv. 4733. 33.

life."[92] We shall treat the paradox of Pamphile's situation more fully below.

In *Stichus* I 2, Antipho visits his daughters to announce his plan to dissolve their marriages; their husbands have been absent on business for three years and have sent no tidings of their existence. Antipho, at first not straightforward about the reason for his visit, at last comes to the point:

> *mi auctores ita sunt amici, ut vos hinc abducam domum.* (128)
>
> my friends advise me thus: that I should take you home from here.

Neither daughter is caught off guard. The younger sister (Soror) is first to insist that they, too, can be *auctores* (129). Her argument is perfectly rational:

> *nam aut olim, nisi tibi placebant, non datas oportuit*
> *aut nunc non aequomst abduci, pater, illisce apsentibus.* (130–31)
>
> For either we ought not, in the first place, to have been given
> to them if they were not agreeable to you,
> or it is not right for us to be led away now, father, when
> those husbands of ours are absent.

There is, of course, no legal basis for Soror's argument; it is, instead, an appeal to fairness which is premised on the immutability of character: the basis for her father's choice of husbands should have been those qualities in them that he had found pleasing; it is not fair to compel divorce when the husbands are unable by their absence to defend that quality. The resemblance of Soror's argument in *Stichus* to one cited without attribution in the *Rhetorica ad Herennium* has been noticed before:[93]

92 Gronewald 1986: 11 suggested the restored readings which I have added into my translation of 817–18: διὰ τοῦτο πότερον ἦλ[θον ἀνδρὶ μόνον ἀεὶ / συνευτυχήσουσ' {ε}ἂν δ' [ἀτυχήσηι, τότ' ἄρα μὴ]. While the restoration is not secure, some such paradoxical notion seems certain from: (1) the appearance of the interrogative (πότερον 817); (2) from the quotation of Pamphile's speech that is given later in the act by Kharisios (920–21): . . . κοινωνὸς ἥκειν τοῦ βίου / κ]οὐ δεῖν τἀτύχημ' αὐτὴν φυγεῖν / τὸ συμβεβηκός . . . (920–22 . . . "I came here as partner in his life [. . . and] I must not flee mishap / when it has chanced to happen"); and (3) from the use of the unusual compound of the participle of συνευτυχέω (817) in a way that resembles the use of the unusual compound of the participle of συναπορέω in the paradoxical statement in the Didot rhesis 25–26 (quoted in text above). Turner in *POxy.* 3532 (p. 11) suggested the name of the god in v. 819 and a slightly different restoration of 817–18: "Then am I who came to his house to share my joy with my husband [now to stay or] to ensure [trouble] for him [sc. by leaving]? By [Hymenaeus (?)], at that moment I entered as partner of his life."

93 Rosivach 1984; N. Lewis 1977; Jocelyn 1969: 274–75; Zucker 1944.

Iniuria abs te adficior indigna, pater;
nam si inprobum esse Cresphontem existimas
cur me huic locabas nuptiis? sin est probus
cur talem invitam invitum cogis linquere? (2. 24. 38)

You treat me to an unmerited injury, Father;
for if you think that Cresphontes is wicked
why did you give me to him in marriage? But if he is good
why do you force me against my will to leave him against his?

Like Soror's argument – and the arguments of the other young women discussed here – this one has no legal basis. The argument is once again based upon an implicit premise of the immutability of character.[94]

Rhetorical treatment is evident in the largely hypothesized structure of Smikrines' and Pamphile's speeches in *Epitrepontes* and in the structure of the Didot *rhesis*. So, too, is it evident in the logical conundrums and rhetorical antitheses of all four pieces; the repetition of the latter in various shapes suggests that these were stock formulations in the presentation of a daughter's arguments. Other motifs are also identifiable: e.g., that marriage is a lasting partnership (*Epitr.* 820 Sandbach *App.* and 920–22; Didot *rhesis* 14–18, *Stichus* 39–46, 142)[95] and that wealth is not a prerequisite for marriage (Didot *rhesis* 22–34; *Stichus* 132–40; possibly *Epitr.* 821–22 Sandbach *App.* – Smikrines has certainly charged Kharisios with squandering money). We have no way of knowing whether such arguments were in fact used by daughters against their fathers in Athens. We can only safely say that the positions taken by fathers and daughters in the scenario were well-known on the comic stage.

2(b)ii Dramatic treatments: rhetoricized contexts

Within the dramatic context of New Comedy, we might productively ask why playwrights chose to rhetoricize this particular domestic situation to such a high degree. My answer is that the delineation of domestic persuasion is another example of New Comedy's interest in

94 The formulation of the premise provides "moral loopholes" for rejoinder; two are easily stated by the author of the treatise; thus (1) "I do not, daughter, treat you to an unmerited injury. If he is good, I have placed you in marriage; but if he is bad, I shall free you from this misfortune by a divorce." (2) "I thought he was a good man. I have made a mistake; Now I know, and since I know, I flee." For arguments of attribution of these lines, see n. 66 above.

95 On this motif, see above all Zucker 1944; for the stock arguments in general, see Rosivach 1984: 218–22.

the informal channels of dispute settlement. The rhetorical aspect of these scenes gives them a formality which masks the sensitive situations lying beneath the plays' surfaces. For all their employment of stock motifs, they are skilfully exploited by the comic poets. This, of course, is only possible to see in those instances for which we know the dramatic context – *Stichus* and *Epitrepontes*.

Stichus

In the opening scenes, the playwright is attentive to modes of dispute settlement. In i 1, Panegyris and her younger sister (Soror) confide to one another their anxieties concerning the three-year absence of their husbands. The younger, more impetuous sister (the "Antigone" of the pair) recognizes the competing *officia* at issue: their father's *officium*, which is now defined as his desire to effect his daughters' divorces (14–16), and their own *officium*, to stand by their husbands in their absence (34–35, 42, 46).[96] Nevertheless, Panegyris appears to have no doubt about the hierarchy of these claims: if their father makes the demand, they will have to comply (68–69). But legal authority is, as usual, only a last resort. Before the young women confront their father in i 2, they devise their own forensic strategy:

> *SOR. quid agimus, soror, si offirmabit pater adversum nos?*
> *PAN. pati*
> *nos oportet quod ille faciat, quoius potestas plus potest.*
> *exorando, haud advorsando sumendam operam censeo:*
> *gratiam per si petimus, spero ab eo impetrassere;*
> *adversari sine dedecore et scelere summo hau possumus,*
> *neque equidem id factura neque tu ut facias consilium dabo,*
> *verum ut exoremus. novi ego nostros: exorabilest.* (68–74)

SOR. What do we do, sister, if our father stubbornly opposes us?
PAN. We must endure

> whatever he does; his *potestas* is the more potent.
> By appeal, not by opposition must our labor be undertaken:
> if we petition him for favor I hope to prevail over him;
> we cannot oppose him without disgrace and singular scandal,
> neither shall I myself do this nor do I counsel that you should;
> instead, we must appeal. I know our father: he is open to appeal.

[96] Arnott 1972 provides the paradigm of Antigone and Ismene for the sororal pair and notes the value-laden terminology as a component of linguistic characterization. On the use of *officium* here, see Zucker 1944. On the concept of (familial) *pietas*, see Saller 1988 and 1991: 146–51.

In the very next moment, Antipho, from the doorway of his house, debates with himself the strategy he should use with his daughters: should he exasperate them with a perplexing speech, pretending that he has no charge against them – or should he take them to task with ferocity if they prefer to stand by their husbands rather than marry anew (76–78, 80)?[97] He rejects the latter strategy – his daughters have done nothing to deserve belligerent treatment; instead, he will frighten them with perplexity and then let them know his mind (81–86). In this none too lucid deliberation, Antipho consciously settles upon a strategy of obfuscation, of perplexing his opponents first and then confounding them into submission as he lays bare his mind. Instead of immediately explaining the purpose of his visit, he therefore begins by asking, as *discipulus* to *magistrae* (105), what character befits the best *matronae* (. . . *quibu' matronas moribus / quae optumae sunt esse oportet*? 105–06); he maintains that his questions have a practical end, to assist in finding a wife now that their mother has died. The catechism that follows is of short duration (111–25); nevertheless, the girls' answers leave no doubt of their diplomatic shrewdness – their skill in maintaining allegiance to their mother while at the same time concealing from their father the offensiveness of his questions.[98] Antipho ends the "test" abruptly and reveals the real purpose of his visit:

[97] The monologue is incoherent; I follow Leo in deleting verse 79 and in altering *leniter* of verse 78 to *saeviter*.

[98] The "test" itself and parts of Antipho's second entrance monologue (75–87) that allude to his strategy of obfuscation are probably Plautine addition with admixture of later accretions into the text. The insertion of the "test" is evident in the manner in which it is prefaced and completed: Antipho abruptly changes the subject at 102 and asks if anyone is eavesdropping; he thereupon introduces the "test" and ends it with the typically Plautine wordplay at 126 (*ingenium ingeni* (cf. *Trin.* 1049 and possibly *Amph.* 899). Immediately afterwards, he announces the real reason for his visit, the advice of friends that he should dissolve his daughters' marriages (127–28). That announcement would fit more easily into the dialogue directly after Soror's remark at 100–01, that it is virtuous for them to exalt the men who took them as their partners. In that case, "Antipho" of the original would respond, "True, but where's the other half of the corporation now? Nowhere in sight! My friends have therefore counselled me thus: that I should take you home from here." Soror's response at 130 would then have a direct connection backwards to 100–01. The "test" itself is offensive and hardly imaginable in a Greek model, but it has the virtue of enlivening what might have been a very dull scene. On the other hand, the "test" could have provided a thematic link with the object of Antipho's visit: just as he is now contemplating a new marriage and the virtues his second (?) wife should have, so his daughters should be contemplating a new marriage and the virtues of a second husband. But Plautus has not developed the "test" in this way; his aim in inserting it is thoroughly Plautine – only consider Antipho's words at 85: *perplexabiliter earum hodie perpauefaciam pectora* ("I'll scarify the living daylights out of them in no enlightening way!")

AN. edepol vos lepide temptavi vostrumque ingenium ingeni.
sed hoc est quod ad vos venio quodque esse ambas conventas volo:
mi auctores ita sunt amici, ut vos hinc abducam domum. (126–28)

AN. By Pollux – what an amusing test I've made of you and your character of character!
But this is the reason why I'm visiting and why I have convened the two of you:
my friends counsel me thus: that I should take you home from here.

What had been, in the question and answer segment of the scene, an explicit oral examination and discussion of character becomes in the subsequent dialogue a real test of character as the daughters demonstrate their mettle to their father, activating, in the process, their strategy of *exorandum*, of appeal to authority. Neither daughter is caught off-guard. We have already heard Soror offer the rhetorical conundrum (130–31) in response to Antipho's report of his friends' advice. The conundrum had been prefaced by mimicry of Antipho's words, in language skirting the law: *at enim nos quarum res agitur aliter auctores sumus* (129: "Yes, but we whose case is being tried counsel otherwise"). Antipho, however, is above all concerned with his daughters' material welfare – is he to allow them, while he is alive, to remain wed to roving mendicants (132)? Why don't they make a first-rate match instead (138)? Both daughters assure him that they are unwilling to marry anyone else. Antipho then asks the most important question of all:

certumne est neutram vostrarum persequi imperium patris? (141)

have neither of you resolved to obey your father's commands?

Panegyris parries the question neatly:

persequimur, nam quo dedisti nuptum abire nolumus. (142)

We do obey it – for we refuse to leave the men to whom you married us.

Antipho, of course, has not explicitly commanded his daughters to divorce – that is the delicacy of his question at 141; and Panegyris' answer manifestly ignores the possibility that such a command could even be made. The daughters thus skilfully avoid the legal issue while Antipho heeds the appeal to sentiment. As he departs, he remarks, "I shall go to my friends and tell them your resolution (*consilia*, 144)." Antipho's decision has been shaped by the separate forensic strategies devised by himself and his daughters: his strategy to delay legal compulsion before testing his daughters in the hope of confounding them into submission, their strategy to make an appeal to persuade him to their view. The daughters succeed: they put their father to the test of fair play – and he passes, *exorabilest*.

Epitrepontes

In this play, the issues are more complicated. Although we do not possess the full text of the debate between father and daughter, we do know that neither individual "won" it: so much is clear from Kharisios' comments (926–32) after he has eavesdropped on the scene and from Smikrines' remarks in Act v when he arrives at Pamphile's house to make one more attempt at persuasion (1062–77). But it is the debate scene that calls for our attention here. I mentioned earlier in discussion of 817–20 (Sandbach *App.*) that paradox would be uppermost in Pamphile's mind; let us recall those lines now:

διὰ τοῦτο πότερον η [
συνευτυχήσουσ' {ε} ἂν δ'
αὐτῶι προίδω; μὰ τόν [
κοινωνὸς ἦλθον τ[οῦ βίου (817–20)[99]

To perceive the paradox, we must keep in mind the situation that Pamphile has found herself in: raped by an unknown assailant before marriage, she has been deserted (not divorced) by her husband upon his discovery that she has given birth far too early for the infant to be the offspring of their marriage. The infant has been exposed; that problem has been solved – for the moment. But how is Pamphile to be treated? With no identifiable rapist to prosecute, Pamphile might even be suspected of having engaged in a consensual, premarital affair. That Kharisios has not divorced her is perhaps a mark of affection or at least of mixed feelings. Possibly he is trying to offer Pamphile a way out of her difficult position, furnishing her with a motive (his taking up with a harpist) to take the initiative in a divorce.[100] The situation should be compared with that in *Hecyra*: there, Pamphilus' wife had been raped before marriage, unbeknownst to her husband; Pamphilus had departed on

[99] See nn. 91 and 92 above and accompanying translation in text.

[100] So Capps 1908: 418–23; Gomme and Sandbach 1973: 292 are perhaps too hasty in their dismissal of Capps' interpretation of Kharisios' conduct. If Pamphile (or her father) were to initiate the divorce, then Kharisios would not be put in the awkward position of revealing Pamphile's secret. While grounds for divorce were not required by law, husbands may have been expected to provide some explanation to the girl's natal family (cf. Is. 2.6–9; *Fab. Inc.* 18).

a long business trip while her pregnancy was still imperceptible. Before his return, she leaves for her parents' house where she gives birth with her mother's (but not her father's) knowledge. When Pamphilus discovers the birth, his wife's mother (Myrrina) begs him to keep it secret – she promises to expose the infant; whether he will take her daughter back is to be his decision (*Hecyra* 382–401).[101] An important difference in the two plays is that in *Hecyra*, the young woman voluntarily leaves her marital house whereas in *Epitrepontes*, she refuses to do so. Grey, murky, ambiguous areas of morality are being explored in these plays as the marriages of the young couples are left in abeyance. What, after all, is the status of the young woman's marriage in *Hecyra*, when she returns to her parents' home? What is the status of Pamphile's marriage in *Epitrepontes* when her husband has "deserted" (not divorced) her? These are surely liminal arrangements, separations betwixt and between marriage and divorce, not legally definable so long as the ambiguities remain unresolved. What, then, is legally right for these young couples to do? What is morally right for them to do? Are Myrrina's pleadings in *Hecyra* legally or morally or socially acceptable?

These are the questions that arise from the plight of the young women in *Epitrepontes* and *Hecyra*, and with these in mind we must return to Pamphile's position in the debate with her father. The latter, of course, wants her to leave her husband; as for Kharisios – even if we do not know his explicit thoughts on the matter, we can conjecture that his wife's "removal" would make his life less complicated; Pamphile, however, stands stalwartly by her marriage. The rhetorical facade of the debate furnishes her a mask behind which all the paradoxes and ambiguities of her position may safely be hidden. At what a price of pain! She calls her husband unfortunate (ἀτυχὼν 813, Sandbach *App.*), surely mimicking her father's speech; she speaks of entering the marriage to share happiness with her husband (συνευτυχήσουσ' *POxy*. 3532, fr. 2. 7 = Sandbach *App.* 818 συνευτυχήσασ', *sic*?), of entering a partnership for life (κοινωνὸς ἦλθον το[ῦ βίου Sandbach *App*. 820); she probably again mimics her father's qualification of Kharisios' conduct when she asks, "he has blundered?" (ἔπταικεν; Sandbach *App*. 821). None of these utterances – whether she picks up the words her father has used or grasps hold of stock motifs of sharing happiness and a life partnership – can

[101] For summary of views of analytic critics, some of whom have conjectured structural changes in Terence's scene, see Ireland 1990: 11–12.

have anything but a special and painful meaning for her. Paradox and moral ambiguity characterize her situation: she will not leave her husband, who, for all intents and purposes, has left her with justification – i.e., with society's sanction, if society only knew what Kharisios knows; she will remain in this partnership, as she would have her husband remain in his – though she has produced an infant conceived outside of marriage and he has, in perplexity, taken up with a harpist.

Is she right to maintain her marriage under these circumstances – even if she is not "at fault"? Was it right for her to marry in the first place? Is Kharisios wrong to take up with a harpist? Who should divorce whom? Morality? Legality? The rhetorical facade – the tripartite plan of Smikrines' speech which may have been answered in triadic form, the adverting to stock motifs and paradox, one long speech set against another long speech (or however many "long" speeches the full text would contain) – all conduce to indirection and concealment. Menander raises questions; he does not answer them. He offers us close looks at individuals at highly pressured moments of their lives, at points where civic, social, family, and individual values intersect and contradict. He suggests, rather than delineates, the grounds for decision – that ambiguous subtext is his partnership with humanity. What he shows us – and shows us in rich clarity – are people acting and in action, without endorsement from an omnipotent ethical genius behind the scenes. This is how life is lived, onstage.

3 CONCLUSIONS

We have examined arguments used by characters of New Comedy in two scenarios of family meetings: discussions of epiklerate marriages and debates over divorce. At the outset, we posed the question, "do these arguments reflect those used 'behind closed doors' in Athens?" Family members who meet to discuss the pros and cons of epiklerate marriages in New Comedy use the same sorts of arguments that we occasionally glimpse in the orators. While sometimes in the oratorical record marriages of sentiment appear to have been pitted against marriages sanctioned by law, we found no reason to believe that epiklerate marriages had become subjected to social disapprobation. New Comedy writers, we argued, preserved that indifference: marriages of sentiment prevail, but sham epiklerate marriages are the vehicle for their execution. For the arguments of daughters who desire to maintain their marriages against fathers who want to dissolve them, we could find no parallel in the orators. While we have no way of knowing whether Athenian daughters ever offered their fathers such arguments as they do in New Comedy, their rhetorical quality nevertheless called for attention. That formality suggested not only that the arguments be viewed as stockpiles of generic motifs, but also that they be seen as a mode of forensic discourse, designed to achieve particular ends – whether that be the conscious deployment of arguments of fairness or the concealment of personal injury.

In the *oikos* disputes discussed in this chapter, forensic strategies are often self-consciously deployed to produce a desirable effect: for some characters, their purpose is to effect an appeal; for others, their purpose is to confound, to intimidate, or to compel a confession. Forensic strategies are oblique strategies of communication that replace more open forms of dialogue. This is obviously true of Micio's *ludus*; but it is no less true of both father and daughters in *Stichus*. The forensic disposition – with its proclivity for making attacks, defenses, and judgments – is most fully developed in the *senes*, slaves, and socially marginal characters of New Comedy, rarely in the young men, occasionally in young married women. These characters second-guess their opponents and argue accordingly; they think "forensically." This does not mean – as should be clear by now – that they think in accordance with the laws, but rather that they think by "formulations": by thinking, e.g., how conduct can be formulated as justifiable, how an end can be attained, how an argument can be most persuasive, how the law can be circumvented, how at times the truth can be explicitly concealed but rendered implicitly self-evident. The "arguments behind closed doors" are essentially no different from many of the arguments used by litigants in court: while the stage is more intimate and confined to *oikos* members, the quality of the act is no less rehearsed, refined, and formalized.

PART III

Playing on the boundaries of the law

CHAPTER 8

Entrapment and framing

Identifying legal or quasi-legal scenarios in New Comedy is a useful tool for interpretation: it provides a context for understanding the not always straightforward conduct of characters on the forensic stage. In this last chapter, I attempt to show how we can apply the paradigms of two scenarios, entrapment and framing, to other situations which are not strictly related to legal or even quasi-legal procedures for settling disputes.

Entrapment, in modern American criminal jargon, takes place when an officer of the law or an undercover agent actively entices an individual to commit an offense in order to obtain evidence to use against him in a criminal prosecution; it is illegal when the methods used to obtain the evidence are such as "to create a substantial risk that the offense would be committed by a person not otherwise disposed to commit it."[1] In ancient Athens, the contours of entrapment are different: there is of course no public prosecutor who might initiate such a plan and hence no law proscribing such conduct on the part of "public servants." But adversaries in Athens did engage in similar unwholesome tactics against one another and their aim in doing so, as we shall see, resembles that of the modern undercover agent: to bring a "past offender" to justice by enticing him to commit a crime for which solid evidence can be presented in a court of law. The "past offender" trapped in this way in Athens need not be a person who has committed an illegal offense before the entrapment; he may have only personally offended his adversary in some earlier dispute. The entrapment of the offender may then be viewed as a radical retaliatory means of coming to terms. There is no specific ancient term for entrapment – nor for the related

[1] New York Penal Law 40. 05 cited in *McKinney's Consolidated New York Law* 1987: 130.

scenario of "framing"; both are often referred to by words connoting "plotting" such as *epibouleuein*.

Framing, unlike entrapment, is not a technical term in modern usage. In contemporary British and American detective fiction, framing often refers to the act of devising evidence in order to convict a person of a crime that someone else has committed or that has not been committed at all. Proving that a person has been framed is another way of proving that he is not guilty of the crime imputed to him. Obviously, any alleged offender – modern or ancient – who claims he is not guilty of an offense might argue, in one way or another, that he has been framed. Athenian law offered no general remedy to innocent victims of such devious plotting; it did, however, provide a specific remedy for framing and possibly for enticement in alleged cases of flagrant *moikheia*.

In the first part of this chapter, I identify specific cases of entrapment and framing in the orators and then turn to their depictions in New Comedy. The writers of the latter genre frequently avail themselves of the two scenarios. Both can be expanded on the comic stage: they allow for the creation of rehearsal scenes in which the frame-up or entrapment can be practiced in advance and for the subsequent enactment of those plays on-stage; attendant opportunities for "meta-theater" can be – and are – exploited.[2] Whether narrated in the orators or depicted by dramatists, however, the scenarios have a definite legal configuration and should be seen as part of the complex interaction of the legal system with individuals engaged in disputes. Modern interpreters of New Comedy frequently designate such scenarios generically as "intrigues." My aim in delineating them here is to create a more specific context for them, to show how they are embedded in the same modes of socio-legal conduct as are observable in the portrayals of certain disreputable and litigious disputants in the orators.

What especially marks the entrapment scenarios is the "plot requirement" that the offender be caught in the act of committing an offense. Only in this way will the offender realize his precarious legal position and so come to terms with his adversaries – either inside or outside the regular court system. Entrapment in crime, however, is not the only type of entrapment to appear in New Comedy. Occasionally, an alleged offender is enticed to commit a

[2] For the notion of meta-theater, see esp. Chiarini 1979; Slater 1985; Muecke 1986.

moral offense which will publicly expose his character; at other times, an entrapment scenario is used with a different aim, to entice an alleged offender to confess a past crime or moral offense. Depictions of "moral" and "confessional entrapment" make up the bulk of the closing sections of this book.

I ENTRAPMENT, FRAMING, AND THE LAW

1 (a) Enticing and framing moikhoi

In Lysias 1, Euphiletos defends himself against the relatives of the deceased Eratosthenes in a prosecution for homicide; Euphiletos claims that the murder was justifiable: he had discovered Eratosthenes naked, in bed with his wife. Euphiletos' defense suggests how the plaintiffs may have argued their case. In cc. 37–46 of the speech, Euphiletos directly argues against what he alleges is the plaintiffs' charge:

> And consider further, gentlemen: for they accuse me of bidding the housemaid on that very day to fetch the young man. (37)[3]

The extended passage is sometimes used by legal historians to argue that "enticement to the act" precluded a husband's right of redress.[4] The law of justifiable homicide as we know it, however, specified only that a man must apprehend another man on or beside his wife (or other specified female member of his household); no conditions are stated in the law other than flagrance and the relationship of the woman to her avenger (chapter 5.1.a). Whether "enticement to the act" is a legal issue in Lysias 1 is therefore questionable. The plaintiffs allegedly claimed that their kinsman had been invited to the house, possibly that he had been dragged there; they might not have added, however, the two final steps, that he had been invited specifically for a rendezvous with Euphiletos' wife and that the meeting had been carried off successfully. Possibly they claimed that

[3] There is a seeming inconsistency between the charges reported in cc. 27 and 37: in c. 27, the speaker alleges that the plaintiffs accused him of dragging (εἰσαρπασθείς) Eratosthenes to the house, whereas in c. 37, he alleges they accused him of sending the maid to fetch (μετελθεῖν) him. But the two verbs could have been used by the plaintiffs as they viewed the action from different perspectives; the "dragging in" might be their own rhetorical exaggeration of a "summoning." Alternatively, the request to the maid to summon the man may have been prelude to the "dragging in" (so Carey 1989: 76).

[4] Harrison 1. 33, citing c. 37, says: "It was a condition of the husband's right of redress that he should not have enticed the adulterer to the act." Similarly Carey 1989: 60, 64 and 81–82; Carawan 1998, chapter 8.

the whole story of an adulterous affair was sheer fabrication; Euphiletos had summoned Eratosthenes to his house and had cold-heartedly killed him for reasons that the defendant now thinks best to shroud in silence. Euphiletos' detailed narrative of the affair between his wife and the murdered man (cc. 8–20), in that case, aims at painting a different story: Eratosthenes was a *moikhos*, he had a history of womanizing – and not only with the defendant's wife.[5] On the other hand, if the plaintiffs had admitted their kinsman's involvement with Euphiletos' wife, then the issue of the husband's part in summoning Eratosthenes to the house might still be extraneous: the law was concerned with the commission of the act under a specific set of circumstances, and in this instance (homicide as a response to flagrant adultery), it was not interested in psychological foreplay. Whether dikasts would take into account the circumstance of enticement is a different issue. It is conceivable that such an argument may have acquired, by usage rather than by law, a persuasive force in court.

The Athenian legal system did, however, have a specific remedy for those who had been detained *adikōs* ("unlawfully," "unjustly") for *moikheia* – and who, unlike Eratosthenes, had survived the ordeal. A difficulty lies in defining what *adikōs* refers to in this instance. The law is paraphrased in [Dem.] 59. 66, in the part of the oration which deals with Neaira's daughter Phano. Crucial for our understanding of the episode is an awareness of the ambiguity surrounding the young woman's identity. Apollodoros, advocate for the prosecutor, claims she is Neaira's, not Stephanos', daughter (c. 50); Stephanos, for his part, may have claimed, as Apollodoros predicts, that she was his daughter, borne by an Athenian wife (cc. 119–20). In our episode, Apollodoros alleges that Neaira's quasi-husband Stephanos plotted (*epibouleusas*, 65) against Epainetos and summoned him to the country, on the grounds that he was offering sacrifice; then, having taken him as a *moikhos* with Phano, he intimidated him and extorted thirty *mnai*, taking as sureties for the sum several men and finally releasing Epainetos in expectation of payment (65). Epainetos

[5] Euphiletos' story might be true or false. It is curious that no witnesses are provided for the narrative of events before the murder; curious, too, that the houseslave is not offered for torture. Wholesale invention, aided by friends who might have given false testimony about the murder scene, is not impossible. For different views about the lack of slave testimony in this speech, see Dover 1968: 188; Thür 1977: 44–45; Carey 1989: 63, n. 11.

reacted by indicting Stephanos before the thesmothetai on a charge of unlawful detainment:

according to the law which bids if anyone detain a man unlawfully as a *moikhos* (ἐάν τις ἀδίκως εἵρξῃ ὡς μοιχόν), the latter may indict him before the thesmothetai on a charge of unlawful detainment; and if he convicts the detainer and is proven to have been plotted against unlawfully (ἀδίκως ἐπιβεβουλεῦσθαι), he is to be let off scot-free and his sureties are to be released from their pledges; but if it be proven that he is a *moikhos*, the law bids his sureties to surrender him to his successful adversary, and the latter, in view of the courtroom, is to treat the man in whatever way he like – provided he does not use a dagger – on the grounds he is a *moikhos*. (66)

Probably an alleged *moikhos* could be detained "lawfully" if he had been caught in the act with one of the female members of a household specified by the law on justifiable homicide (wife, mother, sister, daughter, or *pallake* kept for the purpose of producing free children).[6] "Unlawful detainment," then, might be thought of as occurring when the lawful conditions had not been met, i.e., when the relationship of the woman to the avenger was not the prescribed one or when the offender had not been caught in the act. A person so detained might be said to have been "framed" or "plotted against unlawfully" (ἀδίκως ἐπιβεβουλεῦσθαι). It might be argued, however, that the law paraphrased by Apollodoros could be understood as implying a proscription against enticing a person to commit *moikheia*. Such a scenario seems to fit Epainetos' case, insofar as Stephanos had invited the man to the country (65), but that is not the argument Epainetos allegedly made. Instead, Apollodoros claims it was as follows: Phano was not Stephanos' daughter, but Neaira's (i.e. Stephanos' lack of relationship to the violated woman made it unlawful for him to detain Epainetos); moreover, she was a prostitute and so Epainetos' act of intercourse could not be construed as *moikheia* (c. 67). Epainetos, then, on Apollodoros' evidence, did not make an argument of enticement. The advocate's presentation, however, is likely to be distorted and tendentious. Emphasis on Neaira's alleged profession and Stephanos' lack of relationship to Phano certainly suits his purpose – which is to convict Neaira of posing as the *aste*-wife of Stephanos. Moreover, Epainetos is not present for corroboration of the arguments ascribed to him. It

6 Detainment for the purpose of extorting financial remuneration appears to be an alternative to the physical abuse or killing of such an offender: Lys. 1. 25, 49; [Dem.] 59. 65; see chapter 5.1.a.

remains conceivable, then, that the law proscribing the unjust detainment of a man as a *moikhos* protected men who were either framed for the offense (as Apollodoros' depiction of Epainetos' argument suggests) or enticed to the act (as the paraphrase of the law, without tendentious context, allows us to infer).

1 (b) A scenario of entrapment in [Dem.] 53 Nikostratos

While the law concerning illegal detainment as a *moikhos* may have provided a remedy to individuals who had been enticed to commit *moikheia*, no general Athenian law known to us prohibits the use of enticement in bringing an offender to justice. Apollodoros narrates a pertinent scenario in [Dem.] 53 *Nikostr.* Here he prosecutes the defendant through an *apographe*, claiming that Nikostratos has in his possession two slaves who in fact should belong to the state because they are the property of his brother Arethousios, a state debtor. Apollodoros makes no effort to conceal his motive for initiating the prosecution – he seeks revenge upon the two brothers for the lawsuits they have involved him in and for the ingratitude exhibited by Nikostratos in particular. After reviewing his past generous conduct toward the latter (4–13, e.g., financial help in ransoming Nikostratos after he had been captured by a trireme and sold in Aigina), Apollodoros begins the tale of wicked repayment: Nikostratos had engineered a summons against him as a debtor to the public treasury – when in fact no summons had been served but Arethousios instead had falsely witnessed the citation – the consequence of which enormity was that Apollodoros was convicted in absentia and fined six hundred and ten drakhmai; Nikostratos then carried off all the furniture from his house, which was worth more than twenty *mnai*. Apollodoros, however, paid the fine and then began to proceed against Arethousios with a *graphe pseudoklēteias* (an indictment for fraudulently testifying to a summons, 14–15). At this point, we shall consider the cat and mouse moves in more detail:

Arethousios came to my farm at night and cut off as many of the best fruit grafts as were there and the vines that grew up the trees as well, and he broke down the nursery of olive trees planted in rows, treating the land worse than even an enemy in time of war would. And in addition to this, during the day they sent a young Athenian boy (*paidarion astos*) – since they were neighbors and our land was contiguous – and bid him to pluck away the flowering rose garden so that, if I were to lay hold of him in anger, and if I were to fetter or strike him on the grounds that he were a slave, they could indict me for *hubris*. (15–16)

Apollodoros' reaction was marked by superior self-control: he did not touch the boy but called witnesses to observe what he had suffered and proceeded with the *graphe pseudoklēteias* against Arethousios. But after the preliminary inquiry (*anakrisis*) had taken place and when the case was about to be heard in court, then:

. . . having watched out for me near the stone quarries as I was coming back late from the Peiraios, Nikostratos struck me with his fist and grabbed hold of me by the waist and was about to throw me into the quarries – but some bystanders came up upon hearing my cries for help and ran to my rescue. (17)

A few days later, the case for false citation came to court and Arethousios was convicted. Apollodoros stops at this point in his recreation of the past and supplies witnesses for the events.

The narrative is of great interest – whether or not it is a true representation of facts – with its lively description of the machinations of pre-trial jockeying and intimidation. The particular interest that it holds for us here, however, is its depiction of entrapment: the way that Nikostratos and Arethousios are alleged to have vandalized Apollodoros' farm at night (an incident which eye-witnesses are unlikely to have viewed) and then to have sent an Athenian boy in daylight to destroy Apollodoros' rose garden (an incident which eye-witnesses most likely had been instructed to observe). The stage had been set to entice Apollodoros to an act of violence; he, however, had recognized the scenario and restrained himself from playing the part that had allegedly been scripted for him by his malevolent neighbors. Of interest are Apollodoros' acuity in recognizing the juvenile delinquent as a free Athenian (*astos*) and even more, his desire to point this out: had he done violence to the boy, his status would have made no difference to bringing an indictment – a charge for *hubris* could be brought in behalf of "any person, either child or woman or man, free or slave" (Dem. 21. 47); but the boy's status might have affected the penalty – injuring a free person in this way could be more severely penalized: "If he is fined for the *hubris*, let the person be imprisoned, if the *hubris* is against a free person, until he pays it" (Dem. 21. 47).[7] Nikostratos' and Arethousios' purpose in contriving the

[7] On the authenticity of the law, see chapter 5, n. 50.

scenario is clear: if Apollodoros had struck the boy, they could have indicted him for *hubris*; the free status of the boy could then have been strategically used in court as an argument to blacken Apollodoros' offense and to demand a heavy fine – a fine which might have landed Apollodoros in prison until he could pay. At the very least, the threat of indictment for *hubris* might have induced Apollodoros to drop the *graphe pseudoklēteias*, regardless of the 1,000 drakhmai fine he would supposedly lose for doing so.[8] The scenario of entrapment failed, however; Apollodoros, proud son of a slave who had been made a citizen by decree, had too well-trained an eye for status to be bamboozled in this way.[9]

Before leaving this account behind, let us sketch its salient features as a scenario:

(1) A plot is devised to entice an individual into committing a crime. Successful execution of the plot entails that the crime be committed and that witnesses be present who could later testify to its commission.
(2) The script entails a mistake in status.
(3) The plot presupposes rehearsal. In this case, a free Athenian is to be instructed what to do and how to act as a slave; presumably, witnesses for the plotters are to be instructed where to be present and what to observe.
(4) The motive for the entrapment is to settle a dispute. Here, it is to intimidate Apollodoros into dropping his case against Arethousios.

The four features listed here are present in the instances of New Comedy that will be sketched below. Probably the second feature (a mistake in status) is coincidental to the scenario and not constitutive of it. The presence of that feature in the instances from New Comedy, however, suggests that the (mis-)identification or (mis-)-representation of status may have been the basis for many different kinds of offense in Athens.

[8] The law on *hubris* also required "the thesmothetai [to] bring the case to the Eliaia within thirty days of the submission of the *graphe*" (trans. MacDowell 1990). Apollodoros' account of the events does not permit us to know whether the *graphe hubreos* would have preceded the *graphe pseudoklēteias* in court. If it did, then conviction for *hubris* accompanied by a stiff penalty might have rendered Apollodoros unable to pursue the prosecution against Arethousios.

[9] Pasion's change of status: Dem. 36. 46–48; [Dem.] 59. 2.

2 SCENARIOS OF CRIMINAL ENTRAPMENT AND FRAMING IN NEW COMEDY

Scenarios of entrapment appear in three Plautine comedies: *Poenulus*, *Persa*, and *Miles Gloriosus*. Each scenario is essential to the plot and so will have appeared in the Greek original. Details of treatment and emphasis are undoubtedly different in the Roman plays.[10] In particular, Plautus appears to have expanded scenes of rehearsal, and he may have made other additions as well.[11] We should not, however, attribute all meta-theatrical aspects to the Roman playwright; the scripted scenarios of *Aspis* and *Epitrepontes* give the lie to such a generalized view.

The following is a tabulation of the components of the scenario in these plays:

(1) A scripted plot of entrapment: In *Poenulus*, the pimp Lycus is tricked into harboring someone else's slave who has been loaded up with cash; Lycus becomes liable to a charge of theft (III 3–6). In *Persa*, the pimp Dordalus is tricked into buying a citizen girl and so becomes liable to a charge of kidnapping or enslaving a citizen (IV 3–9). In *Miles*, Pyrgopolynices is enticed to engage in illicit sexual relations (IV–V).

(2) A mistake in status: In *Poenulus*, the pimp Lycus is liable to indictment only if Collybiscus is a slave and so he is misled to believe that he is a foreigner; the latter's true status (as a slave) is revealed when the charge is made against the pimp (III 5). In

[10] Detailed treatment of the relationship of the Greek originals to the three Roman plays is beyond the scope of this chapter. For discussion of Plautus' adaptation of the entrapment scenario in *Persa*, see Scafuro 1993: 64–74; I now am much more convinced of large Plautine additions in IV 4 (see Lowe 1989b: 392–97); on IV 9, see App. 4. 2. In the Greek original of *Poenulus*, the *advocati* may not have had so vocal a role (Lowe 1990); on III 5, see App. 5, add. 4. Earlier theories of contamination to explain the plot of *Miles* have been discredited and replaced by a unitarian view which tends to see Plautus as making additions (sometimes quite important ones) to certain sections of the Greek original (Williams 1958a; Gaiser 1967; Lefèvre 1984b).The last author, for example, argues that the rehearsal scene (III 3) is largely Plautine addition.

[11] Plautus' repetition in two plays (*Persa* 465–66; *Poen.* 581) of the analogy between acting in an entrapment scenario and acting in a play, for example, is likely to be his own handiwork. Fraenkel 1960: 9, n. 2 shows that the comparison of two elements from different spheres is typically Plautine. Not every explicit association of theater plot with forensic plot, however, is necessarily to be ascribed to the Roman poet. The attention that Aristotle bestows on delivery (ὑπόκρισις) in the third book of *Rhetorike*, and the analogies between stage acting and courtroom acting that appear there, are sufficient indicators that this nexus of ideas was familiar and explicitly articulated in fourth century Athens, even before Menander exploited it.

Persa, the pimp Dordalus is only liable to a charge of illicit enslavement if the parasite's daughter is an Athenian citizen and so he is misled to believe she is a foreign captive; Saturio reveals his daughter's true identity at the moment of court summons (IV 9). In *Miles*, Pyrgopolynices is more likely to bite the bait of enticement if Acroteleutium is living alone and so he is misled to believe that she is a divorced woman (1276–78); the woman's (alleged) marital status is revealed only at the moment of flagrant discovery (1402).

(3) Rehearsal and witnesses: In *Poenulus*, the witnesses, the famed *advocati*, are brought on stage and rehearsed (III 1); Collybiscus has practiced his role off-stage (578–81). In *Persa*, both Saturio's daughter (III 1 and IV 2) and Sagaristio arrive on-stage (IV 2), fully instructed and dressed for their parts; the only witnesses will be their fellow conspirators. In *Miles*, Acroteleutium is instructed in her role on stage (III 3) and then retires off-stage for further rehearsal; the witnesses will all be fellow-conspirators.

(4) Motive: In *Poenulus*, the pimp, has refused Agorastocles access to his beloved (157–58); providing payment does not seem to be a problem for the rich young man (165–66). Conviction for the theft of slave and money will supposedly result in the pimp's household being adjudged to Agorastocles (185–86) – he will obtain possession of his beloved (see App. 5, cat. no. III. 14). In *Persa*, the motive appears to be revenge. Toxilus plans the entrapment because of the hard terms imposed by Dordalus for the sale of his beloved slave: either the money was to be paid on that very day and Lemniselenis freed, or else she would remain a slave forever (34–34a, and cf. 81–82, 783–85, 431–32). In *Miles*, the motive is to deflect the soldier's affections from the courtesan he carried off from Athens to Ephesos; the courtesan's Athenian lover will thereby be able to bring her back to Athens.

In both *Poenulus* and *Persa*, the entrapment of the offender is perfectly contrived: Collybiscus is really a slave and the parasite's daughter is really a citizen – entrapment might be a "play," but the offense is not. While, in a Roman court, Lycus or Dordalus might hope to win acquittal by claiming the truth, that he did not commit the crime *sciens dolo malo*, neither of them would have witnesses to support that defense. The scenario in *Miles* is different: the woman who is cast for the role of "respectable divorced woman discovered to be still married" is really a courtesan. A framing scenario in *Miles* has thus been superimposed upon the entrapment. No offense will in fact have been committed – the audience is aware of this from the outset but Pyrgopolynices will never know. The soldier's situation is almost exactly parallel to what Epainetos had allegedly claimed against Stephanos in [Dem.] 59. 66–67: he is unlawfully detained as a *moikhos* since *moikheia* cannot be committed with a prostitute.

A plot to entice an individual to commit a crime, a mistake in status, rehearsal and witnesses, motive: these are the components of the entrapment scenario. The scenario necessitates staging, and the playwright in each instance calls attention to its staginess. The criminal plot becomes dramatic plot, the plotter becomes director, the perpetrators of fraud become actors. The transformation is a natural one; it happens in "real life" whenever anyone – compare Nikostratos, for example – avails himself of the entrapment scenario. This is not quite the "staginess" of "law-in-action" that was adumbrated in the first chapter of this study, where the family council of Lysias 32 *Diogeiton* was characterized as a kind of theatrical performance; here it is rather the "staginess" of proceeding on the law's boundaries and sometimes taking a few steps beyond them. Composing an entrapment scenario entails knowing the lawful scenario – one can only trick someone into breaking the law when one knows the law. That each of these instances involves different laws – of theft, of sale and enslavement, of justifiable homicide – and that each of them relies on a mistake in status to effect the commission of the crime – demonstrates a very sophisticated capacity for exploiting the law; it also reveals a remarkable aspect of the legal systems of Athens and Rome, the effects and defects of very marked status systems.

3 MORAL ENTRAPMENT IN *ASPIS*

The entrapment scenario in *Aspis* has a slightly different shape. In the comedies under discussion in the last section, the plotters had scripted their plays to entice adversaries to commit criminal offenses; in *Aspis*, they script a play in which Smikrines is enticed to commit a moral offense. Smikrines, we recall (see chapter 7.1.b), after hearing the news of the death of his nephew Kleostratos, decided to exert his right as oldest paternal uncle and to claim his niece as an *epikleros*. To prevent Smikrines' marriage, Daos, clever and trusty slave of Kleostratos, devises a plan, to pretend that Khairestratos, younger brother of Smikrines, has died. His death would make his daughter an *epikleros*, too – and a far richer one than Kleostratos' sister; Smikrines would then renounce his claim to the poorer *epikleros* in order to marry the richer. The plot thus requires a mistake in status of a very special kind: Smikrines must mistake a dummy of his brother (σχῆμα νεκροῦ, 345 εἴδωλον, 359) for a corpse. Moreover, he will be enticed to make that mistake; the bait is Khairestratos' wealth. The success of the plan depends on the absolute predictability of Smikrines' character which has been carefully delineated thus far: a materialistic man of no genuine sentiments, who in the first scene of the play appears more excited over the details of Kleostratos' war-booty than saddened by the news of the young man's death. Now, in his eagerness to acquire a more lucrative estate, he will too readily accept the evidence of death and too quickly believe what he wants to believe. "He knows neither kin nor friend," Tukhe tells the audience in a delayed prologue, "and has not the least inkling of his own shameful way of life, but wants to have it all" (117–20 . . . οὗτος οὔτε συγγενῆ / οὔτε φίλον οἶδεν οὐδὲ τῶν ἐν τῶι βίωι / αἰσχρῶν πεφρόντικ' οὐδέν, ἀλλὰ βούλεται / ἔχειν ἅπαντα· . . .).

We shall focus here on the theatrical qualities of Daos' script. But first some comments on its "shortcomings." Critics have pointed out that Daos has not foreseen a problem that will inevitably arise upon the successful execution of his plan: what is to happen when Smikrines renounces the one *epikleros* (Kleoskratos' sister) and claims the other (Khairestratos' daughter)? Is the "deceased" Khairestratos expected to allow Smikrines to marry his daughter? Surely not. Then, if Khairestratos "rises from the dead," what is to stop Smikrines from reinstituting his claim to Kleostratos' sister? Even if she had quickly married Khaireas, would she not be compelled to leave her husband and marry Smikrines? Has our playwright nodded?[12] If so, then he has nodded no differently from the way he apparently did in the *Andria*, nor differently from the way Apollo-

[12] MacDowell 1982: 49–50 solves this problem by asserting that the play provides us "new information about Athenian law" and that "a basic assumption of Daos' plan is that, once the girl is married to Khaireas, Smikrines will not be able to reclaim her when he discovers that he has been tricked. We may draw the conclusion that, unlike a father, a relative who gave away in marriage an epikleros of the lowest income-class did not have the legal right to take her back again." Brown 1983: 418–20 argues against MacDowell's thesis on similar grounds as I do ("Does the world of comedy look further ahead than the short-term thwarting of its villain's plans?" 419–20).

doros presumably did in the Greek original of *Phormio*. In both of those plays, the plan of the clever (or not so clever) slave is a short-term one that solves a problem for the immediate future but creates a second problem in the long run. In Terence's version of the *Andria*, Simo wants his son Pamphilus to marry Chremes' daughter, although his son has no desire for that marriage and his love interests lie elsewhere. When Davos has correctly deduced that Chremes has refused to betroth his daughter, he urges Pamphilus to agree to the wedding (II 3, 387–98); Davos, however, has provided no sure-fire guarantee that Simo will not contract a marriage for Pamphilus from some other quarter or that Chremes will not change his mind; he has only a glib feeling that the *senex*, if he sees his son amenable and obedient, will take his time in finding him another bride (397–98). In *Phormio* IV 3, Geta reports the bargain he has allegedly struck with the parasite: Phormio will marry Phanium, currently the wife of Antipho, with a dowry of thirty *mnai*. The plan provides the cash needed to buy a mistress for Phaedria but puts Antipho's marriage to Phanium in jeopardy. Geta has no fool-proof plan to prevent the latter's marriage to Phormio; he relies upon his feeling that the wedding can be delayed long enough for the young men to borrow money to return the dowry (IV 4, 696–710). In *Aspis*, Daos' plan prevents the marriage of one *epikleros* by creating the opportunity for marriage to a sham *epikleros*. The problem created by the availability of the first *epikleros* for marriage, when the second is discovered to be a sham, is apparently left hanging, as is the problem of Pamphilus' availability for marriage in the *Andria* and the parasite's availability as a husband in *Phormio*.

In the *Andria* and *Phormio*, however, there had been some attempt to address the new problem – no matter that the remedy in each case was not one to warrant much confidence. Did Menander – or Daos – make no similar attempt in *Aspis*? Examination of the slave's plan, particularly the part that envisions the aftermath of Khairestratos' sham death, provides an answer. Smikrines will claim the new *epikleros* and give the other to the first comer "before three thousand witnesses" (354–55); moreover, "he'll start managing the entire house, he'll go about with the keys, putting seals on the doors – a dream of wealth" (356–59); meanwhile, Daos and conspiring actors (Khairestratos' wife, daughter, and Kleostratos' sister, cf. 383–85) will sit in a circle around the sham corpse and prevent Smikrines from approaching too closely (360–61). Daos' plan clearly entails the close observation of Smikrines' conduct – every post mortem action is to be duly noted – whether by the "three thousand witnesses" or by the circle of kin surrounding the dummy. The record-keeping looks to the unstated but obvious dénouement of the plot: Khairestratos' resurrection and Smikrines' realization of his kinsmen's ruse. But what offensive act, in particular, will Smikrines have committed and Khairestratos observed? And what action on the part of Khairestratos and company might compel Smikrines to forego a claim to the first *epikleros* now that the second one is as demonstrably sham as her father's dummy corpse? Daos has already answered the first question: Smikrines will be going about the house, keys in hand, putting seals on the doors (357–58). Seals are put on doors to prevent the removal of property, and they are especially put on doors when an inventory is to take place prior to an adjudication of property (e.g., [Dem.] 42. 2, 6, 8). We might well ask, what purpose would an inventory serve at this point in Menander's play? If, as Daos envisions it, Smikrines is preparing to make a claim on the new *epikleros*, then he must still be awarded the estate and the *epikleros* by the court (see chapter 2, n. 7); his sealing of the house and inventory of its goods anticipate both lawful entry to the estate and a desire to protect it from the encroachments of kin, possibly of the women in particular (cf. 465–67, also 182–84). Smikrines, then, will be caught in the act of attempting to appropriate the entire estate, in a manner fully in accord with his usual zeal for adhering to the letter of the law – but for one serious mistake – Khairestratos is not dead.

Daos' further remarks about the aftermath of sham death might provide an answer to our second question: how do the plotters foresee preventing Smikrines from renewing his claim upon Kleostratos' sister? Unfortunately, a few verses are missing after 361, and the following six are badly mutilated. The latter, however, appear to envision a testing (πεῖραν, 364) of a visitor or visitors (?) to the house (365); one is imagined as a debtor (366), possibly he (or someone else) steals something (conjecture, 366–67), in return for which the speaker suggests that a "doubling" or "twice the amount" (διπλάσιον) be exacted (367). Khairestratos then compliments the plan as being "after his own heart" (368).[13] Any interpretation of these lines is speculative. I suggest the following: Daos (if he is the speaker of

[13] *Aspis* 363–68:]ν τοὺς φί[λους /]υ πεῖραν ἔσται τιν[/]πως ἦλθεν ἐπὶ τὴν οἰκίαν /]τις γέγον' ὀφείλων· εἴ τινι /]διπλάσιον εἰσπράττει πάνυ /]ιν ὃ λέγεις, Δᾶε, τοῦ τ' ἐμοῦ τρόπου

364–67) is not proposing that Khairestratos should actually surprise any "debtor" – including Smikrines himself – in the act of removing property, nor that he should then proceed to prosecute that person for theft (for which the law allowed a penalty that was double the value of the stolen goods: Dem. 24. 114).[14] Smikrines has been envisioned as sealing off the house (358) – neither he nor anyone else will be removing its "furniture." Moreover, Smikrines, unlike the hypothetical petty debtor-thief of verses 366–67, is not trying to make off with a few expensive baubles, he aims at appropriating the entire estate. Rather than a literal plan, what verses 364–67 might convey is a metaphorical blueprint for action against Smikrines. The petty theft will be a metaphor for Smikrines' grand larceny; the double penalty for theft a metaphor for the exacting of a painful punishment. Thus: "if you see a petty thief making off with a few choice goods, you exact for yourself twice the amount."[15] The obvious and grand analogue is left unstated: "Now, when you see your brother getting his hands on your entire estate, you put it to him with a double punch." Khairestratos in 368 shows that he has understood Daos' meaning: "] what you mean, Daos, and after my own heart" (]ιν ὃ λέγεις, Δᾶε, τοῦ τ' ἐμοῦ τρόπου). Khairestratos, who earlier in the same scene had been slow in perceiving the legal

[14] Contra Lloyd-Jones (1971: 183–84) who suggests that Daos, envisioning Smikrines as claiming his brother's property and perhaps removing some of it, makes a recommendation: "Chairestratos should emerge from hiding and threaten to prosecute him for theft." He finds confirmation for his suggestion in the remark about "vengeance" (palmary supplement) in verse 369: "no punishment would hurt Smikrines more than a heavy fine." Lloyd-Jones' suggestion is attractive speculation but must be rejected: (1) It overlooks the importance of verses 357–58. A man who is viewed as sealing a house is not likely to be viewed as simultaneously stealing from it. (2) It is inconsistent with the earlier depiction of Smikrines as law-abiding and knowledgeable of the law; even if he manipulates the law in his favor, he works through lawful channels, adhering, indeed, to the very letter of the law (184–87). It is hard to imagine that Daos would bank his entire plan on Smikrines turning into a lawbreaking burglar especially when he ascribes to the old man an expectation of a lawful means for appropriating all the property. (3) It fails to suggest how a prosecution for theft might keep Smikrines from renewing his claim for the first *epikleros*. More detail is needed for such a plan; the verses devoted to it do not allow for that. Cf. Milphio's far more detailed plan for framing Lycus for theft at *Poen.* 165–87.

[15] If διπλάσιον εἰσπράττει in 367 were to mean "you exact for yourself a double penalty", we would expect the feminine adjective διπλάσιαν, with or without the noun ζημίαν. Since διπλάσιον might be either a masculine or neuter adjective or else an adverb, then we cannot "understand" the object of the verb and must conjecture what was "doubled". For Lloyd-Jones' interpretation to work, the missing noun might be χρῆμα or ἀργύριον or χρυσός or something similar. Those words would work equally well with my interpretation; a gesture might help to convey the analogue. The possibility remains, however, that the missing noun was of a different order, conveying something along the lines of "a double load of fists"; if so, then εἰσπράττει appears παρὰ προσδοκίαν.

implications of Daos' plan (346–47: μανθάνεις / ὃ λέγει;), finds it much easier to understand a reference to private settlement. The younger brother, who had acted above the law in offering Smikrines an unlawful bargain in Act II (see chapter 7.1.b), will readily exact a heavy punishment in private from his "letter of the law" older brother.

It will be a happy moment of vengeance. Consider Daos' exchange with Khairestratos after the slave's "blueprint for action":

<ΔΑ> τιμωρί]αν δὲ τοῦ πονηροῦ τίν' ἂν ἔχοις
] σφοδροτέραν;

(ΧΑ) λήψομαι, νὴ τὸν Δία,
ὧν] μ' ὠδύνηκε πώποτ' ἀξίαν δίκην·[16] (369–71)

<DA>: What greater [vengeance] could you [take]
] on this scoundrel?

(KHA): By Zeus! I'll impose
a fitting punishment for all the pain he's ever caused me.

Smikrines will have a well-deserved punishment, inflicted not only for the "grand larceny" but for all his previous conduct – the near disruption, for instance, of Khairestratos' plans for his stepson's marriage to Kleostratos' sister. The successful execution of Daos' plan thus ultimately aims not at the replacement of one *epikleros* by another, nor at the prosecution of a chance petty thief, but rather at the private humiliation and punishment of Smikrines: the gruff old man is to be caught in the act of being himself (keys and seals in hand!) and all his kinsfolk are to be present as witnesses. Utterly humiliated, quite possibly physically abused in the uproar attendant upon his brother's resurrection, Smikrines will slink away to the solitude of his own house, without ever a whimper of a wish to be connected with his kinsmen in the future by a renewal of his claim upon the first *epikleros*. So the plotters have contrived. What neither Daos nor his fellow conspirators have foreseen, however, is Tukhe's plot, the resurrection of Kleostratos. The soldier's return from the dead at the end of Act IV – when Khairestratos is still a corpse (500–01) – will cause a change – but not a total disruption – of Daos' original plan. Smikrines will be faced with the resurrection of two

[16] It is unclear whether μ' ("me") or σ' ("you") is to be read in verse 371; unclear, too, is the assignment of speakers; see Gomme and Sandbach 1973 ad loc.

corpses – the humiliation will be twice as great. Tukhe herself had envisioned the conclusion of her own script in Act I:

> . . . μάτην δὲ πράγμαθ' αὑτῶι καὶ πόνους
> πολλοὺς παρασχὼν γνωριμώτερόν τε τοῖς
> πᾶσιν ποήσας αὑτὸν οἷος ἔστ' ἀνὴρ
> ἐπάνεισιν ἐπὶ τἀρχαῖα . . . (143–46)
>
> . . . In vain: creating a great deal of trouble
> and toil for himself, and having made evident
> to all what sort of man he is,
> he will revert to his former ways.

Save for its double dose of humiliation, Tukhe's dénouement is no different from the one envisioned by Daos. Interpreted in this light, Menander has not nodded; he has laid bare the tactics of a family feud: a zero-sum game in which the winners take all and the loser must be left with nothing.

We return now to the theatrical aspects of Daos' plot. He had begun its composition at verses 329–30. "You must stage a tragedy of a different sort" (δεῖ τραγωιδῆσαι πάθος / ἀλλοῖον ὑμᾶς 329–30), he tells Khairestratos who is depressed and distracted because of his older brother's conduct (305–07). Daos' plan takes its cue from Khairestratos' ailments: he will become very ill indeed; a doctor will have to be summoned; he will die; a shrouded dummy will be put on view (330–46). The slave refines the plan further: Khairestratos is asked to provide a foreign doctor (374–75). Since he is unable to furnish one, Khaireas offers to find a friend who can speak with a foreign accent; he will supply the costume and props – wig, cloak, and stick (376–79). As father and stepson leave the stage to prepare for the "tragedy," Daos comments to the audience before his exit, "Our calamity will doubtless offer some fine entertainment and agonistic exhibition" (388–89).[17]

The script has been composed and the players informed of their parts. No rehearsal is mentioned; that may be due to the loss of much of the text, or possibly there was none – Khairestratos had no need to practice grief and depression. In Act III, Daos announces the calamity to Smikrines and the performance begins. As if to heighten the moment of tragedy within the performance (i.e., the onset of Khairestratos' fatal illness) and at the same time to call attention to

[17] The text is difficult; I have followed the interpretation of Gomme and Sandbach 1973 ad loc.: ἕξει τιν' ἀμέλει διατριβὴν οὐκ ἄρρυθμον / ἀγωνίαν τε τὸ πάθος . . .

the notion of performance itself, Daos lards his ill-tidings to Smikrines with quotations from tragedy.[18] Sham foreign doctor quickly makes his appearance (430), enters the patient's house (431), and returns again to announce the dim prognosis: no hope for Khairestratos (447–49). Most of the act is missing, but we do obtain a glimpse of Smikrines' predictable response. Apparently deliberating over whether he should follow the doctor inside his brother's house, he says, "If they see me, they will immediately say / that I have come in joy – this I know for certain – and he himself would not be glad to see me" (433–35). Possibly at this point, Smikrines may have ruminated on his new financial prospects. Certainly his thoughts are directed toward his brother's wealth by the end of the scene: after the doctor has reported his prognosis and has left the stage (464), Smikrines suspects that the women of the household are plundering its stores and communicating to neighbors through the water ducts (465–67).

Little of Acts IV and V is extant. In the former, the entrapment scenario is apparently still underway; Khairestratos' death was probably announced near the end of the act (469); Smikrines accepts the testimony: possibly he speculates about an enriched future and the betrothal of Kleostratos' sister to Khaireas (*enguan*, 484); finally, he exits. Kleostratos then makes his return – from captivity, not death – and arrives at Khairestratos' door (491). His first exchange is with Daos, through the closed doors of the house; neither recognizes the voice of the other; the returning soldier, as if he were a stranger, is informed of the death of the master of the house (500–01). Finally, Daos opens the door and the two recognize each other; presumably, Daos explained recent events. The loss of the scene is regrettable: the situation invites exploitation of paradoxical greetings as the thought-to-be-dead soldier encounters the scripted corpse of his uncle. At the beginning of the final act, someone announces a double wedding (521); at this point, Khairestratos probably betrothed his daughter to Kleostratos and the latter probably betrothed his sister to Khaireas. Smikrines may have learned only now of the plot that had been hatched against him. Defeated and utterly humiliated in this family feud, "having made evident to all what sort of man he

[18] 407 = Eur. *Stheneboia* fr. 661 Nauck²; 411 = Khairemon *TGrF* 71 fr. 2; 412–13 = Aiskh. *TrGF* 3 *Niobe* fr. 154a15–16; 415–18 = Karkinos (?) *TGrF* 70 fr. 5a; 424–25 = Eur. *Orestes* 1; 425–26 = Eur. fr. 944a Nauck² (possibly Khairemon: *TGrF* 71 fr. 42); 432 = Eur. *Orestes* 232. See Gomme and Sandbach 1973 ad loc. for details.

is," he will return to his solitary life. Daos and fellow slaves may have protracted his exit with physical blows.[19]

The staging of the entrapment scenario began in Act II with Daos composing the tragedy and assigning the parts; it was in full swing in Act III with Daos' announcement of Khairestratos' illness and the arrival of the doctor who reported the pessimistic prognosis to Smikrines; in Act IV, Khairestratos' death was announced and Kleostratos then returned; the performance of the double resurrection as a double dose of humiliation for Smikrines may have been reserved for the final act. The entrapment scenario of *Aspis* is as extensive as those in *Persa* and *Miles Gloriosus*. It shares with them the requisite components: a script of enticement (but to a moral not a criminal offense), a mistake in status (but a mistake in the condition of "being alive" rather than a mistake in the civic or marital status of an individual), costuming and witnesses, vindicative motive. It is possibly the most theatric – or, to be more precise, the most metatheatric.

Menander called special attention to this quality. Review of the careful structuring of the two opening acts of *Aspis* confirms that statement. The play begins with the grand spectacle of the homecoming of Kleostratos' war-booty and badly buckled shield; Daos gives the opening speech, an apostrophe to the dead Kleostratos and a lament over his death. Dialogue follows between Daos and Smikrines; the slave explains in detailed battle narrative the way that Kleostratos died. Tukhe mirrors that account in the "delayed prologue speech"; she corrects Daos' report and the misconceptions created by the spectacle of a homecoming without a (living) hero. Tukhe herself has been in charge of the preliminary production:

λοιπὸν τοὔνομα
τοὐμὸν φράσαι· τίς εἰμι, πάντων κυρία
τούτων βραβεῦσαι καὶ διοικῆσαι; Τύχη. (146–48)

It remains to tell
my name. Who am I, mistress of all these events,
their arbiter and director? Tukhe.

Tukhe is responsible, then, for the whole chain of events which led to the production of the first *epikleros* – for the fact that a friend wore Kleostratos' shield and died, for the fact that Daos made a mistake

[19] See Arnott 1979: 91–93 and Lloyd-Jones 1971: 188–89 for speculation about the play's ending.

when he thought the friend's corpse, unrecognizable and bloated in death, was his master's – as Tukhe herself says, "that one made a mistake" (οὗτος διημάρτηκεν, 110). Daos' script in the following act for the production of a sham *epikleros* entails that Smikrines should make a similar mistake (cf. 110 διημάρτηκεν and 324 διημαρτηκότ'); a living man is to be thought dead:

> ὃ βούλεται γὰρ μόνον ὁρῶν καὶ προσδοκῶν
> ἀλόγιστος ἔσται τῆς ἀληθείας κριτής. (326–27)
>
> A man who only sees and thinks about his own desires
> will be an unreliable judge of truth.

The creation of the second *epikleros* is thus self-consciously staged by the plotting characters in Act II of *Aspis* and fortuitously replicates the effect of Tukhe's creation of the first *epikleros* by the misidentification of a corpse in Act I. Daos produces a sham *epikleros* – just as Tukhe had; he devises a script according to which a living man will be thought dead – just as Tukhe had. In Daos' plot, it is Smikrines who makes the mistake; in Tukhe's plot, it was Daos. The parallels are undeniable.

What is Menander's point? Surely it is to compare the character of the two men. Both are astute manipulators of the law, but beyond that, there is a world of difference. When Tukhe tricks Daos and entices him to misidentify a corpse, his subsequent conduct is exemplary: he proves himself a loyal and trustworthy slave who returns his deceased master's property to his family, who does not think to advantage himself from it, who genuinely laments the young man's death. When Smikrines is tricked and learns of the fatal illness of his brother, rather than expressing any fraternal concern, he hearkens to materialistic instinct. Menander's cosmic meta-theatrics in *Aspis*, the cosmic staging of Kleostratos' death as parallel meta-script for the human staging of Khairestratos' death, has been harnessed to the juxtaposed demonstration of the characters of the two victims of entrapment.

But that's not all. We seriously underestimate our playwright if we overlook the grand wit in his creation of two sham deaths. In the last chapter (7.3.a and n. 54), I pointed out that much of the wit of Acts III and IV of *Samia* derived from the parallel scenes in which first Demeas (265–66) and then Nikeratos (535–36) infer that a woman who "gives her breast" (*didonai titthion*) is the mother of the infant she holds in her arms. Demeas' misidentification of the mother is due to his subversion of a famous stock example of a *tekmerion* ("necessary sign") from the philosophical and rhetorical tradition. Correctly stated, it runs: "if a woman has milk, she has borne a child or been impregnated"; incorrectly stated, it might run: "if she has milk" (or, more ambiguously, "if she gives her breast"), "she is the mother of the particular infant she holds or nurses." The doubling of inferences in *Samia*, the presentation of a flawed *tekmerion*, suggests that Menander is playing with the tradition as he poses the question, how is the mother of an infant to be identified? There is similar playfulness in *Aspis*; here Menander poses the question, how is a corpse to be identified? We can well imagine that the identification of corpses posed problems in ancient societies: how can one know that bloated and mutilated corpse *X* is the body of soldier *Y*? how can one know that a body is really dead? The latter problem in particular exercised Greek doctors, scientists, and philosophers.[20] The Athenian Stranger in Plato's *Laws* gives a relevant prescription and rationale for the "wake" of the dead:

> The laying-out at home should not last longer than is necessary to confirm that the person really is dead and not just in a faint; in average cases, it will be reasonable for the body to be taken to the tomb after two days. (*Laws* 959a, trans. Saunders)

While we do not know whether the Athenian Stranger's "law" represents an actual feature of Athens' lawcode, the rationale for the laying-out of the body is not fabricated out of thin air. Greek "wakes" provided opportunity not only for intimate grieving among close kin, but also for vigilance: was the body really dead? The circle of conspiratorial kin surrounding Khairestratos' *eidōlon* in *Aspis* therefore had an important role to play in preventing Smikrines from carrying out what must have been deemed, at least, a moral duty; but Smikrines' failure to observe the "corpse" at close quarters, willy-nilly, was a neglect of that duty – he too quickly believes what he wants to believe. Death, like maternity, might be fallibly inferred. While Act IV is too scrappy for reconstruction, it cannot be doubted that Menander's playful attention in this comedy was focused upon the (mis)identification of the dead. The issue of the marriage of one *epikleros* or another played but a secondary role, subordinate to the gleeful havoc produced by scripting two living men as corpses, one

[20] See Lonie 1965: 126–43; Grmek 1987: 129–44.

in a battlefield of Lykia and the other in no less a battlefield, the *oikos* of a feuding family.

4 CONFESSIONAL ENTRAPMENT IN *ADELPHOE* AND *EPITREPONTES*

Confessional entrapments in New Comedy exploit the same analogue between plotting a scenario and scripting a play as the criminal and moral entrapments depicted in the last two sections. The most significant shared feature is a plot requirement for "flagrance": in the scenarios discussed here, a confession of a past offense must be made in public. The admission of guilt is a prerequisite for settlement; it renders the offender vulnerable to lawful punishment or public disapprobation – and provides opportunity for reparation and forgiveness. We may rightly suspect that scenarios of confessional entrapment were not infrequent preliminaries to out of court settlements in Athens. All we need think of are the preparations made by Diogeiton's daughter and her son-in-law before their confrontation with her father in the failed arbitration of Lysias 32. Confession of Diogeiton's abuse of his guardianship would have led, presumably, to a successful private reconciliation.

Micio in *Adelphoe* IV 5 (638–98) extorts a confession from Aeschinus. His *ludus* is brief, but is clearly marked in its own dramatic frame. He sets it in motion when Aeschinus equivocates in response to Micio's inquiry into his presence before Sostrata's house:

> *MI. tune has pepulisti fores?*
> *(tacet. quor non ludo hunc aliquantisper? melius est,*
> *quandoquidem hoc numquam mihi ipse voluit credere.)* (638–40)

> MI. Have you been knocking at these doors?
> (He is silent. Why not play a little trick on him? A rather good idea,
> since he himself would never trust me in this affair.)

Micio's *ludus* is a fiction in which he dons the role of his friend's *advocatus* in the latter's lawful claim to marry Sostrata's daughter as an *epikleros*; the aim of the *ludus* is to extort Aeschinus' confession that he had raped the girl. After Aeschinus breaks down in tears, Micio gives him a proper scolding and ends by announcing that he can marry the girl; the *ludus* then comes to a close:

AE. pater,
obsecro, nunc ludi' tu me? MI. ego te? quam ob rem? . . . (696–97)

AE.: Father,
please, are you making game of me now? MI.: I, do that to you? Why? . . .

The confessional aspect of the scene was discussed in detail in chapter 7.1.b; it is one of a type which is more extensively dramatized in other Menandrian and Menandrian-based plays.

In *Epitrepontes*, such a scenario is devised to extort a confession – of rape and paternity once again. In the third act of the play Onesimos, the slave of Kharisios, has made a brilliant deduction worthy of any detective in modern day criminal fiction). A ring has been found together with an exposed infant; the ring is similar to one lost by Kharisios. The slave quickly reasons that if he shows it to his master, he makes him the infant's father (448–50).[21] He then explains in more detail to his bewildered companion, the slave Suros: "He lost that ring at the Tauropolia – an all-night festival attended by women – logically, this means the rape of a maiden, and she bore this infant and exposed him – it's obvious. Accordingly, if anyone were to find her and show her the ring, then he'd have a piece of clear evidence. But at this point, all we have is suspicion and distress" (451–57).[22] The *psaltria* Habrotonon, who has overheard Onesimos make the deduction, informs the slave that she knew of a girl who had been raped at that festival but does not know her name (473–81). The two decide to look for proof that Kharisios was the infant's father – the case against him is only circumstantial so far; later, they will search for the mother. To carry out the plan, Habrotonon casts herself as the girl who had been raped; she will wear the ring, carry the infant before Kharisios, and elicit a confession:

[21] The conventional function of the ring in comedies of rape is not so fantastic as it might seem. I quote from *The Providence Journal* (November 15, 1990): "A Providence man accused of raping a 25-year-old Woonsocket woman in Lincoln Woods State Park was found guilty of first-degree sexual assault yesterday by a Superior Court jury . . . [Special Asst. Atty. Gen. Jay] Sullivan said the victim pulled Monteiro's ring from his finger during the assault. Later that morning, state police went to the scene of the crime and found the ring which had Monteiro's name engraved on it, Sullivan said. The police then ran a check and got Monteiro's license number. Monteiro returned to Lincoln Park about 1 p.m. that day to look for his ring and a watch he had also lost during the assault and was arrested by state police, Sullivan said."

[22] 451–57: Ταυροπολίοις ἀπώλεσεν τοῦτόν ποτε / παννυχίδος οὔσης καὶ γυναικῶν. κατὰ λόγον / ἐστὶν βιασμὸν τοῦτον εἶναι παρθένου· / ἣ δ' ἔτεκε τοῦτο κἀξέθηκε δηλαδή. / εἰ μέν τις οὖν εὑρὼν ἐκείνην προσφέροι / τοῦτον, σαφὲς ἄν τι δεικνύοι τεκμήριον· / νυνὶ δ' ὑπόνοιαν καὶ ταραχὴν ἔχει.

ἐὰν οἰκεῖον ἦι
αὐτῶι τὸ πρᾶγμ<α δ'>, εὐθὺς ἥξει φερόμενος
ἐπὶ τὸν ἔλεγχον καὶ μεθύων γε νῦν ἐρεῖ
πρότερος ἅπαντα καὶ προπετῶς· ἃ δ' ἂν λέγηι
προσομολογήσω τοῦ διαμαρτεῖν μηδὲ ἓν
προτέρα λέγουσα. (520–25)

If he's tied up
in this trouble, he'll immediately rush in and be carried away
to the proof and, tipsy with wine as he is just now, he'll spill out
everything before I speak – with reckless abandon, too. Whatever he says,
I'll say yes, that's true, so as not to make any mistake by speaking first.

Habrotonon plans her gestures and tears (530–32, 35) and rehearses her lines (517–19, 526–29, 533–34) with Onesimos.

The entrapment scenario (Kharisios' confession) was apparently not dramatized on-stage; its results were probably reported by Karion the cook, who bursts from Khairestratos' house where the meeting between the two had taken place, angry and upset because his carefully prepared luncheon has broken up precipitately. Habrotonon was successful: Kharisios believes himself to be the infant's father.[23] Eliciting the confession from Kharisios, however, is only the "first scene" of the script prepared by the two slaves. The "second scene," entailing Habrotonon's discovery of the girl who had been raped at the Tauropolia, is improvised with great subtlety at the end of Act IV. All that had been foreseen in the earlier "scripting session" was that Habrotonon should make inquiries among well-born acquaintances about the victim. Now, as Habrotonon carries the infant out from Khairestratos' house, she comes upon that very girl by chance. The latter will turn out to be Khairestratos' estranged wife, Pamphile – although Habrotonon is still unaware of her identity as that particular person. Questions are now asked by one of the other, but the questions are only guardedly answered if answered at all as each tries to elicit more information.[24] There is no explicit

[23] That the cook reports what happened is a conjecture based on a number of fragmentary verses. Since Smikrines appears to know at 645 that Habrotonon is the mother of Kharisios' baby, Gomme and Sandbach 1973 suggest that at 621, Smikrines, who may be eavesdropping on the courtesan's speech, might be the speaker of "a surprised or indignant exclamation, e.g., Χαρισίωι παῖς γέγονεν ἐκ τῆς ψαλτρίας;" See further Gomme and Sandbach apud 615–21, and the notes in Arnott 1979: 467–71. Habrotonon's success in extorting a confession of paternity from Kharisios is guaranteed by the preserved text, in Onesimos' monologue at 895–900, in Kharisios' monologue at 915, and in the dialogue of Kharisios, Onesimos, and Habrotonon at 944–58. Kharisios' response to Habrotonon was probably reported earlier.

[24] See Turner 1980, about the way Menander uses questions and answers in general; Scafuro

confession of maternity in this scene; Habrotonon will tell Pamphile "the rest of the story" off-stage (877); on-stage, she limits her information to the identity of the infant's father. Boundaries between public and private spheres are preserved with the utmost delicacy.

The players had designed their two scenes in order to discover the identities of the infant's parents. The dénouement had been sketched earlier by Habrotonon in Act III: if the infant's mother was free-born, Kharisios should be informed (495–96). Apparently, she had blithely envisioned a divorce; Kharisios would leave Pamphile and marry the girl who had produced an heir.[25] Onesimos had viewed the same ending with trepidation at the close of the scripting session (566–71). The two slaves, however, have no control over the conclusion of Menander's comedy. The playwright reasserts command over the script in the final act after Kharisios has confessed paternity and Pamphile has learned the identity of her rapist. Now Onesimos, transgressing beyond the limits of knowledge that might reasonably be ascribed to household slaves, alludes to the larger world of theater, and in particular, to the theater world of New Comedy and its Euripidean roots. First, as Smikrines, the father of Pamphile, approaches the house in one last attempt to bring his daughter home, the slave addresses him:

> καὶ νῦν μὲν ὁρμῶντ' ἐπὶ πονηρὸν πρᾶγμά σε
> ταὐτόματον ἀποσέσωκε, καὶ καταλαμβάνεις
> διαλλαγὰς λύσεις τ' ἐκείνων τῶν κακῶν. (1107–09)

> Even now, while you are rushing headlong to disaster,
> chance has come to the rescue and you arrive to find
> reconciliations and unravellings of those woes.

Here, while the language is not technically that of the stage, it verges on it. Behind "chance" (ταὐτόματον), we might sense an abstract notion of a *deus ex machina* (cf. *Sam.* 163–64); in the "reconciliations" (διαλλαγὰς) of verse 1109, we perceive the basic meaning "changes" and, conjoined with the following genitives (ἐκείνων τῶν κακῶν), we see a variant of "reversals of fortunes"; in the "unravellings of those woes" in the same verse (λύσεις . . . ἐκείνων τῶν κακῶν), we come closest to the terminology of dramatic

1990: 150–51 discusses the curious questioning in *Epitr.* IV. The exchange of questions at *Epitr.* 861–73 most closely resembles Turner's "rally type" (p. 7).

[25] Thus Gomme and Sandbach 1973 apud 495–96.

criticism: *lusis* as the dissolution of a play's intricacies.[26] Later, in the same scene, Onesimos will say: "And now the identification (ἀναγνωρισμὸς) has taken place for them and all is well" (1121–22). While the slave's use of the term *anagnōrismos* acknowledges Habrotonon's dramatic staging of the identification of the two parents, the happy conclusion, unanticipated by Habrotonon and Onesimos, points to Menander's expert hand.[27] The household slave gives explicit directions in the next two verses: he quotes Euripides' *Auge* (1123–24) to aid Smikrines in unravelling the mystery that has eluded him so far. The plot is a well-known one – well known, at least, to theater-goers. Smikrines had been addressed once before in this play as a theater-goer: another slave had recalled the plots of tragedies to aid him in deciding the fate of infant and tokens (325–33). The two moments of theatrical allusion are now united as Smikrines, standing on the threshold of his son-in-law's house, will be reconciled with his daughter's family. Menander thus closes the play with the ending unreflectively hinted at by Habrotonon (495–96) and fearfully envisioned by Onesimos (568–71) – but for one significant detail: while Kharisios is married to the girl he raped, he has been married to her all along. The essential ingredient of the plot has been in Menander's hands – and the tradition of New Comedy – all along.

5 THE FAILURE OF ENTRAPMENT IN THE *ANDRIA*

Moral and confessional entrapment are combined in the *Andria* as Simo tries to entice his son to commit a moral offense and at the same time to elicit a confession of his former transgressions. Simo will receive much attention in the analysis that follows. He is unique among the *senes* of New Comedy in attempting to trap his son rather than himself becoming a victim of filial schemes.[28] That the deception he deploys against his son should take the form of entrapment is a mark of his forensic personality. So thoroughly, indeed, does this forensic quality show up in all his dealings – he treats his son as a prosecutor would a criminal, gathering clues and evidence, formulating arguments and counter-arguments – that the play might justly

[26] For *lusis*, see chapter 4.3, n. 55 above, and R. L. Hunter 1985: 135–36.

[27] As Gomme and Sandbach 1973 observe apud 1121, ἀναγνωρισμός is used for the more usual ἀναγνώρισις, but Aristotle uses the former term at *Poetics* 1452c16.

[28] Steidle 1973: 315 and n. 53 points out that Chremes' suggestion in *HT*, that Menedemus allow himself to be tricked into providing money for his son's beloved, is hardly comparable.

be considered a paradigmatic depiction of the forensic *persona*. As such, it is a fitting subject with which to conclude this study. I begin with a presentation of the play's argument – one that differs from conventional summaries because it attends to its forensic strategies. I then examine the father's account of the son – first for what it tells us of the son, and then for what it tells us of the father.

Some words first about the relationship between Terence's play and the Greek original. Terence tells us (in a round-about way) that he based his play on Menander's *Andria* but borrowed material from his *Perinthia* when it was convenient – two plays, he says, that are so similar that whoever knows one of them, knows both (9–14).[29] Donatus provides information about two major changes that Terence made in his adaptation of Menander's *Andria*. Terence added the freedman Sosia to the opening scene with the result that the *senex* participates in a dialogue; in the original *Andria*, "Simo" had spoken a monologue; in the *Perinthia*, he had addressed his wife (Don. apud *prol.* 14). Terence also added the characters of Charinus and Byrria (Don. apud 301.2 and 977). While the additions are firmly attested, their source is disputable – whether they derive from Menander's *Perinthia* or from Terence's own imagination.[30] I have chosen to be optimistic about Donatus' reports about this play,[31] and I assume there are no other major alterations except for the possibility that expository material from Menander's (hypothesized) prologue may have been dispersed in an opening scene – probably in I 3 rather than in I 1.[32] This does not mean that all the details of

[29] For reconstructions of the *Perinthia*, see Körte 1909 and Schoell 1912.

[30] The freedman Sosia is probably Terence's invention; for a collection of scholarly views, see Gaiser 1972: 1077f. As for Charinus and Byrria: Ludwig 1968: 173 and n. 8 thinks they have been imported from the *Perinthia*; Fantham 1975: 52–53, n. 25, argues that "all the minor awkwardnesses of their scenes (*e.g.*, Byrria's unseen entry, eavesdropping, and exit in 2. 5) suggest the *ad hoc* invention of characters, rather than borrowing of fully-rounded roles from the second Menander-play." Fantham further suggests that Charinus' knowledge of Chremes' daughter, like Clitipho's knowledge of certain young women in *HT* (1061–62, 1065), reflects Roman society and that the marriages of both Charinus and Clitipho are Roman additions. Earlier partisans of one view or the other are annotated by Marti 1963: 61–62.

[31] Donatus additionally compares Terence's play to Menander's at: *prol.* 10.1; 204. 4; 406. 1; 483. 1 and 3; 592. 1; 611. 3; 726. 1; 801; 891. 1; and 919 (where he reports that the *sententia* of 919 was transferred from Menander's *Eun.*).

[32] Oppermann 1934 made the most important contribution to analytic scholarship on the question of the prologue when he argued that a portion (215–24) of Davos' monologue in I 3 (206–25) contained elements that belonged to the eliminated expository prologue. Most scholars have accepted this view. Exceptional is Büchner (1974: 48–50); he has made a convincing rebuttal of every point in Oppermann's argument. (Büchner also believes that none of Terence's six plays had a divine expository prologue in its original.) What Büchner

Terence's play – excluding, of course, those indicated as the Roman poet's additions by Donatus – derive from Menander's *Andria*. In my discussion below, I try to indicate where the Menandrian play might have differed from Terence's, but I do not offer any full-scale reconstruction. I focus to a large extent on Simo's *narratio* in I 1; most of what Simo says there in dialogue was spoken by the "Simo" of Menander's play.[33]

Commentators on the *Andria* (both Terence's and the Greek original) have frequently designated Simo as a lenient and indulgent father – at least for the greater part of the play. "Leniency" and "paternal indulgence" offer them easy rubrics for Simo's behavior in permitting Pamphilus a premarital affair and in letting him off the hook both after viewing his conduct at Chrysis' funeral and after hearing Chremes' report about his relationship to the foreigner. But such an assessment of Simo's character encounters the following problems: (1) it is inconsistent with the father's passionate and zealous inquisitiveness into his son's premarital affairs; (2) it is inconsistent with his deviousness and vehemence in setting the trap of the *falsae nuptiae* for his son (would a lenient father exert himself in this way?); and (3) it is inconsistent with the angry Simo of the last act. Those who see an indulgent, lenient Simo ignore the first two problems; for the third, the alleged change of character at the end of

has shown, however, is not that 215–24 in fact belonged to the slave's monologue in the original play, but rather that Oppermann's proof is not a sufficient demonstration that 215–24 did not. Iron-clad proof, however, is impossible.

Lefèvre's (1971: 21–48) treatment is unsatisfactory. On the basis of his analysis of the effects of the omission of an expository prologue in Terence's play, he has reconstructed a Menandrian original in which the issue of citizenship plays a relatively insignificant role; conversely, the prominence given to citizenship in Terence's play is seen to be an incidental consequence necessitated by the omission of the prologue. Steidle 1973 has cogently rebutted all the major points of Lefèvre's argument. For other treatments of the Menandrian prologue and Terence's "dispersal" of it in the opening scenes of his play, see the following note.

33 That Terence may have taken details from the hypothesized prologue and put them into the narrative of Simo is argued, e.g., by Rambelli 1939: 79–104 (esp. 81–93); Lefèvre 1969: 49–59 takes the most radical view and ascribes verses 50–136 of Simo's narrative to a divine prologue; see Gaiser 1972: 1051f. and n. 102 for quick but sufficient rebuttal. As a parallel to Simo's opening narrative, one should compare Moskhion's opening speech in *Samia*; see further n. 49 below. In my view, the Menandrian prologue may have been limited to details of the true relationship of "Glycerium" to the courtesan, the amount of time that has passed since the latter's funeral, and the announcement that today "Glycerium" would give birth. Possibly a divine prologue speaker, in the manner of Auxilium in *Aulularia*, would also decide to hasten on the girl's marriage by assuring the appearance of "Crito" in Athens for the girl's identification by her father. There is no need to insist that a prologue speaker would provide the detailed account of the young man's upbringing that his father gives in the opening scene.

the play, they have a complicated answer: the change, they say, is due to Terence's addition of the *Perinthia*; Terence has installed the father of that play in Act v of the *Andria* without smoothing over the differences.[34] Such violent hypothesis is unnecessary; it is based on two errors: (1) an incorrect assessment of Simo's character in I 1 and (2) a failure to recognize the crime that Simo in Act v suspects his son intends to commit. The second error has been eradicated by Steidle's persuasive demonstration that the citizen status of "Glycerium" played an important role in the original – it is not a motif introduced by Terence into the Latin play.[35] In the remainder of this chapter, we shall eradicate the first error by demonstrating that Simo is a complicated character from the outset of the play – an *iniquus pater* posturing as an *aequus pater* who masks rigorous moralism beneath a thin liberal veneer; his devious and stern nature makes him a fit character to contrive the *falsae nuptiae* against a son whom he deems a tricky dissembler. With Simo's "leniency" and "paternal indulgence" relegated to the realm of mere pretence (and transparent, from the outset, to all, it seems, but Pamphilus – although he has his rude awakening), Simo's character is consistent throughout – or consistent at least until his anger subsides in v 4 when he finally recognizes the error of his ways.

A good part of the evidence for Simo's character comes from his *narratio* – hence, the *gnati vita* as testimony to the *patris vita*.

5 (a) The argument of the play

In I 1 of the *Andria*, Simo provides an account of his earlier attempts to scrutinize his son's behavior. In the course of a long *narratio*, it becomes clear that he has gathered substantial evidence for supposing Pamphilus guilty of a number of offenses – first, he has a foreign courtesan's sister (Glycerium) for a girlfriend who, it will turn out, is pregnant; secondly, he has been refused as a son-in-law by Chremes on the grounds that he esteems the foreigner as a wife. These offenses entail another – and in Simo's eyes a more serious one: Pamphilus has deceived him. Simo, however, is unable to contrive a persuasive case for punishing his son – and he wants very much to punish him. He therefore carefully sets the stage to trap Pamphilus in another offense – the refusal to marry the girl he has

[34] Büchner 1974; V. Martin 1964. [35] Steidle 1973 contra Lefèvre 1971.

chosen for him. If Pamphilus commits the offense and refuses the marriage, he will be forced to explain his reasons and confess his past transgressions. With confession extorted, Simo will at last be able to vent his righteous anger. Pamphilus, however, accepts the wedding proposition and Chremes likewise agrees to it. But the latter pulls out once again when he hears a report that Glycerium is a citizen and has borne a son to Pamphilus. In v 2–4, Simo himself suspects that his son is about to commit an offense far more serious than any he has imagined so far – marriage to a foreigner, which entails the faking of Glycerium's citizen status and the falsified acknowledgment of a legitimate citizen heir. Pamphilus, of course, does not intend to commit any such crime. But the fear and expectation that he might do so powerfully pervade the play and affect the action and speech of all its major characters.

The fear of the lesser offense (the refusal of the marriage) is dispelled by Pamphilus' apparent agreement to the marriage (II 5, 420) and by Chremes' approval (III 3, 572–73), fought hard for and won at last by Simo. But even before this fear is dispelled, fear of the more serious offense casts a shadow, small at first, but looming larger as the play proceeds. The offenses – both the expected (refusal of marriage) and suspected (marriage to a foreigner) – provide a neatly parallel, paradoxical, and ironic structure for the play: Simo, who creates the plan of the *falsae nuptiae* to entrap his son in an offense which he refuses to commit, finds himself, at the last, suspecting the commission of a serious crime that has likewise been the creation of his own imagination.

This account of the *Andria* differs substantially from other accounts – or plot summaries or interpretations – of the play.[36] It differs because it takes into account the legal scenarios and forensic strategies that figure in it. The creation of the expectation and suspicion that offenses and crimes have been and will be committed is fuel for the play's progress. Symptomatic of the forensic disposition, it is intellectually founded: where an offense or crime is thought to have been committed or to be in the making, clues must be gathered and investigated, sources of information carefully scrutinized, proofs deduced and persuasively presented.

[36] Steidle 1973 comes closest to formulating this interpretation; but his essay is articulated almost as a point-for-point refutation of Lefèvre rather than as a full-scale interpretation of the play.

A pedantic word concerning the use of "crime" words before beginning my analysis. In the preceding argument and in what follows, I have tried to be careful in calling a "crime" only an act that is criminal before the law; and by that I usually mean, criminal in Athenian law. I have used the word "offense" to denote an act that has a disputable legal status. Thus whereas it is a "crime" in fourth-century Athens for a citizen to marry a foreigner, I have called a son's refusal to marry the girl of his father's choice an "offense" or "transgression."[37] Having an affair with a non-*aste* girl or a courtesan, impregnating one or the other (keeping in mind, of course, that she is not a citizen), entering into *pallakia* (concubinage) – none of these actions are crimes. Nor would they be considered despicable moral transgressions by most fathers. But Simo, as will be shown below, is no ordinary father. Morally upright, stern behind a liberal facade, he most certainly does conceive of these activities as offenses and transgressions.

But a *caveat* is in order, too: language – as all speakers, listeners, writers, and readers know – sometimes has a life of its own – just when we thought we had pulled the reins and brought it under control, off it goes, galloping on its own. But a gallop, too, may be part of a daily exercise plan. Forensic thought and language course through the *Andria*; characters (even the one who delivers the opening prologue) defend their actions, accuse others, construct proofs that a crime or offense will or will not happen, has happened or has not. Moral offenses and transgressions may be spoken of as if they are in fact crimes in a legal sense – and often they are far more serious and of greater import than their legal counterparts – as any reader of, e.g., *Oidipous Turannos* knows. Donatus, belonging to an age perhaps more attuned to forensic rhetoric than ours, sees Simo creating a defense for his son in which the latter imputes to his father an intention to convict him of a terrible crime on the order of homicide;[38] he sees Pamphilus as treating his father's demand that

[37] It is a matter of debate whether it was a legal requirement in Athens that a son should have his father's consent to marry; Paoli 1976: 377–83 (= 1952) adduces *Fab. Inc.* to demonstrate that it was, but the evidence is inconclusive. While paternal consent appears to have been required (at least) in practice, a father could probably not lawfully compel his son to marry; see Gomme and Sandbach 1973: 32. In Roman law, the consent of *paterfamilias* was required for a man's marriage; the bridegroom's consent was likewise required – whether he was *sui iuris* or in *patria potestas*. Nonetheless, as Watson 1971: 21 points out, "it was socially proper for the man to obey his father's directions." For detailed discussion and citation of relevant bibliography, see Treggiari 1991: 170–80 and Watson 1967: 41–47.

[38] Donatus on 139. 3.

he marry Chremes' daughter likewise as a crime;[39] and he sees Simo as treating Pamphilus' final (suspected) crime in the last act as parricide.[40] Although we are not likely to agree with all of Donatus' precious distinctions, his commentary is a useful measure of an ancient rhetorical perspective the focal point of which is legal argumentation. It is, I think, the shape of thought throughout. But legal and illegal, right and wrong, is and is not, may not be so important, in the end, as the perfection of the argument that proves the case. The *Andria* stages the meeting ground of law, morality, and rhetoric.

In "The Argument" presented above, the offenses of the son were taken for granted – as was Simo's reaction to them, his strategy of entrapment. The analysis offered below will justify that formulation.

5 (b) The 'gnati vita' as testimony to the 'patris vita'

The first scene of the *Andria* begins with preparations for a wedding.[41] Simo bids his slaves to carry newly purchased items inside the house and then asks his freedman Sosia to remain outside for a few words; after assuring himself of his former slave's loyalty, he confides a surprising piece of information: the wedding that Sosia believes is to take place that day is a sham one (*quas credis esse has non sunt verae nuptiae* 47). Simo then addresses a *narratio* to Sosia as an explanation of why that is so – and at the same time conveys much information that is essential for the plot of the comedy. His *narratio* is

[39] Donatus on 236. 2 and 238. 2.

[40] Donatus on 869. His comments on V 5, which he envisions almost as a courtroom scene, are quite interesting.

[41] Drexler 1938: 40–41 argues that in Menander's originals, the *senex* would enter from the house and would not leave for the market with his slave until after the first scene; the purchase of the goods and their arrival on-stage in the opening scene is therefore Terentian addition. Drexler's strongest arguments are that (1) the purchases in I 1 of Terence's play are inconsistent with Davus' remark to Pamphilus in II 2, 359–61: *redeunti interea ex ipsa re mi incidit suspicio "hem / paullulum opsoni; ipsu' tristis; de inproviso nuptiae: / non cohaerent"* ("while returning, I became suspicious: 'Aha! There were very few provisions; master himself was gloomy; a sudden wedding: the pieces do not fit' ") and that (2) beginning a play with a plan underway breaks a technical rule of New Comedy. Drexler's argument (endorsed by Biggott 1939) is inconclusive. Against his first point: Davos in II 2 has observed that the preparations are not on a scale for a wedding feast, not that there were none; against his second point: as Marti (1963: 61) pointed out, Sostratos has already acted on the plan he announces to Khaireas in the long opening scene of *Duskolos*; moreover, we can add that *Phormio* begins after the parasite has orchestrated a prosecution against Antipho, and *Aspis* begins with Tukhe's scene of entrapment (the announcement of Kleostratos' death) already set in motion.

divided into three parts: an assessment of his son's character (*gnati vitam*, 51–153), an explanation of his plan (*consilium meum*, 155–67), and a description of the task he wants his freedman to carry out (*quid . . . velim*, 168–70):

> *SI. rem omnem a principio audies:*
> *eo pacto et gnati vitam et consilium meum*
> *cognosces et quid facere in hac re te velim.* (48–50)

> SI. You will hear the whole story from the beginning:
> in this way you will learn both the life of my son and my plan –
> and what I would like you to do in this affair.

The *narratio* extends from verse 48 to verse 163 and is interrupted on sixteen occasions by Sosia, seven times with one or two verses, nine times with four words or less. This is truly Simo's scene, Simo's *narratio*. Among the ancients, Cicero admired it for its pleasing *partitio* and for carrying out the division articulated in verses 48–50 in the body of the speech.[42] Modern scholars have likewise admired the *narratio*, for a different reason – its brilliant depiction of Simo.[43] Here, only those portions that are pertinent to the entrapment scenario will be taken up.

Simo begins his explanation of the sham wedding with an account of his son's character. That he begins thus – and not, for example, with a depiction of a capricious future father-in-law who withdraws from a betrothal agreement at the last moment – is significant. We, as readers or spectators, are immediately led to suspect that responsibility for the fact that the *nuptiae* (wedding) is not *verae* (real) will be imputed to Pamphilus, either as the result of some flaw in his character or because of some exceptional circumstance that has befallen him. The important point to observe at the outset, therefore, is that Simo's *narratio*, as an answer to Sosia's question –

> *SO. quor simulas igitur? SI. rem omnem a principio audies* (48)

> SO. Why then do you pretend? SI. You will hear the whole story
> from the beginning –

is designed, in the part that treats the *gnati vita*, to reveal why the *nuptiae* is not *verae*, designed, therefore, to assign responsibility. The assessment – or audit, even – of the son's life, then, is no ordinary *narratio* – no simple description of the past – but a carefully argued –

[42] Cic. *de inu.* 33. The use of an explicit *partitio* is also evident in *Epitr.* 719ff.
[43] E.g., Oppermann 1934: 270; Büchner 1974: 31; Goldberg 1981–82: 137.

we may imagine, even, often rehearsed – speech that will present the case for the son's involvement in the recasting of the *nuptiae*.

Simo's *narratio* is the presentation of the case – so far – against his son. As prosecutor, he must be able to formulate a charge that can be substantiated by hard evidence and that can stand up to any argument offered by the defense. When he describes his own past behavior, he almost always appears as sleuth, making inquiries into his son's conduct, always hot on the trail for any new clue, ready with deductions and theories constructed from circumstantial evidence. When he presents the case that is the product of these activities, he sometimes assumes the role of defendant's advocate, offering justifications for his son's activities or trying to put his son's conduct in the best possible light.[44] The apparent role of advocate should not fool us; it is part of the prosecutor's arsenal as he prepares to make the strongest case against his opponent's strongest argument. Such forensic habit might be devastatingly effective in overseeing the conduct of a young man; in Simo, it turns out to be comical.

As the *senex* describes his son's early and exemplary post-ephebic career, already the description of the auditor contains elements of defense:

> *sic vita erat: facile omnis perferre ac pati;*
> *cum quibus erat quomque una is sese dedere,*
> *eorum obsequi studiis, adversus nemini,*
> *numquam praeponens se illis . . .* (62–65)

So was his life: he was easy going and tolerant of everyone;
with whatever friends he associated, he always devoted himself to them,
a follower of their pursuits, hostile to no one,
never putting himself ahead of anyone . . .

Simo subsequently views the same estimable quality of "obsequiousness" as the motivating force behind Pamphilus' visits to the courtesan's house:

> *qui tum illam amabant forte, ita ut fit, filium*
> *perduxere illuc, secum ut una esset, meum.* (80–81)

[44] Cf. Lysiteles' debate on *Amor* vs. adult responsibilities in *Trin.* II I, 223–76, in which the young man plays the roles of judge and pleader: *de hac re mihi satis hau liquet; nisi hoc sic faciam, opinor, / ut utramque rem simul exputem, iudex sim reu'que ad eam rem* (233–34: "The issues are not sufficiently clear to me – unless I do this, I think – examine each side of the case at the same time, acting as judge and pleader at the trial").

the young men who happened to be her lovers at that time,
as it turns out,
they brought there – that he might be together with them – my son.

The son's conduct is defensible, even virtuous: he yields to friends.[45] While Simo, in his revisionary account, thus allows innocent motives for Pamphilus' presence in the courtesan's house, the record of his reaction at that time invites scrutiny of his own motivation: *egomet continuo mecum "certe captus est: / habet"* (82–83: "Immediately I thought to myself, 'surely he is caught; she has him' "). Simo, however, does not jump to conclusions or utter public complaints; instead, he acts as prudent sleuth – he questions witnesses:

. . . observabam mane illorum servolos
venientis aut abeuntis: rogitabam "heus puer,
dic sodes, quis heri Chrysidem habuit?" . . . (83–85)

I kept observing their young slaves early in the morning
coming or going: I kept asking, "Hey, boy,
tell me, please, who had Chrysis yesterday?". . .

Only when those witnesses give the names of Pamphilus' friends does he at last ask about his son in particular:

. . . "eho quid Pamphilus?" "quid? symbolam
dedit, cenavit." gaudebam . . . (88–89)

. . . "Well, what about Pamphilus?" "What? He paid
his chit, he dined." I was full of joy. . .

Simo now makes a mistake – he uncritically accepts the slaves' evidence. Donatus observes their trick when he comments on the slaves' response: "Admirably executed: no denial of action has been made in Pamphilus' behalf, but all is told in puerile simplicity; and what is kept silent does not seem so much hidden as not to have been done."[46]

[45] Donatus on 62.1 observes how the assessment in 62–66 anticipates the apology in 80–81: *latens argumentum, quare filium ad meretricem commeasse errans pater non ad corruptelam filii sed ad obsequium amicorum traxerit* ("A hidden argument: thus the erring father has ascribed his son's visit to the prostitute not to his depravity but rather to his yielding to friends"). Pamphilus' "obsequiousness" is all the more virtuous since he acts against his own wishes. Donatus on 81 points out the forensic color of *perduxere* when he observes that the verse signifies that "Pamphilus came unwillingly, since those who are compelled by necessity are 'brought'; so *iudices* customarily use the verb" (*invitum isse Pamphilum his verbis significat; perducuntur enim necessitate coacti. hoc etiam verbum iudices pronuntiare solent*). Büchner 1974: 35 sees another purpose in verses 80–81 which he treats as a doublet for 55–61: they introduce Pamphilus as helpmate to his friends – especially Charinus (and hence these verses are Terentian).

[46] Donatus on 88. 4: *mire nulla pro Pamphilo negatio facti est posita, sed per puerilem simplicitatem omnia gesta narrata sunt. et quod tacitum est, non celatum sed et non factum esse ita videtur.*

Why, one wonders, does Simo not question the one individual who could tell him what he wants to know – his son? Donatus supposes that he does not wish to offend Pamphilus.[47] A modern critic, troubled by the same question, supposes that Terence simply wants to disperse necessary information about Pamphilus' past to the audience; there is no need to read any characterization of Simo into his *narratio*.[48] The second explanation, representative of the more colorless and "scientific" spectrum of German analytic scholarship that pre-dates the discovery of the bulk of our longer fragments of Menander, must be cast aside; one need only recall Moskhion's expository monologue that opens *Samia*.[49] In that play, Menander uses the monologue not only to inform the audience of the background of father and son, but also to characterize its speaker: he is a modest young man, grateful to his adoptive father, actively supportive when he had learned of his passion for a foreign woman (some of the twenty or so verses missing from the text at this point must have dealt further with his father's activities), but remorseful and ashamed of his own conduct toward the girl next door. Moskhion's monologue appears to have been a (comically distorted?) mirror image of the one that opened Menander's *Andria*: in the latter play it is the father who reviews the life of the son, who reacts adversely to his acquaintance with a foreign courtesan, who puts his own conduct and character on display as he reveals the results of his investigations. That he does not question his son directly is part of his *persona*: it is not because he fears to offend his son (à la Donatus), but because he refuses to approach him without having sufficient evidence to support his suspicions – hence his sleuthing activities. As the *narratio* proceeds in Terence's version, however, it becomes more and more

[47] Donatus on 82.1: *ut appareat nihil temere constitutum vel prolatum foras, <sed> hoc ipsum satis quaesitum esse, quod statuit de falsis nuptiis, ut inoffensus esset filio* ("[he uses this expression] so that it appears that nothing has been decided recklessly or made public, <but> this itself has been nicely achieved, viz., what he has planned concerning the false wedding, so that he does not offend his son").

[48] Drexler 1938: 41–42.

[49] The descriptive parts of Simo's *narratio* of his son's life (esp. 51–59) are strikingly similar to Moskhion's monologue at the opening of *Samia*; see esp. 10–16: . . .] ἐγράφην οὐδὲν διαφέρων οὐδενός, / τὸ λεγόμενον δὴ τοῦτο "τῶν πολλῶν τις ὤν" / . . .]α μέντοι, νὴ Δί', ἀθλιώτερος· / . . .] γάρ ἐσμεν. τῶι χορηγεῖν διέφερον / καὶ τῆι] φιλοτιμίαι· κύνας παρέτρεφέ μοι, / ἵππο]υς· ἐφυλάρχησα λαμπρῶς· τῶν φίλων / δεομένοις τὰ μέτρι' ἐπαρκεῖν ἐδυνάμην· ("[After that, I was enrolled in my deme?] just like anyone else – indeed, as the saying goes, 'just one of the crowd' – but, by Zeus, [did I turn into?] a sad case – [I can say that?] for we are [. . .]. I excelled when I was *khoregos* and in displays of generosity; he raised hounds for me, horses, too. I served brilliantly as commander of my tribe's cavalry regiment; to friends in need I was able to give some moderate assistance.")

apparent that the "sleuth" has misconstrued some of the clues. Whether, in the instance concerning the testimony of slaves, we attribute Simo's mistaken interpretation to any particular psychological motive, we can surely say that the playwright is calling attention to a short-coming in the critical abilities of the father. This, indeed, is the point of the characterization of Simo in I I: a depiction of a forensic *persona* that comically falls short of the perfect and paradigmatic prosecutor.[50]

There are other occasions, in the course of the *narratio*, that show Simo the sleuth misreading the evidence; we cannot consider all of them here, but we shall notice those which directly pertain to the issue of the son's guilt. Simo had attended the funeral of the courtesan. There, he watched the sister of the deceased woman approach the pyre's flames too closely for the comfort of a certain bystander:

> *ibi tum exanimatus Pamphilus*
> *bene dissimulatum amorem et celatum indicat:*
> *adcurrit; mediam mulierem complectitur:*
> *"mea Glycerium," inquit "quid agis? quor te is perditum?"*
> *tum illa, ut consuetum facile amorem cerneres,*
> *reiecit se in eum flens quam familiariter!* (131–36)

> . . . there and then a terrified Pamphilus
> makes manifest a passion that had been well disguised
> and concealed:
> he runs to her; he embraces the woman's waist;
> "My Glycerium," he says, "what are you doing? why are you
> about to destroy yourself?"
> Then she – so that anyone might easily see that this was an
> intimacy of some standing,
> threw herself against him in tears – how familiarly!

The wonderful speed and clarity of the passage call to mind the reports of tragic messengers who deliver vivid news of lamentable events. Indeed, Sosia, acting here almost as a tragic chorus, had

50 Simo's most proximate analogue in extant Menandrian comedy likewise appears in *Samia* – Moskhion's father, Demeas. He, like Simo, is filled with suspicion concerning his son's conduct but will not bring that suspicion into the open until he has further evidence (270–71; cf. 704–06); he, too, misinterprets the evidence of slaves about his son's conduct (244–79, 313–24); he, like Simo in the *narratio* and later in the play, misinterprets visual evidence (265–67); nevertheless, Demeas is ready to supply defenses for his son (328–47) and does not directly confront him until the climax of the play in Act IV. The two fathers, then, appear to be a "type," but the two dramas run different courses; the wrinkles in their characters have quite distinct physiognomies. See n. 57.

commented before the description, *quam timeo quorsum evadas!* (127: "how I fear where you are leading!").[51] The lamentable event is that Pamphilus has been caught, red-handed, as it were: "He makes manifest a passion that had been well disguised and concealed" (132). Pamphilus' conduct is viewed as "providing evidence" that he has carried on a secret love affair with Glycerium.[52] Donatus points out Simo's emphasis upon the obviousness of that evidence in 135: "he has not said *suspicerare* ('one might suspect') but rather *cerneres* ('one might see')"; the ancient commentator also details the meaningful specificity of diction in 131–32: the use of *indicat* ("he makes manifest") rather than *ostendit* ("he shows"), *accurrit* ("he runs") rather than *accedit* ("he comes"), *mediam mulierem* ("the woman's waist") rather than *vestem* or *manus* ("clothing," "hand"), *complectitur* ("he embraces") rather than *tenet* ("he holds"). We should note, in addition, the careful emphasis Terence gives to Pamphilus' embrace in the repetition of the soft and gliding *-m* and *-l* sounds in 133–34:

. . . mediam mulierem complectitur:
"mea Glycerium," . . .

Finally, we should note the adverb that rounds off this section of the *narratio*: *reiecit se in eum flens quam familiariter!* (136, and cf. 111).

While it cannot be demonstrably proven, what may explain Terence's attentiveness to detail in the creation of this tableau-like scene that so masterfully portrays Simo's moment of discovery is the opportunity it provided for the close inspection of Glycerium's waist, of this *bene dissimulatum amorem et celatum*. How long ago the funeral took place is not precisely indicated in the play; without knowing that for certain, it is impossible to calculate the extent of Glycerium's loss of girlish figure at this time.[53] The audience learns of her

[51] Cf. Büchner 1974: 37.

[52] *Indicare* in verse 132 can have forensic overtones: elsewhere in Terence and Plautus it is used in this way – of revealing specifically incriminating evidence. Cf. *Eun.* 657–59, where Pythias explains to Phaedria how it could possibly happen that a eunuch rape a girl: *ego illum nescio / qui fuerit; hoc quod fecit, res ipsa indicat. / virgo ipsa lacrumat neque, quom rogites, quid sit audet dicere* ("I don't know who the man was; as for the offense he committed, events themselves make that manifest. The girl herself is in tears and, when you ask, she does not dare say what is the matter"). In Ciceronian orations, the verb is sometimes used similarly, of revealing incriminating evidence, e.g., Cicero *Clu.* 180; but at *Sul.* 51 and *Flac.* 92, "to lay information." In strictly juridical Latin of a later age, the verb means "to carry on a judicial process to conviction"; e. g., *D.* 50.16.197.

[53] The few time indications are these: (a) Chrysis arrived in Athens three years ago (69); (b) the wedding of Pamphilus and Chremes' daughter according to the original agreement was to have taken place this day (102); (c) within a few days of the "engagement," Chrysis died (104); (d) Chremes came the day after the funeral and cancelled the wedding agreement

pregnancy in I 3, and she gives birth in III I. But if we allow for the possibility that she may have been visibly *gravida* at the time of the funeral, then we must also grant the possibility that Simo had viewed the sight but had chosen to ignore it. In support of this view, the following points can be raised:

(1) A short time lapse (two to four weeks) between the funeral and Glycerium's birth-giving is not inconsistent with the time indications in the play (see n. 53) and is more likely than a longer lapse (more than two months) – Simo is not likely to have delayed his response to his son's conduct for any lengthy time.

(2) The appearance of a visibly *gravida* Glycerium at the funeral might explain the grounds for Chremes' cancellation of the betrothal of his daughter to Pamphilus on the very next day: *comperisse Pamphilum / pro uxore habere hanc peregrinam* (145–46: "he had discovered that Pamphilus was treating this foreigner as a wife"). Presumably, Chremes has heard a report of the funeral. A young man's arm around the waist of a courtesan's sister and his honeyed words "*mea Glycerium*" will not easily add up to a *peregrina pro uxore* unless, perhaps, an expanded waistline is introduced into the equation. A young man might have a love affair with a courtesan (or a courtesan's sister), but having a child with her – and not deserting her – is proper treatment for a wife (see n. 58).

(3) While in Terence's play, the audience does not learn that Glycerium is pregnant until I 3, that information may have been provided by Menander in an expository prologue.[54] In that case, the Greek audience would already know of the girl's pregnancy when they hear the description of her at the funeral. If funeral

(144); (e) Davos in I 2, under the impression that the wedding agreement has been reinstated, comments that "after the [original] wedding had been cancelled, Simo made no complaint . . ." (177–78) and suggests that Simo wanted them to be caught off-guard *ne esset spatium cogitandi ad disturbandas nuptias* (182: "so there would be no time for planning the disruption of the wedding"); (f) Glycerium gives birth this day (473); (g) Crito arrives from Andros to claim possession of Chrysis' estate – and apparently learned of her death before his arrival and came for this very purpose (IV 5, 796ff.). The shortest time that could have elapsed between the funeral and the present day is two weeks – this allows time for a letter to be sent to Crito in Andros and for his trip to Athens (g) and it makes sense of Davos' mention of Simo's prevention of the *spatium cogitandi*. A shorter rather than a longer time would suit Simo's character better – he always acted immediately in the past – e.g., attending the funeral, questioning slaves. The combination of these bits and pieces of evidence do not make more than, at most, "a probable but unprovable case" that the funeral was recent; but if it was, Glycerium might certainly have lost her waist.

[54] See nn. 32–33.

and day of giving birth are in close proximity, then the old man's account displays his characteristic treatment of evidence – ignoring or misinterpreting it.

(4) Obviously Terence changes the effect of the Greek original if he has delayed the insertion of material from the hypothesized prologue until I 3 when Glycerium's pregnancy is explicitly made known to the Roman audience. But it may be the purpose of Terence's remarkably vivid description of her waist (made emphatic, as pointed out earlier, by the repetition of *-m* and *-l* sounds in 133–34) to mark it as distinctly as possible while at the same time letting its weightiness escape Simo's attention. When Terence's audience learns of the pregnancy at 216 (*si[ve] ista uxor sive amicast, gravida e Pamphilost*) – 85 verses later, only a few "stage minutes" – Simo's description of Glycerium's appearance at the funeral has been so vivid that it is not likely to have been forgotten by everyone. It might appear, in retrospect, as another example of Simo's ineptness as sleuth; in III 1 and 2, Simo will hear Glycerium's labor shrieks and then construct an argument that her birth-giving is a sham – the man capable of ignoring aural testimony is capable of ignoring visual.

(5) If "Simo" had seen a pregnant "Glycerium" at the funeral in the Greek original, it may offer an explanation for a remark the *senex* makes at the end of III 2, after consigning Glycerium's labor shrieks to the realm of mere stage-acting. Now, as Davos has helped him further along the road of self-deception (that Glycerium's pregnancy has been faked to obstruct Pamphilus' marriage to Chremes' daughter), he says:

non inpulit me haec nunc omnino ut crederem;
atque haud scio an quae dixit sint vera omnia, (524–25)

He has not so convinced me now that I utterly believe all this –
and yet I do not know whether what he's said may all be true.

Simo, so adamant in the course of III 1 and 2 that the birth has been faked, now betrays some doubts. Why? Could it be because somewhere in the craggy recesses of his selective memory he has a glimmering recollection of Pamphilus embracing *mediam mulierem* and saying "*mea Glycerium*"?

The argument offered above must remain inconclusive: whether the girl's pregnancy was marked in the Greek play (no. 3 above) depends on the amount of time that has passed since the courtesan's funeral and on whether a prologue had conveyed the information to the audience. But even if Terence had not inherited such a text and had not himself intended to mark Glycerium's waist in the way suggested here, a focus on Simo's description is still not without point: by stressing the vividness of Simo's account of an event that made a great impression on him (and arguably, on Chremes' informants), we can more fully appreciate how deceptive the defense is that Simo later creates for Pamphilus.

He had left the funeral angry – but without good enough cause for rebuking his son (*nec satis ad obiurgandum causae*, 138). As prosecutor, he lacks a strong case – since as advocate, he can provide Pamphilus the following self-defense:

> . . . *diceret*
> *"quid feci? quid commerui aut peccavi, pater?*
> *quae sese in ignem inicere voluit, prohibui*
> *servavi"* . . . (138–141)

> . . . He would have said,
> "What crime have I committed? What offense or wrong, father?
> A girl who wished to hurl herself into flames – I prevented
> I rescued."

The verbal triad in 139 covers a semantic range of offenses that might include criminal activity, moral transgressions, and lesser faults.[55] Simo allows his son to deny guilt on all three levels; so far from committing any sort of wrongful act, Pamphilus' deed can be viewed as the heroic rescue of an endangered individual – there is not the least suggestion that he knows the girl.[56] Simo comments on his own short masterpiece: *honeste oratiost* (141: "a creditable speech").[57] The remark betrays a cynical appreciation of rhetoric –

[55] Cf. Donatus on 139. 3: *Et "feci" quasi facinus dixit, – f a c e r e enim quis et homicidium dicitur –, "commerui" minoris culpae est, "peccavi" multo minoris vel levioris* ("And he said 'I have committed' as if it were a crime – for a person is said 'to commit' (*facere*) even homicide –, 'I have committed an offense' (*commerui*) is used of a lesser transgression, 'I have committed a wrong' (*peccavi*) of a much lesser, even more trivial transgression." Cf. Donatus apud *Ad.* 101.

[56] As Donatus observes on 140: . . . *mira dissimulatio, tamquam illam praeter periculum nesciat* ("Admirable dissimulation – as if he does not know her except for the present danger").

[57] Cf. Demeas' comment in *Samia* which precedes his defense of Moskhion's conduct (330–47). After asserting that his son has not wronged him (even though, by Demeas' misinterpretation of the evidence, that son has cuckolded him), he recognizes how flimsy that assertion appears at first sight: "the argument is perhaps desperate (*parabolos*), gentlemen, but nonetheless true" (328–29). Demeas, to be sure, is the epitome of the forgiving father.

of its ability to manipulate appearances and conceal reality. As we shall see, there is a reason for Simo's creation of such a defense.

Simo next reports Chremes' withdrawal from the marriage arrangement; the latter had visited the day after the funeral. He had cried out:

> *indignum facinu'; comperisse Pamphilum*
> *pro uxore habere hanc peregrinam. ego illud sedulo*
> *negare factum. ille instat factum. denique*
> *ita tum discedo ab illo, ut qui se filiam*
> *neget daturum.* (145–49)

> "Unworthy deed!" – he had discovered that Pamphilus
> was treating this foreigner as a wife. I diligently
> deny the fact. He insists on it. Then at last
> I leave him in such a state that he refuses
> to give away his daughter as a bride.

Although Chremes' report appears to confirm Simo's eyewitness account in 131–36, Simo tells us that he diligently (*sedulo*) denied it, or, more specifically, that he denied *Pamphilum / pro uxore habere hanc peregrinam*. The subject of the dispute between the two men appears to concern the nature of Glycerium's relationship to Pamphilus.[58] But why does Simo deny the relationship itself? Surely he has not forgotten what he had seen the previous day? Honesty, however, is not a quality that can easily be ascribed to Simo; he is, after all, the inventor of the *falsae nuptiae*. In his encounter with Chremes his thoughts are riveted on the preservation of his son's reputation and the restoration of that son to his own high moral standards. No need to consider these thoughts as the personal property of a lenient

[58] If, in the Attic original, "Glycerium" has entered into an intimate, quasi-marital relationship with "Pamphilus," she would be considered a *pallake*. The question debated by the fathers might be whether the couple have indeed taken that step. Büchner 1974: 38, n.12 compares *HT* 98 and 104, where, once again, the young woman in question is (allegedly) a foreigner. Possibly Terence's audience will think of these women as *concubinae*, although Terence, unlike Plautus, never uses the term. (For discussion of Plautus' *concubinae*, see Watson 1967: 1–10.) It may be, however, that Terence implies no technical status of concubinage when he uses the phrase *pro uxore habere*. In *And.* 146, as suggested above, the phrase might simply allude to the fact that Glycerium is pregnant and that Pamphilus has not deserted her – i.e., he is treating her as if she were a wife. *Pro uxore habere hanc peregrinam* is, in that case, a paradoxical statement, a representation of an impossible social reality, similar to Demeas' (likewise hostile) depiction of Khrusis at *Samia* 130 as *gamete hetaira*. Such a non-technical interpretation can be supported by Chremes' later depiction of Pamphilus as a young man *in alio occupatus amore, abhorrens ab re uxoria* (829: "entwined in a different love affair, shrinking from the marital state").

father overcome by paternal affection.[59] They are just as much the property of a stern, upright father, possibly, even, of a devious and stern, upright father who already has a plan to set his son on the morally straight path.

Notwithstanding Chremes' withdrawal from the engagement, Simo the prosecutor still lacks sufficiently strong grounds for rebuke (*ne haec quidem / sati' vehemens causa ad obiurgandum*, 149–50). The advocate has once again supplied a defense for Pamphilus, pointing out a shortcoming in the prosecutor's case. The son is now imagined as imputing to his father inconsistent behavior – taking away his license to act as he liked before marriage:

> "*tute ipse his rebu' finem praescripsti, pater:*
> *prope adest quom alieno more vivendumst mihi:*
> *sine nunc meo me vivere interea modo.*" (151–53)

> "you yourself prescribed the end for these affairs, father;
> the time is nearly at hand when I must live in different style;
> now allow me in the interim to live in my own way."

The poverty of the defense is worth examination; its omissions should be compared with those of the first (139–41): there, Pamphilus was allowed to gloss over any personal acquaintance with the girl; now, in the second defense, he can refer to the relationship in the phrase *his rebus* – as if it were one of any number of casual flings. Are these the omissions and circumlocutions that Pamphilus would have been likely to make had he been asked to formulate his own defense at this time? The answer is decidedly "yes." Concealment and deception have been Pamphilus' *modus operandi* thus far: he has concealed from Simo both his knowledge of Glycerium and the degree of their attachment. Simo's defenses have been cut to suit the character of his son – as he has come to know him through his own investigations.

To Sosia's reasonable question, "what grounds are there left for rebuke?" (154), Simo replies:

> *si propter amorem uxorem nolet ducere:*
> *ea primum ab illo animum advortenda iniuriast;*
> *et nunc id operam do, ut per falsas nuptias*
> *vera obiurgandi causa sit, si deneget;* (155–58)

[59] Donatus (146.3) on *ego illud sedulo: quanto affectu pater factum quod viderat negabat* ! ("With how much affection did the father deny a fact which he had seen!"). The comment seems to have triggered the modern view of Simo as so overcome by paternal affection (*Vaterliebe*) that he denies what he has seen with his own eyes, not only in I 1, but in later scenes (III 1–3) as well: Oppermann 1934; V. Martin 1964; Büchner 1974.

> If on account of his love affair he should refuse to take a wife –
> first and foremost he must pay for that outrage of his;
> and now I'm working on this – that through the pretended marriage
> there may develop a real cause for rebuke, if he should refuse it.

Simo the prosecutor has stepped in with his final assessment of the case: one last piece of incontrovertible evidence has been deemed necessary. So a test of a sort has been designed for Pamphilus – if he should pass it (by accepting the wife that Simo has chosen for him), then Simo will seek Chremes' agreement to the marriage once again and all will be well (165–67); but if he should fail it (by refusing the marriage because of his current love affair), then *ea primum ab illo animum advortenda iniuriast* (156). The language belongs to the courtroom: Pamphilus' failure is an *iniuria* that will have to be punished; refusal of the marriage will constitute the *causa*. What I called a "test of a sort" is really of a very special sort – a scenario of enticement designed to catch the "criminal" in the act, to extort a confession, and to bring him to justice for past and present offenses.[60]

Let us now review Simo's search for and ultimate discovery of a *vera obiurgandi causa*. He first sought one after the funeral, but could not find a satisfactory one. Chremes then gave an incriminating report about his son; Simo denied it; Chremes cancelled the earlier marriage agreement. Simo then sought another *causa*, but it was not sufficiently *vehemens*. He finally decided to create the opportunity for one by inventing the *falsae nuptiae*. If his son were to refuse the marriage, then at last there would be a *vera obiurgandi causa*. What explains Simo's inability to find a *satis causa* and *satis causa vehemens* until he sets the stage for one? Surely not a paternal leniency or love that could only see an ideal son who had no faults. Explanation along those lines overlooks Simo's forensic disposition, his need for evidence, for irrefutable proof that can, in the end, come only from the "criminal" himself, his son. It is, arguably, the act of deception in perpetrating his "offenses" that has enraged Simo to such a degree – not simply that Pamphilus has had an intimate relationship of some long standing with a foreign courtesan's sister (although that is provocative enough to the *iniquus pater*) – but that he has concealed the affair from him, that he has eluded the master inquisitor who insists on frequent occasion that he is not to be – and cannot be –

60 Simo, like Micio in his *ludus* in IV 5 of *Adelphoe*, is certain of the guilt of his son before beginning his "play"; Simo explicitly says at 172: *Non dubiumst quin uxorem nolit filius* ("It is certain that my son does not want a wife").

deceived.[61] What Simo wants is his son's acknowledgment of his deceitfulness; since Pamphilus will not provide this of his own accord, he will force him to the admission by putting him in a position so threatening that there is no more possibility of concealment, equivocation, or cowardice. Pamphilus himself – not Chremes nor any other witness – must come forward and say, "I have been concealing my relationship with Glycerium – that is why I cannot marry Chremes' daughter." The *falsae nuptiae* is the means by which confession will be extorted.

Simo will be soothed, for a time, by Pamphilus' surprising (and deceitful) acceptance of the wedding arrangement (II 5); and, though baffled by his son's acquiescence, he will nevertheless cling to it even in the face of obvious contrary evidence – Glycerium's labor shrieks:

> *sed parvi pendo: illud mihi multo maxumumst*
> *quod mihi pollicitust ipsu' gnatu'* . . . (526–27)

> But I think little of that: this to me is far the greatest thing –
> what my son himself has promised me.

In Act v, Simo's rage will have its venting – and diffusion – when Pamphilus finally steps forward. But at that point, Simo is under the impression that his son has committed a far more serious crime – not that his affections are attached to Glycerium, but that he is passing her off as his citizen wife. The anger that he expresses there is exactly what we expect from the disappointed father and moral prosecutor of the opening scene of the *Andria*.

Simo's *narratio*, then, serves multiple purposes. It depicts the characters of both father and son. The father has acted as sleuth in the past and acts as auditor/prosecutor, defendant's advocate, and judge in the present. The son is portrayed as having concealed his own "immoral activities" behind a veneer of easy-going acquiescence and casual heroics. The message of the *gnati vita* is inseparable from its style. The *narratio*, set up as an audit or assessment of character and enhanced by forensic language and attitude, assigns blame for the breakdown of the wedding agreement and supplies the perfect vehicle for the prosecutor's invention of the *falsae nuptiae.*

The assessment of Simo's character offered here differs from earlier treatments in which Simo is depicted as a lenient father whose *Vaterliebe* leads him astray and causes him to overlook the

[61] See 204, 492–94, 867.

faults of his son. It may perhaps be objected that by focusing on the first scene of the play, support for the *opinio communis* has been tendentiously neglected. That objection will be met now.

5 (c) *The 'aequus pater': the rhetoric of indulgence*

Simo's "lenient" attitude reverberates throughout the play. When Davos first appears on-stage in I 2 after having heard the surprising news that the marriage is to take place, he remarks:

> *mirabar hoc si sic abiret et eri semper lenitas*
> *verebar quorsum evaderet.*
> *qui postquam audierat non datum iri filio uxorem suo,*
> *numquam quoiquam nostrum verbum fecit neque id*
> *aegre tulit.* (175–78)

> I kept wondering if it would turn out so and I kept fearing
> where master's "leniency-on-every-occasion policy" would lead –
> who, after he had heard that a wife would not be given to his son,
> never uttered a word to anyone of us nor took it ill.

Donatus' observations on *semper* (175) are of interest here. He first asks whether *semper* modifies *verebar* or *lenitas*, "so that it would be a single word" (*ut sit* ὑφέν); as an example, he cites Lucretius I. 125, *semper florentis Homeri* ("ever-flowering Homer"). He apparently decides in favor of the latter and explains the phrase in this way: "and so [he means] by this a leniency that has been simulated continuously up to the present moment; for no one can be 'ever-lenient' in diverse circumstances unless he happens to be a crafty and shrewd dissembler."[62] The description, "crafty and shrewd dissembler" (*fictus adsimulator et callidus*), perfectly suits Simo, the fabricator of the *falsae nuptiae* (recall Sosia's question at 48: *quor simulas igitur?*). If we accept Donatus' opinion of *semper* as a modifier of *lenitas* at 175, then 175–76 can best be interpreted by understanding the expression "*semper lenitas*" with quotation marks around it, as if Davos were citing Simo's own words, words which he may have used so often to describe his policy toward his son that they have become a kind of slogan: "I kept fearing where master's 'leniency-on-every-occasion policy' would lead." Davos' next two

[62] *ac per hoc simulata usque nunc lenitas. nam nemo in diversis actibus semper lenis est nisi forte fictus adsimulator et callidus.*

lines (177–78) and following speech (180–83) show how well he understands his master's hypocrisy.[63]

If there is any doubt about Simo's hypocrisy, about his appropriating the rhetoric of leniency as a pose, certainly his speeches in I 2, 185–91 should dispel it. First he announces to Davos: *meum gnatum rumor est amare* (185: "my son is rumored to be in love").[64] Davos, of course, will not be tricked into saying anything that would incriminate his young master, and Simo then shifts his ground:

sed nunc ea me exquirere
iniqui patris est; nam quod ant(e)hac fecit nil ad me attinet.
dum tempus ad eam rem tulit, sivi animum ut expleret suom;
nunc hic dies aliam vitam defert, alios mores postulat: (186–89)

But for me to continue these inquiries at present
is the part of an unjust father. For what he did before now
does not at all concern me.
While his age favored the affair, I allowed him free rein;
this day now brings a different life, demands a different morality.

Simo does not permit his former leniency to be forgotten. His expression in 188 of his earlier stance of leniency recalls (as Donatus reminds us) his words at 151–52 where he had created Pamphilus' "second defense." Simo's leniency is ever on the tip of his tongue. We shall return to this passage shortly.

Pamphilus, too, alludes to Simo's earlier leniency in the midst of his display to Mysis of heartfelt anxiety and divided loyalties in I 5:

tot me inpediunt curae, quae meum animum divorsae trahunt:
amor, misericordia huiu', nuptiarum sollicitatio,
tum patri' pudor, qui me tam leni passus est animo usque adhuc
quae meo quomque animo lubitumst facere. eine ego ut advorser? ei mihi! (260–63)

So many cares hold me fast and pull me in different directions:
love, sympathy for the girl, anxiety about the wedding,
then shame before my father, who in his leniency has allowed me up until now
to do whatever pleased me. Am I to oppose him? Alas for me!

[63] 180–83: *id voluit nos sic necopinantis duci falso gaudio, / sperantis iam amoto metu, interoscitantis opprimi, / ne esset spatium cogitandi ad disturbandas nuptias: / astute* ("he wanted us to be just like this: so off our guard, led away by false joy, so full of hope now, with fear banished, so overcome with gaping yawns there would be no time for planning the disruption of the wedding – clever man!").

[64] Donatus at 185. 1 and 2 points out Simo's hypocrisy. The commentator, it appears, would agree with an interpretation of entrapment; he attributes Simo's withholding of knowledge to a desire to catch out his son, *ne amittat vim vindicaturi* ("lest he weaken the grounds for punishment").

Donatus, once again and not surprisingly observes that 262 looks back to the opening *narratio*, the defense created by the father for his son: "*tute ipse his rebu' finem praescripsti, pater*" (151). In Pamphilus' remark at 262 (*usque adhuc*!), perhaps we are even to hear an echo of the father's "*semper lenitas*" policy. Most striking of all, however, is Davos' quotation of Simo in II 6, the scene in which Simo appears somewhat disappointed by Pamphilus' apparently unhesitant acceptance of the marriage. Nonetheless, Simo persists in his inquiries, seeking to discover the degree of his son's suffering. Davos insists that it is only a "two or three day sorrow," that Pamphilus is now on the right track (440–42). He expatiates:

> *dum licitumst ei dumque aetas tulit,*
> *amavit; tum id clam: cavit ne umquam infamiae*
> *ea res sibi esset, ut virum fortem decet.*
> *nunc uxore opus est: animum ad uxorem adpulit.* (443–46)

> While it was permitted and his age favored it,
> he loved; at that time it was a secret – he was wary, as suits
> any red-blooded fellow, lest the affair should taint his reputation.
> Now that a wife is required, upon a wife he's fixed his mind.

In 443, Davos triumphantly returns (as Donatus once again observes) Simo's own words that were spoken to him at 188, *dum tempus ad eam rem tulit* . . .

The casting of Simo as "lenient father" has been his own production, his own say-so, pompously paraded about by himself before Sosia, naively iterated by Pamphilus, and mimicked by Davos (175, *semper lenitas*, and 443). The liberal veneer was most transparent of all in Simo's words that followed his probing of Davos about the rumor of his son's love affair:

> *sed nunc ea me exquirere*
> *iniqui patris est; nam quod ant(e)hac fecit nil ad me attinet.*
> *dum tempus ad eam rem tulit, sivi animum ut expleret suom;* (186–88)

"But for me to continue these inquiries at present [i.e., the very day a wedding is supposedly taking place] is the part of an *iniquus pater*. For what he did before now does not at all concern me [i.e., as an *aequus pater*]. While his age favored the affair, I allowed him free rein." The verses are dense with hypocrisy; some of it can now be specified by pointing out the way that Simo has chosen to make a distinction between the *iniquus pater* and his implied counterpart. The *iniquus pater* makes inquiry into his son's premarital conduct; for the implied *aequus pater*, such inquiry is irrelevant – he allows an unmarried son to behave as he likes. Yet Simo, as we know from his own *narratio* in I I, made diligent and persistent inquiries before his son's wedding – when, for example, he sought the testimony of *servoli*, when, furthermore, he followed his son to the funeral of a courtesan. Nevertheless, he has bandied about claims of permitting his son freedom. Since we have seen Simo performing the duty of the *iniquus pater*, but doing so only in concealment – that is, by narrating his past sleuthing activities to his freedman in confidence (34, and in Menander's play, he provided his account in a monologue), by keeping his suspicions to himself (82), by confronting *servoli* rather than addressing his son – we are led to the conclusion that Simo's "liberal" or "lenient" character is superimposed, a role he plays in public to his son and his allies. "*Semper lenitas*" is the slogan of the liberal facade. Behind that, Simo has ever held fast to definite ideas about his son's behavior – that he should not be excessive in his interests (56–59), that he should be "obsequious" to friends (63–66), that he should be a *magnum exemplum continentiae* (92) in his relationships – with courtesans! The last requirement (evident in Simo's praise of his son's presumed virtue) especially gives the lie to Simo's liberal pose. When, in the early part of his *narratio*, Simo had praised Pamphilus for "following the pursuits of others (*eorum obsequi studiis*), for being averse to no one, for never putting himself ahead of anyone – in such a way that one could most easily find praise without malice and ready friends" (64–66), Sosia's cynical and ironic response had more pertinence for the father than the son:

> *sapienter vitam instituit; namque hoc tempore*
> *obsequium amicos, veritas odium parit.* (67–68)

> He has organized his life wisely; for in this day and age
> obsequiousness wins friends, truth hatred.

The *obsequium* lauded in the son is the public *modus operandi* of the father, a master at concealing his true designs – the fabricator of the *falsae nuptiae*. Terence's Sosia knows his former master well. The plot of the *falsae nuptiae* is Simo's response to the discovery that his son has availed himself of the *semper lenitas* that had been proffered in name only.

6 CONCLUSIONS

Once again, we see the characters of New Comedy acting in accordance with forensic modes of conduct that are evident in the orators. They entice their adversaries to commit crimes (adultery in *Miles Gloriosus*, purchase of a citizen girl in *Persa*, theft in *Poenulus*) and moral offenses (a display of greed in *Aspis* and of disobedience in *Andria*); they create stratagems to elicit confessions (of sexual violations in *Epitrepontes* and *Adelphoe*, of intimacy with a courtesan's sister in the *Andria*). The most salient feature of this conduct is what I indicated in the first chapter – its "staginess," the notion that conduct is staged to achieve a certain effect, even among close friends and kin. Staginess is most evident in the scenarios of framing and entrapment that have been presented in this chapter. When the more formal modes of dispute settlement appear of no avail, the characters of New Comedy cross the boundaries of the law but recreate its operation, seeking witnesses to supply false testimony, framing their enemies for offenses they did not commit or enticing them to commit crimes – or to confess to past ones – which can then be penalized in the regular court system of Athens or satisfied by private negotiation. The scenarios of framing and entrapment are explicitly plotted, often rehearsed in advance, and acted before an audience – no matter that the audience might be limited to the members of their own *oikos* or related *oikoi*.

To consider these scenarios as mere "intrigues' or "tricks," and not to see them as extensions of the forensic conduct of real or potential litigants, is to ignore the cultural context of contemporary Athenian audiences. Greek New Comedy dramatized the ways in which the Athenian legal system touched the lives of *polis* inhabitants, on and off the forensic stage. The outlines of that interaction are still visible in Roman Comedy, but with significant transmutations. In an earlier chapter, we saw Plautus dilute the arbitration scenarios of Greek New Comedy; Italic folk justice proved to be a livelier means to even the score, an irresistible conclusion for a play. The framing and entrapment scenarios in the Roman plays of this chapter likewise have a rambunctious vibrancy that goes beyond what can be envisioned in the Greek originals (e.g., the rehearsal scenarios of Plautus) – although a costumed doctor's diagnosis of terminal depression and the play-acting of Khairestratos' death in *Aspis* should give us pause before designating Menander's dramaturgy as moribund in comparison. Sometimes, too, the Roman scenarios are transmitted with a breathtaking mastery of verbal manipulation and nuance (e.g., the juxtaposition of ontological and epistemological language in Terence's *verae* and *falsae nuptiae*). That the transmission of the genre to Rome, with all the differences, inventiveness, and inconcinnities it displays there, should breathe so lively is testimony not only to the creativity of Roman dramatists in adapting plays for their audiences, but to the durability of the human delight in getting the better of one's adversaries, in playing litigious games, in stepping onto the forensic stage, whether in the sunlight of the marketplace or the shade of one's own courtyard.

Appendices

APPENDIX I

Official arbitration in the Attic orators

Official arbitrators received their cases from the Forty, and *AP* 53.1 reports that the Forty are the officials "from whom plaintiffs obtained a hearing in the other private suits."[1] It is now generally thought that "the other private suits" refer to a specific set of *dikai* under the jurisdiction of the Forty (and hence of the official arbitrators) distinct from the *graphai* and *dikai* heard by other magistrates.[2] Jurisdiction over *dikai* underwent changes during the fourth century; certain *dikai* which are "confirmed" for official arbitration in the middle of that century appear as *emmēnoi* and under the jurisdiction of the *eisagogeis* in *AP* 52. 2 (thus *dikai proikos* and *aikeias*, and possibly *aphormes* and *trapezetikai*; see Rhodes 1981 ad loc.). The date of the change of jurisdiction cannot be determined, but most scholars have accepted Gernet's (1939) arguments that *dikai emmēnoi* did not exist during the first half of the fourth century. *Dikai emporikai* (a subset of *dikai emmēnoi*) came into existence sometime between 355 and 342 (see MacDowell 1990 apud Dem. 21. 176); dates for other *dikai emmēnoi* cannot be specified beyond saying that they were introduced at some point between the early 340s and the composition of the *AP* (see E. Cohen 1973: 186–91; Harrison 2. 21).

While our limited sources attest to only nine or ten *dikai* (and the identification of some of these is disputable) under the jurisdiction of the Forty,[3] modern authorities usually assume that they were responsible for

[1] For the procedure by which private cases are passed from the four tribal judges to official arbitrators, see *AP* 53. 1–2.

[2] For cases heard before other specified magistrates, see *AP* 52 (Eleven, *eisagogeis*, *apodektai*); 56. 6–7 (*arkhon*); 57. 2–4 (*basileus*); 58. 2–3 (*polemarkhos*); 59. 2–6 (*thesmothetai*). On the jurisdiction of the Forty, see MacDowell 1978: 207; Bonner and Smith 2. 97–116; Harrell 1936: 36–38; Thalheim *RE* s.v. διαιτηταί, col. 315; Lipsius 227–28.

[3] *Dikai* with attestation: see section (a) below and cf. Harrell 1936: 37–38, duplicated in Bonner and Smith 2. 115–16. The Forty's jurisdiction in *dikai arguriou*, *engues*, and *exoules* is nowhere attested but is inferred generally from *AP* 53. 1 (see opening paragraph above). Inference can be bolstered by further inference (see, e.g. the argument of Wyse 1904: 449 on Is. 5. 31). For the so-called *dike lipomarturiou* (correctly excluded by Harrell and Bonner and Smith) and the appearance of the official arbitrator in [Dem.] 49. 19, see Harrison 2. 141–42.

most private suits (cf. Isokr. 15. 237).[4] Modern authorities thus tend to assign to the Forty all *dikai* which are not specifically assigned to other magistrates. I take issue with neither the general assumption nor the tendency outlined here. The purpose of this appendix is to suggest the significance which litigants attached to official arbitration. Accordingly, I begin by setting out the explicit evidence for the jurisdiction of the Forty in the Attic orators; I then demonstrate the extent to which litigants refer to official arbitration in private trials within that jurisdiction, and I identify verdicts in these arbitrations.

(A) EVIDENCE FOR THE JURISDICTION OF OFFICIAL ARBITRATORS IN THE ORATORS

It will be convenient to break the evidence for attested *dikai* into three groups: (1) private orations in which a speaker refers to the official arbitration that belongs to the trial in which he is now taking part; (2) orations in which a speaker mentions an earlier arbitration that does not belong to the preliminary stages of the current trial; and (3) orations which mention suits that belong to the Forty. About one quarter of the 49 trials represented by the 52 extant private orations belongs to the first group.[5] Additionally, the speaker of Isaios 12 reports earlier arbitrations in the dispute over his half-brother's deme membership. The status of this suit (whether public or private) remains indeterminable; the trial is included in the list below but is not incorporated into the statistics for private orations in sections b and c. Seven types of *dikai* and one uncertain case (Isaios 12) are thus represented by this evidence (chapter numbers locate the reference to the official arbitration; probable dates for the orations are given in parentheses):

dike aikeias 1. [Dem.] 47 *Euergos* 5–6, 12–16, 45 (mid 350s; Schaefer 3.2: 197). The speech is a *dike pseudomarturiōn*, arising out of a trial for assault (*aikeia*). Two arbitrators are mentioned in c. 45; the anonymous plaintiff of [Dem.] 47 had sued Theophemos for assault, and the latter counter-sued the former on the same charge. Theophemos postponed the arbitral decision in the speaker's case against him (45), which is apparently still pending (c. 8), but proceeded

[4] Isokr. 15. 237 is speaking of the *sanides* (wooden tablets) used by different magistrates to publicize the names of offenders under their jurisdiction: ". . . on the tablets posted by the thesmothetai are both the public offenders (τούς τε τὴν πόλιν ἀδικοῦντας) and the sykophants; on those of the Eleven are both the *kakourgoi* and their instigators; on those of the Forty are both the private offenders and those who prosecute unlawfully (τούς τ' ἐν τοῖς ἰδίοις πράγμασιν ἀδικοῦντας καὶ τοὺς μὴ δικαίως ἐγκαλοῦντας)"; cf. n. 7 apud fin. Isokrates' speech is datable to 354 (c. 9, and see Münscher *RE* s.v. "Isokrates," cols. 2150, 2208–09).

[5] In three instances, we possess two speeches belonging to the plaintiff during the same trial: (1) Dem. 27 and 28; (2) Dem. 30 and 31; and (3) Dem. 45 and [Dem.] 46.

with (and won) the case against the speaker. See Harrison 2. 131.

2. Dem. 54 *Konon* 26–33 (355? 341?; see Schaefer 3. 2: 251 and Carey and Reid 1985: 69).

dike aphormes (?) 3. Dem. 36 *Phormion* 18 (a *paragraphe* in response to a *dike aphormes*; see c. 12 and Lipsius 725–26; type of suit rejected by Gernet 1. 202–04 who proposes that it was a *dike blabes* (350/49; Trevett 1992: 48, n. 28). Dem. 45 and [Dem.] 46 *Stephanos* are part of a *dike pseudomarturiōn* arising from the trial to which Dem. 36 belongs; further references to the official arbitration for the original suit appear in 45. 8, 10, 17, 24–25, 58, 60 and in 46. 5.

dike blabes 4. Dem. 39 *Boiotos* 22, 37–38 (348; Carey and Reid 1985: 160). There may have been two arbitrations (see section c).

5. [Dem. 48] *Olymp.* 48 (between 343 and 341; Schaefer 3.2: 239).

6. Dem. 55 *Kallikles* 2 and 6 (no date).

7. Dem. 41 *Spoudias* 12 (no date, possibly early; Schaefer 3.2: 228). The type of *dike* is contested; Lipsius 496–97 suggests a *dike arguriou.*

dike epitropes 8. Lysias 32 *Diogeiton* 2 (399/98; MacDowell 1971a: 271–72).

9. Dem. 27 *Aphobos* 51–53 (364/63; MacDowell 1990: 294). Dem. 28 is the second plaintiff speech in the same trial; Dem. 29 is a *dike pseudomarturiōn* arising from the trial for the mismanagement of guardianship and refers to the official arbitration in cc. 20–21, 31, 58 (cf. Dem. 30. 6 and see Bonner 1907: 413–15).

dike kakegorias 10. Lysias 10 *Theomnestos* 6 (384/83; see c. 4 of the oration).

dike proikos 11. [Dem.] 40 *Boiotos* 17–18 (347; Carey and Reid 1985: 160).

dike khreos (?) 12. [Dem.] 49 *Timotheos* 19, 21, 43–44, 55–56, 65–67 (362?; Trevett 1992: 35–36, n. 19). Cf. Lys. fr. XIX B–S (after 399/98, the year in which the *nomos* about the *diaitetai* was instituted; MacDowell 1971a).

status civitatis et familiae (?) 13. Isaios 12 *Euphiletos* 11–12, and cf. 22 (after 346/45?; Bonner and Smith 2. 113). See Bonner and Smith 2. 112–14 for summation of earlier views of the type of suit; the authors suggest the trial was a *dike blabes*. There are probably two arbitrations involved; see n. 8.

References to official arbitration in the second group extend the range of cases handled by official arbitrators to one certain category (*dike klopes*); the type of *dike* represented by nos. 20 and 21 is uncertain.

dike blabes	14. [Dem.] 52 *Kallippos* 14 (369/68; Trevett 1992: 31–32, n. 15).
	15. Dem. 55 *Kallikles* 2 and 31–34 (no date).
dike kakegorias	16. Dem. 21 *Meidias* 81–101 (347/46; MacDowell 1990: 9–11).
dike klopes	17. Dem. 22 *Androtion* 27 (355).
	18. Dem. 24 *Timokrates* 114 (353).
dike proikos	19. [Dem.] 40 *Boiotos* 17 and 31 (347; Carey and Reid 1985: 160).
status civitatis et familiae (?)	20. Dem. 39 *Boiotos* 2–5 (348; Carey and Reid 1985: 160) and [Dem.] 40. 9–11. Bonner and Smith 2. 108 suggest the trial was a *dike blabes*.
	21. [Dem.] 59 *Neaira* 60 (between 343 and 340; Trevett 1992: 48–49 and Schaefer 3.2: 183). Bonner and Smith 2. 112 suggest the trial was a *dike blabes*.

Allusions to the jurisdiction of the Forty add one more action, the *dike biaiōn*, which is mentioned together with the *dike aikeias*:

dike biaiōn	22. Dem. 37 *Pant.* 33 (347 or 346; Schaefer 3. 2: 206). Harrell 1936: 37 classifies the suit mentioned (together with a *diaitetes*) at [Dem.] 25. 55 and 58 in this category. For discussion of the authenticity of that oration (which has been questioned on the grounds of inaccuracies of Attic law), see Hansen 1976: 144–52 and Sealey 1993: 237–39.

(B) REPRESENTATION OF OFFICIAL ARBITRATION IN THE ORATORS

In chapter 1. 1, I suggested that speakers may regularly have alluded to their own hearings before the official arbitrator in trials that fell to the jurisdiction of the Forty. It is impossible to gauge the precise percentage of such allusions in the extant orations on account of the lack of positive evidence for the extent of the Forty's jurisdiction and for the precise dating and definition of certain *dikai emmēnoi*; nevertheless, it is possible to bolster my conjecture. In order to calculate a percentage, a pool of trials that were first heard by an official arbitrator (whether a litigant alluded to the arbitration or not) must be created. Starting from the figure of 49 as the number of trials represented by the 52 extant private orations, the following trials should be excluded from the pool:

(1) Trials that are known with certainty to have been presided over by magistrates other than the Forty: three trials brought by a *dike phonou* (Ant. 1 and 6; Lys. 1); two by a *dike traumatos* (Lys. 3 and 4); eight *diadikasiai* ([Dem.] 42 and 43; Is. 1, 4, 7, 8, 9, and 10). Some of these trials pre-date the institution of official arbitration at the end of the fifth century. Excluded trials: 13.

(2) *Dikai pseudomarturiōn* which emerge from trials that were presided over by magistrates other than the Forty:[6] Excluded trials: 4 *dikai pseudomarturiōn* arising from *diadikasiai* (Dem. 44; Is. 2, 3, and 6).
(3) *Dikai pseudomarturiōn* which emerge from trials that were presided over by the Forty in cases where we possess speeches from the original trial. This affects two trials: Dem. 29 and Dem. 45 and 46 (from the same trial). While the orations thus excluded contain ample reference to the official arbitration before the original trial (see nos. 3 and 9 in the first list above), their inclusion would duplicate the evidence of Dem. 27 and 36. Excluded trials: 2.
(4) Trials which are likely to have been presided over by magistrates other than the Forty: Dem. 50, which Lipsius 775 reasonably designates as a *dike epitrierarkhematos* presided over by the *strategoi*. Excluded trials: 1.
(5) *Paragraphai* which are in response to *dikai emporikai* and *metallikai*, both of which are *emmēnoi*; preliminary hearings before an official arbitrator were eliminated from these cases (*Lex. Seg.* 310. 17; see Isager and Hansen 1975: 85; E. Cohen 1973: 10–40; Lipsius 228 and n. 32). Excluded trials: 6 (Dem. 32 and 37; [Dem.] 33, 34, 35, and 56).[7]
(6) Trials pre-dating the institution of official arbitration which do not belong to any of the groups excluded thus far: Lys. 23 (a *paragraphe*) and Isokr. 18 (another *paragraphe*, in response to a *dike blabes*); for the dating of these trials, see MacDowell 1971a: 270, and cf. Harrell 1936: 31, n. 94 on Isokr. 18). Excluded trials: 2.
(7) Trials brought before the Forty which cannot be evaluated since the orations derived from them are incomplete (it is possible that in the missing narrative sections, reference to official arbitration appeared). Excluded trials: 3 (Isokr. 16, a *dike blabes*; Isokr. 20, a *dike aikeias*, and Hyp. 5, probably a *dike blabes*). Lys. 32 is also fragmentary, but there is a brief allusion to official arbitration in c. 2.

The total number of trials of private cases that can be excluded from the

[6] It is generally assumed that suits for false witnessing came before the magistrates who had jurisdiction in the original action; exceptional were alleged commissions of the offense before the Areopagos: these cases were introduced by the thesmothetai (*AP* 59. 6). Possibly *anakrisis* rather than arbitration was regular even in false witnessing cases which fell to the Forty; in [Dem.] 47. 10, an *anakrisis* is mentioned as preceding the trial for false witnessing that had emerged from a trial for assault (in which the Forty – and official arbitrators – had jurisdiction at the time). Whatever preliminary procedure may have been required, it need only have been formal after the introduction of written evidence.

[7] Many scholars believe that *paragraphai* would not be heard by official arbitrators; for extensive presentation of this view, see Bonner and Smith 2. 91–96 and MacDowell 1990: 306 for relevant bibliography. The appearance of an official arbitrator in Dem. 36. 18 and 33 has created problems. A minority view, formulated by Calhoun 1919a and now endorsed by MacDowell 1990: 307–08 is that a *paragraphe* (as an "objection to the legality of a prosecution") could be submitted to an arbitrator and would follow the usual course of arbitration. Possibly this is what Isokrates is referring to in 15. 237, when he says that the names of "those committing private wrongs and those prosecuting unjustly (τοὺς μὴ δικαίως ἐγκαλοῦντας)" were inscribed on the tablets of the Forty.

pool of trials that were first heard before an official arbitrator is 31. The pool therefore consists of 18 trials; in twelve of these (all instances from the first group excluding Isaios 12 on the grounds that it is probably not a private trial), a litigant refers to the official arbitration; in six, he does not:

(1) and (2) Isokr. 17 and 21: both are *dikai parakatathekes*, possibly *dikai blabes*.

(3) Dem. 30 and 31 (same trial): *dike exoules*.

(4) Dem. 38: a *paragraphe* in response to a *dike blabes*.

(5) [Dem.] 52: *dike arguriou*.

(6) Isaios 5: *dike engues*.

Based on this assessment, then, litigants refer to the preliminary hearing before the official arbitrator in the extant private orations in 66 percent of the trials that fell to the jurisdiction of the Forty. This is a conservative estimate. It should be kept in mind that there is no explicit evidence that connects any of the six trials listed directly above with the jurisdiction of the Forty except for the fourth, a *dike blabes*: the type of suit to which items 1 and 2 belong is uncertain. In these cases, a connection with the Forty is an inference.

(C) VERDICTS

Speakers report verdicts of official arbitrators in ten cases listed in section a: nos. 4, 6, 8, 9, 11, 13, 15 (two different hearings), 16, 19, 20. In six cases, they report the verdict of their own preliminary hearings: nos. 4, 6, 8, 9, 11, and 13. If we exclude no. 13 on the grounds that it might represent a public case, then almost a third of the speakers mention their own verdicts within the pool of private trials that fell to the jurisdiction of the Forty. Additionally, in four cases, speakers plead in such a way that it appears all but certain they lost the verdict: no. 1 (see Harrison 1. 131); no. 2 (see Dem. 54. 33 and Carey and Reid 1985 ad loc.); no. 3 (see Dem. 45. 60); no. 12 (see [Dem.] 49. 19–21 and 65). These sometimes extensive accounts appear in passages where the litigants (presumably "losers") are arguing against the evidence used in making that decision or explaining the circumstances under which the decision was made.

One tendency is clear in announcing the verdict in one's own case: it is usually the winner who offers the information; only in one case (no. 6) does the "loser" do so. In five cases (nos. 4, 6, 8, 9, and 11), the defendant was condemned; in one (no. 13, the latter involving two arbitrations), he was acquiitted – and that acquittal appears as explicit precedent for the ongoing trial.[8]

At least three of the condemnations were executed in absentia (nos. 4, 6, 11, and probably 8); in one instance, the litigant appears to have appealed

[8] Wyse 1904: 716 and 720 accepts the traditional view that the first acquittal was given in absentia and then rendered null and void; the second arbitration may have lasted for two years.

the case immediately to the dikasterion (no. 6); in the other instances (nos. 4, 8, and 11), the verdict may have been declared null and void (*mē ousa*). Wyse 1904 apud Is. 12. 11 suggests that "Boiotos" was probably successful in having the verdict in no. 4 rendered null and void (Dem. 39. 37–38); Mantitheos (the plaintiff) may have lost the second arbitration (see Dem. 39. 22) – he does not mention an adverse verdict. It is unclear what happened to the verdict in [Dem.] 40 *Boiotos* 17–18 (no. 11). Mantitheos reports that in the suit which he brought against "Boiotos" for the recovery of his mother's dowry, the *diaitetes* condemned "Boiotos" by default, but the latter made some sort of objection (by what means is not specified) to the effect that the verdict had not been against him, "since his name was not 'Boiotos' but 'Mantitheos.'" Since "Boiotos" did not appeal the verdict to the dikasterion, he probably managed to have the arbitration declared null and void. Mantitheos waited more than a decade to reinstitute the suit; see chapter 3, n. 38.

There is evidence that three arbitral verdicts were acccepted by litigants; the first is least certain:

(a) [Dem.] 59 *Neaira* 60 (no. 21 above): When Phrastor sued his *gennetai*, the Brutidai, for not registering his son, "they challenged him before the *diaitetes* to swear by full-grown victims that he truly believed the boy was his son, born of an *aste* who was pledged to him according to the law. When the *gennetai* tendered this challenge to Phrastor before the *diaitetes*, Phrastor refused the oath and did not swear." On the basis of the account in [Dem.] 59. 60, we can assume that the procedure being described is an official arbitration (as Carey 1992: 117 does, on account of "the absence of any indication of an agreement to arbitration, the mention of a single arbitrator, and the failure to provide any name"), but we cannot assume the truthfulness of the report. While the deposition that follows the report may well be authentic (two of the three witnesses are known from inscriptions; see Carey 1992: 118), the witnesses testify only that they are *gennetai* and that they prevented Phrastor from introducing his son; there is no mention of the suit, the arbitrator, and the challenge. On the other hand, it might just be possible that Phrastor's *dike* is "non-technical" and refers to an "internal hearing" before the *gennetai* themselves according to their own established procedure (cf. *IG* II^2 1196.11 where the demesmen from Aixone are said "to decide" [*dikazein*] in deme arbitration); if so, an arbitration might be implicit in the testimony of the *gennetai* – they had won their case.

(b) Dem. 39 *Boiotos* 2–5 and [Dem.] 40 *Boiotos* 9–11 (no. 20 above): Mantitheos' half brother "Boiotos" brought suit against his father Mantias, alleging that "he was his son by the daughter of Pamphilos [Plangon] and that he was being treated terribly and was robbed of his civic rights" (39. 2). Mantias is alleged to have feared political repercussions in court and so, during the official arbitration, he tendered a challenge to Plangon, which (we infer) would end the suit (39.3). Plangon accepted the challenge, which was to swear an oath in the Delphinion concerning the paternity of the boy; accordingly, she swore (allegedly breaking a private agreement with Mantias), that he was indeed the father of both "Boiotos" and his brother (39.3–4 and 40. 10–11). "And so," claims Mantitheos, "my father was compelled to abide by the arbitration (ἀναγκασθεὶς ἐμμεῖναι τῆι διαίτηι) on account of his own challenge" (40. 11).

Carey and Reid 1985: 170 argue that "Plangon's oath was decisive not because as mother she should know the father of her children (for at Isae. 12.9 we are told that the plaintiff's mother swore to his paternity, but the oath decided nothing) but because it was sworn as a result of Mantias' challenge. Either Mantias' *proklesis* laid down that Plangon's oath was to be binding on him or Mantias felt that his position was almost helpless when Plangon accepted the *proklesis* (*prokleseis* in Attic litigation were almost always refused) especially as he would not dare to reveal his deal with Plangon." A refinement of Carey's argument is in order: in Is. 12. 9, the speaker reports that Euphiletos' mother was willing to swear an oath before the arbitrator at the Delphinion – not that she did swear one (πρῶτον μὲν ἡ τοῦ Εὐφιλήτου μήτηρ . . . ὅρκον ὀμόσαι ἐπὶ τοῦ διαιτητοῦ ἐβούλετο ἐπὶ Δελφινίωι); the speaker goes on to say that his father also was willing to swear one, both at that time and now. Possibly the offer of oath-taking was rejected by the opponents (cf. offers of mother's oaths, although not on the question of paternity, at Dem. 29. 26 and 55. 27). If so, then in Is. 12. 9 the refusal of the oaths may have been decisive factors of persuasion – the arbitrators (there were two arbitrations; see Wyse 1904 on 12. 11–12) voted against the deme (12. 11–12). In Plangon's case, the acceptance of the challenge may have been decisive – not necessarily because it was "lawfully binding" upon the arbitrator, but because it was a factor of (powerful) persuasion (cf. Todd 1990: 35, n. 29). A final note: there is no need to buy, lock, stock, and barrel, Mantitheos' story of the compact between Plangon and Mantias; regardless of what information was conveyed in the depositions at 39. 5, the testimony can only have been hearsay.

(c) [Dem.] 40 *Boiotos* 17 and 31 (no. 19 above): After Mantias' death, "Boiotos" and his brother sued Mantitheos for recovery of Plangon's dowry, and Mantitheos sued "Boiotos" and his brother for recovery of his mother's dowry. After an abortive private arbitration (16), the suits were instituted again. Mantitheos reports that in the suit brought by his half-brothers, the official *diaitetes* found against them (17 and 31); "Boiotos" did not appeal the case to the dikasterion (17 and 31), and he abided by the arbitration (ἐνέμεινέ τε τῆι διαίτηι, 31).

The evidence presented thus far suggests that official arbitration played a more important role in trials than has hitherto been thought. While detailed analysis cannot be presented here, further studies should take into account: (1) the significant proportion of speakers who mention their own arbitrations (66 percent) and their own verdicts (28 percent) within the pool of private extant speeches belonging to the jurisdiction of official arbitrators (sections b and c); (2) the understandable reluctance of speakers to announce their condemnations (or the acquittals of their opponents) before dikasts; and (3) the absence of opposing speeches: had we extant speeches from both sides of each case, we might better appreciate how litigants deployed references to arbitration against one another.

(D) EVIDENCE FOR THE BINDING QUALITY OF OFFICIAL ARBITRATION

The evidence is slim but secure: (1) Dem. 21 *Meid.* 81: Demosthenes says that he lodged a *dike exoules* against Meidias after an official arbitrator condemned him in absentia for slander; that he has not been able to get the suit tried does not impugn the testimony for the availability of the remedy. (2) The procedure set up for overturning an official arbitrator's verdict made in the absence of a litigant (see Harrell 1936: 33–34 and MacDowell 1990: 309–10) does not make sense unless the verdict can be enforced at that point. (3) In addition, it can be argued that official arbitration was included in the law cited in Dem. 24 *Timokr.* 54 (and paraphrased in abbreviated form in Dem. 20 *Lept.* 147): Ὅσων δίκη πρότερον ἐγένετο ἢ εὔθυνα ἢ διαδικασία περί του ἐν δικαστηρίωι . . . μὴ εἰσάγειν περὶ τούτων εἰς τὸ δικαστήριον . . . ("In cases where there was previously a lawsuit or audit or adjudication about any matter in a place of judgment, [no magistrate] is to bring the matter into the [heliastic] court"). Wolff 1966: 92 objected that the words *en dikasterioi* excluded verdicts of official arbitrators which had been accepted by litigants, on the grounds that these were not brought before the court. But *dikasterion* can mean "place of judgment" (see Boegehold 1995: 146–47, 150, 183–84), and some "places of judgment" were movable in Athens: *IG* II^2 1641. 25–30, for example, reports the acquittal of a man and explicitly says "the dikasterion was the Stoa Poikile." Official arbitrations took place at various locations, e.g. in the Stoa Poikile (Dem. 45. 17); [Dem.] 47. 12 reports that *diaitai* for the tribes Oineis and Erekhtheis were held in the *Heliaia*; Pollux 8. 126 reports that official *diaitai* were carried out in temples (cf. [Dem.] 40. 11 and Is. 12. 9: the *diaitai* take place or are envisioned as taking place in the Delphinion – temple, sanctuary, "place of judgment"?). We might conclude that, wherever the arbitrator gave his verdict, that place was a "place of judgment" and hence a *dikasterion*; the *dikai* pronounced upon by official arbitrators and accepted by litigants therefore become binding (but not, of course, the verdicts of private arbitrators, since they do not pronounce verdicts on *dikai*). "Binding" in this instance refers to the prescription against retrying the case; presumably the remedy was a *paragraphe*.

(E) THE INTRODUCTION OF OFFICIAL ARBITRATION

A law cited at And. 1 *Myst.* 87 probably was enacted as part of the Amnesty in 403/02: τὰς δὲ δίκας καὶ τὰς διαίτας κυρίας εἶναι, ὁπόσαι ἐν δημοκρατουμένηι τῆι πόλει ἐγένοντο· τοῖς δὲ νόμοις χρῆσθαι ἀπ' Εὐκλείδου ἄρχοντος ("All judgments and arbitrations are to be authoritative which occurred when the *polis* was under democratic rule; but the laws are to be enforced from the time of Eukleides"). If official arbitration did not begin functioning until 399/98, then the *diaitai* mentioned in this law, as MacDowell noted in his commentary on the speech, must refer to private arbitrations or arbitrations by the thirty deme judges – or, in my view, both. Apparently, the law was meant to validate decisions produced under the democracy and to invalidate decisions made under the Thirty – as is clear from a law cited at Dem. 24. 56. Presumably the legislation (whether it was one or more laws) would have provided a mechanism by which the "validated" or "authoritative" decisions of *dikai* and *diaitai* were to be protected; cf. the language used in the law cited at Dem. 24. 54 (quoted in section d above), where magistrates are explicitly forbidden to bring a *dike* that has already been heard into the dikasterion.

The institution of official arbitration should probably be seen in relation to private arbitration at the end of the fifth century. If MacDowell's (1971a) argument in support of a suspension of private suits from 404/3 until 401/0 is correct, then private arbitration might be seen as having been given a boost during the period of the court's abeyance:[9] how else was one to settle a private dispute when there was no alternative? Surely private arbitration was the route to take when the courts remained closed. When they opened once again in 401/0, there may have been numerous cases (such as Kallimakhos' first suit against the speaker of Isokr. 18) brought by dissatisfied parties who had accepted the verdicts of private arbitrators because there had been no alternative; presumably, they would be blocked by *diamarturiai*. Athenians in 401 were in the midst of experiencing what it meant to maintain the verdicts of private arbitrators. If dissatisfaction ran high during 401/0–400/399 (e.g. the courts jammed with *dikai* that are blocked by *diamarturiai*), the procedure of private arbitration would come under review. Official arbitration may have been the solution. The speculative scenario envisioned here is entirely in keeping with MacDowell's chronology: that official arbitration was instituted in 400/399, and that the first official arbitrators took office in 399/98. It furthermore offers an explanation of why Arkhebiades refused to refer his case to arbitration until "the law about arbitrators" was passed (Lys. fr. xix B–S): private arbitration had become suspect during the suspension of the courts; there was no way to bring arbitrators to account, and yet there was no other way to end a private dispute.

[9] See chapter 3, n. 28.

APPENDIX 2

Private arbitrations and reconciliations in Athens

(A) LISTS OF PRIVATE ARBITRATIONS AND RECONCILIATIONS IN THE ORATORS

A. Compromise during trial
1 Is. 5. 1, 17–18, 29–30 (executed).
2. [Dem.] 48. 3 and 48 (offer).

B. Private arbitrations or reconciliations
1. Ant. 6. 20–24 and 37–39.
2. Lys. 32.2, 11–18.
3. Lys. fr. XIX B-S.
4. Lys. 4. 1–4.
5. Lys. 8. 9–13.
6. Is. 5. 31–33.
7. Is. 1. 2, 16, 28, 35, 51.
8. Dem. 41. 4, 28.
9. Dem. 41. 1, 14.
10. Dem. 38. 3–9.
11. [Dem.] 52. 15.
12. [Dem.] 52. 30.
13. [Dem.] 52. 20–21.
14. Dem. 29. 58 (cf. Dem. 27.1).
15. Is. 2. 28–30, 38.
16. Dem. 36. 14–17.
17. [Dem.] 40. 44.
18. [Dem.] 40. 16.
19. Aiskhin. 1. 62–64.
20. [Dem.] 59. 45–48.
21. [Dem.] 59. 65–71.
22. [Dem.] 33. 14–17.
23. Hyp. *Athen.* 1–5.
24. [Dem.] 34. 18–21.

C. Rejected offers of private arbitration
1. And. 1. 122.
2. [Dem.] 47. 43–45, 80.
3. Dem. 55. 9, 32, 35.
4. [Dem.] 40. 39.
5. Dem. 21. 104–19, 122.
6. [Dem.] 56. 11–18.

D. Private arbitration on stated terms
1. Isokr. 18. 9–15.
2. Isokr. 17. 17–19.

(B) ARBITRATION DURING TRIAL

Arbitrations in list A are treated separately from those in B since the former definitely occur during trial. Steinwenter 1925: 123–28 thinks that B8 belongs to A; that conjecture is disputable. The procedure in A1 is uncertain. Possibly it was a compromise presided over by the arkhon, as Is. 5. 18 might suggest: συγχωρούντων γὰρ ἡμῶν τῶι ἄρχοντι μὴ συναριθμεῖν ἀλλὰ συγχέαι τὰς ψήφους ("when we consented to the arkhon, not to count the votes but to mix them together"). Possibly the dikasts then acted as a panel of arbitrators, making an award that was agreed upon by the disputants, as 5. 29 suggests: ἡμεῖς δέ, ὦ ἄνδρες, ἐπὶ τοῦ δικαστηρίου, ὅτε ἠναγκάζομεν αὐτὸν ἀφίστασθαι τούτων, . . . ἀφεῖμεν αὐτῶι τοὺς καρπούς, οὕτω τῶν δικαστῶν γιγνωσκόντων ("Now, gentlemen, we in court, when we were compelling him to withdraw from the property, . . . remitted to him the profits, since this was the decision of the dikasts"). Alternatively, the dikasts had nothing to do with the award, and the final clause is to be translated: "seeing that the dikasts were (i.e., still) making their decision."[10] A subsequent (extra-judicial?) agreement is further implied, but vaguely, in the very next sentence: ὕστερον δ' οὐκ ἀναγαζόμενοι ἀλλ' ἑκόντες ἔδομεν αὐτῶι . . . ("and later, under no compulsion but voluntarily we gave him . . .").

As speculative explanation, I propose that there may have been a regular procedure for compromise in trials without fixed penalties after a verdict on the offense was given (i.e., before, during or after the penalty speeches). The appearance of the verb συγχωρεῖν in Is. 5. 18 is perhaps significant: the plaintiff in the *dike pseudomarturiōn* has been asked "to give his consent" or "to concede" to an arrangement. The same verb appears in [Dem.] 47. 43 (see section d apud fin.) when the speaker reports his consent to a lesser penalty, after the *boule* had given its verdict on the offense. It appears again in [Dem.] 53. 26 when Apollodoros reports that the defendant in a trial for having falsely attested to a summons (*graphe pseudoklēteias*) "asked the dikasts to impose a fine and asked me to concede (συγχωρῆσαι)"; Apollodoros claims that this happened "when the dikasts wanted to impose the death penalty on Arethousios" – the words need mean nothing more than that the dikasts had already voted (perhaps overwhelmingly) to condemn the man. Finally, comparison might be made to the use of συγχωρεῖν in Ptolemaic documents (see Pringsheim 1950: 32–33).

The allusion to compromise (or "concession") on penalties after a verdict has been reached (or all but reached in the case of Is. 5. 18) in three different trials thus suggests that there may have been a genuine procedure involved. In view of these instances, the request which the shady plaintiff of A2 makes for a reconciliation at the opening and closing of his speech (a *dike blabes*) might be more than an empty rhetorical topos. Furthermore, that same plaintiff makes clear that the proposed reconciliation is to precede the verdict on the offense ([Dem.] 48. 3 and 58). It might not be anomalous that in Is. 5. 18 the compromise is offered before the verdict on the offense is announced. We may have an instance of a difference of procedure in public and private cases: in the latter, litigants may have been offered the opportunity to compromise before the vote on the offense was completed, whereas in the former, compromise might only have been allowed after that vote (thus [Dem.] 47. 43 and 53. 26).

The courtroom agreement reported in A1, though accepted at the time by both parties (and hence successful), must have disintegrated quickly: there are no indications of any considerable lapse of time between the trial against Leokhares for false witnessing and the initiation of the suit for failure to carry out suretyship. Before that case (the *dike engues*, which is the subject of Is. 5), there was another attempt at extra-judicial settlement (B6).

[10] Wyse 1904 apud 29. 4, 5 understands the clause in the first way, i.e., the dikasts formulated the reconciliation, and compares the *dikastai* of a third-century Athenian inscription (*IG* II²1289) who διέλυσαν a dispute; while those *dikastai* might be arbitrators (so Thür 1987: 473), the context is too bare to warrant a conclusive interpretation.

(C) SUCCESSFUL PRIVATE ARBITRATIONS AND RECONCILIATIONS

The figures provided in chapter 1.1 and used again in chapter 3.1 are based on the lists presented above. In chapter 1.1, figures were reported in answer to three questions that arose during my examination of private arbitration in the orators: (1) How many private arbitrations were successful? (2) How many were initiated after a *dike* had been lodged or a *diadikasia* set in motion? (3) How many plaintiffs (in comparison with defendants) initiated *dikai* and then entered into private arbitration? A separate pool of arbitrations was created to calculate the figures for each question, depending upon the kind of information required by the question and the amount of relevant information provided by each instance of arbitration. Excluded from all three pools were cases which did not concern an issue which could be resolved in a court of law (although cases are included even if the rubric under which the case might be brought to court is vague, e.g. B17 and 20). One case (B23) was excluded immediately. Two other cases might, at first glance, be thought worthy of exclusion on the same grounds (B1 and C5). In these, a reconciliation is effected or requested in order to end ill-will between two parties; in B1, the request is made after one party has dropped a suit against the other; in C5, the request is made after one party has stopped threatening to bring the suit. Since in both cases the suit was a *dike phonou*, it seems possible that the reconciliations were requested in order that the former or would-be plaintiff in the *dikai phonou* might avoid trial for *kakegoria* (see chapter 3, n. 55). The two cases are therefore included among those concerning an issue which could be resolved in a court of law.

There are two further requirements for inclusion in a statistical pool which will help us determine an answer to our first question, the number of successful arbitrations. First, the negotiations must have passed the preliminary stage and preferably have reached the point at which a verdict was to be given or terms of compromise offered (i.e., the offer to negotiate was not refused at the outset and the negotiation itself was taken seriously – allusion to it in a speech is not a mere rhetorical ploy to depict an opponent as *philodikos*). Cases which are excluded on these grounds have been placed in list C. Secondly, the success or failure of the arbitration cannot be ambiguous. In order to be considered successful, the settlement must be accepted by both parties at the conclusion of the negotiation; the success of the settlement must be clear and beyond dispute. On these grounds, four of the twenty-four cases in list B must be excluded as ambiguous: nos. 3, 4, 22 and 24. In B3 (= Lys. fr. XIX B–S), it is not even clear whether a private arbitration did in fact materialize; the possibility that one did take place, however, remains viable on the basis of the ἕως clause (ταῦτ' ἐμοῦ προκαλουμένου οὐδεπώποτ' ἠθέλησε συνελθεῖν οὐδὲ λόγον περὶ ὧν ἐνεκάλει ποιήσασθαι οὐδὲ δίαιταν ἐπιτρέψαι ἕως ὑμεῖς τὸν νόμον τὸν περὶ τῶν διαιτητῶν ἔθεσθε). In B4, the plaintiff in the current suit alleges that a reconciliation had been effected between him and his opponent – but the latter apparently denied it. In B22, a verdict was given in default, but the surety for the losing party disputes its validity. Since the preliminary arrangements for the verdict appear to have been under dispute, and since the arbitral verdict is under dispute in the current case (a *paragraphe*, brought in response to a *dike engues* brought as a *dike emporike*), we can make no reasonable estimate concerning the success or failure of the arbitration. In B24, the arbitration is carried to an end, but the *diaitetes* apparently refused to give a verdict: "he did not acquit him of the charge, but he referred us to the court; for while he was not willing to convict Phormion on account of their friendly relationship (as we later learned), yet he shrank from acquitting him of the charge lest he commit perjury" ([Dem.] 34. 21). One party did heed the advice (decision?) of the *diaitetes*, and the case was re-initiated in court. While in one respect we can say the arbitration was successfully concluded, we can also say that it failed to find a solution for the dispute between the two parties. Additionally, B23 has already been excluded since it does not involve a legal issue – although we might note that it was a successful reconciliation.

Of the remaining nineteen arbitrations and reconciliations in list B, seven misfired at the final stage (verdict-giving or compromise acceptance: nos. 2, 6, 7, 9, 12, 14, 17); three others misfired, possibly at an advanced stage: nos. 11, 18, and 19. In no. 11, one party apparently died before the verdict was given or compromise offered; in no. 18, the *diaitetes* died; in no. 19, the *diaitetes* allegedly delayed, in connivance with one of the parties, until the other gave up his claim. Eight were successful: nos. 1, 8, 10, 13, 15, 16, 20, and 21. It is probable that no. 5 was also successful, even though it left the losing party in an unsatisfied, not to say angry, state of mind. Some of these arbitrations were successful for limited periods of time: no. 10 was successful for 14 years; no. 15 may have been successful for only a brief period; no. 16 lasted between 11 and 15 years; and in the case of no. 20, we may infer that a later arrangement was made, as the original reconciliation permitted. The temporary success of these agreements is in accord with the view expressed in chapter 3.1.a.

(D) INITIATING *DIKAI* AS A MANIPULATIVE STRATEGY

Five cases in list B (4, 5, 9, 14, and 17) do not furnish enough information to pinpoint the timing of the offer to refer the case to private arbitration (question 2); these are omitted from the statistical pool here. Moreover, B23 is once again excluded. Among the remaining eighteen cases in list B, only on two occasions (B2 and 7) is the offer probably extended before any legal action is taken; on sixteen occasions, the offer is made after a legal action has been initiated or a legitimate self-help remedy applied (B1, 3, 6, 8, 10, 11, 12, 13, 15, 16, 18, 19, 20, 21, 22, 24). In six of these cases (B1, 18, 19, 20,

21, 22), the request for arbitration emerges in a sequence of actions: after disputant *X* initiates an action and disputant *Y* counters with a *dike* or *graphe*. Figures from the other lists show the same trend: in list C ("rejected offers"), one offer was certainly made before filing the *dike* (no. 2) and another probably was as well (no. 6); one offer (no. 4) was probably made after the filing, and two offers were made after counter actions were initiated (nos. 1 and 5). The mutual agreements that formed the basis of the so-called "arbitrations on specified terms" (list D: *diaitai epi rhetois*) both followed the initiation of legal actions. While our quarry of evidence is limited, these figures nevertheless suggest that disputants used the court system to intimidate opponents into entering extra-judicial negotiations.

Different qualifications about the evidence are necessary concerning the figure for the much higher percentage of plaintiffs who initiate the proposal for private arbitration (question 3). In most instances, we do not have a full account of the proceedings. If we put together the twenty-three cases of private arbitrations and reconciliations in list B (omitting no. 23 once again) and the six cases of "rejected offers" in list C, we find ten cases in which the initiator of the proposal is not specified as accuser or accused, or as friend of one or the other (including B20 and 22 where unnamed *epitedeioi* and "those who were present" do not assist us in deciding whether these groups are to be identified as supporters of the accusing or accused party; C3 is ambiguous). In six of the remaining nineteen cases, the real or potential defendant initiates the proposal (B3, 6, 14, 24; C2 and 4). In nine cases, the real or potential plaintiff initiates it (B2, 9, 11, 12, 13, 15, 16, 17, and C6). In the four remaining cases where the initiator of arbitration is named, the proposal follows a counter-action (B1 and 21; C1 and 5); in each of these instances, the initiator is the accuser in the counter-action. It is the accuser, then, who most often initiates the request for private arbitration.

Among the cases in which the defendant initiates the proposal, C2 ([Dem.] 47. 43 and 45) is the most interesting. The anonymous speaker had earlier impeached Theophemos before the *boule*, charging him "with impeding the dispatch of the squadron and with defiance of public authorities" (Hansen 1975: 120, a succinct summary of 47. 42). After the *boule* had convicted him, but before the vote on the penalty (whether Theophemos was to be fined 500 *drakhmai* or whether his case should be heard by a dikasterion), Theophemos and his supporters offered an inventory of the equipment and promised "to submit the question of the blows" to any Athenian whom the prosecutor named (47. 43: it is unclear whether this issue was part of the actual accusation before the *boule*). The prosecutor thereupon consented (*sunekhōrēsa*) to a penalty of 25 *drakhmai*. The speaker later reports that Theophemos refused to submit the "question of the blows" to arbitration; hence he initiated an action for assault, whereupon Theophemos initiated a cross-action against him (45). Theophemos thus initiated the proposal for arbitration as part of a penalty-bargaining strategy when he was a defendant in a related case, but rescinded the offer when he was out of danger from the impeachment.

(E) TERMINOLOGY OF PRIVATE ARBITRATION IN OLD COMEDY AND TRAGEDY

Ar. *Wasps* 1417–1426 provides the first traces of the terminology that becomes associated with private arbitration in the fourth century:

> ΚΑ. οἴμοι κακοδαίμων. προσκαλοῦμαί σ' ὦ γέρον
> ὕβρεως. ΒΔ. ὕβρεως; μὴ μὴ καλέσηι πρὸς τῶν θεῶν·
> ἐγὼ γὰρ ὑπὲρ αὐτοῦ δίκην δίδωμί σοι
> ἣν ἂν σὺ τάξηις, καὶ χάριν προσείσομαι.
> ΦΙ. ἐγὼ μὲν οὖν αὐτῶι διαλλαχθήσομαι
> ἑκών· ὁμολογῶ γὰρ πατάξαι καὶ βαλεῖν.
> ἀλλ' ἐλθὲ δευρί· πότερον ἐπιτρέπεις ἐμοί,
> ὅ τι χρή μ' ἀποτείσαντ' ἀργύριον τοῦ πράγματος
> εἶναι φίλον τὸ λοιπόν, ἢ σύ μοι φράσεις;
> ΚΑ. σὺ λέγε. δικῶν γὰρ οὐ δέομ' οὐδὲ πραγμάτων.

Accuser: "How I suffer! Old man, I summon you to court on a charge of *hubris*." BD.: "*Hubris*? No, by the gods, don't summon him! Really – I'll pay the penalty for him – whatever amount you fix, and thank you besides." PH.: "No – I shall be reconciled with him of my own volition. For I admit I struck and knocked him about. Come over here. Tell me, do you refer the case to my decision – how much I ought to pay for this offence before I am your friend in the future, or will you make the pronouncement?" Accuser: "You make it – for I've no need of lawsuits or trouble."

MacDowell 1971b: 316 comments on ἐπιτρέπω in verse 1423: "here it does not refer to a formal arbitration, which could not be conducted by the accused." True, but the words (not only ἐπιτρέπω but also the "friendship terminology," χάριν προσείσομαι and εἶναι φίλον τὸ λοιπόν) do make use of the language of formal arbitration (see chapter 3.1.b); possibly the joke is that Philokleon is misapplying usual procedure.

Disputes are settled on-stage in tragedy, but not by adverting to the formal language of arbitration. Aiskhylos uses *diallakter* once (*Septem* 908) and Euripides uses *diallaktes* once (*Phoen.* 468); neither instance is technical. The closest we come to a private arbitrator is in Eur. *Phoinix* fr. 812 Nauck²: ἤδη δὲ πολλῶν ἡιρέθην λόγων κριτὴς/ καὶ πόλλ' ἁμιλληθέντα μαρτύρων ὕπο/ τἀναντί' ἔγνων συμφορᾶς μιᾶς πέρι./ κἀγὼ μὲν οὕτω, χὤστις ἔστ' ἀνὴρ σοφός,/ λογίζομαι τἀληθές, εἰς ἀνδρὸς φύσιν/ σκοπῶν δίαιτάν θ', ἥντιν' ἡμερεύεται . . . ("Many times before now have I been chosen judge and many times have I decided the arguments of witnesses in conflict about the same event. And I – just as any wise man – reckon up the truth, by examining the nature of a man and his day-to-day activities"). Aiskhines, who reports the speech (1 *Tim.* 152) also interprets it for his audience, drawing pedagogical analogy between the *krites* of Euripides and the *dikastai* in the dikasterion (153). For *krites* used of a private arbitrator, see Men. *Epitr.* 223 and 226.

(F) TERMINOLOGY OF PRIVATE ARBITRATION IN *AGORA* I. 3244 = SOKOLOWSKI 19

Ferguson 1938: 48–49 offers a discussion of the terminology of arbitration in his study of the first inscription concerning the Salaminioi (= *Agora I.* 3244). Some of his observations are incorrect. Since his discussion is still cited in modern literature, it seems worthwhile to correct the errors. The arbitrators, as he points out (p. 48), are called *diaitetai* (line 3) and *diallaktai* (line 83); "the latter name," he says, "is descriptive of their function: they mediated (διήλλαξαν) and their findings are appropriately called *diallagai* (No. 1, line 83)." The natural inference, of course, is that the *diallagai* are the terms of a reconciliation (see discussion in chapter 3.1.a of the most renowned *diallagai* in Athens); but for Ferguson (p. 49), they are "an arbitral order" and "δίαιτα and διαλλαγή were synonyms." The error that Ferguson makes is his assimilation of private arbitration to official arbitration: he assumes that the first step in a private arbitration is an attempt at reconciliation; hence he misinterprets *gignōskein* in line 5, about which he says (p. 48): "formal proceedings had to be taken (ἃ ἔγνωσαν οἱ διαιτηταί)", i.e., the preliminary reconciliation had failed and a verdict had to be given. The sentence in question runs (lines 2–8): ἐπὶ τοῖσ[δ]/ε διήλλαξαν οἱ διαιτηταὶ Σαλαμινίος τὸς ἐκ τῶ/ν Ἑπταφυλῶν καὶ Σαλαμινίος τοὺς ἀπὸ Σονίο ὁμο/λογοῦντας ἀλλήλοις καλῶς ἔχειν ἃ ἔγνωσαν οἱ δι/αιτηταὶ (names follow in text, lines 6–8). Trans. Ferguson: "The arbitrators (*diaitetai* [names follow]) settled the disputes between the Salaminioi of the Heptaphylai and the Salaminioi from Sounion on the following terms, both parties being in mutual agreement that *the decision* of the arbitrators was good" (italics, mine). For Ferguson, *gignōskein* can only mean an arbitral verdict; that is wrong. While the verb can and often does mean that (e.g. *AP* 53. 2), it can also be used of proposals made in the course of reconciliations and mean "think," or "propose," or even "decide," without implying that what is thought or offered as a decision is a verdict (cf. [Dem.] 41. 14: βουλομένων ἡμᾶς τῶν φίλων διαλύειν καὶ πολλῶν λόγων γενομένων, οὐχ οἷος ἦν ἐμμένειν οἷς ἐκεῖνοι γνοῖεν, "when friends wanted to reconcile us and after many discussions took place, he was unable to abide by whatever they proposed"). The terms recorded in the inscription, moreover, argue against the usage of *gignōskein* as implying a verdict; they are clearly terms of compromise, as, e.g. in lines 12–14, where both the successors to priests and priesthoods are to be selected by lot "from both groups taken together." If anything, the inscription demonstrates the usage of *gignōskein* to denote a proposal of reconciliation.

APPENDIX 3

Remedies for enslavement, kidnapping, and slave stealing in Athens and Rome

1 ATHENS

Two Athenian procedures call for our attention first: *aphairesis eis eleutherian* and the *dike exaireseōs*. In *aphairesis*, a third party removes an alleged slave into freedom.[11] This is an extra-judicial, self-help remedy. In the few references to *aphairesis* in the orators, the remedy (or alleged intention to use it) almost always occurs in response to the action of a self-proclaimed owner who attempts to seize (*agein*) his alleged slave; the usual sequence is therefore: seizure (*agein*) into slavery followed by removal into freedom (*aphairesis eis eleutherian*).[12] With the exception of two problematic instances of *aphaireseis* (which might represent abuses of the remedy), the individual who is seized appears to have been living in freedom before seizure; nevertheless, it is likely that one could also be "removed into freedom" while living as a slave.[13] If the alleged owner does not dispute the claim to freedom, then the *aphairesis* is successful and no further action need be taken. There is no instance of such an undisputed *aphairesis* in the orators. Instead, the alleged owner usually disputes the claim to freedom and initiates a *dike* against the third party rescuer which is called, apparently interchangeably, either a *dike exaireseōs* or *dike aphaireseōs* (an action for unlawful removal into freedom).[14] Probably at the time of the disputed *aphairesis*, the alleged owner requires the rescuer to supply three sureties

[11] There is no technical name for the third party who removes the alleged slave into freedom. Some scholars designate him by the Latin term *adsertor*; I have called him the "third party" or "rescuer."

[12] There are seven cases of *aphairesis* (including one "intended" case and one general reference) in the orators: Lys. 23. 9–11; Aiskhin. 1. 62–63; [Dem.] 58. 19; 59. 31–40; Is. frs. XVI. 1 and 2 B–S; Isokr. 17. 14 and 49 and a general reference in Isokr. 12. 97. In [Dem.] 58. 19, the preliminaries to the *aphairesis* are not recorded; we do not learn whether Theokrines' father "removed" the woman "into freedom" in response to a "seizure." In the passages from Isokrates, seizure does not appear to precede *aphairesis*; but these instances may represent abuses of the procedure (see n. 21).

[13] The two exceptions in which individuals appear to be living in slavery before removal into freedom are Isokr. 17. 14 and 49 and the general reference in Isokr. 12. 97. In Aiskhin. 1. 62–63, Hegesandros seizes Pittalakos (whom Aiskhines has described as a public slave) and claims him as his own slave; thereupon Glaukon "removes him into freedom." How a public slave could be seized as a private slave and then removed into freedom is problematic. MacDowell 1978: 83 suggests that the status of a public slave may have been "something like status of a metic."

[14] The terms are used without distinction in Isokr. 14. 8; see further Lipsius 640 n.15. Harpokration discusses the suit under *exaireseōs dike* and there refers to a lost speech by Isaios concerning an *aphairesis*, Ἰσαῖος ἐν τῆι ὑπὲρ Εὐμάθους εἰς ἐλευθερίαν ἀφαιρέσει ("Isaios in his speech, 'the removal into freedom on behalf of Eumathes'").

before the polemarch to guarantee the appearance of the alleged slave at the ensuing trial.[15] The defendant in these suits is probably the rescuer rather than the alleged slave.[16] If the defendant (the rescuer) is convicted of "unlawfully effecting a removal into freedom" (ὃς ἂν δόξηι μὴ δικαίως εἰς ἐλευθερίαν ἀφελέσθαι), presumably the slave is returned to the owner and the court assesses a penalty, half of which is paid to the state.[17] In instances reported in the orators occasionally the *dike exaireseōs* is concluded by a private arbitration before the case comes to court.[18]

One other Athenian procedure and offense should be mentioned in the present context: *apagoge* for *andrapodismos* (arrest for kidnapping or enslavement). An alleged *andrapodistes* could be arrested as a *kakourgos* and haled before the Eleven. If the alleged *andrapodistes* confessed his guilt, he would be treated as other *kakourgoi*: the Eleven would execute him. If he did not confess, then his accuser would indict him with a written *apagoge* and the Eleven would bring the case to court; if he were convicted there, he would be executed by the Eleven (see chapter 2.2.a).

Andrapodistai appear in our sources as one of the most frequently attested categories of *kakourgoi*.[19] Historians of Greek law usually state that the offense entailed the kidnapping of citizens and occasionally question whether the remedy could also be used in behalf of non-citizens.[20] In fact, the evidence is stronger for the latter category. The point is worth clarification since the interpretation of arrests in a number of plays

15 Information in our sources is limited. Probably rejection of the *aphairesis* and summons to the polemarkhos would occur at the same time, provided that witnesses were on hand for the summons. It is unclear whether the rescuer or the alleged slave supplies the sureties; cf. Lys. 23. 12, [Dem.] 59. 40, and Isokr. 17. 14.

16 Harrison 1. 178 takes the opposite view, that the alleged slave was the defendant.

17 The evidence for the financial assessment comes from [Dem.] 58. 21. The return of the slave is probable from Lys. 23. 12 (see Lipsius 641 and n. 18). Harrison 1. 22 n. 1, followed by MacDowell 1978: 80, thinks that the penalty "will be the assessed value of the slave, as settled by the jury, doubled," on the assumption "that the issue is simply the depriving the owner of ownership of the slave."

18 Aiskhin. 1. 63 (abortive); [Dem.] 59. 45 (apparently successful).

19 E.g., *AP* 52.1 (repeated in Pollux 8.102; Photios s.v. ἕνδεκα; Schol. Ar. *Wasps* 1108; *Lex. Seg.* 314–17); Lys. 10. 10; Isokr. 15. 90; Dem. 4. 47; Hyp. 5. 12; Adesp., *CGF* 239, 10–11; Men. *Sik.* 272. For a full catalogue of *kakourgoi*, see Hansen 1976: 37–44; in most of the twenty passages in which *andrapodistai* are specifically mentioned, the term forms part of a list of offenders; there is no definition of the offense. The exceptions, which are discussed above, are Hyp. 5. 12; Men. *Sik.* 272; and Lys. 10. 10 (repeated in Lys. 11. 6). Hansen (p. 46) has collected evidence that suggests that *leistai* (pirates or brigands) were also treated as *kakourgoi*. On the meaning of *leistes* and related terms, with citation of earlier bibliography, see Pritchett 1991: 315–22; Pritchett's presentation demonstrates that the terms *leistai* and *peiratai* are used interchangeably – i.e., there is no distinction, as in English, between piracy (by sea) and brigandage (by land).

20 Harrison 1. 165–66: "We have no evidence whether this procedure was available for the protection of other than Athenian citizens"; MacDowell 1978: 80: "Anyone who tried to enslave a free person was liable to arrest . . . as an enslaver"; similarly Todd 1993: 186–87; E. M. Harris 1994b: 181–82: "The meaning of *andrapodistes* poses no problem; the word refers to the person who makes a free person into a slave." On the other hand, Lambertini (1980: 3–8), a Roman legal historian, has interpreted the material correctly.

discussed in this book (see esp. App. 4 and 5) depends on our understanding of the charge of *andrapodismos*. While numerous references in fifth and fourth-century literary and epigraphical sources indicate that free men were victims of kidnapping, there is no unambiguous reference to an *andrapodistes* who is depicted as a kidnapper of an Athenian citizen.[21] Few passages which mention *andrapodistai* in legal contexts specify the status of the victim; the following provide information of varied value concerning the offender and his victim:

(1) In Hyp. 5 *Athen.* 12, the term is applied by a crowd to an Egyptian businessman in response to his treatment of a citizen in regard to a contract; this is clearly non-technical language.

(2) In Men. *Sik.* 272, the term is applied to a self-proclaimed citizen and his companions in response to their treatment of a girl whose identity is yet to be proven; she had been kidnapped from Athens and sold in a slave market in Karia to a "Sikyonian captain" (*Sik.* 13–14), possibly to the same man who is designated as one of the *andrapodistai* in 272.

(3) In Lys. 10 *Theomn.* 10 (repeated in Lys. 11 *Theomn.* 6), the victim of a hypothetical kidnapper is called a *pais* (boy); the term is ambiguous and might refer to a slave or citizen child.

(4) Harpokration's quotation (s.v. ἀνδραποδιστής) from a speech of Lykourgos limits *andrapodistai* to slave-stealers, but the definition need not be exhaustive: Λυκοῦργος ἐν τῶι κατὰ Λυκόφρονος 'θαυμάζω δ' ἐγὼ εἰ τοὺς ἀνδραποδιστὰς, τῶν οἰκετῶν ἡμᾶς ἀποστεροῦντας μόνον, θανάτωι ζημιοῦμεν' ("Lykourgos in his speech against Lykophron: 'I marvel that we punish *andrapodistai* with death – men who have robbed us only of our slaves . . .' ").

(5) Plato *Laws* 879a formulates a statute by which a man who takes possession of someone else's slave in fraudulent circumstances is to be prosecuted for *andrapodismos*; 955a formulates a statute by which a man who prevents a free man from appearing as a litigant or witness is likewise to be prosecuted for *andrapodismos*. We are only concerned here with the use of the term *andrapodismos* to refer to the kidnapping of free and slave alike.

(6) Pollux 3. 78 defines the victim as either slave or free: ἀνδραποδιστὴς δ' ἐστὶν ὁ τὸν ἐλεύθερον καταδουλούμενος ἢ τὸν ἀλλότριον οἰκέτην ὑπαγόμενος ("An *andrapodistes* is an enslaver of a free man or a stealer of someone else's slave").

The admissibility of the following evidence is questionable for determining the status of victims in fourth-century Athens but is nevertheless interesting:

(7) In Lys. 13 *Agor.* 67, the speaker alleges that Agoratos' brother was

[21] A computer-based study of Aristophanes and the orators of *andrapodismos* and *andrapodizō* (and compounds) shows that, with two exceptions, the words are always used of the enslaving of a *polis* or its population. The two exceptions are Isokr. 17. 14 and 49. In both instances, the status of the allegedly "kidnapped" man is under dispute: the speaker alleges the man is the slave of Pasion (his opponent) and that Pasion has made up the story that he stole the slave (whom Pasion claims is free); in fact, the speaker claims, it is Pasion who has hidden away his own slave.

convicted of abducting a *paidiske* (slave girl) from Corinth and that he died in prison; while the offense and conviction may have taken place in Corinth and the term *andrapodistes* is not used, nevertheless, the scenario conforms to "slave-stealing."

(8) In Lukian *Dis Kateg.* 13 and 16, Loose-Living (*Methe*) prosecutes the Akademy for *andrapodismos* (whether by a *dike* or *graphe* is not specified); the former alleges that the latter has stolen her former slave, Polemon.

Among the ancient testimonies, item no. 5 demonstrates that the term *andrapodistes* was used to refer to kidnappers of free and slave alike, but cannot be used as the basis for a definition of the legal offense of *andrapodismos.* Item no. 4, however, justifies the inference that "slave-stealing" was an offense under the law (no. 3 is ambiguous).[22] The offense of slave-stealing conforms to the general substance of other offenses committed by *kakourgoi*, if they are viewed as offenses against property (cf. *lōpodutai* and *kleptoi*, "clothes-stealers" and "thieves"). The threatened arrest of Athenogenes as an *andrapodistes* in Hyp. 5. 12 should warn against interpreting every occurrence of the word as technical terminology; in such a case (and Men. *Sik.* 272 may be another), the phrase might mean no more than a disparaging "Arrest the rat!" and *andrapodistes* might denote any low creature typified by the loathsome slave-stealer. The lack of ancient attestation of an *andrapodistes* depicted as a kidnapper of an Athenian citizen is curious; but probably we should accept the evidence of Pollux and other late sources that such a scenario was possible.[23] Athenian legal sources rarely define offenses. Athenians knew what they were.

It is conceivable that other means, in addition to executing an *apagoge*, were available for bringing an *andrapodistes* to justice. Neither a *graphe* nor a *dike*, however, is certainly attested (see Harrison 1. 166 n.1). The title of a lost speech of Antiphon (*peri andrapodismou*, fr. II 7 B–S) suggests the existence of a *dike* but is tenuous evidence. Two comic scenarios are best explained if there were private suits for *andrapodismos* (Men. *Kolax* 130–32 and Ter. *Ad.* 248–49, App. 5, cat. IX. 2 and III. 22 respectively). A trial for *andrapodismos*, mentioned above (no. 7), appears in Lukian *Dis Kateg.* 13 and 15–17; it appears to be subsequent to a summons rather than an arrest: note that Lukian's phrasing in c. 13, ἕπου, μιαρέ πρὸς τὸ δικαστήριον ("follow, oh brute, to court!") translates a Roman *in ius vocatio* (cf., e.g. Plautus *Asin.* 490 and *Curc.* 721) and does not replicate an Athenian one.

These procedures (*aphairesis*, the *dike exaireseōs*, and *apagoge* against *andrapodistai*) pertain to Athenian inhabitants (or to those pretending to be) who have been enslaved or stolen in Athens. But Athenians might very well

[22] Deinarkhos composed a speech ὑπὲρ ἀνδραπόδων (fr. LXVI B–S); Lipsius 640 and n.14 thinks this refers to a *dike andrapodōn* (attested in *AP* 52. 2 but without definition) and that it concerned the disputed ownership of a slave; for the view that it concerned damage done to or by a slave, see Harrison 2. 22 n. 10. For a general survey of the usage of the term *andrapodon* with citation of earlier bibliography, see Pritchett 1991: 170–73; ancient references on p. 173 might nurture different speculations about a *dike andrapodōn*.

[23] Late sources: Schol. Ar. *Plut.* 521; *Lex. Seg.* 219. 2 and and 394. 11.

find themselves enslaved elsewhere: (1) pirates might capture them as they travelled on the open sea or brigands might seize them, whether dwelling on Attic soil or living abroad;[24] (2) foreign soldiers or sailors might capture them as an act of war; (3) foreigners (acting out of personal motives or in behalf of their *poleis*) might seize (*sulan*) Athenians travelling abroad as an act of reprisal (a retaliatory seizure in response to a "first unjust seizure of goods or person").[25] As a result of any of these scenarios (which might in fact be hardly distinguishable from one another), an Athenian might be sold in a foreign slave market (if he or she had not been killed on the spot). Judicial redress might be available if an agreement existed between Athens and the foreign *polis* where the Athenian is sold, or if a special grant of protection had been conferred upon the individual by the foreign *polis*.[26] In the absence of such agreements, the only hope of freedom would depend on the slave-buyer's willingness to accept a ransom for the individual;[27] there was no legal requirement that he should do so. If he agreed, then relatives or friends might come to the financial assistance of the victim,[28] or else a wealthy citizen in the foreign *polis* might intervene and pay the ransom, perhaps as a gesture to gain political influence in the victim's home *polis* and to acquire prestige in his own.[29] Ancient authors refer to such ransoming as Hellenic in spirit and numerous inscriptions honor the private ransoming of captives and kidnapped persons.[30] Nevertheless, successful acts of ransoming may not have been common. W. K. Pritchett offers this assessment of epigraphical sources: "Considering the incessant warfare and the activity of pirates, this limited evidence suggests that, once

[24] For the extensive and frequent occurrence of plundering by pirates and brigands in the Greek world in the fourth–first centuries BC, see bibliography cited in Davies 1984: 285–90, to which add McKechnie 1989: 101–41 (with focus on the fourth century) and Pritchett 1991: 312–48.

[25] See Davies 1984: 287 for succinct description of retaliatory *sulan*; Gauthier 1972: 210–19 distinguishes four kinds of *sulan* from a "judiciary" standpoint. For a survey of the full range of meanings of *sulan* and *rhusiazein*, see Pritchett 1991: 73–132 and 358–63.

[26] For a survey of the protections offered by treaty agreements and individual arrangements (*asulia* and proxeny), see Davies 1984: 285–90, with citation of relevant bibliography.

[27] On the ransoming of captives of open warfare or piracy, see Pritchett 1991: 245–97. He furnishes a catalogue (pp. 272–83) of forty inscriptions relating to "ransoming either during warfare or by piracy."

[28] E.g., [Dem.] 53. 8–13; cf. Wyse 1904: 556 (apud Is. 7. 8). The speaker of [Dem.] 53. 11 quotes his opponent's statement, " 'don't you know' he said, 'that the laws bid that a person ransomed from the enemy becomes the property of the ransomer, if he fails to pay the ransom price?' " The legal mechanism by which such enslavement could occur in Athens (and occur without fraud) is not self-evident. The existence of such a law is usually accepted by legal historians (e.g. Harrison I. 165), but the context of the law's paraphrase in [Dem.] 53.11 is suspicious.

[29] For instances of foreigners paying ransoms for Athenians, see, e.g. *IG* II^2 283, 2; 284; 399, 10f.; 844.

[30] Polybios 9. 42. 8 (210 BC): P. Sulpicius Galba (cos. 211) agrees to allow the Aiginetans to send envoys to kindred *poleis* for ransom money, ἐπεὶ τοῦτο παρ' αὐτοῖς ἔθος ἐστίν ("since this was their custom"). Cf. Men. *Mis.* 315–16. Honorary inscriptions: e.g. *IG* II^2 283; 284; *IG* IV. 756; *IG* XII. 5. 36; 7. 5; 8. 3.

captured or abducted, the chance of being ransomed was slight, particularly in the light of the fact that, next to funerary inscriptions, honorary ones comprise our largest collection of epigraphical documents, and, relatively speaking, we have so few examples of ransoming throughout several centuries."[31]

2 ROME

The *vindicatio in libertatem* (a claim to establish freedom) is traditionally said to take place when an *adsertor* claims in court the freedom of a man living in slavery against the claim of his alleged owner; the *vindicatio in servitutem* (a claim to establish slave status) is said to take place when an alleged owner claims in court that a person living in freedom is his slave against an *adsertor*'s contrary claim that the man is free. It is likely, however, that under the *legis actiones* there was no formal distinction between the two actions.[32] In the late Republic, such claims were heard before the *decemviri stlitibus iudicandis*; the presiding magistrates in the earlier Republic are unknown.[33] The form for such claims is assumed by legal historians to be similar to that of an ordinary *vindicatio in rem* in which the dispute would concern ownership (e.g. whether a particular slave belonged to one or the other claimants) rather than status: the claim of the *adsertor libertatis* was probably "*HUNC EGO HOMINEM EX IURE QUIRITIUM LIBERUM ESSE AIO*" ("I say that this man is free by Quiritary right"), while the alleged owner claimed "*HUNC EGO HOMINEM EX IURE QUIRITIUM MEUM ESSE AIO*" ("I say this man is mine by Quiritary right").[34] The fine for losing such a case was set at fifty *asses* by the *XII Tables*; the limit on the fine (regardless of the value of the alleged slave) illustrates one way in which the *causa liberalis* was exceptional under the *legis actiones* system of law. Gaius explains that the disparity between the costliness of other set fines and the cheapness of this one was *favore scilicet libertatis, ne onerarentur adsertores*

[31] Pritchett 1991: 283.

[32] Franciosi 1961b: 53–87 persuasively argues that the *causa liberalis* should be seen as a variation of the ordinary *actio sacramento in rem* since the claim of the alleged owner does not correspond to an equivalent claim on the part of the *adsertor* (see n. 34 below for the phrasing of the competing and equivalent claims in an *actio in rem*); furthermore, the two actions (*vindicatio in libertatem* and *vindicatio in servitutem*) were indistinguishable under the *legis actiones*, "esse non sono azioni autonome, bensì i due momenti, opposti ma equivalenti, della dialettica dell' *actio in rem*" (p. 71).

[33] See chapter 2.2.b, n. 52.

[34] This, in general, is the view of Roman legal historians, e.g. Franciosi 1961b: 52ff.; Kaser 1966: 75; Watson 1967: 220f.; Jolowicz and Nicholas 1972: 134. The probable Latin formula for the *adsertor* is based on the regular formulae for *vindicatio* which are supplied by Gaius 4. 16, according to which the plaintiff says, "*HUNC EGO HOMINEM EX IURE QUIRITIUM MEUM ESSE AIO SECUNDUM SUAM CAUSAM. SICUT DIXI, ECCE TIBI, VINDICTAM IMPOSUI; et simul homini festucam inponebat. adversarius eadem similiter dicebat et faciebat*" ("'I affirm that this man is mine by Quiritary right according to his proper title. As I have declared, so, look you, I have laid my staff on him', and at that moment he laid his rod on the man. His opponent spoke and did the selfsame thing." Trans. Zulueta).

("obviously in order to favour freedom by not burdening assertors of freedom").[35] Two other features of the *causa liberalis* made it exceptional under the *legis actiones*: a representative (i.e., the *adsertor*) could sue and defend and such cases were allowed retrial.[36]

What action preceded appearance in court? Watson supposes that any citizen could act as an *adsertor ad libertatem* and summon the alleged owner before the magistrate.[37] Repeated phrases for a symbolic seizure (*manu adserere liberali causa*, "to make a claim of freedom") used of or by the *adsertor* occur in Roman Comedy; the phrases are also attested in legal contexts in other sources.[38] Franciosi is right in arguing that the various expressions (e.g. *liberali causa manu adserere*) used in these texts do not provide evidence for the formulaic words used in making the claim before the magistrate; rather, they represent words used by the *adsertor* during the extra-judicial seizure into freedom. The preponderance of this language suggests that Watson's view of the preliminaries to a *vindicatio in libertatem* is correct, that the *adsertor* made a symbolic seizure and summoned the self-proclaimed owner to court. That this language when first used by Plautus and Terence is not simply translation (i.e., without any legal reality in contemporary Rome) of the language used for the Athenian procedure of *aphairesis eis eleutherian* is guaranteed by its use in a Plautine joke at *Rudens* 971–74.[39]

An alleged slave would become free by his *adsertor*'s success and the alleged owner's failure in the *vindicatio*. The action protected citizens of Rome (whether Roman citizens or citizens of allied cities) who had been enslaved in Rome; it also protected such citizens of Rome who had been enslaved in cities that had treaties of friendship or *hospitium* with that city. Roman citizens (in the extended sense, i.e., citizens of Rome or of her allied cities) who were enslaved abroad in a country which had no treaty with Rome had no legal redress. Conversely, foreigners who had been seized by a Roman in Roman territory could be enslaved; these would have no legal redress unless their native cities had treaty arrangements with Rome.[40]

Whether there was any specific legislation against kidnapping in the Plautine period is a matter of debate. A *lex Fabia de plagiariis* ("Fabian law on kidnappers") is the subject of *Digest* 48. 15 and *Coll.* 14. 2–3. Legal historians are generally agreed that two chapters of that law are conveyed

35 Gaius 4. 14, trans. Zulueta.

36 On the rarity of representatives allowed to sue: Gaius. *Inst.* 4. 82–87; on re-trial of these suits: Cicero *de domo* 29. 78.

37 For discussion of the limited – and tricky – evidence, see Watson 1975: 96–97, and esp. n. 76; Franciosi 1961a and 1961b: passim and esp. 7–8 and 162–67; cf. Kaser 1966: 75 n. 63 and 98 n. 45.

38 *Poen.* 905, 964, 1102, 1348, 1392; *Curc.* 491, 668, 709; *Rud.* 973; *Ad.* 194. For other sources, see Franciosi 1961b: 142–47.

39 For interpretation of these verses, see Franciosi (1961b: 145), who argues that *manu adserere* here does not refer specifically to *vindicatio in libertatem*, but rather to an ordinary *legis actio sacramento in rem.* Cf. another joke at *Miles* 961 which mentions the *festuca* in the context of manumission.

40 Watson 1967: 161–64, citing *D.* 49. 15. 5. 2 (Pomp.).

by extracts from Ulpian (*Coll.* 14. 3, 4–5) and Callistratus, a late classical jurist (*D.* 48. 15. 6. 2).[41] Lambertini, the author of a recent monograph on *plagium*, argues that the latter's version adheres more closely to the original wording of the law.[42] The extract is as follows: "It is laid down by the *lex Fabia* that a freeman who hides another, freeborn or freed, against his will, or keeps him in fetters or buys him, knowingly and with malicious intent, or who is an accomplice in any of these things, and anyone who persuades another's slave, male or female, to run away from his master or mistress, or conceals him or her against the will or without the knowledge of the master or mistress, or keeps him in fetters, or buys him, knowingly and with malicious intent, or who is an accomplice in the matter, is liable to the penalty [of the statute]."[43] While the sources report a variety of penalties, a number of scholars have accepted the fine of 50,000 sesterces, to be paid to the public treasury (Ulp. *Coll.* 14. 3. 4–5), as belonging to the early period of the law's existence; these scholars differ, it should be noted, in defining that "early period."[44]

Cicero *pro Rab.* 3.8 (63 BC) contains the first explicit reference to the law (*de servis alienis contra legem Fabiam retentis*, "about his having detained another man's slaves contrary to the Fabian law"); the date of the law's inception can only be conjectured. Some scholars (e.g. Voigt) have dated it as early as 209 BC, after the battle of Cannae; others (e.g. Mommsen) have dated it as late as events after the Social War.[45] Most recently, both Molè and Lambertini have supported Mommsen's date, and this date appears to hold sway now.[46]

[41] The sources for the law (fuller than those mentioned here) are discussed by Lambertini 1980 and Molè 1966 with full bibliographic citation. Among earlier treatments, those of Voigt (1885: 328–32), Huvelin (1915: 108–14), and Berger (*RE*, Suppl. VII, cols. 386–94, s.v. "*Lex Fabia*") should be consulted. A "third chapter" of the same law, cited only by Ulpian (D. 11.4.1.2), provides the means for making searches for runaway slaves. Lambertini 1980: 16 thinks it is a gloss on the second chapter. Both Voigt and Huvelin identified a legal scenario based on this chapter in *Merc.* III 4, 663–65; Molè 1966: 120–23 demonstrates the weakness of their arguments, but is not, in my view, conclusive.

[42] Lambertini 1980: 13–14. A majority of scholars have favored the extract from Ulpian; see Molè 1966: 123–24. The arguments for neither side are conclusive.

[43] *D.* 48. 15. 6. 2, trans. Watson. *Lege Fabia cavetur, ut liber, qui hominem ingenuum vel libertinum invitum celaverit invinctum habuerit emerit sciens dolo malo quive in earum qua re socius erit, quique servo alieno servaeve persuaserit, ut a domino dominave fugiat, vel eum eamve invito vel insciente domino dominave celaverit, invinctum habuerit emerit sciens dolo malo quive in ea re socius erit, eius poena teneatur.*

[44] E.g., Voigt 1885: 333 n. 34 and Huvelin 1915: 112 both put the law's inception at the end of the third century BC; Lambertini 1980: 37 puts the law after the Social War. Lambertini is right to see the penalty in line with other penalties of the first century BC; but there is no reason, in my opinion, to think that that penalty was attached to the offense when it was first formulated.

[45] For a date in 209 BC: Voigt 1885: 319–27; at the end of the third century: Huvelin 1915: 114–16 (p. 116 n. 4 citing the dates of earlier scholars); 183 BC: Pernard 1900: 167; after the Social War: Mommsen 1899: 780 n. 4.

[46] Molè 1966: 119–41; Lambertini 1980: 34–37; Robinson 1995: 33. Only Molè examines the evidence for dating in detail. It should be noted that he addresses only the two Plautine passages (*Curc.* 620 21 and *Merc.* 663 65) which Voigt 1885 had adduced and accepted. A pity.

The strongest reason adduced by the two Italian scholars for the later date concerns the penalty: a penal law which threatened a fixed pecuniary fine would require the establishment of a standing *quaestio* or the prior existence of the *quaestiones perpetuae.*

Scholars supporting a date in the late third century brought forward Plautine scenarios which seem to use the language of the law. Voigt and Huvelin both adduced *Merc.* 663–65, in which they saw references to the so-called "third chapter" of the law (see n. 41); Voigt saw another reference in *Curc.* 620–21, this time to the first chapter of the law, concerning the selling of *ingenuae.* Voigt took the wind out of his own sails, however, when he refused to argue for allusions to the law in *Poen.* In regard to Hanno's claim that the pimp has stolen (*subripere*) his *liberas ingenuasque filias* (*Poen.* [1343–44]), Voigt argued that Hanno as a foreigner would not be allowed to plead in court; in regard to the plot against the pimp to entice him to conceal Agorastocles' slave in his brothel, Voigt pointed out that the pimp himself was acting *in bona fide* (*Poen.* III 5). Voigt's juristic sense prevented him from following through the linguistic logic of his argument: the essential point is not whether these cases could in fact be brought into a court of law in Rome (the pimp has been framed and has not a single witness to prove that he has not acted *sciens dolo malo*; whether Hanno is or is not capable of bringing a case into court, he can still make a threat that will refer to a real charge). The essential point is the use of particular language in a specific legal scenario. This was seen by Gratwick in his 1969 dissertation: the language of *Poen.* 1100 ff., 1239ff, and 1245 ff. does not "reproduce Greek law or represent a compromise between Greek laws and Roman." The pimp "could be called *in ius* because *sciens dolo malo* (cf. 899) *liberas ingenuas* (cf. 900, 1240) *emerit* (896) *celaverit* (1239)."[47] Gratwick's conclusion stands: if the *lex Fabia* was not in existence during Plautus' time, then a law, very much like it, was.

Conjecture alone can provide a date for the "similar law." As mentioned earlier, only the penalty in the *lex Fabia* requires a date after the mid-second century BC. It is clear, however, that the penalties for the offenses covered by the law changed over time, while the basic substance of the offenses remained in place. Death (Ulp. *D.* 48.15.1), labor in the mines (Hermog. *h. t.* 7; Paul. *Coll.* 14.2.2.), crucifixion (Paul. *Coll.* 14. 2.2), confiscation of property and deportation (Paul. *Coll.* 14.2.2) are all attested. The phenomenon is not unique. The praetorian edict on *iniuria*, for example, does not appear to have altered the substance of the earlier law in the *XII Tables* but rather to have created an estimatory machinery for the penalty.[48] I suggest that the "similar law" concerning the stealing of free men and slaves may have entered existence, as Voigt argued, in 209 in the wake of Cannae; possibly it entered as a delict, and possibly with a fixed monetary penalty – far less than the 50,000 sesterces reported by Ulpian but more than the 50 asses of

[47] Gratwick 1969: 411–12 with notes. [48] See chapter 5.2.b.

the freedom process. At a later stage, possibly in the aftermath of the Social War, the offense was fully criminalized and the penalty magnified.

My hypothesis cannot be proven (nor can Molè's and Lambertini's). I allow the plausibility of mine to hang on one Plautine passage in particular, leaving the others as back-up support. The passage is *Poen.* 1239–40, clearly a Plautine joke, clearly a Plautine addition, in which Hanno explains to his daughters why "*in ius vos voco*" (1232): "*quia annos multos feilias meas celavistis clam me / atque equidem ingenuas leiberas summoque genere gnatas*" ("because for many years you have concealed my daughters from me – and indeed free-born and native daughters to boot, born from the very best family"). If this passage does not specifically allude to the "similar law," then we must be prepared to believe that Plautus has fortuitously anticipated by a century the language of the *lex Fabia.* That supposition, in my opinion, is tantamount to believing in the tooth fairy.

APPENDIX 4
Controversial summonses in Rudens *and* Persa

In *Rudens* and *Persa,* the slave-owners are summoned to court in highly dramatized fashion: in the former, the pimp Labrax has been held at bay by *lorarii* (floggers) for the greater part of Act III before Plesidippus appears on-stage and hales him, plaintively calling for assistance, to court; in *Persa,* the court summons in IV 9 is the climax of the "legal plot" scripted and rehearsed by Toxilus and his friends. In each play, the alleged criminal reappears on-stage in the last act of the play. What happened in the interim – between the march to the courtroom and the reappearance of the accused on-stage? Are we to imagine, via the brachiology of dramatic time, that the praetor heard the claims and assigned the case (*in iure*) and that a hearing took place at which a verdict was given (*apud iudicem*)? That imagined sequence, however, is fraught with problems: do the procedures and penalties match the offense in each play? and are we to imagine the same sequence in the Greek originals – or is it possible, or even necessary, that different resolutions appeared in them?

1 *RUDENS*

1 (A) PRELIMINARIES

Rudens, while set in Cyrene, has a number of Athenian characters: Daemones, an exile from his homeland after losing his fortune there (33–38), Plesidippus, apparently residing in Cyrene (43) for reasons never told us, and Palaestra, who was kidnapped from home as a child, sold to the pimp Labrax, and brought to Cyrene (39–40). Daemones either rents or owns land, and certainly owns slaves. Plesidippus apparently has access to the court system and also owns slaves. The two Athenian men, therefore, must have been accorded some sort of lawful status in Cyrene, whether as individuals (through grants of *asulia* or proxeny) or as citizens of Athens (by treaty) is indeterminable. Palaestra, on the other hand, could be protected by law in Cyrene under one circumstance only: if Athens and Cyrene have an agreement.

Plays set in foreign cities have complicated legal issues. The legal rights of foreigners, to a great extent, depend upon treaty relations between the foreigner's homeland and the city in which he sojourns.[49] Did Diphilos, the author of the Greek original of *Rudens*, assume a precise knowledge in his audience of treaty arrangements between Athens and Cyrene? Was redress in fact available for the Athenian girl who has been kidnapped, sold to a pimp, and brought to a foreign *polis*? Unfortunately, this question, even if posed of any Greek play with a similar scenario, cannot be answered; e.g. we cannot say that Greek playwrights, as a matter of practice, (1) assumed the existence of treaties, even where there were none; or (2) adhered to the particular historical situation, taking into account the treaty or non-treaty relationships between *poleis*. We do not possess a single Greek play of an international complexity for which we could substantiate either the first or second practice with positive external evidence.[50]

Reconstructing the international situation depicted in the Greek original will then depend on our treatment of the Roman adaptation. In *Rudens*, it has sometimes been assumed that treaty relations are in operation: once the girl is alleged to be free, redress is available in the court system of Cyrene. *Curculio* and *Poenulus* also center on the plight of kidnapped individuals in foreign *poleis*. Gratwick, who incorporated a detailed study of legal problems associated with kidnapping in his 1969 dissertation on the *Poenulus*, iterated his general conclusion in 1982: "Greek dramatists took care to arrange things so that a former citizeness of City One is, through exposure or kidnapping, in the power of a *leno* in City Two which has no reciprocal arrangement regarding civil rights with One, precisely to prevent the mere demonstration of the truth about the girl's origin from

49 For discussion of individual grants of *asulia* and proxeny and judicial remedies which are granted in interstate treaties, see Davies 1984: 285–90 and, in more detail, Gauthier 1972.

50 Men. *Sik.* 133–35 mentions a Sikyonian man who incurred a penalty in a lawsuit with a Boiotian *kata sumbola* ("in accordance with the treaty"); if the last words do represent what Menander wrote (see Gomme and Sandbach ad loc.), then we have at least one explicit reference in New Comedy to an inter-state treaty; whether one in fact existed between the two *poleis* at this time is a different question. Some plots that seem to involve the intermarriage of citizens of different *poleis* might be explained by reference to the existence of historically attested cleruchies (settlements of Athenians in other states who retain their citizenship). In *Ph.*, Phanium, born of an Athenian father and a woman who lived on Lemnos, can marry the Athenian Antipho since her mother was probably an Athenian (i.e., a daughter of an Athenian *klaroukhos* settled in Lemnos). The mother is nowhere said to be "Lemnian" (see esp. 873, 942, 1004). For the vicissitudes of Athenian cleruchies (Lemnos, Imbros) during the period of New Comedy, see Ferguson 1911: 49–65. Wyse 1904 on Is. 6. 13 is open to misinterpretation and Ogden 1996: 178–79 is confused.

seeming sufficient to ensure her release and her owner's punishment."[51] My own view is slightly different from Gratwick's but cannot be argued here: it is possible (and indeed plausible for the Greek original of *Curculio*) that Greek playwrights allowed for the operation of treaties in their plays of foreign setting, even without explicit allusion to them – whether or not such treaties in fact existed – in order to ensure the operational logic of the plays for their audiences.[52] Comedy, on this view, allows for legal fictions (cf. Roman law's "legal fictions," such as the *actio Publiciana*). But for *Rudens*, no decision on this question is necessary: as we shall see, the charge on which the pimp is summoned to court need not be interpreted as one against international law.

I (B) OFFENCE AND PROCEDURE

Before the play begins, the pimp Labrax had accepted a part-payment from Plesidippus for the sale of Palaestra and then had taken ship with her and other slaves to sell in Sicily. Labrax, however, suffered shipwreck; when he first appears on-stage, still wet from the sea (II 6), he is ignorant of the whereabouts of Palaestra. Plesidippus, having been apprised of Labrax's departure and having searched the harbor in vain, leaves the stage during I 2 to find the pimp who has not appeared for his appointment to complete the sale. The distraught lover returns to the stage in III 6, discovers Labrax, and summons him to court:

ego hunc scelestum in ius rapiam exsulem.
age, ambula in ius. LA. quid ego deliqui? PL. rogas?
quin arrabonem a me accepisti ob mulierem
et eam hinc abduxti? (859–62)

I shall drag this criminal to court, the outlaw.
Come, march along to court. LA.: What have I done? PL.: You ask?
Did you not accept a part-payment from me for the woman
and then abduct her from here?

The pimp is forcibly haled off-stage and returns at V 1, 1281ff. to announce the verdict of the *recuperatores*: *abiudicata a me modo est Palaestra* (1283: "Palaestra has just now been taken away from me by judicial decision").

"Part-payment" was a Greek practice (*arrhabōn* or *arrha*) which, while widely attested in Hellenistic papyri, appears rarely in Athenian sources.[53]

[51] Gratwick 1982: 108–09; 1969: 407–93.

[52] If "Therapontigonus" and his sister are not Epidaurians in the Greek original of *Curculio*, then the girl's freedom and marriage to "Phaedromus" (who is not explicitly said to be an Epidaurian but is likely to be one) depend on treaty arrangements which permit *epigamia* between Epidauros and her natal homeland. See App. 5, add. 3.

[53] Millett 1990: 176: there is only one "concrete example" drawn from Athens (Is. 8. 23); a "metaphorical reference" appears in a late fourth-century comic fragment, *hetairas arrhabōn* (Athenaios 586d, 596b).

The practice (*arrabo* in early Latin) may have been known in Rome in the second century BC; whether it had any legal significance there during this period, however, is a matter of dispute.[54] Greek *arrha* imposed a liability on both buyer and seller: if a buyer who had furnished *arrha* withdrew from the sale, he forfeited the amount of the *arrha*; if the seller refused to accept the remaining payment, he was liable to a penalty. Theophrastos *Nomoi* F 21. 6 (S–M) reports that in Thourioi, the penalty for the refusing seller was the full price of the object for sale and in special cases (it appears) both the full price and the *arrha*; in some places, he reports, the laws bid that an action be brought against a seller who did not accept full payment. Pringsheim, on the basis of his study of Hellenistic papyri, concluded that in "Greek law," the refusing seller was liable to pay the potential buyer twice the amount of the *arrha* received; in the papyri, the penalty is usually made actionable by a clause of execution.[55]

The *opinio communis* maintains that in the Diphilan original of *Rudens*, the pimp is summoned to court for failure to execute the sale. Opinions diverge, however, concerning Plautus' treatment: has he depicted a Greek or Roman legal scenario? Pringsheim, upon examining the different contours of Greek and Roman sale, concluded that the scenario was Greek and has not been adapted to Roman law.[56] MacCormack, on the other hand, argued that the part-payment scenario is Roman: "Plautine texts permit the inference that if *arra* is given, the seller is bound to deliver the object sold, and that the buyer may obtain a judgment which in some way allows him to enforce the obligation against the seller."[57] Watson maintains a different position, but nonetheless a Roman one. His starting point is an argument which dates the introduction of consensual sale in Rome to the late third century; since consensual sale created enforceable obligations, there was no need for part-payment after its introduction (cf. Gaius 3. 139). Accordingly, *arrabo* did not have a legal function in Rome in the second century BC; nevertheless, Watson argues, it did have a social function (similar to a handshake) and Plautus exploits this in a way that would be

54 See Pringsheim 1950: 415–29; Kaser 1971: 547–48; Watson 1965b: 46–59; further bibliography is cited by these authors. Watson 1965: 47–49 argues that *arra* would be well-known to a Roman audience; Williams' proviso (1956: 425–26), should be kept in mind: Roman familiarity with *arra* might stem from familiarity with Greeks from Magna Graecia and does not demonstrate that Romans had in fact adopted the practice for themselves.

55 Pringsheim 1950: 412–15; he discusses the evidence at length on pp. 333–428. "Greek law" is a notion that must always be scrutinized carefully.

56 Pringsheim 1950: 416–23.

57 MacCormack 1971: 364 with n. 20, alluding to judgments in *actiones in personam*, which might have allowed the recovery of an object and hence the enforcement of an obligation against a seller. The argument is based on an interpretation of Gaius 4. 48 where the *iudex* of "former times" (*sicut olim fieri solebat*) is said to condemn the defendant to hand over the actual property. While Gaius had ascribed the judgment to *legis actiones sacramento in rem*, nevertheless, MacCormack argues (and is bolstered by Kaser's adherence to the view) that Gaius was referring "not to *actiones in rem* but to *actiones in personam*." See further n. 67 apud fin. below.

recognizable to his audience. Plautus has thus adapted the Greek scenario so that it represents Roman law: the buyer can bring an action "to *compel him [i.e., the seller] to perform*", and "*arra* would not enter into it at all."[58]

While the scholars just mentioned have offered reasonable interpretations of Plautus' depiction of the *arrabo* transaction, they falter when it comes to explaining the verdict: whether a Greek or Roman scenario is depicted, a monetary penalty is expected – not the surrender of a material object (Palaestra) as happens in the play. Nonetheless, each has provided an ingenious explanation by which the verdict reported in 1283 can be made to fit the offense he has perceived in 861–62.[59] The endeavor is perhaps misconceived. The fact that so much ingenuity must be expended to explain the verdict is symptomatic of a deeper complexity in Plautus' depiction of offense and remedy. A more compelling explanation is that the legal scenario of the Diphilan play was incapable of easy adaptation to Roman law and that Plautus was not overly concerned about resulting disjunctions in his depiction of offense, procedural remedy, and verdict.

A starting point for demonstration of this last view is Paoli's reconstruction of the Greek scenario. Focusing upon the procedure used to bring Labrax to justice, Paoli concluded that the pimp's offense was the enslavement of a free woman; in the Greek original, the pimp was not summoned to court, he was arrested as an *andrapodistes* (= enslaver).[60] Paoli developed his interpretation accordingly:

(1) The forced summons addressed to Labrax (859–60; cf. 853, 868, 876, 777–78) represents *apagoge* (arrest).
(2) The grounds for the *apagoge* in the Greek original cannot be the pimp's failure to carry out the sale of "Palaestra," which the pimp had guaranteed by accepting an *arrha* from "Plesidippus" (861–62), for the simple reason that that is not cause for arrest in Athens. Rather, the grounds must be wrongful enslavement (*andrapodismos*), which is alluded to by Trachalio in his claims of Palaestra's Athenian and freeborn birth at 736–39 and by Labrax' protests of ownership at 711–12 and 723.
(3) Plesidippus only learns of Palaestra's free status at 1285ff.; therefore, when he makes the arrest for *andrapodismos* in the part of the Greek original that corresponds with 859–60, he must be basing his claim on

[58] Dating of consensual sale: Watson 1965b: 40–41. Social function of *arrabo* in Rome: Watson 1965: 46–51 and 1971: 131–32. Compulsion to perform: Watson 1965: 52, citing *D.* 19. 1. 13. 23 and 30; and 19. 1. 6. 1, in which the "significant thing is that in all of them we are told not that an action for damages can be brought if the defendant fails to fulfil the obligation, but that an action can be brought to *compel him to perform.*"

[59] Pringsheim 1950: 423 explained the verdict thus: "Labrax was not condemned to perform a contract; he was condemned to pay back the arra. Being penniless he could not pay and therefore, to evade personal execution, voluntarily handed over the slave to the plaintiff. If this was the consequence, though not the tenor, of the judgment a poet might express it in the words of the leno '*abiudicata est*'." The gist of MacCormack's and Watson's explanations of the verdict are given in the two preceding notes.

[60] Paoli 1976 (= 1951): 119–23 and nn. 22–25.

his own intention to free the girl upon the execution of her sale (a common enough practice in Athens) – which the pimp has thwarted by abducting the girl after accepting the *arrha*. "Plesidippus" therefore would be claiming that the girl was "freed."[61]

(4) Labrax' report of the legal proceedings at 1281ff. does not square with the results of an *apagoge*: if he had not confessed his guilt and if the Eleven had then brought his case to trial where he was subsequently found guilty, he would be penalized with death (as foreseen in 777–78); instead, we learn that his penalty is the surrender of Palaestra (1283). Possibly the Eleven, while not believing "Labrax," found the young lover's case against the pimp doubtful and so ordered the case to be heard before an official arbitrator as a *dike exaireseōs* (see App. 3. 1).

The most significant and attractive feature of Paoli's reconstruction is the recognition that the forced summons of the Roman play might represent an arrest in the Greek original; once that point is granted, then it follows that *arrha* cannot have been the offense. Paoli's interpretation, however, requires that an Athenian's claim to freedom would be protected in Cyrene. While, in my view, such a presupposition is not, in theory, illegitimate for reconstructing the operative logic of a play, it is unnecessary. A few modifications of Paoli's depiction of the offense, procedure, and verdict in the Greek original will demonstrate this and at the same time avoid the special pleading required for the third point of his argument.

First, concerning the offense: *andrapodismos* is not limited to the enslaving of a citizen; in fact, it is better attested as "slave-stealing" (App. 3.1). There is no need, therefore, to incorporate "Plesidippus's plans to free Palaestra" as a desideratum for the arrest or to presuppose the existence of a treaty between Athens and Cyrene. "Plesidippus" can claim that "Palaestra" is his slave and "Labrax" can be arrested as an *andrapodistes* (here "slave-stealer") on the hypothesis that the internal lawcode of Cyrene is portrayed as a replica of that in Athens (i.e., slave-stealing would be penalized). Necessarily the abused *arrha* would be taken into account when each party presented his case: the means (*arrha*) by which "Plesidippus" claims to own "Palaestra" is inextricably bound up with the charge of slave-stealing; hence we are to understand that juxtaposition of means (*arrabo*) and charge (abduction) when Plesidippus, in Plautus' play, summons the pimp in III 6, 861–62: *quin arrabonem a me accepisti ob mulierem et eam hinc abduxti?*

As mentioned earlier, *arrha* appears but seldom in Attic sources; its rare appearance provides grounds for doubting its widespread use there. While we can only speculate about remedies for its abuse in Athens, Diphilos' audience may not have been much better informed. If there was a specific suit against violators of *arrha* in Athens, then "Plesidippus" could have

[61] Paoli 1976 (= 1951): 121 n. 25, citing: [Dem.] 48. 53; 59. 30; Men. *Epitr.* 568–71 (Sandbach); Plautus *Epid.* 243–44; *Merc.* 531–32; *Most.* 22–24; *Persa* 33–36; *Poen.* 360–63; Athenaios 590d.

summoned "Labrax" to court for that offense; but he also may have felt he had a good chance of success (and a more expedient means) for convicting him if he arrested him on the charge of slave-stealing. A potential plaintiff in Athens would in many cases have alternative remedies available and would choose what seemed best for him (see chapter 1. 1); his decision might prove good or bad. But Diphilos as playwright was not interested in presenting an airtight case for the magistrate's or dikasts' approval; he chose a spectacular means to bring the pimp to justice in a manner that made sense in Athens.

We do not know how Diphilos conceived of the legal consequences of *arrha*. We should consider, then, what other (i.e., non-legal) function *arrha* served in his play. Why, for example, part-payment – and not full payment? If "Plesidippus" had paid in full, he could expect to receive "Palaestra" immediately, in the way, for example, that Toxilus receives his beloved from the pimp Dordalus in *Persa* (II 3 and IV 3). Full payment entails immediate possession, part-payment does not. In *Rudens*, part-payment creates an interval of the utmost dramatic importance for the action of the play: it allows Labrax to abscond with Palaestra. In Diphilos' play, this may have been the major function of *arrha*: to create that interval.

Let us strengthen Paoli's case that arrest underlies the summons of Plautus' play. Paoli had pointed out, in the passages indicated above (no. 1), that the pimp is haled to court by a forced summons amidst threats of imprisonment and execution. All the allusions to prison and the executioner (778, 857, 872, 876, and 889) foresee immediate action, and do not refer to a more distant future, e.g. to execution or imprisonment after a court hearing. Thus, e.g. at 777–78, Trachalio tells Daemones to guard the pimp carefully, *nam promissimus / carnufici aut talentum magnum aut hunc hodie sistere* ("for we have promised the executioner either the production of an Attic talent or the man himself this very day"). The only Athenian procedure by which an accuser could expect the immediate participation of an "executioner" was arrest to the Eleven. There is no Roman counterpart: an executioner would play no role in handling a charge for failure to perform a contract nor in exacting the penalty for such an offense. Another detail points to the Athenian procedure: the executioner is located in the harbor, and the harbor is part of the city in the Roman play (856–57). But a Roman executioner must dwell outside the city limits; there appears to have been no such prescription for the Eleven in Athens.[62]

A close examination of a series of passages in the play, moreover, suggests that the meeting with the executioner, implied in III 4, 777–78, was a formal denunciation of the pimp's crime; in the original, *apagoge* was preceded by *endeixis* (chapter 2. 2. a). Consideration of the action that took place before the play's beginning will clarify:

[62] Roman executioner: Mommsen 1899: 48 and n. 1, citing Plautus *Pseud.* 331 and Cic. *pro Rab.* 5. 15. For speculation about the location of the Parabuston, the court at which the Eleven presided in Athens, see Boegehold 1995: 178–83.

(1) Undesignated persons (*alii*) had informed Plesidippus of the pimp's departure (64–65); the *alii* are undoubtedly the friends of the young man who appear with him on-stage in I 2.

(2) Plesidippus and his slave, upon hearing the report, had immediately gone to the executioner, taking along with them the friends who had observed the pimp's departure (cf. 65, 89–93, 778). Plesidippus and companions promised "either the production of an Attic talent or the man himself this very day" (778). The meeting with the executioner represents the denunciation or *endeixis* to the Eleven in the Greek original. *Endeixis*, we should recall, apparently did not require that the criminal be caught in the act (chapter 2.2.a, at nn. 30–40). Labrax was not caught in the act of stealing Palaestra, nor did Plesidippus himself see him carry her off – but his friends did. Plesidippus' friends are therefore witnesses to the crime. Their testimony is essential for the denunciation, and will be essential once again when, in the scenario envisioned by the Greek playwright, the arrested *andrapodistes* is brought before the Eleven.

(3) After the meeting with the executioner, Plesidippus had remained in the harbor with his friends to search for and arrest the *andrapodistes* (89–93). Trachalio, instead of accompanying the search party, had begun a slow return to the shrine of Venus (II 1. 306).

In the course of Plautus' play, Plesidippus first appears on-stage with his friends in I 2, to see whether the pimp has arrived at the shrine of Venus. He and his friends depart almost immediately for the beach when survivors from the shipwreck are spotted in the distance. Plesidippus and Trachalio do not encounter one another during this scene (hence the designation of the slave's return as "slow") and the two do not meet again until the interval between III 4 and III 6. Trachalio, upon reaching the shrine in II 2, had remained there, while Plesidippus had persisted in the search at the beach. But at the end of III 4, Trachalio leaves the stage to fetch Plesidippus and to announce the capture of Labrax. When he returns in III 6, Plesidippus accompanies him without his friends; apparently, in haste to apprehend the pimp, he neglected to collect and notify them.

The friends are not, however, entirely forgotten; indeed, their presence is essential for the legal scenario of the Greek original. In the midst of his forcible seizure of the pimp (III 6, 855–57), Plesidippus sends Trachalio to the shore with the following instructions:

> *abi sane ad litus curriculo, Trachalio,*
> *iube illos in urbem ire obviam ad portum mihi,*
> *quos mecum duxi, hunc qui ad carnuficem traderent.*
> *ego hunc scelestum | in ius rapiam | exsulem.*
> *age, ambula in ius.* (855–60)

> Go full speed to the shore, Trachalio,

tell them to head toward the city and meet me at the harbor –
the men I took with me – to hand this fellow over to the executioner.
I shall drag this criminal to court, the outlaw.
Come, march along to court!

Who is to carry out the arrest in the Diphilan original? Lefèvre, who thinks that the offense pertains to *arrha* and that the procedure envisioned is a summons and not arrest, supposes that "Plesidippus" does not himself go before the magistrate; the friends deliver the pimp and carry out the prosecution.[63] That reconstruction is impossible on Lefèvre's own premise, that the offense has to do with the *arrha*: only the injured party could bring such a suit. But the remedy, we have seen, is *endeixis* followed by *apagoge*. It is conceivable that a third party (i.e., not the injured party) could make an arrest for slave-stealing; but "Plesidippus" must nonetheless be present to claim that he is the owner of the stolen slave. Thus in the Greek scene corresponding to III 6, "Plesidippus" plans to meet his friends in the harbor, to inform them to appear before the magistrates with their testimony and possibly to ask them to carry out the arrest themselves – or else to assist him in so doing. The presence of the witnesses obviates the need for the girl's appearance before the Eleven; if the case were to come to trial, however, her attendance would undoubtedly be necessary. While Plautus has tried to adapt the scenario to a forcible summons, the traces of the Greek scenario remain in the awkward pastiche of 855–59: the backward reference to the executioner's role, the new instructions for Plesidippus' friends, the forced summons.

Let us turn now to the verdict. If my modifications of Paoli's reconstruction of the offense and remedy are correct, it is clear, once again, that the verdict given by Plautus could not have stood in the Greek original. Diphilos' audience would expect some explanation of how the pimp, as a convicted *andrapodistes*, had escaped the death penalty. Paoli's reconstruction of the verdict can be modified. Let us consider the circumstances of the pimp and "Plesidippus" at the moment of arrest: the pimp is in great danger; "Plesidippus," for his part, perhaps realizes that his claim to own "Palaestra" is not irrefutable since it rests on the *arrha*. In this situation, the most expedient solution is for the two men to reach a private agreement on their way to the Eleven, either by themselves or with the assistance of a third party – the friends in the harbor would be a likely choice. Plesidippus' instructions to Trachalio to gather up the friends to meet him in the harbor (855–57) is then a remnant of the far more prominent role that Diphilos in the Greek comedy intended them to play – even if that role was performed off-stage. The two men were then reconciled: the pimp would give up the girl and the young man would drop his charges in return. Probably "Labrax" explained some of the

[63] Lefèvre 1984a: 27–28.

details in a monologue upon his return to the stage (corresponding to *Rudens* 1281ff.).[64] Alternatively, some other character (Trachalio, for instance) may have furnished the report.[65]

According to this interpretation, the offense (*andrapodismos*), remedy (*endeixis* followed by *apagoge*), and conclusion (a private arrangement) of the Greek original are incapable of easy and accurate adaptation. Plautus has transformed the arrest into a forced summons, but he has not made the offense clear in terms of Roman law. As for the verdict, only ingenious explanation can make it fit whatever specific offense is hypothesized for the Roman play. Nonetheless, the verdict does make evident the upshot of the Greek reconciliation without burdening the finale with finer detail – such as the role played by the friends of "Plesidippus" in the Diphilan play. Would Plautus' audience understand the action of the play? Jurists might scratch their heads in bewilderment, but the average spectator would undoubtedly understand that Labrax had committed an offense and then was made to pay for it: he had absconded with a girl who rightfully (whether by Greek or Roman law) should have been put in Plesidippus' hands.[66] Some in the audience might have recognized in the verdict a solution that was perhaps appropriate for an ordinary *vindicatio in rem* concerning the ownership of a slave (cf. Gaius 4. 16 and 48); few would recall that the girl had not been present for the trial.[67] The choice of magistracy might pose a difficulty: why has Plautus assigned the verdict to *recuperatores* rather than to a *iudex*? *Recuperatores* appear elsewhere in Plautus only in *Bacchides* 270; these are the two earliest literary references to the magistrates. In *Bacchides*, the *recuperatores* are said to have executed a judgment concerning a debt (and may have given the verdict) in a case between an Athenian (= *civis*) and Ephesian (= *peregrinus*). If *recuperatores* had jurisdiction in private disputes between *cives* and *peregrini*, then their

64 A parallel for such a monologue appears at *Curc.* 679 ff.; see chapter 4.2.d and App. 5, cat. no. II. 1.

65 It is clear that Plautus has made considerable alterations to the last act of the play; Daemones, in particular, has suffered change – he is now a first-class swindler. I do not think it possible to reconstruct the final scenes, beyond positing the following: the conclusion of the legal scenario would be reported; "Palaestra" would be betrothed to "Plesidippus"; a decision would be made about the trunk, probably with "Daemones" presiding – the contestants may have been "Trachalio" and "Gripus" if the pimp did not return to the stage (and esp. if an immediate departure from Cyrene had been one of the terms of the agreement). This is pure speculation, but far less radical than Lefèvre's (1984a) and Kuiper's (1936).

66 For juristic bewilderment: cf. Broggini 1957: 69–70.

67 The regular formula for *vindicatio* is supplied by Gaius 4.16 (cited in App. 3, n. 24). That a verdict in an *actio in rem* might have been a condemnation *in ipsam rem* during the middle Republic can be argued on the basis of Gaius 4. 48 (albeit a corrupt and much disputed passage); in favor of this interpretation, see Zulueta 1953: 264 and Kelly 1966: 69–71 (contra MacCormack: see n. 57).

appearance at *Rudens* 1282, as Paoli suggests, would not be incomprehensible to the Roman viewers.[68]

2 *PERSA*

In *Persa*, which is set in Athens, the pimp Dordalus unwittingly buys a citizen girl disguised as a foreigner who is alleged to have been abducted from deepest Arabia (*furtivam, abductam ex Arabia penitissuma*, 522). The sale is part of an intricate plot scripted and directed by Toxilus. All goes according to plan. When the sale of the disguised citizen girl is completed, her father, the parasite Saturio, appears on cue to claim her (IV 9). The following exchange takes place between pimp and parasite after the latter has made himself known as the girl's father:

> *SAT. age ambula in ius, leno. DO. quid me in ius vocas?*
> *SAT. illi apud praetorem dicam. sed ego in ius voco.*
> *DO. nonne antestaris? SAT. tuan ego caussa, carnufex,*
> *quoiquam mortali libero auris atteram,*
> *qui hic commercaris civis homines liberos?*
> *DO. sine dicam. SAT. nolo. DO. audi. SAT. surdus sum, ambula.*
> *sequere hac, scelesta feles virginaria.*
> *sequere hac, mea gnata, me usque ad praetorem – VI. sequor.* (745–52)

> SAT.: Come – march to court, pimp. DO.: Why do you summon me to court?
> SAT.: I shall tell you there before the praetor. Right now, I am summoning you to court.
> DO.: You're summoning a witness, too, aren't you? SAT.: Listen, murderer,
> shall I rub the ears of any living freeman for your sake –
> you who buy up freeborn citizens?
> DO.: Let me speak! SAT.: Forget it. DO.: Hear me! Sat.: I'm deaf,
> follow along this way, you criminal polecat devourer of marriageable girls.
> Follow along this way, my daughter, to the praetor – VI.: I'm following.

Dordalus returns to the stage at the beginning of V 2 to lament his situation in a canticum:

> *perii, interii! pessumus hic mi dies hodie inluxit corruptor,*
> *ita me Toxilu' perfabricavit itaque meam rem divexavit.*
> *vehiclum argenti miser eieci [amisi], neque quam ob rem eieci, habeo.* (779/80–82)

[68] It is possible that the Greek scenario corresponding to the (fictive) trial before the *recuperatores* in *Bacch.* 261–73 was concluded by a private arbitration presided over by "Pelagon" (see App. 5, cat. x. 4). Cf. Franciosi 1961b: 20–21; Kelly 1976: 47–48 on *Bacch.* 270.

I'm dead, done in! The worst most rotting day of my life dawned today,
so awfully has Toxilus tricked me and destroyed my estate.
Wretch that I am, I have shelled out a cartload of money nor have
I anything wherefore I shelled it out.

Scholars have offered two competing reconstructions of the Greek legal scenario in IV 9. The first is Wilamowitz' and is endorsed by Paoli and Witt.[69] Wilamowitz supposed that the parasite in the Greek scene corresponding to IV 9 availed himself of two self-help remedies: first he removed his daughter into freedom (*aphairesis eis eleutherian*);[70] he then arrested the pimp as an *andrapodistes* (here, an "enslaver of a free person") and haled him away to the Eleven.[71] The parasite's description of the pimp conforms to that of an *andrapodistes*: *qui hic commercaris civis homines liberos* (749: "you who buy up freeborn citizens"; cf. 845). After pimp, parasite, and entourage leave the stage, the following events take place off-stage: before arriving in the presence of the Eleven, the parasite accepts a bribe from the pimp – in return for a tidy sum, he will forget about the arrest. The parasite does not return in the final act because he has gone home with his daughter to enjoy a private feast purchased with his newly-acquired earnings.

According to this view, Plautus has adapted the hypothesized legal situation of the original in this way: (1) he has omitted the *aphairesis* entirely; (2) *apagoge* (arrest) on a charge of *andrapodismos* has become a summons (*in ius vocatio*, with a Roman legal joke in the accused's question about the presence of witnesses). The Roman summons might have been understood as a preliminary to a charge of kidnapping or as the initial step in a *vindicatio in libertatem*.[72] Upon the pimp's arrival on stage in the final act, the Greek and Roman audiences will have different expectations: after the summons, the Roman audience will expect some indication of the pimp's acquittal or else the fine he paid upon condemnation, whereas after the *apagoge*, the Greek audience will await an allusion to the pimp's acquittal or means of escape from the death penalty (i.e., the private agreement between the pimp and the parasite). Plautus has omitted specific details from his adaptation.

Partsch raised two objections to Wilamowitz' hypothesis – neither of them fatal: (1) the pimp is ignorant of the girl's free status when he buys her

[69] Wilamowitz 1971 (= 1893): 260–74; Paoli 1976 (= 1951): 118; Witt 1971: 234; similarly Huvelin 1915: 221 n. 1.

[70] See App. 3.1.

[71] If the scenario is to operate fully in accord with Athenian law, "Saturio" must appear in Athenian rather than Arabian garb; an Arabian would not have access to the remedy. "Toxilus" exits at the end of IV 8, immediately before the arrest. The pimp will surely know that he has been duped; but he has no witnesses to prove it. On the other hand, if "Saturio" were to appear in Arabian garb, the audience will probably not pause to consider whether he has a legal right to carry out the arrest; the scenario will proceed according to the legal fiction that he does. The director of the play will make the decision.

[72] See App. 3. 2.

– a charge of enslavement or kidnapping cannot be seriously entertained; and (2) if "Dordalus" in the Greek original had paid out a large sum of "hush-money" to Saturio, which does not seem to be the case from 782, Plautus would not have omitted its mention.[73] Against Partsch's first objection: the pimp has not a single witness to the sale who is not also one of the conspirators; regardless of the truth, it is impossible for him to prove ignorance of the girl's status. He has been successfully "framed" for the crime. Against Partsch's second objection: Dordalus' remark at 782 must be examined, *vehiclum argenti miser eieci [amisi], neque quam ob rem eieci, habeo* ("Wretch that I am, I have shelled out a cartload of money, nor have I anything wherefore I shelled it out"). The verse cannnot support Partsch's interpretation. *Vehiclum argenti* defies precise assessment (cf. 781, *meam rem divexavit*), but it surely could entail a great sum. *Quam ob rem*, literally, "for what cause (or thing)" might refer to any reason, cause, or material object on account of which the pimp "shelled out" his money; the indefinite reference might very well be to an extorted sum (large or small) in addition to the sham Arabian captive and the sixty minae expended on her – or it might not. The verse is, without question, vague. Plautus is undoubtedly abbreviating the Greek original at this point in his hurry to dramatize the ensuing party scene.

Partsch himself offered an alternative reconstruction which has been endorsed by recent commentators:[74] In the Greek original corresponding to IV 9, the parasite had only availed himself of one remedy, an *aphairesis eis eleutherian*, as was foreseen in 163, *continuo tu illam a lenone adserito manu* ("immediately make a formal claim on her from the pimp"). After the parasite performed the *aphairesis* or "removal," no further legal action (e.g. a *dike exaireseōs*) was necessary, since the pimp accepted the parasite's claim. When the pimp appears subsequently in the Greek play, he makes no mention of the events following the *aphairesis eis eleutherian* because no judicial action was initiated. According to this view, Plautus has introduced the summons to represent an Athenian extra-judicial procedure for which there is no precise counterpart in Roman law; the summons initiates a *vindicatio in libertatem* – a judicial (rather than extra-judicial) remedy. Plautus omits all details about this trial because none took place in the Greek model.[75]

Partsch's reconstruction is, in my opinion, the more problematic one and should be rejected. It entails a scene in the Greek original that is even more abbreviated than the one in Plautus – and yet this scene should be the dramatic climax of all the rehearsal and contrivance that has preceded it. Are we really to expect that the pimp was threatened with no retributive

[73] Partsch 1910: 613.

[74] Partsch 1910: 612; Müller 1957: 25–29; Woytek 1982: 37.

[75] Partsch 1910: 611–13 only alludes to the possibility of such a trial; Müller 1957: 25–29 assumes that one took place during the interval between IV 9 and V 2. Partsch, Woytek, and Müller discount the charge of kidnapping made in 749 as mere bluff.

action in the Greek original and that he himself allowed the girl's removal, admitted he was wrong, shook hands with his adversary, and left the stage in abject but peaceful defeat?

The reconstructions of both Partsch and Wilamowitz, however, indirectly call attention to an oddity in the Roman play that is worth consideration. Why is there no claim made of the girl's freedom – no equivalent to a "removal" through a symbolic seizure – in *Persa* IV 9, the very scene in which both accounts of the Greek model concur in envisioning such a removal – in Partsch's view, as the main fare, in Wilamowitz', as the appetizer to the banquet of arrest? Preliminaries to a Roman *vindicatio in libertatem* are represented elsewhere as being similar to *aphairesis eis eleutherian.*[76] Yet none of these preliminaries appear in the scene under discussion. Unless the scene has been abbreviated in transmission (and I do not think that is a necessary inference), the absence of a claim to freedom allows three observations about Plautine dramaturgy. (1) Plautus is not concerned to present a scene which accords with the legal expectations he has created elsewhere in the play (cf. Toxilus' planning of the stratagem at I 3, 163 and the pimp's foreshadowing of the event at IV 7, 716–17). The neglect of expectation is similar to the one that occurs in *Poen.* III 5 (App. 5, add. 4), where a scenario of *furtum manifestum* is depicted to create a dramatic effect of short duration which is inconsistent with the scenario of *furtum nec manifestum* depicted in the slave's plan at I 1, 183–84. In *Persa* IV 9, the neglect of expectation is evident when the preliminaries to a *vindicatio* are eclipsed and only a summons for one is depicted (Partsch) or when the *vindicatio* is eclipsed entirely and a summons for kidnapping is presented (Wilamowitz). (2) The effect of this neglect (like that in *Poen.* III 5) is to economize dramatic effect. Attention is focused on the action of the summons, a telescoped climax for the preceding masquerade. (3) The focal point of the scene, the summons, provides opportunity for a Plautine joke, which should be added to the treasury of humor that is dependent on the *antestatio*-motif.[77] Dordalus at 747 asks, *nonne antestaris* ("aren't you going to summon a witness?"). According to the *XII Tables* I 1, if the accused resists a summons, the accuser is to appeal to witnesses and then apply force. Dordalus' question, which has been interpreted by Woytek as a strategy for buying time, should instead be interpreted as Plautine metatheatrics.[78] In the culmination of the legal scenario that had been scripted by Toxilus and rehearsed by the actors, Dordalus reminds Saturio that he has forgotten an important line: the call for witnesses. But Dordalus, perhaps the gentlest of pimps in Roman Comedy, appears to know from the moment of Saturio's arrival that the game is up for him (740, 741–43); he himself has not resisted. Plautus retains control: the legal scenario is itself parodied. Humor

[76] See App. 3.2, n. 38.
[77] See Zwierlein 1990: 281–83.
[78] Woytek 1982: 399. Metatheatrics in *Persa*: Slater 1985: 37–54.

is of course added by the fact that all the potential witnesses – the fellow conspirators – have left the stage.

3 CONCLUSIONS

This examination of the summonses in *Rudens* and *Persa* demonstrates the problems of reconstructing the original Attic legal scenarios from "incomplete adaptations" (see chapter 2. 2. c). It is worth noting that while the hypothesized Greek originals in both cases conclude with extra-judicial settlements, Plautus has not treated them in the same way. In *Rudens*, he has created a trial before the *recuperatores* (cf. *Bacch.* 261–73); in *Persa*, he has left the aftermath entirely vague – readers and spectators might conclude that a trial did in fact take place, or that Dordalus made a private settlement. The dénouement of the legal scenario and its conformity to the preceding action does not interest Plautus so much as does the brou-ha-ha of a march to court.

The reconstructions of the Greek models offered here have a bearing on the larger thesis of chapter 2 – i.e., that arrests and summonses in Athens were often executed with a view to out of court settlements. We now have two more cases in which arrests are commenced but not carried out. In the Greek original of *Rudens*, the distraught lover planned in advance for the pimp's arrest (cf. 777–78); his later plan to meet his friends in the harbor (cf. 855–57) entailed an intention to prepare them to act as witnesses, possibly as prosecutors – or even as extra-judicial mediators. Whether "Plesidippus" planned to settle in advance or not, his subsequent agreement with the pimp shows the capacity of arrest to effect out of court settlement. In the Greek original of *Persa*, the entire scenario by which the disguised citizen girl was sold to the pimp and then reclaimed by her father was carefully planned and rehearsed. Given that circumstance, it would be highly unlikely that the plotters should want their case to come before the magistrates. Nonetheless, an arrest is made. Surely here we can point to a case where the intention of the arrester is to settle in private. The parasite of the Greek original may have had more sykophantic coloring than the avid eater of Plautus' play. The scenario of arrest followed by private agreement is analogous to the scenario of suits and indictments being dropped before being decided in court, with this important difference: once an arrest is made but before it is carried out before the Eleven, it would be in the interest of the *kakourgos* to settle as quickly as he could in private – the stakes of trial were far too high for him. Men who make arrests are using a weapon of powerful manipulative value. The arrester of an alleged *kakourgos* can give him a choice "give me what I want or put your life on the line in court". It is not surprising that we do not hear more about the abuse of such a primitive self-help measure in the orators: the criminals who appear there can afford to hire logographers and are usually "higher-class" criminals than the footpads, thieves, slave-stealers, and enslavers who make up the category of *kakourgoi*.[79] But these are the very characters whom we find, not infrequently, running across the stage of New Comedy and occasionally haled away to prison. That they come to agreement with their arresters rather than risk execution at the hands of the Eleven may be a mark of the comic genre; but it may also be a reflection of an Athenian propensity to use the law to settle their disputes extra-judicially.

APPENDIX 5
Threats of lawsuits and self-help remedies in Graeco-Roman New Comedy

A. CRITERIA FOR ASSESSING THE PROVENANCE OF LEGAL SCENARIOS IN ROMAN COMEDY

Situations which pertain to threatening, initiating, or carrying out lawsuits or lawfully endorsed self-help measures in New Comedy are catalogued below.[80] The catalogue is the raw material for the analysis in chapter 2 of pre-trial intimidation and manipulation in New Comedy. In each instance of a threat from a Roman play, I have attempted to determine its provenance ("probably Greek," "Roman," "indeterminable"). The designation "probably Greek" does not mean that the threat in the Roman play is articulated in the same way as it was in the (hypothesized) Greek original; it means that a threat which adverted to the operation of the Athenian legal system or to self-help remedies sanctioned by law probably appeared there. The designation thus includes passages in which the Roman playwright has adapted the threat to Roman law and legal terminology – but it excludes threats which are arguably wholesale Roman additions. Only threats of the latter sort are designated "Roman."

An obvious objection to this endeavor must be stated: there is no guarantee that a threat or summons in a Roman play appeared in the Greek original; the threat or summons might be Roman addition, a spooning of spicy Roman legal sauce to satisfy the unquenchable Roman palate with its own home-grown recipes. The rejoinder: it is true that we can never know for certain whether such utterances represent similar ones

79 Hansen 1976: 54. We have scant evidence for the actual arrests and trials of *kakourgoi*: only Lysias 13. 67–68 (a *lōpodutes*), Is. 4. 28 (a *kleptes*); [Dem.] 25 *hypoth.* and 87 and Dein. 2. 12 all refer to the same case (a *hierosulos*). See chapter 2, n. 35.

80 Kelly 1966: 62–64 attempts to approximate a "cause list" from Roman Comedy, and includes situations in which "one character summons or threatens to summon or is advised to summon another before the praetor; though once or twice a lawsuit is reported from the past (whether truly or falsely)." He uses his list of thirteen instances to show (p. 64) that "it is remarkable how generally comic litigation conforms to the hypothesis that inferiors do not tend to sue superiors, but only superiors inferiors, or persons of equal status." Costa 1890: 419–62 catalogues Plautine evidence for judicial magistrates and competencies, procedures under the *legis actiones*, and stages in a trial (e.g. *in ius vocatio*, pp. 445–47).

in the Greek original unless we possess the original itself; nevertheless, any of five criteria may establish such a strong likelihood in a given case that a threat or its application in a Roman play did or did not belong to the Greek original, that we are justified in working with the resulting reconstruction, always keeping in mind its tentative nature. The criteria (some of which are more persuasive in combination) are the following:

(1) The threat itself is an integral part of the original play. (a) This criterion is applied below when characters explicitly design a strategy, organic to the plot, to bring an alleged offender (including an alleged offender whom they have framed or "entrapped") to justice, as happens, e.g. in the strand of plot that deals with rape in *Adelphoe* (cat. III. 23). (b) This criterion is also applied when the threat or its application depends on a Greek offense or institution for which there is no Roman counterpart; the most obvious case is the prosecution that took place before the opening of *Phormio* which depends on the existence of the epiklerate system (cat. I. 3).

(2) If a threat or a summons takes place in a scene for which we have independent or quasi-independent evidence that (a) the threat or (b) the entire scene belonged to the Greek original, then we may be reasonably certain that the threat appeared in the Greek original in cases of (a), less certain in cases of (b). Under independent evidence, I count Donatus' comment on *Ph.* 668 (cat. VI. 6); under quasi-independent, I count Terence's prologue statement in *Ad.* 6–11 (cat. III. 21).

(3) If a threat is dispensable to the play and is found in a passage that is demonstrably Plautine, by virtue of a combination of such features as its metrical shape and linguistic style, its resemblance to similar verses in other plays, and its obvious expansion of the role of a socially marginal character at the expense of the unity of a particular scene (see esp. Fraenkel 1960: 105–202), then it is likely to be a Plautine addition.

(4) If a threat is dispensable to the play and is found in a passage which (a) refers to a Roman institution for which there is no Greek counterpart, or (b) is applied in a fantastical scenario, the threat might be Roman adaptation or addition; the likelihood that it is an addition (rather than an adaptation of a Greek threat) is increased if the threat is found in combination with other criteria (nos. 3 or 5), or if it is used to enhance an aspect of the ethos of a stock character, in a way that differs from that character's treatment in Greek plays (see Lowe 1985b: 85–86, 101–02).

(5) If the threat is found in a passage that is identifiable as altered from the original on "structural grounds," then the threat is likely to be Roman adaptation or addition; on the other hand, consideration of the same grounds may help to identify an unaltered passage. Structural grounds are sometimes discoverable by accounting for exits and entrances, act division, the number of speaking characters on stage, the omission of an expository prologue, and by the observation of awkwardnesses (such as lengthy stays on stage by silent characters) or inconsistencies (e.g.

repetition of exit motifs) which can best be explained as the result of adaptation or addition (see Lowe 1992: 156–57 and 1983b: 428–31).

These are the criteria that I (or the critics to whom I refer) have used when trying to determine whether a Roman summons or threat of legal action is derived from some similar utterance in the Greek model. I have not made the assumption that the absence of a positive pointer to a Greek scenario or the use of Roman legal terminology automatically renders a threat a Roman addition; in some cases, the possibility remains that a Greek threat underlies the Roman one; the provenance of such cases may be indeterminable.[81] Nor have I assumed that the use of Greek terminology renders a threat Greek (see Fraenkel 1960: 126 on the *agoranomus* of *Captivi* 824, the general skepticism of Fredershausen 1906, and the careful, methodological exposition of the problem by Rotelli 1972). Sometimes Roman depictions of Greek legal scenarios which have an obvious Greek coloring may be better explained as parodies rather than as Roman replicas of the original (see, in more generalized context, R. Hunter 1993: 237).

The catalogue is not meant to be a substitute for an examination of the arguments for attribution to a Greek original in each individual case, but rather a summary of the results of such examination. Criteria 3–5 might appear the most arbitrary, especially since I endorse (or eliminate), in many cases, certain arguments of analytic critics whose capacity for creating consensus in any individual instance is dubious (cf., e.g. Jachmann 1931 and Thierfelder 1935; Lefèvre 1971 and Steidle 1973). My response to criticism on this score is to reiterate that these attributions are tentative. True, the twenty-nine instances in Roman plays that have been designated as "probably Greek" in origin have been used in creating the larger canvas of Athenian pre-forensic and extra-judicial strategies presented throughout this book; but they have been used in conjunction with the fifteen Greek instances and the evidence of the Attic orators. My aim, in the end, has been to point out general trends and patterns of behavior; that I have labored to provide statistics is not because I think that eight occurrences of one phenomenon and two of another is necessarily vital and telling information in and of itself, but because I wanted to make utterly clear the foundations (weak and strong) of the evidence I have used.

The hypothesized provenance of the scenarios listed below are designated as "probably Greek," "Roman," or "indeterminable"; an asterisk indicates that the hypothesis is very tentative. The criteria used in formulating the designation are given in short-hand manner – simply, e.g. "criterion 1b," followed by a brief explanation or reference; "add." plus a number refers to an addendum at the end of the catalogue. For each threat that appears in a Greek play, I have tried to determine the offense and

[81] It should be pointed out that some of the scenarios in Greek plays do not conform with criteria 1a; a threat of legal action might appear in a Greek play without being essential to the plot or without motivating stage action, and it might replicate a feature of Roman law.

procedure that would be followed if the threat were carried out. In the Roman scenarios that are "probably Greek," I have attempted to identify what the offense may have been in accordance with both Greek and Roman law in cases where the language and context are specific enough to make a reasonable conjecture. Particularly tentative identifications (of provenance or offense) are discussed in the addenda attached to the catalogue and in earlier sections of this book which are referred to below. I have designated as bluffs or hyperbole those threats which appear to be non-negotiable blusterings or momentary ventings of anger or jokes, i.e., threats which aim neither at judicial nor extra-judicial settlement (see chapter 2. 3 at nn. 110–12). Verse numbers printed in bold type indicate that the phraseology of *in ius vocatio* is used. Square brackets indicate that the passage might be an interpolation. When I refer to a character in the Greek original of the Roman play, I use the name of the Roman character within double quotations, even in cases where we know the name of the character in the Greek play. The rationale for the division of the scenarios into ten categories is given in chapter 2. 3 at n. 99; likewise provided there are the total number of scenarios for each of the four groups (Greek, probably Greek, Roman, indeterminable).

B. TABLE OF THREATS PRESENTED IN CATALOGUE AND ADDENDA

I.
1. *Aul.* II 4, 316–19
2. *Rud. prol.* 35–38
3. *Ph.* I 1, 124–36n.

II.
1. *Curc.* V 3, 679–86
2. *Pers.* IV 9, **745**–51 and V 2
3. *Rud.* III 6, **859–60**, 867–69

III.
1. Com. Adesp., *CGF* 239. 10–11
2. *Misgune* fr. 279 K–T
3. (i) *Samia* IV 576
   (ii) *Samia* IV 577
4. *Sikyonios* IV 272
5. *Asin.* I 2, 131–33
6. *Asin.* II 4, **480**
7. *Aul.* III 2, 415–17
8. *Aul.* IV 10, 760
9. *Capt.* III 1, 492–95
10. *Capt.* IV 2, 791–826
11. (i) *Curc.* V 2, 619
    (ii) *Curc.* V 2, 620–**21**, cf. **625**
12. *Curc.* V 3, 686–729
13. *Poen. prol.* 16–45
14. *Poen.* III 6, 800
15. *Poen.* V 4, **1225**, **1229**, **1232**
16. *Poen.* [V 6, **1342**, **1343**, **1349**]
17. *Poen.* [V 7, 1399, 1408]
18. *Pseud.* I 2
19. *Truc.* IV 2, 759–63
20. *Truc.* IV 3, **840**
21. (i) *Ad.* II 1, 163
    (ii) *Ad.* II 1, 193–95
22. *Ad.* II 2, 248–49
23. *Ad.* III 2, 348–50 and 4, 497–98
24. *Eun.* IV 7, 806–07
25. *Ph.* II 3, 407–08
26. *Ph.* II 3, 436–39
27. (i) *Ph.* V 8, **936**, **981**
    (ii) *Ph.* V 8, 983–84

IV.
1. *Samia* V 717–18
2. *Amph.* II 2, 852
3. *Amph.* IV: (i) fr. XV; (ii) fr. XVI

4. *Bacch.* IV 8, 917–18
5. *Miles* V 1
6. *Poen.* V 5, 1301–02
V.
1. *Most.* IV 3, 1036–38
and V 1, 1099–1101
VI.
1. *Aul.* III 3, 456–58
2. *Miles* II 5, 453
3. *Rud.* III 4, 712–14
4. *Rud.* V 3, 1380–82
5. *Ph.* II 3, 403–06
6. *Ph.* IV 3, 668
7. *Ph.* V 8, 984
VII.
1. *Perikeiromene* III 499–503
2. *Curc.* I 1, 28–32
3. *Ph.* II 2, 333–36
VIII.
1. Alexis *Epikleros* fr. 78. 4–8 K–A
2. *Samia* IV 506–13
3. *Most.* III 1, 557
4. *Pers.* I 3, 163
5. *Poen.* IV 2, 905–06, etc.
6. *Poen.* V 5 [**1336**], [1337]
7. *Eun.* IV 6, **768**
8. *Eun.* IV 7, 809–10
9. *Ph.* II 4, 450–52
IX.
1. *Aspis* II 270–73
2. *Kolax* 130–32
3. *Sikyonios* 133–35; 138–40
4. *Amph.* I 1, 155
5. *Aul.* IV 7, 700
6. *Pers.* IV 3, 530–31, 534–35
7. *Poen.* [V 7, 1403–04]
8. *Pseud.* I 3, 303–04
9. *Rud.* II 5, 474–77
10. *Trin.* V 2, 1145–46
11. *Truc.* IV 3, 818–20
12. *And.* IV 5, 810–16
13. *Hec.* III 1, 333–35
X.
1. *Aspis* 365–67
2. *Fab. Inc.* 44–45
3. *Perikeiromene* II 356–57
4. *Bacch.* II 3, 270–72
5. *Pers.* II 4, 288–89
6. *Rud.* III 1, **608**
7. *Eun.* V 4, 952–57 and 5, 992–93
8. *Ph.* IV 3, 626–31
Addenda
1. *Misgune* fr. 279 K–T
2. *Tresviri* in Plautus
3. *Curc.* V 2, 619–**21**, **625**
4. (i) *Poen.* III 5, 782–84;
(ii) *Poen.* III 5, 785
5. *Poen.* 5, [6], and [7]
6. *Ad.* II 1, 193–95
7. *Ad.* II 1 and 2
8. *Ad.* III 2 and 4: Hegio
9. *Eun.* IV 7
10. *Ph.* V 8–9
11. *Most.* V 1 and *Hec.* III 1
12. *Ph.* II 3, 403–06
13. *And.* IV 5, 814–16

CATALOGUE

I A character appears on stage after undergoing a prosecution or after trying to initiate one before the action of the play begins (cf. cat. II and X. 3)

(1) *Aulularia* II 4, 316–19. Roman: criteria 3 and 4b (Lowe 1985b: 88).

pulmentum pridem eripuit ei milvos: / homo ad praetorem deplorabundus venit; / infit ibi postulare plorans, eiulans, / ut sibi liceret milvom vadarier ("Once a kite snatched a bit of sauce from him; / the man went off sobbing to the praetor; / there he begins, howling and yowling, demanding / that the kite be bound over for trial").

Strobilus depicts Euclio's litigiousness as an aspect of his miserliness; cf. cat. nos. III. 7, 8, and VI.1. On *vadimonium*, see cat. X. 5 below.

(2) *Rudens prol.* 35–38. Probably Greek: criterion 1 (Marx 1928: 63–64).

senex, qui huc Athenis exsul venit, hau malus; / neque is adeo propter malitiam patria caret, / sed dum alios servat se impedivit interim, / rem bene paratam comitate perdidit. (["Daemones lives there . . .], an old man who came here in exile from Athens – not a bad man; and it's not for any wickedness on his part that he lacks a fatherland, but in assisting others he meanwhile entangled himself, he lost his well-earned fortune out of kindliness.")

Marx suggests that "Daemones" became *atimos* (disfranchised) as a result of standing surety for others who left him in the lurch; unable to pay and convicted in a trial for failing to carry out the suretyship (*dike engues*), he became a state-debtor. See Lipsius 705–15; Harrison 2. 171–76; MacDowell 1978: 167 and n. 380 and 1962 apud And. 1. 2 and 44.

(3) *Phormio* I 1, 124–36. Probably Greek: criteria 1a and b above; see also Donatus on 281.

129–32: *ad iudices veniemu' . . . quom tu horum nil refelles vincam scilicet* . . . ("we shall appear before the *iudices* . . . ; when you fail to contest anything [i.e., our statements of relationship], I shall of course win"). 135–36: *persuasit homini: factumst: ventumst: vincimur: / duxit* ("he [Phormio] persuaded the man [Antipho]; [a summons] was issued; [the case] was brought to court; we were defeated; he married the girl").

In the Greek original, "Antipho" had been convicted of failing to carry out his obligations to an *epikleros* (see chapter 7 n. 45 contra Lefèvre 1978a). In the Roman play, Geta reports the law at 126, the indictment at 127 (*tibi scribam dicam*), Phormio's words at 129–32, and the consequences of the trial at 135–36.

II A character returns to the stage after being arrested or summoned to court during the play; in the interval between his exit and reappearance, he may have undergone prosecution or arbitration

(1) *Curculio* V 3, 679–86. Probably Greek: criterion 5 (see chapter 4. 4 nn. 45–49).

683–85: *ille in ius me vocat; / pessume metui ne mihi hodie apud praetorem solveret. verum amici compulerunt: reddit argentum domo* ("he summons me to court; I was horrified to think that he would settle with me today before the praetor. But friends used compulsion – he repaid the money at home").

In both the Roman play and its model, the pimp had been summoned to court by the banker, perhaps for a bankruptcy proceeding; the precise legal action is not clear. The case is settled extra-judicially.

(2) *Persa* IV 9, 745–51 and V 2. Probably Greek: criterion 1a (see App. 4. 2). In the Roman play, the pimp is summoned to court (**745–46**), apparently for "kidnapping" or a *vindicatio in libertatem*; in the Greek model, he is arrested for *andrapodismos* (for the Greek and Roman charges, see App. 3). The pimp later returns to the stage: in the Roman play, the dénouement of the legal scenario is unclear; in the Greek model, the pimp probably settled out of court.

(3) *Rudens* III 6, **859–60**, 867–69. Probably Greek: criteria 1a and 5 (see App. 4. 1). In the Roman play, the legal scenario is unclear: Labrax is summoned to court for failure to execute a contract of sale (initiated with *arra*) or for an ordinary *vindicatio in rem* or for "kidnapping" (**859–60**, 867–69); he is told, *in iure caussam dicito* (866, "plead your case in court"); he later returns to the stage and reports the verdict of *recuperatores* at 1283, *abiudicata a me modo est Palaestra* ("Palaestra has just now been taken away from me by judicial decision"). In the Greek play, "Labrax" is denounced by *endeixis* (778–79) and arrested as an *andrapodistes* (here, "slave-stealer"; cf. 736–39, 711–12 and 723); he may have settled out of court.

III A character is arrested or summoned to court or is threatened with these procedures during the course of the play. The outcome of such threats in Greek or probably Greek scenarios is indicated below: (a) the accused comes to a private agreement with his accuser (outcome: agreement); (b) a temporary impasse precedes agreement (outcome: eventual agreement); (c) the charge is dropped upon the acquisition of new information which reveals that no offense has been committed (outcome: dropped charge); (d) the outcome is unknown because the text is fragmentary (outcome: unknown)

(1) Comica Adespota, *CGFP* 239, 10–11.

δίωκε, Σωσία, συνάρπασον / τὸν ἀνδραποδιστήν, λαβὲ λάβ' αὐτόν οὐ μενεῖς ("Follow [that man], Sosia, seize the *andrapodistes*, take him, take him! Stop!").

One character attempts to arrest another as an *andrapodistes* ("slave-stealer" or "kidnapper"). Outcome: unknown.

(2) *Misgune* fr. 279 K–T.

ὄμνυμί σοι τὸν ἥλιον,/ ἦ μὴν ἀποίσειν σοι γραφὴν κακώσεως ("I swear by the sun that I shall bring an indictment against you for maltreatment").

One character threatens to indict another for maltreatment of an undefined sort; for different charges of maltreatment (of parents, orphans, and *epikleroi*, see *AP* 56. 6). In another fragment from the play (fr. 278 K–T), the *parastasis* (court fee) is mentioned; see add. 1. Outcome: unknown.

(3) *Samia* IV 576–78. Series of threats; see chapter 2. 3.

(Ni.) πρότερος ἅπτει μου σὺ νυνί· ταῦτ' ἐγὼ μαρτύρομαι/ (Δn.) σὺ δ' ἐπ' ἐλευθέραν γυναῖκα λαμβάνεις βακτηρίαν/ καὶ διώκεις (Ni.: "You are the one who strikes first – I call on witnesses to the act!" De.: "But you are taking a stick against a free woman and pursuing her!").

Nikeratos depicts Demea's conduct as assault and the latter responds by depicting the former's conduct as *hubris*. Outcome: agreement.

(4) *Sikyonios* IV 272.

τοὺς ἀνδραποδιστὰς ἀπαγαγεῖ[ν ὑμᾶς ἐγώ – ("You, *andrapodistai*, I . . . arrest you!").

Moskhion (?) attempts to arrest Stratophanes (?) and others as *andrapodistai*. While it is conceivable that the term *andrapodistai* refers to slave-stealers or kidnappers here, it is also possible that it is applied in a non-technical way; see App. 3. 1. Outcome: unknown.

(5) *Asinaria* I 2, 131–33. Provenance is indeterminable; adaptation from the Greek model is not impossible (see add. 2).

ibo ego ad trisviros vostraque ibi nomina / faxo erunt, capiti' te perdam ego et filiam, / perlecebrae, permities, adulescentum exitium ("I shall go to the *tresviri* and I shall report your names there, I shall destroy you and your daughter on a capital charge – you enticements, blights, ruin of youth!").

Argyrippus threatens in hyperbolic fashion to denounce the courtesan and her mother before the *tresviri*. Cf. cat. nos. III. 7, 19, and IX. 4.

(6) *Asinaria* II 4, **480**. Provenance is indeterminable. The trader bluffingly summons Leonida to court (apparently in response to the slave's threat of violence against him).

(7) *Aulularia* III 2, 415–17. Roman: criteria 3 and 4 (see Lowe 1985b: 88 and add. 2). The Plautine context rather than the term *tresviri* suggests that the verses have been added and not merely adapted.

EUC.: Redi. quo fugis nunc? tene, tene. CO.: quid, stolide, clamas? / EUC.: quia ad trisviros iam ego deferam nomen tuom. CO.: quam ob rem? / EUC.: quia cultrum habes . . . (EUC.: "Come back! Where are you running now? Stop him, stop him!" CO.: "Why are you shouting, blockhead?" EUC.: "Because I am ready to report your name to the *tresviri*." CO.: "Why?" Euc.: "Because you're holding a knife!").

Euclio threatens in hyperbolic fashion to denounce Congrio the cook to the *tresviri*. Cf. cat. nos. III. 5, 19, and IX. 4.

(8) *Aulularia* IV 10, 760. Probably Greek*: criterion 1 (for Plautine addition in this scene, see chapter 6.2.c).

iam quidem hercle te ad praetorem rapiam et tibi scribam dicam ("by Hercules, I'll drag you to the praetor and bring an indictment against you").

Euclio threatens to sue Lyconides for theft if he does not return his pot of gold. While the scene is essential to the Greek model (Ludwig 1961: 65–68), the particular threat is not; nonetheless, the threat is likely to have appeared there. In three other instances in the play, Euclio is depicted as litigious (316–19, 415–17, 458); in yet another, he allegedly takes the law into his own hands (465–69). Plautine bluff is observable in 415–17 and 458 (no. 7 above and VI. 1 below); Plautine fantasy is responsible for the two other instances (see cat. I. 1 for 316–19); none has a toehold on legal soil deep enough to convince a magistrate to give an action. But the threat in 760 is realistic and fits into the context of the scene. The Greek terminology might, in this instance, point to the model. Outcome: dropped charge.

(9) *Captivi* III 1, 492–95. Roman: criterion 3 (see Lowe 1989a: 164 and Fraenkel 1960: 101–02, 237).

nunc barbarica lege certumst ius meum omne persequi: / qui consilium iniere, quo nos victu et vita prohibeant, / is diem dicam, inrogabo multa, ut mihi cenas decem / meo arbitratu dent, quom cara annona sit. sic egero ("Now it is resolved in accordance with a foreign law to pursue my full rights: whoever has entered a plot to keep us from sustenance and life, for them I shall appoint a day in court, I shall impose penalties: they are to give me ten dinners on my say-so, when the price of grain is dear. So I shall act.")

The parasite bluffingly threatens to sue the young men who are no longer inviting him to dine; the remedy is represented as a *barbarica lex* (= Roman) at 492. Cf. (a) Alexis *Lebes* frr. 130 and 131 K–A; (b) Diphilos *Emporos* fr. 31 K–A; (c) Diphilos *Enagizontes* fr. 37 K–A ; (d) Timokles *Philodikastes* fr. 34. 5–6 K–A; (e) Plautus *Merc.* 1015–24; (f) Plautus *Persa* 65–74: all these are references (a) to laws attributed to lawgivers or (b) to a foreign *polis* or (c–f) to laws created by the speaker; there is no direct threat made against any specific individual. The parasite in *Capt.* 492–95, however, has created a more personal scenario and so has been included in the catalogue; similarly, the edicts created by characters in nos. 10, 13, and 18 below.

(10) *Captivi* IV 2, 791–826. Roman: criterion 3 and 4b (Rotelli 1972: 109–12 and Fraenkel 1960: 102, 124–27, 175, 238–39). The parasite produces *edictiones aediliciae* (823) as he threatens all those who obstruct his passage. Both Rotelli and Fraenkel compare the passage with *Curc.* 280–88 which, however, is not presented as an edict – a point which Phaedromus takes note of in the latter play: *recte hic monstrat, si imperare possit* (299, "he sends out his warnings in proper fashion – if only he had authority!"). Cf. nos. 13 and 18 below.

(11) *Curculio* V 2, 619–**21**, cf. **625**. Threat and counter-threat are probably

Greek*, with much adaptation (see add. 3); against Lefèvre's view, see chapter 4, n. 36.

TH.: quam ego pecuniam quadruplicem aps te et lenone auferam. / PH.: qui scis mercari furtivas atque ingenuas virgines, / ambula in ius (TH.: "I shall get my money four times over from you and the pimp!" PH.: Come, you expert buyer of kidnapped and freeborn girls – off to court!").

(i) The soldier threatens a fourfold penalty against Phaedromus and the pimp. The penalties may be exaggeration, or might represent the double penalty for *furtum nec manifestum* in Roman law (Gaius 3. 190) or for theft in Athenian law (Dem. 24. 105, 114), one double penalty to be exacted from the young man, the other from the pimp (so Gratwick 1969: 481: n. 1). (ii) Phaedromus counters with a bluff, a summons for kidnapping (Voigt 1884: 320; Huvelin 1915: 221 contra Molè 1966: 120–21). The Plautine passage has been thoroughly Romanized: Phaedromus calls for a witness at 621 (*antestari*: see Tandoi 1961 and Zwierlein 1990: 283–84) and there is a Roman pun on *intestatus* at 622 (see Daube 1969: 74). In the Greek original, the summons would be an arrest for *andrapodismos* (Witt 1971: 236–37, n. 51; Paoli 1976 [= 1951] 118) and "Phaedromus" would supply or fabricate a reference to the girl's homeland which would be the same as the soldier's. Outcome: dropped charges.

(12) *Curculio* v 3, 686–729. Probably Greek*, with much Roman adaptation (see chapter 4.2.e). In the Roman play, the young man and soldier threaten the pimp with violence in order to recover the soldier's money; a forced summons is thinly veiled behind the threats (693, 695, 707). In the Greek play, a summons may have been issued for recovery of the sum. An arbitration ends the dispute. Outcome: agreement.

(13) *Poenulus prol.* 16–45: Roman: criterion 3 (Watson 1974b: 49–50). Prologue speaker parodies a praetorian edict as he bids the audience to settle down and threatens penalties for disobedience. Cf. nos. 10 and 18.

(14) *Poenulus* III 6, 800. Probably Greek: criterion 1a.

cras susscribam homini dicam ("I shall bring an action against the man tomorrow!").

In the Roman play and its Greek model, the young man is directed to sue the pimp for "concealing" his slave bailiff and a considerable sum of money (180). For problems connected with 782–86, esp. 785, where Agorastocles claims he has caught Lycus as a *manufesto fur*, "red-handed thief," see add. 4. Milphio had contrived the plan earlier and predicted the consequences at 185–86, *ubi in ius venerit, / addicet praetor familiam totam tibi* ("when he comes to court, the praetor will award his entire household to you"). The "award" (in Roman terms) is to be understood thus: the pimp will be convicted of theft; unable to pay the penalty with ready cash, he will become a judgment debtor (cf. Watson 1965: 231 and Gratwick 1969: 404). Outcome: eventual agreement (apparently).

(15) *Poenulus* v 4, **1225** (*in ius vos voco* is Camerarius' emendation for the *in ius vos volo* of *codex Ambrosianus*), **1229**, and **1232**. Roman: criterion 3 (see Gratwick 1969: 409; Zwierlein 1990: 281–83; App. 3.2, apud fin.). Hanno jestingly summons Adelphasium and Anterastilis to court for "kidnapping" – for concealing themselves, his own free-born daughters, from him.

(16) *Poenulus* [v 6]. Provenance is indeterminable (see add. 5). Lycus is issued summonses (a) by Agorastocles for theft [**1342**], (b) by Hanno for "kidnapping" [**1343**, and cf. 1344–48], and (c) by Antamoenides for recovery of *arrabo* [**1349**].

(17) *Poenulus* [v 7]. Provenance is indeterminable (see add. 5). Lycus is threatened with imprisonment by Antamoenides if he does not return the *arrabo* [1399] and by Agorastocles if he does not return the stolen money [1408].

(18) *Pseudolus* I 2. Roman: criterion 3 (Fraenkel 1960: 138–41). Ballio the pimp, in a long canticum which is largely Plautine invention, parodies edictal language as he threatens slaves with punishment if they fail to carry out the tasks assigned to their *provinciae.* Fraenkel analyzes the passage in detail; while a kernel of 133–70 appeared in the Greek original, the block of verses extending from I 2, 170 (*i, puere, prae*) through I 3, 240 (*i prae, puere*) is Plautine invention. Cf. nos. 10 and 13.

(19) *Truculentus* IV 2, 759–63. Provenance is indeterminable (see add. 2).

iam hercle ego tibi, inlecebra, ludos faciam clamore in via, / quae advorsum legem accepisti a plurumis pecuniam; / iam hercle apud novos [omnis] magistratus faxo erit nomen tuom, / postid ego te manum iniciam quadrupuli, venefica, / suppostrix puerum . . . ("Now I swear I shall make sport of you, seductress: I shall shout in the streets that you have accepted money illegally from many men; I shall ensure that your name is put before the new magistrates; after that I shall seize you for a quadruple penalty, you poisoner and buyer in the baby bazaar!").

Diniarchus bluffingly threatens to denounce the courtesan before the "new magistrates." Cf. cat. nos. III. 5, 7, and IX. 4.

(20) *Truculentus* IV 3, **840**. Provenance is indeterminable (see chapter 6.3.b). Diniarchus is summoned to court for rape by the victim's father (for legal remedies, see chapter 5.2.b).

(21) *Adelphoe* II 1, 163 and 193–195. Threat and counter-threat. (i) Probably Greek (Diphilos, not Menander: prol. 11): criterion 2b (Rieth 1964: 42–59 and Fantham 1968: 200–01, following Marx 1928: 293–96). (ii) Probably Greek*: criterion 2b (see add. 6).

163: *ego meum ius persequar* ("I shall pursue my legal right").
193–95: *neque vendundam censeo / quae liberast; nam ego liberali illam adsero*

causa manu. / nunc vide utrum vis, argentum accipere an causam meditari tuam (" . . . nor do I think that a free woman should be sold; for I make a formal claim of her freedom. Take your choice: either accept the money or start rehearsing your case").

(i) The charge which "Sannio" threatens in the Diphilan original is perhaps *hubris* (*iniuria* in Rome); thus Rieth 1964: 53–54 argues, pointing to the excuse which the pimp foresees the young man will offer: *hanc iniuriam mi nolle / factam esse* (162–63, "you did not intend an injury to me"; cf. 165–66; on "lack of intention" as exculpatory grounds for *hubris*, see chapter 6.2.c). (ii) The young man then "removes the girl into freedom," and challenges the pimp to sue him with a *dike exaireseōs* (App. 3. 1). In Terence's play, Aeschinus claims the girl is free (194) and challenges Sannio to make a counter-claim in court (195), probably in a *vindicatio in libertatem*; intimidation is uppermost (see Gratwick 1987: 238–39). Outcome: unknown – as a Diphilan scene inside a Menandrian play, but eventual agreement in the Terentian play.

(22) *Adelphoe* II 2, 248–49. Probably Greek (Menander): criterion 5 (cf. Rieth 1964: 42–59; Gaiser 1964: 136–41; Fantham 1968; see add. 7 concerning the relation of this scene to II 1).

utut haec sunt acta, potiu' quam litis sequar, / meum mihi reddatur saltem quanti emptast, Syre ("However the situation has evolved, rather than my pursuing him with suits, at least, Syrus, let her cost price be returned to me.")

In both the Roman play and its model, the pimp contemplates suing Aeschinus, probably for the return of his slave (a *vindicatio in rem* in Rome: Gaius 4. 16; perhaps a *dike* for *andrapodismos*, "slave-stealing," in Athens); but the pimp must leave Athens on a business trip and there is no time for a suit. For the offense in the Greek model, cf. *Kolax* 130–32 (cat. IX. 2 below). In Terence's play, in a long aside, the pimp reflects that if he postpones a suit, then *refrixerat res . . / . ut sit satius perdere / quam hic nunc manere tam diu aut tum persequi* (233–35: "the case will have cooled off . . . so that it's better to lose [her] than to linger here longer or sue later"). Rieth 1964: 45–46 points out that the metaphor, *refrixerit res*, is found at Dem. 21. 112, καὶ ἀδικήματα ἕωλα τὰ τούτων ὡς ὑμᾶς καὶ ψυχρὰ ἀφικνεῖται ("and their offenses are stale and cold when they come before you" trans. MacDowell). The pimp then addresses the slave in the verses quoted above, with bluffing allusion to his potential to bring suit at the same time as he agrees to settle in private; cf. *Ph.* 408, no. 25 below. Outcome: agreement.

(23) *Adelphoe* III 2, 348–50 and 4, 497–98. Probably Greek: criterion 1a (see chapter 2.4). In both plays, "Sostrata" and "Hegio" threaten to sue for rape (for remedies: see chapter 5. 1–2). Donatus on *Ad.* 351 reports: *apud Menandrum Sostratae frater inducitur* ("in Menander, he ["Hegio"] is

introduced as Sostrata's brother"); the report has been called into question; see further, add. 8). Outcome: agreement.

(24) *Eunuchus* IV 7, 806–07 ("siege scene"). Probably Greek*: criterion 5 (see Ludwig 1973 [1959]: esp. 356–57 with n. 8; 380–89; 406–07 and add. 9 below).

miles, nunc adeo edico tibi / ne vim facias ullam in illam (806–07: "I prohibit you, soldier, from using any violence against her").

That the threat alludes to a lawsuit (for *iniuria* in Rome, a *graphe hubreos* or *dike aikeias* or *biaiōn* in Athens) is demonstrable by Thais' explicit recommendation at verse 768 (cat. VIII. 7 below). If we accept (with Ludwig) at least 792–97a, 804b–808a, 810, followed by the departure of the soldier (i.e., without his dialogue with the parasite) as the Menandrian kernel in the corresponding scene of *Eunoukhos*, then the rival is immediately diverted from his preconceived plan of violent action. Outcome: agreement.

(25) *Phormio* II 3, 407–08. Probably Greek: criterion 1b.

etsi mihi facta iniuriast, verum tamen / potius quam litis secter ("even though I have been treated with contumely, rather than sue you . . . ").

Demipho bluffingly offers to forego a lawsuit (for which there appears to be no justifiable grounds) in order to coerce the agreement of Phormio to an out-of-court settlement (cf. 620–35 and *Adelphoe* 248–49 [no. 22 above]). The legal action potentially at hand for "Demipho" in the Greek original was a *dike* for bearing false witness (*dike pseudomarturiōn*) against the parasite's witnesses in the earlier trial against "Antipho" (cat. I. 2 above); that *dike*, however, is technically unavailable. To bring such a suit, "Antipho" would have had to put in a protest (*episkepsis*) at the trial; thus Phormio reminds the *senex* at 399–401: *dilucide expedivi quibu' me oportuit / iudicibu' : tum id si falsum fuerat, filius / quor non refellit?* . . . ("I gave a clear explanation to the judges who were the appropriate ones to hear it; if it had been false at that time, why didn't your son object?"). Demipho proposes to dower the girl with five *mnai* (409–10), precisely the sum that accords with the law regulating dowries of poor *epikleroi* ([Dem.] 43. 54; see Arnott 1970: 41). Outcome: impasse, eventually, agreement.

(26) *Phormio* II 3, 436–39. Probably Greek: criterion 5 (see Steidle 1975: 376–81).

DEM.: *sati' verborumst: nisi tu properas mulierem / abducere, ego illam eiciam. dixi, Phormio. /* PH.: *si tu illam attigeri' secu' quam dignumst liberam / dicam tibi inpingam grandem. dixi, Demipho* (DEM.: "Enough of words! unless you quickly remove the woman, I shall eject her. I have spoken, Phormio." PH.: "If you touch her in any way that is unworthy for a free woman [to be touched], I shall slam you with a great indictment. I have spoken, Demipho").

In the Roman play and its Greek original, "Phormio" threatens legal action (for *iniuria* in the Roman play, a *graphe hubreos* [cf. *Samia* 577, no. 3 above] or *eisangelia* for maltreatment of an *epikleros* in the Greek model). The threat momentarily stymies Demipho and brings the scene to an end (cf. nos. 21 and 27 for counter-threats at end of scenes). Outcome: agreement.

(27) *Phormio* v 8, 935–**36**, **981**, 983–84. Threat and counter-threat are probably Greek: criterion 5 (see Steidle 1975: 376–77; against the arguments of analytic scholars who ascribe considerable Terentian rewriting to the last two scenes of the play, see add. 10).

935–**36**: *quin tu mi argentum cedo. / PH.: immo vero uxorem tu cedo.* DE.: *in ius ambula* (DEM.: "Hand over the money." PH.: "No, you hand over my wife." DEM. "Go to court").
983–84: *una iniuriast / tecum . . . . alterast tecum, Chreme* ("that's one charge of assault against you ... and that's another charge against you, Chremes").

(i) 935–**36**: While there were actions for recovery of dowry in both Athens and Rome, the threat cannot be taken seriously; its purpose is intimidation. The summons is repeated at **981**. (ii) 983–84: Phormio responds with a movement toward the house: *in ius? huc, siquid lubet!* ("To court? Court is in this direction, please!"). When Demipho and Chremes, one after the other, lay hands on Phormio, he responds with charges of assault (*iniuria* in Rome, *aikeia* or *hubris* in Athens) at 983–84. Outcome: impasse, eventually, agreement.

IV A character, depicted as a sexual offender, is threatened with self-help remedies that are permitted by law or custom (cf. cat. X. 2, 3, and 7). In some cases, he undergoes physical punishment; in others, a private agreement is reached

(1) *Samia* v 717–18.

. . . τίς δ' ἐάσει, μοιχὸν ὄντ' εἰλημμένον,/ ὁμολογοῦντ'; ἤδη σε δήσω, μειράκιον, οὐκ εἰς μακράν; ("And who will allow him [to go abroad], when he's a self-confessed *moikhos*, caught in the act? I'll fetter you right now, young man, with no delay!").

Nikeratos' threat comically exaggerates the young man's offense: Moskhion, the young man, has *not* been caught in the act. Whether *moikhos* means "rapist" or "seducer" here is not certain: (1) the nature of Moskhion's violation is not made explicit in the play (but see chapter 6, n. 48); (2) Nikeratos might not himself know (or care) whether Moskhion had raped or seduced his daughter; (3) Nikeratos is not a good witness for precise application of legal terminology; he is inaccurate when he says that Moskhion was caught in the act and he extravagantly misapplies legal procedure at 506–13 (cat. VIII. 2).

(2) *Amphitruo* II 2, 852. Roman: criterion 4a (see chapter 6. I. a).

numquid causam dicis quin te hoc multem matrimonio? ("you can't plead any reason, can you, why I shouldn't penalize you with divorce?").

Amphitruo, suspecting that his wife has committed adultery, proposes a meeting with Alcumena's kinsman (*tuom cognatum*, 849) to determine whether she is lying about the man with whom she spent the night. The formulation of divorce as a penalty to be imposed after the "family council" has met and established the facts conforms to Roman practice.

(3) *Amphitruo* IV. Provenance of threat and counter-threat is indeterminable (see Fantham 1973 for reconstruction of the fragmentary Roman act).

fr. XV (IX) *(IU.) manufestum hunc oporto collo teneo furem flagiti.* fr. XVI (X) *(AM.) immo ego hunc, Thebani cives, qui domi uxorem meam / impudicitia impedivit, teneo, thensaurum stupri.* (JU.: "I've collared the thief for his scandalous outrage – caught in the act!" AM.: "He lies! Help, Theban citizens! I've caught that treasure-trove of lust – the one who has entwined my wife in illicit acts in my very own house!").

(4) *Bacchides* IV 8, 917–18. Probably Greek: criterion 5 (Lefèvre 1978b: 522–24, 531).

miles Mnesilochum cum uxore opprimeret sua / atque optruncaret moechum manufestarium ("The soldier would have caught Mnesilochus with his wife and slain him as a *moechus* caught in the act").

In both the Roman play and its Greek original, "Nicobulus" compensates the alleged husband "Cleomachus" with a sum of money when he is led to believe that his son has been caught as an adulterer.

(5) *Miles Gloriosus* V I. Probably Greek: criterion 1a (contra Lefèvre 1984: 41–42; cf. the final act of *Samia*). The soldier is treated as an adulterer by the alleged husband (see chapter 6.I.a). Athenian and Roman practice are similar in this instance. There may be Plautine elaboration in the role of the cook who threatens the soldier with castration; the punning use of *testes* is certainly Plautine (1416–17, 1420, 1476); see Lowe 1985a.

(6) *Poenulus* V 5, 1301–02. Provenance is indeterminable.

non pudet puellam amplexari baiiolum in media via? / iam hercle ego illunc excruciandum totum carnufici dabo ("Isn't the maiden ashamed to embrace a porter in the middle of the street? I shall hand him over to the executioner for punishment!").

The scenario is not an accurate portrayal of a lawful Athenian remedy (unless *ho boulomenos* was permitted to arrest a *moikhos*) nor of a Roman practice (see chapter 5.I and 2). It resembles *Misoumenos* III 216–21 (Getas sees Krateia embracing an old man and threatens violence in 220, but is stopped by Krateia's information that the old man is her father). The hyperbolic threat in *Poen.* is inessential to the scene; it might be parody of a Greek motif.

V A character begins an examination of slaves under torture as a preliminary to trial – but he aims to settle in private

(1) *Mostellaria* IV 3, 1036–38 and V 1, 1098–1100. Probably Greek: criterion 1b (see chapter 4, n. 60 for arguments against Stärk 1991).

1036–38: *TH. nunc te opsecro ut me bene iuves operamque des. / SI. quid vis? TH. i mecum, opsecro, una simul. / SI. fiat. TH. servorumque operam et lora mihi cedo.* (TH.: "Now, please, lend a hand and help me out." SI.: "What do you want?" TH. "Please, come with me." SI.: "Sure." TH.: "Give me the use of your slaves and whips.")
1098–1100: *TH. quia enim id maxime volo, ut illi istoc confugiant. sine: / tanto apud iudicem hunc argenti condemnabo facilius. TR. quod agas, id agas. quid tu porro serere vis negotium? / nescis quam meticulosa res sit ire ad iudicem?* (TH.: "Yes, that's what I want above all – that the slaves take refuge there. Allow it! All the easier shall I get him condemned to pay a penalty before the judge." TR. "Follow the plan you were going to follow. Why do you want to sow further trouble? Don't you know how fearful a thing it is to go before a judge?")

The legal scenario makes use of two practices which are not Roman: asylum (Mommsen 1899: 458–59: not a part of Roman law in the Republic) and *arrha* (for succinct explanation of the amalgamation of an *arrha* transaction with a Roman contract of sale, see Lowe 1985c: 14–16 and App. 4.1.b); moreover, slave torture, though practiced in both Athens and Rome, fits the Athenian pattern more precisely here: Thür 1977: 172 on *Most.* 1084–87. In both the Roman play and its Greek model, the old man arranges with his neighbor to have the use of his slaves for torture (cf. 1038 and 1086–87; also 1091–92); he pretends that the torture is a preliminary to a trial (contra Fredershausen 1906), as is clear from *Most.* 1099 and 1100. Possibly, the (bluffing) Roman plaintiff envisions using a lawsuit (an *actio ex empto*) to compel a sale or to obtain a pecuniary *condemnatio* from the defendant (Watson 1965b: 52–53); the Greek law envisioned in the original is not clear – possibly a suit for the recovery of *arrha* or a *dike arguriou*, or some sort of *dike* against a fraudulent claim of owning property (cf. [Dem.] 40. 59 and 48. 45 and see MacDowell 1978: 146).

VI One character challenges another to sue him in court

(1) *Aulularia* III 3, 456–58. Roman*: criterion 4b.

CO.: heus, senex, pro vapulano hercle ego aps te mercedem petam. / coctum ego, non vapulatum, dudum conductus fui. / EUC.: lege agito mecum (CO.: "Listen, old man, I swear: I'll get compensation from you for this beating." I was hired to cook, not to be beaten. EUC.: "Plead your case in court").

Euclio tauntingly challenges the cook (who is a slave, 309–10) to proceed against him for the beating (Watson 1965: 101); the challenge cannot be acted upon by a slave. It should be noted that such jokes (i.e., the pretence that slaves could act in their own capacity) are not absent from Greek plays; similar humor forms the parodic backbone of the arbitration scene in *Epitrepontes* and culminates in Suros' final remark there, "It seems I must quit all else and practice pleading; this is how everything's kept safe nowadays" (417–18). The "inconsistency" in *Aul.* (a slave is incompetent to enter a private suit), however, is probably not a remnant of the Greek original (where the cook can be expected to be free and hence able to sue for compensation for an assault: Athen. 14. 658f), but an instance of the meanness of Euclio. Plautine addition is suggested by the use which Plautus (not the Greek playwright) has made of Euclio's litigiousness elsewhere in the play, sometimes as an appendage to his miserly traits, as at 318–19 (cat. I. 1) and 469, and sometimes not, as at 416–17 (cat. III. 7) and here. Cf. *lege agito* at nos. 2 and 7 below.

(2) *Miles Gloriosus* II 5, 453. Provenance is indeterminable.

lege agito ("plead your case in court").

A slave (Sceledrus) bluffingly challenges the (Athenian) courtesan Philocomasium to proceed against him (for force or violence) in Ephesos. There is no pointer to the provenance of the challenge, as there is in the preceding entry. Lefèvre 1984b: 32–37 attributes the motif of the twin sister to Plautus; the entire scene is therefore Plautine addition. According to Lefèvre, the plot device by which *X* is made to think that *Y* (person) is *Z* (person) is Roman; but Menander *Phasma* illustrates the same logic at work.

(3) *Rudens* III 4, 712–14. Roman*: criteria 3 and 5 (cf. Jachmann 1931: 91–95, Drexler 1934: 50–51, and Lefèvre 1984a: 17–18).

<habe iudicem> / de senatu Cyrenensi quemvis opulentum virum, / si tuas esse oportet nive eas esse oportet liberas ("<Have as *iudex*> any rich man from the Cyrenian senate to decide whether the girls rightfully belong to you or whether they are free").

[n.b.: *Rud.* 708–12 are illegible in *Ambrosianus*; the final two words of 712 were apparently supplemented in *codex Turnebi* as *habe invicem* (?). Lindsay (OCT) has supplemented or emended the text in 712 (*habe iudicem*) without notation in the app. crit. See the comments of Marx 1928 ad loc. Cf. *Men.* 587: confusion in mss. between *apud aedilem* (*A*) and *ad iudicem* (P).]

This is Trachalio's response to the pimp's claim that he has been deprived of his rights since his slaves have been taken away from him (711–12). Trachalio's language mimics *in iure* procedure by which an *arbiter* or *iudex* is selected to hear a case; as a slave, Trachalio himself cannot act in court. Apparently a *vindicatio in libertatem* (App. 3. 2) is envisioned. Drexler had argued that these verses (together with Labrax's response in 719) belonged to the Greek original since the claim and challenge fulfill Daemones' dream, which is reported in Act III 1 (see cat. X. 6) and gives the essentials of the Diphilan plot. But the dream (likewise regarded as Diphilan by Lefèvre) gives no part to a third actor, such as Trachalio plays in the Plautine scene. The verses resemble the undeniably Plautine verses 1380–82 (see next entry); the dynamics here are Plautus' (cf. also *Vid.* 60).

(4) *Rudens* V 3, 1380–82. Roman: criteria 4b and 5 (Lefèvre 1984: 21–22).

cedo quicum habeam iudicem, / ni dolo malo instipulatus sis sive etiamdum siem / quinque et viginti annos natus ("Name someone with whom I can share a *iudex*, to see whether you didn't make a fraudulent contract or if I'm already twenty-five years old").

Labrax claims that an agreement with the slave Gripus was not valid, and challenges him to find someone to represent him in court. The *lex Laetoria* (or *Plaetoria*, see Bruns[7] 45), dated by Watson to 193 or 192 BC, offered a special protection in the form of "an *actio popularis* (that is, an action which could be brought by anyone) for a fine against a person who cheated someone under twenty-five. Condemnation in the action involved *infamia*. The *lex* also provided an *exceptio* for a person under twenty-five who was sued on a contract which he had fraudulently been persuaded to make" (Watson 1971: 42, with nn. 9–14). Cf. cat. IX. 8. Daemones' swindling conduct in this scene is inconsistent with the character he has displayed throughout the play and is contrary to the Diphilan description of him in the prologue (35–38); it is possible that Labrax did not return to the stage after his arrest in the Greek original.

(5) *Phormio* II 3, 403–06. Provenance is indeterminable, although Terentian adaptation is probable; see add. 12.

at tu qui sapiens es magistratus adi / iudicium de eadem causa iterum ut reddant tibi, / quandoquidem solu' regnas et soli licet / hic de eadem causa bis iudicium adipiscier ("But you're a smart man – go to the magistrates and have them set up a re-trial for this very same case since you're sole monarch and it's allowed to you alone here to obtain a second hearing of the same case").

Phormio challenges Demipho to seek a re-trial concerning the *epikleros*.

(6) *Phormio* IV 3, 668. Probably Greek: criterion 2a.

sescentas perinde scribito iam mihi dicas: / nil do ("let him bring six hundred indictments against me – it's nothing to me").

Donatus reports on 668, *μυριάς dixit pro multis* ("Apollodoros said 'innumerable' for 'many'"; = Apollodoros fr. 28 K–A; see Headlam 1899: 7). "Demipho," exasperated by the amount of dowry that

"Phormio" is trying to extort from him, challenges him to bring charges for maltreatment of an *epikleros*.

(7) *Phormio* v 8, 984. Provenance is indeterminable.

lege agito ergo! ("go ahead and plead your case!").

Demipho's challenge to Phormio to proceed against him in court for assault is not essential to the Greek original, although Phormio's charges probably appeared there (cat. III. 27). Donatus on 984 reports that the phrase was said to a person *cuius intentio contemptibilis adversario videbatur* ("whose intention [to prosecute] was held in contempt by his adversary").

VII *A character warns a friend that he is likely to be sued by an adversary or subjected to a self-help remedy*

(1) *Perikeiromene* III 499–503.

(ΠΟ.) ὁ δὲ διεφθαρκὼς ἐμοῦ / ἀπόντος αὐτὴν οὐκ ἀδικεῖ με; (ΠΑ.) ὥστ' ἐγκαλεῖν / ἀδικεῖ σ' ἐκεῖνος, ἄν ποτ' ἔλθῃις εἰς λόγους. / εἰ δ' ἐκβιάσει, δίκην ὀφλήσεις· οὐκ ἔχει / τιμωρίαν γὰρ τἀδίκημ', ἔγκλημα δέ (PO.: "Doesn't the man who corrupted her in my absence *do me a wrong*?" (PA.): "Yes, the man does, so that you might *bring a charge* [or "complain"], if ever you speak with him; but if you use force, you will be *liable to a penalty* since his *offense* [or "wrong"] provides no grounds for *private retaliation*, but a *lawful complaint* [or "complaint"]").

The language concerning offense and redress is ambiguous (so Gomme and Sandbach 1973 ad loc.) and is italicized. The preceding dialogue in which Pataikos outlines to Polemon his legal position strongly suggests that the ambiguities should be resolved in favor of full legal connotation: Pataikos here warns Polemon that if he uses violence against Moskhion, he himself will be liable to a suit (e.g. a *dike aikeias* or *biaiōn*). Polemon is living with Glukera and only becomes betrothed to her at the end of the play. But he considers her as a wife (*ego gametēn nenomika tautēn*, 489; cf. *Mis.* A 35. 6 Sandbach App.; Makhon 15. 220 Gow). If she is in fact a *pallake* (she is nowhere designated as such in the extant remains), it is possible to interpret verses 499–503 as follows: Polemon had no grounds for (lawfully sanctioned) private retaliation against the alleged *moikhos* (Moskhion was not caught in "the ultimate act" – he was observed only kissing the girl out of doors), but he did have grounds for a prosecution (a *graphe hubreos*?). This interpretation assumes that the internal lawcode of Corinth (where the play is set) is depicted as similar to that of Athens.

(2) *Curculio* I 1, 28–32. Roman: criterion 3.

PA. ita tuom conferto amare semper, si sapis, / ne id quod ames populus si sciat, tibi sit probro. / semper curato ne sis intestabilis. PH. quid istuc est verbi? PA. caute ut incedas via: quod amas amato testibus praesentibus. (PA.: "If you're smart, always conduct your love life in such a way / that you'll not be disgraced if people find out about your affairs. / Always take care that you do not become incapable of bearing manful testimony." / PH.: "What do you mean?" PA.: "Make sure that you keep to the road: have your love life but keep your testifiers intact.")

Palinurus warns Phaedromus against engaging in illicit affairs and suffering a self-help remedy as a consequence. The punning use of *intestabilis* and *testis* (cf. 622; *Miles* 1416–17, 1420, 1426, *Poen.* 862) is purely Roman.

(3) *Phormio* II 2, 333–36. Roman: criterion 4a (Lowe 1989a: 163).

aliis aliundest periclum unde aliquid abradi potest: / mihi sciunt nil esse. dices "ducent damnatum domum": / alere nolunt hominem edacem et sapiunt mea sententia, / pro maleficio si beneficium summum nolunt reddere ("Others undergo risk from other sources – if they have anything that can be extorted; they know I have nothing. You will say 'they shall lead you home a condemned man'; but they don't want to feed a hungry man and, in my opinion, they're wise, if they're unwilling to pay a handsome dole for my offense").

In the preceding verses, Geta expresses a fear that Phormio will wind up in jail (325); the sykophant-parasite responds that the risk has been taken (*factumst periclum*) and the solution is clear (326). Then, boasting of the number of men he has thrashed, he asks, "Come now, have you ever heard that a suit for assault has been lodged against me?" (329: *cedo dum, enumquam iniuriarum audisti mihi scriptam dicam?*). He continues at 333–36 with the verses quoted above. The *periclum* of 326 suggests an Athenian context, a prosecutor's risk (*kindunos*) of undertaking a trial by *graphe* and of paying the 1000 dr. penalty if he fails to obtain a fifth of the votes; unable to pay, he would become a state debtor. *Periclum* is used in a similar context (i.e., risk of trial) at *Persa* 63. A technical Athenian legal joke may lie behind 326: the trial that Phormio had orchestrated before the play's beginning, an *eisangelia* for maltreatment of an *epikleros*, was risk-free for the prosecutor – a perfect risk for a *sukophantes* (cf. Is. 3. 46). Terence may have been inspired by the Athenian "risk scenario" to add the Roman joke about the judgment-debtor in 333–36. The Roman addition might begin at 329 (with the Greek idiom *scriptam dicam*!): Geta is not to suppose that Phormio will be sued for assault, lose the case, and, that, being too poor to pay the fine and unable to provide a *vindex* to dispute the plaintiff's subsequent *manus iniectio*, he will be led to the house of the plaintiff in chains (see Gaius 4. 21). Instead, wise men will think twice before they bring a parasite near their household stores.

VIII *One character suggests to another (usually a friend) that the arrest or prosecution of a third party is an appropriate response to a situation*

(1) Alexis *Epikleros* (fr. 78. 4–8 K–A).

ἀναγκάζει τ' εἶτ' ἐπάν τις ἐκδυθῆι, / τηρεῖν ἕωθεν εὐθὺς ἐν τοῖς ἰχθύσιν· / ὃν ἂν δ' ἴδηι πρῶτον πένητα καὶ νέον / παρὰ Μικίωνος ἐγχέλεις ὠνούμενον, / ἀπάγειν λαβόμενον εἰς τὸ δεσμωτήριον ("And whenever anyone has been stripped of his cloak, straightaway at dawn he must be on the watch at the fishmarket. And the first young down-and-outer he sees buying eels from Mikion – he must seize him and hale him to prison").

4 ἀναγκάζει τ' Kaibel: ἅπαντας· εἶτ' ACE: vide *PCG* app. crit.

Cf. Alexis *Lebes* frr. 130 and 131 K–A; Diphilos *Emporos* fr. 31 K–A. Hansen 1976: 51 uses the Alexis fragment cited here to show "how it had gradually become possible to arrest a supposed λωποδύτης on suspicion only." The inference is unjustifiable; the statement is obvious comic hyperbole and may well represent the speaker's stretch of the law rather than actual Athenian practice. Of interest in this and the other fragments cited here are the allusions to prison or an executioner; thus Alexis 130. 5–6: εἰς τὸ δεσμωτήριον / εὐθὺς ἀπάγεθαι ("immediately he is to be haled to the prison"); Diphilos 31. 11: τῶι δημίωι παρέδωκαν αὐτὸν ("they hand him over to the public executioner"; cf. *Rudens* 857).

(2) *Samia* IV 506–13.

ἀνδράποδ[ον εἶ, Δημέα. / εἰ γὰρ ἐμὸν ἤι[σχυνε λέ]κτρον, οὐκ ἂν εἰς ἄλλον ποτὲ / ὕβρισ' οὐδ' ἡ συγ[κλ]ιθεῖσα· παλλακὴν δ' ἂν αὔριον / πρῶτος ἀνθρώπων ἐπώλουν, συναποκηρύττων ἅμα / ὑόν, ὥστε μηθὲν εἶναι μήτε κουρεῖον κενόν, / μὴ στοάν, καθημένους δὲ πάντας ἐξ ἑωθινοῦ / περὶ ἐμοῦ λαλεῖν λέγοντας ὡς ἀνὴρ Νικήρατος / γέγον' ἐπεξελθὼν δικαίως τῶι φόνωι ("You're a slave, Demeas. For if he had shamed my bed, he would never commit an outrage against another nor would his partner do so, either. I'd be the first man up in the morning, selling my *pallake,* disinheriting my son at the same time – no barber's shop, no stoa would be empty – everyone would sit about from early morning talking about me, saying that Nikeratos, a real man, acted justifiably in prosecuting his son for homicide").

Nikeratos suggests (with hyperbole) how he would treat a son who had fathered an infant upon his *pallake.* We perhaps have a (comic) echo of Eur. *Hipp.* 1041–44, where Hippolytos addresses his father after he has consigned him to exile: καὶ σοῦ γε ταὐτὰ κάρτα θαυμάζω, πάτερ· / εἰ γὰρ σὺ μὲν παῖς ἦσθ', ἐγὼ δὲ σὸς πατήρ, / ἔκτεινά τοί σ' ἂν κοὐ φυγαῖς ἐζημίουν, / εἴπερ γυναικὸς ἠξίους ἐμῆς θιγεῖν. ("In you, too, father, I find this same thing marvellous indeed. For if you were my son and I your father, I would have killed you and not be penalizing you with exile, if indeed you had presumed to touch my wife.")

(3) *Mostellaria* III 1, 557. Roman*: criteria 4a and b.

cape, opsecro, hercle, cum eo <tu> una iudicem ("By Hercules, get a *iudex* with that man!").

While the scene is probably derived from the Greek original (see Lowe 1985c: 6–18 for Plautine changes), the slave's recommendation is not essential to it. Tranio bluffingly suggests that there might have been something fraudulent about the original contract of sale when Theopropides first bought his house – the owner did not mention that it was inhabited by a "ghost"; possibly he envisions that his master should apply for an *actio ex empto.* The whole scenario (the ghost in the house) is, of course, Tranio's invention; his advice to go to court is bravura, a seal of "truth" for his fiction. There are a number of (Plautine) legal jokes in the scene (Lowe 1985c: 13, 16–18 on verses 575b-610, 632, and 670b–672); it seems likely that this is another, added by Plautus to enhance Tranio's role. In Athens, there was no remedy for a fraudulent contract; consider the "analogous laws" which the plaintiff in Hyp. 5 *Athen.* presents in order to demonstrate the unfairness of his contract with the Egyptian businessman (chapter 1.3).

(4) *Persa* I 3, 163. Probably Greek: criterion 1a (see App. 4.2).

continuo tu illam a lenone adserito manu ("immediately make a formal claim on her from the pimp").

Toxilus instructs Saturio to assert his daughter's freedom as a preliminary to a *vindicatio in libertatem* against the pimp; in the Greek original, the slave advises the parasite to avail himself of a self-help remedy, an *aphairesis eis eleutherian.* While the pimp worries that the girl might thus be claimed free (IV 7, 716–17), and while the parasite does summon the pimp to court (IV 9), the parasite does not, in the Roman play, use the language of an *adsertor.*

(5) *Poenulus* IV 2, 905–06; cf. V 2, 964, 1102; [V 6, 1348]; [V 7 1392]: "the second trick". Provenance is indeterminable (see add. 5).

omnia memoras quo id facilius fiat: manu eas adserat, / suas popularis, liberali caussa. tacitu's? ("Your information makes it all the easier: let him claim them as free, his own countrymen, in a suit for freedom.")

Synceratus suggests to Milphio that Agorastocles should act as *adsertor* and make a symbolic seizure of the two girls as a preliminary to a *vindicatio in libertatem* or perhaps as a preliminary to a charge of "kidnapping" (App. 3.2) against the pimp. In V 2, 964, Milphio makes that suggestion to Agorastocles (*eas liberali iam adseres caussa manu*). At the end of the same scene (1102–03), Milphio suggests to Hanno that he be the *adsertor* (*manu liberali caussa ambas adseras / quasi filiae tuae sint ambae*).The pimp, upon being summoned to court, wonders why no one has made the claim before this ([v 6, 1348] and [v 7, 1392]). For argument that the entire episode of the "second trick" is Plautine expansion, that the episode in verses 1086–1110 is Plautus' insertion of Men. *Sik.* 343–60, and that the lawsuit is a legal absurdity, see Gratwick 1982: 98–101. For argument that the "second trick" belonged to the structure of the original *Karkhedonios*, see Zwierlein 1990: 138–58 (with extensive argument against proponents of the contamination theory).

(6) *Poenulus* v 5, [**1336**], [1337]. Provenance is indeterminable (see Zwierlein 1990: 70–71 and add. 5 below). The two recommendations to summon the pimp to court are not essential to the plot; they appear in a passage of Roman wordplay and possibly are interpolated.

(7) *Eunuchus* IV 6, **768**. Probably Greek: criterion 5 (see Ludwig 1973 [1959]: 383–85; 406–07; cf. cat. III. 24 above).

si vim faciet, in ius ducito hominem ("if he uses violence, bring the man to court").

In both the Roman play and its Greek model, the courtesan first points out that the rival is a foreigner and thus disadvantaged (759–60) – an observation that implies a lesser chance of success in the case of a lawsuit (cf. IX. 7 and 12); if he should use force, "Chremes" should summon him to court, presumably for assault (*iniuria* in Rome, a *dike aikeias* or *biaiōn* or a *graphe hubreos* in Athens).

(8) *Eunuchus* IV 7, 809–10 ("siege scene"). Provenance is indeterminable; see add. 9.

. . . *GN.: audin tu? hic furti se adligat: / sat[is] hoc tibist* (. . . GN.: "Are you listening? He's making himself liable to a charge of theft – that's enough for you!").

(9) *Phormio* II 4, 450–52 ("*advocati* scene"). Roman: criteria 4a and 5 (Lefèvre 1978a: 15–20).

sic hoc videtur: quod te absente hic filius / egit, restitui in integrum aequomst et bonum, / et id impetrabi'. dixi ("This is the way it seems: since your son acted when you were absent, it is fair and just that matters be restored to their pre-existing condition, and you will accomplish this. That is my opinion").

This is Cratinus' advice to Demipho concerning his son's marriage. There is no remedy in Athens that is equivalent to the Roman *in integrum restitutio*; about the remedy, see Jolowicz and Nicholas 1972: 241 and the article in *D.* 4. 4. While Lefèvre's argument that Terence invented the trial that precedes the play's opening (cat. I. 3) in order to showcase the new remedy is unlikely, the entire scene (and not simply the mention of the remedy) must be ascribed to Terence's witty invention. The scenario parodies a Roman institution, the *consilium* of advisers who offer their advice on legal matters; for a second century BC parody of a *consilium* in the entourage of a *iudex*, see C. Titius 51 F 2 *ORF*[3].

IX *A character fears that he will wind up in prison or be involved in a future court action or subjected to a self-help remedy*

(1) *Aspis* II 270–73.

ἐγὼ λάβω / τὴν οὐσίαν, τούτωι δὲ τὴν κόρην ἀφῶ / ἵν', ἂν γένηται παιδίον, φεύγω δίκην / ἔχων τὰ τούτου; ("Am I to take the estate and leave the girl to him so that if ever she has a child I must defend myself in court for possessing his property?").

Smikrines fears that the tendered estate will become subjest to dispute, perhaps a claim in a *diadikasia*; see chapter 7.1.b.

(2) *Kolax* 130–32.

. . . δέδοικα δ' οὕτω λαμβάνειν· / ἐκ τῆς ὁ]δοῦ γὰρ ἁρπάσονθ', ὅταν τύχηι, / αὐτήν.] δικάσομαι, πράγμαθ' ἕξω, μάρτ[υρας . . . ("I fear they will seize her – for they'll grab her in the street when chance allows; I shall sue; I shall have trouble; witnesses . . . ").

A charge of slave-stealing; cf. cat. III. 22 above.

(3) *Sikyonios* 133–35; 138–40.

. . . καὶ δίκην δέ τωι / ὤφλεν ὁ πατήρ, ὡς ἔοικε, ζῶν σὸς βοιωτίωι - / . . . πολλῶν ταλάντων, Στρατοφάνη, κατὰ σύμβολα. / . . . / . . . / ὄντ' ἀγώγιμόν σε τούτωι πυθομένη τῶν τοὺς νόμους / εἰδότων τήν τ' οὐσίαν σου, τοῦτο προὐνοεῖτό σου / καὶ τελευτῶσ' ἀπεδίδου σε τοῖς ἑαυτῶν εὐλόγως. (. . . "Indeed, Stratophanes, your father, while alive, incurred a penalty of many talents, owed to a certain Boiotian, in accordance with a treaty. / . . . / . . . / Your mother, upon learning from the legal experts that you were liable to the man – and your property as well, looked after your interests in the matter, and she, when she died, tried to restore you, as was reasonable, to your own family").

Much is unclear in this interesting passage. It seems that Stratophanes' putative Sikyonian father had lost a suit to a foreigner; perhaps unable to pay the sum, he had become a state debtor; he thus may have become liable to arrest (if he had not been imprisoned) and his property liable to seizure; apparently, those liabilities would be inherited by his son until the debt was paid off. Stratophanes' putative mother, fearing those consequences, provided documents of his true parentage upon her death. In Athens, merchants and shipowners who were convicted in certain mercantile suits were imprisoned until the penalty was paid ([Dem.] 33. 1; 35, 46–47; 56, 4). Since a treaty between Sikyon and Boiotia appears to be involved in Menander's play

(135), the terms of that treaty are likely to have dictated in which polis the case was to be heard (probably the defendant's) and where and under what conditions arrest, imprisonment, and seizure were permissible. For discussion, see Gomme and Sandbach 1973: 643–45 and Gauthier 1972 on *sumbola* and their judicial remedies.

(4) *Amphitruo* I 1, 155. Roman: criterion 3 (Rotelli 1972: 101–06: Fraenkel 1961: 171–75; Langen 1886: 91; add. 2).

quid faciam nunc si tresviri me in carcerem compegerint? ("What am I to do now if the *tresviri* should lock me up in prison?")

Sosia fears being imprisoned by the *tresviri* because he is walking on the streets at night. Cf. cat. nos. III. 5, 7, and 20.

(5) *Aulularia* IV 7, 700. Provenance is indeterminable.

ibo intro, ubi de capite meo sunt comitia. – ("I shall go inside, where the court is deciding my fate.")

The young man fears that his maternal uncle, who is betrothed to the girl whom he has violated, will take punitive measures against him (cf. no. 11 below). While there are no grounds for arguing that Lyconides' expression of fear has been adapted from the Greek model, the larger scenario depicted here (the fiancé's repudiation of the girl upon learning that she has been violated) derives from it (cf. cat. X. 2). See chapter 6.2.b for discussion.

(6) *Persa* IV 3, 530–31, 534–35. Provenance is indeterminable.

530–31: *nil mi opust / litibus neque tricis* ("I've no need / of lawsuits or subterfuges").
534–35: *metuo hercle vero. sensi ego iam compluriens, / neque mi haud inperito eveniet tali ut in luto haeream* ("Good grief – of course I'm afraid. I've learned these lessons many times already, and it will be no greenhand who'll be stuck in such a swamp").

Dordalus objects to buying the girl at his own risk (*suo periclo*, 524) and without a guarantee (*mancupio neque promittet neque quisquam dabit*, 525; on *promittet*, see Woytek 1992 ad loc.). Partsch (1910: 605–11) argues that the law of sale envisioned here has a Greek model for its basis. The guarantee (which is refused) would have made the Persian or Timarchides (pace Partsch) a πρατήρ, that is, a "co-vendor," who would have been responsible if need arose for warranty of title (cf. Pollux 8. 99). A Roman *mancipium* would also have provided a guarantee against eviction (see Partsch 1910; Watson 1965b: 44 and 73). In regard to the absence of a guarantee, the pimp's later statement in IV 7, after paying for the girl, is patently out of place: . . . *qui ego nunc scio / an iam adseratur haec manu? quo illum sequar? / in Persas? nugas!* ("How do I know now whether a claim of freedom will be made in her behalf at once? Where am I to pursue him? To Persia? Absurd!"

716–18). The pimp in fact needs no guarantee against this contingency – an Arabian girl's claim of freedom has no validity in Athens. Verses 716–18 are likely to be Plautine addition, anticipating Saturio's appearance at the end of the scene. The verses call attention to the entire superfluity of the "guarantee": it is mentioned, only to be withdrawn; even if offered and accepted, it is unnecessary for the one case feared by the pimp. The guarantee is inessential to the plot; it is impossible to determine whether the Greek author or Plautus invented it; hence the provenance of the passage under discussion (in fact, the entire "guarantee motif") is indeterminable.

(7) *Poenulus* [V 7, 1403–04]. Provenance is indeterminable (see add. 5).

si volo hunc ulcisci, litis sequar in alieno oppido, / quantum audivi ingenium et mores eiius quo pacto sient ("If I want vengeance on this man, I shall be suing him in a foreign town, with all the special spirit and customs I've heard the townspeople have").

The particular motif here, a foreigner's fear of bringing suit in a foreign city, might be anyone's (misplaced?) replica of a Greek scenario (cf. VIII. 7 and IX. 12).

(8) *Pseudolus* I 3, 303–04. Roman: criterion 4a (other Roman additions in I 3 are noted by Williams 1956: 427–32).

CALL.: perii! annorum lex me perdit quinavicenaria. / metuont credere omnes. BA.: eadem est mihi lex: metuo credere (CALL.: "I'm undone! The law about twenty-five-year-olds destroys me! Everyone fears to give credit." BA. "The law is the same for me: I fear to give credit").

The reference is to the *lex Laetoria* (see cat. VI. 4).

(9) *Rudens* II 5, 474–77. Provenance is indeterminable. Sceparnio fears that a trap has been set for him, that he will be caught carrying a sacred vessel from Venus' shrine, and that any magistrate who sees him thus will put him in chains. Athenian and Roman law are similar in regard to such criminals. Under Athenian law, temple robbers were probably treated as *kakourgoi*; if arrested and convicted, they would be put to death (see chapter 2.2.a). In early Roman law, sacrilege was penalized with death (Mommsen 1899: 769 n.3). Lefèvre 1984: 11 and 13 thinks that Sceparnio is a Plautine creation, likewise Ampelisca, likewise this scene. The hypothesis is one of many.

(10) *Trinummus* V 2, 1145–46. Roman: criterion 4a.

neu qui rem ipsam posset intellegere, [et] thensaurum tuom / me esse penes, atque eum [a] me lege populi patrium posceret ("[I arranged that he deliver the money . . .] so that Lesbonicus might not learn the very truth, that your treasure was under my control, and then demand it from me under public law as part of his paternal property").

Callicles explains to Charmides why he had devised the circuitous means of obtaining the dowry for his daughter. The remedy referred to here might be the *lex Laetoria* (see cat. VI. 4 and IX. 8); the designation *lex populi* is a pointer. Lesbonicus had sold his father's house to Callicles while his father was out of town; Callicles fears that Lesbonicus could sue him for taking advantage of him fraudulently – he had intentionally concealed the buried treasure from him. There is no precisely equivalent remedy in Athens. While it is possible that Plautus is adapting an Athenian's fear of impeachment for maltreating an orphan (a public charge: *AP* 56. 6; [Dem.] 43. 75), that is only a remote possibility: the application of the remedy would require that "Charmides" be dead.

(11) *Truculentus* IV 3, 818–20. Provenance is indeterminable (see chapter 6.3.b).

lapideus sum, commovere me miser non audeo. / res palam omnis est, meo illic nunc sunt capiti comitia. / meum illuc facinus, mea stultitia est. timeo quam mox nominer. ("I've turned into stone – I dare not make a move in my wretched condition. Everything is out in the open, now the court is deciding my fate.")

Diniarchus, like Lyconides in *Aul.* IV 7 (no. 5 above), fears that Callicles will take punitive measures against him for the rape of his daughter.

(12) *Andria* IV 5, 810–14. Probably Greek: criterion 5 (see Büchner 1974: 100–01; Lefèvre 1971: 41–44).

nunc me hospitem / litis sequi quam id mihi sit facile atque utile / aliorum exempla commonent. simul arbitror / iam aliquem esse amicum et defensorem ei; nam fere / grandi[us]cula iam profectast illinc: . . . ("The experience of others is fair warning how easy and profitable it is for me to go to law as a stranger! At the same time, I bet she has a friend and protector; for she was already a big girl when she left: . . . ").

Crito has just arrived in Athens from Andros, hoping to take undisputed possession of Chrysis' estate (799); he has found out, however, that Chrysis' putative sister (Glycerium) has not yet discovered her true parents and he assumes that she is in possession of the estate; he will now, so he thinks, have to dispute the case in court with a woman who might have more influential support – and a much better case: if Glycerium's advocates are convincing in the claim that she is Chrysis' sister, she would automatically exclude Crito from the estate by the rules of intestate inheritance – in both Athens (lex apud [Dem.] 43. 51) and Rome (*XII* Tables 5. 4–5). In the Greek original, "Crito" in 810–12 imagines the difficulties he will encounter in summoning "Glycerium" to appear before the polemarch for the adjudication of the estate (see MacDowell 1978: 102–03 and lex apud [Dem.] 43. 16). For an argument that the concluding verses (814–16) of the speech are Terence's addition, see add. 13.

(13) *Hecyra* III 1, 332–35. Probably Greek: criterion 5 (see Büchner 1974: 131; add. II on torture).

servom ilico introisse dicent Sostratae, / aliquid tulisse comminiscentur mali / capiti atque aetati illorum morbu' qui auctu' sit: / era in crimen veniet, ego vero in magnum malum ("they will immediately say that Sostrata's slave entered the house; they will invent a story that he carried something fatal to the girl's life and limb which caused the illness to worsen; my mistress will be accused, I'll suffer terrible trouble").

The slave Parmeno explains his lack of desire to accompany Pamphilus as the latter enters the house where his wife lies sick: he thinks his mistress will be charged with murder (or plotting to murder); he will be an accomplice and tortured in the subsequent investigation.

X *A character dreams, wishes for, or invents a story about a summons, a trial, or a self-help remedy*

(1) *Aspis* 365–67

]πως ἦλθεν ἐπὶ τὴν οἰκίαν /]τις γέγον' ὀφείλων· εἴ τινι /]διπλάσιον εἰσπράττει πάνυ

Interpretation of the fragmentary verses is speculative. Possibly Daos uses the exacting of a twofold penalty from a petty debtor-thief as a "blueprint" for retribution against Smikrines: Thus: "if you see a petty thief making off with a few choice goods, you exact for yourself twice the amount." The analogue is left unstated: "Now, when you see your brother getting his hands on your entire estate, you put it to him with a double punch." Lloyd-Jones 1971 thinks that Daos is actually suggesting that Smikrines himself will be caught red-handed as a thief and that Khairestratos should follow up with a prosecution for theft. For discussion of both views, see chapter 8, nn. 13–15.

(2) *Fabula Incerta*. In the first part of the fragment (at least verses 1–31), Lakhes is apparently led to believe that his son Moskhion has been caught in the act of raping a girl and imprisoned until some form of compensation can be arranged (Körte 1937: 69; Gomme and Sandbach 1973: 683); Khaireas, pretending to be fiancé or husband (the text is ambiguous), meets with Lakhes. Fear of a violent mode of redress ( ] ἐ[κ τηλι]κούτων νῦν φόβων / τὸν ὑὸν ἐκ[λυσά]μενος 44–45) explains Lakhes' eagerness to persuade Khaireas to accept his daughter in (compensatory!) return for the raped girl. To modern eyes, the proposed exchange is crude; to Athenian eyes, it must have been, at least, unusual: physical violence or monetary compensation would be the expected form of redress. Above all, the exchange is a comical riff in the rape plot. We may be missing an important clue from the opening of the dialogue between the two men. As Robert (1915: 279) first

suggested, Khaireas may have envisioned obtaining Lakhes' daughter as part of the plan.

(3) *Perikeiromene* II, 356–57.

. . . ἀκαρές δέω δὲ φάσκειν καταλαβεῖν / τὸν μοιχὸν ἔνδον, ἵν' ἀναπηδήσας τρέχηι – ("I'm dying to say that I detected the *moikhos* inside, so that he'll run in with a flying leap").

The slave envisions that Polemon will inflict a self-help remedy on Moskhion. Whether such a remedy was sanctioned by law in the case of violators of *pallakai* is not known (on Glukera's status, see cat. no. VII. 1 above). The phrase, however, might be comic *katakhresis*; see Gomme and Sandbach 1973 apud *Perik.* 499–503 and *Samia* 509; Bushala 1969: 65; Konstan 1995: 111.

(4) *Bacchides* II 3, 270–72. Provenance is indeterminable.

postquam quidem praetor recuperatores dedit, / damnatus demum, vi coactus reddidit / ducentos et mill' Philippum ("Well, after the praetor assigned *recuperatores*, he lost the case and was compelled to pay twelve hundred coins").

The hearing before the *recuperatores* is part of a fictive narrative (251–336) woven by a sly slave for his master's consumption. The narrative is essential to the plot since it provides Mnesilochus access to his father's money; the particular details, however, of Archidemides' refusal to pay the debt and the subsequent hearing are not. While other details are confirmed by a fragment from *Dis exapaton* (cf. *Bacch.* 306ff. and *Dis exap.* 54–56) and while it is plausible that Plautus has given a more or less accurate adaptation of the false tale (Primmer 1984: 44, n. 86), there can be no certainty in regard to all thc details. For discussion of *recuperatores* in this passage from a Roman perspective, see esp. Kelly 1976: 47–48. Barsby 1986 ad loc. suggests that the *recuperatores* might represent an official arbitrator in the Greek original, to whom the tribal judges assigned the case. A different possibility is that a private arbitration appeared in the original, with "Pelagon" as *diaitetes* (261–68). In that case, the scenario involving the *recuperatores* is Plautus' wholesale invention.

(5) *Persa* II 4, 288–89. Roman: criteria 3 and 4a.

PA. at tu domum: nam ibi tibi parata praestost. / SAG. vadatur hic me. PA. utinam vades desint, in carcere ut sis. (PA.: "You, go home: trouble has been guaranteed for you there ." SAG. "He's binding me over by bail!" PA. "May your sureties desert you – so you'll wind up in prison.")

Both slaves use the terminology of *vadimonium* (a promise of court appearance secured by a *vindex*); see chapter 2 at n. 59 and cat. I. 1 above. Woytek 1982 ad loc. discusses the Roman wordplay; on the connection between *praes* and *praesto*, see Skutsch 1910.

(6) *Rudens* III 1, **608**. Provenance is indeterminable. Some critics have accepted the dream in which the summons appears as based on the Diphilan original: the dream anticipates the action in the ensuing scenes; the summons of the dream is acted out by the pimp at 718 and 719; and Daemones explicitly recognizes the dream's fulfillment in III 4, 771–73 (for detailed argument, see Drexler 1934: 41–51 and, more succinctly, Lefèvre 1984a: 17–18; for dreams in New Comedy and their relation to Greek predecessors, see references in Leo 1912: 162–65 and add Alexis fr. 274 K–A and Men. *Dusk.* 410ff.). The dream is similar to the one in *Merc.* II 1 (cf. esp *Rud.* 593–97 and 611–12 and *Merc.* 225–28 and 252–54); both use animals as human characters; in both, a monkey threatens the dreamer – but in *Merc.*, without recourse to the law. If we accept dreams as a Greek motif by which the action of the play is anticipated in riddle form (on the Greek origin of *Merc.* II.1, see Brown 1980: 65, n. 7), the court summons in *Rudens* might be part of the original – but in that case, there will have been considerable alteration in III 4 (see cat. VI. 3). The most economical explanation is that Plautus has spooned on the dream's legal sauce – he has added the summons to court.

(7) *Eunuchus* V 4, 952–57 and 5, 992–93. Probably Greek: criterion 5 (cf. Büchner 1974: 296–98; Ludwig 1973 [= 1959]: 400).

957: *nunc minatur porro sese id quod moechis solet* ("now he's threatening the punishment that is customary for *moechi*").

In both the Roman play and its Greek model, the maid informs a slave that his master's son is about to suffer physical punishment at the hands of the violated girl's brother. An Athenian legal context is suggested by 960–61 (cf. [Dem.] 59. 67). The slave subsequently reports the (false) tale to his master (cf. 992–93). In the end, the young man is betrothed to his victim.

(8) *Phormio* IV 3, 626–31. Probably Greek: criteria 1a and 2b (see Donatus on 647 and 668; discussion in chapter 4.2.b).

"*an legibus / daturum poenas dices si illam eiecerit? / iam id exploratumst: heia sudabis satis / si cum illo inceptas homine: ea eloquentiast. / verum pone esse victum eum; at tandem tamen / non capitis ei(u)s res agitur sed pecuniae.*" ("Or under the terms of the law will you say that he will have to pay a penalty for expelling the girl? This has already been investigated. Ah! – You'll be the one sweating horribly if you pick a quarrel with that man: he is eloquence personified. But suppose he lose the case; in the final analysis, his life's not at stake – only his money.")

Geta acts out a dialogue that he pretends to have had with Phormio: should the parasite sue his master for maltreating the heiress, an out-of-court settlement will be more profitable for him.

ADDENDA

1 CAT. III. 2: *MISGUNE* FR. 279 K–T

The term *graphe* occurs only in this fragment of Menander. While its usage here is vague (and that may be due to the loss of surrounding context), it does not appear to be incorrect. The phrase *graphen apopherein*, which refers to the bringing of the physical document (whether in a public or private action), is first found in the Demosthenic corpus: 18. [54], [105]; 19. 257; 23. 5; [26. 8, 11]; 27. 12; [58. 32, 46]; also, in Aiskhin. 3. 217, 219 (bis), and 227; see Calhoun 1919b: 177–78 and 188–89 for discussion. As for *graphe* here: while there was a public action (*eisangelia*, "impeachment") for maltreatment, a *graphe* in the strict sense may not have been available for that offense (Harp., s.v. *eisangelia*; MacDowell 1978: 94; Rhodes 1981: 629 on *AP* 56.6); but *graphe* might be used in the fragment in its wider sense and so refer to any kind of public action (cf. *AP* 56.6, [Dem.] 58. 32, and Is. 11. 28, 31, 32, 35 where the remedy for maltreatment is designated a *graphe* – and Is. 11. 6 and 15 where it is referred to as *eisangelia*). Elsewhere, Menander uses *dike* at *Aspis* 272 and *Perik.* 502 to refer to what were probably private lawsuits (cat. nos. IX.1 and VII.1); at *Sik.* 133–34, *dike* refers to a penalty incurred as the result of a lawsuit.

2 CAT. III. 5, 7, 19 AND IX . 4: *TRESVIRI* IN *ASIN.* 131–33, *AUL.* 415–17, *TRUC.* 759–63, AND *AMPH.* 155

The existence of the *tresviri* in the third century is attested by the *lex Papiria de sacramentis* (Bruns[7] 47; for recent treatment, see Cloud 1992); their early sphere of competency and/or jurisdiction (i.e., judicial capacity) is much debated and to a large extent depends on the interpretation of the four passages cited above and additionally, *Pers.* 68–74. Determination of the provenance of all five passages is of the utmost importance for Roman jurists. Both Mommsen (1899: 159 n. 2, 690, 860) and Kunkel (1962: 68–69) accept the Plautine *tresviri* as depictions of Roman magistrates.

Kunkel, who argues that the *tresviri capitales* exercised a summary criminal jurisdiction (i.e. a judicial capacity) over the Roman lower classes, found evidence in the *Aul.* passage (cat. III. 7) for the early existence of the substance of the Sullan *lex Cornelia de sicariis et veneficis*. Nippel 1988: 42, however, points out that the reporting of names does not require any subsequent action, such as the bringing of a charge by the informant or the presiding over a court by the *tresviri*. The passages from *Aul.* and *Amph.* depict "police functions" of the *tresviri* at most and have been designated in the catalogue as Plautine additions; the two passages appear in contexts that are demonstrably Plautine (see bibl. cited in cat.).

Some legal historians have also used the other three passages (from *Asin.*, *Pers.*, and *Truc.*) as evidence for the judicial capacity of the *tresviri*. Before we examine that issue, let us consider the origin of the passages. *Pers.* 68–74, which is part of the pimp's monologue extending from 53–80, has been subjected to much critical scrutiny (esp. the significance of the notorious *quadrupulator* in verse 70); see Cloud 1992: 175–86 for discussion and survey of earlier treatments (to which add the discussions of Partsch 1910: 598–602 and Huvelin 1915: 231–36, and see add. 13 below). Re-examination of the passage is not called for here. Attempts to explain verses 68–74 in terms of Roman law have been unsuccessful (see Cloud 1992: 177–79). The arguments of Partsch 1910, Leo: 1912^2: 123–25, and Paoli 1976 (= 1953b) which conclude by acknowledging the Greek background of the passage are surely correct in general. Saturio's proposal (verses 68–69) to require the successful prosecutor to give half his award to the state suggests the Attic procedure of *phasis* (see MacDowell 1991, with discussion of ancient sources). Saturio's additional proposal (verses 70–72) is best explained by Paoli: the *quadrupulator* (= *sukophantes*) who arrests his former victim (now condemned and *atimos*) as a state debtor is to undergo the same treatment: the victim is to arrest his arrester as a state debtor, for failing to hand over half his award to the *praktores*. Cf. the legal joke at Ar. *Birds* 1664–66: first the law offers hope of gain, then it takes it away. Plautus has translated the complicated Greek scenario which is imaginary and full of nonsense: he has not adapted it to Roman realia.

Attribution of *Asin.* 131–33 to a source is less certain: while the metrical context of the passage and its similarity to the content of *Truc.* 759–63 lend plausibility to an argument for Plautine addition, translation or adaptation of the Greek original of *Asin.* cannot be ruled out. The particular offense for which the prostitute and her mother are to be denounced is not named, but the over-charging of clients fits the context (*Asin.* 1 3); possibly a similar offense lies behind one of Diniarchus' charges, viz., that the prostitute has "accepted money illegally [i.e., beyond the regulated price] from many men." The *astunomoi* of Athens saw to it "that the girls who play the pipes, the harp, and the lyre are not hired out for more than two dr., and if several men are eager to get the same girl, they draw lots and hire her out to the winner" (*AP* 50. 2). Rhodes 1981 ad loc., referring to the "girls," comments, "no doubt they might also be called for to provide sexual entertainment"; pointing to the absence of *orkhestrides* from the list, he suggests that it is incomplete. In Hyp. 3 *Eux.* 3, two men are impeached before the *boule* for hiring out female pipers at a price higher than the lawful one; context suggests that while the offense was not unusual, the procedure used in this instance was (for details, see Hansen 1975: 108–09). Suda 1. 254. 4–5 (Adler) reports that the *agoranomoi* (perhaps a mistake for *astunomoi*?) kept a list of *hetairai*, citing "how much each was to receive" (presumably from clients). Since prostitutes were taxed in Athens (Aiskhin. 1 *Tim.* 119–24; Pollux 7. 202 and 9. 29 cites a *pornotelones* mentioned by the comic poet Philonides), some scholars have supposed that the *agoranomoi* might have kept a list of *hetairai* for tax purposes (see Lenschau *RE* s.v. *Pornikon telos*). There is at least an analogous Athenian context, therefore, for magistrates who oversaw brothels, keeping a list of prostitutes and regulating their pay, from which Plautus could have made a Roman translation or adaptation rather than a wholesale addition in *Asin.* 131–33.

Treatment of the *Truc.* passage is more problematic because of the uncertainty regarding its relation to a Greek model (see chapter 6.3.b and n. 56). But whether one hypothesizes that the play has little resemblance to its Greek original or whether one assumes there was none, the passage might still be regarded as adaptation of *Asin.* 131–33; on that hypothesis, *Truc.* 759–63 might ultimately depend on the Greek model for *Asin.* Alternatively, the passage might simply replicate a commonly known Greek scenario.

Thus far: *Pers.* 68–74 is a Roman translation of a Greek scenario with little concern to adapt that scenario to Roman realia; *Asin.* 131–33 might be translation or adaptation rather than addition, and *Truc.* 759–63 might have a more remote relationship to a Greek original. To what extent might the latter two passages represent Roman realia? Do they provide evidence that the *tresviri* – or the aediles – possessed a regular jurisdiction over prostitutes or only a competency to oversee them (i.e., as part of a general directive to keep order in the city)? It should be noted that the *tresviri* are not named in *Truc.*; the officials are called *novi magistratus* and might represent the aediles. The passage from *Asin.* is the only one that associates (in asyndeton) the *tresviri* with jurisdiction. A common feature shared by both the *Asin.* and *Truc.* passages, however, is that the young men threaten to denounce the women's names to officials. Tac. *Ann.* 2. 85 reports that a woman published her *licentia stuprum* to the aediles, *more inter veteres recepto, qui satis poenarum adversum impudicas in ipsa professione flagitii credebant* ("since it was the custom among our ancestors, who thought that a public declaration of her shameful conduct was sufficient punishment for an unchaste woman"). Mommsen 1899: 159 n. 2 interprets the Plautine passages in the light of the Tacitean one: the aediles or their help-mates the *tresviri* kept a list of prostitutes. Note that Plautus' naughty women are already prostitutes or bawds; presumably there is no (Tacitean) need to report their names – they are not posing as *matronae.* Moreover, the young men hope to exact penalties greater than the public humiliation implied by Tac. *Ann.* 2. 85. It seems, then, that Tacitus' "antique" denunciations of prostitutes serve quite a different function from those of Roman Comedy. See McGinn (1992: 281–84) who cogently argues against accepting Tacitus' statement as evidence for the antiquity of a "list of prostitutes." An economical hypothesis that suits the evidence (the comic passages in conjunction with later evidence) might propose that the *tresviri* worked alongside the aediles in overseeing brothels while the latter on occasion introduced extraordinary public trials involving scandalous immoral conduct (see chapter 5.2). The young men's desire for severe penalties is (unrealistic) comic exaggeration: so egregious is the conduct of the women, that exceptional public trials are called for. Cf. Cloud 1992: 181 on *Truc.*: "His [Diniarchus'] words are part of an explosion of rage against her [Phronesium]: he means no more than that he will sue her in every court in the land for every penny he can squeeze out of her." There is no specific allusion – Plautine persiflage. Cf. Nippel 1988: 27–47.

In sum, both *Asin.* 131–33 and *Truc.* 759–63 might be adaptations of a Greek model (but a more remote one in the case of *Truc.*) rather than wholesale addition. Both passages, however, show Plautine elaboration in the comic exaggeration of penalties. The Plautine passages support the evidence for the existence of the *tresviri* in the late third century, but the passages should not be used to create an argument for their judicial capacity.

3 CAT. III. II: *CURC.* V 2, 619–**21**, **625**

The soldier has entered the stage in search of Phaedromus, with the explicitly articulated intention of recovering his money or the girl his money has purchased (612, and cf. 586). The soldier's quest is embedded in the plot structure of the play: first he makes the demand of the banker (IV 3), then of the pimp (IV 4), and now of Phaedromus (V 2). There is thus a steady progression as he moves toward his goal and that progression is surely part of the Greek original. The provenance of Phaedromus' response to the soldier's threat is not so easily determined. Tenuous dramatic grounds, however, might suggest a Greek origin: Phaedromus must resist the soldier's demand and at the same time elicit information about the origin of his ring; given this dramatic situation, the only feasible way for "Phaedromus" to act in the Greek original is to put "Therapontigonus" in a defensive position by making a counter-threat.

A problem lies in Phaedromus' articulation of the charge. If the scenario in the Greek original is to operate other than as a "legal fiction" (see App. 3.1), then "Phaedromus" must know the girl's homeland; moreover, the girl's homeland (if it is not Epidauros) must have a treaty with Epidauros (where the play is set). Unless these conditions are met, the girl will have no legal redress in Epidauros – and will be unable to marry "Phaedromus" at play's end. But Planesium herself does not appear to know where she was born (Plautus never informs us) and Phaedromus appears to have learned only shortly before the soldier's appearance that she was born free (607). Possibly the Greek playwright supplied the necessary details (see Gratwick 1969: 472–81). Even so, the threat would remain a bluff: its grounds (viz., that the girl's freedom would be protected in Epidauros) would be incapable of proof – except for one tenuous piece of evidence of unknown value – the ring which the soldier had lost and which the girl claims her father wore. All would hang on the ability of the soldier to trace the ring back to an earlier owner who may be the girl's father. The soldier knows nothing of the ring's evidentiary value yet. But if "Phaedromus" claimed the girl was an *aste* of Epidauros or of a city granted *asulia* by Epidauros, then surely at this point the latter would prick up his ears and be receptive (cf. Daemones' response in *Rudens* when he first learns that Palaestra claims Attic birth, *mea popularis, opsecro, haec est?* 740): the girl is a candidate for marriage and not concubinage. That such changes in female status (from sought-after *pallake* to pledged wife) are not unwelcome to the lovers of New Comedy is evident from the plots of *Perikeiromene* and *Sikyonios*. If "Phaedromus" in the Greek original of *Curculio* were to state boldly the girl's *polis* of origin, whether fortuitously improvising (which should not be ruled out) or as knowing it for certain, then his "arrest" would be a cogent dramatic strategy to persuade the soldier to listen and to supply the information about the ring's origin. The arrest is a bluff and its purpose is manipulative, to attract the soldier's attention and sympathy as expeditiously as possible.

4 CAT. III. 14: TWO PROBLEMS WITH *POENULUS* III 5, 782–85

(a) In III 5, 782–84, Agorastocles asks the pimp to hand over the purse containing the 300 *philippi*; it is usually assumed that Agorastocles "seizes" the gold (Jocelyn 1992: 131; Lowe 1990: 287; Zwierlein 1990: 287–88). In V 7, however, the gold is still in the pimp's hands. The "inconsistency" has occasioned various explanations (see the two authors cited last). The simplest solution is that Agorastocles does not pick up the gold (if the pimp in fact sets it down: cf. *omitte* at *Poen.* 784 and *Rud.* 1015); Agorastocles then leaves the stage empty-handed to search the house for his slave and expects the *advocati* to attend to the gold during his absence. Cf. Dordalus' brief exit at the end of *Pers.* IV 7, 722–23: just as Agorastocles exits briefly, leaving the money on-stage, so Dordalus exits briefly, leaving the Arabian captive behind (without credible motivation as noted, e.g. by Langen 1886: 180). Both exits are dramatically effective; Agorastocles' neglect of the money allows the pimp to abscond with it in the interim; Dordalus' neglect of the Arabian girl makes it all the easier for the parasite's arrival and removal of his daughter.

(b) On the basis of III 5, 785, *manufesto fur es*, modern scholars have sometimes assumed that the legal scenario envisioned in this scene is *furtum manifestum* (e.g. Huvelin 1915: 179 ff.; Watson 1965: 230: apparently Jocelyn 1993: 131). Gaius 3. 184 is testimony to considerable fuzziness concerning the definition of *manifestum furtum*; while he does not provide a date for the different opinions he cites (e.g. "so long as the thief is carrying the thing to the place to which he planned to take it" or "whenever the thief is seen with the thing"), there is no reason to think that the concept was pellucid in Plautus' era. Since the *advocati* have witnessed the pimp's reception of slave and money and since the pimp is seen holding the latter, spectators might well have viewed the offense as *furtum manifestum* (for discussion, see Watson 1965: 230). The penalty for a free man convicted of this offense under the *XII Tables* was scourging and *addictio* to the plaintiff; the severity of the penalty was lessened by the praetor's edict, which prescribed a fourfold penalty for free and slave alike (Gaius 3. 189); the date for the introduction of the praetorian offense is not known (Huvelin 1915: 236 concludes there is no trace of it in Roman comedy of the second century). At 654, the *advocati* predict that the pimp will suffer *addictio*; in 1341, the pimp fears he will suffer this penalty (in language recalling his exit line at 795); and at 1361–62 (a probable interpolation), he prefers to make himself *addictus* to Agorastocles rather than to appear *in ius* (cf. *Truc.* 840–41).

A problem arises, however, when the scenario of *furtum manifestum* in III 5 is contrasted with 183–84 and 1351 where the penalty envisioned for Lycus is a twofold one; whereas the latter verse is probably interpolated, the former is not. (It should be noted that the *addictio* implied in 186 is that of a judgment debtor: see cat. III. 14 above; it is not the personal *addictio* of early *furtum manifestum*, contra Huvelin 1915: 185–90.) A twofold penalty is attached, not to *furtum manifestum*, but to *furtum nec manifestum* (Gaius 3. 190). If the offense in III 5 is *furtum manifestum*, why is the penalty for *furtum nec manifestum* mentioned in 184? Witt 1971: 240–41 conjectures that in III 5 (see esp. 790), Plautus is translating an Athenian remedy, *apagoge* (arrest), that has no Roman counterpart: the pimp is taken as a thief *ep' autophōroi*, but he escapes before he can be haled to the Eleven. "Agorastocles" must now content himself with bringing a *dike klopes* for which the penalty is twofold. The transformation of the arrest into a summons in the Athenian play occasions the change in penalty (from death to a fine that equalled twice the value of the stolen object – a "twofold penalty").

Witt's solution will not work. Milphio in 184 foresees a twofold penalty as the outcome of the plan; *furtum nec manifestum* is envisioned from the beginning. Would the Greek "Milphio" have planned a *dike klopes* or an arrest at the outset? Which penalty would he have foreseen at this point? Certainly not the penalty for a thief who was convicted in a trial initiated by arrest: the penalty would be the pimp's death; the girls would presumably become the property of the pimp's heirs. But the twofold penalty of the *dike klopes* would lead to consequences similar to those of the twofold Roman penalty: while the pimp might restore the slave and give up the two girls (as "twice the value" of the stolen slave), he would be forced to sell his household in order to acquire 600 *philippi* (double the 300 he stole).

Manufesto fur es is therefore a verse composed – whether by Plautus or by the Greek poet (cf. *Samia* 717, *Sik.* 272, and Hyp. 5. 12) – for dramatic effect; the designation frightens the pimp – indeed, it motivates his exit from the stage. Plautine origin, however, is more likely: the notion of *manifestum furtum* allows for the introduction of the motif of personal *addictio* in accordance with the prescription of the *XII Tables* 8. 14 (cf. 795 and 1341). Thus Gratwick 1969: 393–407: the words *manufesto fur es* are for dramatic effect; moreover, the motif of personal *addictio* is Plautine addition – it certainly would have no part in an Athenian arrest or a *dike klopes*. That interpretation, in turn, supports Lowe's hypothesis (1990: 286) that the witnesses of the Greek original had a much smaller role to play: they might not have witnessed the bailiff's surrender of the money to the pimp; their allusion to the *addictio* of the pimp himself in 564 will be Plautine addition. If Plautus did not himself add 785, he certainly exploited it beyond what can be conjectured for the Greek original. The creation of a scenario of *furtum manifestum* in III 5 (with tentacles in III 1, 564 and V 6, 1341) for dramatic effect at the expense of consistency is harmonious with the dramaturgic creativity of Plautus.

5 CAT. III. 16, 17; VIII. 5 AND 7; IX. 6: THE CONCLUDING SCENES OF *POEN.* AND THE "SECOND TRICK"

I have no confidence in identifying which parts, if any, of the final scenes (starting from the end of V 5) are genuinely Plautine; I have bracketed passages from this portion of the play as possible interpolation. See Zwierlein 1990: 56–94 for a summary of earlier views and p. 59 for a tabulation of passages regarded as spurious by earlier scholars. Zwierlein argues that V 7 is the genuine Plautine ending of the play. He supports this view, in part, by pointing out the "jurististic implications" of the "genuine" (V 7) and "spurious" (V 6) scenes. The basis of this particular argument is unsound and certainly unproven: it assumes both that we can reconstruct Roman procedure on the basis of Roman Comedy in the absence of other evidence and that Plautus would not have presented legal scenarios that were juristically absurd from a Roman standpoint (cf. add. 2 and 4!). Zwierlein (e.g. 91 and nn. 168–70) accepts the hypotheses of Witt's 1971 dissertation and pursues them beyond the limits set by the latter author.

Reconstruction of the Greek original is also problematic. The legal scenario envisioned in the "second trick" is viewed by some scholars as too implausible for an Attic poet to have invented: a Carthaginian contemplating a suit – whether for kidnapping or in behalf of the girls' free status (cat. VIII. 5 and IX. 7) – against a pimp who had bought his daughters in a slave market in a Greek city (Gratwick 1982: 99–100; Jocelyn 1993: 134). The international complexity of the legal problems in this play may be beyond resolution.

6 CAT. III. 21: *ADELPHOE* II 1, 193–95

On the difficulties that arise from Aeschinus' claim that the abducted girl is "free" at verse 194 (she remains a slave in the "Menandrian plot"), concomitant with the offer to purchase her at verse 195, see Rieth 1964: 57 and Fantham 1968: 202 for various solutions. Lloyd-Jones 1990 (= 1973): 90 suggests that when Aeschinus vindicates the girl's freedom in 194, "he may make joking allusion to the procedure of *manumissio* by saying that he vindicates her liberty 'with his hand', meaning 'by force.'" This is the most economical interpretation of Terence's text – Aeschinus has, after all, carried her off by force and he thus calls attention to the effect of his power, actual possession of the girl. If this solution is adopted, then the young man's claim of the girl's freedom and his subsequent challenge to the pimp might still have appeared in the Diphilan original: while the pun is neater in Latin (and Terence's capacity for adding legal jokes ought not to be underestimated – see cat. nos. VII. 3 and VIII. 9), it might still be an adaptation of the young man's (Greek) boast that he had "removed the girl" into freedom, perhaps a euphemistic expression for a kidnapping.

7 CAT. III. 21 AND 22: *ADELPHOE* II 1 AND 2

Most commentators have ignored the subject of the pimp's aside in *Ad.* II 2, 228–35 (where he reflects upon the feasibility of a suit) and the indirect (bluffing) threat that is evident in 248–49 (e.g. Drexler 1934: 8–12; Fantham 1968; Büchner 1974: 373–75). Is the content of his aside and the indirect threat Terentian stitching, added to unite the Menandrian scene to the Diphilan? Or did the pimp contemplate a suit in the Menandrian play as well? Knowledge of the immediacy of the business trip to Cyprus is integral to the slave's successful dealing with the pimp in II 2; the immediacy of the trip renders futile any lengthy dealings between the pimp and the young man; and a suit would entail lengthy dealings. The immediacy of the trip is thus required to cancel the possibility of a suit (cf. Dem. 33. 25 and 47. 30). Unless we are prepared to drop much of the slave's dealing with the pimp in II 2 and the motif of the trip to Cyprus in its entirety (cf. II 3, 277), then the contemplation of a suit and the indirect threat of one were part of the Menandrian original. The mediating role of the slave (see chapter 4.2.a) and the pattern of entering into negotiation at the same time as threatening a suit support this view. Gratwick 1987: 240 suggests that the pimp's aside "sounds like material transferred from the Menandrian entrance-speech replaced by 197ff." Thus the pimp in Menander's scene corresponding to Terence II 2 will have contemplated a suit – and the suit will have been for slave-stealing (232–34: we must assume that the object of *perdere* is the girl), not for the hubristic assault at the opening of the Diphilan scene (162 and 163, with Rieth's interpretation reported in cat. III. 21). There are thus loose threads in Terence's stitching: the suits contemplated in II 1 (Diphilos) and II 2 (Menander) do not quite match.

8 CAT. III. 23: HEGIO AND SOSTRATA IN *ADELPHOE* III 2 AND 4

Donatus on 351: *apud Menandrum Sostratae frater inducitur* ("in Menander, he is introduced as Sostrata's brother"). The report has been called into question. Golden 1985: 11–13 inventively suggests that Donatus has transliterated φράτηρ by *frater* since there was no equivalent Latin term. The strongest support he offers is Varro's use of *fratria* as a transliteration of φρατρία. But acceptance of Golden's suggestion is difficult: it requires not only accepting the notion that women were introduced into phratries (on Is. 3. 79, see Cole 1984: 235–38; Sealey 1987: 18) or that a phratry member would be called a woman's (fellow-) *phrater* (for which there is no attested evidence), but also attribution of linguistic obtuseness verging on incapacity on the part of Donatus in treating a Menandrian play entitled *Adelphoi* (= *Fratres*!).

Gaiser in Rieth 1964: 72 n.109 and 145, on the other hand, focuses upon Menander fr. 6 K–T: "It's a difficult feat for the poor to find a kinsman (συγγενῆ); for no one admits that a person in need of assistance is his relation (αὐτῶι προσήκειν), since he instantly expects to be asked for a donation." Gaiser argues that the words would inappropriately describe "Hegio" if he were brother of "Sostrata" since a brother could hardly have been so distanced from his sister's affairs (see also Rieth 1964: 73); Gaiser thus suggests that "Hegio" was brother of "Simulus"; perhaps "Micio" could have spoken the verses in a brief entrance monologue before he meets with "Hegio" (p. 145). Gaiser ignored the most significant consequence of his solution: "Hegio" as brother of "Simulus" has a very close legal relationship to the daughter of "Sostrata" – a father's brother would be first in line to marry or dower a poor *epikleros*. "Hegio" as brother of "Sostrata" is likewise in the *ankhisteia* – only much further down the ladder; nonetheless, he, too, in the absence of paternal kin, has an obligation to marry or dower the girl. Gaiser's solution (which might, in the end, be right) intensifies the problem.

The complication of the legal responsibilities of "Hegio" might explain the reason for Terence's change from "Hegio" as brother (whether of "Sostrata" or of "Simulus") to Hegio as distant relation and close friend of Simulus. A trace of the change might be evident in the story that Micio tells Aeschinus in IV 4, that the closest relative has just arrived from Miletos and plans to marry the girl in accordance with the laws (i.e., concerning poor *epikleroi*: 650–54). Gratwick (1987: 251 apud 652) notes that Terence has lost "the neat point . . . that there really was someone indoors with the right to the option claimed by the 'visitor from Miletus.'" The "neat point" can be pressed further: "Hegio" might very well have just arrived from Miletos – to dower or even to claim the *epikleros* (cf. the plot of *Aul.*, in which a nephew competes with his maternal uncle for the same bride, likewise a victim of the young man's sexual assault). Note the phrasing for "closest relative" in 650–51: *haec virgo orbast patre; / hic meus amicus illi genere est proxumus* ("the maiden has lost her father: my friend here is closest to him in family"); translated thus the words might be used to strengthen Gaiser's argument that "Hegio" in the Greek original was brother of "Simulus" (cf. 352). The legal complexion of the uncle's relationship to his niece in the original play might explain the abruptness with which Terence introduces Hegio's name at III 2, 351–52: he has omitted allusions to Hegio's arrival from Miletos. Terence has streamlined the play by ridding it of a further Greek complication inessential to the plot.

9 CAT. III. 24 AND VIII. 8: *EUNUCHUS* IV 7, "SIEGE SCENE"

The question of attribution is complicated by Terence's admission in the prologue (25–34) that he has transferred the parasite and *miles gloriosus* from Menander's *Kolax* to his *Eunuchus*. The part of the parasite in IV 7 has probably been added from *Kolax*; cogent arguments have been made that the rival in *Eunoukhos* could have been a *miles*. For different views of Terence's use of Menander's *Kolax*, see Ludwig 1973; Gomme and Sandbach 1973: 420–21; Steidle 1973: 326–47; and Barsby 1993: 160–79. In my view, while Chremes' threat against the rival can be plausibly hypothesized as part of the Menandrian *Eunoukhos*, no such claim can be made for the appearance or non-appearance of the parasite in the scene. Whether Terence has added the parasite here from *Kolax* or has created the dialogue wholesale, his purpose, as suggested in chapter 2.3, may have been to parody the efficacy of legal threats to settle disputes in Greek plays.

10 CAT. III. 27: *PHORMIO* V 8–9

Terence *Phormio* v 8–9: Büchner 1974: 356–60 and 479–81 and Lefèvre 1978a see considerable Terentian re-writing and addition in the last two scenes (v 8–9) of the play. Büchner argues that the parasite deserved no beating (it is Terentian addition) and that in the original play "Nausistrata" would not be informed of her husband's Lemnian relationships. Lefèvre (p. 78) argues similarly: in the Greek ending, "Demipho" must be reconciled with his son so that his marriage can be celebrated; his authority cannot be called into question (yet it is the authority of "Chremes" that is called into question); Nausistrata remains uninformed (in fact, she does not appear in Lefèvre's reconstruction). Against Lefèvre's view, see Fantham (1982: 369) who refutes the technical objection concerning the number of speakers in the final scene and offers comparanda for none-too-respectful treatment of old men elsewhere in Greek New Comedy (*Aspis* and *Epitr.*).

Concerning the appearance of Nausistrata in the final scene, we might ask: is "Nausistrata" of the Greek original a richly dowered wife or an *epikleros*? If she is the latter, the ending of the play, with its transfer of adjudication from wife to son, is neatly integrated with the concerns of the play. In that case, Chremes' abuse of the Lemnian property that had belonged to his rich wife's father (1012–13, and cf. 679–81 and 786–93) entails the diminution of their son's inheritance: the Lemnian property in fact belongs to him (or rather, will belong to him soon). Nausistrata's choice of *iudex* is the injured heir. If "Phaedria" is son of an *epikleros*, why then is he not in possession of the Lemnian estate already? The answer is simple: he is not old enough. According to a law cited at [Dem.] 46. 20, sons of *epikleroi* take possession ἐπὶ διετὲς ἡβῆσαι ("two years past puberty": see Wyse 1904: 610–11; M. Golden 1990: 28–29). "Phaedria", then, must be under eighteen. Nothing in the play suggests behavior unfit for a seventeen-year-old (on the varied ages of the *adulescentes* of comedy, see chapter 7.1.a).

There is, however, no demonstrable proof of Nausistrata's *epikleros* status in Terence's play. Allusions to Nausistrata's wealth in the course of the play accommodate equally well the depiction of a "richly dowered wife." Thus Chremes at 585 says he fears the consequences if his wife learns about his daughter; if she finds out: *ut me excutiam atque egrediar domo / id restat; nam ego meorum solu' sum meus* (586–87: "my only recourse is to take myself off and leave home; for I am the only possession I have"). Donatus on 587 gives a Greek translation (= Apollodoros fr. 25 K-A) and tags on the name Apollodoros (a much emended text): ἐγὼ γάρ εἰμι τῶν <ἐμῶν> ἐμὸς <μόνος> ("for I am the only possession I have": text of K–A). Phormio refers to Nausistrata as among "the richly dowered" at 940 – but he also in the same sentence refers to the poor *epikleros* as "the undowered" (938). Nausistrata's father is probably dead and she probably has no brothers – if these kinsmen were alive, she would hardly wish she were a man to rectify the losses her Lemnian property has suffered through her husband (792). Geta refers to Chremes as the "older brother" (63) – a detail that would explain his success in claiming the *epikleros* (as older brother, he has priority). The details do not add up to a conclusive case. I submit, then, merely as an hypothesis, that "Nausistrata" in the Greek original was an *epikleros* and that Terence has changed her status to that of a richly dowered wife, to rid himself of a Greek complication which was not essential (but how pretty!) for the plot. If we accept Donatus' evidence (see add. 8 above) that in Menander's *Adelphoi*, "Hegio" was brother of "Sostrata," we have evidence of a similar Terentian change. Gratwick (1993: 29–30) conjectures that Matrona, wife of Menaechmus I in *Menaechmi*, may have been an *epikleros* in the Greek original of Plautus' play.

The hypothesis has interesting consequences. While the beginning of the play focuses attention on the sham undowered *epikleros* whom "Antipho" is compelled to marry, attention at play's end is upon "Nausistrata," the rich *epikleros* whom "Chremes" once upon a time claimed by law. It may very well be that the title of Apollodoros' play, *Epidikazomenos* is double-edged: as a middle-voiced participle, it means "the one making a claim (for an *epikleros*) at law," as a passive-voiced one, "the one to whom an *epikleros* has been assigned" (cf. [Dem.] 43. 55 for the middle and 16 for the passive). *Hekura*, another Apollodoran play, has the same double-edged quality: there are, after all, two mothers-in-law. In *Epidikazomenos*, "Chremes" at play's beginning is set on dissolving his nephew's compulsory marriage to a "poor *epikleros*" whereas he himself as a young man had probably jumped to claim a rich one.

To return to the original point claimed in cat. iii. 27 above: Phormio's threats at the end of v 8 are necessary because they turn the focus of the dramatic action to Nausistrata – the one person (aside from her son), who is appropriate to end the dispute.

11 CAT. v. 1 AND IX. 13: *MOST.* v 1 AND *HEC.* III 1

There are numerous references to the examination of slaves by torture in New Comedy: an owner threatens to beat his slave on-stage to acquire information at *Sam.* 304–25; slaves are brought on-stage after having been tortured off-stage at *Truc.* 777–79; a wife acknowledges that she tortured her houseslaves when she suspected them of stealing her mantle at *Asin.* 888–89; a courtesan offers her slaves for torture at *Hec.* 773; Hegio recommends such an examination (and the slave offers to comply) at *Ad.* 479–83. In none of these instances is slave torture (or its suggestion) used explicitly as a preliminary to trial; instead, it is used either to acquire information as an end in itself or as a spur to out-of-court settlement.

Only at *Most.* v 1 is slave torture explicitly viewed as a preliminary to trial – even though Theopropides has no intention of going to court. *Hec.* 327–35, however, might be another instance. There a slave fears *magnum malum*; the reference to torture (cf. Donatus apud 335) might be envisioned as a preliminary to a homicide trial under Athenian law. To consider these two scenarios in reverse order:

(i) *Hec.* III 1: In Rome, the use of slave torture as evidence in trials may have been rather limited in the pre-classical period; exceptions to the norm of restricted use seem to increase in the classical era (*D.* 48. 18 passim; Mommsen 1899: 414–18). At least one broad restriction, that slaves could not be tortured against their masters in capital cases, was probably in effect during the middle Republic; Cicero ascribes it to *maiores nostri* (*pro. Mil.* 59) and *mos maiorum* (*pro Deiot.* 3); Tacitus ascribes it to *vetus senatus consultum* (*Ann.* 2. 30); see Dareste 1902: 169–71. If the slave's words at *Hec.* 335 do refer to torture as a preliminary to trial (even before a domestic tribunal), then the scenario does not accord with Roman law.

(ii) *Most.* v 1: Another restriction, this one forbidding slave torture in private cases on pecuniary issues unrelated to inheritance (Paul. *Sent.* 5. 15. 6), appears to have been granted exceptions (*D.* 18. 48. 18. 9 Marcianus), possibly within Paulus' own generation. If the trend of the law was to admit more and more occasions for slave torture (Fredershausen 1906: 28), the restriction noted here may have existed in Plautus' era. If so, then there is additional support for ascribing the scenario in *Most.* v 1 to its Greek original: the torture is preliminary to a trial over a sum of money, and inheritance is not at issue.

12 CAT. VI. 5: *PHORMIO* II 3, 403–06

The evident sarcasm of the verses is explicable only if re-trial is not permitted in this instance. Re-trial was permitted in Rome and Athens only in exceptional cases: in Rome, in *vindicationes in libertatem* (Cic. *de domo* 29. 78), which has no relevance whatsoever to the situation portrayed in the play; in Athens, it was permitted in a situation relevant to that dramatized here: if a rival claimant (of equal or closer proximity of kinship) for an *epikleros* appeared on the scene after the arkhon had already awarded her to a claimant, the case could be re-opened (*lex apud* [Dem.] 43. 16). While the original trial in Apollodoros' play was not a *diadikasia* but rather an impeachment for maltreatment of an *epikleros* (see chapter 7, n. 45), nevertheless, it had the same result as one: the award of an *epikleros*. A *diadikasia* might be permitted in this instance, and such a trial might be spoken of, loosely, as a "retrial of the very same case."

It is unlikely that Apollodoros would have overlooked this detail of Athenian law (or "conveniently suppressed" it – pace Arnott 1970: 40). While some sort of challenge from the parasite may have appeared in the Greek original at this point, the particular content of 403–06 is probably Terentian. In Apollodoros' play, "Phormio" would be aware that there was no rival or late claimant on hand and that only bribery and false testimony could provide one; if "Demipho" decided to find such a claimant, he would be forced to disclose his brother's plight to a third party – something that the two men have taken pains to avoid (579–87) – and involve that third party in a deception that would probably be expensive to effect. If a challenge appeared in the Greek original, I would expect it have some such form as follows: "But you're a smart man – go to the arkhon and have him set up another hearing about this *epikleros* – and be sure you prepare the new claimant by telling him who 'Stilpo' is." (Cf. And. 1. 122: εἶπον αὐτῶι καὶ κατηγορεῖν καὶ παρασκευάζειν ἄλλους "I bid him to go forward with his accusation and to rehearse other men [for assistance].") According to this speculative interpretation, Terence has changed the Greek original in order to rid his play of a technicality that would be incomprehensible to the Roman audience.

13 CAT. IX. 12: *AND.* IV 5, 814–16

Terence may have added 814–16 to adapt the scenario to Roman law – while smoothing over (!) the adaptation with a Greek term (*sycophanta*): *clamitent / me sycophantam, hereditatem persequi / mendicum. tum ipsam despoliare non lubet* (" . . . they'll say that I'm a sycophant, that I go after impoverished estates. If that's the case, I don't want to rob her"). Crito imagines bringing suit under the *lex Furia testamentaria* (Gaius 2. 225 and 4. 23) for making a fraudulent claim to an estate; if successful, he will exact a fourfold penalty as the law allows (for interpretation of the *l. Furia* along these lines, see Cloud 1992: 185–86). The verses can be compared to *Persa* 62–64: *neque quadrupulari me volo, neque enim decet / sine meo periclo ire aliena ereptum bona / neque illi qui faciunt mihi placent. planen loquor?* ("I have no desire to exact fourfold penalties [i.e., to become a sycophant], nor do I think it decent to go about snatching the estates of others without risk to myself, nor do I like those who do so. Do I speak plainly?"). While the meaning of the verb *quadruplor* is controversial (see Cloud 1992: 175–86), the conjunction of the two passages (along with some scholarly consensus that the noun *quadrupulator* of *Persa* 70 is Plautus' term for συκοφάντης) suggests that in *Andria* 814–16, Terence has combined a Greek term with a Roman legal scenario; cf. *dicam scribere* in cat. VII. 3. Crito's final remark (*tum ipsam despoliare non lubet*) might be sardonic admission of his anticipated failure – rather than Terentian remodelling of Crito into a sympathetic character (so Lefèvre). The remark might easily have appeared in the Greek original before the Roman addition of 814–16 (*clamitent* . . .).

APPENDIX 6
Ambiguous arbitri *in Roman Comedy*

Lady Caroline. John, the grass is too damp for you. You had better go and put on your overshoes at once.
Sir John. I am quite comfortable, Caroline, I assure you.
Lady Caroline. You must allow me to be the best judge of that, John. Pray, do as I tell you. (Oscar Wilde, *A Woman of No Importance*, Act I)

The purpose of this appendix is to provide a brief survey of the use of the terms *arbiter* and *iudex* in Plautus and Terence, and to assess the frequency with which those terms are used in a technical sense. By a technical *arbiter* or *iudex*, I mean either a judge who belongs to the judicial system (*iudex unus* or an *arbiter*, e.g. in an *actio finium regundorum* or in a *bonae fidei iudicium*) or a private arbitrator who resolves a legal dispute outside the court system. By a non-technical *arbiter* or *iudex*, I mean an individual who is depicted as having a judging capacity, but not in areas usually associated with judicial or arbitral practice, e.g. a judge of a good piece of cake – or of the effect of dampness on a husband's feet. Usage of the terms often is metaphorical or verges on the metaphorical ("You be the judge of my complaint!"). Metaphorical usage may be technical or non-technical; in the former case, while the judging agent clearly lies outside the usual judicial or arbitral sphere, notions of courtroom judging and of the adversarial process may be more or less explicit in the larger linguistic context (e.g. *Ad. prol.* 1–5).

I PLAUTINE *ARBITRI*

I (A) TECHNICAL OR NON-TECHNICAL?

In *Casina*, Chalinus, dressed as the young bride whom Lysidamus plans to deflower, threatens to obtain an *arbiter* (here, a metaphor for a club, cf. 967 and 971) to decide a punishment for his rival:

nunc ego tecum aequom arbitrum extra considium captavero. (*Cas.* 966)[82]

Now I'll get a fair *arbiter* with you – outside the courtroom!

In *Truculentus*, Cyamus agrees to fight his master's rival, Stratophanes, after he has obtained an *arbiter* (here, a metaphor for a sword or dagger, cf. 627), presumably to decide which of the two men is more powerful:

† *abo domum*† *ego tecum, bellator, arbitrum aequom ceperim.* (*Truc.* 629)

† . . . . † let me get a fair *arbiter* with you, warrior!

Neither passage is easily attributable to a Greek original: the particularly Roman treatment in each instance (i.e., the metaphorical use of *arbiter* in a humorous situation) makes it unlikely that the adjectives are translations of Greek originals (e.g. *isos*, cf. Men. *Epitr.* 227) – or transference of Attic notions of fair play that may have been involved in the private arbitral decisions of *diaitetai*. Scholars who think the metaphorical *arbitri* refer to Roman technical arbitrators believe the *arbitri* of the two passages are private ones;[83] their argument is based on the belief that the judicial *arbiter* must be appointed by the magistrate without involving the agreement of the disputants and that *captare* and *capere* must denote "choice" (i.e. on the part of the disputants). So doctrinaire a position concerning the appointment of the judicial *arbiter* is difficult to maintain; while the evidence on the point is inconclusive, it seems to point in the opposite direction.[84] Plautus' language, however, is ambiguous: (1) *captáre* in the first instance suggests violence – "seizure" rather than "choosing"; what is depicted is neither judicial nor formalized extra-judicial practice but questionable conduct; (2) *capere* need not mean "to choose" or "to select"; it can mean "to get" or "to obtain" – without implying whether the person or item so "gotten" or "obtained" was imposed upon the subject or chosen by him.[85] The *arbitri*

[82] I have translated *extra considium* (if that is the correct reading of *Ambrosianus*) as "outside the courtroom" (understanding the hapax *considium* to be a formation similar to *praesidium*), following MacCary and Willcock 1976 ad loc. It is also possible to translate the phrase as "outside the assembly [of senators]", understanding *considium* to be a folk etymological formation of *consilium*. Ahrens 1970: 26 understands *considium* in the second way. Verses 966–72 are missing from the Palatine recension.

[83] See chapter 4, nn. 29–31.

[84] See chapter 2, n. 76.

[85] *OLD s.v. capio* no. 9a offers "to choose, select (for a stated or implied purpose)" and under 9b "(with pred. acc.) to choose, appoint (in a particular capacity)," citing inter alia *Merc.* 736: *de istac sum iudex captus*. Under no. 11, it offers "to get, obtain, be given, win." I have preferred to use the meaning cited under no. 11, since it allows for the ambiguity I have suggested in the text above. In the case of *Merc.* 736, both meanings converge. There, Lysimachus says: *de istac sum iudex captus* ("I have been gotten as *iudex* in her case"); his wife, surprised by the subsequent irruption of cook and assistants, asks at 752, whether the intruders have been sent by the men *quos inter iudex datu's?* ("for whom you have been given as *iudex*"). Cf. the wording of the *legis actio p. i. a.ve i.* (chapter 2, n. 76) and the following passages: *Most.* 557–58: *cape, opsecro hercle, cum eo <tu> una iudicem, / (sed eum videto ut capias, qui credat mihi)*" ("I beseech you, get a *iudex* along with him – but make sure you get one who will believe me"); *Rud.* 1380: *cedo quicum habeam iudicem* ("Name someone [as *patronus*] with whom I may have a *iudex*").

of *Cas.* 966 and *Truc.* 629 might then be either judicial or private, at least insofar as the verbs are concerned.

But can we be so certain that the metaphors allude to technical *arbitri* – whether judicial or private? The only argument that has been adduced concerns the epithet *aequus*: the *arbiter* (whether judicial or private) is one who specifically bases his decision on the *bonum aequum*. Plautus uses the collocation *aequus arbiter* on three occasions (*Amph. prol.* 16 in addition to *Cas.* 966 and *Truc.* 629). There is no reason to believe that *aequus* in any of the passages carries a particular technical significance. In *Amphitruo*, Mercury as prologue speaker addresses the audience:

itaque aequi et iusti hic eritis omnes arbitri. (16)

and so you all shall be fair and just *arbitri.*

The verse should be compared with two in *Captivi*, where the prologue speaker ends his speech:

abeo. valete, iudices iustissumi
domi, duellique duellatores optumi. (67–68)

I'm off. Farewell, most just *iudices*
at home, and best combatants in battle.

Arbitri and *iudices* appear to be interchangeable in these verses. In Plautus, alliterative effect rather than precision of meaningful referent might be the decisive factor for preferring one noun (or adjective) to the other. The two verses, *Cas.* 966 and *Truc.* 629 (which are, in any case, doublets of one another), cannot be used as evidence for a private Roman arbitrator who bases his decisions on the *bonum aequum*. It is best to conclude that the *arbitri* of the two verses have no technical referent at all.

A less ambiguous reference to an *arbiter* appears in the final scene of *Trin.* Charmides insists that the rich Lysiteles accept a dowry along with his daughter; a brief exchange follows between Callicles and Lysiteles:

CA. ius hic orat. LY. impetrabit te advocato atque arbitro. (1161)

CA.: Charmides' plea is fair. LY.: He shall win it with you as advocate and *arbiter.*

The verse is a wonderful run of a trochaic septenarius with resounding emphasis on *-tr-* and *-a-* sounds. Does it have meaning beyond sound effects? The collocation of *advocatus* and *arbiter* is, at first glance, somewhat odd. Yet Callicles might reasonably be said both "to advocate" Charmides' position and at the same time "to act as an *arbiter*" when he offers his approving *sententia*. His dual role, impossible of execution in a courtroom, nonetheless refers (metaphorically) to courtroom *personae.*[86] Lysiteles

[86] If an *arbiter* had ever, even in his pre-primeval existence, acted as *advocatus*, those days are long bygone in the Plautine era; cf. Broggini 1957: 40–43 and Ahrens 1970: 22–24.

similarly shoulders a dual (metaphorical) role in II 1; there he chooses between a life given over to love affairs and one devoted to business: the only way to decide the matter, he says, is for him to "examine each side of the case at the same time, to be *iudex* and *reus* in the trial" (234). The linguistic context, the specifying of forensic roles, points once again to the courtroom sphere of judging as the referent of metaphorical usage.

1 (B) *VIDULARIA*

While it is commonly thought that an arbitration takes place in the play, no fragment can be assigned to one. At some point, a slave named Cacistus appears to have fished up a trunk from the sea (fr. VII). Gorgines, like Daemones in *Rudens*, has been made aware of the find; he himself will "sequester" it until the matter is adjudicated: *Animum advortite ambo sultis. vidulum hic apponite; / ego servabo, quasi sequestro detis; neutri reddibo, / donicum res diiudicata erit haec* (fr. V: "Please, the two of you, pay attention. Set the trunk here; / I shall guard it as if you were leaving it with it a depositary; I'll give it to no one / until this matter is decided").[87]

Of interest is the figure of the *sequester.* When Trachalio alights upon Gripus and the trunk in *Rudens* IV 3, he asks him four times to enter into arbitration; on two of those occasions, he adds, as an alternative (?), that he deposit the trunk with a *sequester* (1004, 1018). In fact, Daemones does end up acting as a *sequester* (see ch. 4, n. 8). Nevertheless, Plautus never applies the term directly to Daemones or to his activity.

There is some debate among Roman legal historians whether the *arbiter* and *sequester* performed the same or different functions in pre-classical Roman law. That they are the same is suggested by Wlassak (*RE, s.v. arbiter* cols. 408ff.); that they are not is argued by Broggini 1957: 120 n. 19 and Ahrens 1970: 39–43. Since the evidence on this issue depends on interpreting Plautus, there can be no decisive answer. "Sequestration" is attested in Attic law (μεσεγγύημα, μεσεγγυηθέν); see Lipsius 714f.

2 TERENTIAN *ARBITRI*

Terence is alleged to refer to technical private arbitrators on two occasions (*Ad.* 123 and *HT* 500); both are problematic. The scenario in *HT* is extensive enough to trace an Attic origin. Chremes in III 1 of the play takes momentary leave of Menedemus, saying: ". . . *Simus et Crito / vicini nostri hic ambigunt de finibus; / me cepere arbitrum*" (498–500: "Simus and Crito, our neighbors here, are disputing their boundaries; they have gotten me as *arbiter*"). Chremes' departure from the stage at first sight does not appear essential to the plot; in fact it disrupts the on-going action to such a degree that he exits only to cancel a previous appointment so that he may return

87 For reconstructions of the play, see Friedrich 1953: 199–208 and Webster 1953: 169–71.

to Menedemus' side at once.[88] What explains such an unusual exit and re-entrance (he is off-stage for less than six lines) is the opportunity it creates for Menedemus to comment upon Chremes' keen aptitude for judging the affairs of others (502–07) – a comment pregnant with irony for the audience aware of Chremes' deficiencies in that very department:

. . . di vostram fidem,
ita conparatam esse hominum naturam omnium
aliena ut meliu' videant et diiudicent
quam sua! an eo fit quia in re nostra aut gaudio
sumu' praepediti nimio aut aegritudine?
hic mihi nunc quanto plus sapit quam egomet mihi!

. . . Gracious gods!
That human nature has been so designed
that all men see and judge the affairs of others better than their own!
Does this come about because we're all hedged in by excessive joy
or grief in our own backyard?
How my neighbor here shows more wisdom in my affairs than I do
in my own!

By the play's end, Menedemus will have cause to revise his opinion of Chremes; his later remarks (922–23) ironically pinpoint the shortsightedness of his earlier view – Chremes is just as obtuse as any mortal when it comes to his own affairs:

nonne id flagitiumst te aliis consilium dare,
foris sapere, tibi non posse te auxiliarier?

Isn't it a disgrace that you counsel others,
show wisdom away from home, but can't help yourself ?

The pattern and structure of this *ethos*-exhibition are clear; the fine detail of Chremes' departure as an *arbiter* at the end of III 1 is very much a part of it. We can be reasonably certain that that detail belonged to the Menandrian original, and that Terence has had to adapt or translate the role of the Athenian private *diaitetes* for his Roman audience.[89]

It is impossible to discern, however, whether the *arbiter* of the Roman play is a judicial or private one. If he is the former, then Terence has adapted the original and envisioned Chremes as an *arbiter* who was "appointed" by the praetor in a *legis actio per iudicis arbitrive postulationem*.[90] If, on the other hand, Chremes represents a private *arbiter*, we cannot tell

[88] See Brothers 1988 apud 508 for examples of other brief exits during which extended stage action must be imagined as taking place.

[89] For a lengthier statement of the Menandrian origin of the passage under discussion, see Brothers 1988: 17 and n. 21, 195–96, with citation of earlier bibliography.

[90] The *iudex* or *arbiter* in this *actio* is technically said to be "given" (*datus*). See chapter 2, nn. 76–77 and chapter 3, nn. 64–65.

whether Terence has adapted the private *diaitetes* of the original to fit the contours of a Roman private arbitrator (we have no evidence – beyond Cato's *vir bonus* – for comparison); nor can we tell whether Terence has simply translated the Athenian *diaitetes* into a Latin *arbiter* (i.e. without having a particular Roman counterpart in mind) – as he translates the Athenian *dikastai* of Apollodoros' *Epidikazomenos* into the *iudices*, not *iudex*, of his *Phormio* (129, 275, 282, 400).

In *Ad.* I. 2, the two brothers Demea and Micio are in the midst of a quarrel: how should Aeschinus' conduct be treated? Demea, natural father of the youth, favors stern measures; Micio, adoptive father, favors leniency. Exasperated by his brother's self-righteousness, Micio ends his tirade with the challenge:

> *postremo aut desine aut cedo quemvis arbitrum:*
> *te plura in hac re peccare ostendam.* (123–24)

> In short, either keep quiet or produce any *arbiter* you like:
> I'll prove that you're more in the wrong about this matter!

The remark is too fleeting (and too neutral) to assign a Greek or Roman origin for it. In the context of the debate itself, it is difficult to interpret the referent of *arbiter* as any sort of technical one. Micio might just as well have asked for an *arbiter* of a good piece of cake. The usage verges on the metaphorical. Demea is not asked to find an *arbiter*, but to find anyone who will act as if he were one – private or judicial makes no difference.

3 *ARBITER*, *IUDEX*, AND *VIR BONUS* IN ROMAN COMEDY: A SUMMARY

Terence's designation of Phaedria as a *iudex* in *Phormio* v 9 was discussed in chapter 4.2.c.; the young man was asked to play the role of a private arbitrator and to settle a dispute that directly concerned his inheritance; it was argued that the scenario was based on the Greek model. A private arbitrator designated as an *arbiter* appears in *Rudens* IV 3; in chapter 4.1.b, it was argued that the scenario was based on the Greek model. All the other scenarios in Plautus and Terence in which a figure, designated as *arbiter* or *iudex*, might be envisioned as having a private arbitral function have been presented in the two preceding sections of this appendix. In *Amph. prol.* 16 and *Ad.* 123, allusions to *arbitri* are non-technical. The Roman and metaphorical *arbitri* of *Cas.* 966 and *Truc.* 629 are also non-technical; no particular significance is to be attached to the alliterative epithet *aequus*. On the other hand, the *arbiter* of *Trin.* 1161 and the *iudex* of *Trin* and 234 are metaphors from the (technical) judicial realm. Chremes' technical role of *arbiter* (whether judicial or private) in *HT* was seen to have an Attic origin. We must now see where the instances of *arbiter* and *iudex* discussed here fit into the overall picture of Plautine and Terentian usage of these terms.

The phrase *vir bonus* occurs fourteen times in Plautus and six times in Terence; only one instance (Ter. *Ad.* 961) might possibly suggest a Catonian *vir bonus*. The term *iudex* appears in Plautus twelve times, in Terence ten times; *arbiter* appears in Plautus twenty-one times, in Terence twice.[91] *Arbiter* has a special meaning of "spectator" or "onlooker" in Plautus twelve times, and these instances will be of no concern to us.[92] We limit ourselves therefore to a survey of the twenty-two instances of *iudex* and the eleven instances of *arbiter* in Plautus and Terence (i. e., excluding the twelve Plautine instances of *arbiter* as "onlooker"). Usage can be summarized under the following headings:

(1) *Iudex* as a technical judge in the judicial system: Plautus, eleven times (twice metaphorical); Terence, six times (once metaphorical).[93]
(2) *Iudex* as a technical third party private arbitrator: Plautus, no instance; Terence, once.[94]
(3) Non-technical usage of *iudex* ("a judge of a good piece of cake"): Plautus, once; Terence, three times.[95]
(4) *Arbiter* as the technical *arbiter* of the *legis actiones* system: Plautus: once (metaphorical); Terence: no certain instance (*HT* 498–500 is ambiguous).[96]
(5) *Arbiter* as a technical third party private arbitrator: Plautus, five times in

[91] I have not counted the interesting *captus arbiter* of *Amph. arg.* II. 7, since the *argumentum* is post-Plautine. I have also not counted the reading of the Palatine recension, accepted by Lindsay OCT at *Men.* 587 (*ad iudicem*), nor Lindsay's unacknowledged supplement at *Rud.* 712 (*habe iudicem*).

[92] *Capt.* 211, 220, 225; *Cas.* 90, 143; *Cist.* 64; *Merc.* 1006 (a pun, see chapter 4.3); *Miles* 158, 1137; *Poen.* 178, 663; *Trin.* 146.

[93] *Non-metaphorical*: Plautus: *Merc.* 736, 752; *Most.* 557, 1099 (*apud iudicem*), 1101; *Pers.* 194; *Pseud.* 645 (*apud iudicem*); *Rud. prol.* 18 (*apud iudicem*) and 1380. Terence: *Ph.* 129, 275, 279, 282, 400. The crucial issue is not whether a case could in fact be brought before a *iudex*, but whether a character in a play envisions the availability (or non-availability) of the *iudex* of the court system. At *Most.* 557, for instance, the slave appears to suggest that there might have been something unlawful in the original contract of sale for the house which might allow for a suit – whether that is true or false is not an issue. In another instance, *Pers.* 194, the speaker's point is that a case could not be brought before the *iudex*; his point of reference, nevertheless, is the *iudex* of the legal system. In other instances, the phrase *apud iudicem* is a definite pointer to the second half of the bipartite procedure in the *legis actiones* system.

Metaphorical: Plautus: *Cas.* 76; *Trin.* 234. Terence: *Ad. prol.* 4. The prologue-speaker of *Casina* offers an explanation of slave weddings in Greece, Carthage, and Apulia (71–74); then he challenges any skeptic to wager (*pignus dare*) a bowl of honey and wine on the truth of his statement – provided the *iudex* be Carthaginian, Greek, or Apulian (75–77). The notion of wagering here (but not the idiom) might call to mind the wager of litigants before the *iudex* in the *legis actio sacramento* (Gaius 4. 16).

[94] Terence: *Ph.* 1055. In some of the passages cited in n. 93, forms of *capere* (which I translate as "to get") appear; some scholars have preferred, by translating "to choose," to see a private arbitrator rather than the *iudex unus*; see the discussion of *Cas.* 966 and *Truc.* 629 above and n. 85. On *Rud.* 712, see n. 91 above.

[95] Plautus: *Capt.* 67; Terence: *HT* 213, 352; *Hec.* 255.

[96] Plautus: *Trin.* 1161.

Rud. (1004, 1018, 1038, 1040, 1043); Terence, no certain instance (*HT* 498–500 is ambiguous).

(6) Non-technical usage of *arbiter* ("a judge of a good piece of cake"): Plautus, three times (twice metaphorical); Terence, once.[97]

We can make several observations on the basis of this summary:

(1) *Iudex* most commonly refers to a judge of the judicial system. For Plautus, who always uses *iudex* in the singular, this means *iudex unus*. Terence, however, who only uses the term in the sense of a courtroom judge in one play (*Phormio*), uses it there four times in the plural. Since the trial he refers to has no counterpart in Rome, we may safely assume that he uses the plural to refer to the *dikastai* of the Athenian legal system.[98]

(2) The judicial *arbiter* of the *legis actiones* system is identifiable in only one metaphorical instance (*Trin.* 1161).

(3) An identifiable private *arbiter* appears only once – in a full-blown (if disrupted) scenario that depends on a Greek original (*Rudens* IV 3).

The evidence cited and analyzed here should put an end to assertions that Roman private arbitrators appear frequently in Roman Comedy.

APPENDIX 7
Moikhos *and* moikheia

1 *MOIKHOS* AS FORNICATOR IN TECHNICAL AND NON-TECHNICAL LITERARY USAGE

In chapter 5.1.a, evidence was adduced to demonstrate that fourth-century authors who allude to the homicide law and to other self-help remedies sometimes use *moikhos* as a technical or quasi-technical term to designate the sexual offender.[99] In some passages the *moikhos* is identifiable as an adulterer, in others, he is a fornicator (i.e. a seducer of an unmarried woman). It will be instructive here to reflect on the technical or quasi-

[97] Plautus: *Amph. prol.* 16. Terence: *Ad.* 123. *Metaphorical*: Plautus: *Cas.* 966; *Truc.* 629.

[98] The trial is discussed in chapter 7, n. 45.

[99] The evidence cited in chapter 5. 1.a, nn. 9–13 was based on an examination of the phrase *moikhon labein* ("to take a *moikhos*") in fourth through early third-century literature; it was thought that study of this phrase would provide the best opportunity for observing the meaning of *moikhos* in technical or quasi-technical contexts. Active and passive forms of *moikhon labein* appear at: *AP* 57. 3; Arist. frr. VIII. 593 (= 611 paragr. 24: Tenedos); 611 paragr. 1 (Athens); 611 paragr. 42 (Lepreon) Rose; Lys. 1. 30–31, 49; 13. 66; Is. 8. 44, 46; [Dem.] 59. 65, 67, 71, 72; Demades fr. II. 31 B–S; Men. *Samia* 717. Additionally, active and passive forms of *katalabein moikhon* appear at Arist. frr. VIII. 593 (Tenedos) Rose and the active form at Men. *Perik.* 356–57. The Aristotelian fragments cited here all appear in the collection of *politeiai* (constitutions) abbreviated or excerpted by Herakleides Pontikos. Only fr. VIII. 611 paragr. 1–8 belongs to the constitution of the Athenians; it is possible that non-Athenian *politeiai* do not depend on Athenian sources and so might not represent Attic usage.

technical usage of *moikhos* against the background of more general usage in the fourth century.

When the *moikhos* appears in fourth-century Athenian literature and where the status of his partner or victim is identifiable, he is usually an adulterer. It has been pointed out, for example, that when Aristophanic characters speak of *moikhoi*, or when Aristotle discusses *moikheia*, adultery is the consistent, if not exclusive, focus of attention.[100] That observation is of great significance, but it does not compel us to eradicate the *moikhos* as fornicator (i.e. "seducer of unmarried women") from Athenian history. Here we shall broaden our purview to literature from the late fifth through third century. The appearance of a fornicator not only in the epitome of the *AP* but in the fourth-century Atthidographic tradition – the *moikhos* whom the last king of the Kodridai found upon his daughter – is an important piece of testimony.[101] Aiskhines refers to the same story in 1 *Tim.* 182 to emphasize the father's punishment of an unmarried daughter as example of sterner morality in days of yore; apparently the locale of punishment was a well-known site – even though contemporary sources allege that the building had been razed. The importance of that detail, provided by the Atthidographic tradition, is not to be neglected: the *aition* had captured the imagination of some segment of fourth-century Athenians. The mythological *moikhoi* (fornicators? rapists?) of Alope and Semele in Aristophanes (*Birds* 559) also deserve mention. Another mythological *moikhos* (rapist? fornicator?), this time, Danae's, is used as analogue by a Menandrian father to exculpate his son's offense (rape? seduction?) against his neighbor's unmarried daughter (*Samia* 591). Another *moikhos* is portrayed as highly sought after by an old woman, surely spinster or widow, in Aristophanes *Thesmophoriazousai* (345, and cf. *Wealth* 959 ff.). Polemon, in the last act of Menander *Perikeiromene*, speaks regretfully of having mistaken the brother of his concubine for a *moikhos* (986); he considered the woman as a wife (*ego gametēn nenomika tautēn*, 489). Makhon reports that the pankratist Leontiskos was irked upon learning that Mania, whom he kept for himself alone "as if she were a wife" (*gametes tropon gunaikos*), was being seduced (*moikheuomenen*) by Antenor (Makhon F 15. 221 Gow). *Moikhos* is not used in these comic passages as technical term; nevertheless, the word is neither widowed of meaning nor applied as blanket epithet of abuse. In

100 D. Cohen 1991b: 107–09.

101 Herakleides' version (Arist. fr. VIII. 611 paragr. 1 Rose) represents the more fully developed, overtly historicized story. In it, the girl's father turns out to be Hippomenes, the last of the Kodridai to rule as king (or as arkhon for life); the story has been transformed into a piece of Attic legendary history. The story of Hippomenes and his daughter probably had appeared, in some form or another, in a number of the Atthidographers (e.g. Hellanikos and possibly Androtion) before it appeared in the (now lost) opening of the *AP* from which Herakleides made his excerpt. Hellanikos' *Atthis* was published after 407/06 BC (see Jacoby *FGrHist* III b I p. 5, 12ff.). Androtion published soon after 344/43 BC (Jacoby 1949: 74). Jacoby (*FGrHist* III b I, p. 45. 5ff.) thinks that Hellanikos is the likely source for the story. For the ending of the story, see chapter 6, n. 69.

fact, the term has the same range of meanings that it has in its technical or quasi-technical appearances in the orators. The *moikhos* of Attic comedic literature can be adulterer or fornicator; the term might conceivably refer to a rapist; it is used of an alleged seducer of a concubine, caught in the act of kissing her, and the verb is used of another concubine's seducer, to denote the act itself. The activity of the *moikhos* can be a serious offense; but it might be thoroughly pleasurable experience for the participants and unrealized fantasy on the part of others – hence its frequent humorous treatment in comedy.[102]

Amidst these mythological and legendary creations, lone Epainetos surfaces as identifiable non-fictive fornicator in the orators ([Dem.] 59. 64–71). Alleged father catches him in the act, fetters him, demands compensation from the foreigner; the latter strikes back with a *graphe* for illegal detainment as a *moikhos*: an exceptional case, all around – but not to be discounted.[103] Speculation can provide plausible reasons why we do not hear of other historical fornicators. The evidence of Aristophanes provides an important clue. The comedian uses *moikhos* or *moikh*-derivatives twenty-one times; in thirteen instances, the marital status of the female partner of the *moikhos* can be plausibly deduced; in twelve of these instances she is married.[104] On the basis of these "statistics," one might be led to conclude that Aristophanes overwhelmingly conceived of *moikheia* as limited to the illicit relations of a man with someone else's wife. Examination of the comedies undermines the superficial conclusion. Most often married women are associated with *moikheia* because the actors or chorus members who speak of *moikhoi* speak in reference to themselves or to comrades in their roles as married women. Choruses of married women appear in

102 The term *moikhos* might not have been used at all by tragedians. Only the verb *moikheuein* appears, and this in a scholiast's paraphrase of the plot of a tragedy by Karkinos (*Alope* Nauck[2] p. 797); see chapter 5, n. 67.

103 D. Cohen 1991b: 108–09 with n. 32 (= 1984) discounts the evidence in the Epainetos-Phano episode, "given the context of accusation (part of a plot of fraud and extortion), and the general nature of that oration." Cohen appears to think that the episode is fabricated in order to replicate an accusation made earlier against Neaira and Stephanos (42 ff.). While details may have been added to the episode to suggest the parallel, the reconciliation between Epainetos and Stephanos is witnessed – and it is a reconciliation that concerns Epainetos' alleged activity with an unmarried woman (70–71). On the other hand, the parallel episode in Neaira's life is unwitnessed – and in the more distant past; embroidery is more likely there than in the report about Phano. The arguments which Epainetos allegedly made when he brought his retaliatory *graphe* against Stephanos for unlawful detainment as a *moikhos* are not witnessed (c. 67); but observe that the alleged arguments do not include the plea that the charge was not tenable when a man was caught with an unmarried woman. The scenario itself must have been believable to dikasts (that a man might be taken as a *moikhos* with an unmarried woman), whether or not it in fact took place. Cf. Carey 1995: 408.

104 Marital status of women unidentifiable: *Akharn.* 265, 849; *Clouds* 1076, 1079; *Peace* 980; *Thesm.* 343; *Wealth* 168; *Daid.* fr. 191 K–A. Women are married: *Birds* 793; *Ekkl.* 225, 522; *Lysistr.* 107, 212, 213; *Thesm.* 392, 397, 417, 488, 501. Specific women are married and unmarried: *Birds* 558. Unmarried: *Thesm.* 345.

Lysistrata, *Thesmophoriazousai* ("Women Celebrating the Thesmophoria"), and *Ekklesiazousai* ("The Assemblywomen"). These plays account for ten of the twelve allusions to the *moikhoi* of married women.[105] A chorus of unmarried women may have made different allusions. No such choruses materialize. The only unmarried Athenian citizen girls who appear on Aristophanes' stage are the lascivious girl at the end of *Ekklesiazousai* (see n. 107), the daughters of Trugaios who lament their father's imminent departure in one brief scene of *Peace* (their entrance is marked at 111 and their exit indicated at 149), and Dikaiopolis' daughter, who enters the stage in *Akharnians* carrying a basket en route to celebrate the Rural Dionysia and who speaks a mere two lines (245–46) – a cameo role. Interpretation of the evidence for *moikheia* must account not, in the first instance, for Aristophanes' almost exclusive portrayal of *moikheia* as adultery – but rather for his almost exclusive dramatization of married women and old widows.[106] That is the "clue" in the Aristophanic evidence.

Unmarried girls of course appear in tragedy – but the Antigones and Elektras of the tragic stage are heroines of a bygone age; the daughters of Trugaios and Dikaiopolis, like the Pamphiles and Philoumenas of New Comedy, might be anyone's daughters. Is the virtual absence of unmarried Athenian girls from the Aristophanic corpus due to comic genre convention? Or does it reflect a social code which proscribes their public exhibition? Surely both protocols operate together; the former reflects the latter. Unmarried Athenian girls may have left their *oikoi* to attend sacrifices and funerals of close kin; those in poorer households without slaves may have shopped and fetched water. They might appear in public – but they were not to be publicized, not to be displayed on stage, theatric or forensic, not to be talked about in public forums. Apollodoros in [Dem.] 59 *Neaira* is convinced that Phano is not Athenian; the exceptional case proves the rule. Book Five of the *Republic* is a remarkable case of audacity, permissible because of its utopian garb; similarly the appearance of the girl at the end

[105] Thus *Ekkl.* 522; *Lysistr.* 107, 212, 213; *Thesm.* 392, 397, 417. At *Thesm.* 488, Mnesilokhos, having costumed himself as a woman and joined the festivity of the married women celebrating the Thesmophoria, speaks in *persona* of a married woman in support of Euripides, confessing "her" own adulterous behavior (488) and another's (501). At *Ekkl.* 225, the situation is similar, *mutatis mutandis*: Praxagora, dressed in man's clothing – in fact, all the women are wearing their husbands' garments (26) and posing as members of the *ekklesia* – addresses their meeting and proposes that women take over the government. In her speech that details the superiority of women (214–40), she clearly has her married and costumed comrades in mind, both when she says, "they celebrate the Thesmophoria, even as before" (223) and when she says, "they keep *moikhoi* indoors, even as before" (225). She uses the third person plural (and not the first or second person plural) because she is addressing "other men" at the *ekklesia* in her *persona* as "man at the *ekklesia*."

[106] Henderson 1987: 107 points out that "it is not until 411 that comedy took advantage of its option to portray citizen women sympathetically: until then we find only disreputable types like market-women or the relatives of 'demagogues.'" Henderson suggests that the new sympathetic roles played by citizen wives might be due to the double constraints of political climate ("volatile and dangerous") and genre (humor).

of *Ekklesiazousai* who peeps out of doors in search of a lover just as the *moikheuomenai* of *Peace* do – except that the regime has changed and *moikheia* – like marriage – no longer exists.[107] Aristotle's tendency to treat *moikheia* as adultery might reflect, not a communal definition of *moikheia* as adultery – nor a prude's aversion to depicting adult men engaging in sexual activity with fourteen-year-old girls, but rather an ingrained habit of avoiding their discussion.[108] We hear so little about historical fornicators because we hear so little about girls and unmarried women in non-utopian Athens.

2 THE *NOMOS MOIKHEIAS* IN [DEM.] 59. 87: ἑλεῖν μοιχόν

In addition to the phrases in the *nomos* cited in [Dem.] 59. 87, we find forms of ἑλεῖν μοιχόν in *Wealth* 168; Arist. frr. VIII. 611. 24. 145 Rose; Aiskhin. 1 *Tim.* 183; and [Dem.] 59. 85 and 86. The phrase τῶι ἑλόντι implies μοιχόν as object at [Dem.] 59. 66 and should be translated there as Gernet 1960: 91 does, as "*son adversaire.*" The instances occurring in [Dem.] 59. 85, 86 and Aiskhin. 1. 183 are paraphrases of the *nomos moikheias*; the verbs in these instances should be translated as technical terms, "to be convicted." The Aristotelian fragment uses the passive (*haliskomai*) and does mean "taken"; but the episode comes from a *politeia* of Tenedos and the source cannot be assumed to be Attic. Aristophanes uses the passive ἁλοὺς μοιχός at *Clouds* 1079 and the expression is more easily understood as "taken as a *moikhos*." The play was produced in 423 BC. If there were only self-help remedies against *moikhoi* at this time, then it makes no sense to speak of a "convicted *moikhos*" and ἁλοὺς μοιχός will be the equivalent of ληφθεὶς μοιχός. Alternatively, the use of forms of ἑλεῖν μοιχόν to mean "to convict a *moikhos*" may only have crystallized in the fourth century regardless of when the law was first introduced.

On one hypothesis or the other, Aristophanes could speak of a "convicted *moikhos*" by the time of the performance of *Wealth* in 388 BC. Indeed, it makes better sense to understand the passage where the expression is used if ἁλοὺς μοιχὸς does mean "convicted *moikhos.*" The verse in question is: ὁ δ' ἁλούς γε μοιχὸς διὰ σέ που παρατίλλεται (*Wealth* 168). The *moikhos* is usually interpreted here as "caught in the act" and so paying a penalty for it by "being plucked" (either metaphorically, "plucked of money" as

107 In the last third of *Ekkl.*, a girl appears, in competition with an old woman over a young lover; the girl is somewhat vexed that the old woman has a headstart in peeping out (με παρακύψασα προὔφθης, 884), probably from second-storey windows or separate doors (for problems of staging, see Dover 1972: 197–98). The "peeping" continues (924, 930). The peeping activity of the women is stereotypical and meant to be recognized as such. The same activity is adumbrated in *Peace* and attributed to *moikheuomenai* (978–85). Neither the old woman nor the girl of *Ekkl.*, however, are labelled *moikheuomenai.* The reason is obvious: their conduct belongs to the new regime of Praxagora in which women have been granted sexual license; there can be no *moikheia* now (neither adultery nor fornication) because old style marriage no longer exists.

108 A notable exception is *H.A.* 7. 1. 581b 11–24; the book, not surprisingly, is considered spurious.

Rogers 1927: 377 and D. Cohen 1985: 385–87 interpret – or literally, "being plucked" as bodily punishment, as the schol. apud 168 interprets; cf. schol. apud *Clouds* 1083). But if ὁ ἁλοὺς μοιχός is translated at *Wealth* 168 as "the convicted *moikhos*," then παρατίλλεται can be translated as a middle (cf. *Akharn.* 31; Men. *Orge* fr. 303.5 K–T) and have its literal meaning; and, most importantly, the pattern of syntax established throughout the passage (162–68) can be retained: (1) the subject of the verb is the agent of profit for himself rather than a passive victim acted upon for someone else's profit (the subject of each of the ten verbs in verses 162–67 is actively doing something "on account of Wealth") and (2) the subject of the verb is viewed as plying a trade (as are the the ten subjects in verses 162–67). In this case, ὁ ἁλοὺς μοιχός simply designates a particular person, possibly a topical allusion to a well-known convicted (and pretty) *moikhos*. Women are the more usual depilators in Aristophanic comedy (e.g. *Lysistr.* 89, *Frogs* 516); the attribute is not indicative of austere respectability. *Moikhoi* are depicted at *Thesm.* 345 as receiving the gifts of old women. The ἁλοὺς μοιχός of *Wealth* 168 might then be a topical reference to an individual who is known to have been convicted of *moikheia*, and who uses that notoriety as a kind of advertisement to win the favors of women. That he is well-shaven is a further inducement (a *moikhos*-like young man is described at Men. *Sik.* 201 as being beardless and smooth-skinned), and at the same time a slurring indication of the effeminacy of this particular *moikhos* (cf. Euripides' expectation that Agathon will have a razor ready to hand in the opening of *Thesm.*; also Men. *Orge* fr. 303 K–T and Timokles *Demosaturoi* fr. 5 K–A). The verse is thus to be translated (in the context of the passage): "yes, and the convicted *moikhos* keeps himself well-shaven because of you."

Works cited

Ahrens, H.-J. (1970) "Arbiter und Iudex in den Plautinischen Komödien." Inaugural dissertation. Kiel.

Aicher-Hadler, G. (1989) "Das 'Urteil' des amtlichen Diaiteten," *RIDA* 3rd ser. 36: 57–73.

Andreau, J. (1968) "Banque grecque et banque romaine dans le théâtre de Plaute et de Terence," *MEFR* 80: 461–526.

Arangio-Ruiz, V. (1968) *Istituzioni di diritto romano.* 14th edn. Naples.

Arangio-Ruiz, V. and Pugliese Caratelli, G. (1955) "Tabulae Herculanenses," *La parola del Passato* 10: 448–77.

Arnott, W. G. (1965) Review of Rieth, *Gnomon* 37: 254–63.

(1970) "Phormio *parasitus.* A study in dramatic methods of characterization," *G & R* 17: 32–57.

(1972) "Targets, techniques, and tradition in Plautus' *Stichus,*" *BICS* 19: 54–79.

(1979) *Menander.* vol. 1. Cambridge and London.

Bain, D. (1981) "Menander, *Samia* 580 and 'Not- und Hilferufe' in Ptolemaic Egypt," *ZPE* 44: 169–71.

Barigazzi, A. (1965) *La formazione spirituale di Menandro.* Torino.

Barsby, J. A. (1986) *Plautus* Bacchides. Warminster.

(1993) "Problems of adaptation in the *Eunuchus* of Terence," *Drama. Beiträge zum antiken Drama und seiner Rezeption.* 2: 160–79.

Bauman, R. A. (1992) *Women and Politics in Ancient Rome.* London and New York.

(1993) "The rape of Lucretia, *Quod metus causa* and the criminal law," *Latomus* 52: 550–66.

Beauchet, L. (1897) *L' Histoire du droit privé de la République Athénienne.* 4 vols. Paris. Reprinted 1976, New York.

Behrend, D. (1975) "Die ἀνάδικος δίκη und das Scholion zu Plato Nomoi 937 d," in Modrzejewski, Nörr, and Wolff, 1975: 131–56.

Behrends, O. (1969) "Der assessor zur Zeit der klassischen Rechtswissenschaft," *ZSS* 86: 192–96.

(1970) *Die römische Geschworenenverfassung. Ein Rekonstruktionsversuch.* Göttingen.

(1976) Review of Ziegler 1971, *Gnomon* 48: 678–89.

(1977) Review of Kelly 1976, *ZSS* 94: 446–62.
Bekker, E. I. (1892) "Die römische Komiker als Rechtszeugen," *ZSS* 13: 53–118.
Berneker, E. (1968), ed., *Zur griechischen Rechtsgeschichte*. Darmstadt.
Bers, V. (1985) "Dikastic Thorubos," in Cartledge and Harvey (1985), 1–15.
Bickerman, E. J. (1956) "Two legal interpretations of the Septuagint," *RIDA* 3rd ser. 3: 81–104.
Bigott, E. (1939) *Die Komposition der Andria des Terenz*. Dissertation. Köln.
Birks, P. (1969) "The early history of *iniuria*," *RHD* 37: 163–208.
(1974) "Lucius Veratius and the *lex Aebutia*," in Watson 1974a: 39–48.
(1981) "Other men's meat: Aquilian liability for proper user," *The Irish Jurist* 16: 141–85.
Biscardi, A. (1970) "La *gnome dikaiotate* et l'interprétation des lois dans la Grèce ancienne," *RIDA* 3rd ser. 17: 219–32.
(1979) ed., *Symposion 1974: Vorträge zur griechischen und hellenistischen Rechtsgeschichte*. Köln and Wien.
Boegehold, A. L. (1986) "Gestures and the interpretation of Greek literature," *AJA* 90: 181.
(1991) "Rhetorical delivery," review of Katsouris 1989, *CR* 41: 355–57.
(1995) *The Lawcourts at Athens* (The Athenian Agora, Vol. 28). Princeton.
Bonner, R. J. (1907) "The Jurisdiction of Athenian Arbitrators," *CPh* 2: 407–18.
(1919) "Apollodorus vs. Phormio, Criminal Assault," *CP* 14: 83–84.
Bonner, R. J. and Smith, G. (1930–38) *The Administration of Justice from Homer to Aristotle*. 2 vols. Chicago.
Braun, L. (1980) *Scenae Suppositiciae oder Der falsche Plautus. Hypomnemata* 64. Göttingen.
Bremer, J. M. (1969) *Hamartia. Tragic Error in the Poetics of Aristotle and in Greek Tragedy*. Amsterdam.
Broggini, G. (1957) *Iudex arbiterve. Prolegomena zum Officium des römischen Privatrichters*. Köln and Graz.
Brothers, A. J. (1980) "The construction of Terence's *Heautontimorumenos*," *CQ* 74: 94–119.
(1988) *Terence the Self-Tormentor*. Warminster.
Broughton, T. R. S. (1951–2) *The Magistrates of the Roman Republic*. 2 vols. Cleveland. Reprinted in 1968.
Brown, P. G. McC. (1980) "Terentian *Imitatio*," review of Lefèvre 1978a. *CR* 30: 194–96.
(1983) "Menander's dramatic technique and the law of Athens," *CQ* 33: 412–20.
(1984) Review of L. B. Brea, *Menandro e il teatro greco nelle terracotte liparese*, Genova, 1981 in *LCM* 9: 108–12.
(1987) "Masks, names and characters in New Comedy," *Hermes* 115: 181–202.
(1990) "Plots and prostitutes in Greek New Comedy," in Cairns, F., ed.,

Papers of the Leeds International Seminar 6: 241–66. (ARCA Classical and Medieval Texts, Papers and Monographs 29.) Leeds.
(1991) "Athenian attitudes to rape and seduction: The evidence of Menander, *Dyskolos* 289–93," *CQ* 41: 533–34.
(1993) "Love and marriage in Greek New Comedy," *CQ* 43: 189–205.
Büchner, K. (1974) *Das Theater des Terenz*. Heidelberg.
Burkert, W. (1979) *Structure and History in Greek Mythology and Ritual*. Sather Classical Lectures. Vol. 47. Berkeley.
Bushala, E. W. (1969) "The *Pallake* of Philoneus," *AJPh* 90: 65–72.
Buxton, R. G. A. (1982) *Persuasion in Greek Tragedy. A Study of Peitho.* Cambridge.
Calboli, G. (1980) "Terenzio, *Andria* 481–8," *Philologus* 124: 33–67.
Calhoun, G. M. (1919a) "Athenian magistrates and special pleas," *CPh* 14: 8–50.
(1919b) "Oral and written pleading in Athenian courts," *TAPhA* 50: 177–93.
Cantarella, E. (1976) *Studi sul' Omicidio in Diritto Greco e Romano*. Milan.
(1987) *Pandora's Daughters. The Role and Status of Women in Greek and Roman Antiquity*. Trans. Maureen Fant. Baltimore.
(1991) "*Moicheia*. Reconsidering a problem," in Gagarin 1991: 289–96.
Capps, E. (1908) "The plot of Menander's *Epitrepontes*," *AJPh* 29: 410–31.
Carawan, E. (1998) *Rhetoric and the Law of Draco*. Oxford.
Carden, R. (1974) *The Papyrus Fragments of Sophocles*. Berlin.
Carey, C. (1989) *Lysias. Selected Speeches*. Cambridge.
(1992) ed. and trans., *Apollodorus* Against Neaira [Demosthenes] 59. Warminster.
(1993) "Return of the radish or Just when you thought it was safe to go back into the kitchen," *LCM* 18: 53–55.
(1995) "Rape and adultery in Athenian law," *CQ* 45: 407–17.
Carey, C. and Reid, R. A. (1985), eds., *Demosthenes. Selected Private Speeches*. Cambridge.
Cartledge, P. A. and Harvey, F. D. (1985), eds., *CRUX. Essays Presented to G.E.M. de Ste. Croix on his 75th Birthday*. Exeter.
Cartledge, P., Millett, P., and Todd, S., eds. (1990) *Nomos. Essays in Athenian Law, Politics, and Society*. Cambridge.
Chiarini, G. (1979) *La recita: Plauto, la Farsa, la festa*. Bologna.
Clairmont, C. (1953) "Danae and Perseus in Seriphos," *AJA* 57: 92–94.
Cloud, D. (1992) "The *lex Papiria de sacramentis*," *Athenaeum* 70: 159–86.
Cohen, D. (1983) *Theft in Athenian Law*. Munich (Münchener Beiträge zur Papyrusforschung und antiken Rechtsgeschichte 74).
(1984) "The Athenian law of adultery," *RIDA* 3rd ser. 31: 147–65.
(1985) "A note on Aristophanes and the punishment of adultery in Athenian law," *ZSS* 102: 385–7.
(1991a) "Demosthenes" *Against Meidias* and Athenian litigation," in Gagarin 1991: 155–64.

(1991b) *Law, Sexuality, and Society.* Cambridge.
(1991c) "Sexuality, violence, and the Athenian law of hubris," *G & R* 38: 171–88.
(1995) *Law, Violence, and Community in Classical Athens.* Cambridge.
Cohen, E. (1973) *Ancient Athenian Maritime Courts.* Princeton.
(1992) *Athenian Economy and Society. A Banking Perspective.* Princeton.
Cohoon, J. W. (1915) *Rhetorical Studies in the Arbitration Scene of Menander's Epitrepontes.* Boston.
Cole, S. G. (1984) "Greek sanctions against sexual assault," *CPh* 79: 97–113.
Corbett, P. E. (1930) *The Roman Law of Marriage.* Oxford.
Costa, E. (1890) *Il diritto privato romano nelle comedie di Plauto.* Turin.
(1893) *Il diritto privato nelle comedie di Terenzio.* Bologna.
Cox, C. A. (1983) "The social and political ramifications of Athenian marriages *c.* 600–400 BC." Ph. D. Dissertation. Duke University.
(1989) "Incest, inheritance and the political forum in fifth-century Athens," *CJ* 85: 34–46.
Cronin, J. F. (1936) *The Athenian Juror and his Oath.* (Part of a Ph.D. dissertation, submitted to the University of Chicago in 1934.) Private edition, distributed by The University of Chicago Libraries.
Crook, J. A. (1967) "*Patria potestas*," *CQ* 17: 113–22.
(1995) *Legal Advocacy in the Roman World.* London.
Dareste, R. (1892) Review of Costa, 1890, *Journal des Savants*: 145–54.
(1902) "Le droit romain et le droit grec dans Plaute," *Nouvelles Études d' Histoire du Droit*: 149–75.
Daube, D. (1939) "*Nocere* and *noxa*," *Cambridge Law Journal* 7: 23–55.
(1956) *Forms of Roman Legislation.* Oxford.
(1969) *Roman Law. Linguistic, Social and Philosophical Aspects.* Edinburgh.
(1980) "Greek forerunners of Simenon," *California Law Review* 68: 301–12.
Davies, J. K. (1971) *Athenian Propertied Families, 600–300 B.C.* Oxford.
(1984) "Cultural, social and economic features of the Hellenistic world. iv: Piracy and its Ramifications," *CAH*² VII. 1: 285–90.
Dorjahn, A. P. (1930) "Extenuating circumstances in Athenian courts," *CPh* 25: 162–72.
(1935) "Anticipation of arguments in Athenian courts," *AJPh* 56: 274–95.
(1946) *Political Forgiveness in Old Athens.* Evanston.
Dover, K. J. (1968a) *Lysias and the Corpus Lysiacum.* Berkeley, Los Angeles, and London.
(1968b) *Aristophanes* Clouds. Oxford.
(1972) *Aristophanic Comedy.* Berkeley and Los Angeles.
(1974) *Greek Popular Morality in the Time of Plato and Aristotle.* Berkeley.
(1980) *Greek Homosexuality.* New York.
Drerup, E. (1898) "Über die bei den attischen Rednern eingelegten Urkunden," *Jahrbücher für classische Philologie* Supplementband 24: 221–366.

Drexler, H. (1934) *Die Komposition von Terenz' Adelphen und Plautus' Rudens.* Leipzig (*Philologus* Supplementband 26, heft 2).
(1938) "Terentiana," *Hermes* 73: 39–98.
Düll, R. (1931) *Der Gütegedanke im römischen Zivilprozessrecht.* Munich.
(1943) "*Iudicium domesticum, abdicatio* und *apoceryxis,*" *ZSS* 63: 54–116.
Ehrenberg, V. (1947) "*Polypragmosyne*: A study in Greek politics," *JHS* 67: 46–67.
Engberg-Pedersen, T. "Is there an ethical dimension to Aristotelian rhetoric?" in Rorty 1996: 116–41.
Epstein, A., ed. (1967) *The Craft of Social Anthropology.* London.
Erdmann, W. (1934) *Die Ehe im alten Griechenland.* Munich. Reprint edition 1979, New York.
Fantham, E. (1965) "The *Curculio* of Plautus: An illustration of Plautine methods in adaptation," *CQ* 15: 84–100.
(1968) "Terence, Diphilus and Menander," *Philologus* 112: 196–216.
(1971) "*Hautontimorumenos* and *Adelphoe*: A study of fatherhood in Terence and Menander," *Latomus* 30: 970–98.
(1973) "Towards a dramatic reconstruction of the fourth act of Plautus' *Amphitruo,*" *Philologus* 117: 197–214.
(1975) "Sex, status, and survival in Hellenistic Athens: A study of women in New Comedy," *Phoenix* 29: 44–74.
(1982) Review of Lefèvre 1978a. *CPh* 77: 365–70.
Ferguson, W. S. (1911) *Hellenistic Athens.* London.
(1938) "The Salaminioi of Heptaphyle and Sounion," *Hesp.* 7: 1–74.
Ferrero, M. G. (1976) "L'asindeto in Menandro," *Dioniso* 47: 82–106.
Fisher, N. R. E. (1992) *Hybris. A study in the values of honour and shame in Ancient Greece.* Warminster.
Fitzpatrick, J., ed. (1939) *The Last Will and Testament of George Washington and Schedule of his Property.* Mount Vernon.
Foxhall, L. (1989) "Household, gender and property in classical Athens," *CQ* 39: 22–44.
(1991) "Response to Eva Cantarella," in Gagarin 1991: 297–303.
Foxhall, L. and Lewis, A.D.E. (1996) *Greek Law in its Political Setting. Justifications not Justice.* Oxford.
Fraenkel, E. (1920) "Zur form der αἶνοι," *RhM* 73: 366–70.
(1950) *Aeschylus Agamemnon.* Vols. 1–3. Oxford.
(1960) *Elementi Plautini in Plauto.* Firenze. Transl. of *Plautinisches im Plautus* (Philologische Untersuchungen 28) Berlin 1922.
Fraenkel, M. (1878) "Der attische Heliasteneid," *Hermes* 13: 452–66.
Franciosi, G. (1961a) "Il processo di Virginia," *Labeo* 7: 20–35.
(1961b) *Il processo di libertà in diritto romano.* Naples.
Fredershausen, O. (1906) *De iure Plautino et Terentiano.* Dissertatio Inauguralis. Göttingen.
(1912) "Weitere Studien über das Recht bei Plautus und Terenz," *Hermes* 47: 199–249.

Friedrich, W. H. (1953) *Euripides und Diphilos. Zur Dramaturgie der Spätformen.* Munich (*Zetemata* 5).

Frier, B. W. (1980) *Landlords and Tenants in Imperial Rome.* Princeton.

(1985) *The Rise of the Roman Jurists. Studies in Cicero's pro Caecina.* Princeton.

Frost, K. (1988) *Exits and Entrances in Menander.* Oxford.

Gagarin, M. (1979) "The Athenian law against *hybris*," in Bowersock, G. W., Burkert, W., and Putnam, M. C. J., eds., *Arktouros: Hellenic Studies presented to Bernard Knox*, 229–36. Berlin and New York.

(1981) *Drakon and Early Athenian Homicide Law.* New Haven and London.

(1986) *Early Greek Law.* Berkeley.

(1989) *The Murder of Herodes. A Study of Antiphon 5.* (Studien zur klassischen Philologie, Vol. 45.) Frankfurt.

(1991) ed., *Symposion 1990: Vorträge zur griechischen und hellenistischen Rechtsgeschichte.* Köln, Weimar, and Vienna.

Gaiser, K. (1964) "Nachwort des Herausgebers," in Rieth 1964: 133–54.

(1967) "Zum *Miles Gloriosus* des Plautus: Eine neuerschlossene Menander-Komödie und ihre literaturgeschichtliche Stellung," *Poetica* 1: 436–61. Reprinted in Lefèvre 1973: 205–48.

(1972) "Zur Eigenart der römischen Komödie: Plautus und Terenz gegenüber ihren griechischen Vorbildern," *ANRW* 1.2: 1027–113.

Gardner, J. F. (1986) *Women in Roman Law and Society.* London.

Garofalo, L. (1986) "La competenza a promuovere 'iudicia populi' avverso donne," *SDHI* 52: 451–76.

Garvie, A. F. (1969) *Aeschylus' Supplices. Play and Trilogy.* Cambridge.

Gatti, C. (1957) "Alcuni aspetti della posizione giuridica della donna ateniese nel v e iv secolo A.C.," *Acme* 10: 57–65.

Gauthier, Ph. (1972) *Symbola. Les étrangers et la justice dans les cités grecques.* Nancy.

Geertz, C. (1980) "Blurred genres: the refiguration of social thought," *The American Scholar* 49: 165–79.

Gelhaus, H. (1972) *Die Prologe des Terenz.* Heidelberg.

Gernet, L. (1920) "La création du testament. Première partie" *REG* 33: 123–68. Reprinted in Gernet 1955: 121–42 as "La loi de Solon sur le 'Testament'."

(1939) "L'institution des arbitres publics à Athènes," *REG* 52: 389–414. Reprinted in Gernet 1955: 103–19.

(1955) *Droit et Société dans la Grèce Ancienne.* Paris.

(1954, 1957, 1959, 1960) *Démosthène. Plaidoyers civils.* 4 vols. Budé edn. Paris.

Girard, P. F. (1893) Review of Bekker 1892, Costa 1890, et alii, *Nouvelle revue historique de droit français et étranger* 17: 789–97.

Glotz, G. (1904) *La Solidarité de la Famille dans le Droit Criminel en Grèce.* Reprinted in 1973, New York.

Gneist, R. v. (1845) *Die formellen Verträge des neueren römischen Obligationenrechts in Vergleichung mit den Geschäftsformen des griechischen Rechts.* Berlin. Reprinted 1970, Aalen.

Goldberg, S. M. (1981–82) "The dramatic balance of Terence's *Andria,*" *C&M:* 135–43.

Golden, L. (1987) "Comic pleasure," *Hermes* 115: 165–74.

Golden, M. (1985) "'Donatus' and Athenian phratries," *CQ* 35: 9–13.

(1990) *Children and Childhood in Classical Athens.* Baltimore.

Gomme, A. W. and Sandbach, F. H. (1973), eds., *Menander. A Commentary.* Oxford.

Graf, F. (1992) "Gestures and conventions: the gestures of Roman actors and orators" in *A Cultural History of Gesture*: 36–58. Edited by J. Bremmer and H. Roodenburg. Ithaca.

Grant, J. N. (1975) "The ending of Terence's *Adelphoe* and the Menandrian original," *AJPh* 96: 42–60.

Gratwick, A. (1969) "The *Poenulus* of Plautus and its Attic original." Ph.D. Dissertation. Oxford.

(1982) "Drama," in *The Cambridge History of Classical Literature* vol. ii: 77–137. Cambridge.

(1987) *Terence. The Brothers.* Warminster.

Greiffenhagen, G. (1966) "Der Prozess des Ödipus. Strafrechtliche und strafprozessuale Bemerkungen zur Interpretation des Ödipus Rex des Sophokles," *Hermes* 94: 147–76.

Grmek, M. D. (1987) "Les *Indicia Mortis* dans la médecine Gréco-Romaine," in *La mort, les mortes et l'au-delà dans le monde romain.* Actes du Colloques de Caen 20–22 Novembre 1985, Caen.

Gronewald, M. (1986) "Menander, *Epitrepontes.* Neue Fragmente aus Akt iii und iv," *ZPE* 66: 1–13.

Gruen, E. S. (1984) *The Hellenistic World and the Coming of Rome,* 2 vols. Berkeley.

Habicht, Ch. (1979) *Untersuchungen zur politischen Geschichte Athens im 3. Jhd. v. Chr.* (*Vestigia,* vol. 30.) München.

Hall, E. (1995) "Lawcourt Dramas: The Power of Performance in Greek Forensic Oratory," *BICS* 40: 39–52.

Halliwell, S. (1996) "The challenge of rhetoric to political and ethical theory in Aristotle," in Rorty 1996: 175–90.

Handley, E. (1990) "The Bodmer Menander and the comic fragments," *Recherches et Rencontres* 2: 123–48. (= *Relire Menandre,* edited by E. Handley and A. Hurst, Geneva.)

Hansen, M. H. (1975) *Eisangelia. The Sovereignty of the People's Court in Athens in the Fourth Century* BC *and the Impeachment of Generals and Politicians.* Odense.

(1976) *Apagoge, Endeixis and Ephegesis against Kakourgoi, Atimoi and Pheugontes: A Study in the Athenian Administration of Justice in the Fourth Century* BC. Odense.

(1983) "*Graphe* or *dike traumatos?*," *GRBS* 24: 307–20.

(1991) *The Athenian Democracy in the Age of Demosthenes. Structure, Principles and Ideology.* Oxford.

Harrell, H. C. (1936) "Public arbitration in Athenian law," *The University of Missouri Studies* 11: 1–42.
Harris, E. M. (1989) "Demosthenes' speech against Meidias," *HSCPh* 92: 117–36.
(1990) "Did the Athenians regard seduction as a worse crime than rape?," *CQ* 40: 370–77.
(1992) Review of MacDowell 1990, *CPh* 87: 71–80.
(1994a) Review of Carey 1992, *CR* : 21–23.
(1994b) " 'In the act' or 'red-handed'? Apagoge to the eleven and furtum manifestum," in Thür 1994: 169–84.
Harris, W. V. (1986) "The Roman father's power of life and death," in *Studies in Roman Law in Memory of A. Arthur Schiller.* 81–95. Edited by R. S. Bagnall and W. V. Harris. Leiden.
Harrison, A. R. W. (1968–71) *The Law of Athens.* 2 vols. Oxford.
Harvey, F. D. (1966) "Literacy in the Athenian democracy," *REG* 79: 585–635.
Harvey, D. (1990) "The sykophant and sykophancy: vexatious redefinition," in Cartledge, Millett, and Todd, eds., 1990: 103–122.
Hazard, G. C., Jr. and Trauffo, M. (1993) *American Civil Procedure. An Introduction.* New Haven.
Headlam, W. (1899) "Critical Notes," *CR* 13: 3–8.
Henderson, J. (1987) "Older women in Attic Old Comedy," *TAPhA* 117: 105–29.
Henrichs, A. (1993) "Response," in *Images and Ideologies. Self-definition in the Hellenistic World*: 171–95. Edited by A. Bulloch, E. Gruen, A. A. Long, and A. Stewart. Berkeley, Los Angeles, and London.
Hillgruber, M. (1988) *Die zehnte Rede des Lysias.* Berlin (Untersuchungen zur antiken Literatur und Geschichte 29).
Hitzig, H. F. (1899) *Injuria. Beiträge zur Geschichte der Injuria im griechischen und römischen Recht.* Munich.
Hofmann, H. (1975) "A new interpretation of certain aspects in Menander's *Samia*," in *Proceedings of the XIV International Congress of Papyrologists*: 167–75. London.
Hubert, B. (1885) *De arbitris Atticis et privatis et publicis.* Dissertatio Inauguralis Philologica. Leipzig.
Hudtwalcker, M. H. (1812) *Über die öffentlichen und privat-Schiedsrichter-Diäteten in Athen.* Jena.
Humphreys, S. C. (1978) *Anthropology and the Greeks.* London.
(1983a) "The date of Hagnias' death," *CPh* 78: 219–25.
(1983b) "The evolution of legal process in ancient Attica," in *Tria Corda. Scritti in onore di Arnaldo Momigliano*: 229–56. Edited by E. Gabba. Como.
(1983c) *The Family, Women, and Death.* London.
(1985a), ed., *The Discourse of Law.* London (= *History and Anthropology* 1. 2).
(1985b) "Law as discourse," in Humphreys 1985a: 241–64.

(1985c) "Social relations on stage: Witnesses in classical Athens," in Humphreys 1985a: 313–69.
(1986) "Kinship patterns in the Athenian courts," *GRBS* 27: 57–91.
Hunter, R. L. (1985) *The New Comedy of Greece and Rome.* Cambridge.
(1993) Review of Lefèvre, Stärk, Vogt-Spira (1991), in *Drama. Beiträge zum antiken Drama und seiner Rezeption.* 2: 235–37.
Hunter, V. J. (1994) *Policing Athens. Social Control in the Attic Lawsuits, 420–320 B.C.* Princeton.
Huvelin, P. (1915) *Études sur le furtum dans le très ancien droit romain. Vol. 1: Les sources.* Lyon and Paris.
Huwardas, S. (1938) "Über die Vergleiche und die privaten Schiedssprüche nach attischem Recht," *Zeitschrift für vergleichende Rechtswissenschaft* 49: 289–335.
Ireland, S. (1990) *Terence* The Mother in Law. Warminster.
Irwin, T. H. (1996) "Ethics in the *Rhetoric* and in the ethics," in Rorty 1996: 142–74.
Isager, S. and Hansen, M. H. (1975) *Aspects of Athenian Society in the Fourth Century BC.* Odense.
Jachmann, G. (1931) *Plautinisches und Attisches.* Berlin. Reprinted 1966, Rome.
Jacoby, F. (1949) *Atthis. The Local Chronicles of Ancient Athens.* Oxford.
Jocelyn, H. D. (1967) *The Tragedies of Ennius: the Fragments.* Cambridge.
(1973) "*Homo sum: humani nil a me alienum puto,*" *Antichthon* 7: 14–46.
(1993) Review of Zwierlein 1990, *Gnomon* 65: 122–37.
Jolowicz, H. F. and Nicholas, B. (1972) *Historical Introduction to the Study of Roman Law.* 3rd edn. Cambridge.
Just, R. (1989) *Women in Athenian Law and Life.* London.
Karabelias, E. (1975) "L'épiclérat dans la comédie nouvelle et dans les sources Latines," in Modrzejewski, Nörr, and Wolff 1975: 215–54.
(1979) "Contribution a l'étude de l'épidicasie Attique," in Biscardi 1979: 201–25.
Kaser, M. (1938) "Der Inhalt der *patria potestas,*" *ZSS* 58: 62–87.
(1943) *Eigentum und Besitz im älteren römischen Recht.* Weimar.
(1949) *Das altrömische Ius. Studien zur Rechtsvorstellung und Rechtsgeschichte der Römer.* Göttingen.
(1962) Review of Franciosi 1961b, *ZSS* 79: 391–98.
(1965) "Typisierter '*dolus*' im altrömischen Recht," *BIDR* 65: 79–104.
(1966) *Das römische Zivilprozessrecht.* (Handbuch der Altertumswissenschaft 10.3.4.) Munich.
(1971–75) *Das römische Privatrecht. Das altrömische, das vorklassische und klassische Recht.* 2 vols. 2nd edn. (First edition, 1955.) Munich.
Katsouris, A. G. (1989) *ΡΗΤΟΡΙΚΗ ΥΠΟΚΡΙΣΗ.* Ioannina.
Kelly, J. M. (1966) *Roman Litigation.* Oxford.
(1976) *The Civil Judicature of the Roman Republic.* Oxford.
Konstan, D. (1983) *Roman Comedy.* Ithaca and London.

(1987) "Between courtesan and wife: Menander's *Perikeiromene*," *Phoenix* 41: 122–39
(1993) "The young concubine in Menandrian Comedy," in Scodel, R., ed., *Theater and Society in the Classical World*: 139–60. Ann Arbor.
(1995) *Greek Comedy and Ideology*. Oxford.
Körte, A. (1909) "Zur Perinthia des Menander," *Hermes* 44: 309–13.
(1937) "Menanders *fabula incerta*," *Hermes* 72: 50–77.
Kuiper, W. E. J. (1936) *Grieksche Origineelen en Latijnsche Navolgingen. Zes Komedies van Menander bij Terentius en Plautus*. Amsterdam (Verhandelingen der Koninklijke Akademie van Wetenschappen te Amsterdam, Afdeeling Letterkunde, nieuwe reeks, deel 38, no. 2).
Kunkel, W. (1962) *Untersuchungen zur Entwicklung des römischen Kriminalverfahrens in vorsullanischer Zeit*. Bayerische Akademie der Wissenschaften. Philosophisch-Historische Klasse Abhandlungen. Neue Folge, Heft 56. München.
(1966) "Das Konsilium im Hausgericht," *ZSS* 83: 219–51.
Lambert, S. D. (1993) *The Phratries of Attica*. Ann Arbor.
Lambertini, R. (1980) *Plagium*. Milan.
(1992) "Ancora sui legittimati a uccidere 'iure patris ex lege Iulia de adulteriis,'" *SDHI* 58: 362–75.
Langen, P. (1886) *Plautinische Studien*. Berlin. Reprinted 1970, Hildesheim and New York. (Berliner Studien für classische Philologie und Archaeologie 5.1.)
Latte, K. (1926) Review of Steinwenter 1925. *Gnomon* 2: 209–12.
Lawless, J. (1991) "Law, argument and equity in the speeches of Isaeus." Ph.D. Dissertation. Brown University.
Lefèvre, E. (1969) *Die Expositionstechnik in den Komödien des Terenz*. Darmstadt.
(1971) "Das Wissen der Bühnenpersonen bei Menander und Terenz am Beispiel der *Andria*," *MH* 28: 21–48.
(1973) ed. *Die römische Komödie: Plautus und Terenz*. Darmstadt.
(1978a) *Der Phormio des Terenz und der Epidikazomenos des Apollodor von Karystos*. Munich (*Zetemata* 74).
(1978b) "Plautus-Studien II. Die Brief-Intrige in Menanders *Dis exapaton* und ihre Verdoppelung in den *Bacchides*," *Hermes* 106: 518–38.
(1984a) *Diphilos und Plautus. Der Rudens und sein Original*. Mainz (Akademie der Wissenschaften und der Literatur, Abhandlungen der Geistes- und sozialwissenschaftlichen Klasse 10).
(1984b) "Plautus-Studien IV. Die Umformung des ὁ Ἀλαζών zu der Doppel-Komödie des Miles Gloriosus," *Hermes* 112: 30–53.
(1991a) "Truculentus oder der Triumph der Weisheit," in Lefèvre, Stärk, Vogt-Spira, eds. 1991: 175–200.
(1991b) "Curculio oder der Triumph der Edazität," in Lefèvre, Stärk, Vogt-Spira, eds. (1991), 71–105.
Lefèvre, E., Stärk, E., and Vogt-Spira, G., eds. (1991) *Plautus Barbarus. Sechs Kapitel zur Originalität des Plautus*. Tübingen.

Leisi, E. (1908) *Der Zeuge im Attischen Recht.* Frauenfeld. Reprinted 1979, New York.

Lenel, O. (1927) *Das Edictum Perpetuum.* 3rd edn. Leipzig.

Leo, F. (1912) *Plautinische Forschungen. Zur Kritik und Geschichte der Komödie.* 2nd edn. Berlin. Reprinted 1966, Darmstadt.

(1913) *Geschichte der römischen Literatur I: Die archaische Literatur.* Leipzig.

Lewis, N. (1982) "*Aphairesis* in Athenian law and custom," in Modrzejewski and Liebs: 161–78.

Lewis, R. G. (1989) "The procedural basis of Sophocles' *Oedipus Tyrannus*," *GRBS* 30: 41–66.

Lipsius, J. H. (1905–15) *Das attische Recht und Rechtsverfahren.* 3 vols. in 4 (continuous pagination). Leipzig. Reprinted 1966, Darmstadt and 1984, Hildesheim.

Lloyd-Jones, H. (1971) "Menander's *Aspis.*" *GRBS* 12: 175–95. Reprinted in *Greek Comedy, Hellenistic Literature, Greek Religion, and Miscellanea. The Academic Papers of Sir Hugh Lloyd-Jones.* 1990. Oxford, pp. 7–25.

(1973) "Terentian technique in the *Adelphi* and *Eunuchus*," *CQ* NS 23: 279–84. Reprinted in *Greek Comedy, Hellenistic Literature, Greek Religion, and Miscellanea. The Academic Papers of Sir Hugh Lloyd-Jones.* 1990. Oxford.

Loening, T. C. (1987) *The Reconciliation Agreement of 403/402 BC in Athens. Its Content and Application.* Stuttgart (*Hermes* Einzelschriften 53).

Lofberg, J. O. (1920) "The sycophant-parasite," *CPh* 15: 61–72.

Lonie, I. M. (1965) "Medical theory in Heraclides of Pontus," *Mnem.* 18: 126–43.

Lorenzi, C. (1991) "Pap. Coll. 4, 8, 1: La figlia adultera e il 'ius occidendi iure patris,'" *SDHI* 57: 158–80.

Lowe, J. C. B. (1983a) "Terentian originality in the *Phormio* and *Hecyra*," *Hermes* 111: 431–52.

(1983b) "The *Eunuchus*: Terence and Menander," *CQ* 33: 428–44.

(1985a) "Cario–A Plautine creation," *BICS* 32: 83–4.

(1985b) "Cooks in Plautus," *ClAnt* 4: 72–102.

(1985c) "Plautine innovations in *Mostellaria* 529–857," *Phoenix* 39: 6–26.

(1989a) "Plautus' parasites and the Atellana," in Vogt-Spira, G., ed., *Studien zur vorliterarischen Periode im frühen Rom* (Tübingen), 161–69.

(1989b) "The *Virgo Callida* of Plautus, *Persa*," *CQ* 39: 390–99.

(1990) "Plautus' choruses," *RhM* 133: 274–97.

(1992) "Aspects of Plautus' originality in the *Asinaria*," *CQ* 42: 152–75.

Ludwig, W. (1961) "*Aulularia*-Probleme," *Philologus* 105: 44–71.

(1968) "The originality of Terence and his Greek models," *GRBS* 9: 169–82.

(1973) "Von Terenz zu Menander" with "Nachtrag 1971" in Lefèvre 1973: 354–408. First published in 1959, *Philologus* 103: 1–38.

MacCary, W. T. (1973) "The comic tradition and comic structure in Diphilos' *Kleroumenoi*," *Hermes* 101: 195–208.

MacCary, W. and Willcock, M. M. (1976) *Plautus* Casina. Cambridge.

MacCormack, G. (1971) "A note on *arra* in Plautus," *The Irish Jurist* 6: 360–66.
MacDowell, D. M. (1962) *Andokides. On the Mysteries*. Oxford.
(1963) *Athenian Homicide Law in the Age of the Orators*. Manchester.
(1971a) "The chronology of Athenian speeches and legal innovations in 401–398 BC," *RIDA* 3rd ser. 18: 267–73.
(1971b) *Aristophanes* Wasps. Oxford.
(1976) "*Hybris* in Athens," *G&R* 23: 14–31.
(1978) The Law in Classical Athens. London.
(1982) "Love versus the law: An essay on Menander's *Aspis*," *G&R* 29: 42–52.
(1983) "Athenian laws about bribery," *RIDA* 3rd ser. 30: 57–78.
(1985) "The length of the speeches on the assessment of the penalty in Athenian courts," *CQ* 35: 525–26.
(1989) "The *oikos* in Athenian Law," *CQ* 39: 10–21.
(1990) *Demosthenes Against Meidias (Oration 21)*. Oxford.
(1991) "The Athenian procedure of *Phasis*," in Gagarin, M. 1991: 187–98.
McDonnell, M. (1983) "Divorce initiated by women in Rome," *AJAH* 8: 54–80.
McGinn, T. A. J. (1992) "The *SC* from Larinum and the repression of adultery at Rome," *ZPE* 93: 273–95.
McKechnie, P. (1989) *Outsiders in the Greek Cities in the Fourth Century BC*. London.
McKinney's Consolidated New York Law (1987). New York.
Maltby, R. (1983) "The last act of Terence's *Heautontimorumenos*," in Cairns, F., ed., *Papers of the Liverpool Latin Seminar* 4: 27–41. Liverpool (ARCA Classical and Medieval Texts, Papers and Monographs 11).
Marti, H. C. (1963) "Terenz 1909–1959," *Lustrum* 8: 5–101, 244–64.
Martin, R. H. (1976), ed., *Terence* Adelphoe. Cambridge.
Martin, V. (1964) "Die Dramaturgie des Terenz in der *Andria*," *Das Altertum* 10: 234–49.
Marx, F. (1926) "De Rudentis comoediae nomine Graeco," *RhM* 75: 128.
(1928) *Plautus* Rudens. Leipzig. Reprinted 1959, Amsterdam.
Maschke, H. (1926) *Die Willenslehre im griechischen Recht*. Berlin. Repr. 1979, New York.
Matthiass, B. (1888) *Die Entwicklung des römischen Schiedsgerichts*. Rostock.
(1892) *Das griechische Schiedsgericht*. Stuttgart.
Meier, M. H. E. (1846) *Die Privatschiedsrichter und die öffentlichen Diäteten Athens, so wie die Austrägalgerichte in den griechischen Staaten des Alterthums. Mit einem epigraphischen Anhang*. Halle.
Meinecke, J. (1971) "Gesetzesinterpretation und Gesetzesanwendung im attischen Zivilprozess," *RIDA* 3rd ser. 18: 275–360.
Mette, H. J. (1962) "Die περιεργία bei Menander," *Gymnasium* 69: 398–406.
(1965) "Der heutige Menander (insbesondere für die Jahre 1955–65)," *Lustrum* 10: 5–211.

Meyer-Laurin, H. (1965) *Gesetz und Billigkeit im attischen Prozess*. Weimar.
Millett, P. (1990) "Sale, credit and exchange in Athenian law and society," in Cartledge, Millett, and Todd 1990: 167–94.
(1991) *Lending and Borrowing in Ancient Athens*. Cambridge.
Modrzejewski, J., and Liebs, D., eds. (1982) *Symposion 1977: Vorträge zur griechischen und hellenistischen Rechtsgeschichte*. Köln and Wien.
Modrzejewski, J., Nörr, D., and Wolff, H. J., eds. (1975), *Symposion 1971: Vorträge zur griechischen und hellenistischen Rechtsgeschichte*: Köln and Wien.
Molè, M. (1966) "Ricerche in tema di plagio," *Archivio Giuridico* 70: 116–66.
Mommsen, T. (1887) *Römisches Staatsrecht*. 2 vols. 3rd edn. Leipzig.
(1899) *Römisches Strafrecht* (Photostat. repr. in 1955). Darmstadt.
Monaco, G. (1947) "La scena dell' arbitrato e del riconoscimento nel *Rudens* plautino," *Parola del Passato* 2: 319–34.
Mossé, C. (1989) "Quelques remarques sur la famille à Athènes à la fin du IVème siècle: Le témoignage du théâtre de Ménandre," in Nieto 1989: 129–34.
Muecke, F. (1986) "Plautus and the Theatre of disguise," *CA* 216–29.
Müller, G. L. (1957) *Das Original des Plautinischen Persa*. Dissertation. Frankfurt am Main.
Murison, A.F. (1934) "The law in the Latin poets," *Atti del Congresso internazionale di diritto romano* 2: 607–39.
Nicolau, M. (1933) *Causa Liberalis*. Dissertation. Paris.
Nieto, ed. (1989), *Symposion 1982: Vorträge zur griechischen und hellenistischen Rechtsgeschichte*. Köln and Wien.
Nippel, W. (1988) *Aufruhr und "Polizei" in der römischen Republik*. Stuttgart.
(1995) *Public Order in Ancient Rome*. Cambridge.
Nixon, P. (1916, 1917, 1924, 1932, 1938) *Plautus with an English translation*. 5 vols. London.
Ogden, D. (1996) *Greek Bastardy in the Classical and Hellenistic Periods*. Oxford.
Oppermann, H. (1934) "Zur *Andria* des Terenz," *Hermes* 69: 262–85.
Osborne, R. G. (1985) "Law in action in Classical Athens," *JHS* 105: 40–58.
(1990) "Vexatious litigation in Classical Athens: sykophancy and the sykophant," in Cartledge, Millett, and Todd 1990: 83–102.
Ostwald, M. 1986. *From Popular Sovereignty to the Sovereignty of Law*. Berkeley and Los Angeles.
Page, D. L. (1970) *Select Papyri, Vol. 3: Literary Papyri. Poetry*. Cambridge, Mass. First printed in 1941.
Paoli, U. E. (1943) "L' ἐπίκληρος attica nella *palliata* romana," *Atene e Roma* 3rd ser. 11: 19–29. Reprinted in Paoli 1976: 103–12.
(1946) "La legittima afèresi dell' ἐπίκληρος nel diritto attico," *Miscellanea Giovanni Mercati*, v: 524–38. Reprinted in Paoli 1976: 363–76.
(1950) "Il reato di adulterio (μοιχεία) in diritto antico," *SDHI* 16: 123–82. Reprinted in Paoli 1976: 251–307.

(1951) "La *in ius vocatio* dans les comédies de Plaute," *Studi Senesi* 63: 283–304. Reprinted in Paoli 1976: 113–27.
(1952) "L'assentiment paternel au mariage du fils dans le droit attique," *AHDO-RIDA* 1: 267–75. Reprinted in Paoli 1976: 377–83.
(1953a) "Les limites juridiques de l'*aphérésis* paternelle dans le droit attique," *Recueil de l'Académie de Législation* ii: 1–6. Reprinted in Paoli 1976: 385–91.
(1953b) "Nota giuridica su Plauto (*Persa*, vv. 67–71)," *Iura* 4: 174–82. Reprinted in Paoli 1976: 151–59.
(1956) "Lo 'Stichus' di Plauto e l'aferesi paterna in diritto attico," in *Studi de Francisci*, 1, Milan: 233–45. Reprinted in Paoli 1976: 161–73.
(1961) "Note giuridiche sul Δύσκολος di Menandro," *MH* 18: 53–62 Reprinted in Paoli 1976: 559–70.
(1962) "Comici latini e diritto attico," *Quaderni di Studi Senesi* 8: IV-82. Milan. Reprinted in Paoli 1976: 31–78.
(1976) *Altri Studi di Diritto Greco e Romano*. Milan.
Parker, R. (1983) *Miasma. Pollution and Purification in Early Greek Religion*. Oxford.
Partsch, J. (1910) "Römisches und griechisches Recht in Plautus *Persa*," *Hermes* 45: 595–614.
Patterson, C. B. (1990) "Those Athenian bastards," *ClAnt* 9: 40–73.
Pernard, L. (1900) *Le droit romain et le droit grec dans le théatre de Plaute et de Térence*. Dissertation. Lyon.
Pickard-Cambridge, A. (1988) *The Dramatic Festivals of Athens*. Reissued with supplement and corrections of revised second edition of J. Gould and D. M. Lewis. Oxford.
Pohlenz, M. (1934) *Antikes Führertum. Cicero de officiis und das Lebensideal des Panaitios*. (*Neue Wege zur Antike* ii.3) Leipzig.
Post, L. A. (1939) "Dramatic infants in Greek," *CPh* 34: 193–208.
Prescott, H.W. (1929) "The comedy of errors," *CP* 24: 32–41.
Primmer, A. (1964) "Zum Prolog des *Heautontimorumenos*," *WS* 77: 61–75.
(1984) *Handlungsgliederung in nea und palliata. Dis Exapaton und Bacchides* (*SBAW*, Phil. Hist. Kl., Vol. 441). Wien.
Pringsheim, F. (1932) "*Bonum et aequum*," *SZ* 52: 78–155. Reprinted in Pringsheim 1961. 1: 173–223.
(1950) *The Greek Law of Sale*. Weimar.
(1961) *Gesammelte Abhandlungen*. 2 vols. Heidelberg.
Pritchett, W. K. (1991) *The Greek State at War*. Vol. v. Berkeley.
Rambelli, G. (1939) "Il prologo e la prima scena dell' 'Andria,'" *SIFC*, N.S. 16: 79–104.
Rhodes, P. J. (1981) *A Commentary on the Aristotelian Athenaion Politeia*. Oxford.
(1984) *Aristotle. The Athenian Constitution*. Trans. London and New York.
Rickert, G. (1989) ΕΚΩΝ *and* ΑΚΩΝ *in Early Greek Thought*. (*American Classical Studies*, Vol. 20). Atlanta.
Rieth, O. (1934) Review of Drexler 1934, *Gnomon* 10: 636–49.

(1964) *Die Kunst Menanders in den "Adelphen" des Terenz.* 1943 Habilitationsschrift, edited by K. Gaiser. Hildesheim.

Robert, C. (1915) Review of Sudhaus, ed., *Menandri reliquiae* (1914) and Sudhaus, *Menanderstudien* (1914), *GGA* 177: 249–92.

Robinson, O.F. (1995). *The Criminal Law of Ancient Rome.* Baltimore.

Rogers, B.B. (1924) *Aristophanes.* 3 vols. London.

Rorty, A. O. (1996) ed., *Essays on Aristotle's* Rhetoric. Berkeley and Los Angeles.

Rosivach, V. J. (1984) "*Aphairesis* and *apoleipsis*: A study of the sources," *RIDA* 3rd ser. 31: 193–230.

Rotelli, G. (1972) "Ricerca di un criterio metodologico per l'utilizzazione di Plauto," *BIDR* 75: 97–132.

Rubinstein, L. (1993) *Adoption in IV. Century Athens.* Copenhagen (Opuscula Graecolatina vol. 34).

(forthcoming) Sunegoroi *and* Sukophantai *in the Athenian People's Court.* Ph.D. dissertation. Cambridge University.

Ruschenbusch, E. (1957) "ΔΙΚΑΣΤΗΡΙΟΝ ΠΑΝΤΩΝ ΚΥΡΙΩΝ," *Historia* 6: 257–74 (repr. Berneker 1968, 350–73).

(1965) "ΥΒΡΕΩΣ ΓΡΑΦΗ: Ein Fremdkörper im athenischen Recht des 4. Jahrhunderts v.Chr.," *ZSS* 82: 302–9.

(1966) ΣΟΛΩΝΟΣ ΝΟΜΟΙ. *Die Fragmente des solonischen Gesetzeswerkes mit einer Text- und Überlieferungsgeschichte.* Wiesbaden (*Historia* Einzelschriften 9).

(1989) "Drei Beiträge zur Öffentlichen Diaita in Athen," in Nieto 1989: 31–40.

Saller, R. (1986) "*Patria potestas* and the stereotype of the Roman family," *Continuity and Change* 1: 7–22.

(1987) "Men's age at marriage and its consequences in the Roman Family," *CPh* 82: 21–34.

(1988) "*Pietas*, obligation and authority in the Roman family," in P. Kneissl and V. Losemann, eds., *Alte Geschichte und Wissenschaftsgeschichte*: 393–410. Darmstadt.

(1991) "Corporal punishment, authority, and obedience in the Roman household," in B. Rawson, *Marriage, Divorce, and Children in Ancient Rome*: 144–65. Oxford.

Sandbach, F. H. (1975) "Menander and the three-actor rule," in J. Bingen, G. Cambier, and G. Nachtergael, ed., *Le Monde Grec. Hommages à Claire Préaux*: 197–204. Brussels.

(1986) "Two notes on Menander (*Epitrepontes* and *Samia*)," *LCM* 11: 156–60.

Saunders, T.J. (1991) *Plato's Penal Code.* Oxford.

Scafuro, A. C. (1987) "Prusias II of Bithynia and Third Party Arbitration," *Historia* 36: 28–37.

(1990) "Discourses of sexual violation in mythic accounts and dramatic versions of 'The Girl's Tragedy,'" *differences* 2: 126–59.

(1993) "Staging entrapment: On the boundaries of the law in Plautus' *Persa*," *Drama. Beiträge zum antiken Drama und seiner Rezeption.* 2: 55–77.
(1994) "Witnessing and false witnessing: proving citizenship and kin identity in fourth-century Athens," in A. L. Boegehold and A. C. Scafuro, eds., *Athenian Identity and Civic Ideology*: 156–98. Baltimore.
Schaefer, A. (1856–8) *Demosthenes und seine Zeit.* 3 vols. Leipzig. Reprinted 1979, New York.
Schaps, D. M. (1979) *Economic Rights of Women in Ancient Greece.* Edinburgh.
Schiller, A. A. (1978) *Roman Law. Mechanisms of Development.* The Hague, Paris and New York.
Schmidlin, B. (1974) Review of Ziegler, *ZSS* 91: 435–43.
Schodorf, K. (1904) *Beiträge zur genaueren Kenntnis der Attischen Gerichtssprache aus den Zehn Rednern* (*Beiträge zur historischen Syntax der griechischen Sprache*, H. 17). Würzburg.
Schofield, M. (1973) "Aristotelian mistakes," *PCPhS* 19: 66–70.
Schöll, F. (1912) *Menanders Perinthia in der Andria des Terenz.* Sitzungsberichte Heidelberg Akad. Wiss. 7. Heidelberg.
Schuhmann, E. (1977) "Der Typ der *Uxor Dotata* in den Komödien des Plautus," *Philologus* 121: 45–65.
Schulze, W. (1933) "Beiträge zur Wort- und Sittengeschichte II," *Kleine Schriften*, 160–89. Berlin. First published in 1918 in *SPAW.*
Schwind, A. (1901) *Über das Recht bei Terenz.* Dissertation. Würzburg.
Sealey, R. (1987) *The Athenian Republic.* University Park, PA.
(1990) *Women and Law in Classical Greece.* Chapel Hill.
(1993) *Demosthenes & his Time. A Study in Defeat.* New York and Oxford.
Skutsch, F. (1910) "Lat. *praesto*," *Glotta* 2: 389–97.
Skutsch, O. (1985) *The* Annals *of Quintus Ennius.* Oxford.
Slater, N. (1985) *Plautus in Performance. The Theatre of the Mind.* Princeton.
Sokolowski, F. (1962) *Lois Sacrées des Cités Grecques. Supplément.* Paris.
Sommerstein, A. H. (1980) "The naming of women in Greek and Roman Comedy," *Quaderni di Storia* 11: 393–418.
Sorabji, R. (1980) *Necessity, Cause, and Blame. Perspectives on Aristotle's Theory.* Ithaca, N. Y.
Stärk, E. (1991) "*Mostellaria* oder *turbare* statt *sedare*," in Lefèvre, Stärk, and Vogt-Spira 1991: 107–39.
Steidle, W. (1973) "Menander bei Terenz," *RhM* 116: 303–47.
(1974) "Menander bei Terenz," *RhM* 117: 247–76.
(1975) "Probleme des Bühnenspiels in der neuen Komödie," *Grazer Beiträge* 3: 341–86.
Stein, P. (1984) *Legal Institutions. The Development of Dispute Settlement.* London.
Steinwenter, A. (1925) *Die Streitbeendigung durch Urteil, Schiedsspruch und Vergleich nach griechischem Recht.* Munich (Münchener Beiträge zur Papyrusforschung und antiken Rechtsgeschichte 8).
Stroud, R. S. (1968) *Drakon's Law on Homicide.* Berkeley and Los Angeles.

Szegedy-Maszak, A. (1981) *The Nomoi of Theophrastus*. New York. Reprinted 1987, Salem, New Hampshire.
Talamanca, M. (1994) "Gli studi di diritto Greco dall' inizio dell' ottocento ai nostri giorni," in *Studi in memoria di Gino Giorni*, Vol. 1, 889–949.
Tandoi, V. (1961) "Un passo del *Curculio* e la semantica di *antestor*," *SIFC* 33: 62–86.
Taubenschlag, R. (1926) "Das attische Recht in der Komödie Menanders *Epitrepontes*," *ZSS* 46: 68–82.
Tellegen-Couperus, O. (1993) *A Short History of Roman Law*. London and New York.
Thalheim, Th. (1906) "Der Eid der Schiedsrichter in Athen." *Hermes* 41: 152–56.
Thierfelder, A. (1935) Review of Jachmann 1931, *Gnomon* 11: 113–52.
Thomas, J. A. C. (1976) *Textbook of Roman Law*. Amsterdam.
Thomas, R. (1989) *Oral Tradition and Written Record in Classical Athens*. Cambridge.
Thompson, W. E. (1976) *De Hagniae Hereditate*. Leiden.
Thür, G. (1975) "Komplexe Prozessführung dargestellt am Beispiel des Trapezitikos (Isokr. 17)," in Modrzejewski, Norr, and Wolff 1975: 157–88.
(1977) *Beweisführung vor den Schwurgerichtshöfen Athens. Die Proklesis zur Basanos*. Vienna (Österreichische Akademie der Wissenschaften philosophisch-historische Klasse, Sitzungsberichte 317).
(1987) "Neuere Untersuchungen zum Prozessrecht der griechischen Poleis. Formen des Urteils." *Akten des 26. Deutschen Rechthistorikertages, 22 bis 26 September 1986*: 467–84. Edited by D. Simon. Frankfurt.
(1994) ed. *Symposion 1993: Vorträge zur griechischen und hellenistischen Rechtsgeschichte*. Köln and Wien.
(1996) "Oaths and dispute settlement in ancient Greek law," in Foxhall and Lewis 1996: 57–72.
Todd, S. C. (1990) "The purpose of evidence in Athenian courts," in Cartledge, Millett, and Todd (1990): 19–39.
(1993) *The Shape of Athenian Law*. Oxford.
(1996) "Lysias against Nikomakhos: The fate of the expert in Athenian law," in Foxhall and Lewis (1996): 101–31.
Todd, S. C. and Millett, P. (1990) "Law, society, and Athens," in Cartledge, Millett, and Todd (1990): 1–18.
Townsend, R. F. (1995) *The East Side of the Agora. The Remains Beneath the Stoa of Attalos*. (The Athenian Agora. Vol. 27.) Princeton.
Treggiari, S. (1981) "*Concubinae*," *PBSR* 49: 59–81.
(1982) "Consent to Roman marriage: some aspects of law and reality," *EMC* 26: 34–44.
(1991) *Roman Marriage. Iusti Coniuges from the Time of Cicero to the Time of Ulpian*. Oxford.
Trendall, A. D. and Webster, T. B. L. (1971) *Illustrations of Greek Drama*. London.

Trevett, J. (1992) *Apollodoros the Son of Pasion*. Oxford.
Triantaphyllopoulos, J. (1989) "Aristotle's equity and the doctrine of the mean," *Syllecta Classica* 1: 43–54.
Turner, E. G. (1977) "The lost beginning of Menander, *Misoumenos*," *PBA* 63: 315–31.
(1979) "Menander and the new society of his time," *Chronique d'Egypte* 54: 106–26.
(1980) "The rhetoric of question and answer in Menander," *Themes in Drama* 2: 1–23.
Usener, H. (1901) "Italische Volksjustiz," *RhM* 66: 1–28.
Voigt, M. (1885) "Über die *lex Fabia de plagiariis*," *Phil. hist. Berichte der königl. sächs. Gesellschaft der Wissenschaften* 37: 319–45.
Volterra, E. (1948) "Il preteso tribunale domestico in diritto romano," *RISG* 2: 103–53.
Wallace, R. W. (1994) "The Athenian laws against slander," in Thür 1994: 109–24.
Watson, A. (1965a) "The divorce of Carvilius Ruga," *Tidj. R.* 33: 38–50.
(1965b) *The Law of Obligations in the Later Roman Republic*. Oxford.
(1967) *The Law of Persons in the Later Roman Republic*. Oxford.
(1971) *Roman Private Law around 200 B.C.* Edinburgh.
(1974a) ed., *Daube Noster. Essays in Legal History for David Daube*. Edinburgh.
(1974b) *Law Making in the Later Roman Republic*. Oxford.
(1975) *Rome of the XII Tables. Persons and Property*. Princeton.
Webster, T. B. L. (1953) *Studies in Later Greek Comedy*. Manchester.
(1960) *Studies in Menander*. 2nd edn. Manchester.
(1967) *Studies in Euripides*. London.
(1974) *An Introduction to Menander*. Manchester.
Wehrli, F. (1936) *Motivstudien zur griechischen Komödie*. Zurich and Leipzig.
Wenger, L. (1940) *Institutes of the Roman Law of Civil Procedure*. Rev. edn. Translation of *Institutionen des römischen Zivilprozessrechts* (1925) by O. H. Fisk. New York.
West, M. L. (1974) *Studies in Greek Elegy and Iambus*. (*Untersuchungen z. antiken Literatur u. Geschichte*, Vol. 11.) Berlin.
Whitehead, D. (1982) Notes on Athenian demarchs. *ZPE* 47: 37–42.
Wieacker, F. (1958) Review of Broggini 1957. *ZSS* 76: 582–92.
Wilamowitz-Moellendorff, U. v. (1875) *Analecta Euripidea*. Berlin.
(1893) "De tribus carminibus Latinis commentatio." *Index scholarum publice et privatim in Academia Georgia Augusta*. Göttingen. Reprinted in *Kleine Schriften* (1971) vol 2: 249–74. Berlin and Amsterdam.
(1925) *Menander. Das Schiedsgericht (Epitrepontes)*. Berlin.
Wiles, D. (1991) *The Masks of Menander. Sign and Meaning in Greek and Roman Performance*. Cambridge.
Wilhelm, A. (1905) "Ἀττικὰ ψηφίσματα," *Arkh. Eph.*, 217–81.
Williams, G. (1956) "Some problems in the construction of Plautus' *Pseudolus*," *Hermes* 84: 424–55.

(1958a) "Evidence for Plautus' workmanship in the *Miles Gloriosus*," *Hermes* 86: 79–105.
(1958b) "Some aspects of Roman marriage ceremonies and ideals," *JRS* 48: 16–29.
(1968) *Tradition and Originality in Roman Poetry*. Oxford.
Winterbottom, M. (1964) "Quintilian and the *vir bonus*," *JRS* 54: 90–97.
Witt, P. (1971) "Die Übersetzung von Rechtsbegriffen," *SDHI* 37: 217–60.
Wolff, H. J. (1944) "Marriage law and family organization in ancient Athens," *Traditio* 2: 43–95.
(1946) "The origin of judicial litigation among the Greeks," *Traditio* 4: 31–87.
(1957) "Die Grundlagen des griechischen Vertragsrechts," *ZSS* 74: 26–72. Reprinted in Berneker 1968: 483–533.
(1962) "Gewohnheitsrecht und Gesetzesrecht in der griechischen Rechtsauffassung," *Deutsche Landesreferate zum VI. Internationalen Kongress für Rechtsvergleichung in Hamburg*: 3–18. Reprinted in Berneker 1968: 99–120.
(1964) "Rechtsexperten in der griechischen Antike," *Festschrift zum 45. Deutschen Juristentag*. Karlsruhe, 1–22. Reprinted in Wolff 1974: 81–102.
(1966) *Das attische Paragraphe. Ein Beitrag zum Problem der Auflockerung archaischer Prozessformen*. Weimar.
(1969) "Methodische Grundfragen der rechtsgeschichtlichen Verwendung attischer Gerichtsreden," in *Atti del II Congresso Internazionale della Società Italiana di Storia del Diritto*: 1–13. Florence. Reprinted in Wolff 1974: 27–40.
(1974) *Opuscula Dispersa* (ed. Wieacker, F.). Amsterdam.
Worthington, I. (1992) *A Historical Commentary on Dinarchus*. Michigan.
Woytek, E. (1982) *T. Maccius Plautus. Persa. Einleitung, Text und Kommentar*. Wien.
Wyse, W. (1904) *The Speeches of Isaeus, with Critical and Explanatory Notes*. Cambridge. Reprinted 1979, New York.
Ziegler, K.-H. (1971) *Das private Schiedsgericht im antiken römischen Recht*. Munich.
Zucker, F. (1944) "*Socia unanimans*," *RhM* 92: 193–217.
Zulueta, F. de (1953) *The Institutes of Gaius*. 2 vols. Oxford.
Zwierlein, O. (1990) *Zur Kritik und Exegese des Plautus. I: Poenulus und Curculio* (Akademie der Wissenschaften und der Literatur, Mainz; Abhandlungen der Geistes- und Sozialwissenschaftlichen Klasse 4). Stuttgart.

General index

Italicized page and note numbers indicate where a Greek or Latin term is given a translation, simple definition, or more extended discussion.

Index locorum